The Complete
Civil War
Road Trip Guide

Ten Weekend Tours and More Than 400 Sites, from Antietam to Zagonyi's Charge

MICHAEL WEEKS

The Countryman Press
Woodstock, Vermont

To my parents, Donald and Karen, the two smartest people I know, who instilled their love of learning in me

and

To my wife, Charlotte, for her patience, encouragement, and love

Copyright © 2009 by Michael Weeks

ISBN: 978-0-88150-860-4

Cover and interior photographs by the author unless otherwise specified
Maps by Mapping Specialists, © The Countryman Press
Book design and composition by Faith Hague Book Design

Published by The Countryman Press, P.O. Box 748, Woodstock, VT 05091

Distributed by W. W. Norton & Company, Inc., 500 Fifth Avenue, New York, NY 10110

Printed in the United States of America

10 9

CONTENTS

THERE IS NO BETTER WAY TO LEARN than through experience. It is easy to read about the Civil War—there have been thousands of books dedicated to its battles, its personalities, its politics, and its impact on history. But none of these books (including this one) can take the place of being there, seeing the landscape, walking the fields, and communing with the ghosts of the people who made this war a defining moment in America's history. Anyone can read about the first battle at Fredericksburg, review the battle maps and troop movements, and understand the tactics and strategies of the battle. But when you are able to stand behind the stone wall at the top of Marye's Heights, with the same view that a Confederate soldier had watching Ambrose Burnside's Union troops storm up the hill, you not only begin to better understand the scenes that played out on these hallowed grounds, but you also begin to ask the really important questions—how could this have happened? Why? Using all your senses to experience history brings the facts together and helps them sink in. It involves you wholly, and you learn in a way that no book, no photograph, and no map is able to teach.

This book is designed to help you get to those places that will help you experience the Civil War in a way that no history book can. It will take you to all the most important sites of the war—whether they still exist or not—and help you understand why these places are important. It will help you to learn more by seeing and feeling, and will hopefully inspire you to want to see more to deepen your understanding. When you're ready for that, this book will help you get to those places, too.

This book is going to give you guidance on what to see. It will help lay out the best way to see the most critical sites of the war. But it is not going to restrict itself to the Gettysburgs and Chattanoogas of the war. It is also going to visit the places that might not be so legendary today, but were just as important—battlefields like Fort Pulaski, Prairie Grove, and New Madrid.

In addition to the battlefields, there are hundreds of other historic sites and places where action took place. In some cases the only indication that these places even existed is a sign or a roadside memorial. In other cases there is no memorial at all. But that doesn't necessarily mean that it's not worth going out of your way for. Some of these places are in absolutely unspoiled country, and with a little information, you can re-create the entire scene before your eyes without any distractions or interruptions.

And yes, some of them are now literally underwater, or are parking lots for shopping centers. But if you are interested in a certain general, or are following a campaign, you might want to see every place on the map. This book will help you get to those places and tell you what to expect.

The book will also give you just enough to know why you might want to see these places, and why they're important. But you won't get a complete history lesson. How much you want to get out of your experience is your decision. Some people can drive up to the edge of the Grand Canyon, look in awe for five minutes, and be satisfied. Others will feel left out if they don't learn the name of every rock formation, study the geology, and hike down to the bottom to camp for three days. You'll get enough to get there, know what you're looking at, and why you're looking at it. What you do from there is up to you, and I hope that you gain from what you learn.

One other note: One of the reasons that I wrote this book is to increase the amount of visitation at all the sites, large and small. The more awareness there is about them, the more likely it is that existing sites will be funded and improved and new sites will be created. When you go, let people know why you're there—stay and have a bite to eat, talk to some of the locals, and show them that having history in their backyard brings dollars into the local economy. If you live in one of the locations described in this book, and little to nothing exists to relate the great history that took place there, I hope that you will be inspired to raise your voice, point it out to your community, and get them started in preservation efforts. There is still much work to be done.

WHERE TO BEGIN

There are a lot of Civil War battlefield guides out there. Most are designed to help you get the most out of your experience at a major battlefield. You are dropped in Gettysburg, Pennsylvania, and told in great detail about the reasons the battle occurred, given a map or two, and shown what you can see. Then you are picked up, dropped in Shiloh, Tennessee, and told similar information.

While these guidebooks are absolutely essential, the book you're holding is different. All the tours recommended in this book can be done in either a weekend or a long (three- to four-day) weekend and will guide you to the most important and well-preserved sites of the war. How much time you want to spend at these sites is up to you. You can pick which ones you see and which you skip. But this book is going to give you so many options that you will be able to tailor your trips to exactly what you want to get out of them.

BEFORE YOU GO: PLANNING YOUR TRIPS

There are a couple of resources you can pick up that can add a lot to your experiences. One of them is even FREE.

> *The Civil War Battlefield Guide, Second Edition*—This book, created by an environmental nonprofit group called The Conservation Fund, is an absolute must-have for anyone wanting a one-volume description of the battles of the Civil War. The book has concise and detailed descriptions of 384 battles, contains wonderful maps, and includes essays by such well-known historians as James McPherson and Ed Bearss. It is well organized, thorough, and would make a valuable addition to any Civil War library.

> *Civil War Advisory Commission Report on the Nation's Civil War Battlefields*— This official report, commissioned by Congress, is a sobering assessment of the great danger facing the integrity of our nation's history. It also happens to be a tremendous resource and provides not only a breakdown of the important battles of the war (the same list followed in this book), but also descriptions for

all of them. Best of all, it is a government document, and you have a right to a copy of it. The report did come out in 1993, and although it's currently being revised, print copies are running low. However, the entire report, along with two volumes of appendixes—one of which contains the battle summaries—is accessible through the National Park Service's Internet site, www.nps.gov. Do yourself a favor and check out the wonderful work that the commission did while magnifying the great need for preserving our national treasures.

So many books have been written on so many different aspects of the Civil War that trying to pick a good place to start can be a daunting task. If you're looking for a one-stop source to learn about the complexities of this war, you can't do much better than Shelby Foote's three-volume set titled *The Civil War*. While Foote's work has had its critics, it has established itself as one of the best and most popular narratives on the war, and Foote was a fantastic storyteller. It's a lot of reading, but your knowledge of the Civil War will be much the better for it. If a single volume will do for you, James M. McPherson's Pulitzer Prize–winning work, *Battle Cry of Freedom: The Civil War Era*, has been regarded as a standard since it came out in 1988. If that's still a bit heavy for you, don't be afraid to get yourself a copy of *The Civil War for Dummies*, by Keith D. Dickson. Hey, we all had to start somewhere, and the Dummies series of books has proved to be a great tool to get moving on a wide variety of topics, from history to finance to baseball. From there I'm sure you'll be inspired to do some further exploration.

Finally, at the beginning of each chapter of the book you are now reading are mini-biographies of a few people who feature prominently in that chapter. Knowing the personalities that were involved and relating to them as actual human beings makes history much more interesting than cold, hard facts from events of nearly 150 years ago. So take time to look up a little bit of extra information on these folks, even if it's just a quick peek on Wikipedia.

GETTING TO THE SITES

The classic gas station road map is a thing of the past. The modern road tripper, if relying on anything at all, is most likely to refer to a global positioning system (GPS) or directions from MapQuest, Google, or Yahoo. With this in mind I have given locations for each site that are as precise as possible. If an exact address is available, it is provided, but be aware that the mailing address used for a facility is sometimes very far away from the actual site. Often markers or locations are found at intersections, also easily entered into a GPS or Internet mapping site.

If you've never used a GPS or Internet mapping system before, you're in for a real treat. These—especially the GPS—are wonderful tools, and aside from finding the place you're going to, they can also help you pick out hotels and restaurants along the way. However, they can also be maddening. If you don't spell out a street name just the way a GPS program likes it—for example, using *Dr.* Samuel Mudd Drive instead of *Doctor* Samuel Mudd Drive—it might tell you you're lost or, worse yet, take you somewhere you don't want to go. If you get a GPS system for your tours, use it and rely on it, but if your gut strongly tells you to do the opposite, listen to your gut. If you do get lost, the GPS will get you where you need to be. And when the GPS does steer you wrong, *don't* throw it out the window; it may be your only chance to get home!

THE BATTLEFIELDS

Over 10,500 military actions occurred during the Civil War, ranging from skirmishes to bloodbaths. However, as cities and towns grow, the sites of these actions are gradually being obscured by progress. Recognizing this, Congress commissioned the Civil War Sites Advisory Commission in 1990, which was tasked with reviewing each of these military actions, evaluating the condition of the sites, and determining which ones were the most important to the outcome of the war. With the help of the National Park Service, state historical societies, local groups, and hundreds of volunteers, the CWSAC created a list of 384 Civil War battles that were deemed "principal battlefields" and prioritized them according to their impact on the course of the war, as well as the need for preserving them.

The CWSAC list of 384 sites was divided into four classes:

> ❯ Class A (45 sites)—having a decisive influence on a campaign and a direct impact on the course of the war

> ❯ Class B (104 sites)—having a direct and decisive influence on their campaign

> ❯ Class C (128 sites)—having observable influence on the outcome of a campaign

> ❯ Class D (107 sites)—having a limited influence on the outcome of their campaign or operation but achieving or affecting important local objectives

The road trips outlined in this book will, for the most part, follow the paths of the Class A and, sometimes, Class B battle sites. If you were to take all 10 tours, you would see 44 of the 45 Class A sites, and many of the other sites as well. But if you so desire, this book will help you get to all 384 battlefields—and then some.

OTHER CIVIL WAR SITES

Think the Civil War was just a bunch of battles? Think again. The Civil War is full of people, stories, and events having nothing to do with combat that are better than the best fiction ever written. Visiting the battlefields would never teach you the whole story.

This book will help you learn about the people by going to see where Frederick Douglass worked so hard to achieve equality for African Americans, where Clara Barton used her Civil War experiences to establish the American Red Cross, and where Robert E. Lee was born into a family with possibly the richest American pedigree of all time. These are the people who shaped the events of the time and had a deliberate hand in creating what we know as America today.

You will also see sites that will help you understand the period. Many of these are museums, but be warned: There are a multitude of museums dedicated to the Civil War, and there is absolutely no way they can all be included in this book. The ones included here are the essential ones, or the ones that offer something unique. Some of these places are also living history sites—you will be able to use all your senses to put yourself back in that time. Some sites in the book were essential to war efforts (for example, the Springfield Armory in Massachusetts). Others are sites with such strange, touching, and wonderful stories that they simply could not be left out (such as the Treüe der Union monument in Comfort, Texas).

BREAKING IT ALL DOWN

The book is divided into three main parts: the War in the East, the War in the West, and the War along the Coasts, along with a final part, the Wide-Ranging War, which captures the sites that, although important, are too distant or remote to be included in the tours. Each part is divided into chapters that further break the war down into manageable pieces that can be seen in a weekend or a long weekend road trip. These tours will hit all the major sites of the war, as well as other sites that might not have been as important strategically but are perhaps very well interpreted, or can't be missed for some other reason. If you are able to take each of these ten tours, you will be at the head of the class as far as knowledge of the War Between the States is concerned.

WHERE TO STAY

There are two prevailing philosophies to the road trip. One is to throw your map out the window and go where the road leads you, hopefully winding up at your final destination, eventually. The other is to plan out every detail, knowing exactly what you're going to see, how long it's going to take to get from point A to point B, and where you're going to stop for the night.

Most people fall somewhere in the middle of that spectrum, so you will be given just a little guidance about where you can bed down for the night. You will be presented with some great options for bed-and-breakfasts that are perfect for Civil War buffs, in case you're the type to plan ahead, and especially if you plan on staying in one place for a while. Some of these can greatly enhance your experience. For instance, if you are studying the battles in the Fredericksburg area for a few days, staying at the

Richard Johnston Inn is a necessity. Ask for the room with the remnants of damage from the battle (but be careful if you're asking about the ghost of the Confederate sniper; some people just don't like to talk about it).

If you're not the B&B type and simply like to drop and sleep wherever you finish sightseeing, you're covered there, too. Usually the tours follow major interstates and highways, and there are plenty of hotels and motels that will suit just about anybody. But some of the places described in this book are *way* off the beaten path, and you might not have a lot of options. If you do plan to stray from the interstates and visit sites that are a little more isolated, this book will let you know if you have to plan ahead.

Of course, another great option, if you're so inclined, is camping. Many of the battlefields are located near national parks, national forests, state recreational facilities, or other great places to pitch a tent or sleep in a lodge. It can be a cheap and very fun way to hit the road.

A NOTE ON NUMBERS, NAMES, AND TERMS

As you read through this guide, you may note some apparent inconsistencies, or wonder what some terms mean or how they are used. One essential term for military historians that is commonly misunderstood is "casualties." Casualties, or losses, suffered in battle are often assumed to mean the number of persons killed, but the term actually includes those killed, wounded, missing, captured, or otherwise "lost" to a force during a battle. For instance, if an army suffered 500 casualties during a battle, perhaps 50 men were killed, 150 were injured, and 300 were captured by the enemy. Other military terms or expressions of the time may seem somewhat mysterious (after all, the Civil War was almost a century and a half ago), but I have tried to keep these to a minimum. For military terms that may be foreign to you (such as "abatis" or "enfilade") *The Civil War Battlefield Guide* by the Conservation Fund contains an excellent glossary that will answer almost all your questions.

Another difference you might notice is in town names. Over time, many towns that ended in the suffix "-borough" (for example, Jonesborough, Georgia) at some point simplified their name by dropping the "ugh," to end simply in "boro" (as Jonesboro is called today). There are several cases of this in towns where Civil War battles occurred. In general, in historical passages I use the spelling of the town that was used during the Civil War; but if I am referring to present-day names and addresses, I use the modern spelling.

Finally, a historical note: After the Civil War began with the bombing of Fort Sumter in April 1861, the state of Virginia seceded and joined the Confederate States of America. However, the mountainous western portion of Virginia was not heavily populated with slaveholders, and for this and other reasons much of western Virginia did not support secession and remained loyal to the Union. Early in the war, the counties in western Virginia essentially seceded from Virginia itself, and in 1863—right in the middle of the war—formed the new state of West Virginia, loyal to the Union. For this reason you may see references to battles in Virginia from 1861 through early 1863 that occurred in what is now West Virginia but was Virginia at the time.

HOW NOT TO USE THIS BOOK

This is a guidebook. Use it as a guide. You can even use it as a checklist, of sorts. But *please*, don't rely solely on this book to tell you exactly where to go. When you visit these places, discover them, appreciate them for the gifts that they are, learn the deep lessons that they teach, and then decide for yourself what is important to experience next. If you stick to that guideline, you will want to see more than anyone could ever outline in any book.

IMPORTANT THINGS TO REMEMBER
WHEN VISITING CIVIL WAR SITES

❭ Many of these battle sites are on private property. If you would like to see a site that is on private property, and contact information is available, be sure to ask before you go *trespassing* through somebody's yard. If you don't know, stay out, or take pictures from the roadside.

❭ Many of the sites in this book that are staffed are done so only seasonally and either reduce their hours in the off-season or close entirely. Other smaller sites (for example, town and county museums) may be open only one day a week or month throughout the year. If there's any chance that a site may not be accessible, be sure to call ahead and find out.

❭ All of these sites, including those overseen by the National Park Service, are desperately short of funding, not only to keep their site open, but to heighten the experience for the visitor and, with some luck, acquire and restore surrounding battlefield land that is currently privately owned. Often the sites that are staffed depend on volunteers. So when you visit, be sure to add a little to the donation box, even if the site is free, and sign the guest book so that when the time comes to ask for funding, they can demonstrate that the site is bringing people like you in to support not only the site, but also the local economy.

❭ You will be going through some very rural areas. Make sure your vehicle is in tip-top shape—you don't want to get stuck with a broken-down automobile in a place where your cellular phone doesn't get any reception. Always plan for the worst—keep an emergency road kit with you, and make sure it includes first-aid supplies. There are also locations in this book that are accessible only by dirt or gravel roads, some of which are not always well maintained. If you have any doubt whatsoever that your vehicle might not be able to handle going up the mountainside on a muddy road, don't try it.

❭ As you go through these tours, you will see some very different parts of the country, each with its unique flavors, customs, and cultures. You may even come to some areas where you feel a little out of place, as if you don't belong.

Although you should always follow your better judgment, do not be afraid to approach the locals and ask for directions, about the town, or where a good place to eat might be. They are usually just as friendly as you are and will almost always be as eager to help as you would be if they visited your neck of the woods. In fact, you will find that most people are proud of the history that surrounds them and will happily share what they know. These conversations will probably be the highlights of your trip.

› Good shoes, water, and insect repellent: Keep these three items with you, and you'll be able to enjoy every site.

PART ONE

The War in the West

1

The Far West

OVERVIEW

Years before the Civil War began in 1861, Missouri, Kansas, and other parts of the West were in turmoil. In the decades before the war, Congress had admitted Missouri as a slave state as part of the Missouri Compromise (1820), then repealed part of the compromise (1850) to pass the Kansas-Nebraska Act (1854), defeated President James Buchanan's attempt to admit Kansas as a slave state (1858), and finally admitted Kansas as a free state (1861). All of this made Missouri and "Bleeding Kansas" the first true battlegrounds of the war. Before its admittance as a state, Kansas was flooded with pro- and anti-slavery activists in an attempt to tip the balance in their favor, and violence erupted all around, spreading into Missouri. The fierce and cold bloodshed drew firm battle lines between towns, families, and all groups of people.

When the war did finally break out, Missouri was truly a border state; it did not secede from the Union, but its residents were deeply divided over slavery and secession. Even within its own borders, citizen and soldier alike fought each other over the same issues that plagued the rest of the nation, but with the added weight of a violent history and old scores to settle. The state's governor even formed his own Confederate fighting units, though the state itself remained in the Union. In many ways the war in Missouri and Kansas was an entirely different conflict from what was happening in the rest of the country. Bloody raids and the cold-blooded murder of civilians, jay-hawking and bushwhacking, made this part of the great conflict extremely personal and truly terrible.

That does not mean that the states of the West had no strategic value to the United States or Confederate governments. This region of the country was referred to by both

Union soldiers' monument, Baxter Springs, Kansas.

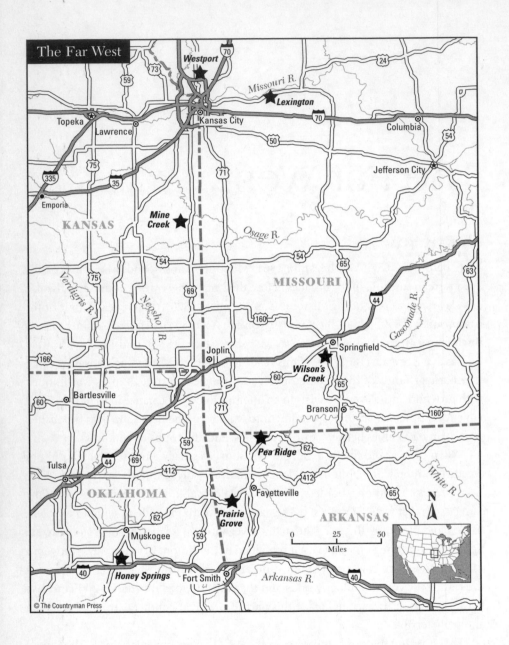

The Far West

Westport
70
73
24
Missouri R.
59
Lexington
70
Kansas City
Topeka
Lawrence
50
Columbia
54
75
Jefferson City
335
35
Emporia
KANSAS
Mine Creek
Osage R.
MISSOURI
54
54
65
63
75
44
Gasconade R.
69
Neosho R.
160
Verdigris R.
Joplin
Springfield
166
60
Wilson's Creek
60
Bartlesville
65
71
Branson
160
60
White R.
Tulsa
44
59
Pea Ridge
62
69
412
N
412
OKLAHOMA
Fayetteville
65
ARKANSAS
62
Prairie Grove
0   25   50
Muskogee
59
Miles
Honey Springs
40
Fort Smith
Arkansas R.
40

© The Countryman Press

sides as the Trans-Mississippi, and it was a tremendous source of fighting men. The eastern borders of Arkansas and Missouri ran along the strategically important Mississippi River, and the western borders were America's frontier. Although Kansas and the Indian territories (in modern-day Oklahoma) were sparsely populated, each side still wanted control, knowing that no matter the result of this war, westward expansion would only continue. All the major trails of the West, including the Santa Fe Trail and the Oregon Trail, had their starting points in Missouri.

Another distinctive aspect of the war in the West was that it featured some largely nontraditional soldiers. A large number of black Union units fought in this area, particularly distinguishing themselves at the battle of Honey Springs in Oklahoma. Several units of immigrants were also formed to fight for the Union; many of these consisted of German Americans, who had fled the oppression of their own country and could not accept slavery or the rejection of the nation that had adopted them. Perhaps the most unusual units in the war belonged to the Confederates, who recruited and organized Native Americans of the so-called Five Civilized Tribes, who fought in several large actions. They were led in large part by Cherokee Stand Watie, who was eventually promoted to brigadier general and was the last Confederate leader of the war to surrender, in June of 1865.

The armies' fight for control of the area started very early in the war, at Wilson's Creek in southern Missouri. Coming only weeks after the first battle of Manassas (Bull Run), the Union defeat here, along with the first death of a major Union field commander in General Nathaniel Lyon, sealed in the minds of many that this would be a long and bloody war. Other large battles, such as Pea Ridge and Prairie Grove, assured the Union's control of at least the soil, if not the hearts and minds, of the area.

In 1864, with the war winding down, the Confederacy decided to launch one last major offensive into Missouri. Major General Sterling Price entered the state hoping to capture St. Louis and the capital at Jefferson City, install a Confederate government, and strike a great blow for the dying cause. However, a combination of disasters led to the ultimate defeat of Price's army at Westport, near Kansas City, and his army disintegrated as it retreated through Kansas. The war in the West was essentially over.

The tour in this chapter will take you through the major battle sites in the Trans-Mississippi. Be sure, though, to see the smaller sites and explore the towns and the people along the way. It is perhaps the best way to begin to understand the conflict in the far West.

» PEOPLE TO KNOW

Sterling Price—The leader of the Missouri State Guard, Sterling Price was born a Virginian in 1809; he moved to Missouri with his family when he was 21. His political career started soon after, as he was elected to the Missouri House of Representatives in

1836 and 1840, eventually becoming speaker. He was elected to the U.S. House in 1845 but left before his term ended to fight in the Mexican War, where he served with distinction and was eventually promoted to brigadier general. In 1853 he became governor of Missouri, serving one term. When the time came for Missouri to consider secession, Price presided over the convention, which voted to remain with the Union.

Price voted with the majority against secession, but when the Federal army seized the state's arsenal at St. Louis, Price was outraged that the government would invade his officially neutral state, and he decided to fight. He led his state guard troops in two major campaigns in the state, despite usually long odds. After the war Price led a colony of Confederate exiles in Veracruz, Mexico, but he eventually returned to his home in St. Louis, where he died in 1867.

Stand Watie—The final surrender of the Civil War came not in Virginia or North Carolina but in Oklahoma, on June 23, 1865. The Confederate brigadier general who held out so long was the highest-ranking Native American in either army—Cherokee leader Stand Watie.

Watie did not have the background of the typical Indian of the time. He was born in Georgia in 1806, was educated in Connecticut, and became a planter and a journalist. When the Civil War broke out and the tribes of the Indian territories (Oklahoma) fought among themselves about which side to support, it was Watie who took command, declaring his support for the Confederacy. Although others left the Indian territories to avoid the fighting, and many of the Indian units that did form did not last long, Watie quickly distinguished himself as a hard fighter and a courageous leader, advancing from colonel to brigadier general during the war. Following his surrender he returned to planting tobacco, and he died in 1871.

William C. Quantrill—One of the most notorious figures of the Civil War was Captain William Clarke Quantrill, leader of the infamous Quantrill's raiders that terrorized eastern Kansas and southwest Missouri. Arriving in Kansas in 1857 during the Bleeding Kansas era, Quantrill soon sought and found trouble, regularly joining in and then leading bushwhacking raids *with* the anti-slavery partisans. The Civil War, however, brought Quantrill more opportunity for trouble.

When the war broke out Quantrill switched his allegiance to the Confederate cause, drawing together a group of men who saw the war as license to commit mayhem. Among these men were "Bloody" Bill Anderson, Cole Younger, and the James brothers, Frank and Jesse. Quantrill's men rampaged through the countryside, angering not only Union but also Confederate leaders, who were embarrassed by his actions. His worst offense came when his men attacked Lawrence, Kansas, in August 1863, with the objective of murdering all the males in the town. Late in the war, as he headed east, allegedly to assassinate President Abraham Lincoln, Quantrill was cornered by Federal troops in Kentucky, who mortally wounded him.

» THINGS TO KNOW

If you stick to the major sites in this chapter, you will be traveling near major highways and frequently near large cities and towns, so lodging and food shouldn't be a problem (although Mine Creek is a bit isolated, Fort Scott, Kansas, contains a couple of motels and restaurants). However, if you stray to some of the other battlefields in this chapter, you may find yourself pretty far from places to stop for the night, so be sure to plan ahead.

Don't forget that at many of the small town or county museums, hours are often infrequent and irregular, so phone before you go to be sure that staff will be there when you are.

Many Missourians, perhaps because of the often very personal nature of the state's violent history, are very proud of their Civil War heritage. In some cases this might even manifest itself in defensiveness, particularly in the case of Quantrill's raiders or some of the other border activities. When you talk to the locals about the history in their area, be sensitive to the fact that many of them may have had not-so-distant relatives fighting and dying on the soil on which you are standing, and remember that what you may have read in a book or on a sign might not tell the whole story. There are plenty of interesting stories in Missouri, and they all deserve to be heard.

» THE CAN'T-MISS SITES

Westport and Byram's Ford

Sterling Price's invasion of Missouri in the fall of 1864 had not exactly gone according to plan. Initially Price's intention was to capture St. Louis, then move to Jefferson City and install a new government, claiming the state for the Confederacy and renewing the war west of the Mississippi. Following his surprising and devastating defeat at Pilot Knob at the outset of the campaign, Price was forced to abandon his plans for St. Louis and Jefferson City and to settle for Kansas City to the west. Still, the campaign had not been a complete loss. Price was able to pick up some recruits (although not nearly as many as he had hoped), and following Pilot Knob the Confederate army had for the most part advanced across the state with little opposition. As the Confederates neared Kansas City, morale was high, even though many of the mostly untrained men were still lacking weapons or proper clothing.

The Union Department of the Missouri, commanded by Major General William Rosecrans, watched as Price's army moved slowly across the state. As the Confederates approached Kansas City, the opportunity to squeeze Price's force in a pincer movement presented itself, and Rosecrans wasted no time. On October 19 Major General James Blunt, with only 2,000 men, met Price at Lexington, and although badly outnumbered and easily pushed back, Blunt gathered valuable intelligence

Jacob Loose Memorial Park, site of decisive fighting at Westport, Kansas City.

about the Confederates' size and movements. Several days later the Confederates pushed another small Union force back at the battles of Little Blue River and Independence, and although the Federals were again easily defeated, the net result was that 13,000 Kansas militia, waiting over the border to protect their own state, recognized Price's army as a direct threat and advanced eastward into Missouri. Meanwhile, Rosecrans had sent 9,000 infantrymen and 7,000 cavalrymen westward after Price. The pincers were about to close.

On October 22, 1864, the Kansas militiamen, led by Major General Samuel Curtis, waited for the Confederates on the west side of the Big Blue River. They were now called the Army of the Border, and they were determined to stop Price's advance to Kansas City. Price, seeing the strong defensive position, sent part of his cavalry, led by Brigadier General Jo Shelby, to find another crossing, which he did at Byram's Ford, southeast of the Union position. Now outflanked, the Union force was forced to withdraw toward the city of Westport, to form another defensive position. Price, meanwhile, brought the rest of his army across Byram's Ford.

After the Confederates had crossed, Price left cavalry commanded by Brigadier

General John Marmaduke to guard the crossing. On October 23, three brigades of Union infantry under Major General Alfred Pleasonton attacked Marmaduke at the crossing, sending the Confederates westward in a rush. In their pursuit the Federals ran into Price's rear and pounced. This was the initiation of the battle of Westport and the downfall of Sterling Price's army. As Pleasonton attacked the Confederate right and rear, Curtis's Army of the Border, now 20,000 strong, lashed at Price from the south. In addition, Major General Andrew Jackson Smith brought 9,000 Union infantry to the fight, attacking Price's left. Price, knowing that he was stuck, quickly began to move southward to avoid the pincers of Rosecrans's forces. Fighting raged all over the area, as almost 40,000 troops were engaged—Pleasonton at Byram's Ford, and the remainder in and around Westport. It was only by an outstanding rearguard action fought by Jo Shelby's troops that the Confederate army was able to escape by the skin of its teeth.

SITE DETAILS

Westport Driving Tour and Byram's Ford Walking Tour—Brochures for a walking tour of the battle of Byram's Ford and a driving tour of the battle of Westport are available from the Civil War Round Table of Kansas City and the Westport Historical Society. They can be picked up at either the society's headquarters at the Harris-Kearney house or online (the method I would suggest, since the hours for the home are irregular). The brochure for Byram's Ford takes you to the ford itself, as well as the rest of the battlefield; unfortunately, most of this is now contained within an industrial park, and the tour is a bit hard to follow. Several memorials have been erected along the way, and you are able to walk down to the site of the ford. As for the driving tour for the battle of Westport, it is probably easy to follow if you live in the area, but if you are from out of town, it can be a nightmare. There are many stopping points on the tour, and the historical interpretation is excellent, but most of the sites are on very busy streets, making stopping to view them difficult and sometimes even dangerous. In addition, the tour is a bit winding, so if you want to follow the tour stops in order, be prepared for a long, confusing ride. Fortunately, there is a bright future for the interpretation of Byram's Ford and Westport. The Westport Historical Society is working on creating a separate visitor's center near the area of Byram's Ford that will contain a museum and interpretation for both battles, in addition to the driving and walking tours. This is slated for completion in the near future, depending on funding, so keep your eye out for it—these battles are much too important to let slip by without recognition. *Brochures—Walking Tour of Battle of Byram's Ford and Driving Tour of Battle of Westport, available online and at Westport Historical Society, 4000 Baltimore St., Kansas City, MO, 64111; 816-561-1821; www.battleofwestport.org. Sites accessible daily.*

Although the Confederates were able to leave Westport without having to surrender, they were badly mauled, and the Federals remained in very close pursuit. Price took his army into Kansas and was hammered again at Mine Creek. By the time Price reached the southern border of Kansas, his army was a shell of its former self, with desertions taking as devastating a toll as Union ordnance. Byram's Ford and Westport, in terms of the number of troops involved, was the largest battle of the Trans-Mississippi, and it proved to be the death throes of the Confederacy in that region.

Mine Creek and Marais des Cygnes

The area around Pleasanton, Kansas, far west of most of the action of the Civil War, saw both the early rise and the late fall of the terrible violence associated with the period. Even before the war began, during the years of Bleeding Kansas, the region was witness to bushwhacking and jayhawking. A signature event took place along the banks of a small river on May 19, 1858, when five men, all local abolitionists, were executed in what came to be known as the Marais des Cygnes massacre. The massacre served as both a rallying cry for the abolitionist movement and an excuse to extend the bloodshed that was taking place all over eastern Kansas.

The unspoiled battlefield at Mine Creek, Kansas.

During the war, although border ruffians and raiders continued to be active, the area was relatively quiet. Located between Kansas City and Fort Scott, the area was under solid Union control. The peace was shattered, however, in 1864, under the chaotic conditions of an army that was running for its life. Major General Sterling Price had entered the southeast corner of Missouri scarcely more than a month before, moving north and then west across the state. His campaign had met none of its military objectives, and the Federals had finally caught up with him just outside Kansas City, defeating his forces soundly at the battle of Westport. Price's army was in great danger, and he immediately crossed over into Kansas to retreat to the south. The Union forces remained on his tail, and it was at Mine Creek that they caught up with him.

In the early hours of October 25, 1864, after a brief midnight rest, Price's army had begun to resume its movement south. At the crossing of the Marais des Cygnes River, Brigadier General John Marmaduke was tasked with delaying the Federal pursuit. The first Union contact occurred at 2 AM, and by 6 AM Marmaduke had his men blocking the crossing with abandoned wagons. Not long after this short delaying action, known as the battle of Marais des Cygnes, Marmaduke left to catch up with the rest of Price's army, still heading south in haste. The Federals simply found another place to cross.

In the meantime, the rest of Price's army was held up. He still had a large force, and only a small crossing of Mine Creek, 10 miles south of the Marais des Cygnes, was available. A portion of the army, in a large-scale rearguard action, was forced to turn to the north and make a stand, while the rest of the wagons and men attempted to cross the narrow ford. Some 7,000 men under Marmaduke and General James Fagan formed a line nearly a mile long to delay the Federals. Most of the men, as they had been throughout the entire campaign, were mounted, as were the Federals chasing them.

At 10:30 the first elements of the Union army began to appear over the shallow crest to the north of the creek. The two Union brigades, commanded by Lieutenant Colonel Frederick Benteen and Colonel John Phillips, totaled 2,800 men. The Union brigades were arranged in a line to counter the Confederates. It would be a classic military duel of line against line, man against man.

The Union charge came at 11 AM, with Benteen on the Union left and Phillips on the right. Both brigades, though outnumbered, advanced down the hill directly toward the Confederates. Many of the Union troops, however, did have the distinct advantage of the repeating Spencer rifle, capable of firing seven shots before reloading. Two of Benteen's units moved to flank the Confederate right, and in no time Marmaduke's Confederates were moving rearward, abandoning their artillery and retreating toward the creek. All along the line the Confederates were overrun. Marmaduke, still on horseback and trying to rally his troops, was eventually captured, along with Brigadier General William Cabell, by two Iowa cavalrymen.

Although most of the wagon train did make it across the creek, and Price's army survived to make a final stand at Newtonia, Mine Creek was a rout and began the

SITE DETAILS

Mine Creek Battlefield State Historic Site—Like many battlefields of the West, the site at Mine Creek is not only superbly preserved, but so is the landscape surrounding it. Although a few scattered residences are visible in the distance or through the trees, it is very easy to picture what took place here in 1864—thanks in part to the Kansas State Historical Society, and also the Mine Creek Battlefield Foundation, which has bought much of the surrounding land. The battlefield doesn't contain easily distinguishable topographical features, or remnants of earthworks dug long ago. It is simply undisturbed. You can follow a self-guided walking trail through the battlefield, with the stops explained by an excellent accompanying brochure and interpretive signs. As the trail winds through the prairie, you can't help but notice the silence. It is remarkably peaceful here, and it is easy to feel very alone with the ghosts of this place. Even the markers that help visitors distinguish where battle lines were or where certain events took place are unobtrusive. Top that off with a visitor's center that is first-rate and an extremely knowledgeable and friendly staff, and you've got one remarkable historical site. There is only one downside: Because of an unfortunately light tourist load and underfunding, the visitor's center is not open daily. But even if you are traveling through the area on a day that the visitor's center is not open, the battlefield itself will still be open, so plan ahead and obtain the brochure. In any case, do not miss this one. There are no markers for the battle of Marais des Cygnes, which occurred just a bit north of the Mine Creek site, but information on that battle can be found here. *Mine Creek Battlefield State Historic Site, near intersection of US 69 and E. 850th Rd., Pleasanton, KS, 66075; 913-352-8890; www.kshs.org/places/minecreek/index.htm; www.minecreekbattlefield.org. Open Wed.–Sun., Mar.–Nov., and Fri.–Sun., Dec.–Feb.; admission charged.*

Marais des Cygnes State Historic Site—Not very far from the Mine Creek battlefield is the Marais des Cygnes State Historic Site. The site is not dedicated to the battle of Marais des Cygnes, but rather the massacre that took place here in 1858. Although the site is not staffed, recently updated interpretive signs and a long-standing memorial to the free-staters who were killed here tell the story not only of the massacre but of the turmoil over the admission of Kansas as a state. The site is located a little ways down the back roads, but follow the signs and you'll be fine. *Marais des Cygnes State Historic Site, east of intersection of E. 1700 Rd. and Young Rd., Pleasanton, KS, 66075; 913-352-8890; www.kshs.org/places/marais/index.htm. Open daily.*

dissolution of Price's army. Within 30 minutes the Confederates had suffered 1,200 casualties, including the loss of two generals, to the Union's 110. The war in Kansas was essentially over.

Honey Springs

In the Oklahoma Indian territories, loyalties had been split throughout the war. Fighting among the tribes who inhabited the area had been heated, and although the Confederacy had been more successful than the Union in forming fighting units from the Indians, the area was still very much up for grabs. Fort Gibson, in the northeast portion of Oklahoma, had changed hands and was under Federal control in the middle of 1863. Not far south was the Indian community of Honey Springs, where 5,700 Confederate troops were stationed, waiting for reinforcements and preparing to retake the fort.

The Union commander in the territory, Major General James Blunt, had 3,000 men at Fort Gibson. Upon hearing that more Confederate troops were headed for

The opening battleground at Honey Springs, Oklahoma.

Honey Springs, Blunt decided to take immediate action, even though his force was only half the size of the Confederates'. Blunt moved his troops—several regiments of Unionist Indians and one black regiment—south out of Fort Gibson toward Honey Springs. The forces he would be facing were also heavily Indian, led by Colonel Stand Watie, along with a contingent of Texans. In the battle to come, there would be more troops of black or Native American origin than there would be white soldiers—a rarity even in the battles of the Trans-Mississippi.

Overall command of the Confederates at Honey Springs was held by Brigadier General Douglas Cooper. Hearing that the Union forces were on their way, Cooper set his men astride the Texas Road, which ran through Honey Springs. The Confederates were dug in along a tree line, with the banks of Elk Creek behind them. The creek had only one bridge, along the road, but also had several shallow crossings.

On the morning of July 17, 1863, Blunt's Union troops reached Honey Springs and formed a line of battle. At 10 AM the advance began, and two of the four Confederate guns were quickly taken out of action. The fighting raged for two hours, with each Union attack repulsed. Finally, in the confusion of the smoke-filled battlefield, the Confederates made a critical error. Mistaking a Union order for one of the units to move as a call for a retreat, the Texans decided that the time was right for a charge. Their bravery led them into slaughter, as the First Kansas Colored Regiment tore into them, sending them reeling and creating a critical weakness in the Confederate center. Cooper, seeing that his line was faltering, ordered a retreat.

The remainder of the day was a running battle, as the Confederates formed several lines to protect the main force as it withdrew. After several hours the Confederates were

SITE DETAILS

Honey Springs Battlefield Park—Operated by the Oklahoma Historical Society, the battlefield park is only a short distance west of Fort Smith, Arkansas. Although the site is lightly staffed, the small visitor's center, the driving tour alongside the still-visible Texas Road, and the interpretive signs are all exceptional, making this an easy piece of history to experience. Along the driving tour are several stops, each with a very short trail and interpretation. Further development of the park is in the works, but what is already there is plenty of reason to visit the scene of this unique battle. In addition to the new facilities, there are several older monuments and memorials; although some have suffered from neglect and vandalism over the years, it is still remarkable to see that the importance of what happened here was recognized early. The site is a little bit out of the way, but you will find it easily if you follow the signs. *Honey Springs Battlefield Park, near intersection of E1020 Rd. and N4232 Rd., Checotah, OK, 74426; 918-473-5572; www.honeysprings.org. Closed Mon.; admission charged.*

gone, and the exhausted Union troops could not pursue them. Honey Springs remained under Union control, even though Blunt took his troops back to Fort Gibson, weary but having suffered only 77 casualties to the Confederates' 134. The grand result of the battle, though, was that the Union now had strong control of the Oklahoma Indian territories and within two months would occupy Fort Smith without much of a fight. In addition to being an important tactical victory, Honey Springs, perhaps more than any other battle of the war, demonstrated that black and Native American troops could fight as hard, as bravely, and as effectively as their white counterparts.

Prairie Grove

After the battle of Pea Ridge established firm Union control of southwest Missouri in March of 1862, northwest Arkansas became the next battleground. By the fall of that year, the Union's Army of the Frontier was now commanded by Brigadier General John Schofield and consisted of two main forces: one division commanded by Brigadier General James Blunt and two divisions by Brigadier General Francis Herron. Blunt, never one to hesitate to start a fight, advanced his division into Arkansas, while Herron kept his men in Springfield.

In late November 1862, Blunt encountered Colonel Jo Shelby's Confederate cavalry at Cane Hill in the Boston Mountains of northwest Arkansas. Knowing that Confederate forces were present but not knowing their intentions, Blunt decided to sit tight at Cane Hill, while sending word to Herron that he should prepare his divisions to join him when needed.

Meanwhile, the Confederates in the area were preparing for another invasion of Missouri. Now commanded by Major General Thomas Hindman, the Confederate Army of the Trans-Mississippi was already at 11,000 men and growing. Although they were short of food and supplies and nowhere near fighting condition, when word came that Blunt was holed up in the Boston Mountains—and potentially trapped—Hindman decided that the time to attack was now, while the Union army was divided. Hindman planned to bottle up Blunt's force in the mountains by moving north and east of him, then defeat him before Herron's divisions could arrive.

Blunt, receiving word on December 2 that the Confederates were on the move, sent a message to Herron to hurry to Cane Hill. The division in the Boston Mountains consisted of only 5,000 men, and Blunt knew he was outnumbered and vulnerable. Herron, receiving the message the next day, immediately put his forces on the move and covered the terrain with incredible speed, leaving by the wayside many a soldier who could not keep up.

Herron reached Fayetteville, just north of Cane Hill, on December 7, only to find what he thought was an advance guard of Confederates. Meanwhile Hindman, realizing that Union reinforcements had arrived, altered his plan: Instead of attacking

The memorial yard at Prairie Grove State Battlefield in Arkansas.

Blunt, the Confederates would fight Herron first, then turn south to meet Blunt. Situated between the two Union forces, Hindman lined up his men facing north on a small hill between Fayetteville and Cane Hill near the Prairie Grove church, surrounded by farmland and a few houses. For the most part he ignored Blunt's division to the south.

Upon reaching the open fields at Prairie Grove, Herron lined up his exhausted men at the bottom of the hill opposite the Confederate line and launched an immediate assault. Still thinking that they had encountered a much smaller force, the Federals opened up with an artillery barrage, taking out several guns, then advanced across the open fields and up the hill toward the Confederate line. Herron soon learned that he was facing not an advance guard but an entire Confederate army, as his men were torn to pieces by the two Confederate divisions waiting at the top of the hill. Devastated, the Union troops fell back to the bottom of the hill, and the Confederates followed, only to be hit hard themselves when they started to cross the open ground.

By this time Hindman realized that Herron's force was much smaller than his and prepared for an all-out assault of his own. However, just as his men began to advance to the bottom of the hill, a sudden burst of artillery came from the northwest. Blunt, who had remained in the Boston Mountains awaiting an attack, had heard the fight break out at Prairie Grove and immediately sent his entire force there. The Confederates, in ignoring the threat to their rear, had allowed Blunt to move completely around them and join Herron in the field. With Blunt's division now on the Union right and Herron's two divisions on the left, the Union line was strong, and they again advanced up the hill. Heavy fighting took place on the hill for the rest of the day, going back and forth, with neither side gaining advantage. The fight raged until daylight ran out. The Confederates, low on ammunition and lacking artillery, withdrew south into the Boston Mountains during the night. Although costly (1,251 Federal casualties), it was another signal victory for the Union in the area. Any Confederate hopes of an invasion of Missouri were again dashed, as they suffered 1,317 casualties, a very high toll for an army that was depleted to begin with. In addition, Confederate desertion increased tremendously after the battle, as Missouri and Arkansas soldiers, seeing their armies suffer repeated defeats on their home soil, returned to their farms and homes.

SITE DETAILS

Prairie Grove Battlefield State Park—Although the state park does not cover every inch of the ground fought over that day, it might as well. The land around the park is still mostly rural, and while there has been some development, most of the surrounding private property is still agricultural, leaving all of the prominent features of the battlefield still easily discernible. The museum at the park's visitor's center contains helpful exhibits, and a driving tour takes the visitor not only through the park (which is positioned from the top of the ridge southward, the scene of the heaviest fighting) but also outside the protected area, offering views of virtually the entire battlefield. Some historic buildings are also present on the property, and living history exhibits often take place. The park is rather large, and the interpretation is excellent, so be sure to set aside enough time for a good visit. *Prairie Grove Battlefield State Park, 506 E. Douglas St., Prairie Grove, AR, 72753; 479-846-2990; www.arkansasstateparks.com/prairie grovebattlefield. Open daily; admission charged for museum.*

Pea Ridge

In early 1862 control of southwest Missouri was still up for grabs. Although Major General Sterling Price had raided Missouri and still had a strong presence there, Union forces had been building up to drive him out for good. Price, building his own force to retake his home state of Missouri, was too large and too capable to be ignored.

Over the winter the Union had named Brigadier General Samuel Curtis commander of the forces in the area, which he quickly consolidated into the Army of the Southwest. In early February he began to pursue Price, eventually driving him into the mountainous region of northwest Arkansas. While Curtis paused to plan a defense for the state of Missouri, Price combined his troops with those of Brigadier General Benjamin McCulloch. In early March additional help was received when the Confederacy appointed Major General Earl Van Dorn commander of all forces west of the Mississippi River. The Confederates now had 14,000 troops at the ready and began preparations to retake the state of Missouri.

Within days Curtis learned of the Confederates' new strength, and he prepared his men for battle. He positioned his men south of Elkhorn Mountain, along the tiny but easily defensible Little Sugar Creek, near a small hamlet around the Elkhorn Tavern. Here Curtis's 10,250 Union soldiers waited, strengthening their positions and

Artillery at the ready, Pea Ridge National Military Park.

SITE DETAILS

Pea Ridge National Military Park—Easy to get to but still remote enough to remain virtually undisturbed, Pea Ridge is one of the most enjoyable Civil War battlefields in the National Park System. The combination of the presentation of information, the intact battlefield, and the beautiful scenery makes this one a must-see. The visitor's center contains an excellent film on the battle, and the driving tour through the park presents all of the battle's prominent features, including a rebuilt Elkhorn Tavern, plus a wonderful mountaintop view of the battlefield that makes the interpretation of the action very clear, while also providing excellent photo opportunities of the surrounding mountains. Make sure that you do not miss this one. *Pea Ridge National Military Park, intersection of US 62 and Boundary Line Rd., Pea Ridge, AR, 72732; 501-451-8522; www.nps.gov/peri. Open daily; admission charged.*

preparing for the hard fight they knew was coming. It was to be a showdown for the possession of Missouri.

First contact was made on March 6, 1862, when the Confederates caught some of Brigadier General Franz Sigel's Federals as they moved into position south of the mountain. Seeing that Curtis's position was strong, Van Dorn decided to move the Confederate army around them—and around the entire mountain—to fall upon the Union right. It might have been a masterstroke if it had worked, but it did not. Price's division made it to their position in good time, but McCulloch's division was so slow that Van Dorn redirected him to come around the south side of the mountain and meet Price at Elkhorn Tavern.

Curtis awoke on the morning of March 7 to find that he had been given a great gift. Although the entire Confederate army was in his rear, they were not only split into two, but the two parts were separated by an entire mountain. The Union soldiers, who had been facing south, turned around to the north and attacked both divisions—McCulloch's division on the west side of the mountain and on the Union left, and Price's division at Elkhorn Tavern, on the east side of the mountain and the Union right.

On the west side of the mountain, the center of McCulloch's division approached the Federal lines, which were still well positioned, despite the fact that they had turned to the north. The Confederates moved across open farmland, approaching the Union line. On the west side of the farms, however, was a tree line where Union skirmishers were hidden. As McCulloch's infantry passed they were suddenly hit hard from the tree line, and McCulloch was killed on the field. He was replaced by Brigadier General James McIntosh, but soon McIntosh also fell dead to Union fire.

Although they had been stopped in the center farmland, McCulloch's Confederates had had success on both flanks and began to push the Union forces back. Eventually, though, Franz Sigel brought additional Union forces to the battle, and the remaining Confederates west of Elkhorn Mountain were driven back in retreat. Sigel now moved his men eastward toward the fighting at Elkhorn Tavern.

The fighting around the tavern was fierce. Although the Union position was strong, Price and Van Dorn were able to hammer at the Federal lines, first with artillery, then with infantry, until the Federal units were forced to fall back. After hard fighting on March 7, ceasing only with the darkness of night, the Confederates had advanced well but knew that the battle was not over. Knowing that Curtis was bringing the rest of his men from the west side of the mountain to strengthen his force, Van Dorn did the same, bringing over what was left of McCulloch's men and forming a strong defensive position around the tavern.

The Confederates had formed a V-shaped line around the tavern. To match this, on the morning of March 8, Curtis lined up his entire army—all four divisions—and advanced northward toward the tavern. Sigel commanded the two divisions on the left, and Curtis the two on the right. As they approached the Confederate position, Sigel began to swing his two divisions around so that they would meet the Confederate right side of the V head-on—in essence, the Federals had created a V of their own, to envelop Van Dorn's.

As the Union infantry moved into position, artillery began to decimate the Confederate lines, which were soon forced back. The Union infantry quickly pursued, and soon the Confederates were on the run, in every direction. It was a rout, and Van Dorn's men scattered to wherever they could. The Union victory was complete. Although they had suffered 1,384 casualties, no small number, they had inflicted 2,000 on the enemy, who had come with far superior numbers. The Confederate defeat essentially ended any hopes for another campaign for Missouri, and the Federals were now in a strong position to take control of Arkansas and the rest of the Trans-Mississippi.

Wilson's Creek

The first major battle of the West, Wilson's Creek, like the first battle of Manassas only a few weeks before, sent shock waves through both North and South. The battle itself, tactically a Confederate victory, was a virtual draw in terms of casualties. The Union, however, had lost the battlefield, and with it a chance to slow or stop the efforts of the Confederacy and the Missouri State Guard in southwest Missouri. In addition, the Union lost its first general in combat. Wilson's Creek served notice to all that the war would be long and hard-fought.

In August of 1861 the Federals, commanded by Brigadier General Nathaniel Lyon, were stationed in Springfield, Missouri, the largest city in this part of the state. Lyon, knowing that the Missouri State Guard had been growing and had now been supplemented by a large Confederate force, had been asking for reinforcements, but they

The spot where General Lyon fell, Wilson's Creek National Battlefield.

were repeatedly refused. He had already been chasing parts of the Missouri State Guard with great success, but with the arrival of the Confederate force, he now faced somewhere between 12,000 and 13,000 men. Deciding that he had to act, Lyon directed a night march from Springfield toward the Confederate camp at Wilson's Creek, just southwest of Springfield.

The Confederates, recently arrived, were commanded by Brigadier General Benjamin McCulloch. They were a welcome addition for General Sterling Price's Missouri State Guard, which had done its best to wreak havoc on Federal activities in the state but needed reinforcement. On the same night that Lyon advanced from Springfield, McCulloch had planned to advance on Springfield, but poor weather and wet gunpowder prevented the assault from taking place. The Confederates stayed in camp.

Early on the morning of August 10, Lyon approached the north side of the Confederate camp with 4,200 men, while Colonel Franz Sigel moved from the south with 1,200 men. At 5 AM Lyon's men advanced southward toward a rise that would later be known as Bloody Hill. The Confederates, caught completely off guard, were driven back to the crest of the hill and down the other side. Sigel, after hearing Lyon's guns open up, hit the Confederates at the south end, driving them out of their camp.

An hour after the battle had begun, just as Lyon had reached the crest of the hill,

Confederate artillery that had been set up to the east opened up, enfilading the Union line. The advance stalled, enabling McCulloch to form battle lines of his own. Lyon sent infantry to silence the batteries and protect his left, but they were repulsed. The fighting raged on Bloody Hill for the next four hours.

One common battlefield problem, particularly early in the war, was that it was often difficult to distinguish friend from foe. Uniforms were not uniform; some Northern units wore gray, and some Southern units wore blue. This was part of the confusion at Wilson's Creek, and it proved to be devastating for Franz Sigel's men at the south end of the field. As gray-clad soldiers approached his position, Sigel, thinking they were the First Iowa Infantry, held his fire. At point-blank range, the soldiers, who were actually from Louisiana, opened fire, tearing Sigel's men to shreds and driving them off the battlefield for good.

On Bloody Hill the fighting remained heavy, as the Confederates and the Missouri State Guard launched several counterattacks. The first two were repulsed, but both were fierce and did considerable damage. During the second, as the fighting grew heavier, General Lyon was struck by a musket ball and killed. He was the first Union general to die in the Civil War. The third and final attack, which involved 6,000 Confederate and Missouri State Guard soldiers lined in battle, was the fiercest of all, and at some points the opposing lines were within 20 yards of each other. But the Union line held, and at 11 AM the Confederates withdrew. The Federals, having lost their commander and being well outnumbered, retreated back to Springfield. The battle was over. Union forces had suffered 1,317 casualties, including their general. The Confederates and the Missouri State Guard fared only slightly better, with casualties totaling 1,222. But the Confederates held the field and, for the next several months, southwest Missouri.

Lexington

Two battles were fought around Lexington, Missouri, at one time a small boom town along the Missouri River. The first was near the outset of the war, when the border state of Missouri was still up for grabs. The second was near the end of the war, when what was once a great army fighting for what it believed to be a just cause began to be crushed to oblivion.

After the Union defeat at Wilson's Creek in August, the Missouri State Guard was more or less free to roam and recruit all over southwest Missouri. Further, the Confederate victory emboldened pro-slavery Missourians all over the state to join the guard, which was led by Major General Sterling Price. They gathered, grew, and trained, and by mid-September were ready to move. Their first target as a large force was the Union outpost at Lexington, just east of Kansas City. Price's army was as large as 12,000 men, while the Union garrison, commanded by Colonel James Mulligan, numbered only 3,500. They did, however, command a strong position and believed they could easily hold out until reinforcements arrived.

After first contact on September 13, 1861, the Federals withdrew into their fortifications north of the town, and while they waited for reinforcements, Price waited for his wagon train. On September 18 Price, now fully supplied, opened fire on the Union works. On the west end of the fighting stood the Anderson house, being used

One of the bullet-ridden rooms of the Anderson House at Lexington, Missouri.

as a field hospital by the Union. The Confederates assaulted it, apparently believing that they were receiving sniper fire from the building. To Mulligan it was an intolerable breach of the rules of war, and for several hours attack and counterattack raged around the home. The matter was not settled until darkness fell, at which time the house was under the control of the Missouri State Guard.

The Anderson house was not the only valuable property controlled by Price's troops at the end of the first day's fighting. Mulligan's men were now completely encircled, with no access to the Missouri River or any source of water. Throughout the next day the heat took a terrible toll on the Union soldiers, while Price's men were able to quench their thirsts as they inched ever closer to the Federal lines.

On the morning of September 20, the Union soldiers, still holding out, saw a strange sight that was not duplicated during the rest of the war. Overnight, Price's men had gathered bales of hemp from the local warehouses, soaked them in water, and set them up along the line of battle. That morning, while some of the Confederate soldiers were assigned to gradually rolling the soaked bales forward, Confederate

SITE DETAILS

Battle of Lexington State Historic Site—This modern, well-maintained, and well-cared-for historic park encompasses a good portion of the original battlefield. The visitor's center contains an excellent collection of artifacts and tells both sides of the story in the Missouri conflict very well, beginning with the origins of the town of Lexington and discussing slavery, the statehood debates, the allegiances of the residents of the town, and finally focusing on the first battle of Lexington. There is also an exceptional film that discusses the battle from the viewpoints of some of those affected by it—the Union's Colonel Mulligan, one of the Anderson daughters, and a German immigrant living in the town. Guided tours of the Anderson house are also available. The home still bears many of the scars of battle, including a bullet-ridden exterior wall and a large hole in the ceiling created by a cannonball. A walking trail through the grounds highlights the important areas of the battlefield; and the Union earthworks, though long gone themselves, are visible through some creative landscaping that shows exactly where they were set up. This is an excellent site and should not be missed. (Also, as you drive through the town, note the old courthouse, which was present at the time of the battle; a cannonball is still very visibly lodged into one of the columns.) As for the second battle of Lexington, some information can be found at the historic site if you ask, but not much, and there is only a one-line blurb about it in the museum. *Battle of Lexington State Historic Site, intersection of Delaware St. and Cottonwood St., Lexington, MO, 64067; 660-259-4654; www.mostateparks.com/lexington/index.html. Open daily; admission charged for tour of Anderson house only.*

riflemen followed close behind the slowly moving barricade. After several hours, as the Union men helplessly pumped bullets into the wet material, the Confederates were close enough to launch a final assault. Although there was confusion in the final stages of the battle, the end was clear enough. The "Battle of the Hemp Bales" was over, and it was a decisive Confederate victory. Mulligan surrendered his command, which was then paroled. Price, meanwhile, saw that several large Union forces were moving toward him, and he took his men back into southwest Missouri.

The second battle of Lexington also involved Sterling Price, but it was more than three years later, just before his doomed Missouri campaign of 1864 was about to unravel. On October 19, 1864, Brigadier General Jo Shelby encountered 2,000 Union troops under Major General James Blunt. Blunt's men could not stop Shelby or the rest of Price's much larger force at Lexington, but they were able to gain valuable information about its size and strength. Within a week Price's once-proud army would be defeated at Westport and would disintegrate as it retreated south through Kansas and southwest Missouri.

OTHER SITES IN THE FAR WESTERN THEATER

Liberty—Just northeast of Kansas City, Liberty, Missouri, was the location of an arsenal and was therefore a recruiting ground for the Missouri State Guard. On September 17, 1861, small forces from each side met here and fought for about an hour, with the Federals eventually withdrawing. It was a small battle, but the consequences were larger, as neither force was able to participate in the battle of Lexington, occurring a short distance to the east.

The battle site at Liberty is now farmland, along with a public sports complex. No monuments or memorials commemorate the battle, but the fighting took place on the land north and west of the intersection listed below. Some information can be found by contacting the Clay County Archives. *Liberty Battlefield (private property), land west of intersection of MO 210 and S. Mick Rd.; Clay County Archives, 210 E. Franklin St., Liberty, MO, 64068; 816-781-3611; www.claycountyarchives.org. Private property, viewable from roadside.*

Independence and Little Blue River—Independence, Missouri, as the trailhead or supply depot for virtually every major trail heading west, was an important strategic location, and several battles occurred in and around the small city. The first was on August 11, 1862, when a small group of the Missouri State Guard attacked the Union garrison there. After a short fight that ended with the Union commander barricading himself in a downtown building and then being forced to surrender, the Federal force was taken prisoner and paroled. In 1864, as Major General Sterling Price's Confederates approached Kansas City from the east, troops under Major General James Blunt supplemented a smaller Union force under Colonel James Moonlight, who had taken up a position east of Independence at the Little Blue River. On October 21, 1864, Brigadier General John Marmaduke attacked the Union force at the Little Blue. Marmaduke was held at the river for a short time, until Brigadier General Jo Shelby's cavalry arrived and drove the Federals back into the town of Independence. The fight resumed the next day in what is known as the second battle of Independence, as the rest of Price's army dug in for the battles of Byram's Ford and Westport to the southwest. Union cavalry under Major General Alfred Pleasonton was able to hit the rear guard of the Confederates, ultimately driving them west through the town. Perhaps the most important result of the battles of the Little Blue River and second Independence was that thousands of Kansas militiamen, who had resisted leaving their own state, saw that Price's army was a threat and joined the larger Union effort against the Confederates.

The Independence Tourism Department has been anticipating an increase in tourist traffic with the war's upcoming anniversary and has responded by creating walking and driving tours for all three battles. The driving tour for the first battle of Independence, which occurred mostly within the existing town, is well put together; although some of the battle's features have been lost, the terrain is still mostly recognizable. The driving tour for the battles of Little Blue River and the second battle of Independence ranges farther outside town (for Little Blue), and the landscape and markers make it very easy to recognize prominent features, including monuments at the river crossing itself and some still-existing buildings from both battles. The brochures are located throughout the town and online. Considering the rich history of Independence, which involves the early Church of Mormon, virtually all the westward pioneer trails, and a United States president, a lot of work and care went into these tours, and they are exceptionally done. (One note: When driving the tour route for the battle of Little Blue River, take care along the roads—they are busy; you might also want to avoid midafternoon, when the roads are jammed as the local school, located at one of the stops, lets out.) *Driving tours—Little Blue River and Independence, Independence Tourism Department, 111 E. Maple Ave., Independence, MO, 64050; 816-325-7111; www.indepmo.org/tourism/civilwar.aspx. Sites accessible daily.*

Lone Jack—On the night of August 15, 1862, a Union force of about 800 men attacked a Confederate camp with twice that number near Lone Jack, Missouri, and drove the Confederates out. The next day, however, another Confederate force in the area of 3,000 men struck back. The Union leader, Major Emory Foster, was killed in the counterattack, and although a heavy and hard fight occurred after this, the Confederates who had been attacked the night before returned. The Union force withdrew, having lost 272 men.

One part of the Lone Jack battle site is at the Lone Jack Battlefield Museum and Soldiers' Cemetery. Although the land dedicated to the site is only a small portion of the battlefield, its position and the interpretive information available through signs and at the museum put you square in the middle of the action. The museum is well run, doing a great job of highlighting Lone Jack's importance, and the cemetery is small but well kept. The volunteers staffing the site are very proud of what they have, and they should be. *Lone Jack Battlefield Museum and Soldiers' Cemetery, 301 S. Bynum Rd., Lone Jack, MO, 64070; 816-697-8833; www.historiclonejack.org. Open Wed.–Sun., Apr.–Oct., and weekends Nov.–Mar.; admission charged.*

Lawrence—Early on the morning of August 21, 1863, as the Reverend S. S. Snyder of Lawrence, Kansas, was milking his cow, a man quietly came up to him and shot him in the head. It was one of William Quantrill's raiders, and that shot began what would be a three-hour rampage of murder and mayhem. Lawrence had its roots in the anti-slavery movement and was incorporated in the years of Bleeding Kansas as an abolitionist city. As such it was regarded with contempt by pro-slavery men such as Quantrill. The official name of the group, of which Quantrill made himself captain, was the Confederate Partisan Rangers, and they practiced guerrilla and terrorist tactics all along the Missouri and Kansas border. The rangers went throughout the town, from building to building and house to house, and killed every man and boy they could find, about 150 in all. When word came that Union troops were on their way, Quantrill and his men ran, leaving only the devastated citizens and survivors of the Lawrence Massacre behind. This infamous act of terrorism made Quantrill a marked man, but also made him a hero among some of the local population, where he and his men were able to find shelter. As a result Union officials ordered the civilian evacuation of four Missouri counties along the Kansas border and burnt houses and farms there to the ground. Kansas was still bleeding.

Even though the town of Lawrence suffered a terrible tragedy only a few years after its founding, today it is as strong a community as ever. Much of the town's attention today is focused on the University of Kansas, but Lawrence has also embraced its history. The "battlefield" here was a very different sort—no prominent features of the landscape, no artillery emplacements, no lines of infantry—so touring it might appear to be a difficult prospect. Fortunately, though, the Lawrence Convention and Visitor's Bureau has created a driving tour of the town that touches on all the scenes of that terrible day. Although most of the homes and buildings that existed at the time of the massacre are long gone, the tour information is interesting and thorough enough that one finishes with a very good idea of what happened. The brochure is available at the Lawrence Visitor's Center, which also shows a video on Lawrence's early history, from its founding to Quantrill's raid. Lawrence is a college town, not to mention a pretty little city, so if you go on the weekends, expect the streets to be a little crowded, but don't let that deter you. *Lawrence Visitor's Center, 402 N. 2nd St., Lawrence, KS, 66044; 785-865-4499; www.visitlawrence.com. Open daily.*

Dry Wood Creek and Marmaton River—These two battles occurred years apart, but both happened in the same area, and both involved the Confederates' Major General Sterling Price. On September 2, 1861, as Price began to advance on Kansas City and Fort Scott, Kansas, he was met at Dry Wood Creek by a small Union force out of Fort Scott. The Union party, outnumbered ten to one, was eventually driven back north, but it was able to scout the size and location of Price's army and went back with enough information to protect both Fort Scott and Kansas City. Price, meanwhile, advanced to Lexington. Price's other large Missouri expedition, which led eventually to his defeat at Westport, brought him back through the area on October 25, 1864, as his shattered army was on a quick retreat to Arkansas. One of the Confederate wagon trains was stalled at the ford of the Marmaton River, and Brigadier General Jo Shelby sent his cavalry to protect it. Union forces eventually caught up, but Shelby's troops were able to hold them off until the wagons were safely across the river.

Although the two battle sites are several miles apart, there is one location, in the parking lot of a truck stop, where interpretive signs have been placed for both battles. The two signs explain the battles in great detail. In addition, in nearby Nevada, Missouri, is the Bushwhacker Museum, where more can be learned not only about the battles, but about the war in Missouri in general. Note that the museum is open only seasonally. *Interpretive signs, parking lot of Emery's Truck Stop, intersection of US 54 and old US 54, Deerfield, MO, 64741; Bushwhacker Museum, 212 W. Walnut St., Nevada, MO, 64772; 417-667-9602; www.bushwhacker.org. Signs accessible daily. Museum open Tue.–Sat., Apr.–Mar.*

Carthage—After the Missouri State Guard and Governor Claiborne Jackson were chased from Boonville, Major General Sterling Price took his state guard toward the southwest corner of Missouri, while Jackson gathered his own men, planning to join with Price. General Nathaniel Lyon sent Federal troops after them under Colonel Franz Sigel, and on July 5, 1861, Sigel's and Jackson's armies met north of the city of Carthage, Missouri. In a 10-mile running battle, the Union force was pressed through the city, eventually withdrawing to Springfield.

The Battle of Carthage State Historic Site is not large and covers only a very small portion of this running battlefield, but it is enough to explain this battle and the situation in Missouri in the early part of the war. There is a well-designed interpretive kiosk, along with some picnic and other park facilities. If you're exploring some of the other battles in the area, you're likely to pass through Carthage, so be sure to pay a visit. *Battle of Carthage State Historic Site, intersection of S. River St. and E. Chestnut St., Carthage, MO, 64836; 417-682-2279; www.mostateparks.com/carthage.htm. Open daily.*

Baxter Springs—Captain William Quantrill and his Confederate Partisan Rangers, who had committed the atrocities at Lawrence, Kansas, only a few weeks earlier, targeted a Federal supply post at Baxter Springs, Kansas, on October 6, 1863. As half of

A lone soldier watches over his comrades at Baxter Springs Cemetery.

Quantrill's men attacked the post, Major James Blunt, moving through the area with 100 Federals, approached Baxter Springs. The other half of Quantrill's men, wearing Union uniforms, went to attack Blunt's party. Because of the uniforms, Blunt thought that they were Union troops from the post coming to meet him. By the time the truth was discovered, another massacre was under way. Although many of Blunt's men tried to surrender, 70 of them were killed in cold blood. Blunt and a few others who were on horseback managed to escape.

A driving tour has been created for the battle of Baxter Springs. A recently redone brochure can be picked up at the Baxter Springs Heritage Center. It is very good, and the story behind the event is well told. Located in town and part of the tour is Fort Blair Park, around which much of the massacre took place. A memorial and several interpretive signs here explain what happened that day. Finally, near the end of the tour, in the Baxter Springs Cemetery just west of town, is an impressive monument to those killed in the masscre. *Driving tour—Battle of Baxter Springs, Baxter Springs*

Heritage Center, 740 East Ave., Baxter Springs, KS, 66713; 620-856-2385; www.baxter springs.us. Sites accessible daily.

Old Fort Wayne—Attempting to strengthen their hold on southern Missouri, the Union sent forces to chase the Confederates out of the area, pursuing them all the way to the Indian territories. Early on October 22, 1862, Brigadier General James Blunt attacked a group of mostly Native American Confederate regiments, led by Colonels Douglas Cooper and Stand Watie, on Beattie's Prairie, near Old Fort Wayne and just west of the Arkansas state line. The Confederates put up some resistance, then retreated south of the Arkansas River. They were forced to leave behind much of their supplies, including artillery, and suffered 150 casualties to the Federals' 14.

There is a historical marker at the site of Old Fort Wayne, although it was recently found to be missing. The site around the marker is farmland and privately owned and should be respected. *Memorial marker, intersection of OK 20 and S-700, Jay, OK, 74346. Site accessible daily.*

Cabin Creek—Just south of the supply depot at Baxter Springs, Kansas, but well into the Indian territories was Fort Gibson. The fort had become a center of supply, as well as a haven, for Unionist Indians who were waiting to return to their homes in the territories. Between Baxter Springs and the fort lay a small fortified ford of Cabin Creek. On July 1, 1863, as a wagon train was passing through the area on its way to supply Fort Gibson, 2,000 Confederates commanded by Colonel Stand Watie attacked the train. The fighting was fierce and lasted for two days, but the Confederates were outnumbered and were not able to stop the train, which made its way safely to Fort Gibson.

The Cabin Creek battlefield site, maintained by the Friends of Cabin Creek Battlefield, is an inviting, quiet place to visit, although remote. Interestingly, the interpretation and markers focus on a later action that happened here, when Watie's force *was* able to capture a large wagon train. But the location is still the same, and some memorials recognize the earlier action. The locals like to make sure that the battlefield is kept in good order, so don't be surprised if during your visit one of the neighbors comes by to say hello (and just to check up on the battlefield). But they are friendly and will be happy to pass some time with you. *Cabin Creek Battlefield, intersection of E0366 and N4420, Adair, OK, 74330; 918-256-4406. Open daily.*

Chustenahlah—Colonel Douglas Cooper, who had been leading a large band of Confederates against the Unionist Indians under Cherokee chief Opothleyahola, was losing men. Many of the Indians of the tribes of the Oklahoma territories who had initially agreed to fight for the Confederacy were now changing their minds, joining bands of Unionist Indians as they moved toward Kansas and peace. His force depleting rapidly, Cooper called for and received 1,400 cavalrymen as reinforcements, and on December 26, 1861, he attacked Opothleyahola's followers in their camp. The

Unionists were routed, suffering 211 casualties to the Confederates' 40. In addition, in the abandonment of their camp, the Indians had lost much of their winter stores. Union assistance was slow to respond, and many of the initially Unionist Indians died on the prairie waiting for help.

A stone monument briefly describing the action and memorializing those who fought here has recently been placed along a roadside near the Chustenahlah battle site by the Oklahoma Historical Society. *Memorial marker, 0.5 mile west of intersection of OK 20 and N. 52nd West Ave., Skiatook, OK, 74070. Site accessible daily.*

Chusto-Talasah—On December 9, 1861, Cherokee chief Opothleyahola's band of Unionist Indians from the tribes of the Oklahoma territories was attacked in camp by a combined force of white and Native American Confederate units. Unlike the camp at Round Mountain, which was difficult to defend, this site had been well chosen, and after a fight lasting several hours, Opothleyahola's Indians were able to drive off the Confederates.

An Oklahoma Historical Society monument has been placed near the Chusto-Talasah battlefield. The monument, accessible by car, is located within a somewhat large public park that has full picnic facilities. *Memorial marker, Nick Taylor Park, intersection of N. Delaware Ave. and E. 96th St. North, Sperry, OK, 74073. Site accessible daily.*

Round Mountain—The situation in the Oklahoma Indian territories was tense, even before the Civil War. The tribes referred to as the Five Civilized Tribes—Cherokee, Creek, Choctaw, Seminole, and Chickasaw—disagreed over the various treaties they had all signed that sent them to the reservations, and when the war broke out, the disagreements turned to open hostility. Many of the tribes were abolitionist and supported the Union; others were hostile to the U.S. government, or supported slavery, and decided to fight with the Confederacy if the territories were invaded. Some 3,500 Unionist Indians, under the leadership of Cherokee chief Opothleyahola, headed north toward Kansas, seeking peace and protection. But on November 19, 1861, as they camped during their move north, they were attacked by several of the Confederate regiments raised by the tribes, along with a large number of Texas cavalry. After a short fight the Unionist Indians set a prairie fire and escaped back to their camp, then withdrew during the night.

When referring to Civil War battlefields, the term "lost" is usually used when the battlefield has lost its integrity or is unrecognizable. However, the battlefield at Round Mountain is truly lost—nobody is certain where the actual battle took place. Nevertheless, there is a very fine stone monument dedicated to the battle, which presumably took place somewhere nearby. If it's not at the exact site of the battlefield, you can well imagine what the scene must have looked like; it is placed on a knoll from where you can see all the terrain for miles. *Memorial marker, 0.3 mile west of intersection of OK 18 and McElroy Rd., Yale, OK, 74085. Site accessible daily.*

Middle Boggy Depot—By 1864 the Union had established control over most of the Indian territories. In February of that year, a Federal expedition attempted to consolidate that control, heading for the Texas border to try to force several of the pro-Confederate tribes to rejoin the Union. On February 13, 1864, part of this expedition ran into a band of Confederates, consisting largely of Native American regiments, near Middle Boggy in southern Oklahoma. The Confederates were outnumbered and routed, suffering 47 casualties. This action, as well as the destructive expedition itself, did little to persuade the pro-Confederate tribes to rejoin the Unionists.

Adjacent to the battlefield of Middle Boggy Depot is the Confederate Memorial Museum and Cemetery. The museum contains exhibits on the battle and the war in this part of the country, and it and the grounds are well taken care of. The site includes a small cemetery with Confederate graves from the battle, plus several interpretive signs and memorial markers. This quiet, out-of-the-way roadside park has full facilities. *Confederate Memorial Museum and Cemetery, 0.6 mile east of intersection of US 69 North and US 75, Atoka, OK, 74525; 580-889-7192. Open Mon.–Fri.*

Devil's Backbone—Following the Union victory at Honey Springs, Major General James Blunt was able to penetrate deeper into the Indian territories and on September 1, 1863, occupied Fort Smith, Arkansas, a commanding position on the Arkansas River. Blunt sent Federal cavalry south to catch the retreating Confederates, and a three-hour fight erupted at a ridge known as the Devil's Backbone. Casualties were low on both sides, but the Confederates were forced to continue their retreat southward.

A small monument, a boulder with a plaque on it, is located at the ridge where the battle took place. It is only a short drive south of Fort Smith, and although what's left of the battlefield is private property, Devil's Backbone is still easily discernible. *Memorial marker, intersection of US 71 South and Hendrix Rd., Greenwood, AR, 72936. Site accessible daily.*

Cane Hill—After pushing Confederate forces out of the southwest Missouri region and into the Indian territories, ending with the rout at Old Fort Wayne, Brigadier General James Blunt began to move his men back to Springfield, Missouri. Major General Thomas Hindman, in an attempt to prevent this, sent Confederate cavalry under Brigadier General John Marmaduke to get in his way. On November 28, 1862, in the mountainous region of northwest Arkansas, Blunt's 5,000 soldiers surprised the Confederates at Cane Hill, and a running fight ensued. The Confederate cavalry was quickly pushed through the Cane Hill area, with Colonel Jo Shelby commanding the rear guard and protecting the larger force of 2,000. Blunt remained in Cane Hill, setting up the battle at Prairie Grove 10 days later.

A historical highway marker has been erected just across from the post office in the tiny present-day town of Canehill. This is a blink-and-you'll-miss-it town, but there was a good deal of action here. *Historical highway marker—Arkansas Civil War*

Centennial Commission (the Battle of Cane Hill), intersection of AR 45 and CR-4764, Canehill, AR, 72717. Site accessible daily.

Newtonia—Two battles, both centered on the Ritchey Mansion property, passed through the small town of Stark City, Missouri, during the Civil War. The first occurred on September 30, 1862, when a small Union force attacked an only slightly larger Confederate force holding the town. However, both Confederate and Union reinforcements soon arrived, and a long battle followed. Eventually the Confederates launched an all-out assault, breaking the Union left and sending them on the retreat to the north; the Federals suffered 245 casualties to the Confederates' 78. The second battle of Newtonia was the last gasp of Major General Sterling Price's army after his disastrous raid into Missouri. On October 28, 1864, as Price stopped what was left of his command to forage for food, 1,000 Union cavalry approached the camp from the north. Price quickly put his men on the retreat, leaving Brigadier General Jo Shelby to hold the Federals off. Although the Union received reinforcements during the day, Shelby was able to hold his position until darkness fell, when he caught up with Price's retreating army. Shelby's action was effective, but it could not prevent Price's army from disintegrating as it retreated, eventually all the way to Texas.

Though the battlefield site is still under development, Ritchey Mansion is available for tours by appointment. The site recently suffered some tornado damage, but dedicated local volunteers were quick to patch up the home and get back to the restoration of the battlefield. Interpretive signs are also accessible at the mansion. Further development is being planned for the site, which now covers several acres. *Ritchey Mansion and Battlefield, 520 Mill St., Stark City, MO, 64866; 417-592-0931. Interpretive signs accessible daily; mansion tours and battle interpretation available by appointment.*

Springfield and Zagonyi's Charge—As the largest city in the area of the fighting between the Union forces and the Missouri State Guard, Springfield, Missouri, with its position as a rail center, was an objective for both armies from the beginning of the war. It was the site of several battles, in addition to the major engagement at Wilson's Creek. On October 25, 1861, as a large Union army was moving north of Springfield, a smaller Confederate force attempted to surprise the Federals. Major Charles Zagonyi, commanding 5,000 Union cavalry troops, discovered the ambush and drove the Confederates off. In addition, he was able to enter Springfield, held by the Missouri State Guard at the time, and rescue a number of Union prisoners. The Union army was able to take control of the city several days later. Another battle occurred on January 8, 1863, when Brigadier General John Marmaduke, leading a large Confederate raid into Missouri, headed into Springfield. Although outnumbered, the Union force was able to supplement its ranks with local citizens, and after burning many of the town's homes in order to clear the field of fire in front of their earthworks, the Federals were able to keep the Confederates out of the city.

The site of the "first" battle of Springfield, Zagonyi's charge, is not preserved, but a monument to the action is located on the front lawn of a local business. Though behind a chain-link fence and a little hard to spot, the monument is easily viewable, and the street it is on, Mount Vernon Avenue, is essentially the route of the famous charge. The "second" battle of Springfield encompassed much more of the city itself, and although most of the buildings of the time have disappeared, the natural features of the landscape remain. The Springfield-Greene County Historical Society has created an excellent driving tour of the sites of this battle, with a well-written brochure and interpretive signs along the route. (Somewhat confusingly, the major battle of Wilson's Creek, which occurred several months before the "first" Springfield battle of Zagonyi's charge, is also often referred to as the battle of Springfield, especially on many Confederate battle flags.) Further information on all these actions, along with the tour brochure, can be found at both Wilson's Creek National Battlefield and the History Museum for Springfield-Greene County. *University Club historical marker No. 17— Zagonyi's Charge (First Springfield), 1724 Mount Vernon Ave.; History Museum for Springfield-Greene County, 830 Boonville Ave., Springfield, MO, 65802; 417-864-1976. Sites accessible daily; museum open Tue.–Sat.*

Clark's Mill—A small Union force stationed at Clark's Mill, near the old town of Vera Cruz, ventured out to pick a fight with a Confederate cavalry force of 1,750 men. On November 7, 1862, the Federals fought with and pushed back elements of the cavalry but then withdrew into the blockhouse at Clark's Mill, where they were surrounded by the rest of the Confederate cavalry. Although they put up a fight, they were eventually forced to surrender.

Nothing remains of the battle site or the mill today except for the old mill pond. It is located at a public fishing access site operated by the Missouri Conservation Department. There are no markers or memorials in any of the nearby towns, and the old town of Vera Cruz, although it can still be found on the map, really no longer exists. *Vera Cruz Public Fishing Access, Missouri Conservation Department, on MO AB, 2.2 miles east of intersection of MO AB and CR AB-217, Vera Cruz, MO, 65608. Site accessible daily.*

Hartville—The battle of Hartville, Missouri, began on January 9, 1863, when a Confederate cavalry brigade captured the small Union garrison posted in the town. The Confederate cavalry, knowing that Colonel Samuel Merrill was en route with 700 Federals, combined with Brigadier General John Marmaduke, who had just left a failed attempt to capture Springfield, Missouri. On January 11 the now combined Confederate force attacked Merrill, who was able to withdraw into the defenses at Hartville and drive off the Confederates.

Several reminders of the battle can still be seen in Hartville, although there is no recognizable battlefield. A monument to the Confederate soldiers who died in the battle was recently erected in the Steele Memorial Cemetery by the Sons of Confederate Veterans and the Wright County Historical Society, along with an interpretive sign and kiosk. A historical marker describing the history of Wright County, including the battle, stands in front of the county library at the center of town. Just across the corner from the library is the Wright County Historical Society Museum, where more information about the battle can be found. *Memorial marker, Steele Memorial Cemetery, intersection of S. Main Ave. and W. South St.; historical highway marker—State Historical Society of Missouri and State Highway Commission (Wright County), 125 Court Square; Wright County Historical Society Museum, 101 E. Rolla St., Hartville, MO, 65667; 417-741-6265. Sites accessible daily; museum open Wed.–Fri.*

Boonville—For several months after fighting broke out in the East, negotiations continued in Missouri regarding the creation of Union and Confederate fighting units. The governor of Missouri, Claiborne Fox Jackson, had formed Confederate units and developed a training camp for them, putting them under the command of General Sterling Price and dubbing them the Missouri State Guard. Meanwhile, Union forces under the command of Brigadier General Nathaniel Lyon took control of the arsenal in St. Louis and disarmed one of Jackson's camps, causing a bloody riot in the streets of St. Louis. Price, Jackson, and Lyon met for a final time to try to work out their differences, but the conference was unsuccessful. Upon leaving the conference, Lyon immediately occupied the capital at Springfield, and Jackson moved the state's operations to Boonville. On June 17, 1861, Lyon led 1,700 men into Boonville and drove off a small Missouri State Guard force there. This was the first true battle of the Civil War on Missouri soil. Although the fight was relatively small, there were two significant results. First, the Federals now had a strong grip on the Missouri River, a major artery through the state. Second, Jackson and Price left for southwest Missouri, where they prepared an army for battle, eventually leading to the conflict at Wilson's Creek.

A memorial marker on the courthouse lawn in Boonville commemorates this first battle in Missouri. Some information on the battle can also be found at the Historic Jail Museum, which displays much of Boonville's rich history. *Memorial marker, Cooper County Courthouse, 200 Main St.; Historic Jail Museum, 614 E. Morgan St., Boonville, MO, 65233; 660-882-7977; www.friendsofhistoricboonville.org. Memorial accessible daily, museum open Mon.–Fri.; admission charged.*

Glasgow—Major General Sterling Price, after his defeat at Pilot Knob, abandoned his plans for capturing St. Louis and installing a Confederate government in Jefferson City. He instead moved westward across the state toward Kansas City. At Glasgow, Missouri, on October 15, 1864, part of the Confederate force attacked the Union garrison in the town. Although the Federals were able to fall back into their earthworks and supplement their force with some of the local residents, they were eventually forced to surrender. Part of the Confederates' spoils was the contents of a full Union supply boat docked alongside the town.

At the former location of the pier on the Missouri River are interpretive signs that describe not only the battle of Glasgow, but also the importance of the river and the town. Several memorials have also been erected in this area. An additional memorial in front of a Catholic church in town marks the end of the Union battle line; among the town's honored citizens whose names are engraved on the monument are Captain Samuel Steinmetz and Aaron Steinmetz, the leader of the town militia and his brother, both of whom were killed in the battle. *Interpretive signs, intersection of Market St. and Water St.; memorial marker, intersection of 3rd St. and Howard St., Glasgow, MO, 65254; 660-338-2377. Sites accessible daily.*

Mount Zion Church—Union forces under Brigadier General Benjamin Prentiss, operating near Hallsville, Missouri, discovered the presence of a band of Missouri State Guard in the area. On December 28, 1861, the Federals attacked the guardsmen, whose main force was established around Mount Zion Church. The very short battle ended with the guard fleeing the field, leaving behind their supplies and their dead and wounded, their casualties totaling 210.

Mount Zion Church is still at its original location, although the present church building postdates the war. In the small church's cemetery is a monument recently erected by the Sons of Confederate Veterans. The cemetery is also the final resting place of seven Confederate soldiers who died during the battle, their graves laid neatly in a row. Mount Zion is still an active church, so be sure to show the respect that any place of worship is due, especially if you visit on a Sunday morning. *Mount Zion Church, intersection of E. Mount Zion Church Rd. and N. Hartley Rd., Hallsville, MO, 65255. Site accessible daily.*

Roan's Tan Yard—The Missouri State Guard had established a training and recruiting base at a location known as Roan's Tan Yard. On January 8, 1862, Federal cavalry forces attacked and destroyed the camp, so that it could not be used again. Following the battles at Mount Zion Church and Roan's Tan Yard, Confederate recruiting in central Missouri slowed to a crawl.

The actual site where the battle of Roan's Tan Yard was fought is near the town of Yates, Missouri, and is on private property; no markers or monuments commemorate the event. The Huntsville Historical Museum, however, is only a short drive away. The museum contains a diorama of the battle, as well as a description and several resources that can help a tourist learn what happened there. The locals here are very engaged in the history of the Civil War in their state and are committed to seeing it commemorated in a way they think fitting, and it is evident at the museum. *Huntsville Historical Museum, 107 N. Main St., Huntsville, MO, 65259; 660-277-3111. Open weekends Apr.–Oct. and by appointment.*

Kirksville—The war in Missouri saw many guerrilla bands of Confederates conducting raids and ambushes throughout the countryside. The leader of one of these bands was Colonel Joseph Porter, who in August of 1862 was on the run with 2,500 men. Finally, on August 6, 1862, Union forces caught Porter's force at Kirksville, in northern Missouri. After a brief fight throughout the town, Porter's command was driven out and, over the next several days, finally defeated.

A historical highway marker stands on the courthouse lawn, which was the center of the fighting. Information about the battle is also available at the Adair County Historical Society Museum (note the limited hours of operation before you go); the historical society has also created a brochure that describes the battle and plans for future development. *Historical highway marker—Adair County Historical Society (Battle of Kirksville), intersection of W. Washington and S. Franklin Sts.; Adair County Historical Society Museum, 211 S. Elson St., Kirksville, MO, 63501; 660-665-6502; www.adrcohs.org. Marker accessible daily; museum open Wed.–Fri.*

» WHERE TO STAY IN THE FAR WESTERN THEATER

Depending on your tastes, lodging along your tour may be hard to come by. That's not to say there aren't plenty of places to stay, because there are. But much of the area you'll be traveling through is rural, and even the larger towns along the way may have only a motel or two.

Of course, Kansas City, Missouri, and nearby Lawrence, Kansas, have plenty of options for lodging, including some nice bed-and-breakfasts, most of which postdate the Civil War. Once you get outside that area, however, your options become limited. There are a few resort casinos in northeastern Oklahoma that provide excellent accommodations. The next stop along the way with any considerable concentration of hotels and restaurants is Fort Smith, Arkansas, which also has a wealth of history and a great downtown. Finally, as you come back up through northwest Arkansas, you won't be far from the entertainment and resort town of Branson, Missouri, only a short drive off your tour.

2

The Middle Mississippi Valley: From Cairo to Memphis

OVERVIEW

At the outset of the Civil War, General Winfield Scott, commander of all Union forces, produced a grand strategy for bringing the rebellious states to submission. Although Scott's involvement with the war would not last long (he was essentially pushed out by General George McClellan), his plan was followed through, and it proved successful. It was called the Anaconda Plan, because it would ultimately divide the Confederacy into pieces and "constrict" each of those pieces until they could no longer function. The plan consisted of two parts. The first part was to gain control of the Mississippi River from source to mouth, cutting the Confederacy in half. The second part was to blockade the coasts and prevent the Confederacy from importing or exporting goods. The South thus would be starved of food and supplies, and eventually its will to make war would be broken; there would be little need for aggressive conflict. Against Scott's advice, however, Union armies made advances upon the enemy and attacked Confederate forces in the field. Nevertheless, the Anaconda Plan played a vital role in defeating the Confederacy. This chapter, along with the next, is devoted to part one of the Anaconda Plan—the fight for control of the Mississippi River.

Gaining control of the Mississippi was critical to keeping open supply and communication lines to Union armies making their way south. The Federals began at Cairo, Illinois, and worked their way south down the river and up its tributaries, win-

The Wizard of the Saddle, Nathan Bedford Forrest, atop his final resting place in Memphis.

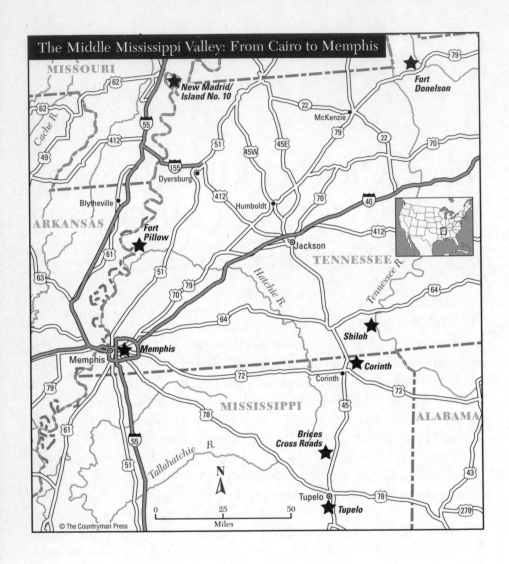

The Middle Mississippi Valley: From Cairo to Memphis

ning major battles at New Madrid in Missouri, Forts Henry and Donelson in Tennessee, and other river strongholds, eventually opening the Mississippi River all the way to Memphis. By opening the Mississippi (as well as the Cumberland and Tennessee Rivers) and preventing their use by the Confederacy, the Northern armies not only were able to quickly transport supplies and troops, but made any northward excursions by Confederate armies almost impossible. The capture of the rivers ultimately made the Confederate positions at Nashville, Memphis, Corinth, and other major ports and railroad centers untenable. Once the rivers fell, those cities were quickly abandoned.

One great battle, though, would have to be fought. The Confederacy knew the importance of the rivers and railroads as well, and needed to make a stand. That stand came at Shiloh, one of the earliest of the war's terrible battles. The news from the Shiloh battlefield shocked the world, sobering the country into the realization that this would be a very bloody war. Although the Union's Ulysses S. Grant, who was quickly building a reputation as a skilled general, almost lost that reputation at Shiloh, the Union victory there led to the capture of the vital railroad center at Corinth, Mississippi.

Control of the upper portion of the river, however, did not prevent Confederate raiding parties from heading north to disrupt Union supply lines. The undisputed champion of this activity was the controversial and colorful general Nathan Bedford Forrest. The "Wizard of the Saddle" conducted numerous excursions northward to disrupt Union efforts all over the western theater. His raids were quick and daring and caused much anxiety in the Union ranks. General William T. Sherman, whose operations to capture Atlanta were constantly disrupted by Forrest, called him "the very devil" and exclaimed that there would be no peace in this part of the country "until that man is dead."

This chapter will focus on the fight to capture the upper part of the Mississippi River in the South—from the Missouri boot heel south to Memphis, Tennessee.

» PEOPLE TO KNOW

Nathan Bedford Forrest—Although Forrest will appear in other chapters of this book, this one is clearly his. We will follow his exploits through Mississippi, Tennessee, and Kentucky. Forrest had little education but amassed a fortune through real estate, cotton, and slaves. He raised and financed his own cavalry battalion, and his amazing successes and daring raids made him celebrated in the South and loathed in the North.

Nathan Bedford Forrest stirs up as much as passion as any figure of the Civil War. He was undoubtedly a cavalry genius (even though he had no formal military training), his bravery, daring, and dedication to duty are the stuff of legend, and he is still revered by many today, with parks and statues in his honor all over the South. He was also a man who made a good deal of his fortune via the slave trade, who was in command during the still-debated "massacre" of black troops at Fort Pillow, and who went on to form what would eventually become the Ku Klux Klan. Whatever it may be that stirs continuing interest about this man, his life and legacy are worth exploring. **Albert Sidney Johnston**—At the outset of the Civil War there was one military leader for the Confederacy who, in the hearts and minds of his countrymen, stood head and shoulders above the rest. His name was not Lee. It was Albert Sidney Johnston.

Johnston had graduated high in his class at West Point and fought bravely for the United States Army, first in the Black Hawk War and then under General Zachary Taylor in the Mexican War. In between he settled in the Republic of Texas, serving as the fledgling nation's secretary of war. When the Civil War broke out, Johnston was confronted with the same decision that all military commanders from the South faced: to fight for the Union or for their state. Like most other Southerners, Johnston chose his state and was given command by the Confederacy of virtually the entire western theater. Within a year of his arrival, he was killed at the battle of Shiloh after being shot in the leg. The Confederacy's high hopes for Albert Sidney Johnston were dashed in one of his first major battles of the war.

Ulysses S. Grant—It was in the West that Colonel Ulysses Simpson Grant started to make a name for himself—his first command in battle at Belmont, Missouri; his first major victory at Fort Donelson; and his ultimate, but debated, success at Shiloh. This is where the story of U. S. Grant and the Civil War begin.

Grant was a virtual unknown at the outset of the war. Although he was a West Point graduate and had fought bravely in the Mexican War, Grant bounced around the country after that conflict, fighting loneliness and alcohol, until he finally resigned from the army in 1854. After trying various occupations without much success, Grant was given a commission soon after the war started and within months was promoted to brigadier general. In both victory and defeat, Grant demonstrated early that he was willing to fight. This tenacity was a virtue that seemed to be lacking in many Northern generals, and it made Grant stick out like a sore thumb. Even after the devastation at Shiloh, when many were calling for Grant's resignation, Abraham Lincoln felt compelled to defend him, saying, "I can't spare this man—he fights." The legendary military career of Ulysses S. Grant begins here in the Mississippi Valley.

» THINGS TO KNOW

This trip is designed as a circle tour—you will begin and end in Memphis, Tennessee. You will cover a lot of ground in between, and because many of the destinations are somewhat isolated, the best routes to get from place to place are usually through the backcountry; you probably won't spend too much time on or around the interstates. You might want to plan ahead at least a little and make your best guesses as to where you're going to stop for the night, because in some cases your hotel choices may be scarce.

Also, because some of these sites are isolated and may not get steady visitors all year, if the site is staffed, take the trouble to phone ahead and make sure someone will be there. Depending on the time of year, the weather, what's going on in town that day, or other factors you cannot possibly anticipate, the dedicated volunteers who staff these sites might close up shop early on some days, or not show up at all. So if there's a museum or visitor's center you must see, phone ahead.

THE TRIP

This trip starts and ends in Memphis. Only two smaller battles took place here, but it is by far the easiest point of your tour to get to. The rest of the trip makes a wide circle that will have you cutting through at least three states (and maybe even five or six, if you tend to wander). It's a big, long circle that covers a lot of ground, but you will also see the places that did much to seal the fate of the Confederacy early in the war.

I suggest heading north from Memphis and starting at Fort Pillow, then continuing clockwise—but going in either direction will work just fine. Either way, plan on covering a lot of backcountry, allowing travel time between sites, and thinking ahead at least a couple of hours on where to stay for the night.

» THE CAN'T-MISS SITES

Memphis

Two battles occurred in Memphis, both Union victories. Although both of them were small in terms of casualties, both are remembered today—one for its military significance, the other for a great escape.

In 1862 the Union had already won significant victories upriver at New Madrid and at Fort Pillow, and Memphis was the next stop on the Mississippi. Although it was a vital river port and one of the Confederacy's major cities, its position became practically indefensible with ironclad Union gunboats approaching. Memphis, along with the major railroad junction at Corinth, Mississippi, was evacuated, and the Confederates left only a token river defense to allow for the military evacuation.

On the morning of June 6, 1862, the Union fleet attacked, and within two hours, seven of the much-inferior Confederate navy's eight river rams had been sunk. The lone casualty on the Union side was Colonel Charles Ellet—the engineer who had designed the Union's rams, which had done so much to ensure previous Union successes on the rivers. His son, Charles Ellet Jr., accepted the surrender of the city from its mayor and raised the United States flag over the courthouse. Memphis was officially in Union hands, and it would remain so for the duration of the war.

The Union possession of Memphis, however, did not prevent the Confederacy from trying to occasionally shake things up. The most celebrated of these counterstrokes came at the hands of the man who had a greater reputation for causing mis-

Mud Island and the Mississippi River from the Confederate battery position at Memphis, Tennessee.

chief than any other leader in the Confederate army. Early in the morning on August 21, 1864, General Nathan Bedford Forrest raided the city, much to the surprise of the Union forces—particularly the three Union generals stationed there, who were reportedly forced to flee in their nightshirts to avoid capture. Forrest spent only two hours in the city before he withdrew, and although two of the objectives of his raid—the capture of the Union generals and the freeing of Confederate prisoners—were not met, he was able to set off enough alarms on the Union side that Federal armies who were operating in northern Mississippi were recalled to Memphis, giving him greater freedom to wreak havoc in the territory. In later years, however, it was the image of General Cadwallader Washburn running in his nightshirt down an alley (later to bear his name) that was most recalled.

Although the actions were small, Memphis was and is still one of the great cities of the South, and there is much to see here related to the Civil War.

SITE DETAILS

Confederate Park—Located along the Mississippi River and adjacent to the former courthouse, this park is on the site of the land batteries engaged during the first battle of Memphis. Along with interpretive signs about the battle, and a wonderful view of the river, there is a statue of Jefferson Davis. *Confederate Park, intersection of Jefferson Ave. and N. Riverside Dr., Memphis, TN, 38103; open daily.*

Mud Island River Park and Mississippi River Museum—This museum has interpretive material on both Memphis battles, along with a life-size recreation of a Union ironclad gunboat. *Mud Island River Park and Mississippi River Museum, 125 N. Front St., Memphis, TN, 38103; 1-800-507-6507; www.mudisland.com. Open Apr.–Oct., closed Mon.; admission charged.*

General Washburn's escape alley—This is the alley that General Cadwallader C. Washburn ran through, allegedly still in his nightshirt, to escape Forrest's men. (Washburn later went on to co-found what would become the General Mills Company.) *General Washburn's Escape Alley, intersection of Sam Phillips Ave. and S. Orleans St., Memphis, TN, 38103. Open daily.*

Nathan Bedford Forrest Park—This city park is the final resting place of General Nathan Bedford Forrest and his wife, Mary. Atop the grave is a large, imposing statue of Forrest on horseback. *Nathan Bedford Forrest Park, intersection of Union Ave. and S. Manassas St., Memphis, TN, 38103. Open daily.*

Forrest's Artillery historical highway marker—This marker, southeast of downtown, marks Forrest's artillery positions during his 1864 raid. *Historical highway marker 4E-39—Tennessee Historical Commission (Forrest's Artillery Positions), intersection of Mississippi Blvd. and E. Trigg Ave., Memphis, TN, 38106. Sign accessible daily.*

Fort Pillow

Strategically, the battle at Fort Pillow in April 1864 was not particularly significant. Nathan Bedford Forrest raided a supply point on the Mississippi River, causing damage, disrupting operations, and moving on. However, in the grand scheme of the Civil War, including basic questions like why the war was fought, and how strongly Americans felt about the issues at stake, the battle here, perhaps as much as any event in the war, is one that forces you to consider all sides of the equation.

Forrest, after raiding Paducah, Kentucky, assaulted Fort Pillow on April 12, 1864; his 1,500 Confederates faced approximately 600 Union troops, half of them U.S. Colored Troops. Before the assault, Confederate sharpshooters were placed to cover the fort, and the attack began. After some time it was obvious that the Union soldiers were outnumbered, and Forrest asked for surrender. Major William Bradford, placed in command after the ranking officer was killed, refused, and the Confederates assaulted the fort. Forrest, uncharacteristically, did not lead the assault but stayed behind the main thrust. The results were nothing short of a disaster for the Union, with 277 men killed. This much is known.

What happened inside the fort after the initial assault, however, is still somewhat in question. Some 64 percent of the black soldiers were killed, along with 32 percent of the white soldiers. There were numerous reports of black soldiers trying to surrender, only to be murdered. After the details of the Fort Pillow Massacre became public, some Confederate officers claimed that although individual Union soldiers were surrendering, no efforts were made to lower the fort's U.S. flag, which may have confused the Confederates as they rushed over the parapet in the heat of battle. Although there are accounts on both sides that substantiate this, no other battle of the war—all of which contained some degree of confusion—resulted in the kind of carnage seen at Fort Pillow. And other reports from Confederate soldiers stated that they were ordered to give the black soldiers no quarter. Forrest wrote shortly after the battle that he hoped the results of the fight would show that Negro soldiers could not match white soldiers in combat. Regardless of the conflicting reports, the battle at Fort Pillow was labeled a massacre, and it galvanized the resolve of many in the North who believed that the war was just.

The high earthen walls of Fort Pillow in Tennessee.

SITE DETAILS

Fort Pillow State Park—The restored original fort, including many of the surrounding earthworks, is in excellent shape and does a wonderful job of teaching why the site was so important, as well as how the battle played out in 1864. There is a small museum at the visitor's center that, while helpful, seems to gloss over the tragedy that took place here. The hiking trails through the park are extensive and lead to every conceivable point of interest, as well as through beautiful forest and views of the Mississippi River. The interpretation here leaves something to be desired, so I advise reading up on the battle before you visit. But do visit. Even though Fort Pillow is off the beaten path, the excellent preservation of the battlefield, as well as the questions raised by considering the event, makes it worth the trip. *Fort Pillow State Park, 3122 Park Rd., Henning, TN, 38041; 901-738-5581; state.tn.us/environment/ parks/fortpillow. Open daily.*

Just as one can debate today whether John Brown's actions at Harpers Ferry were justified, one can also look back on Fort Pillow and try to get into the minds of the men who were there, consider the beliefs of the time, and use history as a reminder what men are capable of. The reputation of Nathan Bedford Forrest, revered by many, is forever tarnished by this event. Are we able to look back so far into the past, truly understand, and fairly judge? We can condemn the institution of slavery, but can we condemn the men who fought for what they believed was a just cause 150 years ago, no matter which side they fought on? The events at Fort Pillow compel one to thoroughly consider the vast complexities of the American Civil War, and how what happened so long ago still shapes our national psyche.

New Madrid / Island No. 10

New Madrid, Missouri, lies on the apex of a long horseshoe bend in the Mississippi River near the Kentucky-Tennessee state line. From the town you can see for miles down the two bends in the river, and any heavy artillery placed here had the opportunity to take a good long look at any boat that passed by. Slightly upriver of the town was a sizable sandbar known as Island No. 10, which also made for a good point for a commanding river defense. If these positions could be fortified and held, the Confederacy could keep the river closed to Union traffic to all points south.

In February 1862 Brigadier General John Pope approached New Madrid and on March 3 laid siege to the town, which was occupied by a moderate Confederate garrison manning the batteries there. After some resistance, Brigadier General John McCown evacuated New Madrid, escaping to Island No. 10, and the town was occupied by Pope on March 14.

Meanwhile, upriver, flag officer Andrew Foote, with six ironclad gunboats and an assortment of mortars, was bombarding Island No. 10 and making little headway. Pope was unable to get any support from his stalled navy; shells flew toward the island for three weeks, with virtually no effect. It was eventually decided that a canal would have to be dug through the peninsula created by the bend in the river, thus allowing boats to simply bypass the Confederate position. The canal was dug, and several shallow-bottom gunboats were able to pass and get downstream of the island, on the side of Pope's forces. Still, more help would be needed to take the island.

In the darkness of night and during a heavy storm on April 4, the ironclad Union gunboat *Carondolet* was able to pass the island, followed by the *Pittsburg* on April 6. Pope now had the firepower he needed to take the island, and the Confederates knew it. On April 7 Pope's troops blocked the only escape route from Island No. 10, and the Confederates quickly surrendered, without putting up much of a fight.

Union casualties totaled only 51 men, while the Confederates surrendered 5,000. It was a major victory for the North, not only in terms of the low price paid in casualties, but because the Union now had access to the Lower Mississippi River. Only the comparatively minor garrisons at Fort Pillow and Memphis stood between them and

The long upstream view of the Mississippi River toward the former Island No. 10 at New Madrid, Missouri.

the Confederate stronghold at Vicksburg, Mississippi, and the Federals would now be able to move troops and supplies up and down the river quickly, to support virtually any military movement.

Fort Donelson and Dover

The Tennessee and Cumberland Rivers, reaching far into the states of Tennessee and Mississippi, were much coveted by the Union army. Like the Mississippi, control of these major waterways would enable the Union to move troops and supplies as quickly as any possible route. Conquering them, however, meant conquering two heavily fortified positions. This daunting task fell to one of the western theater's younger generals: the expendable Ulysses S. Grant.

Fort Donelson was one of two Confederate forts guarding river access to the heartland of Tennessee. Commanded by Brigadier General John Floyd, Donelson controlled the Cumberland River, while Fort Henry, 10 miles to the west, commanded the Tennessee River. Grant saw the importance of gaining these two great waterways and was finally given reluctant approval to attempt to capture the forts.

Fort Henry was taken on February 6, 1862, without much effort. It so happened that the fort was being inundated by the river anyway, and the garrison, after putting up a token defense, eventually made its way east to the much stronger position at Fort Donelson. Grant also moved his troops east, while sending flag officer Andrew Foote's gunboats back up the Tennessee to come around and approach Fort Donelson on the Cumberland, from the north. Taking the mighty defenses at the fort would require naval support.

On February 13 Grant's troops began to surround the fort, probing the Confederate lines and testing their strength. The fortifications at Donelson were formidable; two batteries of heavy naval guns overlooked the river, and the garrison was protected by 2 miles of heavy earthworks. In addition, after Fort Henry's garrison retreated to Donelson, the Confederates' strength exceeded 21,000 troops. Grant's force of 27,000, although considerable, was not nearly enough for a direct assault on a fortified position.

Foote's six gunboats, four of which were ironclads, began to shell the fort on February 14. At Fort Henry they had reduced the fort within hours; at Fort Donelson the result was very different. The flotilla received heavy damage when it came within range of the fort's guns. Foote was wounded during the assault, and the boats were quickly sent back downriver, barely making a dent in the Donelson defenses.

By this time the Federals had completely enveloped the works. On the morning of February 15 the Confederates pushed back the Union right, attempting a breakout, but Union reinforcements were able to stop the assault and push them back. It was the Confederates' last real chance to escape overland, and they returned to their original lines, knowing that the end was near. Over that night Floyd relinquished his command to Brigadier General Simon Buckner, third in command, and escaped upriver with 2,000 troops, not willing to surrender the fort personally. Colonel Nathan Bedford Forrest also broke out with his cavalry, and the remainder of the Confederate garrison was left high and dry.

When Buckner offered terms to surrender the fort, Grant responded with a message that would begin to cement his legend as a great military leader. His short note

The commanding Confederate artillery position on the Cumberland River, Fort Donelson National Battlefield.

read: "no terms except immediate and unconditional surrender can be accepted." Although Buckner was outraged by what he considered an unacceptably improper response from a fellow military officer, he had no choice but to comply. From that moment on, "Unconditional Surrender" Grant was recognized as a fighter, not just by the army, but by the public.

The Dover Hotel, Fort Donelson National Battlefield, where "Unconditional Surrender" Grant earned his famous nickname.

SITE DETAILS

Fort Donelson National Battlefield—Although many of the outer siege lines have been lost to time, much of the original earthworks still exist and are well preserved, including the Confederate river batteries that were critical in stopping the Union's ironclad gunboats. The visitor's center has an interpretive film and a small museum covering the assaults of both Fort Henry and Fort Donelson. A driving tour through the park showcases the most prominent features of the battlefield, as well as the Surrender House, or Dover Hotel, where Grant accepted the surrender of the fort. Many of the earthworks and other features present during the 1862 battle of Fort Donelson were also used during the 1863 battle of Dover; information on this battle can be found at the visitor's center. *Fort Donelson National Battlefield, intersection of US 79 and Fort Donelson Park Rd., Dover, TN, 37058; 931-232-5348; www.nps.gov/fodo. Open daily.*

In addition to the accolades received by Grant, the blow to the Confederate cause resulting from the fall of Fort Donelson was significant. The Union, almost 10 months into the Civil War, finally had its first major victory. Upstream, the Confederates were forced to evacuate the city of Nashville, the first Confederate capital to fall. Finally, the Union now controlled the Tennessee and Cumberland Rivers, opening middle Tennessee to Union shipping all the way to Alabama.

Dover, Tennessee, and nearby Fort Donelson were also the objectives of an attack on February 3, 1863, by Major General Joseph Wheeler and Nathan Bedford Forrest, by this time a brigadier general. The attack was poorly coordinated, and the Confederates were easily repulsed. Forrest, who had considered Wheeler a friend, refused to ever serve under his command again after the battle.

Shiloh

On April 6 and 7, 1862, the world changed. In an isolated, quiet part of the American countryside, in western Tennessee, two great armies met on a field of battle. The result of that battle was carnage on a scale that shocked not only America, but the entire world. The battle at Shiloh was unprecedented in its devastation; in two days of fighting, 23,746 casualties were suffered. The American Civil War was, in many respects, the beginning of modern warfare, in tactics, technology, and the scope of its destruction. Shiloh was the first indication that this war would be different, more terrible than any other war fought in history.

The Union army was in the process of occupying western Tennessee and Arkansas. Having gained the Tennessee River for the Union, Grant took his army up the river to Pittsburg Landing, just northwest of the next Union target, the crucial railroad junction at Corinth, Mississippi. Major General Don Carlos Buell's army, positioned in Nashville, began making its way to Pittsburg Landing to join forces with Grant in preparation for taking the railroad hub.

Major General Albert Sidney Johnston, commanding all the Confederate western armies, did not want to wait for Grant to get to Corinth; he was not the type to wait for the enemy. Instead he decided that with Grant's army scattered and divided, the time was right to attack. North of the federal encampment was a creek and swampy area; Johnston planned to separate Grant's army from the safety of its river landing to the east, push it back into the swamps, and defeat it, then turn on Buell as he approached. Johnston gathered over 44,000 men from the forces around Corinth and his own command at Murfreesboro and began to march toward Pittsburg Landing.

Early on April 6, 1862, the Confederates quietly approached the Union encampment from the south. Although the Confederates were discovered by a Federal patrol just south of Shiloh Church, the attack on the main body of the Union army was a complete surprise, remarkable considering that the Confederates had encamped only

One of several Confederate burial trenches at Shiloh National Military Park.

2 miles away the night before. The Union troops, scattered and encamped wherever they could find dry ground, were not even entrenched, and the Confederates hit them hard, driving them back toward Pittsburg Landing. Johnston began to concentrate his army on the Union left, hoping to separate the Federals from the river to the east, but the Union forces fought fiercely, and the assault became general across the entire line. Along the Confederate left, after early success, fighting stalled in a dense grove of trees, later to be known as the Hornet's Nest because of the buzzing of the bullets flying through the trees.

Meanwhile Grant was at his headquarters—9 miles away. He would receive considerable criticism for this afterward; had he been in the field to command during the first two hours of the battle, it was thought, the outcome might have been different.

Fighting was fierce over the entire field throughout the day, but the Confederates eventually pushed the Union lines back toward Pittsburg Landing. They had also captured Brigadier General Benjamin Prentiss's division, which had fought hard throughout the day and had stalled the Confederate advance on the Union right. By the early evening of April 6, the Confederates held most of the battlefield, with the Union forces consolidated at the landing. Although the fight had been costly, victory seemed imminent for the Confederates. However, two events had occurred that would completely shift the momentum of the battle. First, General Albert Sidney Johnston,

SITE DETAILS

Shiloh National Military Park—Nestled in the quiet backcountry of Tennessee, this National Park Service property captures every significant element of the two days of battle at Shiloh Church and encompasses virtually the entire battlefield. The landscape is relatively undisturbed. Scattered throughout the park are monuments representing units from the various states, as well as markers interpreting the battle. Also prominent are markers where commanders fell, including at the site of General Albert Sidney Johnston's death, also marked by the preserved stump of the tree he died under. The museum at the visitor's center and the interpretive film there are somewhat outdated but still informative and effective. A driving tour through the park leads past the most prominent sites of the battle, and hiking trails lead to other well-known scenes of the fighting. The park also contains Shiloh National Cemetery, as well as five trenches dug at the time of the battle for the Confederate dead, all now prominently marked and memorialized. Just as its name implies, it is a calm, peaceful place, and you will wonder how such an event could have occurred here. *Shiloh National Military Park, 1055 Pittsburg Landing Rd., Shiloh, TN, 38376; 731-689-5696; www.nps.gov/shil. Open daily; admission charged.*

the promising leader in whom the Southern cause had placed so much hope, lay dead from a bullet wound. Second, unknown to the Confederates, General Don Carlos Buell's army had arrived from Nashville and was being ferried over the Tennessee River during the night.

On the morning of April 7, this time to the complete surprise of the Confederates, Grant and Buell attacked. Now numbering over 40,000, the Union forces were able to push the Confederates back over the same ground that had been fought over the day before. Although the fighting was again severe, the Confederates, with their morale fading, could not hold off the waves of Union attackers. Finally, Major General P. G. T. Beauregard, who had taken command after Johnston's death, sounded a retreat in the early afternoon, and the army moved back toward Corinth. The Federals, exhausted from two days of hard fighting, did not pursue until the next day, and when they did, Confederate cavalry quickly convinced them it was not worth the effort.

News of the fighting at Shiloh stunned the nation. All remaining hopes that this war, now almost one year into the fighting, would be quick and relatively bloodless were dashed. Strategically, the battle at Shiloh led to the capture of Corinth and strengthened the Union hold on western Tennessee and the middle Mississippi. Psychologically, even though other terrible battles would follow, Shiloh served as a wake-up call to both North and South that this would be a long, hard-fought war and would bring suffering that was previously inconceivable.

Corinth

During the Civil War, control of the railroads was a strategic necessity. Rail and ship were the only ways to move soldiers or large amounts of supplies with any speed. That is why Corinth, Mississippi, a small town that had suddenly sprung up at the junction of two critically important railroads, was a focus for both armies. Whoever held Corinth had control of not only the Mobile & Ohio Railroad, but also the all-important Memphis & Charleston—the only significant east–west railroad line through the Confederate states.

After the carnage at Shiloh, neither army was eager to get into another bloodbath. Major General P. G. T. Beauregard gathered 70,000 Confederate troops at Corinth, which was already heavily fortified, and waited as the Union army slowly advanced toward the city. Major General Henry Halleck, taking personal command of Grant's force after Shiloh, began to close in on the east and north sides of the city, building approach entrenchments daily that gradually brought the army closer to the Confederate stronghold. Although some heavy fighting occurred along the lines, the strategy was to besiege Corinth, rather than take it by force. For over a month the Union army crept closer, and the Confederates could only watch from their defenses. Finally, on May 29, 1862, Beauregard evacuated his army overnight, and Federal troops occupied Corinth the next day.

The vital rail crossing at Corinth, Mississippi.

SITE DETAILS

Corinth Civil War Interpretive Center—This center, developed by the National Park Service as an extension of Shiloh National Military Park, opened only recently and contains an outstanding presentation of the importance of this railroad junction, along with up-to-date, high-tech, interactive interpretations of the two battles that occurred here. The center is located at the former Battery Robinett, the sight of much fighting during the second battle. In addition to being an outstanding teaching center and museum, the center employs creative architecture; the walkway leading to the front doors is a winding path scattered with the leftover elements of battle (a soldier's cap, a cartridge box, and so on), and behind the center is a very moving memorial water sculpture that not only depicts a timeline of the events of the Civil War, but also why it was fought—at the beginning, the preamble to the United States Constitution, and near the end, parts of the 13th, 14th, and 15th Amendments, related to abolishing slavery and guaranteeing equal rights under the law. Also available at the center is a driving tour of Corinth, outlining several prominent and still-existing features of the two battles and the Civil War era, including Battery F from the second battle, and a walking path through a former "contraband" camp. This site is not to be missed. *Corinth Civil War Interpretive Center, 501 W. Linden St., Corinth, MS, 38834; 662-287-9273; www.nps.gov/shil/historyculture/corinth.htm. Open daily.*

Crossroads Museum—The railroad junction at Corinth, so important during the war, is still used today, and a small railroad museum is located right next to it. While the museum's focus is on more than just the battles, seeing the crossing does emphasize just how critical the railroads were. It has been called, in terms of blood, the smallest and costliest square footage fought over during the Civil War, and its significance begs one to take the short drive into town to see it. *Crossroads Museum, 221 N. Fillmore St., Corinth, MS, 38834; 662-287-3120; www.crossroads museum.com. Closed Mon.*

Over the following summer, after Halleck had already constructed additional fortifications around Corinth, Major General William Rosecrans took command. Rosecrans decided to further bolster the city's defenses, constructing a more compact but substantial inner line that could more easily be manned by his army, giving them freedom to move quickly to wherever reinforcement was needed. He knew that the Confederates would have to make an attempt on Corinth.

Meanwhile, President Jefferson Davis replaced Beauregard with Major General Braxton Bragg, who began a campaign to penetrate deep into the heartland of Kentucky. Bragg expected the armies left in northern Mississippi—commanded by Generals Sterling Price and Earl Van Dorn, both of whom had been driven out of Arkansas earlier in the year—to support him by invading western Tennessee. Van Dorn, the senior of the two generals, decided to attack Corinth and attempt to regain the Memphis & Charleston, which the Union had spent considerable effort rebuilding, and then move north to support Bragg's efforts.

On October 3, 1862, Van Dorn approached Corinth from the north and west. Rosecrans first met the attack at the outermost defensive line, which had been the original Confederate line during the earlier siege. He then pulled his men back to Halleck's line, compacting his army and moving closer to the city, as the continued Confederate assaults were repeatedly repulsed. By the end of the first day, the entire Union force was within the inner defenses that Rosecrans had built—a line 2 miles long, with heavily fortified batteries at key points. Although the lines still covered a considerable distance, the number of troops at Rosecrans' disposal allowed him great freedom in his defense.

When the Confederates attempted to take the works the next morning, they were repulsed at all points and were forced to withdraw by midday. The Federals, exhausted from the two days' fighting, gave only a half-hearted pursuit, having held their vital railroad junction. In the end the Union had suffered 2,350 casualties, the Confederates 4,800. Corinth remained in Union hands until the end of the war.

Brices Cross Roads

The battle at Brices Cross Roads, though relatively small when compared to some of the great battles of the Civil War, has become a focus for military students around the world. Not only is the battle the premier example of Nathan Bedford Forrest's genius

A trailhead near Brices Cross Roads National Battlefield, Mississippi.

SITE DETAILS

Brices Cross Roads Visitor and Interpretive Center—Make sure that this is your first stop. The small museum here, developed and maintained locally (with assistance from the National Park Service), does a fantastic job of interpreting the battle. Not only are there artifacts and displays, but also an interpretive film that thoroughly explains Forrest's masterpiece. Also available is a driving tour of the battle sites that will take you through all the most important locations of the action, which are all well marked along the roadway, and some of which are developed. It is locally run, and the hours are not always regular, so call first just to be sure; it is also closed on Monday. *Brices Cross Roads Visitor and Interpretive Center, 607 Grisham St., Baldwyn, MS, 38824; 662-365-3969. Closed Mon.; admission charged.*

Brices Cross Roads National Battlefield Site—This unit of the National Park Service is located at the crossroads itself and consists of several memorials, as well as interpretive signs. It is included as part of the driving tour issued at the interpretive center. *Brices Cross Roads National Battlefield Site, intersection of MS 370 and CR-231, Bethany, MS, 38824; 1-800-305-7417; www.nps.gov/brcr. Open daily.*

as a field commander, but it is also an ideal case study in military precision. It has been called by some "the perfect battle" because the battle plan was not only executed perfectly, but also worked, something that happens only on very rare occasions in any war. More commonly, however, Brices Cross Roads is known as "Forrest's finest hour."

In early June of 1864, at the command of Major General William Tecumseh Sherman, who was driving for Atlanta, Brigadier General Samuel Sturgis left Memphis to find Forrest and bring him to battle, to keep him out of Sherman's hair. On June 10 the Union cavalry broke camp early in the morning and headed for Brices Cross Roads, well ahead of the infantry. Blowing through some harassing fire from a small band of Confederates, they passed the crossroads at about 9:45 AM in pursuit. Suddenly, about a mile down the road, the Union cavalry was attacked by one of Forrest's brigades, dismounted and lying in wait. Although the fighting was fierce, the Confederates pounded the Union cavalry. Step one of Forrest's now-textbook plan had been accomplished; the Union force had been split, and the cavalry had been effectively taken out of the fight.

Step two of the plan also happened just as Forrest had predicted. Like clockwork, the Union infantry, upon hearing about the beating the cavalry was taking, was sent up the road double-quick by Sturgis. Running hard, the Federals raced to save their fellow soldiers. By the time they reached the fighting (by now, back near the crossroads), the soldiers were exhausted—and vulnerable. The Confederates, now having reunited and at full force, drove the Union infantry back, pursuing them down the road.

The victory was decisive. It cost the Union 2,612 killed and wounded and the loss of 250 wagons, 18 pieces of artillery, and 5,000 stands of small arms. By comparison, Confederate casualties totaled 493 killed and wounded. It was a harvest for the Confederates, and the largest feather in the cap of the Wizard of the Saddle.

Tupelo

By the summer of 1864, William T. Sherman had had quite enough of Nathan Bedford Forrest. His previous attempt at containing him had ended in a disaster for the Federals, and Forrest was constantly disrupting the supply lines that were critical to the Union drive for Atlanta. Sherman sent several other expeditions out to catch Forrest, but none of them were successful. But Forrest had to be contained, so the Federals tried again.

On July 5, 1864, Major General Andrew Jackson Smith set out from Memphis into northern Mississippi with a force of 14,000 to get Forrest, as well as do some damage to the main Confederate railroad in the area, the Mobile & Ohio. Smith had also been authorized by Sherman to lay waste to the countryside, waging the "total war" that

Tupelo National Battlefield sits amid the sprawl of the city.

SITE DETAILS

Tupelo National Battlefield—Within the city of Tupelo sits Tupelo National Battlefield. It is less than a half acre and contains interpretive signs, as well as several memorials to the battle. The area surrounding the national battlefield is completely suburbanized, with virtually no indication of the large action that was fought here. It takes quite a bit of imagination to picture the scene. *Tupelo National Battlefield, intersection of W. Main St. and Monument Dr., Tupelo, MS, 38801; 1-800-305-7417; www.nps.gov/tupe. Open daily.*

Natchez Trace Parkway Visitor's Center—This center, one of several placed along the Natchez Trace Parkway, offers limited information about the battles of Tupelo and Brices Cross Roads. The center (as well as the parkway) is maintained by the National Park Service. *Natchez Trace Parkway Visitor's Center, 2680 Natchez Trace Parkway, Tupelo, MS, 38804; 1-800-305-7417; www.nps.gov/natr. Open daily.*

Sherman had been preaching, designed to sap the Confederate will to fight. Several towns and miles of railroad track were destroyed as part of Smith's campaign.

Forrest had been awaiting Smith's advance and, along with Lieutenant General Stephen D. Lee, had been gathering troops. They knew the strength of the Union force but not its exact location. Each side was aware the other was there, but they danced with each other for several days trying to gain an advantage and pick a proper place for battle. The two armies finally met at Harrisburg, Mississippi, just west of Tupelo.

On the morning of July 14, the armies confronted each other in a line of battle almost 2 miles long, with the Union troops dug in and facing the west and north. The Confederates opened the attack at 7 AM, charging the Union line. Similar assaults were made against the Union line throughout the day, but the attacks were uncoordinated and were repulsed each time. By the afternoon, most of the fighting had eased, although firing continued throughout the night. Meanwhile the Union troops behind the lines destroyed the town of Harrisburg, burning it to the ground.

The next morning Smith's Union army began to move north, with some detached Confederate units harassing its rear the entire time. By the end of the day on July 15, the Confederates held the field, but not without paying a high price. Their casualty total of 1,326 was almost twice that of the Federals, and Forrest, almost always at the front of his lines during battle, had been shot in the foot (although the wound was minor and he was raiding Memphis a month later). Most important for the Union, however, was that the Confederates were temporarily unable to disrupt Sherman's supply line to Atlanta, and as a bonus, Union troops tore up a considerable amount of railroad track and ravaged much of the countryside during the expedition, leaving a lasting impression on the Southern civilians.

» OTHER SITES IN THE UPPER MISSISSIPPI VALLEY

Chalk Bluff—General John Marmaduke, after a failed attempt to take Cape Girardeau, Missouri, quickly bridged the St. Francis River and started moving his Confederates into Arkansas on May 1–2, 1863. The battle at Chalk Bluff consisted mostly of a rearguard action, as well as Marmaduke's guns, placed on the bluff, firing into the pursuing Union troops. Marmaduke's army was able to escape, although some Texans, stranded on the Missouri side of the river, had to swim for it.

Although the Chalk Bluff Battlefield Park is a bit difficult to find, it is a gem. Interpretive signs at the park also give the history of the former town of Chalk Bluff, and a paved trail leads to the site of Marmaduke's river crossing. The park is north of the town of St. Francis, and the county roads used to reach it are unpaved; still, the local effort put into developing the park makes it worth the hunt. *Chalk Bluff Battlefield Park, intersection of CR-347 and CR-368, St. Francis, AR, 72464; 870-598-2667. Open daily.*

Cape Girardeau—Cape Girardeau, Missouri, was recognized early as an important river port and supply point on the Mississippi and was occupied quickly by Federal forces. Four forts—designated A, B, C, and D—were built to protect the town from a land attack. On April 26, 1863, General John Marmaduke began to test the fortifications, and the action escalated into a battle. Upon learning that Union reinforcements were on the way, Marmaduke quickly withdrew to the south.

The Cape Girardeau Convention and Visitor's Bureau has created a driving tour that outlines the 1863 action, as well as other Civil War–era points of interest in the town. Although the battle sites themselves have been largely lost, the tour brochure is an extremely thorough interpretation of the events and makes picturing the action very easy. The highlight of the tour is Fort D, which has been restored and is a public park; although it did not take an active part in the battle, it is an excellent example of the fortifications existing at the time. Brochures are available at the Cape Girardeau Visitors Center, as well as at most tourist information centers throughout town. *Cape Girardeau Convention and Visitors Bureau, 400 Broadway, Cape Girardeau, MO, 63701, 573-335-5421; www.visitcape.com. Open daily.*

Fredericktown—On October 21, 1861, some 5,000 Federal troops converged upon Fredericktown, Missouri, in the hopes of catching a division of the Missouri State Guard, 1,200 men under the command of General M. Jeff Thompson. Told that the guard had left the previous day, the Union soldiers began to pursue, when suddenly they found themselves in a fight. Thompson had ordered his division to return to Fredericktown and attack. After a two-hour fight, the outnumbered Missourians finally withdrew to the south, anxious to protect their supply wagons, which held large amounts of lead and other stores taken from the surrounding country.

Today, because of strong local support, the story of the battle here and the battlefield itself are receiving a lot of attention. The Fredericktown Civil War Museum recently opened in a vintage building near the town square. The museum contains information on the battle and the town during the war years. The Fredericktown Foundation for Historic Preservation, which also runs the museum, has taken an active role in preserving the battlefield, acquiring several acres where the most severe fighting took place and erecting an interpretive sign at the site, with the help of the Missouri Department of Natural Resources Parks Division. They are also hoping to host reenactments on the battlefield, with the cooperation of the farmers who own the surrounding property. Finally, the foundation is preparing the War Eagle Trail to honor Old Abe, the bald eagle mascot of the Eighth Wisconsin Volunteer Infantry, who was present at 36 of that regiment's battles, including New Madrid, Corinth, and Vicksburg. The idea of Old Abe as a mascot resonated with many, including the current 101st Airborne Division, which adopted Old Abe the War Eagle as its mascot in 1942. Fredericktown was Abe's first battle, and there is a monument and sculpture of him on the town square. *Battle site at cemetery located at intersection of S. Main St. and John Holt Dr., Fredericktown, MO, 63645; Fredericktown Civil War Museum, 156 S. Main St., Fredericktown, MO, 63645; 573-576-8528; www.fhphistory.org. Battle site open daily; museum open by appointment.*

Fort Davidson—As the Civil War wound down in 1864, the Confederacy launched several efforts to help prolong the fight. One of these was an invasion into Missouri, led by Major General Sterling Price, to attempt to turn Missouri from a neutral into a Confederate state. Price had an eye on capturing St. Louis, then recruiting volunteers in the state. In late September, as he advanced northward with 12,000 men, Price learned that a small Union force of 1,500 was holding Fort Davidson at Pilot Knob, Missouri, in order to protect the St. Louis Iron Mountain Railroad. Price, thinking he had easy pickings, decided to take the fort. Much to his dismay, however, the Union commander, Brigadier General Thomas Ewing, would not give. Acting against his orders, Ewing decided to hold out to delay the Confederate advance on St. Louis. On September 26, 1864, Ewing crammed his men and 11 cannon into the tiny earthworks, while Price set artillery on the commanding hills nearby. However, the overconfidence of subordinates led Price to approve an all-out assault on the fort. Unfortunately for the Confederates, the attacks were wholly uncoordinated and were conducted by green troops. The small Union force repulsed every furious assault through the next day, taking advantage of the fort's deep moat and high walls. Finally, early in the morning of September 28, Ewing skillfully withdrew his troops, undetected, through Price's army. The Confederates lost up to 1,000 men to the Union's 200, along with any initiative to approach St. Louis. Price's humiliation here would set the stage for the rest of his disastrous Missouri expedition, which ended with the ultimate disintegration of his army after the battles of Westport and Mine Creek.

The remnants of the exploded powder magazine at Fort Davidson State Historic Site in Pilot Knob, Missouri.

Fort Davidson State Historic Site contains the extremely well-preserved Union earthworks from the original fort, as well as an outstanding interpretive center, which not only includes museum exhibits, but also a short film and a fiber-optic electronic map illustrating the movements during the battle. From the park, the other features of the landscape that helped shape the battle are easily visible. The park also contains picnic and play areas, and the 78 acres of open fields and beautiful scenery make it a nice place to stop and rest the family. *Fort Davidson State Historic Site, 118 E. Maple St., Pilot Knob, MO, 63663; 573-546-3454; www.mostateparks.com/ftdavidson.htm. Open daily Mar.–Nov.; closed Mon., Dec.–Feb.*

Belmont/Columbus—Confederate fortifications at Columbus, Kentucky, were blocking Union passage of the Mississippi River. Ulysses S. Grant, newly appointed brigadier general, set out in a movement to capture the town of Belmont, Missouri, across from the fort. On November 7, 1861, Grant's troops attacked a Confederate encampment on the Missouri side of the river, with the Union troops eventually driving through the Confederates. However, while the Union soldiers stopped to celebrate their victory and loot the encampment, the Confederates were reinforced from the fort. Now receiving fire from both the rallied Confederates and the heavy guns at Columbus, Grant's troops were caught in a crossfire and retreated in haste to their river transports. Although Belmont was not captured, Grant, in his first engagement of the Civil War, was recognized as a commander who was willing to fight.

Columbus-Belmont State Park is located in Columbus, Kentucky, across the river from the actual battlefield but on the site of the original fortifications. The park contains a recently refurbished museum, as well as hiking trails, remnants of earthworks, wonderful views of the Mississippi River, and a portion of the chain and anchor that was stretched across the river at this point. However, be sure to note that the park is open only from May through September, and weekends in April and October. The town of Belmont was long ago washed away by the Mississippi River. *Columbus-Belmont State Park, intersection of Cheathem St. and Back St., Columbus, KY, 42032; 270-677-2327; parks.ky.gov/findparks/recparks/cb. Open daily May–Sep., open weekends Apr. and Oct.; admission charged.*

Paducah—On March 25, 1864, Nathan Bedford Forrest, as part of a raid to draw troops away from Sherman's armies in northern Georgia, occupied the city of Paducah, Kentucky, sending the Union troops into Fort Anderson, just north of the city. While Fort Anderson did hold back the attacks made on it, during its assault Forrest's men took supplies and destroyed military stores and property in Paducah. After the battle, Northern newspapers let slip that the raiding army had not captured a large number of Union horses at Paducah. Forrest sent back a small detachment to capture the horses, which they promptly did—not only to complete the job, but also to serve as a diversion to Forrest's attack on Fort Pillow.

Fort Anderson itself is gone; a historical highway marker stands at the former site, near the Paducah Convention Center. There is a Downtown Paducah Civil War Walking Tour that focuses on the Union occupation of Paducah, but interpretation of the 1864 battle is limited. The walking tour is available through the visitor's center run by the Paducah Convention and Visitor's Bureau. *Visitor's center, 128 Broadway; historical highway marker (Fort Anderson), at Convention Center, Kentucky Historical Commission / Kentucky Department of Highways, near intersection of 4th St. and Park St., Paducah, KY, 42001; 1-800-723-8224; www.paducah-tourism.org. Open daily.*

Fort Henry—Just as Fort Donelson guarded the Cumberland River from Union use, Fort Henry, its counterpart 10 miles to the west, guarded the Tennessee River. Grant's army, along with Navy flag officer Andrew Foote's ironclad gunboats, assaulted the fort on February 6, 1862, and took it within an hour and a half. The fort's commander, Brigadier General Lloyd Tilghman, had already sent most of his men to Fort Donelson and left a token defense to stall the Union fleet.

In one sense, Fort Henry today looks much as it did during the battle; the fort was flooding prior to and during the Union assault. Today, the job is complete, and you will need scuba gear to explore the original site, which lies under the waters of Lake Kentucky, formed by the damming of the Tennessee River in 1944. The only remnants of the fort that were not swallowed by the lake are a few rifle pits, along with a small Confederate cemetery. These are all located within the Land Between the Lakes National Recreation Area and can be seen by exploring the Fort Henry hiking trails. Trail maps can be obtained from one of the area's welcome centers, or at the area's Internet site. The trailhead itself is somewhat difficult to find, and you have to take unpaved roads to get there. A historical marker can be seen along the highway. Information on the battle is best obtained at Fort Donelson National Battlefield. *Trail information—Land Between the Lakes, trail information at South Welcome Station, intersection of The Trace and Fort Henry Rd., unincorporated Stewart County, TN, 1-800-448-1069; www.lbl.org. Historical highway marker 3C-35 (Fort Henry), Tennessee Historical Commission, along US 79 at Fort Henry Rd., Fort Henry, TN. Open daily.*

Johnsonville—The town of Johnsonville, on the Tennessee River, became an important point of transfer for Union supplies, with a rail line running from here to Nashville. Nathan Bedford Forrest made this the objective of one of his raids, and on November 4, 1864, he opened fire on the supply depot with well-placed artillery on the opposite bank of the river. The Union lost four gunboats, transport ships, and millions of dollars of supplies. Forrest's cavalry escaped without a scratch.

This engagement is actually represented by two separate Tennessee state parks. Nathan Bedford Forrest State Park, on the west bank at the location where Forrest set his artillery, offers a sweeping view of the river. Along with a memorial to Forrest, there is interpretive material, as well as a small museum. On the east bank, at the former site of the town of Johnsonville (just north of the present town of New Johnsonville) is Johnsonville State Historic Park, where earthworks and rifle pits can still be seen. There is a small museum here, but it is open by appointment only. *Nathan Bedford Forrest State Park, 1825 Pilot Knob Rd., Eva, TN, 38333; 731-584-6356; state.tn.us/environment/parks/nbforrest. Open daily. Johnsonville State Historic Park, intersection of McAdoo Rd. and Old Johnsonville Rd., New Johnsonville, TN, 37134; 931-535-2789; state.tn.us/environment/parks/johnsonville. Park open daily, museum open by appointment.*

Parker's Cross Roads—As Brigadier General Nathan Bedford Forrest concluded his raid through western Tennessee, the Union army moved to trap him before he could leave. At Parker's Cross Roads on December 31, 1862, Union troops attempted to block Forrest's escape route. The outset of the battle had the Confederates pushing Colonel Cyrus Dunham's Union brigade back through the crossroads, but before long Forrest discovered Colonel John Fuller's brigade coming up on his rear. Faced with Union armies to his north and south, Forrest famously ordered, "Charge them both

A monument along the Parker's Crossroads Battlefield driving tour, in Tennessee.

ways!" Whether or not he actually issued this command, that is exactly what his army did, and they escaped to cross the Tennessee River the next day.

Brochures for a self-guided driving tour put together by the Parker's Crossroads Battlefield Association can be found either at the town's visitor's center (exit 108 off Interstate 40) or at the association's Web site. The tour covers the entire scope of the battle, the sites are well preserved, and the interpretation found in the brochure and at the tour stops is excellent. *Parker's Crossroads Battlefield Park, Log Cabin Welcome Center, south of I-40 on TN 22 at exit 108, Parkers Crossroads, TN, 38388; 731-968-1191; www.parkerscrossroads.com. Open daily.*

Jackson—On a raid through western Tennessee, Nathan Bedford Forrest met with Federals at the town of Jackson on December 19, 1862. He launched an attack on the Union force and pushed it back, but the attack was actually a diversion to allow the rest of his cavalry to tear up railroad track around the city.

Some of the battle site is preserved at Salem Cemetery, northeast of the city, and a kiosk interpreting the battle, along with several memorials, is located there. *Salem Cemetery Battlefield, 35 Cotton Grove Rd., Jackson, TN, 38305; 731-424-1279; www.salemcemeterybattlefield.com. Open daily.*

Hatchie's Bridge (Davis Bridge)—Following the second battle at Corinth, Grant ordered a pursuit of Van Dorn's army, which was attempting to escape to the west over the Davis Bridge. On October 6, 1862, the Federals caught Van Dorn and General Sterling Price at the bridge, and although it looked for a time as if the Confederates would be trapped on the east side of the Hatchie River as planned, Confederate scouts eventually found another crossing, and the armies escaped.

South of the town of Pocahontas, two scenes of the battle are nicely preserved, including the former site of the Davis Bridge, long since washed away, and Metamora Hill, west of the bridge, where Union troops captured some of Price's army. The two sites are not adjacent to each other, and getting to them both will require some backtracking and circuitous driving. But although it takes a little effort to find them, the available interpretation and relatively untouched landscape make this battlefield a hidden gem. *Davis Bridge Battlefield—Metamora Hill site, 1.1 miles south of intersection of Wolf Pen Rd. and Pocahontas Ripley Rd. on Pocahontas Ripley Rd.; Davis Bridge site, 1.1 miles south of intersection of Wolf Pen Rd. and Pocahontas Ripley Rd. on Essary Springs Rd., Pocahontas, TN, 38061; 731-254-0461. Open daily.*

Iuka—Grant tried to trap General Sterling Price's army here as Price prepared to join General Earl Van Dorn's army and attempt to capture Nashville and, it was hoped, Kentucky. Price was able to evacuate on September 19, 1862, but not before a battle had occurred south of the town.

A county museum interprets the battle, and nearby is a memorial to the Confederates who fought here. *Old Tishomingo County Courthouse Museum, 203 E. Quitman St., Iuka, MS, 38852; 662-423-3500; www.rootsweb.ancestry.com/~mstchgs/museum.htm. Museum open Wed.–Sat., admission charged; memorial accessible daily.*

Okolona—General William Smith's Union cavalry force, heading south from Memphis toward Meridian, Mississippi, in February 1864, found itself caught by Forrest's cavalry. On February 22 the two forces clashed in a running battle through Okolona, about 20 miles south of Tupelo. Notable in this battle is the death of Colonel Jeffery Forrest, who led a brigade against the Union forces.

There is a Confederate cemetery in town, the site of some of the battle, as well as a memorial and a historical highway marker. *Okolona Confederate Cemetery, intersection of S. Church St. and Park Lane Dr.; memorial and historical highway marker (Okolona in the Civil War), Mississippi Department of Archives and History, intersection of W. Main St. and Gatlin St.; Okolona, MS, 38860; 662-447-5913. Sites accessible daily.*

Collierville—Several battles occurred at this depot, the site of a small railroad center, including one on November 3, 1863, when Confederates attempted to raid the Memphis & Charleston Railroad while Sherman was moving his troops from Vicksburg to Chattanooga.

A small museum on the town square is dedicated to the importance of the railroads, and outside the museum is an interpretive sign about the 1863 battle. There is also a historical marker on the town square. *Main Street Collierville Depot, 125 N. Rowlett St., Collierville, TN, 38017; 901-853-1666; park and sign accessible daily.*

» WHERE TO STAY IN THE UPPER MISSISSIPPI VALLEY

Because many of the major sites on this tour are off the beaten path, finding somewhere to sleep for the night might take a little bit of extra effort if you're expecting to stay in motels. For some parts or the tour you will likely either have to plan ahead or drive a little bit out of the way to find a motel. Some of the exceptions are Memphis, which has many lodging options, Tupelo, and Corinth.

If you are looking for a historic bed-and-breakfast, some outstanding options are available. In Memphis is the **Inn at Hunt Phelan,** built in 1828. The home is rich in history, and its previous guests include both Union and Confederate generals and politicians, not to mention several presidents of the United States. General Grant used the home as a headquarters during his Vicksburg campaign, and it is suspected that while Jefferson Davis was conducting business in the home, his wife, Varina, actually planted some of the original garden. The *Inn at Hunt Phelan, 533 Beale St., Memphis, TN, 38103; 901-525-8225; www.huntphelan.com.*

Bolivar, Tennessee, is a little bit off the tour path, but the short drive from the Shiloh battlefield may be well worth the effort. The **Magnolia Manor Bed and Breakfast** is not only witness to history, but holds some great stories as well. Among the Union generals who stayed here were Grant, Sherman, James McPherson, and John Logan. It is quite possible, even probable, that preliminary planning for the battle at Shiloh occurred in the home. The home even still shows some evidence from its famous guests. The story holds that Sherman, while dining in the presence of the owner, a Mrs. Miller, may have made a remark that all Southern gentlemen should be "exterminated." Mrs. Miller, upset, went to the back porch of the home and began to cry. Grant, who was also at the dinner table, went back to find out what had happened. Grant had not heard the remark but nevertheless ordered Sherman to apologize to the woman, which he did. However, Sherman was apparently unhappy with the order, because he slashed at the banister with his sword on his way upstairs to his room. The mark is still there for guests to enjoy. *Magnolia Manor Bed and Breakfast, 418 N. Main St., Bolivar, TN, 38008; 731-658-6700; www.magnoliamanorbolivartn.com.*

In Dover, Tennessee, on some of the land that was fought over during the battles of Fort Donelson and Dover, is the **Riverfront Plantation Inn,** built in 1859. It partially burned during the war, but some of the home did survive, and it has been restored on a grand scale. It was also used as a field hospital during the war. Located on the banks of the Cumberland River, the inn provides fine views of the great waterway. *The Riverfront Plantation Inn, intersection of Crow Lane and Rose Dr., Dover, TN, 37058; 1-877-660-5939; www.riverfrontplantation.com.*

For the camping set, the backcountry locations of most of the tour sites mean that you will have plenty of opportunities for experiencing the outdoors. Conveniently, numerous state and county parks can be found along the route. One of the larger ones among the many options is the **Land Between the Lakes National Recreational Area.** This sprawling area is located between Lake Kentucky and Lake Barkley, two artificial lakes created by the damming of the Tennessee and Cumberland Rivers. The park not only contains campsites and lodges, but also offers many opportunities for water activities, as well as herds of bison and elk. The park straddles the Kentucky-Tennessee state line, and Fort Donelson National Battlefield is only a few miles from the south entrance. Within the park, technically, is the Fort Henry battlefield—most of which is under Lake Kentucky, but some of which is still visible. *Land Between the Lakes National Recreational Area, South Welcome Station, Stewart County, TN, 1-800-448-1069; www.lbl.org.*

3

The Lower Mississippi Valley: Vicksburg and the Red River Campaign

OVERVIEW

The Mississippi River was a critical artery for both sides during the Civil War. For the Union it was a means of splitting the Confederacy in half and advancing General Winfield Scott's Anaconda Plan. For the Confederacy, control of the Mississippi meant not only the survival of their armies by keeping a means of supply open, but also the survival of their economy, as Southern farmers needed to get their goods to the world market.

The Mississippi was also an avenue into the farthest reaches of the Confederacy. Earlier Union victories along the river and its tributaries in 1862 had opened the way to Tennessee. The southern part of the river provided access to the Red River, a long waterway stretching northwest from Alexandria, Louisiana, all the way to Shreveport and beyond into Texas. For the South the Red River was a major shipping artery; for the Union it was an avenue of invasion into the far West.

By the end of 1862, the Union had made great headway toward gaining and keeping control of the Mississippi. The upper part of the river was under solid Union control southward to well past Memphis, Tennessee. Near the river's mouth at the Gulf of Mexico, New Orleans, the South's largest city and its major port to the world,

The grand monument to the soldiers of Illinois at Vicksburg National Military Park.

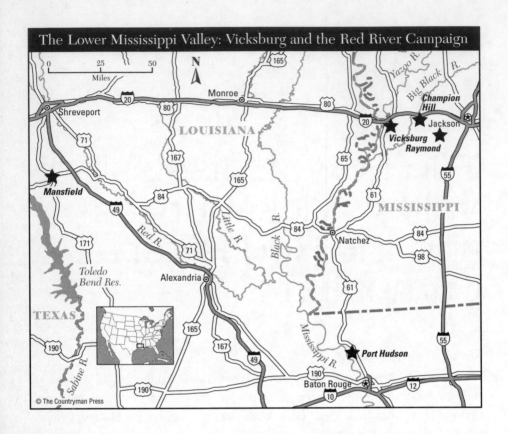

The Lower Mississippi Valley: Vicksburg and the Red River Campaign

was also under Union control, shutting down the primary Confederate lifeline to foreign markets. The only portion of the river that remained under Southern control was a stretch from the port city of Vicksburg, Mississippi, to a Confederate stronghold at Port Hudson, Louisiana.

Although this was only a very small portion of the great river's length, it was enough to put a major crimp in the Union's war strategy. For starters, it meant that the Confederate armies of the West still had a safe means of passage for troops and supplies from the West (also known as the Trans-Mississippi) to the East. Second, control of either one of the two strongholds, let alone the river in between, meant that enemy shipping could not pass. This applied not only to military river traffic such as the transport of Union troops and supplies, but also to shipment of goods from the North down to the port of New Orleans. By 1863 Northern farmers were raising an uproar about not being able to get their goods to market, and the Union army was under considerable pressure to get the Mississippi River open.

Taking either of these two strong ends of the Confederate stretch of the Mississippi River, however, was a daunting task. Both Vicksburg and Port Hudson, besides being extremely well fortified, held commanding positions on the river and could see any action on the water in either direction from miles away. Taking either of these strongholds would have to be done with limited help from the ironclad riverboats that had served so well in previous actions. In addition, both forts still had open supply lines, so conducting a siege would take careful planning and cautious strategy. Finally, both were surrounded by swampland and thick growth, making troop movement difficult.

In October of 1862 the task of clearing the river for the Union was given to Major General Ulysses S. Grant. Grant attempted several maneuvers to capture Vicksburg, trying to cut supply lines, march through the bayous, and even, at one point, attempting to avoid the city altogether by digging a canal and redirecting the Mississippi River. None of these attempts were successful. Finally, in April of 1863, Grant began to move his army south through Louisiana, recrossed the river south of Vicksburg, and then moved north to invest the stronghold. After fighting a series of battles that put Major General John Pemberton's Confederates on the defensive, Grant made a decisive move at Raymond, Mississippi, and instead of heading north to Vicksburg, moved to Jackson, took the Mississippi capital, and then turned to approach Vicksburg directly from the east. After another important and decisive Union victory at Champion Hill, the Confederates were forced back into their defenses at Vicksburg, and the Federals besieged the city. Finally, on July 4, 1863, Pemberton surrendered his army to Grant, and Vicksburg belonged to the Union.

Meanwhile, downriver, Union forces had begun another siege at Port Hudson. The Union commander was Major General Nathaniel Banks, who had prepared by cutting supply lines from the West in a series of small battles. Over the coming weeks,

Banks inched ever closer to the Confederate works, digging new trenches around the clock. Finally, word reached both sides that Vicksburg had fallen, and the writing was on the wall. Port Hudson surrendered, and the Mississippi River was under the full control of Federal forces.

After the Mississippi fell, the Trans-Mississippi operations of the Confederacy were greatly weakened. The headquarters of these operations was in Shreveport, Louisiana, far up the Red River. In March of 1864 Banks had set his sights on taking Shreveport, and ultimately Texas and the West, putting an end to the Confederacy in that part of the country. His campaign began well, and he steadily moved up the Red River, supported by the powerful ironclad riverboats of Rear Admiral David Porter.

However, two major obstacles conspired against the Union effort. The first was that the water level of the river was low, and Porter's gunboats had trouble maneuvering. The other was Major General Richard Taylor. Taylor certainly had fight in his blood; his father was Zachary Taylor, the great hero of the Mexican War and 12th president of the United States. As Taylor retreated up the Red, he patiently waited for an opportunity and a place to make a stand. Finally, just south of Shreveport, Banks decided to turn away from the river and the protection of Porter's fleet to take advantage of the available roads to the city. Taylor saw his opportunity and turned to face the Union army at Mansfield, Louisiana. In a decisive fight that ended in a rout, Taylor sent the Union army on the run back to the river and the protection of the gunboats. After being chased back down the river, Banks's campaign mercifully ended in Yellow Bayou. A sister campaign originating in Arkansas, intended to support Banks's movements, finished with similarly unsuccessful results. The Red River campaign is still often regarded as one of the most poorly conducted military campaigns not only of the Civil War, but in American history.

These great struggles for control of the waterways, so important to the survival and the cause of both sides of the Civil War, are stories of bravery, drama, and ingenuity. This chapter will take you through the decisive campaigns for Vicksburg, Port Hudson, and the Red River.

» PEOPLE TO KNOW

John Clifford Pemberton—General John C. Pemberton is something of an oddity among Confederate leaders. He was born in Pennsylvania to a Quaker minister as part of a family of antiwar abolitionists. But Pemberton wanted a military career, and his father's friend, President Andrew Jackson, got him into West Point. A career soldier, Pemberton was decorated in the Mexican War, after which he married into a wealthy Virginia family. When the Civil War came, he sided with his state, instantly drawing the suspicion of both his relatives and his fellow Confederate leaders.

Nevertheless, Jefferson Davis commissioned the experienced Pemberton as a brigadier general, and he was eventually given command of the Department of Mississippi and Louisiana. After the surrender of Vicksburg, many Southerners blamed Pemberton for the loss, rather unfairly accusing him of Northern sympathies. Pemberton resigned his commission, and after the war he eventually returned to Pennsylvania.

Nathaniel Prentiss Banks—General Nathaniel Banks will long be remembered for his disastrous Red River campaign, but to be fair, he has a number of other military failures to account for. Born in Massachusetts and mostly self-educated, Banks entered politics at the age of 35, serving in the state legislature. He was later elected congressman, then governor of Massachusetts, leaving office after only one term to become president of the Illinois Central Railroad. When the war broke out, Banks immediately volunteered his service and, despite having no military experience whatsoever, was commissioned a major general.

Banks began his military career by being thrown into the fire, commanding troops in the Shenandoah Valley opposite Stonewall Jackson. Thereafter Banks bounced around until relieving the locally despised Major General Benjamin Butler in New Orleans. Here Banks was remarkably successful, managing the isolation, siege, and capture of Port Hudson. Following this, however, was the Red River campaign, and his military reputation was sealed. Banks returned to politics after the war and died in Massachusetts in 1894.

Joseph Bailey—Truly one of the most underappreciated parts of the army (by civilians, anyway) are military engineers, and it takes some incredible work to get a mention in the history books. One of the few to be so recognized is Joseph Bailey, who saved Rear Admiral David Porter's fleet of Union gunboats during the Red River campaign. A short time later Bailey would quickly construct a half-mile-long bridge at Yellow Bayou out of gathered boats and timber that would save Nathaniel Banks's army from defeat during the same campaign. Bailey was promoted to brigadier general after the campaign, and the story of Bailey's Dam is one of the highlights of the Red River campaign—and certainly the only highlight on the Union side.

» THINGS TO KNOW

In case you haven't heard, it gets hot in the South. Sometimes very hot. So when you plan your trip, know what to expect when you go. If you go in July or August, expect hot, humid, muggy weather. Of course this may be the best time to go if you want to get some deals on hotels or air fare. In any case, be prepared; keep water in the car, and bring sunscreen.

Another critical item that should be in your luggage is insect repellent. Many of the areas you will visit are swampland or are near it, and they are home to all varieties and sizes of bugs, many of which will bite you or, at least, be extremely annoying. If you are not prepared for this, you will be swatting your way through your tour.

Finally, when traveling through Louisiana, know that many of the pronunciations of place names along the way are not what you might expect. For instance, Natchitoches, which many nonnatives might pronounce "natch-eh-tow-chez," is actually pronounced as something closer to "na-kah-tish." So, if you do stop to chat with the locals, whether it's to ask for directions or just to make friendly conversation, don't be surprised if you miss a word or two; simply ask them what they meant, and they'll help you. Not only are they extremely friendly, but they are also very proud of their unique heritage.

THE TRIP

This is designed as a circle tour. Probably the easiest way to take the tour, if you stick to the major sites, is to start and finish in New Orleans, heading north first to Port Hudson. Flying into Baton Rouge, Shreveport, or Jackson, Mississippi, is also an option; if you expand your tour into Arkansas, flying into Little Rock or even Memphis, Tennessee, offers other alternatives.

If you do start in New Orleans, the distance between there and the final stop in Mansfield, Louisiana, makes for a fairly long drive. But there are plenty of interesting, lesser-known sites between the two cities that are associated with the Red River campaign and are easy to get to, so get off the interstate and explore a little if you have the time.

» THE CAN'T-MISS SITES

Port Hudson

Following the battle of Baton Rouge in August 1862, the Confederates moved north upriver to the site of Port Hudson, Louisiana. The commander at the time, Major General John Breckenridge, a former U.S. vice president, ordered that a fortified position be built here along the Mississippi. Soon, Port Hudson, Louisiana, would present as strong an obstacle to Union control of the Mississippi River as Vicksburg. Over the course of the next year, the Confederates dug in, built strong fortifications and gun emplacements, and took advantage of the thick vegetation and variable terrain in the area. Port Hudson was going to be a hard nut to crack.

While Grant was busy trying to come up with a way to capture Vicksburg, Major General Nathaniel Banks had the assignment of taking Port Hudson. Banks began by cutting supply lines coming from west of the position, seizing control of the Red River south of Alexandria during a series of battles in April 1863. From here he approached Port Hudson from the north, while Major General Christopher Augur's division approached from the south. After a battle at Plains Store, Louisiana, on May 21, 1863, the Confederates were driven back into their positions at Port Hudson. Cut off from supplies and with no hope for reinforcements (thanks in part to conflicting orders to

A view of the battlefield from the observation tower at Port Hudson State Historic Site.

evacuate from Major General Joseph Johnston and to hold from President Jefferson Davis), Port Hudson was now surrounded, and Banks began his siege of the stronghold on May 22.

Port Hudson was now held by 7,500 Confederates under the command of Major General Franklin Gardner. Surrounding them were 40,000 Union troops, eager to seize the bastion. But hopes of taking the fortifications by assault were dealt their first blow on May 27, when Banks ordered an attack along the entire length of the line. It didn't quite happen that way; confusing orders led to uncoordinated assaults, and the attack, which ended up beginning on the Union right and ending on the left, was repulsed at all points. Banks's men suffered 2,000 casualties, with virtually nothing to show for it on the map. However, one notable victory for the Union on this day was the bravery displayed by several black units, some composed of freed slaves and others organized in New Orleans by free black men. Their willingness to fight proved to many that the decision to use black soldiers to aid the Union cause was a wise one.

After the failed assault, the Union began a constant bombardment of the Port Hudson fortifications and resumed the siege. On June 14, after a demand for surrender

SITE DETAILS

Port Hudson State Historic Site—Although a good deal of the original Port Hudson fortifications have been lost to the Mississippi River and surrounding development, much still can be seen at the Port Hudson State Historic Site. Even a short walk on the extensive trails here will demonstrate just what the Union was up against; besides the strong earthworks, the terrain is a mess of undergrowth and ravines. The trails lead to some of the remaining earthworks and other important points of the battle, and interpretive signs are placed along the way. However, if you do plan on exploring, be prepared—the trails can be strenuous and are dirt and mud, and you will be hiking through junglelike conditions, so at the very least bring good shoes, water, and insect repellent (lots of it). If you don't plan to hike, there is still plenty to see at the site. The visitor's center and museum is outstanding, covering the siege in great detail and containing a number of outstanding artifacts. An observation tower next to the visitor's center offers a bird's-eye view of the landscape, and several of the important battle locations inside the park are drivable. Also available at the visitor's center is a short driving tour to points of interest outside the park's boundaries; although they are on private property, they are viewable from the roadside. *Port Hudson State Historic Site, US 61 and Robert Newport Lane, Jackson, LA, 70748; 1-888-677-3400; www.crt.state.la.us/parks/ipthudson.aspx. Open daily; admission charged.*

was refused by Gardner, Banks ordered another assault of the defensive works. The results were much the same as before; 1,805 more Union casualties, with no ground gained.

From this point onward Banks stuck to siege tactics. Trenches inched closer and closer to the Confederate lines, while the bombardment continued. Conditions in the Confederate works were terrible, but the defenders held firm until word reached them that Vicksburg had surrendered on July 4. With no hope to hold out and with his force decimated, Gardner finally agreed to terms, and the formal surrender of Port Hudson occurred on July 9, 1863. The cost to the Union was high—10,000 casualties, half due to disease—but they had captured the entire Confederate force. More important, though, the Mississippi River was now under full Union control from its source to its mouth.

Raymond

The battle at Raymond, Mississippi, was not extraordinary in terms of casualties. However, the consequences of this battle are extremely important when telling the story of the Vicksburg campaign. Because of the fight at Raymond, Ulysses S. Grant's Union army altered the course of its plans in a way that ultimately spelled a quick end to Confederate control of Vicksburg and the Mississippi River.

After the battle of Port Gibson on May 2, Grant brought his entire fighting force back east across the river into Mississippi. After Major General William T. Sherman brought his force across the river, Grant decided to advance north to Vicksburg, splitting his army into three: the left commanded by Major General John McClernand, the center by Sherman, and the right by Major General James McPherson.

As Grant prepared his strategy, he knew that Confederate troops were gathering east of him at the Mississippi capital of Jackson. He also knew that those troops would be commanded by Major General Joseph E. Johnston. Johnston, who had been commander of the armies in Virginia until he was severely wounded at the battle of Seven Pines in the spring of 1862, was a capable, experienced, and respected commander. What was unknown was the size of the force gathering in Jackson, and how quickly the Confederates were coming in. Still, Grant decided to head north.

In nearby Raymond, Mississippi, which was to be the starting point of the Union right and the destination of McPherson's men, was a group of 4,000 Confederate troops under the command of Brigadier General John Gregg, coming from Port Hudson, Louisiana. On May 12, 1863, as McPherson's force of 12,000 marched up the Utica Road toward Raymond, Gregg, who had been alerted that the enemy was approaching, was ready for them. As the Union army neared a small stream known as

A crossing of Fourteenmile Creek along the trail at Raymond Military Park, Mississippi.

Fourteenmile Creek around midmorning, the Confederate artillery opened fire. The Union troops advanced to the creek and the woods around it, and the Confederate soldiers poured in to meet them. Heavy fighting occurred here, with several uncoordinated attacks launched by both sides. Finally, the Union right was able to break through, and Gregg ordered a withdrawal and began heading for the defenses at Jackson. The Confederates had lost 514 men to the Union's 442.

When Grant saw what was happening at Raymond, he changed his strategy for the campaign. Now suspecting that the Confederates were gathering in much larger numbers at Jackson than he had anticipated, Grant swung all three parts of his army around to head east toward Jackson rather than north to Vicksburg. This way he could attempt to hit Johnston's army before it had come to full strength, and keep them from reinforcing Vicksburg. The result was that Johnston, arriving in Jackson late on May 13, determined that he and the 6,000 men currently gathered in the capital were greatly outnumbered, and he ordered the evacuation of the city. Grant attacked and occupied Jackson the next day, taking Johnston out of the fight, and swung back west toward Vicksburg. Had he not changed his strategy at Raymond, Grant would quite possibly have chased Pemberton out of Vicksburg but not captured his army, and may have been exposed to Johnston in his rear. The outcome of the war in the West may have been prolonged for some time.

Champion Hill

After Jackson, Mississippi, had been captured, Grant swung his army back toward Vicksburg, while still keeping an eye on Major General Joseph Johnston's Confederates northeast of the city. While Major General William T. Sherman was preparing to burn and then evacuate Jackson, Grant sent Major General James McPherson and 32,000 men west to meet Major General John C. Pemberton's 22,000 Confederates. While both armies were strung out over lines 4–5 miles long, they would both use the same area as a centering point—a crossroads located near a small ridge known as Champion Hill.

On the morning of May 16, 1863, the Confederates were already there. Aware that a Federal force was approaching, Pemberton ordered a brigade and artillery to the crest of Champion Hill. As McPherson's corps approached, they spotted the Confederates and prepared their lines of battle. Passing the Champion house, where Grant set up his headquarters, the Federals advanced on the hill with two divisions. Seeing that they were outnumbered, the Confederates on the hill were quickly reinforced as the Union troops moved ever closer. Finally, at approximately 11:30, the Union pressed the Confederate left, quickly driving them back, and eventually pressed the entire Confederate line behind the crossroads. The Federals now had a commanding position on the battlefield.

Several miles south of this action, several Confederate divisions were guarding the Raymond–Vicksburg road. Pemberton called two of them up quickly to attempt to stop the Union push. Hurrying to the fight, Brigadier General John Bowen's Confederates came up on the right and forced the Union soldiers back through the crossroads, recapturing it (along with several pieces of artillery the Confederates had previously lost). Bowen's men pressed on until they had recaptured Champion Hill.

Monument to General Lloyd Tilghman, mortally wounded at Champion Hill.

SITE DETAILS

Champion Hill Battlefield—Touring the battlefield at Champion Hill can be either an extraordinary or an extremely frustrating experience. The battlefield has been wonderfully preserved, with the exception of the loss of the buildings that were present at the time. However, almost all of it is private property. While this may be irritating to those who would like to walk the grounds, you have to remember that no one asked Sid Champion if they could hold a major battle on his property in 1863. However, you can ask his great-great-grandson, Sid Champion V, and he will be happy to take you on a private guided tour of the battlefield. Although this is probably the most expensive of all the major battlefields in the country to tour, the fee is very low, considering that you are receiving a private tour from a descendant of living history. Very recently a driving tour was available online, but the tour only skirted the edges of the battle and didn't cover many of the important sites. It doesn't really matter anymore, because the tour map has been taken off the Web site in order to promote the private tour. You could probably get some old battle maps and make up a driving tour of your own from the existing roads, but if you want to see the real thing, take the private tour. *Champion Hill Battlefield Private Tour, Edwards, MS, 39066; 601-316-4894; www.battleofchampionhill.org. Tours arranged by appointment (minimum two persons); admission charged.*

In response, Union reinforcements were brought up, including sixteen pieces of artillery, and soon the Confederates were being pounded. Pemberton had few reserves to maintain the fight, with the remaining men still holding the Raymond–Edwards road to the south. Soon the Federals again pushed the Confederates back through the crossroads, although the fighting was extremely heavy. The field belonged to the Union.

To the south, Brigadier General Lloyd Tilghman's Confederate brigade was the only unit left to guard the Raymond–Edwards road. Tilghman was killed by Union artillery fire, and his men began to retreat with the rest of the Confederate force.

By midnight what was left of Pemberton's army was on its way back into the defenses at Vicksburg. They had taken a terrible beating, suffering 3,840 casualties and losing 27 cannon. The Union victory was not cheap, as they lost 2,441 men of their own. But Pemberton's army was on its last legs and was now forced to hole up at Vicksburg. It was a major success for the Union and set up what would be ultimate victory at Vicksburg.

Vicksburg

As a result of the devastating defeat at Champion Hill on May 16 and Grant's skillful maneuvering to keep Joseph E. Johnston's men from providing reinforcements, Major

General John C. Pemberton led what was left of his army back into the fortifications at Vicksburg, Mississippi, on May 17 and 18, 1863. The Union army followed right behind and began to invest the city in earnest. With the threat of Confederate help from the east virtually eliminated, supply bases were established at Snyder's Bluff and Chickasaw Bayou, just north of the city, and Rear Admiral David Porter's Union gunboats were brought back into the action. But if the Union forces thought that the siege and capture of Vicksburg would be an easy endeavor, they were in for a rude awakening.

Union probing of the fortifications began on May 19, when Major General William T. Sherman advanced toward the city, testing the outer defenses. Although heavy Union reinforcements from Major Generals James McPherson and John McClernand eventually helped push the Confederate defenders back into the city, the Federals had taken a beating. It was a clear indication that not only did Pemberton still have an army, but that they were going to fight.

Grant took three days to more carefully organize an assault, arranging his units and artillery around the Vicksburg defenses. Early on the morning of May 22, an artillery

The partially reconstructed USS Cairo, *Vicksburg National Military Park.*

barrage began from both the land batteries and the gunboats on the Mississippi River. After several hours the guns stopped, and the Union launched an all-out assault on the works. McClernand gained some ground, but Sherman and McPherson's men were repulsed easily. Grant ordered another assault later in the day, and the only result was that the ground gained earlier in the day was lost. The Union had lost almost 3,200 men to the Confederates' 500.

In the following days, Grant's grip on Vicksburg tightened. All possible supply lines to the city, by land and water, were closed. The Union soldiers began to dig approach trenches, inching ever closer to the Confederate lines. The bombardment of the Confederate fortifications and the city itself was now almost without cease, pausing only at 8 AM, noon, and 8 PM so that the artillerymen could eat their meals. More Union troops began to stream toward the siege, and within three weeks the Federal force numbered 77,000 men. For Grant, everything seemed to be under control.

For the Confederates in the trenches and the citizens of Vicksburg, conditions worsened by the day. Soldiers were put on siege rations, and food was scarce among the populace as well; soon, any substantial meal being eaten in Vicksburg consisted of horse or mule meat. The artillery barrage took its toll, and many of the city's inhabitants began to dig caves in the hills around the city rather than risk the wrath of a Union cannonball. The July Mississippi heat also took its toll on the defenders, and many fell ill. Morale decreased rapidly, especially as the soldiers realized that no help would be coming from Joe Johnston or any other Confederate forces. Any remaining hopes that Vicksburg could hold were fading fast.

SITE DETAILS

Vicksburg National Military Park—Without any doubt, Vicksburg National Military Park is one of the nation's true historic treasures. The driving tour through the winding hills of the park is almost deceiving in its stillness and is only occasionally disturbed by monuments, cannon, and interpretive signs. The main visitor's center and its staff are exceptional in helping visitors understand the siege and the campaign. There is also a second visitor's center, near the national cemetery at the north end of the park. It is centered on the USS Cairo, raised from the depths of the Yazoo River, where it had struck a mine in the months before the siege. Although what is left of the boat is just a skeleton of its former self, walking around and through the timbers, iron plates, and machinery that are left is an experience that is truly memorable. Of the many battlefields and historic sites in our country, Civil War–related or otherwise, Vicksburg is on the short list of places that are not to be missed. *Vicksburg National Military Park, 3201 Clay St., Vicksburg, MS, 39183; 601-636-0583; www.nps.gov/vick. Open daily; admission charged.*

On July 3, after being convinced by his subordinates that his men could not fight their way out, Pemberton contacted Grant to discuss surrender terms. After some negotiation, Pemberton finally accepted Grant's terms, and on July 4, 1863—the same day that Robert E. Lee was rapidly marching south after his defeat at Gettysburg—the Confederate army at Vicksburg surrendered, with a total loss of 32,697 men during the siege and surrender. For Grant, it was an exceptional campaign that established him as the nation's premier military commander. For the Confederacy, the fall of Vicksburg (and the resulting surrender of Port Hudson, Louisiana, several days later) meant the loss of the Mississippi River and the division of the South. Coupled with the defeat at Gettysburg, it was a severe blow to their cause. The American Civil War had truly reached its turning point.

Mansfield

Once the Mississippi River was under Federal control, Confederate activity in the West greatly diminished. The forces that remained, however, did what they could to disrupt activities and keep Union troops occupied. The operational headquarters for the Confederate Trans-Mississippi Department was Shreveport, Louisiana, on the Red River far upstream of its confluence with the Mississippi and far away from most Federal activity. Still, Union authorities thought enough of what was left to try to eliminate any threat once and for all.

In addition, the Red River was an avenue into Texas, which not only was a source of fighting men for the Confederacy, but also provided a maritime outlet at Galveston and a suspected conduit of supplies from south of the border. Mexico was in upheaval, with the French arranging the ascendance of Maximillian as emperor there. It was widely thought that French influence in Mexico might lead to eventual collaboration with and support for the Confederacy.

In March of 1864 the Union Red River campaign began. Major General Nathaniel Banks led the land force of 30,000 soldiers, while Rear Admiral David Porter's powerful river fleet of 60 gunboats and transports steamed upstream alongside the army. After meeting some resistance but easily taking Fort DeRussy near Marksville on March 14, the joint operation continued its advance virtually unopposed for several weeks. Before long the Confederate headquarters at Shreveport was within striking distance.

In overall command of the Confederate Trans-Mississippi forces was Major General Kirby Smith. Smith's domain was wide, covering Texas, Arkansas, Louisiana, Missouri, and the Oklahoma territories, but he had few men or resources. He did have one exceptional asset, however, under his command: Major General Richard Taylor. Taylor had done much of his fighting in Louisiana, his adopted home state, but had also served under the tutelage of Stonewall Jackson in the Shenandoah Valley of Virginia and fought during the Seven Days Battles around Richmond. Taylor was the son

A trailhead at Mansfield State Commemorative Area, Louisiana.

of another great general—Zachary Taylor, hero of the Mexican War and 12th president of the United States. His military heritage, training, and experience made him invaluable, and Smith needed him to oppose Banks's force as best he could, despite the long odds against holding the Trans-Mississippi.

As Banks approached Shreveport, Taylor, with only 8,800 men and growing increasingly frustrated with continuously having to give up Louisiana soil to the superior Union force, waited patiently for any opportunity that he might take advantage of. Banks obligingly offered him that opportunity just before reaching his goal at Shreveport.

For almost the entire campaign, the Union army had marched up the west bank of the river, under the protection of the guns of the naval force. Banks, however, decided that the best way into Shreveport by land was via the town of Mansfield, Louisiana, just north of which three roads led directly to Shreveport. Although Mansfield was almost 20 miles west of the river, having three available roads would make for the easy movement of troops, and Banks would be out of the protection of his gunboats for only a very short time. That short time was exactly what Taylor had been waiting for.

On April 8, 1864, just southeast of Mansfield, Taylor set his force across the Old Stage Road, south of the forks that Banks was marching for. Banks, meanwhile, had virtually his entire army strung out along the road as it advanced. Taylor's men were mostly set along a tree line, with the open field of a plantation in front of them and an easy view of the Union force as it advanced. Infantry held the middle of the Confederate line, while both flanks were held by cavalry. Finally, around noon, the Union soldiers began to appear across the field. The Federals encountered a small force of Confederate skirmishers and formed a line, advancing until they reached a ridge known as Honeycutt Hill. Suddenly, Confederate infantry under Brigadier General Jean Jacques Mouton opened fire. The Union men, mostly cavalry, were hit hard, and they took position in the trees behind them and along a rail fence and waited as reinforcements, still strung along the Old Stage Road, could be brought up. Meanwhile, the Confederates inflicted as much damage as they could across the open field.

Finally, at approximately 3:30, the Union had set a line forming a 90-degree angle across the road. As the afternoon passed, Taylor decided that the time had come to launch an all-out assault. Mouton's infantry began the charge across the field at 4 PM, suffering heavy casualties (including Mouton himself), but as the other brigades and cavalry joined in, the Federals were quickly compelled to fall back. The Union formed a second line, but before long it too had been routed, and the Federals were on the run, leaving many of their supply wagons on the Old Stage Road.

A final Confederate assault was made late in the day, and Banks's army retreated southeast to the town of Pleasant Hill, having lost 2,235 men, 20 cannon, and 150 wagons; because of their position on the road, they were only able to bring 7,000 men to the fight. Taylor had chosen his spot well, and Mansfield became a sudden and unexpected turning point for the Red River campaign. Not only would Banks not capture

SITE DETAILS

Mansfield State Commemorative Area—The Mansfield State Commemorative Area covers only a small portion of the original battlefield, but it is enough to see exactly what happened here and why. Louisiana Highway 175 is essentially what the Old Stage Road was in 1864, and the field and the tree lines have not changed much from what they were, making it easy to see the problem the Union army was faced with. There are walking trails with interpretation through the park, and plans for further development are slowly unfolding, including the development of Honeycutt Hill. The visitor's center contains an excellent video on the battle, and the museum interprets the entire campaign; the staff is knowledgeable and extremely helpful. Mansfield is the obvious place to start any tour of the Red River campaign sites, and this park is up to the challenge. *Mansfield State Commemorative Area, 15149 LA 175, Mansfield, LA, 71052; 318-872-1474; www.crt.state.la.us/parks/imansfld.aspx. Open daily; admission charged.*

Shreveport or conquer the Trans-Mississippi, but he was in danger of losing his entire army to a force less than a third the size of his.

» OTHER SITES IN THE LOWER MISSISSIPPI VALLEY

Plains Store—The Confederates holding Port Hudson learned that Major General Nathaniel Banks was approaching from the north and that Major General Christopher Augur was approaching from the south. In an attempt to prevent these two forces from meeting and surrounding Port Hudson, a group of Confederates 600 strong was sent to defend the crossing of the Plains Store and Bayou Sara Roads. On May 21, 1863, Augur's division met the Confederates at the crossroads and after some intense fighting drove them back into the defenses at Port Hudson. Banks arrived early the next morning, and the long siege of Port Hudson began.

A historical highway marker customarily stands at the Plains Store crossroads. Unfortunately, from time to time it has been damaged or has disappeared. However, information on the Plains Store engagement can easily be obtained from the nearby Port Hudson State Historic Site. *Historical highway marker—Plains Store, intersection of LA 964 and E. Plains–Port Hudson Rd., Zachary, LA, 70791. Site accessible daily.*

Grand Gulf—After months of failed plans and setbacks, the Union army finally decided to march down the opposite side of the Mississippi, recross the river well downstream of Vicksburg, and advance on the city from the south. The point of landing was determined to be the small town of Grand Gulf, Mississippi. Two Confederate batteries—Fort Wade and Fort Cobun—held commanding views of the Mississippi here, so the first order of action was to knock out these guns. On April 29, 1863, Rear Admiral David Porter's ironclads began shelling the emplacements. Fort Wade was put out of action, but Fort Cobun, high on the bluffs overlooking the river, would not be silenced. The Union could not cross here. But this was not enough to stop Grant, and in a movement characteristic of his tactics, he simply moved a bit farther south, and his men crossed at another location—but only after his remaining gunboats and transports had run past the still-hot guns of Grand Gulf.

Grand Gulf Military Park now maintains the land where the two river batteries were located. The park also contains an observation tower, the view from which might cause one to agree with Admiral Porter that Grand Gulf was "the strongest place on the Mississippi." An extensive museum not only addresses the battle and the Vicksburg campaign, but also highlights local history and exhibits artifacts dating to prehistoric times. The grounds contain several buildings from the original town of Grand Gulf, and other facilities include full campsites and an amphitheater. The staff is extremely knowledgeable, helpful, and friendly, and really cares about your visit to their park. While the site might seem a little bit out of the way if you're centered in Vicksburg, it is worth making the drive to visit. *Grand Gulf Military Park, 12006 Grand Gulf*

Rd., Port Gibson, MS, 39150; 601-437-5911; www.grandgulfpark.state.ms.us. Open daily; admission charged.

Port Gibson—After the action at Grand Gulf, the Confederate troops who had done so well to hold their position were forced to withdraw inland following Grant's landing. However, even though Major General John Pemberton had been told that Grant was crossing the river to the south, he was still preoccupied with other events around Vicksburg that Grant had set up as diversions, and would not reinforce his troops to the south. On May 1, 1863, some 24,000 Union soldiers who had just crossed the Mississippi met 8,000 Confederates a few miles west of the town of Port Gibson, Mississippi. It should have been an overwhelming Union victory, but the Confederates' knowledge of the thick forests and rough terrain in the area helped them hold Grant's men at bay for over 18 hours. Despite the slow going, however, the Federals advanced inland, and before long the full Union strength was upon the Confederates. By the time darkness fell, the Confederates were on the retreat, having lost 787 men to the Union's 875.

Getting to the battle site at Port Gibson, although extremely rewarding, is tough; if you plan on going, please read this carefully. The roads leading to the site are mud and gravel, and you must travel several miles of them to get to the site. With even a little bit of rain, it would be very easy to get stuck in the mud with anything but a four-wheel-drive vehicle, and there is no cell phone reception here. In addition, the site is difficult to find—the roads are not marked and branch off numerous times. However, if you are able to make the effort, the site is exquisite. The Shaifer House,

The Shaifer House, at the heart of the Port Gibson battlefield.

around which much of the fighting occurred, still stands, and numerous interpretive signs fully explain the battle and the Vicksburg campaign. There are also several memorials around the grounds. Being here makes it very easy to appreciate how difficult the fighting must have been through the thick surrounding growth. The roads to the site are not on most maps or even GPS systems; your best bet for getting here is to ask for directions at Grand Gulf Military Park or the Port Gibson Chamber of Commerce. *Shaifer House, on Rodney Rd. east of intersection with Bessie Weather Rd., Port Gibson, MS, 39150; 601-636-0583; www.portgibsononthemississippi.com. Open daily.*

Jackson—After his victory at Raymond, Grant quickly turned east to capture the capital at Jackson, Mississippi, and head off Major General Joseph E. Johnston before Johnston could reinforce Pemberton's forces at Vicksburg. Johnston had arrived in Jackson on May 13, but upon learning of the battle at Raymond the previous day and that Union forces were descending upon him, he decided to withdraw his 6,000 troops, convinced that he could not hold the city. The next day, May 14, 1863, the Federals attacked while the Confederates, in the process of evacuating the city, fought a delaying action. By the afternoon the Union army was in control of Jackson, and before long much of the city was in flames. More important than the capture of the capital, however, was the fact that the Confederate force in Vicksburg was now effectively cut off from all hope of reinforcement from the east.

Within the city of Jackson lies Jackson Battlefield Park, a city park that contains, among other things, remnants of the earthworks that protected the city, as well as several memorials and monuments. Most of the park is devoted to recreational use, with playgrounds and picnic areas, but what is here is all that remains of the battlefield. *Jackson Battlefield Park, 801 W. Porter St., Jackson, MS, 39204. Open daily.*

Big Black River Bridge—While withdrawing into their fortifications at Vicksburg after the defeat at Champion Hill, the Confederates left 5,000 troops on the east bank of the Big Black River to hold the bridges open for other Confederate forces in the area. On May 17, 1863, behind hastily thrown-together fortifications of abatis and cotton bales, the Confederates attempted to defend a poor position against an advancing Union force. A Union charge sent the Confederates in quick retreat across the river, abandoning 18 pieces of artillery in the process. The Union force captured almost 1,700 troops and continued its advance to Vicksburg.

No signs or monuments memorialize the battle of Big Black River Bridge, and the land itself is privately owned. However, the scene of the action can be viewed from the roadside near the original bridge, where the railroad still crosses the river. There isn't much room to pull off the road, so take care if you visit the site. Information about the battle can be found at Vicksburg National Military Park. *Big Black River Bridge battle site, 0.2 mile south of intersection of US 80 and Warriors Trail, Vicksburg, MS, 39180; 601-636-0583. Private property; site viewable from roadside.*

Chickasaw Bayou—Just north of Vicksburg lies Chickasaw Bayou, a natural water obstruction to any force approaching the city from that direction. However, Grant's first plan to seize Vicksburg involved Major General William T. Sherman crossing Chickasaw Bayou with 32,000 soldiers. Lieutenant General John Pemberton had already constructed strong fortifications around the city, including at Chickasaw Bayou, and when the combined Union land and naval forces arrived on December 26, 1862, the Confederates were ready for them. Fighting was heavy, and the Federals, probing the lines for a point of weakness, could not find one. Finally, on December 29, Sherman ordered an all-out assault. Artillery fire began early in the morning, and at noon the Union troops advanced. The results were disastrous for the Union; the attack was repulsed at all points. At the end of the four days' action, the Union had lost 1,176 casualties to the Confederates' 187. This attempt at Vicksburg was a decisive failure, and Sherman's men returned to their base at Memphis.

The battlefield lies just north of the city of Vicksburg, and a driving tour brochure written by local Terrence Winschel is available for purchase at Vicksburg National Military Park. The site is now completely privately owned and is occupied by private homes and small industry. The tour brochure, though, contains a very thorough retelling of the battle, along with maps of the troop movements; for 50 cents, you can't beat the price. *Chickasaw Bayou Driving Tour, available at Vicksburg National Military Park, 3201 Clay St., Vicksburg, MS, 39183; 601-636-0583; www.nps.gov/vick. Open daily.*

Snyder's Bluff—On April 29, 1863, as Grant's army prepared to cross the river and land in Mississippi, Major General William T. Sherman assaulted several fortified positions north of Vicksburg as a diversion to keep Confederate troops occupied. One of these positions was Snyder's Bluff, on the Yazoo River. The Union troops played with Confederate forces in the area for two days before returning to their encampment at Milliken's Bend.

There is a well-hidden memorial to the battle located on the bluff itself. The stone monument is on an isolated road in an overgrown park, which has its own parking lot and a somewhat-obscured view of the Yazoo River. It's only a short drive north of Vicksburg, and even though it's very easy to get to, it is one of those battle sites that make you feel rewarded just for finding it. Information on the battle, of course, can be found at Vicksburg National Military Park. *Snyder's Bluff historical marker, on MS 3, a mile north of intersection of US 61 and Redwood Rd., Redwood, MS, 39156. Open daily.*

Milliken's Bend—While Grant had Vicksburg under siege, his main supply base at Milliken's Bend remained active, serving as a refugee camp, a recruiting center for troops (many of them escaped slaves), and a hospital. After a reconnaissance mission out of Milliken's Bend encountered some unexpected resistance, Union troops under Colonel Hermann Lieb withdrew back into the camp and requested reinforcements, which were promptly sent, including the Union gunboat *Choctaw*. Very early on June

7, 1863, the Confederates charged the Union lines, inflicting heavy casualties. The Federal troops withdrew behind the levees of the Mississippi River and under the protection of the *Choctaw*'s guns. When a second Union gunboat (the *Lexington*) arrived, the Confederates withdrew. Although the Confederates inflicted 652 casualties to their 185, the Union held the ground and the day.

A historical highway marker near the site tells of the camp and the battle, but getting to the site of the battle at Milliken's Bend can be difficult. If you approach from Vicksburg, be prepared to travel on winding gravel roads that are not well maintained, and make sure your car's suspension is in good shape and that you have a spare tire in the trunk—there are some huge potholes. It might be better to drive north of Tallulah, Louisiana, and approach from the west. *Historical highway markers (Battle of Milliken's Bend and Grant's March), 1.1 miles north of intersection of Thomastown Rd. and Airport Rd., Tallulah, LA, 71282. Site accessible daily.*

Goodrich's Landing—Only days before the Confederates surrendered Vicksburg to the Union, a small Confederate force from Arkansas headed to Lake Providence, Louisiana, to attack Union fortifications protecting plantations that had been given to freed slaves. The fortifications were also heavily manned by freed slaves who had been trained to fight. On June 29, 1863, the much larger Confederate force approached the fortifications and demanded an unconditional surrender. They received it, with one glaring exception—that the white officers would be granted all their rights and privileges as prisoners of war. The next day the Confederate force was driven off by Union reinforcements who had landed nearby. In the meantime, the Confederates had only barely succeeded in their mission of slightly disrupting the Vicksburg operations.

A park in Lake Providence has some signs related to the Vicksburg campaign and Grant's canal but nothing dedicated to the battle that took place here. The park is across the street from the town visitor's center at the Byerley House, but again, there is little battle information here. *Byerley House, 600 Lake St., Lake Providence, LA, 71254; 318-559-5125. Open daily.*

Old River Lake—Even after the Federals gained control of the Mississippi River, Confederate units would still make opportunities to fire at Union river traffic from time to time. One such unit was the small Confederate cavalry brigade stationed in Lake Village, Arkansas. Major General Andrew Smith, after being freed up from the Red River campaign and while on his way to help the Union drive for Atlanta, decided to try to silence the Confederate guns here and left a force of 3,000 men near Lake Village to undertake the task. On June 6, 1864, the Union force headed west toward Lake Village, passing just south of Lake Chicot and through the swampy area of Ditch Bayou. Although the Union troops drove the Confederates back toward the town, they were slowed and eventually stopped by the bayou. The 600 Confederates, with their six pieces of artillery, were able to form a line and hold the Federals back until they ran out of ammunition and had to withdraw. The next day the two Union brigades were back with Smith's main force and on their way to Atlanta.

A brochure outlining an excellent driving tour of the battle, also known as the battle of Ditch Bayou, is available at the Arkansas Welcome Center in Lake Village. As part of the tour, there are also interpretive signs and memorials at the bayou, the scene of the heaviest fighting. *Self-Guided Civil War Tour—Chicot County, Arkansas, Welcome Center, intersection of Arkansas Great River Rd. and S. Lake Shore Dr., Lake Village, AR, 71653; 870-265-5480. Open daily.*

Arkansas Post—Although Union efforts to open the Mississippi were focused largely on Vicksburg, there were other complicating Confederate outposts in the area. One of these was Fort Hindman, on the Arkansas River at Arkansas Post. The fort was heavily armed and manned and served not only to keep Union gunboats from approaching the capital at Little Rock, but also as a point of operations for Confederate riverboats to disrupt Union shipping on the Mississippi, 50 miles downstream. On January 9, 1863, a joint Union expedition headed by Major General John McClernand and Rear Admiral David Porter, with 33,000 troops and a number of gunboats, including three ironclads, approached the 5,000 Confederates at Fort Hindman. The attack was opened by the gunboats, which inflicted heavy damage on the fort while the army approached. The Union troops assaulted the fort on January 11, and after heavy fighting the Confederates surrendered.

Arkansas Post has a rich history that dates to long before the assault on Fort Hindman. The French and Spanish both had trading posts here, and this heritage, as well as that of the battle, is retold at Arkansas Post National Memorial. Fort Hindman itself, unfortunately, is a victim of time and erosion, and the site of the original fortification now sits in the middle of the Arkansas River. However, some of the original earthworks are still undisturbed, and the tale of the battle is well told at the museum in the visitor's center. The park's other features, which include extensive nature trails through the surrounding marsh, offer many opportunities for peaceful picnicking or wildlife watching. *Arkansas Post National Memorial, AR 169 and Old Post Rd., Gillett, AR, 72055; 870-548-2207; www.nps.gov/arpo. Open daily.*

St. Charles—A small town overlooking the White River, St. Charles was a good spot to place a Confederate battery to guard against Union traffic on the river, which was a supply line to armies in northwest Arkansas. Arkansas itself was lightly defended, with most of the troops there having been transferred to the fighting in Tennessee. But on June 17, 1862, the two heavy guns atop the bluff made their mark. Four Union gunboats, two of them ironclads, and several transports were steaming past St. Charles when the Confederate batteries opened fire on them. One cannonball, in a one-in-a-million shot, entered a port hole of the USS ironclad *Mound City* and found the ship's steam drum.

The ship was instantly filled with scalding steam, and 105 of the 175 sailors aboard were killed, with another 44 injured. Soon after, the transports landed, and Union troops took the town of St. Charles and the Confederate artillery. But the loss of the *Mound City* was a heavy blow to the Union river fleet. The deadly shot that came from the St. Charles battery has been called the single most destructive shot in the Civil War.

St. Charles has a town museum that has interesting current and period information on the battle there, including some well-done drawings and models of the action. There is also a monument outside the museum to the soldiers and sailors of both sides who died in the fighting, as well as a historical marker near the point in the river where the *Mound City* was struck. *St. Charles Museum, 608 Broadway St., St. Charles, AR, 72140; 870-282-3425. Open Mon.–Fri. Historical highway marker—Arkansas Civil War Centennial Commission (Engagement at St. Charles), intersection of CC Camp Rd. and Belnap Rd., St. Charles, AR, 72140. Site accessible daily.*

Helena—On July 4, 1863, the day of the formal surrender at Vicksburg, the strong Union position at Helena, Arkansas, was attacked by a force of 7,600 Confederates. Helena was a major supply depot for Grant's operations and was held by 4,100 Union soldiers entrenched in heavy fortifications. The Confederates made coordinated, direct assaults on the Federal works and captured a number of positions and Union prisoners. However, by midmorning it was clear that the assault had failed, and the Confederates withdrew. Helena remained an important point of Union operations in Arkansas for the rest of the war.

Although remnants of the fortifications around Helena still exist, the best place to see and interpret what happened here is at the Delta Cultural Center. From here a climb onto a platform on the levee gives a view of the entire city, with an interpretive sign that points out the most important landmarks of the battle. The museum itself is fantastic, and although only one room is dedicated to the battle of Helena, the telling of the story is thorough, interesting, and vivid. The center is also working to acquire and interpret other locations around the town that featured prominently in the battle. Much of the rest of the two-building museum complex is dedicated to the city's rich musical heritage and is truly entertaining; it is obvious that a great deal of care went into its creation. *Delta Cultural Center, 141 Cherry St., Helena, AR, 72342; 1-800-358-0972; www.deltaculturalcenter.com. Closed Sun. and Mon.*

Hill's Plantation—Because Union supply boats assigned to his army could not get up the shallow White River, Major General Samuel Curtis, advancing through Arkansas, was forced to detour to meet the boats. As Curtis marched his army down the river on July 7, 1862, a small Confederate force attacked him at Hill's Plantation near Cotton Plant, Arkansas. Although the Confederates outnumbered the advance unit they faced, their uncoordinated attacks were repeatedly repulsed, and they retreated when Union reinforcements began arriving. Although the attacks did not slow

Curtis much, he did arrive at his destination only to find that the supply boats had already left. He took his army to Helena, Arkansas, which he occupied.

No marker or memorial commemorates the battle of Hill's Plantation, and the site is on private property. Cotton Plant, Arkansas, is just south of the battle area, but trying to get near the battlefield involves some heavy travel on dirt roads to an unsure destination. Hopefully, some monument to the battle can be placed and accessible at a later date. *Hill's Plantation, battle site on private property.*

Bayou Fourche—In 1863 the Union controlled the borderlands of Arkansas; they held sway on the Mississippi River to the east and had a strong grip on the northern part of the state. They did not, however, have the capital of Little Rock, almost directly in the center of the state. After the fall of Vicksburg, Major General Frederick Steele decided to take hold of Arkansas and marched on Little Rock. Steele left Helena with 12,000 Union troops, while Major General Sterling Price waited with 7,700 Confederates. Knowing that he could not hold the capital when Steele attacked, Price began preparing to evacuate the city. His first step was to release Brigadier General John Marmaduke from prison—Marmaduke had been jailed for killing another general in a duel—to lead the Confederate cavalry. Beginning in late August, Marmaduke's cavalry began fighting delaying actions against Steele's troops, while Price prepared to leave Little Rock and head southwest. Finally, on September 10, 1863, Steele's force approached the capital. Marmaduke fought one more effective action east of the city at Bayou Fourche, and although the Confederates were driven back to Little Rock and the rest of Price's army, it allowed enough time to complete the evacuation. The capital of Little Rock, however, now fell under Federal control.

Pratt Remmel Park commemorates the battle of Bayou Fourche and contains several interpretive signs, as well as a picnic area and other facilities. Not far from the park is a bridge crossing Fourche Creek, where several monuments memorialize the fighting that took place here. Also, the Central Arkansas Civil War Heritage Trail Association has created a very good driving tour that highlights all the major sites of Steele's campaign as he approached Little Rock. The brochure should be available at any local tourist stops or rest stops along the interstate as you approach the city. *Pratt Remmel Park, 0.2 miles south of intersection of Lindsey Rd. and Fourche Dam Pike (I-440 exit 4), Little Rock, AR, 72206; 501-371-4770. Bayou Fourche monuments, west side of bridge at intersection of E. Roosevelt Rd. and Fourche Dam Pike, Little Rock, AR, 72206. Little Rock Campaign Tour, Central Arkansas Civil War Heritage Trail Association; available at tourist facilities and rest stops. All sites open daily.*

Pine Bluff—After the capture of Little Rock, Union forces began to reach southward to strengthen their hold on Arkansas. On October 25, 1863, Major General Sterling Price decided to send Brigadier General John Marmaduke and 2,000 Confederates against the town of Pine Bluff to test Federal resolve. Pine Bluff, held by only 550 men, would have been an easy target, but the Union force threw up strong defenses around the small town and augmented their fighting force by 300 "contraband" slaves who were eager to prove they could fight. Marmaduke's cavalry rushed the town several times, centering their attacks on the town's courthouse, but they eventually withdrew.

Memorial markers can be seen on the town square at the courthouse, where most of the action took place. Also, the Jefferson County Historical Museum, located nearby, contains an exhibit on the battle. For a small museum, it has a fine collection of artifacts, including original battle maps and flags. *Pine Bluff Courthouse, 101 W. Barraque St.; Jefferson County Historical Museum, 201 E. 4th St., Pine Bluff, AR, 71601; 870-541-5402. Courthouse memorials accessible daily; museum closed Sun.*

Jenkins' Ferry—Major General Frederick Steele's Union army was running for its life, trying to reach Little Rock, Arkansas, and safety. The army was nearly out of food, and after the loss of several wagon trains, along with the realization that the Red River campaign they had intended to support had met with disaster, the Union soldiers were severely weakened, and morale was low. Also, the Confederates had greatly reinforced their units in the area. On April 29, 1864, Steele reached the Saline River at Jenkins' Ferry. The next day, while his army was trying to complete its crossing, Major General Kirby Smith attacked the rear of the Union force. Although hungry and tired, the Federals had not lost all their fight, and they were able to hold off the Confederate attack until the last of them had crossed, taking the bridge with them. The Confederates, who had been chasing Steele for days, were also exhausted, and they gave up their pursuit here. Steele's army made it back to Little Rock two days later, beaten but still intact.

Although the Jenkins' Ferry State Park does not include much of the surrounding land on which most of the fighting took place, it does contain the site of the ferry crossing. There are memorials and interpretive signs here, as well as some very short trails to the crossing site. The park also includes picnic facilities and a swimming area. *Jenkins' Ferry State Park, near intersection of AR 46 and CR-540, Leola, AR, 72084; 1-888-287-2757; www.arkansasstateparks.com/jenkinsferry. Open daily.*

Marks' Mills—Already in trouble because it was desperately short of supplies, the Union force under Major General Frederick Steele was trying to reach Shreveport, Louisiana, to support the Red River campaign of Major General Nathaniel Banks. What Steele did not know was even worse: Banks's army in Louisiana was in full retreat, and the Confederates had begun to shift troops northward in order to defeat Steele's own force. The new Confederate troops reached the main party on April 19, and Confederate command was shifted from Major General Sterling Price to Major General Kirby Smith. Smith sent his cavalry north of the Union army to cut its avenue of retreat, as well as its supply lines from Pine Bluff, Arkansas. On April 25, 1864, at Marks' Mills, Arkansas, the Confederate cavalry attacked a fully loaded wagon train bound for Steele's army. The result was decisive, not only for the battle, but for Steele's campaign. The Confederates captured the entire Federal force, including their 240 wagons of supplies. Steele's army was now in deep trouble, and he was forced to try to make it back north to Little Rock with his army intact.

The Marks' Mills Battleground Historical Monument is only a small area set aside at a fork in the road, but this is the junction where the wagon train was caught. The state site contains several monuments and interpretive signs, along with a picnic area. *Marks' Mills Battleground Historical Monument, intersection of AR 97 and AR 8, New Edinburg, AR, 71660; 1-888-287-2757; www.arkansasstateparks.com/marksmills. Open daily.*

Poison Spring—Major General Frederick Steele's Union army, trying to reach Shreveport to support the Red River campaign, was having trouble living off the land, thanks to Major General Sterling Price, whose Confederates had destroyed anything that might have helped the Federals. A foraging party was sent out by Steele, and they collected almost 200 wagons with provisions. However, on their way back to the main force on April 18, 1864, the Union party was attacked by Confederate cavalry at Poison Spring, Arkansas, and was forced to abandon the wagons and their desperately needed supplies. The Arkansas expedition to support the Red River campaign was in serious trouble.

Poison Spring Battlefield State Park contains extensive interpretation, as well as several monuments and markers. In addition, following Arkansas Highway 76 south of the park will take you along the road on which the Union wagon train was drawn out and hence the scene of the battle. There are also picnic facilities at the site. *Poison Spring Battlefield State Park, intersection of AR 76 and CR-175, Chidester, AR, 71726; 1-888-287-2757; www.arkansasstateparks.com/poisonspring. Open daily.*

Prairie D'Ane and Elkin's Ferry—An important part of the plan of the Red River campaign was for Major General Frederick Steele to join Nathaniel Banks's force at Shreveport, Louisiana. Confederate plans were to send most of their troops against Banks in Louisiana; the rest of the soldiers, 7,500 in all, were under the command of Major General Sterling Price, whose job it was to slow Steele's Federals as they advanced. On April 3, 1864, the fight began, as Confederate cavalry struck the rear of Steele's force, without much result. The next day, at a crossing of the Little Missouri River known as Elkin's Ferry, near Okolona, the Confederates hit again, eventually withdrawing. Steele was soon reinforced by 5,000 troops; however, while the cavalry stalled the Union, Price had been tearing up the countryside, making sure that the Federals would have a hard time finding forage. Several days later, on April 10, 1864, Price opposed the Union force with 5,000 entrenched men at Prairie D'Ane, again not far from Okolona. Although the Confederates were eventually pushed back, the Union army was having a hard time living off the countryside and was forced to move east instead of south. Price had not only slowed the Federals but had forced them to alter their campaign and begin to think twice about advancing farther south to Shreveport.

The stories of both the Elkin's Ferry and the Prairie D'Ane battles are told at the Nevada County Depot and Museum, where there is also a memorial to the battle at Prairie D'Ane. The battlefield at Prairie D'Ane is on private property; it can be viewed by driving along Interstate 30 and looking northwest. The site of Elkin's Ferry is now a public boat launch on the Little Missouri River. The roads leading to it are gravel and not always in the best condition, so be cautious as you proceed—if you get stuck here, your cell phone may not be able to help you. There is no memorial or marker at the site. *Nevada County Depot and Museum, 403 W. First St. South, Prescott, AR, 71857; 870-887-5821; www.depotmuseum.org. Closed Sun. Elkin's Ferry Boat Launch—Arkansas Game and Fish Commission, 2.7 miles north of intersection of CR-37 and CR-211, Prescott, AR, 71857. Open daily. Prairie D'Ane battlefield is private property.*

Pleasant Hill—Just south of the Mansfield battlefield, Pleasant Hill was the scene on April 9, 1864, of a follow-up to that battle, although the results in terms of casualties came much closer to a draw. The Federals, exhausted from a 17-mile retreat, had camped at Pleasant Hill, their positions scattered about. Meanwhile, Major General Richard Taylor had reinforced his force by 4,000 men and saw an opportunity to at the very least send the Union army running again, and possibly even capture it. Unfortunately for the Confederates, their forces could not be organized until midafternoon, and what was planned as a coordinated attack went awry. The first attack did

Entrance gate at Pleasant Hill Battle Park, Louisiana.

not begin until 5 PM, and although some ground was gained, the confused movements of the Confederates led to uncoordinated assaults. When the fighting stopped as darkness fell, the Confederates had lost 1,626 men and had inflicted 1,369 casualties. The Union held the field but retreated back toward the Red River during the night.

Pleasant Hill Battlefield Park occupies only a very small portion of the battlefield, but enough is here to warrant a visit. The site is only a short drive south of the Mansfield battlefield, and although it is unstaffed, the parklike grounds and beautiful gardens are well cared for and make for a pleasant (no pun intended) stop. Several interpretive markers and memorials can be seen inside the grounds, and they are enough to explain the battle; the surrounding land is private property. *Pleasant Hill Battlefield Park, 23271 LA 175, Pelican, LA 71063; 318-796-2777. Open daily.*

Blair's Landing—After the battle at Pleasant Hill, the Union army was on the retreat, but the naval force had already advanced up the Red River toward Shreveport. Hearing of the Union defeat at Mansfield, and with the level of the Red River rapidly falling, the fleet started to make its way back downstream. On April 12, 1864, some of the gunboats and transports were stalled at a place called Blair's Landing and took fire from Confederate forces on the riverbank under the command of Brigadier General Thomas Green. Eventually the Confederates withdrew, but not before General Green had been killed.

A brand-new historical highway marker at Blair's Landing tells of the action there and also commemorates the death of General Green in the battle. The landing is on a levee along a road leading to one of the Red River's dams. *Historical highway marker—Louisiana Society Order of the Confederate Rose (C.S.A. Brigadier General Tom Green), on road for Lock and Dam #4 (0.3 mile north of intersection of LA 1 and LA 174, then 1.5 miles along Dam Rd.), Coushatta, LA, 71019. Site accessible daily.*

Monett's Ferry—After spending some time dug in on the banks of the Red River at Grand Ecore, Louisiana, Major General Nathaniel Banks began to move his Union troops back down the river toward the safety of the Mississippi. The Confederates' Major General Richard Taylor, who had just had part of his force reassigned to confront Major General Frederick Steele in Arkansas, sent 1,600 of his remaining men and artillery to a crossing of the Cane River known as Monett's Ferry, hoping to oppose the Federals as they retreated. However, the Union force simply found another crossing and on April 23, 1864, hit the Confederates on both flanks, causing them to retreat.

During this period of Banks's retreat, it is interesting to note the trials of the U.S. naval flotilla. Rear Admiral David Porter was struggling to get his gunboats over the falls at Alexandria, Louisiana, because of low water in the river. Fortunately for the Union, Lieutenant Colonel Joseph Bailey, a resourceful engineer, was able to raise the level of the river by constructing makeshift dams extending from either side of the river, creating a water chute in the opening between them. The dams sent the water of the Red rushing through the gap, and Porter's boats were shot through to safety. Had Bailey's dams, the result of quick thinking and extraordinary engineering, not been constructed, the Union fleet would certainly have been doomed.

The only physical reminder today of the battle at Monett's Ferry is a very small sign on the east side of the bridge that now crosses the former ferry site. The state highway marker customarily here has been repeatedly vandalized and replaced, and it is not known if it will be replaced again. Still, the site is easy to get to, and pulling to the side of the road will give you a good view of the crossing and the site of the battle. *Monett's Ferry site, bridge at intersection of LA 1 and Marco Rd., Cloutierville, LA (unincorporated); 1-800-259-1714. Site accessible daily.*

Fort DeRussy—A fairly strong earthwork fortification located upriver from Simmesport, Fort DeRussy was the only Confederate position between the main Union force under Major General Nathaniel Banks and Admiral David Porter and the city of Alexandria. The fort was garrisoned by 350 Confederates, and the sides of the earthworks were plated with steel to protect them from the powerful artillery of the Union riverboats. Shortly after landing his force at Simmesport, Banks marched his troops up the west bank of the Red River, while Porter followed alongside with his massive fleet. On March 14, while the gunboats shelled the fort from the river, Brigadier General Andrew Smith led his Union troops around the rear of the fort to assault it. Late in the day, as the naval bombardment continued, Smith's troops attacked, quickly overwhelming the heavily outnumbered Confederates and taking the fort. The Confederates retreated up the Red River and did not stop until General Richard Taylor made his decisive stand at Mansfield. The battle at Fort DeRussy was the only significant action between the two forces while moving up the Red.

Today the Fort DeRussy State Historic Site is under the care of the Louisiana State Park system. The site itself is unstaffed, and information on the battle is best obtained from the nearby Marksville State Historic Site. But the earthworks are largely intact, and several monuments are located on the grounds, including one to the black slaves who built the fort, many of whom died during the effort. The state has bought up much of the land surrounding the site, and big plans are in the works, including a staffed interpretive center and marked trails. The site also receives outstanding local support from the Friends of Fort DeRussy, and in recent years an annual reenactment has been established at the site. While some of the funding has been derailed by the Hurricane Katrina recovery efforts, it shouldn't be long before this becomes a can't-miss site for interpreting the Red River campaign. *Fort DeRussy State Historic Site, 425 Fort DeRussy Rd.; Marksville State Historic Site, 837 Martin Luther King Dr.; Marksville, LA, 71351; 1-888-253-8954; www.fortdrussy.org. Open daily.*

Mansura—While Major General Nathaniel Banks was burning the city of Alexandria, Major General Richard Taylor had slipped his Confederates south to the town of Mansura. Now down to only 5,000 men, Taylor attempted to make a show at Mansura and stall the Union retreat, but when the whole of the Union army approached on May 16, 1864, the outnumbered Confederates were forced to withdraw after only a short artillery duel.

A Louisiana historical highway marker near the center of town in Mansura marks where the Confederate line crossed the Union retreat route. A very limited amount of information can be gathered at the Mansura State Historical Site. *Historical highway marker—Louisiana Department of Commerce and Industry (Battle of Mansura), intersection of Baton Rouge Ave. and Leglise St., Mansura, LA, 71350. Site accessible daily.*

Yellow Bayou—On May 18, 1864, the Union army was finally within sight of safety—the other side of the Atchafalaya River at Simmesport, Louisiana. Unfortunately for them, though, the river was too wide, and a makeshift bridge had to be constructed (again thanks to the engineering prowess of Lieutenant Colonel Joseph Bailey). As the bridge was being built, the Confederates were still approaching, and the Federals sent a small force to stall them at Yellow Bayou. They held the Confederates back, and by May 20 the Union army had crossed the river. The disastrous Red River campaign was over.

The site of the battle has been preserved at the Yellow Bayou Civil War Memorial Park. Although the park is largely for community use and contains facilities such as softball fields, playgrounds, and picnic areas, the remains of earthworks run the length of the park. A state historical marker and other memorials offer some interpretation of the battle. *Yellow Bayou Civil War Memorial Park, LA 1 and W. Bernard Rd., Simmesport, LA, 71369; 1-800-833-4195. Open daily.*

» WHERE TO STAY IN THE LOWER MISSISSIPPI VALLEY

Although the tour will take you through some rural areas, finding a place to stop won't be too difficult. Vicksburg and Jackson have a wealth of hotels, so any exploration of the battlefields around those areas will keep you close to lodging. Finding a stop in Louisiana while retracing the Red River campaign might prove a little more difficult, but Shreveport has plenty of hotels, and there are places to stop along the interstate, such as Natchitoches.

The **Cedar Grove Inn** in Vicksburg, right in the downtown, dates to before the war. Although the house survived the siege, it took some battle damage, some of which can still be seen, including a Union cannonball lodged in the parlor wall. The home survived after the siege mostly due to the fact that it was used as a Union hospital, and the original owners actually had personal ties with the Sherman family, for which the wife received considerable backlash from her neighbors. Many of the furnishings predate the war and are original to the home. *Cedar Grove Inn, 2200 Oak St., Vicksburg, MS, 39180; 1-800-862-1300; www.cedargroveinn.com.*

4

America's Heartland and the Drive for Atlanta

OVERVIEW

Early in the war it was recognized that whoever controlled the heartland of the country—Kentucky and Tennessee—would be well on their way to winning the war. From these central states, each side could easily strike deep into the other's territory. Regarding his home state, Lincoln remarked that "I think to lose Kentucky is nearly the same as to lose the whole game." While great attention was focused on the two armies maneuvering in Virginia between Richmond and Washington, a critical chess match was taking place in middle America to see who would control the hearts and minds of the people.

After several invasions by each side, Kentucky was finally decided at the battle of Perryville in October of 1862. The Confederate armies began to pull southward, and the Union had a new goal: to capture the critical rail center at Chattanooga and, eventually, the most valuable and grand city of the South—Atlanta. The armies continued to face each other, coming together several times, with the Union forces drawing closer and closer to the Confederacy's major industrial center. Finally, after the battle of Stones River near Murfreesboro, Tennessee, the Confederate armies pulled back toward Atlanta. However, Union miscommunications and timely intervention by an army from Virginia, rushed in by rail, gave the Confederates a great victory at Chickamauga in

The Illinois Monument, at the site of Confederate General Braxton Bragg's headquarters on Missionary Ridge, Chattanooga.

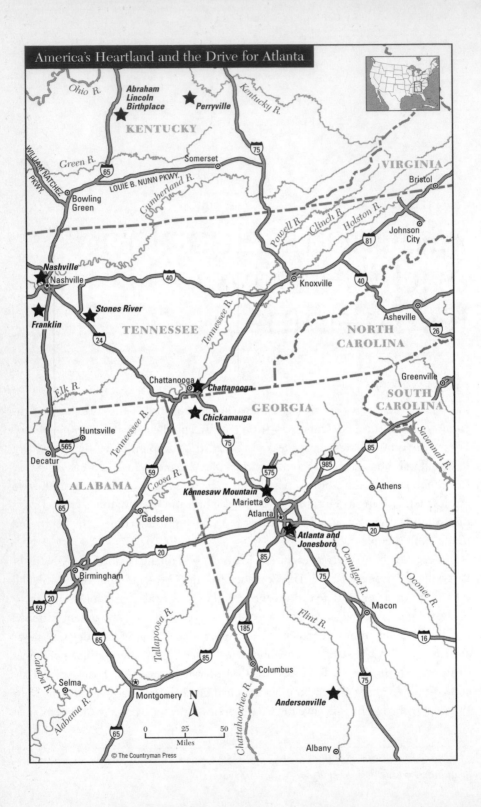

America's Heartland and the Drive for Atlanta

Ohio R.

Abraham
Lincoln
Birthplace

Perryville

KENTUCKY

Kentucky R.

Green R.

Somerset

75

VIRGINIA

Bristol

WILLIAM NATCHEZ PKWY.

LOUIE B. NUNN PKWY.

Cumberland R.

Powell R.

Clinch R.

Holston R.

Bowling
Green

81

Johnson
City

Nashville
Nashville

40

Knoxville

40

Asheville

26

Stones River

Tennessee R.

NORTH
CAROLINA

Franklin

24

TENNESSEE

Elk R.

Tennessee R.

Chattanooga

Chattanooga

Greenville

SOUTH
CAROLINA

GEORGIA

Savannah R.

Huntsville

Chickamauga

75

565

Decatur

ALABAMA

59

Coosa R.

575

985

85

Athens

Kennesaw Mountain

Marietta

Atlanta

Gadsden

65

Atlanta and
Jonesboro

20

85

Birmingham

Tallapoosa R.

20

75

Ocmulgee R.

Oconee R.

59

65

Flint R.

Macon

Cahaba R.

185

16

Selma

65

85

75

Columbus

Montgomery

N

Chattahoochee R.

Andersonville

Alabama R.

0   25   50
Miles

© The Countryman Press

Albany

northwest Georgia, and the demoralized Union army was suddenly in danger of being trapped at Chattanooga.

Then, in October of 1863, General Ulysses S. Grant arrived, followed shortly by his trusted friend, General William Tecumseh Sherman. Quickly coming up with a plan, the Federals were able not only to break out of Chattanooga, but to snatch victory from the jaws of defeat and put the Confederate army on the defensive. After the victory Grant was made general-in-chief of all Union forces and went to oversee the action in Virginia, leaving the capable Sherman with the task of taking Atlanta. The Confederates opposing him, now with General Joseph Johnston commanding, were up to the challenge, and months of constant maneuvering and hard fighting followed. Finally, in September of 1864, Sherman entered Atlanta and burned it to the ground, not only destroying the most important industrial and rail center in the South, but driving a deep nail into the coffin of the Confederacy. Sherman's concept of total warfare—"War is cruelty, and you cannot refine it"—would soon lead to his famous march to the sea and the capture of Savannah.

There was, however, still one chapter remaining to be written in this part of the country. General John Bell Hood, who commanded the Confederate armies in the last battles of the Atlanta campaign after Johnston had been removed, collected his force and boldly invaded Tennessee. Although the fighting was bloody for both sides, the Union victories at Franklin and Nashville were complete and devastating, and Hood's army dissolved, crushed and beaten.

This chapter will take you through the heartland of Kentucky and Tennessee and the great battles leading to Sherman's drive for Atlanta, as well as the aftermath of that campaign.

» PEOPLE TO KNOW

William T. Sherman—By the time the Atlanta campaign and his infamous march to the sea came around, Major General William Tecumseh Sherman had more than proved his worth as a commander. He had been with Grant at Shiloh and Vicksburg and had taken part in the great battle at Chattanooga. But in the first years of the war, the verdict was still out on Sherman. Born in Ohio in 1820, Sherman was raised by foster parents—one of whom was Senator and cabinet member Thomas Ewing. Through his adoptive father, Sherman gained admittance to West Point, and subsequently he served in the Mexican War. He tried several occupations after he resigned from the army in 1853, and when the Civil War broke out, he was the superintendent of a military academy in Alexandria, Louisiana (which would later be known as Louisiana State University). Believing in the Union, he refused an offer to serve as an officer in the Confederate army, and moved back to his family in Missouri. Eventually, however, the war caught up with him, and he was given a command by the time the first battle of Manassas came around.

Sherman was soon promoted to brigadier general, but doubts about his mental toughness and even his sanity arose when he was given a command in the western theater. But after proving himself in the field at Shiloh, Corinth, and Vicksburg, Sherman had established himself as indispensable, especially in the eyes of General Ulysses S. Grant. He and Grant would become good friends, and they supported each other both behind the scenes and on the field of battle. When Grant was finally made commander of all Union forces, he left Sherman with the daunting task of taking Atlanta. Sherman followed through with a brilliant campaign, waging "total war" with a ferocity for which he is still cursed in the South. William Tecumseh Sherman will forever be linked with both the glory of the Union's victory and the devastation caused by the Civil War.

Joseph E. Johnston—Joseph Eggleston Johnston, born in 1807 in Virginia, is unfortunately not a name that is often remembered with the great generals of the Civil War, North or South. However, he appeared all over the map for the Confederate army, and although he could not get along with President Jefferson Davis on any terms, he was loved by the men who served under him and continually proved himself a worthy adversary to all who faced him.

Early in the war Johnston fought in Virginia, and he was in command of the forces that faced the quick rotation of Union generals who led the Army of the Potomac. When General George McClellan attempted to take Richmond with his campaign up the York Peninsula in 1862, Johnston was severely wounded at the battle of Seven Pines. He was replaced by Robert E. Lee, who went on to command the Army of Northern Virginia until its surrender in 1865. When Johnston recovered, he was given command of the scattered Confederate forces in the western theater, all the while bickering with Davis over everything from military strategy to rank. Eventually he replaced Braxton Bragg at the helm of the Army of Tennessee, immediately reorganizing it and reestablishing its morale. When the Federals finally moved, it was Johnston who continually checked their advance, until again removed by Jefferson Davis just before the final decisive battles for Atlanta. Johnston would be given one more appointment by Davis before the end of the war, to try to stop Sherman's advance through the Carolinas in 1865, but the effort was futile, and he was eventually forced to surrender after Lee had done so at Appomattox. Johnston lived a varied and successful life after the war, dying shortly after catching pneumonia—after removing his hat, as a sign of respect, at Sherman's funeral.

John Bell Hood—Absolutely no one, North or South, could dispute the fact that John Bell Hood was a hard-fighting general and a brave man. He fought in the defense of Richmond during the Seven Days Battles, lost the use of an arm at Gettysburg, and lost a leg at Chickamauga; still, even though he needed to be strapped to his horse by his aides every morning, he fought on. However, this exceptional courage and dedication could not hide the fact that Hood, as a tactician and commander, was reckless and deficient.

During the Atlanta campaign Hood served under General Joseph Johnston, who was slowly being backed into Atlanta in what was, in retrospect, brilliant defensive maneuvering. However, Hood and President Jefferson Davis did not agree with this assessment, and after several months Johnston was replaced by Hood. Upon hearing the news, General Sherman was thrilled, knowing that Hood would fight him out in the open, rather than from a defensive position; it was what Sherman had longed for throughout the campaign. Sure enough, within days of taking command, Hood did go on the attack, and Sherman promptly took advantage, putting the finishing touches on a hard-fought campaign. After Atlanta fell, Hood decided that rather than attack Sherman, who eventually marched on to the sea, he would invade Tennessee. Despite the repeated objections of his officers, Hood moved north, and the decisive Confederate losses at Franklin and Nashville effectively destroyed his entire army. Still, Hood was regarded as a hero until his death during an epidemic of yellow fever in New Orleans in 1879—at the age of only 48.

George H. Thomas—George Henry Thomas, the "Rock of Chickamauga," was involved in the issues of the war long before it started. During the slave uprising led by Nat Turner, Thomas, a boy at the time, rode through the Virginia countryside to warn the local inhabitants of the trouble. His courage earned him a spot at West Point, and he later became an instructor there. When the Civil War broke out he remained with the Union, to the horror of his friends and family; in fact, even the Union leadership was surprised, to the point that some were initially suspicious of his motives. Thomas soon proved his value, however, with decisive action and bold victories on the battlefield.

Thomas's worth proved itself at Perryville, Murfreesboro, and other large battles, but it was his remarkable defensive stand at Chickamauga in the face of certain defeat that earned him his fame. Soon after, he was given command of the Army of the Cumberland, and his bold (and slightly unauthorized) charge at Chattanooga took the day, earning him greater respect. The final feather in his cap was his destruction of John Bell Hood's Confederate Army of Tennessee at the battle of Nashville, effectively ending the war in the western theater. Thomas remained in the army until his death in 1870.

William Rosecrans—William Rosecrans was a career military man, and although many will remember him for a lack of aggressiveness and the near loss of his army at Chickamauga, Rosecrans was actually an accomplished leader with many significant victories under his belt.

Brought out of retirement to serve in the Union army, Rosecrans preserved Union possession of the critical rail crossing at Corinth, Mississippi, with his defensive realignment there in 1862. Pressed into taking action while the Confederate army sat at Murfreesboro, Rosecrans advanced on Braxton Bragg's force, ultimately winning the battle at Stones River. His campaigning in the following spring would drive the Confederates out of Tennessee, leading to the capture of the extremely important city of Chattanooga. At Chickamauga, however, Rosecrans's micromanagement led to a fatal error in troop placement, and by sheer luck the Confederates were able to take full advantage, consequently routing the Federals. After the war Rosecrans remained in the military, then returned to civilian life as a miner in California, along the way serving two terms in the U.S. House of Representatives. He died in 1898.

Braxton Bragg—It is probable that there was no other officer in the entire Confederacy more universally disliked than General Braxton Bragg. A tactical genius on paper who continually proved to be an excellent military strategist, Bragg was abhorred by the men who served under him in the field.

In June of 1862 Bragg planned and successfully carried out an invasion of Kentucky that gave the Confederacy a much-needed stronghold in that critical area of the country. But before long Bragg began to falter, and his defeat at Perryville in October of that year was the last sign of a Confederate presence in Kentucky. Pushed back to Murfreesboro, he attacked again at Stones River in December, only to pull back again. In mid-1863 he was driven back to Chattanooga, and soon after into northern Georgia. While he gained a significant victory at Chickamauga, he still lacked the confidence of his troops and field commanders. However, despite repeated calls for his removal, he did have the confidence of President Jefferson Davis, who not only left him in command, but removed the naysayers. Davis's decision proved costly; Bragg suffered a total and embarrassing defeat at Chattanooga only two months later. He finally resigned, becoming Davis's chief of staff. Bragg died in 1876, still remembered mostly for his incompetence in the field and for his own soldiers' complete lack of faith in him.

» THINGS TO KNOW

Although this trip does cover some distance, most of the route will be along interstate highways, and Louisville, Nashville, and Atlanta are only the bigger cities along the way. Even if you stray a bit from the trail, you won't ever be far from food or lodging.

THE TRIP

This trip starts at Perryville, in central Kentucky, and ends at the infamous Confederate prison camp at Andersonville, Georgia. Although both of these bookends are somewhat isolated, they are not that far from Louisville and Atlanta, respectively. Also, since most of the route will be along interstate highways, and since most of the battle sites tend to concentrate around Nashville, Chattanooga, and Atlanta, the time spent to get from one point of interest to another is usually relatively short.

It would also be very easy to reverse this trip and start in Atlanta; but by starting in Kentucky and heading south, the tour will more or less progress chronologically, with the exception of the battles of Hood's Nashville campaign. In addition, if the tour proves too long (this drive covers a lot of very important and thoroughly interpreted sites), it can easily be broken into two between Stones River and Chattanooga.

» THE CAN'T-MISS SITES

Perryville

In August of 1862 General Braxton Bragg began an offensive into Kentucky. After victories at Richmond in August and Munfordville in September, the Confederate army had established itself and was determined to win the hearts and minds of the people of this critical border state. Yet although many Kentuckians did join the Confederate cause, many others did not. Bragg's intention of establishing a Confederate government at the capital in Frankfort was not met with the enthusiasm he had hoped for.

In October, while Bragg was in Frankfort, Major General Don Carlos Buell, who had resisted engaging Bragg's army, finally decided to act. Feinting toward Frankfort, Buell led his army southward from Louisville; Bragg, in response, kept half his army in Frankfort, leaving the other half with Major General Leonidas Polk.

The rolling hills of the Perryville battlefield in Kentucky.

For an army in the field, a source of fresh water is always critical, and Kentucky happened to be in the middle of an extreme drought. Creek beds throughout the state had run dry. So it happened that, near Perryville on October 8, 1862, two armies, each heading toward one of the few water sources in the area, met and fought a battle that would determine the fate of Kentucky for the rest of the war.

Early on October 8, with each army positioned near a creek called Bull Run, the fighting started over the water. In the morning, at the south end of the battlefield, Brigadier General Philip Sheridan gained an early advantage and pushed the Confederates back but, despite his advance, was unexplainably called back to his original position on the line. Buell, because of an odd acoustic phenomenon, did not hear the action, even though he was only 2 miles away.

By 10 AM Bragg had received reinforcements from Polk, and he immediately sent them to the right side of the line. Now bolstered by Polk's men on the north end of the field, the Confederate right slammed into the Union line in the early afternoon. However, the Union left, under Major General Alexander McCook, held firm in a remarkable show of defiance, although two Union generals were lost. As more Confederates joined the fight, McCook was only very slowly pushed back, taking several

SITE DETAILS

Perryville Battlefield State Historic Site—The battlefield at Perryville, in central Kentucky far from any interstate highways or major cities, is one of those destinations that truly reward the effort taken to get there. Although the complete battlefield is not part of the historic site, the beautiful Kentucky landscape has changed little over the years, which not only makes interpretation of the battle easy, but helps transport visitors back in time without the distractions of modern buildings marring the landscape or the sound of cars continually whizzing by. The site does contain the scene of the most intense fighting, where McCook established his defensive positions, and a driving tour of other areas of fighting located outside the park is available. One unique feature of the park, which can be either a blessing or a curse, is that the wonderful tour of the battlefield is via unpaved walking trails, rather than by driving, as at other large battle sites. The guides at the visitor's center, however, can help you pick out which of the trails tell the story of the battle the best. While at the visitor's center be sure to watch the outstanding video about the battle, filmed in 2006. If visiting anytime other than summer, be sure to call first; off-peak hours for the park are short and irregular. *Perryville Battlefield State Historic Site, intersection of Mack Rd. and Park Rd., Perryville, KY, 40468; 606-332-8631; http://parks.ky.gov/findparks/histparks/pb; open daily Apr.–Oct., call for other times of year. Admission charged.*

hilltop positions in a rearward movement. Finally, Buell, now fully informed of the danger his army faced, reinforced McCook late in the day, and the Union left held as darkness approached.

Meanwhile, at the south end of the battlefield, Sheridan was finally given permission at 4 PM to reenter the fighting, and again he pushed the Confederates back, this time through the small town of Perryville. As evening came, Buell brought up the rest of his forces, which had been kept in reserve because he did not know that the battle was occurring. Although Bragg held the field on the evening of October 8, he knew that he was now outnumbered, and he started his army south toward Tennessee.

The costs for both sides, in terms of casualties, had been extremely high—4,211 Union, and 3,396 Confederate. But the greatest loss for the Confederacy was Kentucky. Never again would a Confederate army threaten this critical border state.

Abraham Lincoln Birthplace National Historic Site

Shrines to Abraham Lincoln can be found all across the United States—even all over the world—but this one, his birthplace, is one of the most recognizable. This is the ground where young Abraham took his first steps, the spring from which his first drink of water came. Not long ago it was discovered that the log cabin, for years purported to be the

The granite shrine protecting the fragile Lincoln cabin at Abraham Lincoln Birthplace National Historic Site, Kentucky.

cabin of Lincoln's birth, is probably not what we all hoped it was; but it doesn't matter. People from all over the world still visit this quiet place in the Kentucky countryside to reflect on this man who has become a universal symbol of the American dream.

Nashville

General George Thomas, hero of the battle at Chickamauga, was in command of the Union armies in Tennessee, a force of about 55,000 troops. In December 1864, with his entire force now concentrated at Nashville, he knew what was coming his way. General John Bell Hood, commanding the Army of Tennessee, had already been engaged at Columbia, Spring Hill, and Franklin before his decimated troops reached the outskirts of Nashville, heavily fortified and in Union hands since shortly after the fall of Fort Donelson in February 1862. Hood's army, by this time fewer than 20,000 troops, dug in south of the city and waited.

On December 15, 1864, after days of cold and wet weather, Thomas did not need to wait any longer. He knew that Hood's army, hungry and ragged, could not hold out. Thomas attacked the Confederate force, the main brunt of the assault coming on the Confederate left, at redoubts numbered one through five, placed along the Hillsboro Pike. Hard fighting continued all along the line throughout the day, and by nightfall the Federals had driven the Confederates back to a more condensed line placed between two commanding positions, Shy's Hill and Peach Orchard Hill.

The next morning the Union forces pressed the attack, now on the two Confederate strongholds holding up Hood's left and right flanks. Thomas went around Hood's left, attacking from the rear, and took Shy's Hill late in the afternoon. Although the Confederate position on the right at Peach Orchard Hill held firm, when news of the fall of Shy's Hill reached the remaining Confederates, this last stronghold was abandoned. Hood's army, in shambles before the battle even started, now effectively disintegrated. Thousands of prisoners were taken, and what was left of the army headed south in tatters. The battle at Nashville had been the death knell for the Confederate Army of Tennessee and was the last major battle of the war in the western theater.

SITE DETAILS

Battle of Nashville driving tour—Even with careful planning, tracking down what is left of the battle at Nashville will try your patience. A brochure for a driving tour of the major sites of the battle is available from the Battle of Nashville Preservation Society; however, getting this brochure is not as easy as it sounds. Don't bother trying at the Nashville Visitor's Bureau, the convention center, or at any roadside rest stops, because you won't find it. It can be picked up at Fort Negley, which debuted a new visitor's center at this city park in 2007, as well as the plantations at Traveller's Rest and Belle Meade. However, not all of these sites are open daily, and they often have short hours. The best way to get the brochure is to contact the preservation society ahead of time—www.bonps.org—and they will be happy to mail one to you. (There is also an excellent book available for sale on the Web site and at local bookstores that will take you through the sites.) The valiant efforts of the BONPS have made possible the preservation of parts of Shy's Hill and Confederate Redoubt No. 1, but other parts of the battle are difficult to imagine, with the growth of the city swallowing up the battlefield. Unfortunately, tourism efforts in the city of Nashville, concentrating on the music industry, have virtually ignored its Civil War heritage, which happens to include one of the largest and most important battles of the entire war. But don't let that stop you from visiting—the more tourists the battle areas bring in, the more momentum can be built for developing these sites. *Driving Tour of the Battle of Nashville, www.bonps.org; 615-352-6384.*

Fort Negley—A new visitor's center was dedicated at Fort Negley in 2007. Although the center has very limited hours, the fort itself is a city park and is accessible daily. *Fort Negley, 534 Chestnut St., Nashville, TN, 37203; 615-862-8400. Park open daily; call for visitor's center hours.*

Shy's Hill—The Battle of Nashville Preservation Society, fighting to preserve what is left of the battle sites, has now developed Shy's Hill, a critical portion of the battlefield. *Shy's Hill, intersection of Shy's Hill Rd. and Benton Smith Rd., Nashville, TN, 37215; 615-352-6384. Open daily.*

Traveller's Rest—This plantation was Hood's headquarters during the battle, and Peach Orchard Hill (now covered by a high school football field) is easily visible nearby to the west. *Traveller's Rest, 636 Farrell Pkwy., Nashville, TN, 37220; 1-866-832-8197. Open daily; admission charged.*

The ruins of Fort Negley, part of the Union defenses at Nashville.

Franklin

On November 30, 1864, one day after General John Bell Hood had missed a golden opportunity to trap a large portion of the Union army at Spring Hill, he quickly advanced northward toward Nashville, hoping to catch the Federals before they could escape. The exhausted Union troops, commanded by Major General John Schofield, had marched throughout the previous night to escape Hood's trap and stopped in Franklin, where strong defensive fortifications had previously been built. The Union lines, facing south toward the Confederates, were formidable, and open fields south of the town afforded a clear view of the advancing army.

Late in the day Hood ordered his 20,000 men to attack the Union lines in a frontal assault against the works. The confident Confederates went forward in a rush, but although confusion in the Union ranks resulted in an early Confederate breach of the line, the gap was quickly filled, and the results for the Confederates were devastating. Still, they continued with their attacks and continued mounting up casualties.

After five hours of fighting, the Federals had held, taking a total of 2,633 casualties; they again marched throughout the night, and reached the safety of the Nashville defenses early the next morning. But of the 20,000 Confederate soldiers in action, approximately 7,300 were lost as casualties, including an unbelievable twelve generals,

SITE DETAILS

Fort Granger Park—The earthworks of this fortress can still be found along the Harpeth River and are located in a larger park named Pinkerton Park. The fort is situated on a high bluff at the north end of the park, and it is well-hidden behind brush and trees. A short hike and climb is required to get there, but the great condition of the site is worth it. Interpretive signs are located throughout the earthworks, explaining both the fort and the battle. The fort was also involved in the first major battle in Franklin on April 10, 1863. *Fort Granger Park, located in Pinkerton Park, 405 Murfreesboro Rd., Franklin, TN, 37064; 615-794-2103. Open daily.*

Carter House—This house in the middle of town, with an accompanying museum, demonstrates vividly just how savage the fighting was in November of 1864. The original home, as well as several outbuildings, still stand, and they are still riddled with bullet holes from the battle. Although much of the original battlefield has been lost to development, the museum here is excellent and will help you interpret the action by looking at the landscape around the house. *Carter House, 1140 Columbia Ave., Franklin, TN, 37065; 615-791-1861; www.carterhouse1864.com. Closed Sun. during Jan. and some holidays; admission charged.*

Carnton Plantation—The home here served as a Confederate field hospital in the terrible aftermath of the battle at Franklin. At one point, four Confederate generals lay dead on its back porch, and the home still bears the bloodstains of those wounded and killed in the battle. The grounds also hold one of the largest private Confederate cemeteries in the United States, with nearly 1,500 interments. There are guided tours of the home and grounds, as well as a self-guided tour. *Carnton Plantation, 1345 Carnton Lane, Franklin, TN, 37064; 615-794-0903; www.carnton.org. Open daily; admission charged.*

Winstead Hill—This hill south of the town gives the best vantage point of the entire battlefield, although it does take some imagination to picture it between the development that has taken place. Still, the interpretation here is very good, and the site provides a fine overview of the battle. *Winstead Hill, intersection of Columbia Pike and Hillview Lane, Franklin, TN, 37064. Open daily.*

Battle of Franklin driving tour—A nonprofit organization called Save the Franklin Battlefield Inc. has developed a 26-stop driving tour of the remaining sites of the Franklin battlefield. Although many of the stops on the tour are still private homes, this is a truly thorough dissection of the battlefield. The tour can be picked up in town, but it is probably best to order one ahead of time at the organization's Web site. *Battle of Franklin Driving Tour, PO Box 851, Franklin, TN, 37065; 615-500-6612; www.franklin-stfb.org. Tour sites viewable daily.*

The earthworks of Fort Granger, which saw action during both battles of Franklin, Tennessee.

An outbuilding of the Carter house still bears the scars of the second battle of Franklin.

six of them being mortally wounded. Hood's bravado, so admired, had again proved fatal in the field. The losses at Franklin were crushing, but still the Confederates pushed on to Nashville, where Hood's army would suffer its destruction.

Franklin was also the site of several earlier battles in the war, the most significant being on April 10, 1863, when General Nathan Bedford Forrest met a small Union force here that had reoccupied the town after having been forced out on a previous raid. Although Forrest was able to dent the Federal defenses, at the end of the day the Confederates withdrew southward, and Union forces held control of the area.

Stones River

Major General William S. Rosecrans, recently placed at the head of the Union Army of the Cumberland, was determined to drive General Braxton Bragg and his Army of Tennessee out of the state. Although Bragg had shown no inspiration as a field commander, he was aggressive and before too long would launch another assault. In late December Rosecrans moved southeast from Nashville with 44,000 troops, heading toward Murfreesboro, where Bragg's army had taken position, expecting an attack.

Though outnumbered, Bragg had decided to take the offensive once the Federals approached. As the Union army had just begun moving early on December 31, 1862, Bragg sent his left flank in a wheeling motion on the Union ranks in an attempt to cut off the Union line of retreat. This movement surprised Rosecrans, who had planned an assault on the Confederate right but was slow to act. The Union right had been outflanked but nevertheless was able to hold the Murfreesboro–Nashville Pike, the Union supply line and line of retreat. Gradually the Union forces rallied and were able to stop the Confederate advance. The advance was also hampered by the rough terrain, as the Confederates had found it difficult to coordinate their assaults.

With the Union line now essentially folded almost in half, like a jackknife, the

SITE DETAILS

Stones River National Battlefield—Although much of the battlefield has been lost, Stones River National Battlefield maintains an excellent interpretation of the fighting here, as well as Fortress Rosecrans, focus of the second battle of Murfreesboro. The difficult terrain experienced during the fighting, as well as the wide-open fields, today give only some indication of the massive slaughter that took place here. Also part of the park is Stones River National Cemetery, which contains the Hazen Brigade Monument, erected in 1863 to honor those who fell in Hell's Half Acre. It is believed to be the first Civil War monument erected in the country. *Stones River National Battlefield, 3501 Old Nashville Hgwy., Murfreesboro, TN, 37129; 615-478-1035; www.nps.gov/stri. Open daily.*

A cotton field along the trail at Stones River National Battlefield.

Confederates directly attacked the angled center of the line yet were unable to gain an advantage, despite inflicting heavy casualties. The ground later came to be known as Hell's Half Acre by those who fought there, and the Union troops would remember proudly their repulse of the Confederate attack.

Later in the afternoon Bragg ordered an attack on the Union left. The Federals had heavily entrenched and had also brought up artillery to support their lines. The Confederates were charging across an open field, and the Union men had a clear field of fire. The result was a disaster for the Confederates, who were forced to limp back to their lines, having taken many casualties.

As darkness fell, the fighting subsided, and the field remained mostly quiet until the afternoon of January 2, when Bragg ordered a final assault on the Union line. The Confederates, after an initial barrage of artillery, again advanced over an open field and again were mowed down by Union fire. The next day, with Stones River rising and threatening to cut off his escape route, and with fresh intelligence of Union reinforcements having arrived, Bragg withdrew toward the south.

Casualties for both sides were high—approximately 13,000 for the Union and 10,000 for the Confederates. More important for the Federals, though, the Confederates had again been beaten south and were forced to give up important ground in

Tennessee. Despite the heavy Union losses here, by the end of the year the Confederates would never again have any real opportunity to gain a foothold on Tennessee soil.

The same ground fought over during the battle of Stones River was also the site of the second battle of Murfreesboro on December 5–7, 1864. In preparation for his assault on Nashville, Major General John Bell Hood ordered an assault on Fortress Rosecrans, built after the battle of Stones River to protect the large Union supply base here. Major General Nathan Bedford Forrest, commanding the Confederate force of 6,000 men, found the defenses too strong for a direct assault and pulled back. On December 7 fighting occurred outside the fortress, ending in a rout of the Confederates and a withdrawal south by most of the troops. Forrest remained near Murfreesboro to keep the garrison there from interfering with Hood's plans at Nashville, although the reinforcement of Nashville proved to be unnecessary.

Chattanooga

To say that Chattanooga was strategically important is an enormous understatement. Although Atlanta was a major industrial center and rail hub, Chattanooga was the northern gateway to the South's major metropolis. A city of only 2,500, Chattanooga was also a major railroad center, with lines stretching not only south to Atlanta, but also to Virginia, the Atlantic, the Gulf of Mexico, and the Mississippi River. It is also located at what was a critical point on the Tennessee River, an enormous loop called Moccasin Bend. To have any hope of controlling the heart of the South, the Union army needed to take and hold Chattanooga.

The first battle of Chattanooga came early in the war and was not so much an attempt to take the city as to harass its defenders. On June 7–8, 1862, Brigadier General James Negley, who had been destroying railroad track in nearby Alabama, set up artillery west of Chattanooga and fired on the city and the Confederate defensive works there. The major result of this bombardment had little to do with Chattanooga; it primarily served notice that the Union army was in heavy force in northern Alabama. That realization ultimately led General Braxton Bragg to decide that the time was right to launch an invasion of Kentucky, which climaxed at the battle of Perryville on October 8.

Major General William Rosecrans, by now at the helm of the Union Army of the Cumberland, finally pulled his army out of Murfreesboro, Tennessee, in June of 1863 and drove the Confederates south to Chattanooga. Moving slowly but skillfully, Rosecrans finally approached Chattanooga with three columns and finally, on August 21, 1863, began an artillery assault on the city, from the same location as Negley had earlier. Bragg, soon realizing the positions of the rest of Rosecrans's army, knew that he was in danger and withdrew from Chattanooga on September 8. Ten days later the two armies met each other at Chickamauga, where the Confederates scored a decisive victory. The Union army, which had been pursuing Bragg, was forced back into Chattanooga. Bragg quickly cut off most of the supply lines to the city, and the Union Army of the Cumberland was soon under siege.

After the Union disaster at Chickamauga, quick action was taken to attempt to right the situation. First, Major General Joseph Hooker and two entire corps of the Army of the Potomac were sent to Chattanooga as reinforcements and arrived southwest of the city in only 11 days. Major General William Tecumseh Sherman was also sent from Mississippi with another 20,000 soldiers. Then, President Lincoln put Major General Ulysses S. Grant in charge of most of the armies west of the Appalachian Mountains; Grant immediately went to Chattanooga to take command. Finally, Rosecrans was replaced with Major General George Thomas, the "Rock of Chickamauga," as leader of the Army of the Cumberland.

When Grant arrived in Chattanooga in late October, it was clear that the first necessary step would be to reopen the supply line; the Union soldiers, under siege now for a month, were on half rations and struggling to hold out. On October 27, 1863, three Union columns—Hooker's men, coming from the southwest, and two Union forces from Chattanooga—converged upon a lightly defended crossing of the Tennessee River known as Brown's Ferry. The Federals surprised the Confederates there, taking the crossing in half an hour and opening a supply line to Bridgeport, Alabama, which was located not only on the Union-controlled Tennessee River, but also had a direct railroad link to Nashville. Hooker's army withdrew back toward Bridgeport to defend the newly opened line, whereupon General Bragg ordered Lieutenant General James Longstreet to drive him out. Although Longstreet was not able to carry out his attack, one Confederate division did launch an attack on a Union division guarding a railroad stop at Wauhatchie Station. The battle of Wauhatchie, occurring on the night of October 28–29, 1863, lasted only three hours and was a decisive Union victory. Most important, it maintained the supply line, now known as the Cracker Line by the grateful Union soldiers who had lasted through the siege.

Even with the Union supply line now open, the Confederates still held all the strong positions surrounding Chattanooga. The most commanding point was Lookout Mountain to the south, and Bragg placed 2,700 troops there, along with artillery. Also prominent was Missionary Ridge, a long, steep hill running along the eastern edge of the city. Finally, in the valley below these points, was a large hill known as Orchard Knob, a patch of very high ground in front of Missionary Ridge. However, two circumstances were working against the Confederates. The first was that although the Confederate positions were strong, they did not work well for the siege that Bragg had decided upon. As Longstreet later noted, "We were trying to starve the enemy out by investing him on the only side from which he could not have gathered supplies." The second was that virtually the entire Confederate Army of Tennessee, from the

The view from atop Lookout Mountain as the Tennessee River winds through Chattanooga.

leadership down to the foot soldier, had lost all faith in the abilities of General Braxton Bragg. Although Bragg was a brilliant tactician, consensus was almost universal that he was a poor field commander, and his failure to destroy the Union army after Chickamauga was the final straw for those under his command.

While the Confederates controlled the high points around the city with 40,000 troops, the Union ranks were quickly swelling, and the soldiers were eager to avenge their embarrassment at Chickamauga. The arrival of Sherman's army in mid-November brought the Union force to 70,000 battle-hardened troops. Grant decided to attack. The design of the battle was that Sherman's men would assault the Confederate right, atop Missionary Ridge. Thomas's army would advance to take Orchard Knob, then hold the center of the Confederate line on the ridge. Hooker's men, still southwest of the city, would take Lookout Mountain, then attack the Confederate left.

For the first two days of the battle, all went as planned for the Federals. On day one, November 23, 1863, Thomas's men moved forward and took Orchard Knob, giving the Union army a critical high point in front of Missionary Ridge. Then, on November 24, Hooker's army climbed Lookout Mountain and overran the Confederate positions there, mostly amassed along a shelf on the mountain around the

SITE DETAILS

Chickamauga and Chattanooga National Military Park (Chattanooga Unit)—The battlefields of Chattanooga are mostly long gone, overtaken by the growth of the city. However, despite this setback, all the battles that took place at Chattanooga are easily interpreted. The reason for this is Lookout Mountain, the natural feature that still dominates the landscape, and it makes this one of the more unusual battlefields to visit. From Point Park, at the peak of the mountain, you can view the entire city below, including Moccasin Bend, from where the first two battles of Chattanooga were started; the great bend in the Tennessee River where Wauhatchie's Ferry was located; and Missionary Ridge, where Thomas's troops made their famous charge. All the while you will be standing on the ground where the fabled Battle above the Clouds took place. The park's visitor's center is located at Point Park, and besides the awesome views of the city, several monuments, interpretive signs, and short but easily walked trails can be found to help you explore the mountain. A bit farther down the mountain is the Craven house, where Hooker's men overran the main body of Confederate troops on the mountain. *Chickamauga and Chattanooga National Military Park (Chattanooga Unit), 110 Point Park Rd., Lookout Mountain, TN, 37350; 706-866-9241; www.nps.gov/chch. Open daily; admission charged.*

Missionary Ridge—Also included as part of the National Military Park is the crest of Missionary Ridge. A road runs along the top of the ridge, with monuments, interpretive signs, and pullouts along the way. The ridge is now part of a residential area, but it is worth the drive to see where the climax of the battle of Chattanooga took place. *Missionary Ridge, road begins at intersection of Chickamauga Ave. and W. Crest Rd., Rossville, GA, 30741; 706-866-9241; www.nps.gov/chch. Open daily.*

Orchard Knob—This large hill in the middle of Chattanooga is still pretty well preserved, even though it is surrounded by a residential area. Numerous monuments have been placed on the hill, and interpretive signs explain the importance of the location, a commanding elevated point in the middle of relatively flat land. *Orchard Knob, intersection of N. Orchard Knob Ave. and Ivy St., Chattanooga, TN, 37404; 706-866-9241; www.nps.gov/chch. Open daily.*

Wauhatchie—The National Park Service is in the process of developing four sites related to Wauhatchie, the small battle that was so critical in ensuring a Union victory at Chattanooga. At the moment, only one of the sites is readily accessible, and it contains only a single monument. It takes a little effort to find the site; it is behind a hotel and a McDonald's, on a road that is usually gated. You will have to drive to the end of the road (which is paved but in poor condition), walk around the gate, and then around a bend in the road to the monument, but it is a very short and easy stroll. *Wauhatchie Site 1, on Parker Lane east of intersection of Browns Ferry Rd. and Parker Lane, Chattanooga, TN, 37419; 706-866-9241; www.nps.gov/chch. Open daily.*

Craven house. Hooker's action and victory on this commanding position became known famously as the Battle above the Clouds. With these two objectives won, the Union army was ready to proceed with the main attack—Sherman and Hooker assaulting the Confederate right and left, while Thomas held the middle to prevent Bragg from reinforcing his flanks.

However, fate would not have it, and the third day of the battle of Chattanooga, November 25, brought on one of the most incredible moments of the Civil War. As the attack opened, Hooker, on the Union right, was slow in getting into position. Meanwhile, on the Union left, Sherman was facing Major General Patrick Cleburne, who was putting up a tremendous fight. But in the center of the line, Thomas's men—who were commanded only to press and hold the Confederate center in place while Sherman and Hooker attacked—advanced in the afternoon, and rather than stop as they had been ordered, instead charged up Missionary Ridge, unauthorized. These brave men—almost wiped out two months earlier, but now unstoppable—drove right through the Confederate line, breaking the center and sending the entire army into flight. The demoralized Confederates would never hold Chattanooga again, and the Union army, having thoroughly avenged their great loss at Chickamauga, was poised to advance on Atlanta.

Chickamauga

In August 1863 Major General William Rosecrans and the Union Army of the Cumberland were finally able to reach Chattanooga, where Major General Braxton Bragg's Confederate Army of Tennessee had holed up. Although Chattanooga was vitally important, Bragg had no choice but to abandon the city on September 8. But Rosecrans was not content; he pursued Bragg into northern Georgia with three brigades, led by Major Generals George Thomas, Alexander McCook, and Thomas Crittenden. For several weeks the two armies danced just south of the city, meeting only incidentally. Bragg, deciding to meet the challenge rather than pull back to Atlanta, devised a plan to hit the Federals and, hopefully, regain Chattanooga.

Calling for and receiving reinforcements from Mississippi and Virginia, Bragg positioned his army east of Chickamauga Creek, opposite the Union position. Rosecrans, fearing an attack, had consolidated his forces and set up a line on the opposite side. On the evening of September 18, 1863, the right flank of the Confederates began to push across the creek, with the rest of the line following. The two lines were now practically on top of each other, separated by thick forest, and the day ended with the two camps practically able to speak to each other.

On September 19 Major General George Thomas, on the Union left, pressed forward into the close Confederate line, and the battle was on. Heavy fighting occurred all along the line, but the bloodiest occurred at the north end, as Thomas faced off against Major General William Walker. All day both armies sent reinforcements to this part of the field, hoping to gain an advantage. Although by the end of the day Thomas's brigade had fallen back slightly, the two armies ended the day's fighting with neither side showing a real gain.

However, during the evening of September 19, as Union forces built formidable breastworks, the Confederates received a much-needed boost from Virginia. Lieutenant General James Longstreet, Robert E. Lee's extraordinary commander in the eastern theater, had brought his army by rail to reinforce Bragg's. Bragg divided his new force into two parts, placing Longstreet's men on the left and Lieutenant General Leonidas Polk on the right. They planned for an assault on the Union lines the next day, beginning again on the north end of the line against Thomas's brigade.

On September 20, despite confusion among the Confederate forces, the attack was finally launched after a four-hour delay. Again Thomas held firm, but called for reinforcements. Rosecrans responded by sending troops from Crittenden's and McCook's brigades to the north to reinforce Thomas. In the heat of battle, Rosecrans thought that by doing this he had created a gap in the center of the Union line, and he sent part of Crittenden's army north to close it. This proved to be a fatal error. There had

The excellent visitor's center at Chickamauga, at the Chickamauga and Chattanooga National Military Park.

been no gap in the Union line to close. Now, with the movement of Crittenden's unit, there was a huge one.

Almost simultaneously, across the field, an unknowing Major General John Bell Hood had organized an assault on the Union center. His men charged—and, bewildered, found themselves in the center of the Union line, with almost no resistance. They had found the gap that had been created by Crittenden's shift and immediately seized upon the opportunity. Rolling the Federals up both to the north and to the south, the Confederates tore down the Union line. The Federals broke and fled rearward, with no other place to go. McCook and Crittenden were routed. Thomas, however, held strong, despite heavy Confederate attacks, and did not budge until finally ordered by Rosecrans to withdraw with the rest of the army at sundown. His actions here forever earned him the nickname of "The Rock of Chickamauga."

The Union army retreated north to Chattanooga, having suffered 16,170 casualties from a force of 62,000. Although the Confederates held the field, the price had been high, with 18,454 casualties out of a force of 65,000. Tactically, it was the last large victory for the Confederates in the western theater. Bragg was able to follow the Federals to Chattanooga, beginning a siege, but the lack of confidence in him by his field commanders, already serious, began to snowball.

Dallas, Marietta, and Kennesaw Mountain

Since early May 1864, General William Tecumseh Sherman had been moving his army in any direction necessary in order to push the Confederate Army of Tennessee south toward Atlanta. Although Major General Joseph E. Johnston had been very successful in finding defensible positions along the way, Sherman's army, despite its large size, was more mobile and was able to force Johnston from every stronghold he chose. However, Sherman did have one restriction: He could not move far from the Western

The view from the strong Confederate position atop Kennesaw Mountain in Georgia.

& Atlantic Railroad, his primary supply line. In mid-May, with Atlanta seeming ever closer, Sherman decided to leave his supply line and move west around the Confederates toward Dallas, Georgia. This movement began a series of battles in which the two forces would continually duke it out over the same ground for over a month.

The Confederates had created a defensive position stretching from Dallas northeast to Pickett's Mill, with the center of the line fixed near the small town of New Hope. On May 25, 1864, Major General George Thomas's Army of the Cumberland attacked Lieutenant General John Bell Hood's force centered at New Hope Church. Hood's Confederates were strongly entrenched, and the Union troops were forced to fight through thick undergrowth. Although they came near the Confederate lines, they were thoroughly repulsed at all points. On the next day, May 26, the other two Union armies—Major General James McPherson's Army of the Tennessee, to the west, and Major General John Schofield's Army of the Ohio to the east—were brought toward the center to try to break the stalemate. The result was continuous fighting around the church that lasted for five days. The heavily entrenched Confederates were able to repel every attack that came their way.

On May 27 an assault was made on the Confederate right near Pickett's Mill. Major General Oliver Howard led his men against the Confederate lines, again through difficult undergrowth and terrain. Johnston, however, had anticipated their movement and had moved a division eastward to extend his line. The Union force, particularly Brigadier General William Hazen's and Colonel William Gibson's brigades, suffered heavily and were forced to fall back in the darkness.

The next day, May 28, the battle shifted westward to the Union right near Dallas. On this side of the line, the fortunes were reversed. The Confederates came out of their lines to attack McPherson's army, which by now was also behind strong breastworks. After approximately two hours of fighting, the Confederates finally staggered back to their lines, having taken heavy casualties and gaining no ground.

The losses during the battles of New Hope Church, Pickett's Mill, and Dallas totaled 2,645 for the Union and as many as 2,300 for the Confederates. The four days of hard fighting convinced Sherman that his previous strategy of flanking and outmaneuvering Johnston was the better choice for his offensive. He slowly shifted his armies back toward his supply line to the east, and Johnston countered his move. For the next several weeks the two forces continued to pick at each other in a number of fierce actions. These battles, collectively called the Marietta operations, occurred during June and early July of 1864 while the Confederates centered their position on Kennesaw Mountain. The operations include the small battles known as Gilgal Church, Noonday Creek, and Ruff's Mill, among others. None of the battles were decisive, but by keeping the Confederate line extended, they still played a part in forcing Johnston to eventually move out of the Marietta area.

After his armies had been resupplied, Sherman attempted to move Schofield's Army of the Ohio around the Confederate left to cut off their supply route. On June 22 Schofield encountered General Hood's men. Knowing his old West Point roommate's tendency to take the offensive, Schofield quickly erected breastworks while sending two regiments forward to lure Hood out of his lines. Hood took the bait and attacked the Union regiments across an open field known as Kolb's Farm. When the Confederates were out in the open, the rest of Schofield's army opened up on the unsheltered soldiers. Hood lost approximately 1,000 men to the Union's 350, although Schofield was unsuccessful in cutting the Confederate railroad.

After a month of constant fighting and little movement, Sherman decided that the time was right for an all-out assault on Johnston's army, intending to defeat it once and for all. With McPherson's army on the left, Schofield's on the right, and Thomas's in the center, Sherman planned to hold the flanks while making a strong assault on the Confederate lines centered on Kennesaw Mountain. Promptly at 8 AM on June 27, the Union artillery opened up on the mountain, continuing the bombardment for an hour. Again the Union troops fought through rough country and thick terrain, barely able to see what was in front of them. What was in front of them was an extremely strong defensive position erected by the Confederates. Sherman had hoped to split the Confederate line in two, but his men were unable to approach the earthworks with

SITE DETAILS

Pickett's Mill State Historic Site—The state historic site maintained here is the best resource for interpreting the battles of New Hope Church, Pickett's Mill, and Dallas, and the action that followed up through Kolb's Farm. The walking trails lead past excellent examples of the sturdy earthworks that the Confederates used during the battle. In addition, the museum is of exceptionally high quality. It not only does a very good job of interpreting the battle of Pickett's Mill, but also goes into other areas that most museums neglect—things as simple as basic military tactics (for example, what is a flanking movement? How big is a brigade?), as well as the role of immigrants in the war, and the archaeological history of battlefields. *Pickett's Mill State Historic Site, intersection of Mount Tabor Church Rd. and Garrison Dr., Dallas, GA, 30157; 770-443-7850; www.gastateparks.org. Closed Mon.; admission charged.*

New Hope Church Monument and Battle Site—A kiosk with interpretive signs, as well as remnants of Confederate earthworks, can be seen near the site of the original New Hope Church, the center of the Confederate line during the four days of battle. There is also an Atlanta campaign relief map and picnic area at the site. *New Hope Church Monument and Battle Site, intersection of Hosiery Mill Rd. and Bobo Rd., Dallas, GA, 30132. Open daily.*

Gilgal Church Battle Site—The Gilgal Church battle site, part of the Marietta operations, presents a very well-maintained example of Confederate reinforced earthworks, along with a small trail, some monuments, and remnants of the original earthworks. *Gilgal Church Battle Site, 667 Kennesaw Due West Rd. NW, Kennesaw, GA, 30152; 770-975-0877. Open daily.*

Ruff's Mill and Smyrna—Ruff's Mill still exists, and although it is on private property, it can easily be seen from the road. Historical highway markers in the area describe the action, and additional markers can be found near the Smyrna Welcome Center. *Historical highway marker 033-77 (Battle of Smyrna), Georgia Historical Commission, in front of Smyrna Welcome Center, 2875 Atlanta Rd., Smyrna, GA, 30080; historical highway marker 032-14 (Battle of Ruff's Mill), Georgia Historical Commission, in front of mill at 10 Concord Rd. SW, Smyrna, GA, 30082. Markers accessible daily.*

Kennesaw Mountain National Battlefield Park—Although much of the battlefield has given way to housing developments, there are still enough landmarks to get a sense of the action, and the view from the top of Big Kennesaw Mountain is not only spectacular, but offers a fine prospect of the battle area. The visitor's center is very well done; being the only unit of the National Park Service that provides any interpretation of Sherman's drive for Atlanta, it provides a comprehensive look at the entire campaign and its importance in the Civil War. The Kolb's Farm battle site is also a unit of the park and is part of the driving tour. *Kennesaw Mountain National Battlefield Park, 900 Kennesaw Mountain Dr., Kennesaw, GA, 30152; 770-427-4686; www.nps.gov/kemo. Open daily.*

any momentum. The battle was over by 10:45. The Union had lost 3,000 men to the Confederates' 1,000. In early July Sherman returned to his strategy of maneuvering rather than direct assaults, and Johnston was forced out of his works on July 2, moving still closer to Atlanta.

Atlanta and Jonesborough

Major General Joseph E. Johnston had done the best he could. Over the course of almost three months, Johnston had directed the Army of Tennessee to one defensive front after another through northwest Georgia, doing everything possible to stall Sherman's advance on Atlanta. Greatly outnumbered, his army was nevertheless able to keep Sherman's progress slow. The reality, however, was that there was little he could do to prevent the eventual fall of Atlanta. Still, it was a brilliant defensive campaign; this was echoed by Sherman himself, who noted later that "No officer or soldier who ever served under me will question the generalship of Joseph E. Johnston."

Still, the Confederate government, and some under Johnston's command, wished for more decisive action. The two major Confederate armies were in danger of both being put under siege, one at Petersburg and the other at Atlanta. So it came about that on July 17, 1864, by order of President Jefferson Davis, Joe Johnston was relieved of his command and replaced by Major General John Bell Hood. Hood, an aggressive and fearless but often reckless general, was a man who preferred the offensive rather than the defensive. This was known by the Union leadership as well (some of whom had been classmates of Hood at West Point), and when they heard of Hood's taking command of the army, they were not entirely displeased. Joe Johnston had repeatedly placed his armies in strong, easily defensible positions, requiring the Union forces to move and flank him out of those positions. These actions not only took a lot of time, but also ate up resources, although the casualty rate was relatively low. John Bell Hood was the type of commander who would bring his army into the open field and fight, and with the combined Union armies' vastly superior numbers, his men would not stand a chance.

It was not three days after taking command that Hood launched his first attack. The Union force, now only 5 miles north of Atlanta, was on the move, and its armies were momentarily separated, with Major General George Thomas's Army of the Cumberland isolated. On July 20 Hood planned to launch an assault at Thomas, hoping to catch Thomas's army as it crossed Peachtree Creek. Learning that Sherman was advancing on Atlanta from the east, however, threw the Confederates into confusion, and they did not attack Thomas until the late afternoon, well after his army had crossed the creek. The Federals quickly threw up an organized defense, while the Confederates charged their lines in an uncoordinated manner through thick brush and undergrowth. The attack was called off after two hours, and the results were astounding—for the Union, 1,710 casualties, and for the Confederates, 4,796.

The death of General James McPherson is memorialized in a quiet neighborhood of Atlanta.

One poorly executed assault was not enough to deter Hood, however. While the Union army began to terrorize the city of Atlanta by beginning a constant bombardment, Hood quickly planned his next attack. Two days later, on July 22, after a grueling night march, Hood's men attacked the Union forces east and north of the city. The battle of Atlanta began around midday, with the Confederates attacking the Union left. Again the Federals were prepared, with Major General James McPherson holding a strong position. Again the Confederate charges were fierce but uncoordinated. This time the Confederate losses were even heavier, with 8,499 casualties. An unfortunate loss for the Union, though, was one of its most promising generals—James McPherson. McPherson had showed Sherman much during this great Atlanta campaign, but in the confusion of the battle of Atlanta, McPherson rode into the enemy's lines and was shot and killed when he attempted to flee on his horse.

Even with the grievous loss of troops from the two previous battles, the Confederates still occupied Atlanta. Sherman began to move his armies westward around city, cutting off the railroads supplying the capital as he went. On July 28, 1864, Hood sent four divisions against Major General Oliver Howard's Army of the Tennessee to stop the destruction of the city's main supply line. These divisions, against orders, attacked Howard's army rather than concentrating on defending the railroad tracks, leading to the battle of Ezra Church. Howard's men repulsed every assault, and although at the end of the day Hood still held the railroad, it had cost him 4,642 casualties to the Union's 700. In the 12 days that Hood had commanded the Army of Tennessee so far, he had fought three major battles and lost almost 18,000 men. Joe Johnston, on the other hand, had lost about 10,000 men in the three previous *months*.

Meanwhile, Sherman continued his westward circle around Atlanta. One important location west of the city was a railroad junction at East Point. On August 5, 1864, the Federals tried to take this position, but the Confederates, expecting their arrival, had already constructed strong defensive earthworks. In what became known as the battle of Utoy Creek, the Union troops were repeatedly repulsed, and when the Confederates fell back to an even stronger position, the assault was called off after three days of fighting.

Sherman was keenly aware that with Grant besieging Petersburg, unable to move, and the presidential elections of 1864 only months away, it fell on his shoulders to bring about the major victory that would propel Abraham Lincoln to a second term.

Present-day Jonesboro, Georgia, location of the final dramatic scenes of the Atlanta campaign.

SITE DETAILS

Battle of Atlanta historical highway markers—Although the entire battlefield has been lost to development, a number of signs mark the most important sites related to the battle. These include the sites where Generals James McPherson and William Walker were killed, troop positions, and other landmarks. *James McPherson Monument, intersection of McPherson Ave. SE and Monument Ave. SE, Atlanta, GA, 30316. William H. T. Walker Monument, Glenwood Triangle, intersection of Wilkinson Dr. SE and Glenwood Ave. SE, Atlanta, GA, 30317. Historical highway marker 044-60 (Noon under the Trees), Georgia Historical Commission, intersection of DeKalb Ave. and Oakdale Rd., Atlanta, GA, 30317. Several historical highway markers on Battery Place NE and Degress Ave. near intersections with DeKalb Ave., Atlanta, GA, 30317. All markers accessible daily.*

Atlanta Cyclorama and Civil War Museum—Perhaps the best place in Atlanta to get an interpretation of the battle and the Atlanta campaign is the Cyclorama, home of what is still the world's largest oil painting. Commissioned by John Logan, a former Union general, and finished in 1886, the painting, along with an audiovisual program and other objects that have been added over the years, is part of a half-hour show that tells the story of the battle. The museum, although somewhat dated, tells in digestible detail the story of the campaign. The centerpiece of the collection, though, is the *Texas*, the railroad engine that chased down another engine, the *General*, which was stolen by Union soldiers in the escapade that became known as the Great Locomotive Chase. *Atlanta Cyclorama and Civil War Museum, 800 Cherokee Ave. SE, Atlanta, GA, 30315; 404-658-7625; www.bcaatlanta.com. Closed Mon.; admission charged.*

Peachtree Creek—Located in Atlanta's Tanyard Creek Park is a set of historical markers telling in detail the story of the battle of Peachtree Creek. Not only is there a map of the battle, but there are also markers describing where elements of the battle took place as they relate to current landmarks such as schools and cemeteries. Although the battlefield is essentially gone, Atlanta's park district has gone a long way in interpreting this critical battle. *Peachtree Creek historical markers, Tan-*

Within a few days of the battle of Utoy Creek, Sherman greatly intensified his bombardment of Atlanta, now using heavy siege artillery that had been brought south from Chattanooga. Then, after seemingly incessant attack, the firing suddenly stopped. The Confederates probed what had been the Union lines and found them empty. The Federals had virtually disappeared. Hood reasoned that Sherman had moved north, and that for the moment the city was safe, although he knew that some small Federal forces were operating south of the city, still trying to disrupt the railroads.

In reality those small Federal forces were virtually Sherman's entire command. Deliberately abandoning supply wagons and his positions north of the city, Sherman

yard Creek Park, intersection of Collier Rd. NW and Walthall Dr. NW, Atlanta, GA, 30309. Site accessible daily.

Ezra Church—Similar in concept to the design of the markers at Peachtree Creek, signs detailing the battle of Ezra Church are located in another of Atlanta's city parks, Mozley Park. The signs are again very detailed, although it seems that some of them are in need of repair. Still, the area is surrounded by a small but lovely park, and the interpretation of the battle, again using current local landmarks as guidelines, is excellent, considering the amount of the battlefield that has been lost. *Ezra Church historical markers, Mozley Park, 1565 Martin Luther King Dr. NW, Atlanta, GA, 30314. Site accessible daily.*

Utoy Creek—Two historical highway markers have been placed on the southwest side of Atlanta near where the battle of Utoy Creek took place. The markers are in a residential area and are easy to find. *Historical highway markers 050-159 (Battle of Utoy Creek) and 060-160 (The Embattled Ridge), Georgia Historical Commission, intersection of Cascade Rd. SW and Woodland Terrace SW, Atlanta, GA, 30317. Open daily.*

Jonesboro Depot—The town of Jonesboro (even though the name has changed slightly) still exists, and some buildings remaining from the time of the battle are still standing, although for the most part the battlefield is long gone. A museum is housed in the former railroad depot. The main focus of the museum, as well as most of the rest of the town's well-developed tourist industry, is related to the Civil War, but not to the battle that took place here. Jonesboro bills itself as the home of the famous epic novel and film *Gone with the Wind,* and along with the museum, there is a trolley ride stopping at related points throughout town, as well as at several grand plantation homes. Although the museum focuses on the famous story, the small section regarding the battle of Jonesboro is very good, albeit dwarfed by the other exhibits. The museum also has handout information on the battle itself for interested tourists. *Jonesboro Depot Welcome Center, 104 N. Main St., Jonesboro, GA, 30236; 1-800-662-7829; www.historicaljonesboro.org. Closed Sun.; admission charged.*

had swung all three of his armies south to finish the job of severing Atlanta's supply lines. Hood finally realized the extent of his trouble on August 30 and directed his forces against General Oliver Howard at Jonesborough. Over the two following days, the battle of Jonesborough was fought, and although the fighting was heavy, the Federals were successful in not only repulsing the Confederate attacks, but also in closing the last remaining railroad into Atlanta. Hood evacuated the city that night. Sherman entered Atlanta triumphantly on September 3 and began preparations for his great march to the sea and Savannah. The capture of Atlanta was a great victory for the Union cause. It was the end of a brilliant and hard-fought campaign. It robbed the

South of its grandest and most strategically important city. Finally, it virtually ensured the election of Abraham Lincoln in the upcoming election. The people of Atlanta still pass down stories of the devastation and destruction that resulted from the terrible fighting and the burning of their city following Sherman's departure. Atlanta's fall was one of the truly defining moments of the Civil War and signaled the beginning of the end for the Confederate States of America.

Andersonville

The conditions for prisoners during the Civil War, on both sides, were horrendous. From Camp Douglas in Chicago to Belle Isle prison camp in Richmond, the harsh realities found at virtually all of them are almost unimaginable; they were centers of disease, starvation, and violence. Among all these prison camps, however, one name has clearly stood out as the symbol of the inhumanity that pervaded these terrible places: Andersonville.

As the Civil War raged on, the Confederacy found that their prisons, particularly in Richmond, were becoming increasingly overcrowded, not to mention in danger of being captured and having their occupants returned to the enemy. So in early 1864 a prison camp, officially known as Camp Sumter, was constructed in Andersonville, Georgia. The small, isolated location was initially chosen because of its abundant food and water supply. However, Andersonville soon had the same problem as all the other prisons of the war: It was overcrowded. Initially designed to hold 10,000 prisoners, at its high point Andersonville held more than 32,000. To make matters worse, the

A reconstructed portion of the stockade wall at Andersonville National Historic Site.

Confederacy, in its waning days, could barely feed or clothe its own soldiers, let alone its prisoners. In the 14 months that Andersonville was in operation, nearly 13,000 Union prisoners died there.

After the war was over and the horrors of Andersonville were made public, the cry went up for justice. It was decided that justice meant the hanging of the prison commander, Captain Henry Wirz, although in reality there was probably little that Wirz could do for the mass of men under his guard. A national cemetery was also soon established at the site, thanks largely to the efforts of Clara Barton.

Throughout the war some 26,000 Confederate prisoners died in prison camps, and 30,000 Union prisoners met a similar fate. But Andersonville, accounting for almost half the deaths on the victor's side, will forever remain the most infamous.

» OTHER SITES IN THE HEARTLAND

Lincoln Boyhood National Memorial—The Lincoln family moved to Indiana in 1816, and this is where young Abraham grew up, staying here from age 7 until he was 21. It was during these formative years that he lost his mother, began to educate himself, and grew into the man he was to become.

The huge memorial located on the grounds is truly impressive, decorated with scenes from Lincoln's life. It holds a visitor's center, which includes displays and a film about Lincoln's early days. Also on the grounds is a small cemetery containing the grave of Lincoln's mother, Nancy Hanks. Finally, there is the excavated site of the Lincoln cabin, located near a living historical farm. Although the site is isolated from other Civil War–related areas, it is worth the diversion. *Lincoln Boyhood National Memorial, 3027 E. South St., Lincoln City, IN, 47552; 812-937-4541; www.nps.gov/libo. Open daily; admission charged.*

Corydon—In July 1863 Brigadier General John Hunt Morgan, already famous for his raids into Kentucky, decided to take it a little further and crossed the Ohio River into Indiana, against the orders of his commander, Braxton Bragg. On July 9 Morgan's Confederates encountered the town militia of Corydon, Indiana, once the state capital. The militia quickly surrendered, and Morgan depleted the town of supplies and cash and moved eastward toward Ohio, where he would eventually be captured.

The Battle of Corydon Memorial Park has been established to commemorate the event. The park is open to the public and contains interpretive material about the battle, as well as picnic facilities. *Battle of Corydon Memorial Park, 100 Old Highway 135 SW, Corydon, IN, 47112; 1-888-738-2137. Open daily.*

Munfordville and Rowlett's Station—Two battles, Rowlett's Station and Munfordville, were fought near Munfordville, Kentucky, over a key bridge spanning the Green River for the Louisville & Nashville Railroad. On December 17, 1861, Union forces attacked a Confederate defensive position here, and the battle of Rowlett's Station resulted, occurring just south of the bridge. Union forces took control of the bridge after that battle, but on September 14, 1862, the Confederates attempted to get it back. Although the initial attacks were repulsed heavily, the Confederates were able to place troops on both sides of the river and asked for the Union force's surrender. Colonel John Wilder, commanding the small force packed into the earthen fortification known as Fort Craig, refused. He was soon reinforced, and the Union strength now numbered approximately 4,000 troops. However, General Braxton Bragg had more forces coming and again demanded surrender. After asking for and receiving the very unorthodox privilege of viewing the strength of the enemy surrounding his fort, Wilder finally surrendered on September 17. The Confederates burned the bridge, by this time an important supply line to Union armies in Tennessee.

The Battle for the Bridge Historic Preserve, in Munfordville, is already a great place to visit, and the local Hart County Historical Society is doing much to make it an outstanding one. Currently, the battlefield at Munfordville consists of a walking trail, with interpretive signs, surrounding the battlefield. Visible from the trail are the remnants of the Green River bridge (the stone piers are still used today) and Fort Craig, although it is on private property and must be viewed from a distance. In the works are a visitor's center and guided tours of the town. The Historical Museum of Hart County also contains information about both the Munfordville and Rowlett's

Station battles. *Battle for the Bridge Historic Preserve, intersection of Charlie Dowling Rd. and Woodsonville Rd., Munfordville, KY, 42765; www.battleforthebridge.org; open daily. Historical Museum of Hart County, 109 Main St., Munfordville, KY, 42765; 270-524-0101; www.historichart.org; closed Sun.*

Jefferson Davis State Historic Site—Within eight months and less than 100 miles from the event of Abraham Lincoln's birth, Jefferson Davis, future president of the Confederate States of America, was born in Fairview, Kentucky, on June 3, 1808. Although it was very early in his life that his family moved south, eventually settling in Mississippi, it was on this site in Kentucky that Davis was born.

The obelisk monument, at 351 feet high, is indeed striking and demonstrates the high regard that the state of Kentucky, the center of many of the war's struggles, holds for this man, who served as congressman, U.S. senator, and as secretary of war under Franklin Pierce. There is a small visitor's center in the base of the monument, as well as an observation area at the top, although these are open only part of the year. *Jefferson Davis State Historic Site, US 68 and Britmart Rd., Fairview, KY, 42221; 502-886-1765; http://parks.ky.gov. Visitor's center and observation deck open May–Oct., admission charged; site open daily.*

Hartsville—Union forces were encamped at Hartsville, Tennessee, to protect a crossing of the Cumberland River there. On December 7, 1862, Colonel John Hunt Morgan, with less than two-thirds of the force that he came with (the rest were stuck on the other side of the river), conducted a daring predawn raid and surrounded the Federal camp, causing them to surrender. Morgan, who would go on to fame for his raids of Kentucky, Indiana, and Ohio, was given the rank of general for his victory here.

A 17-stop driving tour of the battle of Hartsville has been developed by the Hartsville-Trousdale Chamber of Commerce, and although copies can be found in town at the Hartsville Train Depot Museum, your best bet is go to the chamber's Web site and print out the brochure, just in case. The tour covers the entire battle, from the river crossing to the cemetery. However, most of the battle sites are on private property, so be sure to view the scenery from the road. *Battle of Hartsville driving tour, Hartsville Train Depot, 240 Broadway, Hartsville, TN, 37074; 615-374-9243; www.hartsvilletrousdale.com; tour sites open daily.*

Vaught's Hill—Union raiders, under Colonel Albert Hall, were pursued by John Hunt Morgan, and on March 20, 1863, near Milton, Tennessee, Morgan caught up with the Union rear guard. The Federals took up a strong position on Vaught's Hill, a ridge running north to south facing the Confederates, and easily repulsed the attack.

A historical highway marker is the only sign that a battle took place here, but Vaught's Hill is easily discernible, and the countryside is relatively untouched. Information about the battle can be obtained at Stones River National Battlefield. *Historical highway marker 3A-107 (Battle of Milton), Tennessee Historical Commission, located on south side of Lascassas Pike, east of intersection of Lascassas Pike and Ruel McKnight Rd., Milton, TN, 37118. Accessible daily.*

Brentwood—Union forces held a garrison at Brentwood, Tennessee, just south of Nashville, along the Nashville & Decatur Railroad. On March 24, 1863, General Nathan Bedford Forrest's Confederates surrounded the garrison and cut off all means of escape. Forrest asked for, and received, surrender the following day.

A historical highway marker, located in front of an office complex, is all that remains to mark the battle. More information can be obtained at the Carter House in Franklin. *Historical highway marker 3D-58 (Forrest's Brentwood Raid), Tennessee Historical Commission, located at 155 Franklin Rd., Brentwood, TN, 37027; accessible daily.*

Spring Hill—A prelude to the battles of Franklin and Nashville, Spring Hill did not result in high casualties for either side. However, the opportunity missed by Confederate forces here ensured doom for Hood's army as he approached Nashville. Major General John Schofield's mission was to stall Hood's army at Columbia to ensure that Union reinforcements reached Nashville before Hood did. Hood, knowing that he needed to break through, planned to circle around Schofield's army and either trap him where he was or break free and approach Nashville. After learning that Hood might be on the move, Schofield sent troops north to join the garrison he already had posted in Spring Hill. While the Confederates outnumbered the Union forces almost two to one when they attacked at Spring Hill on November 29, 1864, there was much confusion among the Confederate ranks, and they did not press their advantage. As the winter darkness quickly fell on the town, the fighting died down, and as the Confederates slept, Schofield, now fully knowing the threat to his army, slipped northward in the night. Hood had missed a golden chance and had set his army up for the disaster at Franklin the next day.

The Civil War Preservation Trust has preserved a section of the battlefield at Spring Hill south of the town, where the heaviest fighting occurred. There are interpretive trails and signs at the site, and unlike at Franklin and Nashville, the landscape is largely untouched, and it is easy to interpret the battle. The Spring Hill site is only a few miles south of Franklin and is worth the effort to see it. *Spring Hill Battlefield Civil War Site, intersection of Kedron Rd. and Old Kedron Rd., Spring Hill, TN, 37174; 931-486-9037; open daily.*

Thompson's Station—Union forces under Colonel John Coburn, heading south toward Columbia, encountered Confederates at Thompson's Station, Tennessee, just north of Spring Hill, on March 4, 1863. After initially taking the advantage, Union forces were pushed back. In hard fighting, the Federal position was seized by Brigadier General W. H. "Red" Jackson, while General Nathan Bedford Forrest blocked off the escape route. The Federals surrendered their force of 1,600.

Two historical highway markers are related to the battle; one describes the battle itself, while another, located at the Homestead Manor historical house, tells the story of 17-year-old Alice Thompson, who ran out of the cellar and retrieved the colors of the Third Arkansas when the color bearer fell. The house also served as a field hospital after the battle. There are plans to develop the house into an attraction, but for now it is private property, so treat it as such. *Historical highway marker 3D-55 (Battle of Thompson's Station), Tennessee Historical Commission, intersection of Columbia Pike and Thompson Station Rd.; historical highway marker (Homestead Manor), Williamson County Historical Society, 4683 Columbia Pike, Thompson's Station, TN, 37179. Accessible daily.*

Columbia—General John Bell Hood's Confederates were approaching Nashville, and Major General George H. Thomas, commanding the Union Army of the Cumberland, knew that he had to stall Hood until his own expected reinforcements arrived. Hood's army, led by Forrest's cavalry, proceeded to Columbia, Tennessee, and was met there on November 24, 1864, by Major General John Schofield and 28,000 Federal troops. Schofield, although outnumbered, knew that his mission was to delay the Confederates, and he was able to hold them around Columbia through November 29, while slowly pulling back toward Nashville.

A historical highway marker at a very busy intersection in Columbia tells only generally about the battle. Information is best obtained at the Carter House in Franklin. *Historical highway marker 3D-13 (Hood and Schofield), Tennessee Historical Commission, intersection of TN-243 and TN-50, Columbia, TN, 38401. Accessible daily.*

Murfreesboro I—Murfreesboro served as a Union supply center for Tennessee operations, especially in the approach to Chattanooga. General Nathan Bedford Forrest launched a surprise attack on Murfreesboro, fighting throughout the town until only one group of Union troops had not surrendered. Forrest led the Union commander through the streets of Murfreesboro under a flag of truce to indicate his strength; in reality, Forrest's troops were moving about the town in order to appear more numerous than they were. The surrender was completed, and Forrest's men proceeded to destroy the supplies there.

While the battle occurred throughout town, the surrender took place at the Oaklands Plantation, site of one of the Union encampments and now a historic house and museum. The grounds are a public park, while a fee is required to see the home and museum. *Oaklands Historic House Museum, 900 N. Maney Ave., Murfreesboro, TN, 37130; 615-893-0022; www.oaklandsmuseum.org. Closed Mon.; admission charged.*

Hoover's Gap—In June 1863 Major General William S. Rosecrans, aware that General Braxton Bragg was sending troops to Vicksburg, Mississippi, decided to attack the Confederate lines just south of Murfreesboro. Rosecrans feinted against the Confederate left, then on June 24 launched coordinated attacks at three fortified mountain gaps on the Confederate right—Liberty Gap, Guy's Gap, and Hoover's Gap—in an attempt to turn the line. Fighting occurred at Hoover's Gap for three days, until the Confederates were driven back; Bragg was eventually forced to abandon his position and retire to Chattanooga.

At Hoover's Gap sits the Beech Grove Confederate Cemetery and Park, just off the interstate. The site contains interpretive signs, push-button audio recordings describing the action and the history of the area, and a small cemetery that contains not only Confederate dead, but the remains of a small community cemetery predating the battle. There are also picnic and restroom facilities. A product of local efforts, this is an easily accessible and wonderful site to visit. *Beech Grove Confederate Cemetery and Park, intersection of Oscar Cromwell Rd. and Cemetery Rd., Beech Grove, TN, 37018; 931-455-9500. Open daily.*

Davis' Cross Roads—Two days after the Confederate army had abandoned Chattanooga, General Braxton Bragg realized that the three Union armies under General William Rosecrans's command were pursuing him—but were also separated from one another. Seeing an opportunity, Bragg halted his march south and attempted to catch General George Thomas's corps in McLemore's Cove, a region in northern Georgia surrounded by mountains with only one escape route. It was a prime opportunity, but poor planning and execution on the part of the Confederates prevented what could have been a major victory. After some initial action on September 10, 1863, the Union forces fell back to Davis' Cross Roads, in the middle of McLemore's cove, and then withdrew back through Stevens Gap toward Lookout Mountain the next day to await reinforcements.

There is a very nice interpretive sign set up at Davis' Cross Roads showing a map of McLemore's Cove and noting what could have been had Bragg's forces seized the opportunity in front of them. More information on the battle can be gathered at Chickamauga National Military Park. *Davis' Cross Roads interpretive sign, 58 Hog Jowl Rd., Chickamauga, GA, 30707. Site accessible daily.*

Ringgold Gap—After the Confederate defeat at Chattanooga, Braxton Bragg's army withdrew south. Worried about his supply wagons and artillery, Bragg ordered Major General Patrick Cleburne to occupy Ringgold Gap and delay any Union pursuit. Early on November 27, 1863, Major General Joseph Hooker's Federals entered the town of Ringgold and approached the gap. Cleburne, a master tactician, had planned well; the Confederate force was well hidden, and the Union column was hit almost without warning. Hooker's men tried to dislodge the Confederates for four hours, but to no avail, and the attempt was finally called off. The Union suffered 507 casualties in the battle, and the Confederates only 221.

The state of Georgia has developed a small park and relief map interpreting the battle of Ringgold Gap and the part it played in the Atlanta campaign. From the town of Ringgold, the gap itself is easily discernible to the east. *Atlanta campaign relief map and picnic area, 8379 US 41, Ringgold, GA, 30736. Site accessible daily.*

Dalton and Rocky Face Ridge—The city of Dalton, Georgia, is surrounded by several ridges, with only a handful of small gaps allowing access to the area from the north or west. For this reason Dalton was often chosen as a defensive position and was the site of several engagements during the war. The first began on February 22, 1864, when Major General George Thomas's Army of the Cumberland approached Dalton to test the defenses of the Confederate Army of Tennessee, which had fallen back to regroup at Dalton after its defeat at Chattanooga. After several days of fighting, Thomas had the information he needed: The Confederate defenses were extremely strong, particularly around Mill Creek Gap and Dug Gap, which were the most direct routes into Dalton. But Thomas had also discovered Snake Creek Gap, south of the city, which was not defended.

Several months later the Union began its advance on Atlanta, and the first step was to drive the Confederate army out of Dalton. On May 7, 1864, Sherman began his offensive, attacking the long line of Confederate earthworks on the ridges surrounding Dalton with two armies, while secretly moving General James McPherson's Army of the Ohio south to Snake Creek Gap in an attempt to sever the railroad. The fighting, known as the battle of Rocky Face Ridge, lasted a week, until Johnston realized that part of Sherman's army was moving toward Snake Creek Gap and Resaca, threatening not only the Confederates' supply line but also their position. The Confederates withdrew to Resaca on May 13, and Union forces occupied Dalton.

Finally, late in the Atlanta campaign, General John Bell Hood, now in command of the Army of Tennessee, sent his cavalry north in an attempt to destroy the railroad that served as Sherman's supply line. On August 14, 1864, the cavalry, under the command of General Joseph Wheeler, attacked the small Union garrison at Dalton and demanded its surrender. Refusing, the Union troops fell back to a fortified position, and Wheeler's troops were driven out of Dalton the next day by Union reinforcements.

Although Dalton was the scene of much activity, most of the battle areas themselves are not accessible, because the actions were primarily defensive and occurred on mountainous ground. There is, however, the Dug Gap Battle Park, located west of the city on Rocky Face Ridge. Also, an Atlanta campaign relief map and picnic area is located in front of the Georgia State Police Patrol station. *Dug Gap Battle Park, on Dug Gap Battle Rd. north of intersection of Dug Gap Battle Rd. and W. Dug Gap Mountain Rd., Dalton, GA, 30720; 1-800-331-3258. Atlanta campaign relief map and picnic area, 2401 Chattanooga Rd., Dalton, GA, 30720. Sites accessible daily.*

Resaca—As the armies of Sherman and Johnston faced each other at Rocky Face Ridge, both were sending elements of their force southward. Sherman had ordered Major General James McPherson to Snake Creek Gap, where he was to enter Resaca to the east, destroy the railroad, and then await Johnston. McPherson, cautiously, suspected that he might be outnumbered and did not advance past the gap. Johnston, meanwhile, had been moving elements of his army to Resaca all along, anticipating a battle there. Eventually Sherman's entire force was also at Resaca, and on May 14, 1864, the two armies finally collided in force, facing each other in a line running north to south. The fighting was bloody, and it lasted until the next day, with neither side gaining real advantage. Finally, near the end of the day on the 15th, the Federals had gained a position south of Resaca that put Johnston's army in jeopardy, and the Confederates withdrew overnight, having lost 2,800 of their men. The Union suffered 2,747 casualties.

A number of historical highway markers note the primary positions of the Resaca battlefield, and an Atlanta campaign relief map describes the action. However, groundbreaking for the Resaca Battlefield State Park occurred in October 2008, and the plans for the park, organized and fought for by the Friends of Resaca Battlefield, include a museum with interactive displays and a theater. The target date for opening is 2010; stay tuned for this one. *Atlanta campaign relief map, intersection of US 41 and Confederate Cemetery Rd. NW, Resaca, GA, 30735. Historical highway markers along Chitwood Rd., east of intersection of US 41 and Chitwood Rd. NE, Resaca, GA, 30735. Accessible daily. Resaca Battlefield Park, near intersection of GA 136 and Taylor Ridge Rd. NE, Resaca, GA, 30735; 1-800-864-7275; www.resacabattlefield.org. Currently under development.*

Adairsville—General Johnston, moving south after the battle at Resaca, chose the town of Adairsville as a good place to make another defensive stand. On May 17, 1864, before he was able to make any preparations, the front of a Union column was surprised by Confederate artillery near the town. General George Thomas, the Union commander, stopped the column as darkness fell; Johnston, meanwhile, had decided that a defensive position at Adairsville was too risky and moved south again that night.

Adairsville, Georgia, is a cute little town, but there are almost no reminders of the battle anywhere near it. Some information can be gathered at the Adairsville Rail Depot, the local visitor information center, but its hours are limited and extremely irregular; call first if you plan to visit. *Adairsville Rail Depot, 101 Public Square, Adairsville, GA, 30103; 770-773-1775. Open Tue.–Fri. and by appointment.*

Allatoona—After General John Bell Hood was driven out of Atlanta, he headed north. His initial plan, before he ultimately decided to invade Tennessee, was to close Sherman's single supply line to Atlanta—the Western & Atlantic Railroad, running south from Chattanooga—and to take Sherman's army. On October 5, 1864, a Confederate division commanded by Major General Samuel French approached the Union garrison at Allatoona Pass, a deep railway cut. The plan was to take the supposedly small Union force there and literally fill the gap with dirt and debris, thereby blocking off the railroad. However, Sherman anticipated Hood's movement (aided by the loose lips of Jefferson Davis during speeches in Georgia and South Carolina), and by the time the Confederates arrived, the Union position had been reinforced. Already strong with two substantial earthen fortifications, now over 2,000 men, most armed with the new Henry repeating rifle, awaited French's division. It was a pitched battle, but the Confederates were not able to take the gap.

Allatoona Pass Battlefield is now maintained by the Georgia State Parks as a unit of Red Top Mountain State Park. Although the location is unstaffed, the relatively untouched fortifications and the stunning pass itself, along with interpretive signs, make this a site worth seeing. Parts of the trails running through the battlefield are somewhat steep and strenuous, but the road through the pass itself is straight and smooth. *Allatoona Pass Battlefield, Red Top Mountain State Park, north of intersection of Old Allatoona Rd. SE and Allatoona Landing Rd. SE, Cartersville, GA, 30121; 770-975-4226; www.gastateparks.org. Open daily.*

Lovejoy's Station—General Sherman had sent his cavalry, commanded by Brigadier General H. Judson Kilpatrick, south of Atlanta to destroy part of the railroad that was still supplying the city. After the Federals had done some damage near Jonesborough, word came that a Confederate force was headed their way. Kilpatrick headed south to Lovejoy's Station and awaited their arrival. On the morning of August 20, 1864, the Union cavalry was attacked on two sides, but Kilpatrick's troopers were able to break free by riding hard with sabers drawn. It was a close call, but Jonesborough was taken in force less than two weeks later, and Atlanta could hold out no longer.

The Nash Farm Battlefield, the site of part of the Lovejoy's Station breakout, is currently open to groups for guided tours for part of the year. It is also being developed for future use for all visitors. The battlefield, unlike just about every other one related to the Atlanta campaign, is relatively unspoiled. *Nash Farm Battlefield, 4361 Jonesboro Rd., Hampton, GA, 30228; 770-288-7300; www.henrycountybattlefield.com. Call to arrange for tours.*

Stone Mountain Park and Museum—In 1958 a group of artists, noting the world's admiration of the famous sculpture on Mount Rushmore in South Dakota, thought that the Confederate States of America would do well to have its own larger-than-life homage to its heroes. So happened the world's largest relief carving on the world's largest piece of exposed granite, Stone Mountain, just east of Atlanta. The carving captures the Confederate president, Jefferson Davis, and Generals Robert E. Lee and Stonewall Jackson riding horseback together among their soldiers.

The image is impressive, and the unbelievable amount of work required to create it is showcased in a museum near the monument. The Stone Mountain Park also contains numerous picnic areas, outdoor activities, rides, and other attractions that make up a very large family entertainment area. If you wish to view the carving only, all that is required is to pay a parking fee and drive up to the monument; a large field in front of the sculpture will give you a grand view. However, if you are interested, there are plenty of other activities available, including a museum that details the carving of the monument, all at additional cost. If you happen to be traveling with the kids, this could be a great place to stop and unwind. *Stone Mountain Park and Museum, 1126 Stonewall Jackson Dr., Stone Mountain, GA, 30087; 770-498-5690; www.stonemountainpark.com. Open daily; admission charged.*

Alexander H. Stephens State Historic Site—Alexander Stephens, vice president of the Confederate States of America, was a unique and interesting fellow. A small and sickly man throughout his lifetime, he was nevertheless widely known for his fearlessness and tenacity. Disliking Richmond (and especially President Jefferson Davis), Stephens spent virtually his entire Confederate term at his home in Crawfordville, Georgia. In fact, Stephens cast only the very last vote for the secession of Georgia from the Union and wished to be remembered for his public service record as a whole (schoolteacher, lawyer, U.S. congressman both before and after the war, and finally, governor) rather than his Confederate service.

The Stephens home, built after the war was over but on the same ground on which he lived throughout his life, is wonderfully preserved as a Georgia State Historic Site. There is a small museum on the grounds, as well as camping and other recreational facilities, but touring the home itself is a must if you visit the site, as the museum does not explain much about Stephens himself. Although this site is a little removed from most of the major Civil War sites, it is just off the interstate and is definitely worth a stop. *Alexander H. Stephens State Historic Site, 456 Alexander St. NW, Crawfordville, GA 30631; 706-456-2602; www.gastateparks.org. Closed Mon.; admission charged.*

Griswoldville—The only significant battle associated with Sherman's infamous march to the sea occurred at the town of Griswoldville, Georgia, just east of Macon. As the Union army, divided into two main bodies, moved toward Savannah, the troops destroyed everything in their path, burning and looting every home and farm they encountered. A rear guard to one of the Union forces was attacked on November 22, 1864, and the Federals quickly entrenched along a strong position, facing an open field. A group of 1,500 Georgia militia charged them across the field, and although the Confederates fought ferociously, they were little match for hardened veterans in an entrenched position. After three charges the Confederates withdrew, and when the smoke cleared, the Federals found to their horror that they had been fighting old men and young boys—all that was left to protect the home front. The Georgians suffered 650 casualties to the Union's 62.

There is a Georgia State Historic Site here, although it is unstaffed. Memorials and interpretive signs are located at a small parking area, and you can walk the open field where the Georgians made their brave but futile charges. The site is maintained by Jarrell Plantation State Historic Site, and information on the site can be found there. *Griswoldville State Historic Site, on Baker Rd., 0.4 mile north of intersection of Baker Rd. and Old Griswoldville Rd., Macon, GA, 31217; 478-986-5172; www.gastateparks.org. Open daily.*

The now-quiet field at Griswoldville, filled with the ghosts of the old men and young boys of the Home Guard.

National Civil War Naval Museum—This museum, in the somewhat isolated city of Columbus, Georgia, has only two drawbacks: It is in a remote location, and no major battles occurred near it. Other than those two small details, the National Civil War Naval Museum is pure gold. This museum leaves no stone unturned, closely examining the naval war on both the rivers and on the open sea. The exhibits include the wooden hull of the CSS *Jackson*, set adrift from its port in Columbus and burned, only to be salvaged years later by preservationists; walking into the hall where it is kept, with a metal frame outlining the missing sections of the ship, will take your breath away. Also leaving a memorable impression is the surround-sound multimedia presentation of an attack on the CSS *Albemarle*, docked at a re-created North Carolina port. Other highlights include full-size mockups of sections of Admiral David Farragut's flagship, the USS *Hartford*, and the turret of the USS *Monitor*; and the rest of the museum's exhibits are all educational and intriguing. Even the gift shop is unique, offering a complete library of titles on the all-too-often overlooked naval side of the Civil War. If you are in the area, this site is not to be missed. *National Civil War Naval Museum, 1002 Victory Dr., Columbus, GA, 31901; 706-327-9798; www.portcolumbus.org. Open daily; admission charged.*

The re-created turret of the USS Monitor *at the National Civil War Naval Museum in Columbus, Georgia.*

Jefferson Davis Memorial Historic Site—As Lee was in the process of evacuating his lines at Petersburg, Jefferson Davis and the rest of the Confederate cabinet fled Richmond. Davis's hope was to reunite with those Confederate armies still left in the field in the western theater and possibly relocate the government to Texas. However, he was heavily pursued by Union troops, and after the assassination of President Lincoln and the suspicion of a Confederate conspiracy, it was only a matter of time before he was caught. On the morning of May 10, 1865, as Davis and his party were camped near Irwinville, Georgia, two separate Union parties approached the group and surprised them. After some confusion, with the two Union patrols firing at each other and killing two soldiers, Davis was captured, thus ending his hopes of reestablishing the Confederate government.

The spot where Davis was captured is memorialized, as is the location where the two Union soldiers were killed. A small but excellent interpretive museum is located on the grounds, as well as a short nature trail. Isolated in the quiet Georgia countryside, this site provides an excellent diversion. Do plan ahead, though; the site is closed on Monday and Tuesday, although the memorial is just off the road. *Jefferson Davis*

Memorial Historic Site, 338 Jeff Davis Rd., Irwinville, GA, 31760; 229-831-2335; www.gastateparks.org. Closed Mon. and Tue.; admission charged.

» WHERE TO STAY IN THE HEARTLAND

With the exception of the two bookends of the trip, Perryville and Andersonville, all the major sites are near not only interstate highways, but large cities also, and lodging will be easy to find throughout your tour. And with a little planning, you can find a few nice alternatives to the interstate motels.

Near the Perryville battlefield, in the town of Lebanon, Kentucky, is the **Myrtle- dene Bed and Breakfast**. The home served as the headquarters of famed Confederate raider John Hunt Morgan for some time. While Lebanon is the nearest large town to Perryville, and several motels are nearby, this bed-and-breakfast does hold a bit of history. *Myrtledene Bed and Breakfast, 370 N. Spalding Ave., Lebanon, KY, 40033; 1-800- 391-1721; www.myrtledene.com.*

On the other end of the route, just east of Atlanta, is the **Village Inn**. The inn was built in the 1820s and was used as a field hospital during the Atlanta campaign. Because it was still in use when Sherman's men passed through, it was spared the torch. Now it serves as a bed-and-breakfast in the historic village of Stone Mountain, near the famed memorial carving. *The Village Inn, 992 Ridge Ave., Stone Mountain, GA, 30083; 1-800-214-8385; www.villageinnbb.com.*

The museum and visitor's center at Jefferson Davis Memorial Historic Site, where Davis was captured while fleeing through Georgia.

PART TWO

The War along the Coasts

5

The Gulf Coast

OVERVIEW

A major part of the Union's war strategy, as outlined in Major General Winfield Scott's Anaconda Plan, was to take away the Confederacy's ability to import the goods needed to make war. This also meant that the Southern states would not be able to export their staple crop—cotton—to the rest of the world, severely slowing down the economy and damaging the morale of many Southern farmers. The involvement of several European countries, which were paying close attention to the contest, was also somewhat dependent on whether they could get the cotton they needed to produce their goods. The Union knew that a successful naval blockade of the Southern shores was vital to winning the war.

Beyond the overall blockade strategy, several strategic points along the Southern coast were critical to the Union effort in other ways. Capturing New Orleans was an early necessity if the Union had any hopes for gaining full control of the Mississippi River. Mobile, Tampa, and Galveston, with their well-protected harbors, were not only shipbuilding and commerce centers, but were also gateways to the South's interior.

Although the Union navy was far superior to the Confederacy's, both in number of vessels and in firepower, gaining control of the coastline was no small feat. Along the Gulf of Mexico, the Confederacy had several important ports that were well protected, courtesy of the strong system of fortifications that the United States had built there after the War of 1812. Although blockade runners were often caught, trying to shut down thousands of miles of coastline was nearly impossible. But because of these high stakes

---

Seven different flags—Spanish, French, British, Confederate, the state of Alabama, the Alabama Militia, and the United States of America—have flown over fortifications at Mobile Point, site of Fort Morgan.

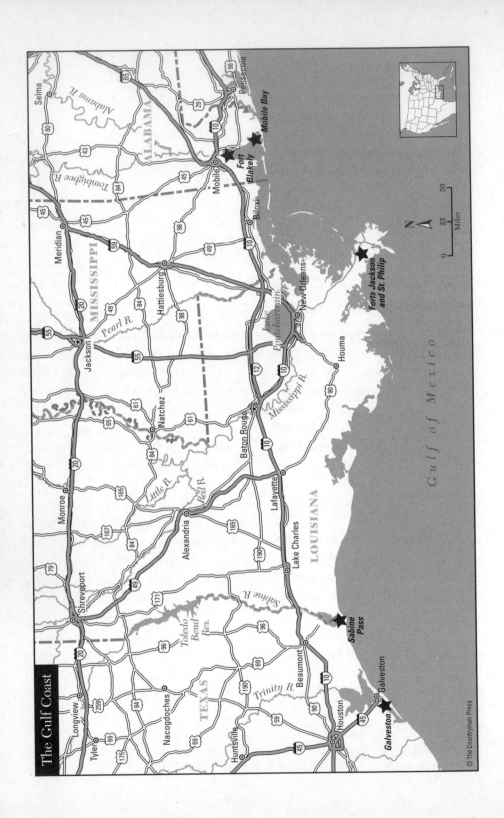

The Gulf Coast

and long odds, the battles along the Gulf Coast provided some of the most memorable and heroic moments of the Civil War, from "cottonclads" to damned torpedoes.

» PEOPLE TO KNOW

David G. Farragut—David Glasgow Farragut was already a naval hero before the Civil War. Beginning his career at sea at the age of nine, Farragut served in the War of 1812 and sailed around the world with the United States Navy, finally attaining a captaincy in 1855. Although he was born in Tennessee and lived in Norfolk, Virginia, Farragut remained with the Union, and he was soon given the assignment of capturing the important port at New Orleans.

Farragut's passing of Forts Jackson and St. Philip, with the assistance of Commander David Porter (whose father, Commodore David Porter, was Farragut's foster father and a naval hero himself), brought New Orleans to the Union. Farragut's later victories on the Gulf and on the lower rivers earned him a reputation as a great fighter. But it was his victory at the battle of Mobile Bay and his (alleged) exclamation of "Damn the torpedoes—full speed ahead!" that made him a legend. Farragut became the United States Navy's first full admiral after the war.

Benjamin Butler—Despite all that could be said about him, fairly or unfairly, no one can deny that Benjamin Butler wasn't afraid of a little controversy. An attorney and a powerful politician before the war, Butler, like many other prominent men, sought and obtained a commission in the Union army. In mid-1861 he was chosen to command Fortress Monroe in Virginia. Butler decreed that slaves captured during the war were contraband and would be freed and immediately employed by the Federal army. His declaration earned him his first jeers from the South.

But that was nothing compared to what was coming. When the Union took possession of New Orleans in early 1862, Butler was put in command of the city and soon began to rack up nicknames like "Spoons," being accused of pilfering citizens' silverware as their property was seized, and "Beast Butler," after he declared that any woman insulting a Union soldier would be considered a "lady of the town" and arrested for prostitution. After his removal from New Orleans, Butler was given one more field command during General Ulysses S. Grant's 1864 campaign for Richmond, but his tactics resulted in his being bottled up in the area known as Bermuda Hundred, and he was effectively taken out of action by the Confederates. After the war, Butler reentered the political arena and was one of the most vocal proponents of a harsh reconstruction policy.

» THINGS TO KNOW

If you've never traveled to this part of the country, there are a few critical things to know before you set out. The first, and maybe most important, is that you will be visiting some very beautiful and popular places. Sure, you'll want to be prepared to possibly run into large numbers of tourists; and depending on where you decide to stop for the night, you may have to pay a bit extra for a hotel, particularly in New Orleans or in Florida. But if you are looking for a "relaxing" Civil War trip, this is probably the place to do it. This trip will provide plenty of opportunities to work on your tan and get some sand between your toes.

Second, know what to expect for the time of year that you go. It's difficult to understate just how hot and humid it can get along the Gulf Coast during the summer months, so if you do decide to go in August, be prepared. Of course, this also means that you might be able to score some cheaper rates if you go during the hotter months. Also, don't forget that the areas covered by this tour are ground zero not only for Mardi Gras in New Orleans, but also the college spring break season along the entire coast.

As noted in Chapter 3: Bring insect repellent and sunscreen. Trust me—they are necessities.

One more note: In the past few years, the Gulf Coast, notably New Orleans and Galveston, have been devastated by hurricanes. Be sure to call first if there's anything important that you would like to see, as these areas are still undergoing major reconstruction. But your traveling to the region will help restore those areas' economies, so don't delay your trip.

THE TRIP

This is a one-way trip. It is laid out from west to east, starting in Galveston and ending in Mobile. But you can easily reverse the direction, and there are some very interesting sites farther along the coast, both in Texas and Florida, that are worth seeing. If you are taking family, especially kids, spending some time on the beach in Galveston or the Florida panhandle should ensure something for everyone.

If you start in Galveston, nearby Houston is usually the easiest and cheapest place to fly to. Finishing in Mobile will put you in a good position to fly out of New Orleans, although flying out of Mobile itself is usually not a bad option. One thing to remember with any of the one-way trips, if you rent a car, is the dreaded drop-off fee, which can be quite pricey. However, because of Florida's popularity as a tourist destination, several companies offer occasional specials on one-way rentals from that state, so check and see if these are available when you go.

» THE CAN'T-MISS SITES

Galveston

There were only a handful of Southern ports where blockade-running could be called anything close to successful. Galveston, Texas, was near the top of the short list. Although it was quite a distance from most of the fighting, and even though it was partially closed by the Union navy, Galveston remained an important Southern port,

Civil War exhibit, Galveston County Historical Museum.

bringing in much-needed supplies. Its sheltered, calm waters had been selected as a defendable haven by the Spanish and the French before them, and the Confederacy took full advantage of these natural attributes.

Two principal battles were fought in short order in Galveston Bay, although blockade running occurred throughout the war. The first took place on October 4, 1862, when a Union fleet under Commander William Renshaw appeared just outside the bay. One ship steamed in under a flag of truce, to demand the surrender of the city. When the ship received no response, other Union ships entered the bay, dueling with the Confederate-held Fort Point at the bay's eastern end. Early in the afternoon, the Confederates sent two officers to meet Renshaw on his flagship, the USS *Westfield*, to discuss surrender terms. Renshaw demanded immediate unconditional surrender, threatening to fire on the city. However, when it was made clear that the Confederates would not agree to the terms, and Renshaw would have to open his guns onto women and children, he agreed to give the Confederates four days to evacuate the citizens of Galveston. It was a handshake deal, and a poor one. In the four days, the Confederates not only evacuated the citizens, but also all their soldiers and weapons. Although it was a somewhat hollow victory, the U.S. Navy did take control of Galveston, temporarily halting the import of goods there.

SITE DETAILS

Galveston County Historical Museum—Operated by the Galveston County Historical Society and housed in a former bank building, the Galveston County Historical Museum is small, but the interpretation of the Galveston battles is well done and simple to understand. The museum is also a great place to visit to get perspective on why Galveston was and is such an important seaport. The story of the area's sometimes tragic relationship with the sea, from the devastating hurricanes of 1900 and 2008 to the terrible destruction of the maritime disaster in 1947 at Texas City across the bay, makes you wonder how Galveston has managed to stay afloat; the museum helps you understand how it couldn't be any other way. (Note: The Texas Seaport Museum, also run by the Galveston County Historical Society, contains no information on the two naval battles that occurred right outside its back door, except for one historical marker outside the museum. It's a neat place to visit, but don't expect to learn about the battles.) *Galveston County Historical Museum, 2219 Market St., Galveston, TX, 77550; 409-766-2340; www.galvestonhistory.org. Open daily.*

Fort Point historical marker—There is a marker near the former site of Fort Point at the east end of Galveston Bay. Many different nations operated fortresses here for years, but there is virtually no sign of any of them today, all washed away by time. However, the views of the bay and the Gulf of Mexico from here are great, and you can see the entire area of the battle. The monument is also located near several beaches, so soak in the sun if you have the time. *Fort Point historical marker, intersection of Seawall Blvd. and Boddecker Dr., Galveston, TX, 77550 (at ferry boarding area). Open daily.*

The Union occupation of Galveston did not last long, however. Less than two months later, on January 1, 1863, Confederate naval and land forces under Major General John Magruder launched an early morning assault on the city in an attempt to retake it. Four Confederate ships approached the Union fleet from within Galveston Bay. Two of the Confederate vessels were steamboats, and two were "cottonclads"—ships that were piled high with cotton bales in order to deaden the effect of Union cannonballs. Infantry also worked eastward into the city, bottling up the entire corps of defenders, the 42nd Massachusetts Regiment, onto a pier in the harbor. The Union infantry soon surrendered, while on the water the Federals suffered great losses. Four Union ships, three of them supply ships, were captured, and one Union steamboat sank after ramming another Union ship. The *Westfield*, Renshaw's flagship, ran aground. While Union sailors were able to blow up the ship to prevent its capture, the premature explosion claimed the lives of several aboard, including Renshaw himself. In the end the Confederates had easily retaken Galveston, and they held it until the end of the war. Although the blockade of Galveston continued, blockade runners still entered Galveston with relative success.

Sabine Pass

At the time of the Civil War, the former town of Sabine City was located near the Texas-Louisiana state line on the Gulf Coast. The mouth of the Sabine River opens up into the Gulf here, and during the war the channels created by the river became a favorite passage for Confederate blockade runners. The small Texas port was important to the Confederate cause during the war, but its significance today is as a source of Texas pride, another shining example of Texans defending their native soil.

Sabine Pass was actually the site of two principal battles during the war. The Confederates, eager to protect their shipping haven, had set up several fortresses along the Sabine pass, a relatively narrow strip of the Sabine River only slightly upriver from the Gulf. However, the defenses were only lightly manned. The U.S. Navy, eager to discourage the blockade runners, decided to take Sabine and on September 24, 1862, opened fire on the defenses with three ships. The Confederate force knew that they could not hold long and soon spiked their cannons and evacuated. By the next day the shore batteries had been destroyed, and Sabine City was surrendered to the Union. While the U.S. Navy did take eight small Confederate boats that were at Sabine, they

The great Texan Dick Dowling stands atop a memorial at Sabine Pass Battleground State Historic Site.

SITE DETAILS

Sabine Pass Battleground State Historic Site—At the site of Fort Griffin is Sabine Pass Battleground State Historic Site, in what is now Port Arthur, Texas. Although most of Fort Griffin itself has been lost to the river, the site contains enough interpretive signs to explain the battle and where the action occurred. A number of historical markers are set along the area, as well as memorials to the First Texas and its commander, Dick Dowling. The park is set deep in the industrial heart of the Texas coast and takes a little effort to get to, but the reward is a quiet, undisturbed view of the channel where the action took place. There are also picnic areas available, and fishing the pass is a common pastime among the locals. Although some of the park's facilities are a little worn, and it's surrounded by major shipping and refinery towers, it's a nice place to visit. *Sabine Pass Battleground State Historic Site, 6100 Dick Dowling Rd., Port Arthur, TX, 77640; 409-463-6323; www.thc.state.tx.us/ hsites/hs_sabine_pass.shtml. Open daily.*

did not have the manpower to garrison the town after its capture, and it was left as it was. The Confederates retook Sabine City, uncontested, soon after, and proceeded to rebuild their defenses along the pass.

One of the improved defenses, known as Fort Griffin, was commanded by Lieutenant Richard "Dick" Dowling. Under Dowling's command were members of the First Texas Heavy Artillery Regiment, particularly a group known as the Jeff Davis Guards. These 46 men, Irish longshoremen armed with only six cannon, were skilled at their craft, and they made sure that they would be ready the next time Union gunboats came around. The Texans set markers along the pass, driving piles into the river to guide their shots, so that they knew exactly where their artillery needed to be set when a ship approached.

The day finally came on September 8, 1863. Major General Nathaniel Banks, under the direction of President Lincoln, had decided on a joint operation to regain Texas. At the time Lincoln was extremely concerned with events in Mexico. France's Napoleon III had just played a major part in overthrowing the Mexican government and putting Maximilian in power as emperor. The Confederacy, desperate for recognition by European nations, would be eager to recognize the new regime in Mexico in exchange for French assistance, possibly even trading arms for cotton across the Mexican border. The Union campaign against Texas was intended to be a warning to the French.

On September 8, 1863, four gunboats approached Sabine Pass to cover the landing of 5,000 troops waiting in transports shortly behind. The patient Texans waited until the gunboats approached the markers set in the river, then opened a deadly fire. The lead Union gunboat was soon struck through the boiler, and the flagship, the USS *Clifton*, had to be surrendered. In no time the rest of the Union ships were headed back toward the Gulf. Not one Confederate soldier was lost in the battle, but the Union lost two ships and 350 sailors. More important, the invasion of Texas was stopped. The legend of Dick Dowling and the First Texas Heavy Artillery still looms large in a state known for big heroes.

Forts Jackson and St. Philip and New Orleans

Anyone visiting New Orleans today cannot help but be engulfed in the city's history; it is everywhere. The French Quarter, with its street names still in that language, harks back to the days before the Louisiana Purchase in 1803. Walking around the quarter, you will see that many of the buildings are built in the Spanish style, remnants of that country's claim on this charming place. Although the city has historically (and recently) had its troubles, New Orleans has remained important throughout the centuries because of its location at the mouth of the Mississippi River. It is not only the end of the riverboat captain's run, but the beginning of the sea captain's journey. New Orleans was the Confederacy's largest city and the gateway from which its goods were transported to the ports of the world.

During the Civil War New Orleans became a critical first target for the Union, not only to stop the Confederacy's industrial and trade activities there, but to open a

Defying time and the elements, the walls of mighty Fort Jackson still stand south of New Orleans.

The Cabildo, in New Orleans's French Quarter and part of the Louisiana State Museum system.

gateway to invasion via the vital artery of the Mississippi. Union control of New Orleans and the Mississippi meant that goods from the South would have a hard time getting to the world market, thus starving the South's economy. Control of the river would also cut the Confederacy in half, essential to the Union's Anaconda Plan.

Though the value of New Orleans was not lost on the Confederacy, early Union successes north of the city, with major armies moving southward through Kentucky and Tennessee and approaching Mississippi, led the Confederates to believe that any attempt on New Orleans would come by land. Therefore the city itself was only lightly garrisoned, with most troops being shipped to where the fighting was. That is not to say that New Orleans was defenseless. Well south of the city, down the Mississippi, were two substantial positions, Forts Jackson and St. Philip. Located across the river from each other, these stone fortifications, along with several naval vessels, commanded a stretch of the Mississippi with over 100 cannon. The Confederate river fleet lay behind the protection of the forts, and in addition, several ships had been sunk in the river as obstacles, and heavy chain was laid across the river to tear apart the hulls of enemy vessels. The only way to New Orleans by sea was to run this seemingly impenetrable gauntlet.

The Union, however, was undeterred and tasked flag officer David G. Farragut with breaking through the passage and taking New Orleans. Backed by Navy commander David Porter and 15,000 troops under Major General Benjamin Butler, Farragut assembled 23 warships and an additional 21 mortar schooners, part of Porter's fleet, at the mouth of the Mississippi. On April 18, 1862, Porter's mortars opened fire on Fort Jackson, located on the west bank, and began to reduce it. In the meantime, Farragut's warships started to work on moving or somehow getting around the obstructions in the river. In the middle of the night on April 24, with a path in the river

SITE DETAILS

Fort Jackson—Fort Jackson still stands on the banks of the Mississippi, in the town of Buras, 75 miles south of New Orleans. In the past it was operated by Plaquemines Parish as a historic site. However, visitors today can only see the fort from the outside. Hurricanes have devastated much of the surrounding town, and although the fort itself is still in pretty good shape, the town is yet in recovery mode. Sharing the park with the fort, for instance, is a half-destroyed football stadium, still waiting for repair (or, more probably, the wrecking ball). The park is still open, though, and from the levee you can see inside the fort. (Trespassing is strictly forbidden, and you probably don't want to swim the moat anyway.) Some outlying areas of the fort are accessible, but these are all from a later era. For now the site is deserted and overgrown, but hope remains that before too long the fort will be back in operating condition. *Fort Jackson, on LA 23 at Herbert Harvey Dr., Buras, LA, 70041; 504-657-7083. Park open daily, but inside of fort not presently accessible.*

The Cabildo—Although it is listed on the Civil War Sites Advisory Commission's list of principal battlefields, there really wasn't much of a battle of New Orleans (at least not during the Civil War). However, there are two excellent museums in the city that have exhibits on the occupation of New Orleans. One is the Cabildo, part of the Louisiana State Museum complex. It also happens to be the same building in which the Louisiana Purchase was signed, well before the war. Not only are the exhibits on the Civil War splendid, but the city's rich history is also displayed in grand detail. Also in New Orleans is the **Louisiana Civil War Museum** at Confederate Memorial Hall. The museum enjoys an excellent reputation as one of the largest collections of Confederate artifacts in the country; unfortunately, it has been closed for renovations for some time, part of a larger restoration project with some of the surrounding museums. Optimism remains that the museum will open by 2009. *The Cabildo, 751 Chartres St., New Orleans, LA, 70116; 1-800-568-6968; http://lsm.crt.state.la.us/cabex.htm. Closed Mon.; admission charged. Louisiana Civil War Museum at Confederate Memorial Hall, 929 Camp St., New Orleans, LA, 70130; 504-523-2522; www.confederatemuseum.com. Currently closed for renovation; call before visiting.*

cleared, Farragut led his warships through the gauntlet under intense fire from the Confederate guns. Miraculously, 14 warships made it past the forts, then engaged the Confederate river fleet and destroyed or captured 13 vessels, while losing only one. With the fortresses passed and Union soldiers now landed nearby, the fall of New Orleans was inevitable. (Both river forts surrendered to Porter four days later.)

Upon learning Farragut had passed the downriver defenses, Confederate troops evacuated New Orleans, in the process destroying millions of dollars of supplies and cotton waiting for export. Farragut's ships reached New Orleans the next day, April 25, and after several days of negotiations (and the arrival of Butler's troops), the city officially surrendered on May 1, 1862. Soon afterward Farragut was promoted to rear admiral, the first in United States history.

Benjamin Butler's prize was the city of New Orleans. Called Beast Butler for his impositions during the occupation of the city, Butler was reviled by the citizens of New Orleans and suffered indignities that even included the emptying of a chamber pot on his head as he walked down the street one day. The people of the city did have specific grievances to point to: Butler issued an order essentially declaring that all unescorted women would be considered "ladies of the town" and famously had a man hanged for taking down the U.S. flag flying over city hall and tearing it apart. However, Butler's "beastly" reputation was largely undeserved, and he quickly restored order in the city, even improving many of the public services already in place. This was partly done in order to encourage Louisiana to reenter the Union as quickly as possible.

Although small in terms of loss of life when compared with other major actions of the war, the passing of Forts Jackson and St. Philip and the capture of New Orleans was certainly a landmark event in the conflict. It greatly advanced the Union effort to control the Mississippi, leaving only Vicksburg and Port Hudson to contend with. It also cost the South a major industrial and shipbuilding center, not to mention its primary outlet to the rest of the world.

Fort Blakely

In early April of 1865, while much of the nation was focused on Robert E. Lee's evacuation of Petersburg and Richmond in Virginia, another large battle was brewing in the swamps of Alabama. While the Union had gained control of Mobile Bay with Farragut's great victory in August of 1864, the Confederates still held the city of Mobile with a sizable force. In order to protect the city, the Confederates had built fortifications at Spanish Fort, on the north end of the bay, and a large set of earthworks just north of Spanish Fort known as Fort Blakely.

The Confederates had had time to construct Fort Blakely well. It consisted of nine strong redoubts, abatis, and minefields and was located in thick, forested swampland that was difficult to fight through. Still, as the war pressed on, and troops were needed

The restored remnants of Redoubt No. 4 at Fort Blakely in Alabama.

in other parts of the country, the force defending Mobile grew lighter and lighter. Finally, in mid-March of 1865, Union forces under Major Generals Edward Canby and Frederick Steele began to march around the bay toward the city of Mobile. As they approached the Confederate strongholds, Canby directed his forces toward Spanish Fort, while Steele's men focused on Fort Blakely.

Blakely was held by approximately 3,800 Confederates under the command of Brigadier General St. John R. Liddell. Steele arrived on April 2 and immediately prepared to lay siege to the earthworks, digging trenches and setting artillery while edging ever closer to the Confederate lines. When Spanish Fort fell on April 8, Canby added his men to Steele's, producing a total of 18,000 Union soldiers. Their forces clearly overwhelming, the Union commanders immediately began preparing for an assault. On April 9, at approximately 5:30 pm, an all-out assault was launched against the whole of the Blakely line. While the Confederates briefly held their positions in the scattered rifle pits and breastworks in front, it was not long before the approaching sea of bluecoats compelled most of them to either fall back to the redoubts or surrender. But the Union troops, slowed only slightly by the abatis and mines, were soon upon the redoubts, taking them by overwhelming force. By the time the day was through, the Confederates had lost 3,700 men, the vast majority of them by surrender, while the Union had lost 775. The fall of Fort Blakely meant the end of the defense of

SITE DETAILS

Historic Blakely State Park—Just north of Spanish Fort, Alabama, Historic Blakely State Park does not contain the entire battlefield, much of which was lost to farming, but it does contain a large enough portion of it to make what happened all along the line understandable. Confederate Redoubt No. 4 is still largely intact, as are the breastworks, many of the rifle pits, and some Union artillery positions. Although the park lacks an interpretive center or even interpretive signs, a driving tour brochure that you can pick up when entering the park gives plenty of information on the battle and what happened around Redoubt No. 4 during the final assault. The park is very quiet and isolated, and the landscape is relatively untouched, making it easy to imagine what the furious Union assault must have looked like. In addition to the battlefield, the park also contains numerous campsites, picnic areas, horseback riding trails, and other outdoor activities, as well as remnants of the original town of Blakely, now long gone as a community. The park is a bit hidden, so keep your eyes out for it, but it is very easy to get to and well worth the visit. *Historic Blakely State Park, on AL 225, 4.5 miles north of intersection with US 31, Spanish Fort, AL, 36527; 334-580-0005; www.blakelypark.org. Open daily; admission charged.*

Mobile, and the city was evacuated by the Confederates on April 12. By this time, of course, Robert E. Lee had already surrendered his army in Virginia. But the Civil War was not quite over. As it turned out, Mobile, Alabama, was the last of the major cities of the South to fall to Union troops.

Mobile Bay

By 1864 Mobile, Alabama, was the only remaining major port of entry into the heart of the Confederacy from the Gulf Coast. Although the U.S. Navy was having some success in its blockade, Mobile and Mobile Bay were still under full control of the Confederacy, and Mobile still had open rail lines to remaining Confederate territory. For these reasons Mobile was a blockade runner's favorite destination, and a good amount of supplies slipped into the city. If a runner could get into the bay, the rest was smooth sailing.

The reason Mobile Bay was still operating in this way was that it was simply too well defended. The entrance to the bay was guarded by two stone fortifications: Fort Morgan, located on Mobile Point to the east, and Fort Gaines, slightly west on Dauphin Island. In addition, considerable earthwork batteries had been constructed to add extra firepower, including Fort Powell farther up the bay on the west side. Between Fort Morgan and Fort Gaines, engineers had driven pilings into the bay so that ships could only pass through a small channel left open under the close guns of Fort

Morgan. This channel was also filled with torpedoes (what today we would call mines) on the western side, leaving only about 400 yards between the fort and the torpedoes. Finally, the Confederate navy had built a squadron of four ships, including the iron-clad CSS *Tennessee*. Any ship that tried to run the bay entrance would face an almost overwhelming defense.

Still, the job had to be done, and the obvious choice was Rear Admiral David G. Farragut. His previous successes at Forts Jackson and St. Philip, along with his work on the Mississippi River, had earned him a reputation for tenacity. Farragut was patient and planned his attack carefully. It would take a large number of ships to run the defenses successfully. Also, with the *Tennessee* waiting inside, Farragut would have to wait for ironclad monitors of his own to be able to counter the threat. And after gaining the bay, Union forces would still need soldiers to silence the forts. It would require a large operation.

Finally, in July of 1864, Farragut had his tools at the ready. His fleet included 14 wooden ships and four monitors. Major General Gordon Granger was at the ready with 1,500 Union soldiers to land and take the forts. The 14 wooden ships were lashed together, in pairs side by side, to run the channel in one long, powerful column of guns. The four monitors, in the meantime, would pass between Fort Morgan and the wooden ships to protect them. The fleet would have to pass through as quickly as possible and get into the open bay in order to have a chance, where they would then have to separate and contend with the Confederate ships.

The interior of Fort Morgan; white posts mark the former location of the citadel, destroyed during the bombardment.

Early on the morning of August 5, 1864, the Union ships began their run through the channel to Mobile Bay. The *Tennessee* waited just beyond the field of torpedoes, ready to take on any ship that got through the channel. The lead ship of the wooden gunboats was the USS *Brooklyn*, while the lead monitor was the USS *Tecumseh*. Farragut's flagship was the USS *Hartford*, just behind the *Brooklyn*. Lashed into the rigging, Farragut watched as his ships made their run and the fort began firing mercilessly on the fleet. Unfortunately for the Confederates at Fort Morgan, their fire soon filled the area of the channel with smoke, making targeting the ships almost impossible. They were passing the channel almost unscathed.

Suddenly, the monitor *Tecumseh*, getting into position to take on the *Tennessee*, struck a Confederate torpedo. The ship was severely damaged and sank within minutes. The commander of the *Brooklyn*, stunned by the loud explosion, began to slow and then back up, not wanting to hit another torpedo. All the other ships were momentarily thrown into confusion, and instantly the entire fleet was in danger of being stuck under the guns of Fort Morgan.

While there is some debate as to how it happened and just what was said, there is no question of the effect: Farragut reportedly commanded, "Damn the torpedoes, full speed ahead!" These may not have been the exact words used (he probably shouted a few expletives), but the orders were crystal clear to everyone. Farragut directed the *Hartford* to the front of the line and steamed through the torpedoes, with the other ships following. Farragut's daring and leadership had won the day, and soon his fleet was past the fort and safely into the bay. The passing of Fort Morgan had taken 45 minutes.

But the battle was not over; there were still four Confederate ships to contend with. The Union ships were able to make quick work of two of the three Confederate wooden ships—the CSS *Gaines* was knocked out and grounded, and the CSS *Selma* was surrendered. The third escaped to the safety of Mobile. This left only the Confederate ironclad *Tennessee*. Farragut's ships unlashed and separated, then went after the *Tennessee*, ramming her and firing on her. After an hour of fighting, a lucky shot broke the *Tennessee*'s steering chains, and she was unable to maneuver. Dead in the water, she was forced to surrender. The naval action was over, and the Union fleet had prevailed decisively.

With no hope of reinforcements, the fall of the forts was just a matter of time. The 140 men at Fort Powell did not wait, blowing up the magazine and abandoning the position on the night of the naval battle. Three days later, on August 8, Fort Gaines surrendered, leaving only Fort Morgan. Although surrounded by reinforced infantry, the entire Union fleet, and the captured *Tennessee*, the fort's commander, Brigadier General Richard Page, refused surrender on August 13. The Union ironclads began shelling the fort while other pieces of artillery were put into place. On August 21 Granger's troops, 25 cannons, and 16 mortars, along with the Union ships, unleashed

SITE DETAILS

Fort Morgan State Park—Fort Morgan still stands proudly at the far western end of Mobile Point, in the same place that the French, Spanish, British, and Americans had established earlier fortresses. Although a tremendous amount of work goes into its upkeep, the fort is still in pretty good shape, despite the beatings it has taken from not only shot and shell, but also weather and several reconfigurations over the years through World War I. An excellent museum outside the fort tells not only of the Civil War battle, but also of the rich history of the point; it also contains an interesting exhibit on exactly what Farragut may or may not have said in the heat of battle, as well as whether sailing through the torpedo field might have been a calculated risk (it was found after the battle that the vast majority of the torpedoes had been in the water too long and did not work). A brochure is provided for a self-guided tour of the fort that is thorough and interesting, leaving no detail out. The view of Mobile Bay and the Gulf of Mexico is wonderful, and visitors can see the entire area of the battle, with a buoy marking the location of the sinking of the *Tecumseh*. This is a must-see site. Note that if approaching from the west, you will either have to drive completely around Mobile Bay or take a ferry from Dauphin Island (site of Fort Gaines, which also still stands) to Mobile Point. While the ferry is convenient, it is also small and infrequent, so call and plan ahead if you expect to cross without waiting a considerable amount of time. *Fort Morgan State Park, 51 AL 180 West, Gulf Shores, AL, 36542; 334-540-7125; www.preserveala.org. Open daily; admission charged.*

a devastating barrage on the fort. Finally, after spiking what guns he had left, Page surrendered Fort Morgan on August 23. Although the city of Mobile was still under Confederate control, Mobile Bay was in Union hands, closing the door on the Confederacy's last significant port on the Gulf of Mexico.

» OTHER SITES ALONG THE GULF COAST

Palmito Ranch—Brownsville, Texas, on the north bank of the Rio Grande close to the Gulf of Mexico, had become a valuable avenue for the Confederacy to export goods through Mexico. The city had changed hands several times, but as the Civil War wound down, the fighting stopped. However, on May 12, 1865, a month after Lee's surrender at Appomattox, 800 Union troops under the command of recently installed Colonel Theodore Barrett advanced on Brownsville and attacked a Confederate camp east of the city at Palmito Ranch. The next day, the 350 Confederates led by Colonel John "RIP" Ford counterattacked, driving the Union force back to the island of Brazos Santiago. The final military action of the Civil War, a Confederate victory, cost 30 Union and 118 Confederate casualties.

The Palmito Ranch battlefield is located in what is now the Lower Rio Grande Valley National Wildlife Refuge. If you head east from Brownsville on what quickly becomes an isolated, lonely road (except for the border patrol checkpoint), you will eventually come to the battle site, which has a highway pull-off, interpretive signs, and a historical marker. When you are out here, you can truly feel the isolation of the place, especially if you go at a time of day when cars are not constantly passing by to reach the beach several miles down the road. Palmito Ranch, the last and perhaps most unnecessary battle of the Civil War, also happens to be one of the most unusual in setting. Yes, it's well off the path of other battlefields, and yes, tourists don't often get an excuse to travel to Brownsville, Texas. But if you do, be sure to take the short drive out to the battle site. *Palmito Ranch Battlefield, Lower Rio Grande Valley National Wildlife Refuge, intersection of Boca Chica Hgwy. and Palmito Hill Rd., Brownsville, TX, 78521; 1-800-626-2639. Open daily.*

Treüe der Union Monument—In 1854 a group of German immigrants founded the town of Comfort, Texas, and the haven soon attracted other immigrants as well. The idea of slavery was unthinkable to these immigrants, so when Texas seceded from the Union, most of the townsfolk, in their hearts, remained loyal to their adopted country and the principles they had embraced. When the state decreed that all males

The Treüe der Union monument, Comfort, Texas.

between 18 and 35 must sign an oath of allegiance to Texas, which amounted to signing up for military service, the young men followed the lead of Texas governor and legend Sam Houston and refused to sign. The immigrants put up with harassment and worse, including lynchings and the burning of their homes, for a year, reminding many of them of the oppression they had fled in Germany. Finally, a large group of the settlers decided to wait out the war in Mexico and hopefully reach U.S. officials there. On their way south, however, the group was attacked twice, once at the Nueces River and again near the Rio Grande. Accounts vary on the number killed (ranging from 40 to 68), but even less clear is the manner in which they died—some were known to have drowned in the Rio Grande, and others were said to have been executed after being taken prisoner. After the war, what remains could be gathered were returned to Comfort for reburial.

The small town of Comfort is less than an hour's drive northwest of San Antonio. The Treüe der Union ("Loyalty to the Union") monument is one of the more moving memorials to the terrible price of war, fear, and hatred in the country. It is very simple; there is no remarkable architecture, no lush setting, and no grand effect to it at all. It is a white stone obelisk, inscribed with the names of the victims, with several small monuments and interpretive signs surrounding it in a modest plot that is well taken care of. Perhaps the story is enough to make this such a special place. If you ever head to San Antonio, be sure to make the short trip up to Comfort to pay your respects to our fallen countrymen. *Treüe der Union Monument, intersection of High St. and 4th St., Comfort, TX, 78013; 830-995-3131. Open daily.*

Vermilion Bayou—Not wanting to stake all on a direct assault on the Confederate stronghold at Port Hudson, Major General Nathaniel Banks decided to besiege it. The first step in his plan was to cut Confederate supply lines, and so in April 1863 he set his sights west of the Mississippi, on the Bayou Teche region and Major General Richard Taylor. After being driven back at the battles of Fort Bisland and Irish Bend, the Confederates under Taylor crossed Vermilion Bayou at what is now Lafayette, Louisiana, set fire to the bridge, and stopped to rest after a week's worth of retreat. Unfortunately for them, a Union column caught up with them on April 17, crossed the still-burning bridge, and began to fight. Although well-placed artillery was able to hold back the Union troops, the Confederates retreated, and Banks's mission was a success—all supply lines to Port Hudson had been cut.

A new bridge stands where the old one once was, and a historical highway marker there memorializes the battle. Although this is at a busy intersection, there are plenty of nearby parking lots where you can leave your car in order to walk up to the sign and the bridge. *Historical highway marker—Lafayette Parish Bayou Vermilion District (Bayou Vermilion), intersection of LA 182 and La Rue France, Lafayette, LA, 70508. Site accessible daily.*

Irish Bend—The day after evacuating Fort Bisland, Confederates under Major General Richard Taylor sent 1,000 soldiers to Irish Bend to protect his retreating supply lines. The Confederates also had the support of the captured gunboat *Diana* and decided to attack, initially pushing the Union troops back. However, as the Union force, 5,000 strong, prepared to counterattack, the outnumbered Confederates fell back to their main force, destroying the *Diana* on their way out.

A historical highway marker commemorates the battle site. Although it is a little difficult to see the bayou where the *Diana* held the Confederate flank, the battlefield is mostly open field and farmland now, and almost the entire area of the fighting is visible. *Historical highway marker—Louisiana Society of the Order of the Confederate Rose (The Battle of Irish Bend), 0.2 mile east of intersection of Irish Bend Rd. and Easy St., Franklin, LA, 70538. Site accessible daily.*

Fort Bisland—Before Major General Nathaniel Banks set out to sever Port Hudson's supply lines from the west, the only real protection the supply lines had was Fort Bisland, where most of Major General Richard Taylor's Confederate army was stationed. On April 12, 1863, Union troops approached the fort, which soon opened fire along with the captured gunboat *Diana*. After a day's fighting, with the *Diana* knocked out of action and word that more Federal troops were approaching, Taylor evacuated Fort Bisland overnight and headed for Vermilionville, now Lafayette. Within a week Taylor's army was driven out of the region for good.

A historical highway marker can be seen near the Fort Bisland site, but it is located alongside busy US 90, so take care as you pull off to read it. *Historical highway marker—Louisiana Department of Culture, Recreation and Tourism (Battle of Bisland), intersection of US 90 and LA 182, Patterson, LA, 70538. Site accessible daily.*

Lafourche Crossing—The Confederates had hoped to distract the Union efforts at Vicksburg and Port Hudson by threatening New Orleans. Near Thibodeaux, Louisiana, on June 20, 1863, Union troops met a Confederate raiding party head-on at Lafourche Crossing. After a day of skirmishing and the arrival of reinforcements, the Federals had built up a well-protected position. The Confederates attacked again the next day but could not budge the Union troops. They moved on to Donaldsonville soon afterward.

A historical highway marker at Lafourche Crossing explains the action there. It is right next to the bayou and is in a small clearing that makes for an easy pull-off to see the area. *Historical highway marker—Lafourche Crossing, intersection of LA 308 and Bartley Lane, Thibodeaux, LA, 70301. Site accessible daily.*

Georgia Landing—Union troops were attempting to establish a point of operations in Louisiana west of the Mississippi near Bayou Lafourche. On October 27, 1862, near the town of Labadieville, Louisiana, at a place called Georgia Landing, Confederate troops waited on both banks of Bayou Lafourche; because there was no bridge nearby, the forces could not unite. The Union troops took them in pieces, first hitting the

Confederates on the east bank, then crossing by pontoon bridge to attack the west bank. The Confederates withdrew to Labadieville when they had exhausted their ammunition, relinquishing control of the region.

There is no marker or sign of the battle of Georgia Landing. The battle site is on private property; to view it from a distance and at least see the lay of the land, an intersection in Napoleonville (see below) isn't too far from where the action was. *Georgia Landing battle site, near intersection of LA 1010 and Georgia Rd., Napoleonville, LA, 70390. Private property.*

Donaldsonville and Kock's Plantation—Donaldsonville, Louisiana, at the confluence of the Mississippi River and Bayou Lafourche, was a center of activity for both armies, and several engagements took place there. As the Union moved up the Mississippi and military river traffic began to increase, sharpshooters would occasionally fire on Union shipping from the town. Rear Admiral David Farragut tried to put a stop to it on August 9, 1862, when he announced to the town that they should evacuate their women and children, then shelled the town from the river and sent landing parties ashore to destroy selected buildings. On June 28, 1863, three Confederate columns converged on the newly built Fort Butler, which was serving as a supply base for Major General Nathaniel Banks as he laid siege to Port Hudson. The fort held, aided by well-built fortifications and a Union gunboat in the river. Over the next two weeks, the Confederates blockaded the Mississippi River in an attempt to relieve the pressure on Port Hudson, but the action came too late. After Port Hudson surrendered, Union forces were sent to Donaldsonville to chase the Confederates out and open up the river. On July 12, 1863, the two forces met at Kock's Plantation, just outside Donaldsonville, in skirmishing that lasted for several days. The Union party was eventually driven back to Fort Butler, and the Confederates escaped relatively unscathed.

In Donaldsonville is the Historic Fort Butler Commemorative Site, where several memorials and interpretive signs have been erected. Although a thorough excavation of the site of the fort has been performed, not much remains of it that is recognizable; but a good view of the river and the fort's location, along with the interpretation, are enough to tell what happened here. Visitors can arrange for a guided tour of the grounds (see phone number below). The Historic Donaldsonville Museum, a short walk from the site of the fort, contains information on the battles. Kock's Plantation, also known as St. Emma Plantation, still stands and is open for tours by appointment. A historical highway marker is outside the front of the home. *Historic Fort Butler Commemorative Site, intersection of LA 18 and Iberville St., Donaldsonville, LA, 70346; 985-369-1950; www.fortbutler.com. Open daily. Historic Donaldsonville Museum, 318 Mississippi St., Donaldsonville, LA, 70346; 225-746-0004; www.historicdonaldsonville museum.org. Closed Sun. St. Emma Plantation, 1283 LA 1 South, Donaldsonville, LA, 70346; 225-922-9225. Home open by appointment only; historical marker accessible daily.*

Baton Rouge—In late July 1862, a Union force of 3,200 under Brigadier General Thomas Williams occupied Baton Rouge, Louisiana. Shortly after, on August 5, some 4,000 Confederate troops, under the command of John Breckenridge, former U.S. vice president, arrived at Baton Rouge from Jackson, Mississippi, to take the city back. An early morning assault eventually crumpled the Union left, and the Federals began to retreat westward through the city toward the Mississippi River and the safety of Union gunboats. One scene of heavy fighting was Magnolia Cemetery, and the battle is often referred to by that name. Williams was killed in the action, but the heavy artillery from the river stopped the Confederates from advancing farther.

Magnolia Cemetery is still operated and maintained, and visitors can pretty much come and go as they please, within certain hours. The only reminder of the battle that remains, however, is a historical marker just outside the gates. Across the street from Magnolia Cemetery is Baton Rouge National Cemetery, which was also part of the battleground. Although there is no interpretation of the battle here, either, any visit to a national cemetery provides a quiet place and opportunity to reflect. *Magnolia*

America's soldiers are remembered on Memorial Day at Baton Rouge National Cemetery, part of the Baton Rouge battlefield.

Cemetery, intersection of Florida Blvd. and N. 19th St., Baton Rouge, LA, 70821; 225-387-2464. Open daily.

Stirling's Plantation—In an attempt to reach into Texas, Major General Nathaniel Banks decided to send Federal troops into the area of Bayou Teche. On September 29, 1863, at Stirling's Plantation near the Atchafalaya River, Confederates attacked a Union cavalry outfit posted there to guard the road to the river. The cavalry was driven off, with some being captured. A Union force attempted to chase the Confederates but was not in time.

The battle site is now private property and cannot be viewed. A historical highway marker on an isolated stretch of road in front of a farm describes the action. *Battle site is private property. Historical highway marker—Louisiana Society of the Order of the Confederate Rose (Battle of Bayou Fordoche), in front of 10594 LA 10, Morganza, LA, 70759. Site accessible daily.*

Spanish Fort—On March 17, 1865, Major General Edward Canby began his advance on Mobile, Alabama, marching up the east side of the bay. After sending Major General Frederick Steele to invest Fort Blakely, Canby concentrated his forces on Spanish Fort on March 27 and began preparing to besiege the Confederate camp there. Soon artillery was picking at the Confederate earthworks, and finally, on April 8, Canby unleashed a complete barrage on the encampment, not only from the 90 pieces of artillery on land, but also from six Union gunboats on the Apalachee River. Union forces did assault the Confederate works, but the fighting was soon stopped by darkness. That night the Confederates evacuated to Mobile, and the next day Canby's men joined Steele in the assault on Fort Blakely.

Unfortunately, most of the earthworks that were present during the siege at Spanish Fort have been lost to a housing community. (Many of the streets have been named after the various participants in the battle.) There is, however, an information kiosk at the visitor's center of the Eastern Shore Chamber of Commerce, located just off Interstate 10 at exit 35. The signs tell of the action at both Spanish Fort and Fort Blakely, and a convenient overlook gives you a decent picture of what the terrain was at the time of the battle. *Eastern Shore Chamber of Commerce, north of I-10 at exit 35, Spanish Fort, AL, 36527. Open daily.*

Santa Rosa Island—The harbor at Pensacola, Florida, was coveted by both sides, and for a time each had a piece of it. The Union held Fort Pickens, standing on the western end of Santa Rosa Island, and controlled the opening to the harbor. The Confederates controlled the harbor itself, erecting batteries around the western side and holding Forts McRee and Barrancas, as well as the Pensacola Navy Yard. Throughout 1861 the two forces sniped at each other and conducted the occasional raid. Finally, on October 9, 1861, Major General Braxton Bragg ordered a raid on Fort Pickens, approaching from the east. The Confederates, advancing in three columns, first encountered Union troops about 1 mile from the fort and quickly pushed them back. However, when the Confederates stopped to loot the encampment they had just overrun, the Federals counterattacked, and confusion quickly ensued. The clamor had aroused the troops stationed at Fort Pickens, who were soon pushing the Confederates back to the east and off Santa Rosa Island.

Fort Pickens still stands today, and the area of the fighting east of the fort is well preserved. It is all part of Gulf Islands National Seashore, a unit of the National Park Service that runs from Florida to Mississippi. Unfortunately, the hurricanes of recent years have taken their toll on the park, and the road that leads out to the fort is still closed. The area is accessible by foot, but you'll have to set aside a day for it if you want to see anything up close, because the hike to the fort is 7 miles each way (although it is through some beautiful scenery). Until the road is restored, there is one other option, which requires a decent set of binoculars: You can drive to Fort Barrancas—also part of the park but located on the Pensacola Naval Air Station—and from there you will have a view across the channel to Santa Rosa Island; Fort Pickens is easily discernible along the shoreline. The interpretation at Fort Barrancas, explaining the American Third System of fortresses built after the war of 1812, is quite interesting and helps to explain why many other famous fortifications of the war were built as they were. *Gulf Islands National Seashore, 1801 Gulf Breeze Pkwy., Gulf Breeze, FL, 32563; 850-934-2600; www.nps.gov/guis. Open daily; admission charged.*

Natural Bridge—In March 1865, just south of the Florida capital at Tallahassee, a joint Union army-navy operation was launched to try to capture the small Confederate force that operated in the area. The expedition ran into problems from the start, gaining and then losing ground, and the rivers leading to Tallahassee were too shallow for the 16 Union ships, with some running aground. On March 6, 1865, some 600 Federal soldiers met 700 Confederate soldiers at a shallow crossing of the St. Marks River known as Natural Bridge. Although the Union troops drove the Confederates back, they could not take the position, and they returned to their boats, having suffered 148 casualties to the Confederates' 25.

Natural Bridge State Historic Site contains memorials and several interpretive signs explaining the battle. There are also picnic areas and some limited facilities. The area itself is not very large and does not encompass much of the original battlefield. Still, the park and its surroundings give a good idea of what the battle was like, and it's worth the small detour off the interstate. *Natural Bridge Battlefield Historic State Park, 7502 Natural Bridge Rd., Tallahassee, FL, 32305; 850-922-6007; www.florida stateparks.org/naturalbridge. Open daily.*

Tampa and Fort Brooke—Two separate actions occurred at Tampa, Florida, both essentially naval actions. The first took place on June 30, 1862, when the USS *Sagamore* anchored in Tampa Bay and demanded the surrender of the city. After receiving a refusal, the ship gave the citizens of Tampa several hours to evacuate, then began shelling the town and continued the next day. This action became commonly known as the Yankee Outrage at Tampa. A year later, on October 16, 1863, the U.S. Navy sent a force up the Hillsborough River at Tampa in an attempt to catch a couple of blockade-running ships at their docks. After the raiding force fired on Confederate-held Fort Brooke as a diversion, a landing party, guided by a local Union sympathizer, marched up the river, found the blockade runners, and destroyed them.

The site of Fort Brooke, which has been fortified for hundreds of years under the flags of several nations, is now in Cotanchobee Fort Brooke Park, near the convention center in downtown Tampa. Although there is no mention of the Civil War action there (much of the history in the park is dedicated to military actions against the Seminole Indians), the park is on the ground where the fort stood and offers a beautiful view of the bay from which the "Yankee Outrage" occurred. Perhaps more exciting to history buffs is the Tampa Bay History Center, which opened its doors in December 2008. The center will reflect all the rich history of the area, from the Seminoles to pirates to the Civil War, and it promises to present an outstanding collection of exhibits. *Cotanchobee Fort Brooke Park, 601 St. Pete Times Forum Dr., Tampa, FL, 33602; 813-228-0097; www.tampabayhistorycenter.org. Park open daily; admission charged for museum.*

» WHERE TO STAY ALONG THE GULF COAST

A lot of fantastic places to stay can be found along the Gulf Coast, but not many of them have direct ties to Civil War history. The exception is New Orleans, where many of the older bed-and-breakfasts predate the war; however, few were involved in specific war-related events, since no combat occurred near the town. Still, the wealth of history in the city results in many great options for lodging.

Also, as you travel along the coast, you will have plenty of opportunities to hit the beach, and that means resorts, scattered all along the coast. The primary stops are near Galveston, Gulf Shores in Alabama, and Pensacola, but many other locations along the way offer plentiful lodging and the lure of great beach time. (Just ask ahead to try to avoid the traffic.)

6

The Atlantic Coast

OVERVIEW

Although the ports of the Gulf Coast were generally closer to the South's king cotton crop, the ports of the Atlantic Coast were closer to the major population centers and the lucrative tobacco crop. They were as essential for the survival of the Confederacy as the Gulf ports were.

These eastern seaboard ports, in general, were easier to defend. The harbors at Charleston, Wilmington, and Savannah were geographically well protected. The natural barriers of the Outer Banks of North Carolina provided security for ports in Albemarle and Pamlico Sounds, as well as superb shelter for blockade-running ships. Venture outside these harbors, however, and rough and hazardous seas waited, as many a shipwreck has lain testament to over the centuries.

At the beginning of the war, most of the major ports of the East Coast were defended by fortifications designed during the period of the Third System of fortifications, begun shortly after the War of 1812 to protect America's coastline against foreign invaders. These massive brick and earthen fortresses, such as Fort Monroe, Fort Pulaski, and Fort Macon, were as imposing as they were thought to be impenetrable, and passage of these fortifications had proven, in the past, to be a very dangerous undertaking. Conquering them would be an almost impossible task. Still, the first shots of the war were fired at one of these behemoths, the surrounded and lightly defended Fort Sumter in Charleston Harbor.

One other significant point along the Atlantic Coast was of vital importance to both the United States and the Confederacy: the great shipyard at Norfolk, Virginia. Besides being a key defensive position for the Confederate capital of Richmond, Nor-

The South Carolina State House, still standing defiantly over Columbia.

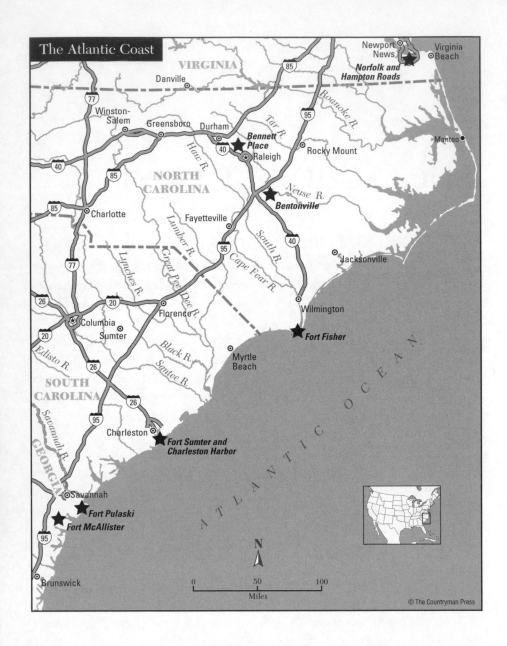

The Atlantic Coast

VIRGINIA

Danville

Newport News

Norfolk and Hampton Roads

Virginia Beach

Winston-Salem

Greensboro

Durham

Bennett Place

Raleigh

Rocky Mount

Manteo

NORTH CAROLINA

Charlotte

Fayetteville

Bentonville

Jacksonville

Columbia

Sumter

Florence

Wilmington

Fort Fisher

Myrtle Beach

SOUTH CAROLINA

Charleston

Fort Sumter and Charleston Harbor

GEORGIA

Savannah

Fort Pulaski

Fort McAllister

Brunswick

ATLANTIC OCEAN

Roanoke R.

Tar R.

Haw R.

Neuse R.

Lumber R.

Cape Fear R.

South R.

Lynches R.

Great Pee Dee R.

Black R.

Santee R.

Edisto R.

Savannah R.

N

0   50   100
Miles

© The Countryman Press

folk had been used for building fighting ships for the United States Navy for decades, and possession of the facilities there could provide a great asset as both a production facility and a point of operations along the coast.

If one single feature tied all the battles for the Atlantic Coast together, it was technology. The naval battles of the Atlantic Coast were the proving ground for what eventually developed into the modern navy as we know it. The first ironclad warships met and fought a great battle at Hampton Roads, Virginia. The first submarine successfully used in warfare, the CSS *Hunley*, was operated (and sank) in Charleston Harbor. And the great fortresses of the Third System, thought to be invincible, were proven not only vulnerable but impractical in a matter of hours by the introduction of the rifled cannon. This in turn led to the use of earthen fortifications, which could take more punishment and be repaired more quickly than their brick-and-mortar counterparts.

There is an additional story to be told along the Atlantic Coast, one that is all too often omitted from our history books. While many are familiar with General William T. Sherman's famous march to the sea, which ended with the capture of Fort McAllister at Savannah, Sherman then turned his troops north through the Carolinas, destroying everything in their path and racing to meet Grant to complete the Union envelopment of Petersburg, Virginia. After tearing through the "Cradle of Secession" of South Carolina with a terrible vengeance, moving quickly through miles of swampland and other nearly impassable terrain, Sherman then faced a Confederate army led by Major General Joseph E. Johnston, as he had done during the Atlanta campaign. The two would meet in battle again at Bentonville, North Carolina, ultimately deciding the Confederacy's fate in that area. But the march itself was a truly amazing feat; Johnston, when hearing of the incredible progress of Sherman's armies, stated that "there had been no such army in existence since the days of Julius Caesar."

Ironclads, great sieges, heroic deeds, and amazing inventions. Your journey along the Atlantic Coast will prove to be one of the more fascinating tours of the Civil War.

» PEOPLE TO KNOW

P. G. T. Beauregard—Although Pierre Gustave Toutant Beauregard's name is attached to many of the Confederate army's great victories, Beauregard never got the high command he sought, thanks in part to his exuberance and in part to his poor relationship with President Jefferson Davis. Though Beauregard graduated high in his class at West Point, he was not the type to mince words, and gained a few enemies along the path of his military career.

Born to a prosperous Creole family, Beauregard joined the Confederate ranks before the war broke out and was in charge of the Charleston defenses and the bombardment of Fort Sumter. He was also in command at the first battle of Manassas, but was soon sent to the West to serve under General Albert Sidney Johnston after Davis felt he should have assaulted Washington. When Johnston was killed at the battle of Shiloh, Beauregard took over and kept command through the evacuation of Corinth. Again, Davis saw Beauregard's actions as timidity and put him back in charge at Charleston, where he repulsed numerous assaults on the city's defenses. In 1864 he was at Richmond and was the general who "bottled up" Benjamin Butler at Bermuda Hundred, then successfully defended Petersburg with 2,500 men as Grant's army began its initial assault on the city. Finally, Beauregard served under Joseph Johnston in North Carolina during the last campaign of the war. When the war was over, Beauregard returned to New Orleans and ran the Louisiana state lottery.

Ambrose E. Burnside—Ambrose Everett Burnside was, by all accounts, a very well-liked man. He was modest and affable and had made many friends throughout his career. Burnside will probably be remembered for three things: his characteristic whiskers, which now bear his name (though scrambled); a bridge at the Antietam battlefield, which also now bears his name; and his terrible losses at the battle of Fredericksburg in December of 1862. However, Burnside was a capable commander, and he proved so along the coast of North Carolina early in the war.

After serving in the military for a while, Burnside left after he patented a well-liked carbine rifle, but lost money manufacturing it and returned to the army when the war broke out. His first command was in North Carolina, where his offensive to gain control of the Outer Banks and push inland along the North Carolina coast had great success. Following his campaign, he was offered command of the Army of the Potomac and would have replaced George McClellan, but he refused twice because McClellan was his friend. When essentially assigned the job after McClellan was dismissed, Burnside remarked that he was not fit for the position. After the disaster at Fredericksburg, many agreed. But Burnside went on to command in other areas, capturing the notorious Confederate raider John Hunt Morgan in Ohio, then saving the city of Knoxville from occupation in December of 1863. His career ended when he commanded the ill-fated attempt at a breakthrough at Petersburg known as the Battle of the Crater. Burnside went on to serve as governor of Rhode Island and then in the United States Senate.

» THINGS TO KNOW

This is a one-way tour, beginning in Savannah, Georgia, and ending in Norfolk, Virginia. However, you could easily make a loop out of it by starting and ending in Norfolk—and if you are visiting some of the other sites in the chapter, this is probably the best way to do it. Flying into Norfolk or even Richmond will be your best option.

Be aware that the roads between all the sites are smaller highways and can sometimes be slow going, although traveling on these back roads makes for a beautiful drive. If you stick to the coast, however, especially during the summer months or on the weekends, be prepared for some traffic tie-ups as people head for the wonderful beaches and resorts there. This is especially true in North Carolina; and if you plan on visiting any of the sites along the Outer Banks, you will need to take a ferry or two at some point. Be prepared for this, because if you're not, you could be stranded somewhere without a place to stay for the night. But don't let that stop you—the sites here, whether they're related to the Civil War or not, are spectacular.

Finally, when visiting Fort Sumter (which *is* a must), make sure that you know when the boats to the fort are operating. Although there are several each day leaving from two different points, you do not want to get to Charleston only to find that you are not able to visit one of the Civil War's iconic sites. Plan ahead and schedule your trip in advance.

THE TRIP

» THE CAN'T-MISS SITES

Fort McAllister

Just south of the port of Savannah, Georgia, on the banks of the Ogeechee River, stood Confederate-built Fort McAllister. It was a strong, formidable earthwork, with several heavy artillery emplacements scattered among the earthen walls. Its face was to the river, and its intention was to prevent Union forces from advancing up the river to approach Savannah and the roads and railroads leading to it. However, for the first three and a half years of the war, Fort McAllister mostly served as a full-scale military laboratory—and an extremely important one, with both sides learning much from their experiments. Finally, in December 1864, Fort McAllister became known as the endpoint to one of the most famous expeditions in all military history—Sherman's march to the sea.

After the fall of Fort Pulaski, which protected Savannah just north of Fort McAllister, the emergence of the rifled cannon and the vulnerability of brick and mortar fortifications to this new weapon became evident. Out of military necessity, an alternative had to be found for coastal fortifications. The Confederates soon realized that it was right under their feet—sand. Contrary to military logic centuries old, the most massive, sturdy, seemingly indestructible structures were no longer the most durable. Sand and mud earthworks, in this emerging age of accurate and powerful artillery, had two distinct advantages over their previous counterparts. First, although earthen fortifications could certainly be battered and destroyed by artillery, they could often take a beating for far longer, with the impact of cannonballs or shells being much better absorbed. Second, during a bombardment, when a brick wall was destroyed, it was destroyed, and repairing it required not only the bombardment to stop, but a crew

Restored earthworks and chevaux-de-frise *at Fort McAllister in Georgia.*

of skilled laborers to rebuild the wall completely, with bricks, mortar, scaffolding, and all. Rebuilding damage done to an earthen fortification, in contrast, could be done quickly, by a small group of unskilled men with shovels. Before long, many Confederate fortifications began to emerge using this model.

The Federal navy had some ideas brewing as well. In early 1862 they had launched their new warship, the USS *Monitor*, and the age of ironclads had begun. After the John Ericsson–designed warship with the shallow draft and revolving turret had proven itself a tremendous success, further improvements were made on the design, and the ships that followed it were termed monitors, even after the original sank in a gale off the Carolina coast late in 1862. When the newest class of monitors came out, Rear Admiral Samuel Du Pont wanted to test the improvements to the ships in preparation for using them in yet another attempt on Charleston Harbor. Fort McAllister was his choice for a firing range.

On January 27, 1863, the monitor USS *Montauk*, accompanied by several other vessels, headed up the Ogeechee River toward the fort. The *Montauk* took a number of hits from the fort's gun but was able to bombard the fortifications for four hours without suffering any major damage. The *Montauk* went back up the river several days later to repeat its experiment, and again it was successful. Finally, on March 3, Du Pont sent three of the monitors up the river to bombard the fort. They did so for seven hours, barely suffering a scratch. Du Pont was convinced, and the monitors were used when efforts to take Charleston Harbor stepped up a month later.

However, in all the hours of bombardment, it did not go unnoticed by either side that despite its inability to do much damage to the ironclads, Fort McAllister had also come through each encounter virtually unscathed. During and following each attack, the fort's earthen defenses were quickly replaced, ready to take another beating. In fact, during all of DuPont's bombing exercises, the Confederates had suffered only one casualty—Fort McAllister's commander, Major John Gallie, during the *Montauk's* second trip up the river. The value and virtue of earthen fortifications had been tested under fire, and they would prove more effective than Du Pont's monitors in his attempts to take the defenses around Charleston.

Fort McAllister did not see action again until late in December 1864, and it was not a naval assault. For the previous month, Major General William T. Sherman had taken what many considered a foolish gamble and marched his invading army toward the Atlantic Ocean. Marching in two wings, Sherman had divided his forces, left a major Confederate army under John Bell Hood in his rear, and, most critical of all, left himself without supply lines or communication to other Union forces. His armies would live off the land—and destroy anything in their path that they did not need. It would be total war, relentless and cruel. Against the advice of many in Washington, Sherman was convinced: "I can make the march, and I can make Georgia howl!"

Sherman's success is well known. He did make the march, and he did make Georgia howl, and the havoc created by his armies is still reviled in the South. But until Sherman completed the march, it was still very much an iffy proposition, despite the successes he had had. Sherman knew that as he approached the sea, he was running out of real estate and, along with that, the ability for his army to supply itself. He would need to open a supply line with Union forces as soon as possible.

On December 9 Sherman approached Savannah, Georgia, which was defended by 10,000 Confederate soldiers. To the south, close to the sea, lay Fort McAllister. Investing Savannah would take time and supplies that he did not have, so Sherman headed for McAllister and its 230-man garrison. The Confederate commander at the fort was Major George Anderson, and although he had some idea that Sherman was in the area, his command was for the most part unprepared and certainly undermanned for any attack. The attack came on December 13, 1864. Union forces under Brigadier General William Hazen, 3,500 men, assaulted the fort just before sundown. Although the fort did have land defenses, consisting mostly of abatis and similar obstructions but also including artillery, the defenders were overmatched. Union sharpshooters first quickly took out the artillerymen, and the Union infantry followed

SITE DETAILS

Fort McAllister Historic Park—Perhaps because it was so resilient, and perhaps because it fell so quickly, Fort McAllister is still in great shape today. Fort McAllister Historic Park is in Richmond Hill, Georgia, just south of Savannah, and visiting it is a real treat. Unlike most of the other wartime earthen fortifications that have been washed away by wind and tide, Fort McAllister is set back from the sea, and its walls, bombproofs, barracks, and magazines are remarkably intact. The park's visitor's center contains a wonderful museum that very concisely explains the importance of the fortification and its place in history, as well as tells some of the interesting stories of the men who manned the fort during the war. The walking trail around the earthworks is fantastic, and the storytelling of the battle superb. There are also many other facilities here, including a picnic area, boat launch, fishing dock, and campground. *Fort McAllister Historic Park, 3894 Fort McAllister Rd., Richmond Hill, GA, 31324; 912-727-2339; www.gastateparks.org/info/ftmcallister. Open daily; admission charged.*

immediately after. Within 15 minutes the fort was taken. Sherman's great gamble was over, and his lifeline to the world was reopened.

Within days Sherman demanded the surrender of Savannah. While the Confederates refused, Lieutenant General William Hardee was able to conduct a skillful night evacuation of the city, and the Federals walked into Savannah the next day, December 21. Sherman sent President Lincoln a telegram. "I beg to present to you, as a Christmas gift, the city of Savannah, with 150 heavy guns and plenty of ammunition; also about 25,000 bales of cotton." Sherman's march to the sea is still rightly celebrated as one of the greatest military accomplishments in history.

Fort Pulaski

Following the War of 1812, President James Madison authorized the construction of a new coastal defense system that stretched from Maine to Louisiana and even included some locations on the Pacific coast. The new group of fortresses became known as the Third System of fortifications, and they were thought to be nearly invincible. Consisting of thick, massive walls of brick and earth and structurally designed to take a beating from any enemy cannon—which would have to be placed so far away from the fortresses' numerous and huge guns that their power would be greatly diminished—Third System fortresses guarded the critical harbors at New Orleans, Charleston, Mobile, and more than 30 other cities. Among these cities was Savannah, Georgia.

Savannah, at the time of the war, was a city of approximately 20,000, and a booming seaport, exporting cotton and other goods to the world. In the middle of the Savannah River lay Fort Pulaski, and soon after the wave of secession, the state of Georgia took control of the fort, eventually ceding it to the Confederate States of America. Fort Pulaski was considered by many to be one of the finest of the Third System fortresses, even though it was not even completed when the war broke out in 1861. As the Union army's chief of engineers, Joseph Totten, put it, "You might as well bombard the Rocky Mountains." This sentiment was also shared by one of the engineers who had helped build the fort, General Robert E. Lee. Lee plainly told the fort's commander, Colonel Charles Olmstead, that even if Union forces were to capture Tybee Island, across the river from the fort, the distance was far too great for artillery to breach the fort's infrastructure, and that he would not have to worry about it.

It just so happened that the Union plan was to do exactly that. After gaining a foothold on the Confederate coast at nearby Hilton Head Island in South Carolina in November 1861, Union forces began preparations for an assault on Fort Pulaski. Anticipating this, the Confederates pulled all their men off Tybee Island and moved them into Fort Pulaski. Soon Union forces landed on the island and began preparing for siege operations, bringing in troops and heavy guns and cutting the fort's supply lines.

The commander of the Union effort was Captain Quincy Gillmore, and his intention was to bomb the fort into surrender. Gillmore brought 36 heavy guns and

The heavy brick arches of the Third System of fortifications, once thought indestructible, at Fort Pulaski in Savannah.

The sally port at Fort Pulaski, Savannah.

mortars onto Tybee Island, setting up batteries on the few spots of dry land—the nearest being well over a mile from Fort Pulaski's walls. Although the Confederates were uneasy with Federal artillery visible from the fort's ramparts, knowing that the tried-and-true smoothbore cannons and mortars would have virtually no impact on the fort's walls at ranges over 1,000 yards gave them comfort.

Gillmore, however, was a believer in a newer but as yet unproved weapon—the rifled cannon. While smoothbore cannons simply launch a cannonball or other projectile, rifled cannon contain spiraled grooves on the inside that match grooves on the projectile, usually a shell. The spiraled grooves give the projectile a spin when ejected from the barrel, and that spin enables the projectile to travel a much greater distance with much more accuracy. Still, no one had successfully used rifled cannon beyond 600 yards. Gillmore thought the time was right, and over several months in early 1862, he had 10 of the rifled cannon quietly installed in the batteries closest to Fort Pulaski, having them dragged across the marshes of Tybee Island with the rest of the heavy artillery.

Inside the fort the 385 Confederates manning the 48 guns (of which fewer than half could be turned toward the Union position) watched the Union buildup in relative comfort, fearing little for their position. On April 11, 1862, the Union guns opened fire. The southeast angle of the fort, the closest to the Union position, was the first target. Gillmore's strategy in the reduction of the fort proved brilliant. As the mortars attempted to land their shells inside the walls of the fort, the highly accurate rifled cannon first began to disable the Confederate artillery one by one, then began to very precisely pick at the tops of Fort Pulaski's walls. While the rifled projectiles, which proved not only to be more accurate but also to have great penetration power, loosened the brick on the outside of the walls, the heavy Columbiad smoothbore cannon would then follow with a mighty blast to destroy the weakened bulwark. This went on for the remainder of the day, and by nightfall it was clear that the fort had suffered heavy damage. Although the Confederates were able to remount some of their guns overnight, the Union rifled cannon quickly redisabled them the next morning, then went on with their piecemeal destruction of the fort. Soon, a large breach in the fort's walls enabled Union artillery to threaten Fort Pulaski's powder magazine. At 2:30 in the afternoon, only 30 hours after the bombardment of the once-mighty Fort Pulaski had begun, a flag of truce was flown, and a stunned Olmstead surrendered the fort.

Although the fall of Fort Pulaski represented an important Union victory, the real significance of the battle lies in the introduction of the rifled cannon. Gillmore had rendered the entire Third System of fortifications obsolete with the weapon in little more than a day. The resounding effect was that strategies for coastal defense were necessarily altered forever overnight, not only by the Confederacy but by the entire world.

SITE DETAILS

Fort Pulaski National Monument—Eighteen miles down the Savannah River from the city, Fort Pulaski National Monument is located well out into the marshland. Even as you approach the fort (or many of the other Third System fortifications, most of which still stand), you cannot help sense that it does seem virtually invincible. Its huge walls, massive structure, and moat system convey a message that conquering a place like this would take years and incredible power. As such, its story is a wonderful testament to technology and the power of man to overcome the seemingly invincible. A small but excellent museum stands outside the fort, and the surrounding marsh serves as a wildlife refuge. Exploring Fort Pulaski reveals that much of the damage caused by Gillmore's rifled cannon is still visible, and a walk on the ramparts to view seemingly distant Tybee Island helps one realize just how improbable a feat this must have been. Great picnic and other recreational facilities are also available. *Fort Pulaski National Monument, entrance near intersection of US 80 and Johnny Mercer Dr., Savannah, GA, 31410; 912-786-5787; www.nps.gov/fopu. Open daily; admission charged.*

Fort Sumter and Charleston Harbor

After Abraham Lincoln's election in November of 1860, although dramatic actions and drastic measures were taken, blustery speeches made and incendiary articles printed daily, everybody in the nation was still in suspense. Would there be a war? South Carolina seceded in December, followed immediately by six other states. Several other states still hung in the balance. Was secession legal? Would the United States attack its own countrymen? Could it allow states to leave the Union? Would it guarantee the rights to slavery that the South demanded, bringing the states back? Debate raged all over the nation, but still no one was sure of the outcome. Most, however, knew that the powder keg that would become the Civil War sat in the middle of Charleston Harbor at Fort Sumter.

Almost immediately following the secession of the first seven states—South Carolina, Georgia, Florida, Mississippi, Alabama, Louisiana, and Texas—local and state militias seized control of most federal operations in the South, both military, such as forts and arsenals, and nonmilitary, such as post offices and mints. The states usually took control first, and after the Confederate States of America formed as a government, these states transferred most of the military property to the new government. There were a very few exceptions, only one of which really became a hot point between the United States and the Confederacy, and that was Fort Sumter. The outgoing administration of President James Buchanan, as it had done through most of the

A sampling of the heavy artillery used to reduce Fort Sumter sits on the fort's former parade ground.

events leading up to the war, sat back and watched as, one by one, federal property was seized in the seceding states. A gentleman's agreement had been made to keep the defenses at Charleston as they were, as the administration waited for diplomacy to settle the issue. But the Union commander of Charleston Harbor's defenses, Major Robert Anderson, saw the South Carolina militia swarming around him and hoped to protect his garrison by abandoning the other three installations around the harbor and moving all his troops to Fort Sumter, the massive Third System fort that towered above the opening to the harbor.

South Carolinians were outraged and immediately took control of Charleston Harbor's other defenses, building new ones as well—all facing Fort Sumter. When a chartered ship, the *Star of the West*, attempted to resupply and reinforce the fort in early January, the ship was fired upon. Anderson, keeping his cool and not wanting to start a war, held his fire, and the ship left the harbor.

Charleston, and the country, remained in this stalemate for several months. During the lull, President Lincoln was sworn in on March 16, 1861. The next day, news came that Fort Sumter was on the verge of giving out. Anderson's men had no more than six weeks' worth of provisions, and they would need to either be resupplied or evacuate the fort. An attempt at resupply would likely be fired upon again and stopped, and retaliation would start a war. Evacuation would mean the surrender of military property to a government whose existence the United States of America refused to acknowledge. It was a lose-lose situation.

Fortunately, Abraham Lincoln was a politician, possibly one of the best ever to hold the office of president, and politicians know how to turn desperate situations to their advantage. Lincoln ultimately decided to resupply the fort, but not reinforce it. Notifying the government of South Carolina of his intentions, he would send a re-supply ship providing only food and other necessities, escorted to the outside of Charleston Harbor by warships and troop transports. If the ship was allowed through, the men would be resupplied and would hopefully last until a compromise for restoring the Union was negotiated. If it was fired upon, the support ships would engage, and history would point its finger at the Confederacy for starting the war. Lincoln had turned lose-lose into win-win.

An outraged but outmaneuvered Jefferson Davis called his new cabinet together, and the conclusion was quick and almost unanimous: Fort Sumter would be taken immediately, before supplies or supporting military force could arrive. In the early morning of April 12, 1861, the batteries surrounding Fort Sumter opened fire, pummeling the walls of the bastion. Although Anderson's men were able to return fire, and were able to hold out through 33 hours of constant bombardment, they had been holed up on the tiny island for over three months. The garrison of 85 men surrendered Fort Sumter with honor on April 14, 1861. Although the Confederacy had gained Charleston

Harbor, Anderson was hailed as a hero in the North, and the Confederacy had clearly committed an act of war. There was no turning back now. The Civil War had begun.

Now in possession of Charleston Harbor, an important and valuable seaport, the Confederacy had to fight to keep it. With Fort Sumter seen as a symbol to both sides, the desire to possess it was fierce, and attempts by the Union to take it lasted throughout the war. While Federal forces immediately blockaded the harbor, attempts to take the harbor and its city were in vain. The Union first tried land approaches in June of 1862, but they failed, culminating in the battle of Secessionville. Confederate defenses, as at the outset, were commanded by Brigadier General P. G. T. Beauregard. The primary Confederate works consisted of Fort Moultrie on the mainland to the east, Fort Johnson on James Island to the west, and Fort Wagner on Morris Island to the south. In addition, numerous land and floating batteries were scattered across the harbor, along with several ironclad ships, torpedoes, and other obstructions. The only way to take Charleston from seaward would be to take these defenses, along with Fort Sumter, out of commission.

In April 1863 Rear Admiral Samuel Du Pont gathered a Union fleet of nine iron-clads, while infantry under Major General David Hunter waited. On April 7 Du Pont's ships steamed toward Fort Sumter in what became known as the first battle of Charleston Harbor. It was a complete mess on the Union side. Du Pont's ironclads took an incredible beating, and one of them, the USS *Keokuk*, eventually sank. As for Hunter's troops, only one small landing was made, without consequence. Both Du Pont and Hunter were eventually replaced for their failure.

The next major effort came two months later. Fort Wagner, a large earthwork on Morris Island, controlled any approach to Charleston Harbor from the south. If Union forces could gain control of Morris Island, they would have a solid base from which to attack the Charleston defenses. On July 10 the new Union commander, Brigadier General Quincy Gillmore, directed an assault on Fort Wagner. As the fort was bombarded by Union artillery and four ironclad warships, 2,500 Union troops landed on the south end of Morris Island and advanced north. The Federals were stopped in their advance by darkness, and the Confederates reinforced the fort overnight. When the Union troops attacked in the morning, although they reached the moat at the base of the fort's earthen walls, they were ultimately repulsed. The Union had suffered 339 casualties; the Confederates, a scant 12.

The second battle of Fort Wagner occurred less than a week later. Gillmore brought more troops onto Morris Island and prepared for an all-out assault of the works. On July 18 Gillmore's artillery and six ironclads opened fire on the fort, which now held 1,620 Confederates. After eight hours of bombardment, the fort was still in-tact; the earthen walls of Fort Wagner were not the brick and mortar of Fort Pulaski, which Gillmore had picked apart so famously the previous year. Finally, late in the

One of the tens of thousands of pieces of solid shot hurled at Fort Sumter in Charleston Harbor.

day, 5,100 Union troops, led by the 54th Massachusetts Colored Infantry, attacked the fort from the beach. Again the Union troops reached Fort Wagner's walls, but again they were repulsed after intense hand-to-hand fighting. The Confederates held the fort. Union losses came to 1,515, while the Confederates had suffered 222 casualties.

In August the attack was renewed, this time all around Charleston Harbor. Bombardment of Fort Sumter began on August 17, from the Union foothold on Morris Island and from the sea. Several weeks later Union ironclads sailed right up to Fort Sumter and fired point-blank for five hours before withdrawing. They had done considerable damage, and although the fort held, it was beginning to crumble after nearly unceasing bombardment. On September 5 Gillmore directed another assault on Morris Island, laying siege to Fort Wagner. General Beauregard, watching the Federals inch ever closer to the fort's walls, ordered the evacuation of Morris Island on September 6. However, the Confederates still held the harbor and had strengthened their previously built defenses. On September 8 some 400 marines landed on the small piece on land that extended from Fort Sumter. The Confederates inside the fort and the surrounding batteries tore the Union troops to pieces, and they were forced to withdraw.

The action in September 1863 would be the last direct assault upon any of the works in Charleston Harbor. Although the blockade continued, Charleston Harbor's

SITE DETAILS

Fort Sumter National Monument—Although only a shell of its former self, Fort Sumter still stands proudly in the middle of Charleston Harbor. The fort can be reached only through Fort Sumter National Monument, which offers boat tours daily to the fort and the island. The ride is approximately 30 minutes each way, and the stay at the fort is one hour, which means you have to plan your visit, but the time allowed at the fort is plenty to see everything there. The boat ride itself, with narration along the way pointing out the locations of the other harbor defenses, is a wonderfully peaceful jaunt across the harbor. It leaves from two locations, one in downtown Charleston and one at the site of Fort Moultrie, which itself is definitely worth a visit. When you arrive at Sumter, an optional short ranger program tells the history of the fort and what to see, after which you are free to roam the grounds. When built, Sumter was a three-level fort; the constant bombardment reduced it to only one, and much of the original damage, including artillery shells still stuck within its bricks, is clearly visible. Although a Spanish-American War–era gun emplacement was ruthlessly built into the middle of the historic fort in 1898, it now serves as an excellent museum and gift shop. If you somehow find yourself unable to take the cruise to the fort, be sure to see the visitor's center in Charleston, which has a very good exhibit on both Charleston Harbor and the causes and consequences of the Civil War. One final note: Much of Morris Island is now privately owned, and although it can be seen from the fort, the location of Fort Wagner has mostly been lost to the sea. It is, of course, often asked about, as the second assault on the fort is the famous final battle depicted in the film *Glory*, which tells the story of the 54th Massachusetts. Although preservation efforts are under way to attempt to secure some land on the island, it will be some time before it happens, if ever. *Fort Sumter National Monument; 340 Concord St., Charleston, SC, 29401; boats to the fort also originate from the Fort Moultrie site, 1214 Middle St., Sullivan's Island, SC, 29482; 843-883-3213; www.nps.gov/fosu. Open daily; admission charged for fort.*

defenses held firm. In 1865, as General William T. Sherman marched his men north from Savannah, Georgia, through the Carolinas, the writing was on the wall, and the Confederates evacuated Charleston on February 17. Although the city was now occupied, the Confederates went virtually the entire war without surrendering Fort Sumter.

Fort Fisher

Gradually, over the four years following South Carolina's secession in December 1860, almost every major Southern port was effectively closed by the Union blockade or was captured. This was directly in line with the Union's Anaconda Plan at the outset of the war—close the Confederacy off to outside influences and diminish or eliminate its capacity for import and export of goods, weakening both its military and its economy. There had been significant Northern victories over that time—New Orleans had been captured, Mobile Bay was under control, and Charleston, Galveston, and other major ports were effectively blockaded. By December 1864 only one major port remained open to the Confederacy: Wilmington, North Carolina.

The port at Wilmington was now critical to the survival of the Confederacy. Not only was it the last remaining outlet for the export of Confederate goods, but it was also the closest major port to Robert E. Lee's Army of Northern Virginia, under siege in Petersburg, Virginia. It was known early that Wilmington would be of great importance, and so in July 1862, what had initially been a few small batteries guarding the mouth of the Cape Fear River began to grow significantly.

The new Confederate commander, Colonel William Lamb, had previously traveled to Russia and had seen the Malakoff Tower, a remnant of the Crimean War. Lamb modeled his construction of the new Fort Fisher after the famous tower, and in addition had learned the lessons of Fort Pulaski: that earthen fortification could absorb heavy artillery bombardment far better than a fort of brick and mortar. Over the next years Fort Fisher grew and grew, until by early 1865 it was a massive and imposing position. The fort was L-shaped, with the longer side of the L extending more than

Artillery emplacement at the massive Fort Fisher in North Carolina.

2,000 yards and facing the Atlantic Ocean. The short side of the L crossed almost the entire width of the peninsula the fort was located on, to protect against an attack from the land side. Armament consisted of 47 pieces of artillery, scattered among a series of batteries that ranged from 12 to 60 feet in height on the sea side, and 32 feet on the land side. Fort Fisher was a formidable defensive work, from land or sea.

It was decided by Union commanders that both land and sea forces would be needed to take the fort and press on to Wilmington. Major General Benjamin Butler and Rear Admiral David Porter, who were not exactly on friendly terms, collaborated on a combined attack on the fort that would involve 6,500 Union troops and Porter's massive fleet, the largest in the U.S. Navy. Although Fort Fisher was garrisoned by only 800 Confederates, overwhelming force would be necessary to take this massive fortification.

Although naval bombardment commenced early in December 1864, the real first assault on Fort Fisher wasn't until December 24—and although it began with quite a bang, it amounted to only a fizzle. Butler had the idea of loading an old ship with explosives, floating it next to the fort, and igniting it, hoping to blow a major breach in the earthworks. A ship was loaded with 200 tons of gunpowder and set adrift toward the fort, and at 1:18 AM the ship exploded in a huge fireball that could be heard for many miles. Unfortunately for Butler, the explosion also occurred many yards from the fort—about 600—and no damage was done, save a few rattled eardrums.

The next day, Christmas morning, as Porter's fleet bombarded Fort Fisher, Butler landed 3,500 troops north of the land face of the fort, approaching cautiously to within 50 yards of the earthworks. Suddenly, after seeing the fortification up close, Butler called off his attack and pulled his men off the peninsula, enraging Porter and ultimately leading to Butler's removal from command. Over the nearly three weeks of operations, virtually no impact was made on Fort Fisher's operations.

Determined as ever to take Wilmington, President Lincoln replaced Butler with Brigadier General Alfred Terry, who had known and worked well with Porter in the past. The two devised a plan for attack, and within three weeks of Butler's failed attempt, a new amphibious assault would be launched on Fort Fisher. On January 13 Terry landed most of 8,000 men north of the fort, unopposed, and quickly began digging approach trenches to the land side of the fort, cutting it off from reinforcement. The next day, Porter's fleet of 59 ships began a devastating bombardment. The fort, which had been reinforced to 1,500 men during the lull between the two assaults, suffered 20 percent casualties from the bombardment alone, many more than during the first battle.

During the bombardment 1,500 marines landed on the peninsula, and on the afternoon of January 15 they began the attack, making a direct assault on the L angle of the fort. The marines, stuck out in the open, took heavy casualties as the Confederates concentrated their fire down the beach. However, the Confederates' preoccupation with the assault on the angle took their attention away from Terry's infantry; the marines had served as a diversion. On the opposite end of the fort, 3,500 troops stormed the works. Confederates rushed back over to this end of the fort and temporarily held the attackers in place, fighting hand to hand. Eventually the sheer number of Union troops proved too much, and the Confederates were pushed eastward down the length of Fort Fisher, with the Federals capturing the works piece by piece. Lamb took what was left of his command to an isolated battery southwest of the fort, Battery Buchanan, but they were forced to surrender the same day. The mighty Fort Fisher had fallen, and the fate of Wilmington was sealed. The city was being occupied by Union forces one month later, and the Confederacy's last major port was closed.

Bentonville

After almost two months of slogging through the Carolina swamps at an unbelievable pace, leaving a 45-mile-wide path of destruction in their wake, Major General William Tecumseh Sherman's armies were advancing confidently, with nothing seemingly in their path. Although several battles had been fought, some slowing their progress, they had for the most part been unchecked. The Union Army of the Tennessee, commanded by Major General Oliver Howard, was on the right, and the Army of Georgia was on the left, commanded by Major General Henry Slocum. Both were converging on Goldsborough, North Carolina, with the objective of meeting even more Federal troops sent north from Wilmington—13,000 men under Major General Jacob Cox.

The Harper House, used as a field hospital, part of Bentonville Battleground State Park.

After meeting virtually no resistance, Sherman and his men thought that with the Confederates on the run and with the Neuse River at their backs, chances of an engagement were slight.

Sherman should have known better, as he knew his opponent well. The commander of Confederate forces in the Carolinas, only recently appointed, was Major General Joseph E. Johnston, whom Sherman had battled for months trying to reach the city of Atlanta less than a year earlier. Johnston, who had been gathering most of his army at Smithfield, North Carolina, finally received the intelligence he had been waiting for. Lieutenant General Wade Hampton, who had dogged Sherman's men in Georgia and continued to do so through the Carolinas, reported that Sherman was not marching for Raleigh, but Goldsborough. Furthermore, Sherman's left wing, Slocum's Army of Georgia, was isolated from the right wing, having been delayed at the battle of Averasborough. Johnston saw his chance to take on Sherman's force, whose number was triple his own, in pieces rather than all at once.

On March 19, 1865, as Slocum's army approached the town of Bentonville, 20 miles from Goldsborough, Slocum sent a dispatch to Sherman, who was traveling with Howard's army. Slocum reported that only a very small Confederate force was ahead of him and that all was well. He then ordered an advance against the still-forming Confederate line. Johnston had centered his line around the Cole plantation, alongside the Goldsborough Road, and the first Federal units to approach the Cole house were

Brigadier General W. P. Carlin's men. Seeing that Carlin was meeting resistance, Slocum ordered an advance along the line. The advance was met with a strong repulse from the Confederate right, sending Carlin's men reeling. The rest of the Union line immediately rushed up to bolster Carlin's divisions, quickly throwing together a defensive line made up of log breastworks. Finally, early in the afternoon, Slocum called for reinforcements, realizing that he was facing more than light Confederate cavalry.

Seeing that he had the advantage, Johnston ordered an assault on the Union left at 3 PM. The charge was devastating for the remainder of Carlin's men, who were forced to make a hasty retreat for more than a mile. The resulting disappearance of the Union left meant that the right was now exposed, and the Confederates were quick to seize the opportunity. A terrible fight was the result, and the battle and the fate of Slocum's army hung in the balance, until the Union line was reinforced by a brigade under General William Cogswell. For the rest of the day, repeated assaults by the Confederates against the Union line were repulsed. Sundown brought an end to the fighting, with the Confederates withdrawing back to the Cole plantation.

The next morning, the Confederates took a defensive position north of the plantation, forming a large V north of the Goldsborough Road. Johnston knew that Sherman and Howard's army would soon arrive, and he anticipated an assault. Sherman did arrive on the afternoon of March 20, and Howard's Army of the Tennessee formed on the Union right. Although there was some heavy fighting on the 20th and 21st, the fate of Johnston's army had been sealed on the first day of the battle. He now faced 60,000 Union troops, and on the night of the 21st he withdrew the entire Confederate force back to Smithfield. Sherman, his army whole again, continued on to Goldsborough.

SITE DETAILS

Bentonville Battleground State Park—The park contains a very good interpretive center, located near the Harper House, used as a Union hospital during the battle. The museum contains a light-map of the battle, clearly explaining the events of the critical first day. The Harper House is also open for tours. From the visitor's center, located behind the position of the Union lines, you drive up the Goldsborough Road through the battlefield, where several interpretive stops have been created along the way. Although much of the land around the road remains private property, the interpretation at the stops is excellent, and the view of the battlefield is quite good. This critical battle of the war, often overlooked, deserves your attention, and it is too well presented and too easily accessible to miss. *Bentonville Battleground State Park, 5466 Harper House Rd., Four Oaks, NC, 27524; 910-594-0789; www.nchistoricsites.org/bentonvi. Closed Sun.*

Johnston's Confederates had suffered heavily, taking 2,606 casualties to their force of 21,000. The Union had taken fewer casualties, 1,527, but had won the battle only by timely reinforcement and had just barely averted a major disaster. With the victory, however, Sherman's march through the Carolinas was complete, a remarkable end to a highly successful expedition. As for the Confederates, it was only a matter of time until they would be forced to give up their fight.

Bennett Place

In March 1865 Union forces under Major General William T. Sherman were tearing their way north through the Carolinas. Although they had fought a major battle at Bentonville on March 19–21, they had survived and were ready to press north. General Ulysses S. Grant still had Robert E. Lee's Army of Northern Virginia besieged at Petersburg, Virginia, and with the Confederates weakening by the day, the addition of Sherman's forces would surely bring the long stalemate to a decisive end.

In Sherman's way was a large Confederate army under the command of Major General Joseph E. Johnston. Mostly composed of the remnants of the armies that had defended Atlanta and took part in the failed campaign against Nashville, Johnston's force was much smaller than Sherman's, but the Confederates were not about to let Sherman join Grant without a fight.

Then, in early April, Union forces were able to break through the lines at Petersburg, driving the Confederates out of their defenses and west to Appomattox. The Confederate capital at Richmond was evacuated and burned, with most of the government fleeing the city. On April 9 Lee surrendered his army to Grant at Appomattox Court House, ending what had been almost four years of constant fighting between the capitals at Washington and Richmond. The surrender, however, did not apply to Johnston's army, nor did it apply to the other Confederate forces still scattered across the country.

On April 11 Johnston met with President Jefferson Davis, who was on his way south in an attempt to somehow re-form the Confederacy and keep it alive. Although Davis hoped to keep the government intact, he also saw the futility of further bloodshed and permitted Johnston to confer with Sherman, should the occasion present itself. Johnston sent word to Sherman, and they agreed to meet on April 17. The two great generals, who had dueled for months in Georgia and again in North Carolina, would finally meet face to face.

As Sherman left for the meeting, he received an urgent dispatch from the War Department. The news was shocking: President Lincoln had been assassinated on April 14. Knowing that releasing the information immediately might have disastrous results, Sherman stuck the dispatch in his pocket and ordered the telegraph operator to tell no one.

The two generals, each accompanied by a large mounted escort, met on the Hillsborough Road near what is now Durham, North Carolina. Johnston had passed a small farmhouse on his way and suggested that they confer there. The two parties headed back west on the road to the modest cabin of James and Nancy Bennett. The Bennetts had seen the Confederate party pass, but that was not unusual; there had been a lot of military traffic on the road lately. But they were naturally a bit surprised when the home was converged on by both a Union and a Confederate group, each led by the commanding officers of the armies. After granting permission for the use of their house, the Bennetts retreated outside, while Sherman and Johnston sat down to begin to discuss terms of surrender.

The first order of business was difficult. Sherman placed the note announcing Lincoln's assassination on the table and slid it over to Johnston. Not yet knowing the details of the event, or whether or not it was an action of the Confederate government, both men realized that Lincoln's assassination could create considerable complications, and that a quick surrender would be best to prevent further bloodshed. The two discussed terms, then agreed to meet again the next day. That day, April 18, they agreed on the surrender terms, then sent dispatches to their governments for approval.

The reply from Washington was immediate and definite: the terms were unacceptable. There were two primary reasons for this. First, unlike the surrender terms

The reconstructed Bennett place, site of the largest surrender of the Civil War.

SITE DETAILS

Bennett Place State Historic Site—Within the city of Durham, which at the time of the surrender was nowhere near the booming metropolis it is today, is the Bennett Place State Historic Site. The original cabin was lost to fire in the 1920s, but local preservationists, in a decades-long effort, had the home rebuilt in the 1960s around the still-standing chimney. The surrender room has been recreated using sketches that were taken during the surrender and is both humble and humbling. A museum also exists on the site that explains the surrender, and parts of the Bennett farm have been recreated around the home; the remnants of the Hillsborough Road also still run past the house. Finally, a peace monument celebrating the union of North and South stands beside the house, signifying the great and historic reconciliation that took place here. *Bennett Place State Historic Site, 4409 Bennett Memorial Rd., Durham, NC, 27705; 919-383-4345; www.nchistoricsites.org/bennett. Closed Sun. and Mon.*

that Grant had offered Lee, Sherman's terms involved more than just military cessation of hostilities. It also included, among other things, recognition of the Confederate state governments and amnesty for many Confederate leaders, both military and civilian. The politicians in Washington felt that anything beyond military terms was out of Sherman's jurisdiction. Second, considering Lincoln's assassination and the events of the previous week, Sherman's terms were considered much too generous. Washington was angry, and the government wanted the Confederacy to pay. Grant was asked to dismiss Sherman from his duties and handle the surrender personally.

Grant, however, could not turn his back on his old friend. Sherman and Grant had been together early in the war and had supported each other through thick and thin. In order to help Sherman save face, Grant asked him to return to Johnston with the same terms that Grant had given Lee at Appomattox. Sherman and Johnston met again at the Bennett place on April 26. Although Johnston had been instructed by President Davis to order the troops home and flee in the hopes of raising another army, Johnston saw the futility in holding out. Under strictly military terms, Johnston surrendered all Confederate forces in the Carolinas, Georgia, and Florida—89,270 soldiers. Although other surrenders of Confederate forces would occur over the next two months, the surrender at the Bennett house was the largest surrender of the Civil War.

Sherman and Johnston, forever linked in history as adversaries, had great respect for each other. Although they did not meet again, when Sherman died in February of 1891, Johnston was one of the pallbearers at his funeral, leading to one of those wonderfully unbelievable stories that only history can create. The funeral took place in New York City during a bitterly cold and wet winter day. The 83-year-old Johnston had kept his hat off during the funeral, even when advised by a friend to replace it to prevent himself from becoming ill. Johnston refused, replying that were Sherman in his place, he would most certainly do the same. Johnston did indeed fall ill, and died of the resulting pneumonia one month later.

Norfolk and Hampton Roads

For decades the city of Norfolk and the area surrounding it had been booming. The region, with its wide, protected harbor at Hampton Roads, was open not only to the rivers reaching into Virginia, but also the Atlantic Ocean and Chesapeake Bay. Over time Norfolk became the destination for the agricultural products of much of Virginia and North Carolina, from where they would be shipped across the globe.

Militarily, Hampton Roads was important for two primary reasons. First, it was home to the Gosport Navy Yard, one of the U.S. Navy's best shipbuilding facilities. Second, it protected the mouth of the James River, the water route to Richmond, future capital of the Confederacy. Control of Hampton Roads meant a great deal to both sides, and it would become not only a battleground, but also ground zero for some of the Civil War's most important events.

In early 1861 the area was a mishmash of different facilities, and although local sentiment favored Virginia over the Union, the region's loyalties would remain somewhat confused for over a year. When Virginia seceded immediately following the bombardment of Fort Sumter, Virginia militia seized the navy yard and many of the surrounding

The re-created deck of the USS Monitor *at the Mariners' Museum in Newport News, Virginia.*

batteries, although Federal forces were able to destroy nine ships during their evacuation. Just across Hampton Roads, however, the Union held the mighty Fort Monroe, one of the massive Third System fortresses that, at the time, seemed virtually impregnable. Furthermore, the Union was able to control much of the Newport News area, erecting artillery batteries there and at other locations across from Norfolk, well out of range but certainly not forgotten. Hampton Roads would be stalemated for over a year.

That is not to say the year was uneventful. The first action at Hampton Roads occurred on May 18, 1861, less than a month after Virginia's secession and the beginning of the naval blockade of the Southern coastline. The Confederates had erected a battery at Sewell's Point, one of the more prominent points on the peninsula, to guard the mouth of the Elizabeth River and access to the Gosport Navy Yard. During what became known as the battle of Sewell's Point, two Union warships, the USS *Monticello* and USS *Thomas Freeborn*, fired on the battery for two days. Seeing that the Confederate emplacements were strong and well-positioned, the U.S. Navy would not attempt another assault on Norfolk or the navy yard for another year.

The Confederates took advantage of their occupation of the shipyard, the only major shipbuilding facility in their possession. Although they could not hope to counter the vast U.S. naval fleet, they would be able to turn out enough ships to make a fight of it. The difference would be technology, and the Southerners thought they had the answer: the ironclad warship. Salvaging the steam-powered frigate USS *Merrimack*, one of the naval ships scuttled at Gosport, the Confederate navy designed and built around its hull a technological marvel: a warship made of iron, able to repel any ordnance Union vessels could throw at it, but still buoyant enough to stay afloat. When finished, the new ship was christened CSS *Virginia*, and the Confederates immediately sent her out to break the Federal blockade that had been choking Hampton Roads and the James River.

On March 8, 1862, the *Virginia* appeared at Hampton Roads in outrageous defiance of the three Union naval vessels in the harbor. This strange-looking new ship must have been an unbelievable sight to the Union sailors, but duty called, and they went after her. *Virginia*'s commander, Captain Franklin Buchanan, steamed immediately for the USS *Cumberland*, ramming and sinking her, then turned toward the USS *Congress*, taking fire all the while not only from the Union ship but also the Federal batteries at Newport News Point, which she had strayed close to. Although the *Congress* put up a fight, her shells just kept bouncing off the slanted iron sides of the *Virginia*, and she was forced to surrender. Finally, the USS *Minnesota*, in her desperation, ran aground, a sitting duck. However, the *Virginia*'s deep draft, required by her weight, prevented her from approaching the shallow waters where *Minnesota* was stuck. It was nightfall, but there was no hurry for the Confederates; the *Minnesota* would be there in the morning.

But just as on the morning before, another strange and unexpected visitor had

Jefferson Davis's barren cell at Fort Monroe, Hampton Roads, Virginia.

steamed into Hampton Roads. In the shipyards of New York City, naval engineer John Ericsson, who had already invented and perfected the remarkable twin-screw propeller that had completely modernized the United States Navy, had been tinkering with an ironclad warship of his own. It was described as a floating shingle, which it essentially was, with a very shallow draft and almost completely flat deck. The only prominent feature above the deck was a rotating turret containing two heavy guns. The necessity of the ship had been realized only after reports of the Confederates' work on their own ironclad had reached the United States Navy. Although Ericsson's design was controversial and even scoffed at by many, the ship was built in fewer than 100 days and was sent steaming down the Atlantic coast. Destiny would introduce the USS *Monitor* to history at the most critical moment.

And so, on the morning of March 9, 1862, the *Monitor* entered Hampton Roads and headed for the *Minnesota* to protect her, coming between her and the *Virginia*. While many Union naval officers had heard the rumors about the *Virginia*, the *Monitor* was a complete surprise. The two ironclads immediately came at each other, firing and bouncing cannonballs off each other's iron plating. The lighter *Monitor* was much quicker and was able to run circles around the *Virginia*, but *Virginia* had a definite advantage in ordnance, carrying 10 guns to *Monitor*'s two. For hours the two ironclads fought it out, with neither side able to inflict much damage. Finally, after Lieutenant John Worden, the *Monitor*'s captain, was injured, the gunboat pulled back. The *Virginia*

SITE DETAILS

Hampton Roads Naval Museum—In Norfolk is the Hampton Roads Naval Museum. Among the area museums, this one is certainly the most comprehensive when it comes to the history of the United States Navy, starting with the colonial period and running through today's nuclear-powered armada. The facility is gigantic and also includes an aquarium and science exhibit. Regarding the Civil War era, there is plenty of information here on the area's battles, history, and the famous clash of the ironclads. Furthermore, the museum is staffed partly by U.S. Navy personnel, who are eager to share their knowledge and pride of their navy's great history. Among the interactive exhibits here, the prize-winner lies outside the museum: Although it has nothing to do with the Civil War, no history buff (or most others, for that matter) will want to pass up a chance to roam the decks of the monstrous Iowa-class battleship USS *Wisconsin,* permanently docked next to the museum. The cost for this wonderful attraction? Nothing. Touring the museum, the exhibits, and the battleship is absolutely free. *Hampton Roads Naval Museum, 1 Waterside Dr., Norfolk, VA, 23510; 757-322-2987; www.hrnm.navy.mil. Open daily, Memorial Day through Labor Day; closed Mon., Sep.–Dec. and Apr.–May; call for hours Jan.–Mar.*

The Casemate Museum at Fort Monroe—Across the water from Norfolk is Fort Monroe, still an active military installation. While Fort Monroe was never involved in any major battles (it was held by the Union for the duration), it certainly does have a strong tie to the Civil War. After the Confederate capital of Richmond was evacuated, President Jefferson Davis, not one to give up easily, fled south with his family, trying to eventually reach Texas and form a new government. He never got there; he was captured in southern Georgia with his family. He was immediately imprisoned in a cold, damp casemate at Fort Monroe and was held at the fort for two years. The Casemate Museum at Fort Monroe brings you into Davis's cell, which is just as cold, bare, and dreadful as it was those many years ago. (Davis, a somewhat sickly man, was eventually moved to healthier quarters at the insistence of the fort's doctor.) Also displayed is a wealth of history, much of it concerning Davis and his imprisonment. There is also a very good exhibit on the battle of Big Bethel, the first land battle of the Civil War in old Virginia, which occurred only a few miles away. To top it all off, you can tour the original fortress itself—and located within the fort is Robert E. Lee's home when he was stationed here early in his career (it is still being used as housing, so do not disturb the current occupants!). *The Casemate Museum at Fort Monroe, 20 Bernard Rd., Fort Monroe, VA, 23651; 757-788-3391; www.army .monroe.mil. Open daily.*

The Mariners' Museum—Located in Newport News, the Mariners' Museum has great exhibits of life on the seas, from the largest cargo vessels down to the smallest ski boats, but this museum's strength lies in its artifacts and its interpretation of them.

The granddaddy of all these artifacts, of course, is the turret of the USS *Monitor*, raised from the Atlantic and being restored to something close to its former glory. For the time being, the turret, along with other components of the ship, is in a laboratory being reconditioned, but all of it is viewable through Plexiglas windows. Several other pieces of the ship are on full display, including one piece of its iron plating that can actually be handled by visitors. Another incredible feature of the museum is its full-scale reproduction of the Monitor; visitors can actually roam the deck and get a feel for the actual scale of the ship. Separate mock-ups have also been made of the gun turret, both in its original and current condition. To top it off, the architecture of the museum is stunning, and the grounds surrounding it contain a lake and several hiking trails. *The Mariners' Museum, 100 Museum Dr., Newport News, VA, 23606; 757-596-2222; www.mariner.org. Open daily; admission charged.*

Hampton Roads—If you don't have time to visit any of the museums, you can still look across the waters to see where the battle of Hampton Roads took place. There are two areas with Virginia Civil War Trails signs that describe the two different phases of the battle. The first, located in Christopher Newport Park facing to the southwest, overlooks the site of the first day of the battle, when the CSS *Virginia* attacked the USS *Congress* and USS *Cumberland*. The second overlook faces southeast of the peninsula from Anderson Park and takes in the area where the *Monitor* and the *Virginia* dueled. *Virginia Civil War Trails—Congress & Cumberland Overlook, Christopher Newport Park, intersection of West Ave. and 26th St.; Virginia Civil War Trails—Monitor-Merrimack Overlook, Anderson Park, intersection of Walnut St. and VA 167, Newport News, VA, 23607. Sites accessible daily.*

Sewell's Point—This is one area of historical interest that is not accessible by land. Sewell's Point lies within the navy base (Naval Station Norfolk) and is closed to the public. Nothing is left of the batteries in any case, and the battle happened over the water, so if you want to be able to say that you saw where the battle of Sewell's Point took place, your best bet is to either satisfy yourself with a good view of Hampton Roads, or even to go so far as to take one of the many boat tours of the harbor.

took advantage of the situation and withdrew into the navy yard. The battle of Hampton Roads was over, a tactical draw. But naval warfare had been changed forever.

Ironically, although the designs of the two ships were multiplied by each navy, *Monitor* and *Virginia* never met again, and neither one lasted very long after their historic encounter. Two months later, on May 10, 1862, Major General George McClellan opened his Peninsula campaign for Richmond by taking control of Norfolk and the Gosport Navy Yard. The next day, because the *Virginia*'s draft was too deep to allow her to withdraw up the James River, her Confederate crew was forced to scuttle and destroy her to prevent her capture. As for the *Monitor*, her extremely shallow draft and top-heaviness—along with the unforgiving seas of the Outer Banks of North Carolina, which have taken many a ship—caused her to founder at Cape Hatteras, where she sank with 16 of her crew on December 31, 1862. Although neither ship was able to survive a year, the great battle of the ironclads will long live on in Civil War and naval lore.

Three outstanding museums portray the experience and the importance of Hampton Roads and its history. Don't bother trying to pick one; try to see all three. If you can't, any one of them will provide a great experience.

» OTHER SITES ALONG THE ATLANTIC COAST

Olustee—In February 1864 some 5,500 Union troops landed at Jacksonville, Florida, and began to move westward across the state, hoping to expand their toehold on the coast. As they approached Lake City, Brigadier General Truman Seymour learned that a Confederate force was gathering in front of them. Rather than follow orders to protect Jacksonville and not engage the enemy, Seymour advanced on the Confederates, hoping to destroy a railroad bridge spanning the Suwannee River. On February 20 Seymour's Federals met the Confederate force of 5,100 led by Brigadier General Joseph Finegan near Ocean Pond. The Union troops made several attacks against the Confederate center but were repulsed each time. When Confederate reinforcements arrived, they were able to flank the Union right, drive the Federals from the battlefield, and send them on their way back to Jacksonville. Although Jacksonville remained in Union hands for the rest of the war, the ultimate goal of bringing the state of Florida back into the Union fold would have to wait for Reconstruction.

Olustee Battlefield Historic State Park is 50 miles west of Jacksonville in what is now Sanderson, Florida. The battlefield has a small visitor's center, numerous interpretive signs, and a number of walking trails (although they are a bit hard to follow sometimes). Several impressive monuments and a small cemetery are also at the site, and full restroom and picnic facilities are available. A side note: One of the units that featured prominently in the battle at Olustee was the 54th Massachusetts Infantry, the African American volunteer regiment that was the subject of the film *Glory*. The Olustee battlefield, with its open pine forests, was also the location for much of the shooting of that film. *Olustee Battlefield Historic State Park, intersection of US 90 and Battle Field Trail, Sanderson, FL, 32087; 904-758-0400; www.floridastateparks.org/olustee. Open daily.*

St. John's Bluff—During the Civil War era, Florida was sparsely populated. But it was a state nonetheless, and President Lincoln was eager for it to return to the Union fold. One major route into the more populated areas of Florida was the St. Johns River, with its mouth near Jacksonville, a city that had shown encouraging signs of pro-Union sentiment. In September 1862 an expedition was launched to take Jacksonville, which was guarded by several Confederate batteries on the St. Johns River. On October 1 some 1,600 Federal infantry landed downstream of the batteries, supported by six gunboats, and began to push the Confederates upriver. The next day they captured the Confederate camp at St. Johns Bluff with virtually no opposition and on October 5 took control of Jacksonville, only to leave it four days later.

The location of the Confederate camp and the battery at St. Johns Bluff is within the boundaries of Fort Caroline National Memorial, just east of Jacksonville. The focus of the park, though, is on the fortifications built by the French and the Spanish long before the Confederates took possession, and there is very little Civil War interpretation at the site. But like at almost every other unit of the National Park Service, the presentation, interpretation, and experience of what is at the historic site make it worth taking the time to visit. *Fort Caroline National Memorial, 12713 Fort Caroline Rd., Jacksonville, FL, 32225; 904-641-7155; www.nps.gov/foca. Open daily.*

Honey Hill—As William T. Sherman's Union army was marching through Georgia on its way to the sea, it was feared that Confederate units might gather enough force to harass this risky advance deep in enemy territory. One possible means of bringing Confederate troops to the area quickly was the Savannah & Charleston Railroad, so Major General John Hatch left the Union base at Hilton Head, South Carolina, with 5,500 men to cut this link. On November 30, 1864, Hatch's force encountered 2,000 entrenched Confederate troops at Honey Hill on Parris Island. Despite repeated assaults on the Confederate line, the Federals could not break through. They returned to Hilton Head after suffering 746 casualties and failing to disrupt the railroad.

The entire Honey Hill battlefield is within Marine Corps Recruit Depot Parris Island and cannot be accessed by the public. The base does have a small museum, which tells the history of the marines on the island, but there is only one very small display on the battle (after all, the marines did not have any part in the action). *Parris Island Museum, 111 Panama St., Parris Island, SC 29902; 843-228-2951; www.pimuseum.us. Open daily.*

Buck Head Creek—While William T. Sherman's infantry was busy tearing up the countryside during its march to the sea, his cavalry was doing most of the fighting. Repeated harassment by Confederates under Major General Joseph Wheeler was countered by Union cavalry under Brigadier General H. Judson Kilpatrick. As

Sherman's army marched, the two cavalry units fought and feinted their way alongside. On November 28, 1864, at Buck Head Creek near the town of Millen, Georgia, Wheeler surprised Kilpatrick's encamped troopers, almost capturing them before Federal artillery began to take a heavy toll on the Confederates, inflicting 600 casualties. Kilpatrick rejoined Sherman following the battle.

Buck Head Church, present at the time of the battle, still stands, and there are several historical highway markers at the site, one of them regarding the battle there. The site is on an isolated dirt back road near Millen. *Historical highway marker—Georgia Historical Commission 082-9B (Cavalry Action at Buckhead Church), 0.2 mile south of intersection of Big Buckhead Church Rd. and Porter Carswell Rd., Millen, GA, 30442. Site accessible daily.*

Waynesborough—As Sherman's Union army approached Savannah, Brigadier General H. Judson Kilpatrick's cavalry was still very busy keeping Major General Joseph Wheeler's Confederate cavalry at bay. Early on December 4, 1864, near the town of Waynesborough (now Waynesboro), Georgia, Kilpatrick's force attacked Wheeler's, quickly outflanking it and forcing the Confederates into the town. The battle was short, and Wheeler was soon forced to withdraw, unable to further harass Sherman's march to Savannah.

A historical highway marker describing the action has been placed south of the town of Waynesboro. The Burke County Museum also has information on the battle, but the museum is open by appointment only, so be sure to call ahead if you want to visit. *Historical highway marker—Georgia Historical Commission 017-15 (Cavalry Skirmish at Thomas' Station), intersection of US 25 South and Idlewood Rd.; Burke County Museum, 536 S. Liberty St., Waynesboro, GA, 30830; 706-554-4889; www.burkecounty ga.gov. Museum open by appointment only.*

Rivers Bridge—Shortly after Sherman's two armies—Major General Oliver Howard's Army of the Tennessee and Major General Henry Slocum's Army of Georgia—began their march northward through the Carolinas, they split into two main columns, with Howard's army on the right and Slocum's on the left. On February 2, 1865, part of Howard's force began to cross the Salkehatchie River near Rivers Bridge in South Carolina. A Confederate force, which had failed to burn the bridge, set up artillery above Rivers Bridge to attempt to prevent the crossing. After a failed assault on the position, the Union troops went around the Confederates, building bridges to get through the swampland, and outflanked and attacked the position the next day. The Confederates were forced to retreat and abandon the crossing.

Rivers Bridge State Park consists of a hiking trail with numerous interpretive signs. The telling of the story of the battle is very good, even without an established visitor's center, and the site is worth a visit. Don't let the somewhat isolated location of the park stop you from going, but be aware that the park is closed in the middle of the week. *Rivers Bridge State Park, 325 State Park Rd., Ehrhardt, SC, 29081; 803-267-3675; www.southcarolinaparks.com. Closed Tue. and Wed.*

South Carolina State House—After making Georgia howl during his march to the sea, William T. Sherman intended his next campaign, in early 1865, to accomplish much of the same—destroy as much property as possible and take away the will of the Southern people to continue the war. This time, however, he would be tearing his way up the Atlantic Coast—and his first stop was the Cradle of Secession, the state of South Carolina. Sherman and the two armies under his command undeniably had a special interest in making the people of South Carolina suffer for being what the North saw as the seed of this terrible conflict. As the armies moved northward, many expected that Sherman's primary target would be Charleston, still holding out as it had the entire war. But instead Sherman directed his army toward the state capital at Columbia. On their approach to the capital, the Federals announced their presence by finding an appropriate target to test the range of their artillery, and there was no more appropriate target than the South Carolina State House itself. The Capitol sustained several artillery hits, but the real damage to Columbia occurred during the night. As the Union armies approached, the evacuating Confederates set fire to cotton and other supply warehouses that might be of military value. In addition, after Union troops had secured the capital, several fires were set by renegade soldiers, against the orders of their commanding officer. Sherman awoke in the night to find the city ablaze and immediately ordered his men to fight the fires. In the morning, however, Columbia lay in ashes, although the proud State House had survived.

The current State House, built shortly before the war, is the same building that Sherman's artillery used for target practice in 1865. The west face of the building is marked with large gold stars that indicate where artillery damage is still clearly visible. The grounds themselves are testament to South Carolina's defiance during the war and the hard feelings that remain—one statue of George Washington has been preserved in its state of disrepair, with a plaque indicating clearly that it was the victim of Yankee vandalism during the occupation. There are also numerous memorials to the Confederate heroes of the state, as well as a memorial to the preceding State House, which stood on the Capitol grounds until it was burned by Sherman's armies (the fire damage from this building is also still visible on the current State House). Parts of the interior of the State House are open to the public, but be aware that this is not the location at which South Carolina voted to secede from the Union; the secession convention took place in Charleston. *South Carolina State House, intersection of Main and Gervais Sts., Columbia, SC, 29201; 803-734-2430; www.scstatehouse.net. Open daily.*

Grimball's Landing—Brigadier General Quincy Gillmore, still attempting to capture the Confederates' Fort Wagner near Charleston Harbor, launched a series of diversionary movements to confuse the defenders. In one of these, 5,400 soldiers under

Brigadier General Alfred Terry landed on James and Sol Legare Islands and settled into scattered camps. On July 16, 1863, the Confederates launched a series of attacks against the camps, but hard fighting, timely reinforcement, and the appearance of Union gunboats forced the attackers back. The hardest fighting occurred around a road through the marshland known as Grimball's Causeway, which changed hands several times; when the Confederates attempted a final assault to regain the area, they found that the Federals were gone, preparing for their second assault on Fort Wagner.

A stone monument has been placed near the site of the fighting at Grimball's Landing memorializing the role of the 54th Massachusetts Infantry in the fighting. Further information can also be found at Fort Sumter National Monument. *Memorial—the Civil War Battle of Sol-Legare Island, intersection of Sol Legare Rd. and Old Sol Legare Rd., Charleston, SC, 29412. Open daily.*

Secessionville—More than a year after the first shots of the Civil War were fired at Fort Sumter, the great Southern city of Charleston was still defiantly flying a Confederate flag. With its magnificent harbor, now guarded by numerous heavy guns, Charleston was a very difficult target. However, the land approaches to the city were vulnerable, and after receiving valuable intelligence in May of 1862, Union forces began preparing to land troops on James Island, just south of the city. Under the overall command of Major General James Hunter, 10,000 Union troops eventually landed on the island, but Hunter, thinking the Confederate positions too strong, called for reinforcements, leaving his subordinate, Brigadier General Henry Benham, with orders not to attack. However, both sides began exchanging fire, and Benham decided that in order to ensure the safety of his force, he needed to capture a small Confederate battery, manned by 600 soldiers, near the small town of Secessionville (which, believe it or not, received its name before the war broke out). Before dawn on June 16, 1862, Benham attacked the battery with 3,500 Federals, supported by Union gunboats. The Union troops made quick progress across the terrain and scaled the earthen walls of the battery but were not able to take the position. As Colonel Thomas Lamar braced his Confederates for a second assault, Union troops shifted their position and began a furious enfilading fire on the battery. However, before the Federals could begin their second assault, Confederate reinforcements arrived, and Benham was forced to withdraw. Union casualties came to 683, while the Confederates had suffered only 204. Within a month Union troops were off James Island, and they did not attempt another land assault on Charleston for the remainder of the war.

After the battle, the previously unnamed battery was christened Fort Lamar by the Confederates, and the small earthwork is now the centerpiece of the Fort Lamar Heritage Preserve, managed by the South Carolina Department of Natural Resources. There is a short walking trail through what remains of the earthworks, along with a paved parking lot and an interpretive shelter. Brochures for the walking tour are available at the shelter. This is an excellent site to visit, and the neighbors are very proud (and protective) of the park. However, before you go, know two things. First, the park is surrounded by saltwater marsh, and parts of the park are frequently wet or even slightly submerged, so be prepared for the possibility of getting muddy. Second, depending on the time of year that you visit, the mosquitoes can be distracting to the point that you don't want to stay, so be sure to bring insect repellent. *Fort Lamar Heritage Preserve, intersection of Fort Lamar and Battalion Dr., Charleston, SC, 29412; 803-734-3886; www.dnr.sc.gov/managed/heritage.html. Open daily.*

Simmon's Bluff—On June 21, 1862, a small Union force landed south of Charleston in an attempt to disrupt one of the railroads leading to the city. The party stumbled upon a Confederate camp, burned it, returned to their boats, and left.

There are no reminders, monuments, or markers regarding the action, or as one National Park Service historian described it, the "nonbattle" of Simmon's Bluff. Information on the battle can be obtained from the park historians at nearby Fort Sumter National Monument. *Fort Sumter National Monument, 340 Concord St., Charleston, SC, 29401; 843-883-3123; www.nps.gov/fosu. Open daily.*

Wilmington—Brunswick, North Carolina, a former trade and political center for early colonial North Carolina, had been a virtual ghost town in the decades leading up to the Civil War. That all changed when the Confederates, as part of a defense system for the prized harbor at Wilmington up the Cape Fear River, built a fortress

The heavy earthworks of Fort Anderson, the final Confederate line of defense for the vital port at Wilmington, North Carolina.

around the ruins of the town, first calling it Fort St. Philip (after the church house that still remained) and then Fort Anderson. Following the fall of Fort Fisher in January 1865, Major General Braxton Bragg pulled his defenses up the Cape Fear River closer to Wilmington, including the large earthworks at Fort Anderson. After landing in early February, Major General John Schofield led 12,000 Federals up the river and reached Fort Anderson on February 16. While Admiral David Porter shelled the fort, Union infantry landed downstream and began to surround the earthworks. The Confederates evacuated Fort Anderson on February 19, moving farther north, and within days both the Union army and navy were closing in on Wilmington. Bragg ordered the city's evacuation on February 21, first destroying cotton and anything of military value, and the Federals occupied the city the next day.

Brunswick Town / Fort Anderson State Historic Site is a history buff's delight. Native American history, British colonial life, a Spanish raid, the Revolutionary War, and the battle of Wilmington are all depicted here, not only in the outstanding museum at the visitor's center but also in the archaeological work that has been performed at the site. The ruins of the town are clearly visible, with some buildings and items still partially intact, and the massive Confederate earthworks are in beautiful condition. A walking tour with interpretive signs takes the visitor through both the town and the fort, and it is time well spent. Very close to both the city of Wilmington and Fort Fisher, this one is worth the stop. *Brunswick Town / Fort Anderson State Historic Site, 8884 St. Philips Rd. SE, Wilmington, NC, 28479; 910-371-6613; www.ah.dcr.state.nc.us/ hs/brunswic/brunswic.htm. Closed Mon.*

Monroe's Cross Roads—On March 10, 1865, a brigade of Brigadier General H. Judson Kilpatrick's Union cavalry was attacked while asleep in camp at Monroe's Cross Roads. The awakened troopers fled into the nearby swampland, but the rest of Kilpatrick's division soon arrived, driving the Confederates off.

The entire battlefield at Monroe's Cross Roads is within the boundaries of the U.S. Army's Fort Bragg. Luckily, the Fort Bragg Cultural Resource Center gives guided tours of the battlefield for small groups on the first Monday of each month. Visits must be coordinated with the office well ahead of time, but the reward is a personal guided tour of a battlefield that is otherwise completely inaccessible. If you can't arrange to make the tour, an exhibit on the battle is available at the Cultural Resource Program office. *Fort Bragg Cultural Resource Center, Fort Bragg, NC, 28310; 910-396-6680; www.bragg.army. mil/culturalresources. Tours given first Mon. of each month; call before visiting.*

Averasborough—The Union Army of the Tennessee, Sherman's left wing during his march through the Carolinas, approached Averasborough, North Carolina, on March 15, 1865. Major General Joseph E. Johnston, now commanding all Confederate forces in the Carolinas at General Lee's urging in Richmond, desperately wanted to prevent Sherman's two armies from uniting, and so he sent Lieutenant General William Hardee and 6,000 men to stop Major General Henry Slocum at Averasborough. Hardee formed his line across the Raleigh Road, with a river anchoring each flank—the Black on his right, and the Cape Fear on his left. First contact was made by Brigadier General H. Judson Kilpatrick's Union cavalry, and realizing that the Confederate lines were very strong, Kilpatrick requested additional forces. The next morning, March 16, Kilpatrick assaulted the Confederate front line, and after four hours of fighting and the timely arrival of an entire corps of reinforcements, the Federals were able to push the Confederates back into their second line of defense. As another Union corps approached, the Confederates fell back again and repulsed repeated Union assaults. Finally Hardee was forced to withdraw his Confederates northward. He had lost 865 men to the Union's 682 but was able to slow Slocum's attempt to unite the two Union armies.

The Averasborough Battlefield Commission, largely through local efforts and private donations, has developed the Averasborough Civil War Battlefield. An outstanding museum contains an impressive display of artifacts, and a driving tour has been developed with interpretive signs, highlighting not only the locations and terrain, but some of the remaining residences that were present at the time of the battle. While most of the waysides are still private property (this includes the homes!), the tour is excellent. Even if you are not able to visit the museum during its operating hours, there is enough interpretation in the parking lot outside to get you well on your way. Not far off the interstate, this is one worth stopping for. *Averasborough Civil War Battlefield, intersection of NC 82 and Arrowhead Rd., Dunn, NC, 28334; 910-851-5019; www.averasboro.com. Museum closed Mon.*

Goldsborough Bridge—The Wilmington & Weldon Railroad, which supplied Robert E. Lee's Army of Northern Virginia, crossed the Neuse River at Goldsborough (now Goldsboro), North Carolina. After being only slightly slowed at battles at Kinston and White Hall, a Union force commanded by Brigadier General John Foster arrived in Goldsborough to destroy the bridge. Foster's campaign was designed to coincide with the campaign of the man he had succeeded in North Carolina, Major General Ambrose Burnside, who was preparing to attack Lee's army at Fredericksburg. On December 17, 1862, Foster's men attacked the 2,000 Confederates stationed at Goldsborough and within three hours had driven them off and set the bridge ablaze. Although Foster's mission was accomplished, the bridge was rebuilt within the month, and Burnside's assault against the Confederate lines at Fredericksburg was a disaster.

Goldsborough Bridge Battlefield, just south of the city of Goldsboro, contains a short walking trail with interpretive signs, as well as preserved earthworks from the battle. The walking tour does take you right up to the site of the bridge, and the other stops make the most of this somewhat small but important battle. *Goldsborough Bridge Battlefield, 0.2 mile east of intersection of Mount Olive Hgwy. SE and NC 117 Bypass North, Goldsboro, NC, 27530; www.goldsboroughbridge.com. Open daily.*

White Hall—After the Federal occupation of Kinston, North Carolina, the Union force moved west toward Goldsborough Bridge, the objective of their expedition. As the Federals approached the small town of White Hall, the retreating Confederates burned the bridge over the Neuse River, leaving troops on the other side to slow the Union advance. On December 16, 1862, as the Union troops occupied the town, they shelled the Confederates on the opposite side of the river, driving them off quickly and continuing their advance to Goldsborough.

In the small town of Seven Springs sits Whitehall Landing Park, which not only covers a small portion of the battle site, but also provides a clear view of the Neuse River where the Confederates burned the town's bridge. The park contains interpretive signs about the battle, as well as several memorials to those who fought there, including one particularly moving tribute that nicely sums up the principles of why these men fought in the first place. *Whitehall Landing Park, intersection of W. River St. and New St., Seven Springs, NC, 28578. Open daily.*

Kinston—In December 1862 some 10,000 Union soldiers commanded by Brigadier General John Foster left their base in New Bern, North Carolina, heading east to destroy a railroad bridge crossing the Neuse River at Goldsborough. In the town of Kinston, directly in the path of the Federals, 2,000 Confederates under Brigadier General Nathan "Shanks" Evans decided to make a stand and made contact with Foster's force on December 13. On December 14, although the Confederates put up a good fight,

View of the Confederate position on the banks of the Neuse River at Whitehall Landing, Seven Springs, North Carolina.

Union troops were able to turn the Confederate left, sending them into a retreat. In their haste to get away, the Confederates burned a bridge crossing the Neuse before their entire force had crossed, resulting in the capture of 400 men.

The First Battle of Kinston Battlefield, lovingly preserved just south of the town of Kinston, contains a walking trail along the Confederate lines, as well as a few interpretive signs describing the battle. The battlefield is a public park at the edge of a quiet neighborhood and is obviously well taken care of. There are also several North Carolina Civil War Trails signs scattered throughout the area describing the battle. *First Battle of Kinston Battlefield, 1400 Meadowbrook Dr., Kinston, NC, 28504. Open daily.*

Wyse Fork—A Union corps of 13,000 men led by Major General Jacob Cox left New Bern, North Carolina, in February 1865 to meet General Sherman's army in Goldsborough. On March 7, near the town of Kinston, Cox's men ran into 10,000 entrenched Confederates commanded by Major General Braxton Bragg; the Confederates also had the support of the ironclad CSS *Neuse* in the Neuse River. The next day Bragg attacked the Union left, pushing it back, but although his men were able to capture approximately 1,000 Federal soldiers, Union cavalry forced the Confederates back to their original lines. Little happened the next day, as Cox awaited reinforcements, but on March 10 the Confederates renewed their assault, again on the Union left and also on the center. The Confederates were able to advance within 50 yards of the Union line but were forced back after heavy fighting. Cox's force then retreated but was able to occupy Kinston unopposed within the week. The Federal occupation led to the Confederates' burning and sinking of the *Neuse* to prevent its capture.

A couple of locations in Kinston are connected to the battle of Wyse Fork. Near the site of the battlefield, the corner of an intersection has been set aside for remembrance of the battle. Several interpretive signs and monuments can be seen here, and although not much of the surrounding land is visible, indications are that more land may become viewable to the public in the future. Also in Kinston is the CSS *Neuse* State Historic Site, which houses the remains of the ironclad, brought up from the river bottom in 1963. *Wyse Fork Battlefield, intersection of US 70 and British Rd., Kinston, NC, 28501; CSS* Neuse *State Historic Site, 2612 W. Vernon Ave., Kinston, NC, 28502; 252-522-2091; www.cssneuse.nchistoricsites.org. Signs at battlefield accessible daily; historic site closed Sun. and Mon.*

Fort Anderson—In 1863 Major General James Longstreet was put in command of all Confederate forces in North Carolina. With Robert E. Lee's Army of Northern Virginia desperately needing supplies, Longstreet was given the mission of gathering what he could to send north—all the while keeping the Union forces, who had established strongholds on the North Carolina coast, in place. At Longstreet's direction, Major General Daniel Harvey Hill attacked the Union stronghold of New Bern, North Carolina, on March 13, 1863, forcing the Union soldiers back into their lines. All the while, Hill's men scoured the countryside for food and supplies to send to Lee's army in Virginia. One of the Union positions, Fort Anderson, was located opposite New Bern on the north bank of the Neuse River. The fort was bombarded for two days, until Union gunboats arrived, forcing the Confederates to withdraw. While the Confederates did not take the fort or New Bern, their foraging mission for the Army of Northern Virginia was accomplished.

If you plan on visiting the site of the battle of Fort Anderson, don't be confused, as even some popular Civil War guidebooks have been. The North Carolina state historic site of Fort Anderson, located near Wilmington, is *not* the site of the battle of Fort Anderson (although it is the site of the 1865 battle of Wilmington, which is *also* sometimes known as the battle of Fort Anderson). The Fort Anderson that was established across from New Bern is no longer there, and there are no markers to commemorate the action. Some limited information can be found at the New Bern Historical Society. *New Bern Historical Society, 512 Pollack St., New Bern, NC, 28563; 252-638-8558; www.newbernhistorical.org. Open Mon.–Fri.*

New Bern—In 1862 New Bern, North Carolina, was the second-largest city in the state and a major objective of the Union army trying to gain control of eastern North Carolina. A joint expedition commanded by Major General Ambrose Burnside and U.S. Navy commander Stephen Rowan approached New Bern in early March, reaching the heavy Confederate defenses on the 13th. The next day the Federals attacked the five forts along the Confederate line, with Brigadier General Jesse Reno finding a gap in the center of the line. Although the Confederates were able to seal the gap, the Union charged the center again, this time breaking it for good. The Confederates retreated northward, leaving the Union with the city of New Bern, its first strong foothold on the North Carolina mainland.

There are big plans for the battlefield at New Bern, although the project has been slowed by construction delays. The New Bern Civil War Battlefield Park will eventually consist of a visitor's center, interpretive signs, monuments, and a walking trail through the property. For the moment, while the rest of the park is being developed, guided tours of the battlefield are available from the New Bern Historical Society. As with any private tour, be sure to call well ahead of your visit. New Bern was the capital of North Carolina during the colonial period, so there is plenty of other interesting history to be experienced here. *New Bern Civil War Battlefield Park, across railroad tracks south of intersection of US 70 and Taberna Way, New Bern, NC, 28563; 252-638-8558; www.newbernhistorical.org/cwbp.html. Open daily.*

Washington—After keeping Federal troops occupied at New Bern during the battle of Fort Anderson, Confederate forces moved north toward Washington, North Carolina. Their mission was the same: keep Union forces from leaving their established strongholds along the Carolina coast while other Confederate parties foraged for supplies for

Robert E. Lee's Army of Northern Virginia. On March 30, 1863, three Confederate brigades surrounded Washington and the approaches by the Tar River, besieging the town for almost three weeks. When a Union ship ran the blockade on April 19 and re-supplied the 1,200 Federal soldiers holed up in the town, the Confederates withdrew.

A North Carolina Civil War Trails marker along the beautiful Washington water-front tells of the siege. Other Civil War Trails interpretive signs are scattered throughout the city telling the story of wartime Washington, North Carolina. *North Carolina Civil War Trails—Siege of Washington, intersection of S. Bonner St. and Water St., Washington, NC, 27889. Site accessible daily.*

Tranter's Creek—After Union troops reoccupied Washington, North Carolina, in May 1862, word soon came that Confederates were operating just west of the town. On June 5 a small party left Washington to investigate and found the Confederates blocking a bridge across Tranter's Creek. The Federals were initially pinned down in an open field, but their artillery drove the Confederates out of their position and killed their commander.

A North Carolina Civil War Trails sign has been newly placed somewhat near the area of the fight, along US 264 in the parking lot of a paint shop. The actual battle-field is privately owned and not accessible to the public. *North Carolina Civil War Trails—Tranter's Creek, parking lot of Paint Production Services Inc., 6149 US 264 West, Washington, NC, 27889. Site accessible daily.*

Plymouth—On April 17, 1864, a joint army-navy operation was launched by the Con-federates to retake the town of Plymouth, North Carolina, on the Roanoke River. The centerpiece of the action was the newly christened ironclad CSS *Albemarle*. Confederate infantry attacked the Union earthworks at Fort Williams on the 17th but did not make much headway. Two days later the *Albemarle* steamed downstream, going straight after the Union gunboats and sinking one of them. The next day the land assault was finally successful when the troops attacked the fort with the support of the ironclad. The Union defenders surrendered, bringing their casualty total to 2,900 to the Confederate's 300. The Confederates held Plymouth until the *Albemarle* was destroyed six months later.

The Port O' Plymouth Roanoke River Museum has a great collection related to the battle of Plymouth and the *Albemarle*, and the interpretation is excellent. Even if you can't visit during the museum's regular hours, the outside of the museum is just as in-teresting. There is a model of the *Albemarle*—not quite actual size, but certainly large-scale—floating in the river behind the museum. There are also several interpretive signs along the riverbank detailing the battle and the destruction of the ironclad. *Port O' Plymouth Museum, 302 E. Water St., Plymouth, NC, 27962; 252-793-1377; www.livinghistoryweekend.com/port_o.htm. Open Tue.–Sat., and Sun. during the summer; admission charged.*

Albemarle Sound—Only a few weeks after the ironclad CSS *Albemarle* had debuted at Plymouth, the Federals got another chance when the *Albemarle* and two other Confederate ships, the transport *Cotton Plant* and the steamer *Bombshell*, entered Albemarle Sound from the Roanoke River on May 5, 1864. While the *Cotton Plant* retreated back up the Roanoke, seven Union warships attacked the *Albemarle*, ramming her and bouncing shot after shot off her armor. Although the *Bombshell* was captured, the *Albemarle* was able to get away after dark, damaged but still intact. The *Albemarle* protected Plymouth for the next six months, until a small raiding party led by Lieutenant William Cushing, on a covert mission, blew her up. It is said that Cushing was avenging the death of his good friend Navy captain Charles Flusser, who was killed fighting the *Albemarle* at Plymouth.

In a small park overlooking Albemarle Sound in Edenton, North Carolina, a North Carolina Civil War Trails sign interprets the action that happened on the water across from you. The pretty little town is a bit busy during the summer months, but just find a good place to park and take a walk down to the waterfront, being sure to make a stop or two in the little shops and restaurants along the way. *North Carolina Civil War Trails—Edenton, intersection of Water St. and Broad St., Edenton, NC, 27932. Site accessible daily.*

South Mills—The Dismal Swamp Canal, which connected Albemarle Sound to Norfolk, Virginia, was a potential route to transfer Confederate ironclads southward to disrupt General Ambrose Burnside's North Carolina expedition. In an attempt to destroy one of the canal's locks, at South Mills, North Carolina, 3,000 Union troops approached the city on April 19, 1862, exhausted after an overnight march. Confronted by 900 Confederate infantry, the Federals took four hours to outflank the smaller Confederate force, only to withdraw back to their base at New Bern.

A North Carolina Civil War Trails interpretive sign has been erected along the canal in South Mills. It is located a little ways along the canal road, but it explains Burnside's expedition and the importance of the canal. *North Carolina Civil War Trails—Battle of South Mills, south of intersection of Main St. and Canal Dr., South Mills, NC, 27976. Site accessible daily.*

Fort Macon—By March 1862 only one inlet through the Outer Banks of North Carolina was not under Union control. Confederate-held Fort Macon, at the south end of the Banks, was a sturdy, massive fortress, but as had been proved at Fort Pulaski in Savannah, it could be picked apart with powerful rifled cannon. Union forces began to cut supply lines to the fort on March 23, 1862, and slowly began their approach, digging trenches closer and closer to the fort's walls. On April 25 the artillery began to take the fort down piece by piece, and soon 17 of the fort's guns were out of commission. By the next day, one of Fort Macon's powder magazines became vulnerable, and the Confederates were forced to surrender. With the exception of the port at Wilmington, the entire North Carolina coast belonged to the Union.

The interior of Fort Macon, last Confederate defender of North Carolina's Outer Banks.

Fort Macon State Park protects the original fortress, and many of the fort's rooms have been converted into museum exhibits depicting the battle, the Civil War, life as a soldier and an officer, and the fort's changing role over the years. A little time spent exploring will reveal some of the fort's more remote corners, so bring a flashlight and check it out. The park also contains a very nice public beach with full facilities, and a new nature center is being built near the fort. This is a great one to take the family to. *Fort Macon State Park, E. Fort Macon Rd. and Picnic Park Dr., Atlantic Beach, NC, 28512; 252-726-3775; www.ncparks.gov. Open daily.*

Hatteras Inlet Batteries—Early in the war the Outer Banks of North Carolina provided an ideal shelter for blockade runners of all sorts. As a result, closing them off was one of the first objectives of the U.S. Navy as it began to hurriedly expand its fleet. Hatteras Inlet, between Hatteras and Ocracoke Islands on the Banks, was the central of the three inlets through which ships could move, and the Confederates built earthen fortifications on both islands—Fort Hatteras to the north, and Fort Clark to the south. On August 28, 1861, Union ships began bombarding the two forts, while 880 troops commanded by Major General Benjamin Butler landed on the beach. Fort Clark was soon abandoned, and despite Confederate reinforcements that had arrived overnight, Fort Hatteras was surrendered the next day.

Virtually nothing remains of Forts Hatteras or Clark—they have been washed away by wind and sea, and their former locations are now underwater. In Hatteras, the Graveyard of the Atlantic Museum contains information on the battle, and several stone monuments in the parking lot tell the stories not only of the battle, but also of the sinking of the USS *Monitor*, which occurred just off the coast. Possibly your best view of the actual battle site would be from the ferry, which operates between Hatteras and Ocracoke Island every half hour. *Graveyard of the Atlantic Museum, 0.2 mile south of intersection of NC 12 and Marina Way, Hatteras, NC, 27943; 252-473-2111; www.graveyardoftheatlantic.com. Museum open Mon.–Fri.; monuments accessible daily.*

Roanoke Island—In the second phase of the Union effort to close off the protected area behind the Outer Banks and secure the eastern part of North Carolina, a combined land and naval force assaulted the Confederate works on Roanoke Island at the north end of the Banks. Four fortifications—Forts Huger, Forrest, Blanchard, and Bartow—were on the northwest portion of the small island. Union warships began to bombard Fort Bartow on February 7, 1862, as 10,000 Union troops landed on the south end of the island and worked their way northward. Overnight the Confederate troops retreated to the works at Fort Huger, and the next morning Major General Ambrose Burnside's men assaulted the works there, eventually driving out the Confederates. Running out of real estate, the Confederates were forced to surrender at the north end of the island, opening the way for the Union to access Albemarle and Pamlico Sounds.

Some interpretive information about the battle of Roanoke Island can be found at Fort Raleigh National Historic Site, where there is a small display on the battle, as well as a memorial to the freedman's colony that was set up in the area. The park staff will also be able to answer questions you might have about the battle. As for the actual sites, what remains of Fort Huger is visible at low tide at the base of the William B. Umstead Bridge on the east side. There are also interpretive signs there describing the battle, as well as some parking. *Fort Raleigh National Historic Site, 1401 National Park Dr.; Fort Huger site, intersection of US 264 and Fort Raleigh Rd., Manteo, NC, 27954; 252-473-5772; www.nps.gov/fora. Open daily; admission charged for National Park.*

Suffolk—Technically two battles, the actions at Suffolk, Virginia, were both part of the Union's defense of the massive shipyard at Norfolk to the east. On April 13, 1863, as part of an attempt to gather food and supplies for the starving Confederate Army of Northern Virginia, the Confederates demonstrated against the extensive earthworks at Suffolk to allow forage parties to take what they could from the surrounding country. In the process the Confederates managed to push the Union right and establish a battery on the Nasnemond River to harass Union shipping. Two days later the Confederates were driven out of some of the positions they had established, but they still maintained some earthworks on the river. In the second battle, on April 19, the Federals took the remaining earthworks in a surprise attack, overrunning the fortification within 10 minutes. During their short stay, the Confederates had been able not only to temporarily disrupt Union activity on the river, but to help supply Lee's army in Northern Virginia. They left Suffolk on May 3 to join Lee in the fight.

In Cedar Hill Cemetery is an impressive Confederate Memorial, newly restored to its former condition. A Virginia Civil War Trails sign interprets both of the battles of Suffolk. *Cedar Hill Cemetery, main entrance at 326 N. Main St., Suffolk, VA, 23434; 757-923-3880. Open daily.*

Big Bethel—Early in the war the Confederates recognized that one possible avenue of invasion for Union forces to reach Richmond was up the peninsula between the York and James Rivers. Fort Monroe, at the tip of the peninsula, remained under Union control and would make a prime landing site for troops. To guard against a possible invasion by this route, the Confederates built earthworks near Big Bethel, several miles up the peninsula. On June 10, 1861, a force of 3,500 Federal soldiers ventured toward the Confederate lines and after some confusion assaulted the position. The attack was not coordinated, and the battle lasted less than an hour, with the Union troops withdrawing back to Fort Monroe.

In addition to a historical highway marker, there is a monument in the Big Bethel Recreation Area to Henry Lawson Wyatt, remembered as the first casualty of the Civil War in Virginia. Unfortunately, most of the battlefield has been lost to the Big Bethel Reservoir, and there is not much interpretive information at the site. However, a good deal of information about the battle can be found at the Casemate Museum at Fort Monroe. *Wyatt Monument, Big Bethel Recreation Area, intersection of Big Bethel Rd. and Semper Farm Rd., Hampton, VA, 23666. Open daily.*

» WHERE TO STAY ALONG THE ATLANTIC COAST

Although Savannah, Charleston, and Wilmington were extremely important strategically, the cities themselves did not see a lot of action. All three offer a choice of lodgings that date back to long before the Civil War period, but not too many that have direct ties to the war. Still, all these cities have rich histories going back to colonial days, and you won't have any trouble finding a good place to stay.

One bed-and-breakfast that does have a tie to the war is Charleston's **Phoebe Pember House**. The home, over 200 years old, was inhabited by young Phoebe Pember, who became chief nurse at Chimborazo Hospital in Richmond and later went on to write a wonderful memoir of her Civil War experiences. The home is not only in the heart of the historic district but also contains gracious rooms and its own yoga studio. *Phoebe Pember House, 26 Society St., Charleston, SC, 29401; 843-722-4186; www.phoebepemberhouse.com.*

Finally, don't miss a chance to spend some time at the beach. Your travels along the coast will take you to or near Myrtle Beach in South Carolina, the Outer Banks of North Carolina, and Virginia Beach. There are hundreds of resorts, bed-and-breakfasts, and other very enjoyable spots along the way, not to mention a wealth of history.

PART THREE

The War in the East

7

The War for the Capitals: Richmond

OVERVIEW

This chapter covers more battles than any other in this book, yet all the battlefields are contained in a relatively small area. They are also virtually all part of only two campaigns of the war. The sites around the Confederate capital of Richmond are among the most important of the war, and not only are they important, but there is a lot to see.

Once the Civil War began, the cry soon went up from the North: "On to Richmond!" Yet each successive commander of the Union forces had trouble making this seemingly straightforward and much-desired objective come to fruition. Many tried, but only two succeeded in coming close to the outskirts of Richmond: George McClellan and Ulysses S. Grant.

Early in the war, the reason was initiative. The Union armies, having been defeated at Manassas (Bull Run) in July of 1861, remained just south of the Potomac due to the unwillingness of Washington politicians to allow them to stray far from the capital. The government in Washington faced the threat of the Confederates' taking the city and forcing an end to the war. Although in reality the Confederacy lacked the resources to capture and hold Washington—nor was it strategically necessary for them to capture the city to win the war—the fear that they would do so remained, and most Union troops remained holed up in the city's defenses until McClellan finally won approval to campaign for Richmond. And although he moved forward with his preparations, he did not exactly go straight on to Richmond. His plan was a convoluted,

Over 18,000 Confederate dead from surrounding battlefields are memorialized by this imposing pyramid at Hollywood Cemetery in Richmond.

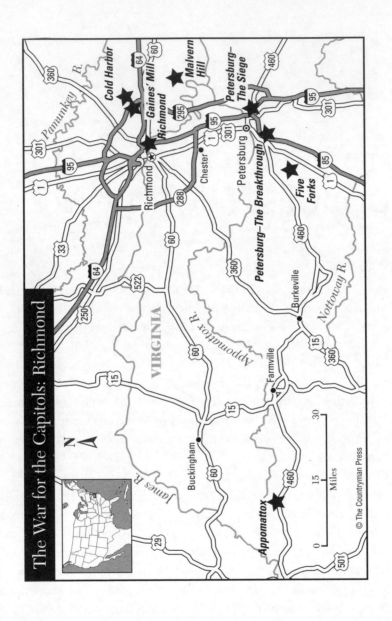

The War for the Capitols: Richmond

backdoor way to the capital, up the Virginia peninsula from the sea and then heading northwest. It became known as the Peninsula campaign, and it was a disaster in every sense of the word. The first two months of the campaign were spent outside Washington, with McClellan taking his time and insisting that he needed more soldiers—even though he outnumbered the Confederates by more than two to one.

As McClellan's Peninsula campaign progressed, the main reason that few approached the Confederate capital from June of 1862 onward emerged: That reason was General Robert E. Lee. When the Confederate commander Joseph Johnston was severely wounded at the battle of Seven Pines, he was replaced by Lee the next day. Within two weeks Lee had completely taken the initiative from McClellan and was driving him out of the area during what became known as the Seven Days Battles. Lee then turned his attention north, defeating every general that the Union could throw at him. Every commander in the Union army respected and feared the capabilities of Robert E. Lee.

Then came Grant. Ulysses S. Grant had proved his worth in the battles of the West, with major victories at Fort Donelson, Shiloh, Vicksburg, and Chattanooga. Soon President Abraham Lincoln put him in charge of all Union forces, and the first order of business for the Army of the Potomac was to move on Richmond. Grant first met Lee at the battle of the Wilderness, and suffered heavy losses. But Grant knew that those losses were necessary for victory. So after the loss, Grant stunned Lee—and his own men—by moving not north, in retreat, but south, putting pressure on the Confederates to defend their capital. Immediately after the Wilderness came Spotsylvania Court House, with even more casualties. But Grant continued south. For almost two months, the Union army moved toward Richmond, with Lee continually maneuvering to keep between Grant and the capital.

Soon Grant realized that a direct assault on Richmond would not work. He then set out to capture Petersburg, the vital railroad hub just south of Richmond. What came of that was 10 months of siege warfare, with both armies facing each other for what seemed an eternity. Finally, after the Federals were able to weaken the Confederates by gradually cutting off all their supplies, they were able to take Petersburg, sending Lee's army fleeing for its life to the west. The Confederates were finally caught at Appomattox Court House, where Lee surrendered his army. Although other armies around the country remained in the field, the Civil War was as good as over.

This chapter will take you through the incredible history in and around Richmond, helping you get to know the most compelling and celebrated military characters of the Civil War—Robert E. Lee and Ulysses S. Grant.

» PEOPLE TO KNOW

Robert E. Lee—Robert Edward Lee, son of Revolutionary War hero "Light-Horse Harry" Lee and not-so-distant relative of George Washington, began his part in the

Civil War in western Virginia, where not much was going on. But he soon proved himself a worthy commander, and before long he would be known and revered as one of the greatest military minds produced in America.

Lee began his military career as an engineer, working on many of the coastal defenses that would later be assaulted by Union forces. When the Mexican War broke out, although Lee did not agree with it, he served his nation and was promoted to colonel by war's end. He then became superintendent of West Point, and subsequently served in the West. When it came time for Virginia to secede, a motion that Lee opposed as much as he did slavery, he remained loyal to his state, resigning his U.S. Army commission from his home at Arlington, Virginia, across the Potomac River from the capital at Washington. Later serving in Richmond, Virginia, when Major General Joseph Johnston was wounded at the battle of Seven Pines, Lee took over the next day and began his rise to fame. His campaigning over the next three years was nothing short of brilliant, all the way through his surrender to Ulysses S. Grant at Appomattox. After the war Lee became president of Washington University in Lexington, Virginia, until his death. The school was later renamed Washington and Lee University in his honor. A truly remarkable figure, Robert E. Lee throughout his life embodied honor, humility, and service, and his reputation is well deserved.

J. E. B. Stuart—James Ewell Brown Stuart, famed cavalry commander of the Confederate army, certainly had flair, with his plumed hat and colorful garb. He was also a brilliant cavalryman, and his extraordinary exploits supporting the Army of Northern Virginia are the stuff of legend.

Stuart spent much of his early career in the West, serving in Kansas while that state bled, and once even being severely wounded fighting the Cheyenne. When Virginia seceded, he went with it and resigned his U.S. Army commission. He was in the thick of the action immediately, fighting at the first battle of Manassas and in the Shenandoah Valley, quickly achieving the rank of brigadier general. When Robert E. Lee was appointed commander of the newly christened Army of Northern Virginia, Stuart served him until his own death and was involved in virtually every battle and campaign that Lee led. He himself led two famous "Rides around McClellan," in which he circled the Union commander's army, and his daring reconnaissance work for Lee earned him the respect of everyone. When the tide of the Confederate cavalry's dominance began to turn with the battle of Brandy Station, Stuart boldly kept up the fight, performing ably, with the notable exception of his absence from the first two days' fighting at the battle of Gettysburg. Stuart was mortally wounded at the battle of Yellow Tavern, north of Richmond, and died on May 12, 1864. It was a great loss to the Confederate cause and to the Confederate army.

George B. McClellan—George Brinton McClellan was, at the outset of the Civil War, a promising general, having early success in western Virginia and earning the respect of his men. But a tendency against aggressive action doomed McClellan's reputation, and his sluggishness—which Lincoln termed "the slows"—eventually cost him his command.

Among those who knew him casually, McClellan had a reputation for arrogance, even snubbing the bona fide war hero commanding the armies, Winfield Scott, and President Abraham Lincoln. But Lincoln nevertheless named him commander of the Army of the Potomac after the disastrous first battle of Manassas, and McClellan whipped his troops into fighting shape, restoring morale. Then, he did very little. Finally convincing Lincoln that the best way to Richmond was the long way, McClellan launched his doomed Peninsula campaign in early 1862, ending ingloriously with the Seven Days Battles. A few months later McClellan won a great victory at the battle of Antietam, only to let Robert E. Lee's army escape afterward. He was soon removed from command after refusing Lincoln's orders to pursue Lee, insisting—as he did throughout virtually his entire career as a military leader—that he had too few men. Lincoln and McClellan would fight it out one more time, when McClellan ran for president on the Democratic ticket in 1864, but he was soundly defeated. He stayed in politics, then later in life went back to his original profession of engineering.

» THINGS TO KNOW

Many of the sites in this chapter are well preserved as parts of parks, while absolutely nothing remains of others. Some of the sites that remain are designated by little more than historical highway markers, simple signs that denote only that history happened nearby. Fortunately, information about almost all these battles is close at hand. The staffs at Richmond National Battlefield Park, Petersburg National Battlefield, and Appomattox Court House National Historical Park know these battles inside and out, since they were all fought relatively close to one another and as parts of the same campaigns. If you have any questions at all, they will be glad to help you out.

THE TRIP

This trip occurs almost entirely within a short drive of Richmond and Petersburg, Virginia, with the exception of the battlefields along Lee's line of retreat to Appomattox. While you will do a lot of driving to see these sites, they will almost all be around these two cities, where lodging and restaurants are plentiful. Your best bet is probably to set up in Richmond and/or Petersburg and do all your exploring from there.

The trip out west to Appomattox takes about two hours and is on smaller highways. It is a beautiful drive, but you won't find nearly as many options for lodging. Unless you plan ahead and have somewhere to stay, expect to drive back to Richmond or Petersburg, or press on to Lynchburg, to find a place to sleep for the night.

» THE CAN'T-MISS SITES

Richmond

The Confederate capital at Richmond, Virginia, chosen by the Confederate government originally seated at Montgomery, Alabama, after Virginia's secession, was once a major, thriving city in America. Since the war, Richmond has been eclipsed in stature, in good part because of the war and its aftermath. But the history of this great city, which begins long before the Civil War and even the founding fathers, is rich with won-

SITE DETAILS

Richmond National Battlefield Park Civil War Visitor Center—The primary center for the vast Richmond National Battlefield Park, the park's visitor's center has recently moved from the old site of the Chimborazo Field Hospital to the restored Tredegar Iron Works, the great producer of guns and cannonballs that armed the Confederacy. The ruins of the works alone are worth a visit; you wander through the remains of old brick buildings, furnaces, and sluices scattered along the shores of the James River, with interpretive signs explaining the function of each as them. The new visitor center contains interactive exhibits, films and audio programs, and exhibits and artifacts from Richmond and the war. Any exploration of Richmond and the many battlefields around it virtually requires that you start here; the maps and explanation of the campaigns that took place are remarkably helpful. The old visitor's center at the Chimborazo site is still open and contains a very good display on medicine during the war. *Richmond National Battlefield Park Civil War Visitor Center, 490 Tredegar St., Richmond, VA, 23219; 804-771-2145; www.nps.gov/rich. Open daily.*

The Museum and White House of the Confederacy—If the Confederate States of America ever had something akin to the Smithsonian Institution, this would undoubtedly be it. Consisting dually of a top-notch museum and Jefferson Davis's home during the time he was president of the Confederacy, this should be a destination for all who have an interest in American history. This is not just an ordinary museum. Yes, the exhibits are well done, the artifacts well presented, and the story of the Confederacy is well told. But even before you step inside, you start to realize that this collection is special. Outside the front door you see parts taken off an old ship, just as you may have seen in other places, and you lean on it, before realizing that it is the propeller shaft of the USS *Monitor*. As you walk through the museum, your experiences are similar. *That's Robert E. Lee's sword from the surrender. Those are Stonewall Jackson's spurs. That's J. E. B. Stuart's plumed hat.* The entire collection is made up of items like these, and it is astonishing. When you finish with the museum, you may take the guided tour of the White House of the Confederacy. The restoration of the home and the tour are truly outstanding, and the guides are knowl-

derful sites and stories. It is in Richmond that Patrick Henry uttered the famous words, "Give me liberty, or give me death!"—and the church where he gave that speech still stands. Just down the street is where a young Edgar Allan Poe began his literary career. And in the heart of the city is the home of John Marshall, the great chief justice of the Supreme Court who was so instrumental in establishing the strength of today's legal system; he is buried in one of the city's cemeteries. But despite these distinctions, Richmond's history will forever be cemented with the Civil War. Civil War–related sites abound in Richmond, and a number of them simply cannot be missed.

edgeable, easily fielding any question thrown at them, whether concerning the materials in the furnishings or the life of the Davis family. Their stories and their relation of how many important events took place in the home are among the best you will ever come across. You may have to work a little to get there—parking in the area is somewhat scarce—but this is a wonderful destination. *The Museum and White House of the Confederacy, 1201 E. Clay St., Richmond, VA, 23219; 804-649-1861; www.moc.org. Closed Wed.; admission charged.*

Hollywood Cemetery—A premier cemetery for Richmond's finest when it opened in 1850, this vast tract eventually became thoroughly linked with the Civil War, as it contains over 18,000 Confederate dead from the surrounding battlefields. A large pyramid monument was constructed in 1869 to remember them. Among the more notable burials related to the Civil War: Jefferson Davis, along with his wife Varina; General J. E. B. Stuart; General Fitzhugh Lee; General John Pegram; and General George Pickett, surrounded by many of the men who were with him during his famous charge at Gettysburg. Other notables not related to the war also happen to be in the cemetery, including two United States presidents, James Monroe and John Tyler. A driving tour brochure of the beautiful cemetery is available at the front gate; be sure you pick one up, or you are bound to get turned around. *Hollywood Cemetery, 412 S. Cherry St., Richmond, VA, 23220; 804-648-8501; www.hollywoodcemetery.org. Open daily.*

Virginia State Capitol—The current Virginia State Capitol building, which recently underwent a massive restoration, was the same building where the Confederate government sat during the entire time it was in Richmond. The Capitol and its grounds are once again open to the public, and besides the beautiful building itself (which was designed by Thomas Jefferson), the surrounding monuments and greenery are a delight. Tours of the interior of the Capitol, as well as the exterior grounds, are available during the week. *Virginia State Capitol, Capitol Square at intersection of Ninth St. and Grace St., Richmond, VA, 23219; 804-698-1788; www.virginiacapitol.gov. Open for tours Mon.–Fri.; grounds open daily.*

General J. E. B. Stuart lies at rest in Hollywood Cemetery, Richmond.

Cold Harbor

Although Robert E. Lee's Army of Northern Virginia and Ulysses S. Grant's Army of the Potomac stood across from each other for the better part of 12 days, the battle of Cold Harbor, the part that people recognize and remember, was not very long at all. For all their strategic importance, Gettysburg is remembered as the bloodiest battle, and Antietam as the bloodiest day, but the battle at Cold Harbor will always be known as the bloodiest hour of the Civil War.

The Union army, continuing its movement south to Richmond, all the while staying east of Lee's army to protect its supply lines, had fought in the region northeast of Richmond for several days, capturing vital crossroads and trying to secure a route to the city, only 10 miles away. At Haw's Shop, Totopotomoy Creek, and Old Church, Union cavalry and infantry had put the Confederates on the defensive. On May 31, 1864, Philip Sheridan's cavalry took possession of the crossroads at Old Cold Harbor. With the capture of this important real estate, Grant now had a position from which he could threaten the Confederate capital to the southwest, protect his supply and communication lines to the east, or lunge at Lee's army to the northeast.

In the previous days both armies had grown, and both from the same source. Grant had ordered Major General Benjamin Butler, bottled up at Bermuda Hundred southeast of Richmond, to send 10,000 men under Major General William Smith to his army. Lee, after much arm-twisting and political maneuvering, was finally able to pull a division from General P. G. T. Beauregard, whose forces were manning the Howlett Line at Bermuda Hundred, the cap on Butler's bottle. The armies' strength now stood at 117,000 for the Federals and 60,000 for the Confederates.

Early on June 1 the Confederates made an attempt to regain the crossroads. Sheridan's cavalry was greatly outnumbered, but he faced green troops, and his men were armed with repeating rifles. The attack failed, and Lieutenant General Richard Anderson pulled his Confederates west, set them up on a north-south ridge, and began to prepare field fortifications. In the ensuing hours two Union corps, under Major Generals William Smith and Horatio Wright, arrived on the field and prepared to assault the Confederate line. At 6 PM the Federals advanced, driving back Confederate skirmishers, but they were slowed once they reached Anderson's strong position. Although they did find a gap in the Confederate line, Anderson was able to seal it, and the Union attackers fell back, forming a line facing west, across from the Confederates.

The view from the Union position at Cold Harbor, once an open field.

Little combat occurred on June 2, but both armies were very active. Lee lengthened his line around Anderson's position, with Lieutenant General A. P. Hill forming on the right, Anderson in the center, and Lieutenant General Jubal Early on the left. Although the Confederates had the Chickahominy Swamp at their backs, Lee was willing to take that risk, deeming it more necessary to keep between Grant's army and Richmond. Wright and Smith kept their positions, with Major General Winfield Scott Hancock forming to the south on the Union left, Major General Gouverneur Warren to Smith's right, and Major General Ambrose Burnside on the far Union right, the northernmost position on the Federal line. The Confederates did attempt to turn the Union right on June 2, but Early's assault against Burnside and Warren's positions did not succeed.

On the night of June 2, both armies knew what was coming. The Confederates improved their field works, making them even stronger than before. They had a clear field of fire to the east virtually all along the line. Union troops prepared for what they knew would be a fierce fight the next morning, with the assault scheduled for 4:30 AM.

The next morning, June 3, 1864, the assault began promptly at the appointed time. While Warren and Burnside held their positions on the Union right, the rest of the

SITE DETAILS

Cold Harbor Unit, Richmond National Battlefield Park—Although much of the Cold Harbor battlefield has been lost, the portion that included Wright's assault of the terrible Union charge is preserved as part of the Richmond National Battlefield Park. The park has established the Cold Harbor Visitor Center here, which serves not only the Cold Harbor battlefield but also the battlefield at Gaines' Mill, just down the road. Unlike the other remote visitor's centers of the park, the Cold Harbor center is open year-round. The center is small, but the interpretation of the battle and the surrounding ground is excellent, complete with a fiber-optic map display showing the events leading up to and including the June 3 assault. From the visitor's center, a walking trail and a short driving tour will take you through the well-preserved earthworks of the battlefield. Just down the street from the visitor's center is Cold Harbor National Cemetery, where many of the battle's dead are buried. The Cold Harbor battlefield is not one that lends itself to complex interpretation or inspection of the works and the terrain; it is also not dotted with great stone monuments dedicated to the armies and their valor. It is a place where one walks the now-quiet field and listens to the ghosts of the men who fought there. Although it is, in comparison to other Civil War battlefields, a simple place, it is one of the most affecting visits you will make in your travels to the sites of the Civil War. *Richmond National Battlefield Park—Cold Harbor Unit, 5515 Anderson Wright Dr., Mechanicsville, VA, 23111; 804-226-1981; www.nps.gov/rich. Open daily.*

line—Wright's, Anderson's, and Smith's corps—directly assaulted the front of the Confederate works. It was slaughter, and it occurred along the entire front. Although the Federals were able to get close to the line, establishing forward positions and entrenching just to survive, the well-protected Confederates fired mercilessly into the oncoming blue wave. The assault that had begun at 4:30 was over, for the most part, by 5. In that 30 minutes of fighting, the Union army had suffered an unfathomable 7,000 casualties.

The assault was called off, and the armies maintained their positions. The Union troops who had been able to advance and entrench were often picked off over the next few days by Confederate sharpshooters or fell victim to an artillery blast, but most of the fighting was over, with the armies pulling out on June 12. Although the Confederates, who could ill afford any losses, had suffered 5,000 casualties, the Union had lost 13,000, most of them during the morning of June 3. Grant, in later years, remarked that he had "always regretted that the last assault at Cold Harbor was ever made" and that "no advantage was gained to compensate for the heavy loss we sustained." Part of Grant's overall strategy for ending the war, knowing that he heavily outnumbered Lee's army, was that as long as he kept inflicting heavy casualties, his army was much better equipped to replace losses. But Cold Harbor was too much. It was remarked by one of his aides that in all the devastation of war that Grant had witnessed, the assault at Cold Harbor was the only occasion that caused the great general to weep.

However, Grant was able to learn from his defeat. Seeing now that there would be no getting around Robert E. Lee, the Union army would no longer attempt to directly assault Richmond. Grant redirected his army to Petersburg, Virginia, just south of Richmond. Petersburg was a major rail center, and taking it would cut the capital off, with the exception of only one railroad, from all possible routes of supply. As Lee had predicted would happen if Grant was able to reach the James River, which he soon did, it would "become a siege, and then it will be a mere question of time."

Gaines' Mill

Major General George McClellan had spent almost three months trying to get his army to a point where it could besiege the Confederate capital at Richmond. Beginning April 5, 1862, the army had spent a month laying siege to the Confederate defenses at Yorktown, then slowly began making its way up the Virginia Peninsula, only to be stalled east of the city at the battle of Seven Pines a month later. Moving north, McClellan began carefully making his plans for the siege, convinced that the Confederates, now called the Army of Northern Virginia by their new commander, Robert E. Lee, outnumbered the Union two to one. (It was actually the other way around.) Finally, on June 25, McClellan attacked the Confederates at Oak Grove. The next day Lee took the initiative, attacking the Union lines at Beaver Dam Creek; on the same

The Watt house on the Gaines' Mill battlefield, part of Richmond National Battlefield Park.

day, Major General Thomas "Stonewall" Jackson arrived, fresh from his successful campaign in the Shenandoah Valley, and went into camp opposite the Union right. McClellan, thinking that his army was suddenly in danger, that his main supply line was about to be cut, and that he was greatly outnumbered—all of which were not true—decided to withdraw south toward the James River, abandoning his plans for Richmond after one day of offensive operations.

On June 27 McClellan had four of his five corps south of the Chickahominy River and moving south. Left north of the river was a Union corps of 30,000 commanded by Major General Fitz John Porter. McClellan ordered Porter to begin his withdrawal across the river, which was still swollen with the spring rains. Although Porter was able to begin sending units across, he still had elements of Lee's army to his west and was forced to turn and face him to enable an orderly withdrawal. After the previous day's fighting, the Union troops had withdrawn to a strong position south of Boatswain Creek. The men were heavily entrenched and held the high ground, with the line extending for 2 miles. The Confederates had formed opposite the creek, with Major General James Longstreet on the Confederate right, Major General D. H. Hill on the left, and Major General A. P. Hill in between them. Lee had decided to bring almost all his army north of the river, leaving only a small force to guard Richmond. With most of the Union army south of the river, it was the only time during the entire campaign that the Federal troops actually were outnumbered.

The day was extremely hot, and the Confederates moved slowly to get their offensive started. The attack began at 2:30 in the afternoon, with men from A. P. Hill's force bursting from the opposite tree line in a rush, headed straight for the center of the Federal line. Union artillery immediately opened up on them as they crossed the open fields before the creek and then went down the ravine of the creek and up the other side, stopping just before the crest. After resting briefly, the unit resumed the charge. They were met immediately by Union troops who countercharged, and after fierce fighting the Confederates were forced back into the tree line along the creek. For four hours the Confederates launched similar attacks against the Union line, with each one being repulsed.

At about 6:30 PM there was a lull in the fighting, and both sides took advantage. Porter, who had called for and received reinforcements, shored up the Union line for another assault. The Confederates prepared for a decisive attack that they hoped would break the Union line and carry the day. Finally, at 7 PM, the Confederates burst forward against the Union center. The attack was led by Brigadier General John Bell Hood, and the Confederates, under orders not to fire until they had reached the Union line, went forward in a giant, unstoppable wave, across the field and through the ravine around the creek. Hood's Confederates broke through two of the Federal lines, and Porter had no choice but to withdraw his entire corps.

As darkness fell, Porter was already on his way south of the Chickahominy River to join the rest of the retreating Union army. Although the Confederates had gained a great victory, they had paid a high price, taking 8,750 casualties. The Federals had lost 6,837 but were retreating from Richmond. Robert E. Lee had seized all control

SITE DETAILS

Richmond National Battlefield Park (Gaines' Mill Unit)—The Richmond National Battlefield Park preserves the area of the Gaines' Mill battlefield where Hood's assault broke the Union line and won the day for the Confederates. There are walking trails and interpretive signs throughout the property, which is only a small part of the battlefield but very well presented. In addition, Gaines' Mill shares a visitor's center with the nearby Cold Harbor battlefield that is open the entire year. The visitor's center contains exhibits on the battle, as well as a fiber-optic map that tells the story of the battle. *Richmond National Battlefield Park—Gaines' Mill, intersection of Cold Harbor Rd. and Wyatt House Rd., Mechanicsville, VA, 23111; 804-226-1981; www.nps.gov/rich. Open daily.*

from McClellan's Union army, which really did outnumber him two to one, and not only had saved the Confederate capital but was now in a position to possibly destroy the Army of the Potomac.

Malvern Hill

On the face of it the battle of Malvern Hill was won by the Union. They certainly had fewer casualties, they held the field, and they had never really been threatened during the entire battle. But on this seventh day of the Seven Days Battles of 1862, with Major General George McClellan's campaign for Richmond coming to an end, neither side could claim victory.

The Union had spent months approaching Richmond, only to have Robert E. Lee's army unravel the entire plan over the course of a few days. The Federals had had to rapidly retreat to the James River just in order to survive, abandoning the campaign that was supposed to end the war. On the Confederate side, Lee had created his own momentum by attacking McClellan at Beaver Dam Creek and had chased the Federals all the way to the James. But the Confederates had also taken heavy casualties along the way, which they could ill afford. Even worse, through bumbled and misinterpreted orders, lack of initiative by many of the commanders, and generally uncoordinated actions, they had also let what might have been their best chance to destroy the Army of the Potomac slip through their fingers.

By July 1, 1862, the Union army had reached the James River and was ready to withdraw to Harrison's Landing, the main Union supply base on the river. The day before, during the battle of Glendale, the Confederates had been unable to coordinate Lee's orders and get their troops onto the field. Major General Stonewall Jackson had also performed uncharacteristically poorly at White Oak Swamp—not his only lapse throughout the Seven Days. Because of the inability of the Confederates to pounce on the Federals while they were vulnerable, the Union army was able to get its entire force atop Malvern Hill by the next morning. The hill, set along the James River and overlooking a vast open field, was the strongest defensive position the Federals had taken during the entire campaign. McClellan set 100 pieces of artillery around the outskirts of the plateau that topped the hill, with four of his five infantry corps forming their line along the plateau's edge. A creek ran along each side of the hill, making any flank attack by the Confederates almost impossible. From this position, McClellan could cover any movement by his troops to Harrison's Landing.

Lee, by this time extremely frustrated with his generals' inability to carry out his orders, could not resist taking one more crack at the Union army. He knew that it could probably no longer be destroyed, but he, along with Major General James Longstreet, had devised a plan that could have a chance to carry the day. Longstreet had found high ground opposite the Union left that, if filled with artillery, could enfilade the Union line, enabling an infantry assault on the center of the line. Lee was willing to try, and they would run at the Federals one more time.

Unfortunately for Lee, the same problems that had plagued his army for days would arise again. It was noon before the Confederates were able to begin forming their attack line in the tree lines around Malvern Hill. Longstreet's artillery position, which was to have held 140 pieces, held only 20 because of the difficulty of getting them through the rough terrain. Even Lee contributed to the loss by issuing attack orders, then changing his mind without telling his generals. The orders read that the attack would begin with Brigadier General Lewis Armistead, who would have the best view of the effects of the bombardment, and that Armistead's attack would trigger a general assault all along the line. After discovering the problem with getting the artillery into place, Lee called off the attack, mulling alternative plans without informing his subordinates.

Soon after the Confederates had placed their 20 artillery pieces on their right, the Union guns opened up, quickly taking out nearly every one of them. Meanwhile, Union skirmishers were firing on Armistead, who counterattacked in an attempt to stop the harassment. Major General John Magruder, seeing Armistead's movement, followed the orders he had been given and assaulted the Union line at 4:45 PM. The Federal artillery, 100 guns, now turned its attention to the charging Confederate

Union artillery placed atop Malvern Hill, Richmond National Battlefield Park.

infantry, switching from solid shot to canister and launching it at the charging men in gray, decimating their ranks.

Shortly before 6 PM Major General D. H. Hill, who was to the left of Magruder, threw his men into the fight. Hill's troops were able to make a running charge to within 200 yards of the Union line, but the Federal infantry opened a deadly fire on them, stopping them in their tracks. Within an hour Hill's men were forced to return to their original position. Magruder had fared only somewhat better—his men got to within 20 yards of the Union line—but his result was the same. The high bluff of Malvern Hill, along with the guns massed atop it, was unforgiving.

The Confederate attacks continued all along the line until nightfall, but no progress was made. Although McClellan's army had suffered 3,000 casualties, it was able to reach Harrison's Landing safely, where it would remain for over a month before heading home. The Confederates, in their desperate attempt to not let the Union army get away, had lost 5,355 men at Malvern Hill. Over the Seven Days, the Confederate casualties totaled over 20,000, and although the threat to Richmond had gone away, the chance to destroy the Army of the Potomac and win the war was lost. As for McClellan, although his much larger army had escaped with 15,849 casualties, his Peninsula campaign had ended in failure, and his reputation for slowness and timidity was now well cemented.

Petersburg—the Siege

After the devastating charge at Cold Harbor, Grant realized that a direct assault on Richmond would not work. Lee would stay between him and the capital, and stalemated slaughter would continue. But there was another way. Just south of Richmond was the city of Petersburg, a major transportation hub that directly fed the city of Richmond. With the exception of the Richmond & Danville Railroad from the west, all other remaining rail links to Richmond passed through Petersburg. As Grant stated, "the key to taking Richmond is Petersburg."

But it was not quite that simple. The Union army was still in its lines at Cold Harbor, and any movement to Petersburg would expose the Army of the Potomac to an attack. On the night of June 12, 1864, the Union army quietly began to sneak south. The corps of Major Generals Gouverneur Warren and Winfield Scott Hancock, who had held the Union left at Cold Harbor, stayed in their positions while the corps of Major Generals Horatio Wright, William Smith, and Ambrose Burnside slipped behind them. When these three had passed, Warren and Hancock acted as their rear guard, following them out of the lines. All five of the corps took separate routes to Charles City, with the exception of Warren, who held a position south at Riddell's Shop as the rest of the army passed behind him. When Lee's Confederates awoke the next morning to find the Federals missing, they moved south to Malvern Hill, assuming that Grant was again trying to outflank the Confederate right. Lee's suspicions were seemingly confirmed by the movement of Brigadier General James Wilson's cavalry, which had been left behind to actively demonstrate in front of the Confederates while the Union army crossed the James.

Hancock's corps was the first to cross the James River and did so by ferry on June 14 and 15. While Hancock crossed, Union engineers built a pontoon bridge across the

The Crater, Petersburg National Battlefield.

river; the bridge was 2,100 feet long and designed to withstand both the strong current and a 4-foot rise and fall with the tide. The engineers completed the bridge in one day, a truly remarkable feat, and the remaining corps were able to cross on foot on the 15th and 16th, as did Wilson's cavalry. Smith's corps, which had initially been with Major General Benjamin Butler's Army of the James, rejoined Butler at Bermuda Hundred, then crossed the Appomattox by pontoon bridge and approached Petersburg from the north. Robert E. Lee had been completely outsmarted and to his surprise learned that the Army of the Potomac was suddenly south of the James River.

When Smith began to envelop Petersburg on June 15, 1864, the city was strongly fortified but lightly defended. The Confederates well understood the importance of Petersburg, but most of its troops had been shifted north to Lee's army to protect Richmond. General P. G. T. Beauregard, in charge of the Petersburg defenses known as the Dimmock Line, had only 5,400 troops to man the 55 redans, artillery batteries that could easily be shifted for either frontal or flanking fire. Smith, moving cautiously,

Reproduction of the legendary Union mortar "The Dictator," Petersburg National Battlefield.

attacked redans numbers five and six at 7 PM and moved down the line for over a mile, capturing redans seven through eleven but stopping after hearing that Lee was on his way to reinforce the defenses. Had Smith proceeded he probably would have captured Petersburg outright, because Lee was still at Malvern Hill. Hancock arrived the next day to take over for Smith's exhausted corps, capturing more of the line but still not taking the city, even though the only reinforcements Beauregard had received were his own, removing the remaining men who were manning the Howlett Line that had bottled up Butler's army at Bermuda Hundred. The Confederate strength at Petersburg was now 14,000. Burnside's corps arrived that night and attacked on the 17th, but by that time Lee's army was rushing to the Petersburg defenses.

By the time the Federals launched their first full-scale assault on June 18, elements of Lee's army were in Petersburg to meet them, and reinforcements continued arriving throughout the day. Lee himself took command at 11:30 AM. The Federals had lost a good chance to take Petersburg by direct assault and possibly end the war very quickly. Instead they would have to lay siege to the city for another 10 months.

Of course, nobody wanted to wait that long. Shortly after the siege began, an idea was brought forward by Lieutenant Colonel Henry Pleasants, commander of the 48th Pennsylvania Infantry, part of Major General Ambrose Burnside's corps. No one is sure whether the idea belonged to Pleasants or one of his men. Had it been carried out as planned and been successful, it likely would have been hailed as genius, but in the end no one wanted credit for it. The 48th Pennsylvania was made up in large part from men who had been coal miners before the war. It was proposed that the miners dig a tunnel beneath the no-man's-land between the trenches all the way to one of the Confederate redans, a distance of over 500 feet. The tunnel would then be packed with explosives, which would be detonated, blasting a huge gap in the Confederate line. Burnside took the plan to Grant and Meade, who were skeptical but gave their approval.

As the miners dug the tunnel, black troops under Brigadier General Edward Ferrero were trained on the operation, which would certainly be a unique one, and how to execute it. The black soldiers would wait for the blast, go around the crater, and advance outward, leading the way for waiting divisions to pour through the gap. In addition, Grant would create pressure on Richmond, drawing troops north of the James River to fight the first battle of Deep Bottom. However, only 12 hours before the assault was to begin, Meade directed a stunned Burnside to withdraw Ferrero's men from the operation and send a white division to lead the attack. Meade had foreseen possible disaster in the assault, which would look politically bad if it were perceived that black soldiers were sent to slaughter. So with Grant's approval, Ferrero's men were out and were replaced by the brigade of General James Ledlie, with no time to train the new men.

On July 30, 1864, at 4:40 AM, the explosives were detonated, blowing a 170-foot-wide hole in the Confederate fortifications. Those Confederates who were not killed or wounded ran in every direction, abandoning their positions. Ledlie's men charged the breach, moving slowly through the Union abatis and other obstructions that were supposed to have been moved but were not. They then reached the crater and jumped right into it. They were quickly followed by two other white divisions, who did the same thing. The problem was that Ledlie's brigade had not left the crater. When they entered they found a 30-foot wall on the opposite side, and they could not climb out. When the new brigades came in, they simply began to fill the crater with Union troops, with no means of escape. Effective command may have been able to lead them out. But Brigadier General James Ledlie, just as he had been at the battle of North Anna, was dead drunk, hiding in a dugout.

By this time the Confederates had begun to return to the area and found the human equivalent of fish in a barrel. They began to fire into the crater, picking off the officers first and then going after the troops, and soon their artillery was brought up. After 8 AM Ferrero's black troops were finally brought in and moved around the crater as they had been trained to do, trying to push the Confederate attackers off the rim. But by now the Confederates were everywhere, and the new troops could do nothing. After hand-to-hand fighting, the Confederates finally took possession of the crater at 1 PM. For the Union it had been a complete disaster. The Confederates had taken 1,491 casualties, 300 or so of them when the mine was detonated. But the Federals had lost 3,798 men in what was regarded afterward as a harebrained scheme. Burnside took the brunt of the blame and was relieved of command, although he did rejoin Grant's army later.

After the battle of the Crater, Grant continued his strategy of extending his siege lines to the west, cutting off roads and railroads and forcing the Confederates to stretch their poorly manned lines even more thinly. Union operations also continued north of the James River so that Lee would be forced to occasionally take troops from the Petersburg lines to protect Richmond. The months passed, then the winter, and by the spring of 1865 the only routes left into Petersburg were the South Side Railroad from the west and the Boydton Plank Road from the southwest. The Boydton Plank Road was Lee's lifeline to the long-since severed Weldon & Petersburg Railroad, which led to the Confederacy's only open port at Wilmington, North Carolina. The train was forced to stop well south of Petersburg, where supplies were then loaded onto wagons that made their way into the city by the road. It was a slow process, but it was all that Lee had.

On the Confederate side of the lines, things had gotten very bad. By spring Lee had lost thousands of soldiers to desertion, surrender, and disease as the futility and stress of holding out took its toll. In addition, Wilmington fell soon after Fort Fisher was captured; and more important, the Shenandoah Valley, the "breadbasket of the Confederacy," had been completely cleaned out by Philip Sheridan's campaign the previous fall and was no longer a source of supply. Lee had weakened his own lines to send troops to defend both the Shenandoah and Wilmington, and now they were gone for good. Knowing that Grant was about to launch his spring offensive, the Confederates saw only one possible option for survival. They would have to attack and temporarily stun Grant, enabling an escape from the Petersburg and Richmond defenses and a quick march south to join Joseph Johnston's army in North Carolina. Their combined forces would then attempt to destroy the Union army under General Sherman, which was making its way north through the Carolinas, and afterward return north and face Grant with renewed strength. It was a desperate plan, but the Confederates were desperate.

The attack would be against Fort Stedman, east of Petersburg on the Union right. Lee positioned nearly half his entire army of 60,000 men in Colquitt's Salient, across from the Union fort. At 4 AM on March 25, 1865, a small group of Confederates with

SITE DETAILS

Petersburg National Battlefield—The sites of the initial assault on Petersburg in June 1864, the battle of the Crater, and Fort Stedman are all within the Eastern Front unit of Petersburg National Battlefield, running east and south of the city. Various smaller pieces of the park are scattered across the city of Petersburg, but this unit contains much of the original siege lines, in addition to the park's main visitor's center. The visitor's center contains museum exhibits and audiovisual programs describing the siege and its effects, and a short walking trail near the center will take you to Battery 5, the first redan of the Dimmock Line captured during the initial assault on Petersburg, as well as past a reproduction of "The Dictator," a monstrous Union mortar that was used during the siege. The driving tour leading from the visitor's center will take you to Fort Stedman, as well as to some of the surrounding batteries used during the battle, and the remnants of the Crater. Also along the driving tour are other well-preserved earthworks, as well as reconstructions of the original siege defenses, complete with abatis, chevaux-de-frise, and other contrivances. Note that the address given by the park will not lead you to the park itself, and the area around the entrance is complicated by the nearby U.S. Army base at Fort Lee. If you're using a GPS system, use the address given here; otherwise it may be best to follow the signs through the city. *Petersburg National Battlefield, 5001 Siege Rd., Petersburg, VA, 23803; 804-732-3531; www.nps.gov/pete. Open daily; admission charged.*

Petersburg Siege Museum—Within the city of Petersburg is the Petersburg Siege Museum, a collection of artifacts and recollections from the citizens of Petersburg about the war, the siege, and reconstruction, as well as some other local history. Also near the museum is the Petersburg courthouse, which survived the war and is recognizable from virtually every collection of Civil War photographs ever published. *Siege Museum, 15 W. Bank St., Petersburg, VA, 23803; 804-733-2400; www.petersburg-va.org/tourism/siege.htm. Open daily; admission charged.*

axes began to cut through the Union obstructions between the two lines, creating a gap through which the Confederates could charge. Just behind them were the rest of the Confederate infantry, led by Major General John Gordon. The Confederates stormed Fort Stedman and were quickly able to create a huge gap in the Union line, nearly 1,000 feet wide and containing three batteries. But even though Gordon kept sending troops through the gap, a Union counterattack against the weakened Confederates was able to stop them. Before long the Federals were taking their line back, and the Confederates were forced to withdraw. Union troops kept after them, using the surrounding positions to put the Confederates in a crossfire and capturing many of them. The day ended with 2,681 Confederate casualties to the Union's 1,017.

The assault on Fort Stedman was the Army of Northern Virginia's last gasp. Lee shifted many of his troops to the Confederate right, knowing that Grant would soon resume his push for the Boydton Plank Road and the South Side Railroad. The writing was on the wall, and it was only a matter of days before the fate of Petersburg, and the Confederacy with it, would be decided.

Five Forks

The intersection of the White Oak Road, Dinwiddie Court House Road, Scott's Road, and Ford's Road west of Petersburg, known as Five Forks, was the site of the final battle outside Petersburg before Robert E. Lee's army was forced to retreat. The result here spelled the beginning of the end of the Army of Northern Virginia, and thus Richmond and the Confederate States of America.

After Major General George Pickett, with the help of cavalry, had kept Union cavalry in place at the battle of Dinwiddie Court House on March 31, developments in his rear forced Pickett to abandon his position. Major General Gouverneur Warren, who had led Federal troops at the battle of White Oak Road the same day, had begun to move 16,000 infantry to support Major General Philip Sheridan's 12,000 men at Dinwiddie Court House. Pickett decided that he had no choice but to withdraw to Five Forks, a crucial intersection that led directly to the South Side Railroad, the final line of supply into Petersburg now that the Federals controlled the Boydton Plank Road. Pickett withdrew from Dinwiddie Court House at 5 AM on April 1, 1865, pulling back to Five Forks, where the Confederates had already constructed formidable earthworks, stretching almost 2 miles along the White Oak Road, with both flanks turned in and well-protected by cavalry, and artillery scattered along the entire front. Pickett ordered his men to strengthen their defenses, and he received orders from Lee to hold the vital crossroads at all costs. Then he left his troops and went to a shad bake, apparently thinking that the situation was under control.

Seeing that Pickett had pulled back, Sheridan's men followed him to Five Forks, anticipating that Warren's infantry would be joining them. Although some elements

The critical crossroads at Five Forks, part of Petersburg National Battlefield.

of Warren's corps did join Sheridan as they advanced along the Dinwiddie Court House Road, Sheridan did not know where the rest of Warren's men were, and by the time he reached Five Forks he was growing impatient with General Warren. Meanwhile, because of poor maps issued by Sheridan's staff, Warren's men were delayed reaching the field and set up for their assault a full three-quarters of a mile east of the nearest Confederate position. It was 4 PM by the time the Union soldiers were in position. Sheridan's cavalry would attack the front of the line, while Warren would flank the Confederate left.

The attack began with Sheridan's dismounted cavalry pressing the Confederate front, while Warren's infantry marched toward the White Oak Road, where they were to wheel to the west and envelop the Confederate flank. Reaching the road and finding no Confederates, the infantry advanced westward until they found some, and began to roll up the Confederate line, with some units even able to pass around the Confederate flank and attack their rear, going all the way around the line to Ford's road and advancing south to the intersection. On the Confederate right, Brigadier General George Armstrong Custer's cavalry was able to outflank this side of the line, driving the Confederate cavalry under Major General W. H. F. "Rooney" Lee out of their position.

The Confederates at Five Forks were now being assaulted on all sides, and by the time Pickett was able to return from his picnic, it was far too late. Most of the Confederates surrendered, while others were able to escape into the woods surrounding the intersection. The Federals had Five Forks, and they now had easy access to the South Side Railroad. The Confederates had lost 3,000 men, mostly captured, to the Union's 830. A still-angry Sheridan, who had been given authorization by Grant earlier in the day to relieve Warren if he felt it necessary, replaced him with Brigadier General Charles Griffin; Warren was given command of Richmond after the evacuation of the city two days later. After 10 months of siege warfare, Petersburg was finally on the verge of falling.

Petersburg—the Breakthrough

It was time. Since the siege of Petersburg began in mid-June of 1864, with the exception of the battle of the Crater, Ulysses S. Grant's army had made no direct assaults on the Confederate defensive line south of the James. But after almost 10 months, the Federals had won the battle at Five Forks on April 1, 1865, enabling them to sever the South Side Railroad, the last line of supply into Petersburg. There was no need to wait. The decisive assault against Petersburg would be launched immediately.

On the night of the Five Forks battle, preparations for a general assault along the entire Confederate line were made. Artillery bombardment of the Confederate works was increasing, softening them up for the next morning's action. The Union troops were put into their formations, forced to wait out the long night knowing what was coming the next day. At 4:40 AM on April 2, 1865, the attack began near the Union left. A mass of 18,000 troops under Major General Horatio Wright, charging in a wedge-shaped formation as if to literally pierce the Confederate line, began the assault. Wright had picked his spot along the line, finding gaps in the obstructions in front of Lieutenant General A. P. Hill's corps. Although Wright lost 1,100 men in the first 15 minutes of the assault, the Union troops were able to break the Confederate defenses and began to move west, rolling up the line. Trying to rally his men, Hill rode frantically among the routed soldiers, until he came upon Union troops and was killed on the spot.

To Wright's left, Major Generals Edward Ord and Andrew Humphreys were also able to overrun the Confederate defenses in the wake of Wright's success. To the right, Major General John Parke assaulted the Confederate works in front of the city but was prevented from breaking the line by Major General John Gordon's Confederates. The other Union corps began to push the Confederates back toward Petersburg and by mid-afternoon had reached the inner defense lines west of the city. There, Confederate Forts Gregg and Whitworth were able to stall the Federals while Major General James Longstreet brought troops into the Petersburg defenses, forming an inner line to hold the city.

Although the Confederates kept fighting, the outcome of the battle was fairly obvious by midmorning, and Lee began to consider his options for withdrawal. He sent word to Jefferson Davis in Richmond, telling him that he should evacuate the

Abatis *and* chevaux-de-frise *at Pamplin Historical Park, site of the Union breakthrough of the Confederate defenses at Petersburg.*

SITE DETAILS

Pamplin Historical Park & the National Museum of the Civil War Soldier—At first glance, this park may seem to some a sort of Civil War theme park, a high-production, high-cost fantasyland. It is not. It is much more; in fact it is outstanding. Your experience begins at the National Museum of the Civil War Soldier, an interactive set of exhibits about life on the front lines of the war that is extremely educational and entertaining. There are also several outdoor classrooms and demonstration areas around the museum. Walking down a trail will lead you to an antebellum farm, and farther on is a reconstructed earthwork exhibit, where you can get close and personal with the fortifications used during the period, as opposed to the "do not touch" approach that most parks must take, Next comes the Battlefield Center, where the battle of the Breakthrough at Petersburg is demonstrated in rich detail by two films, one short and one long, which are both very well done, as well as artifacts and other exhibits. Finally, the highlight of the park is a trail system winding through the actual location of the breakthrough of the Confederate lines on April 2, 1865. The trails are divided nicely so that you can take either a very short or a very long walk through the remaining earthworks. All the exhibits mentioned above can be seen either through self-guided observation or guided tours. Finally, through prior arrangement, the park offers limited tour opportunities of the Civil War sites in the area, as well as "Civil War Adventure Camp," available to all ages and families, and varying from day experiences to overnight stays. Pamplin Historical Park is a wonderful surprise, is great for families, and is a necessary stop on your Civil War journey. *Pamplin Historical Park & the National Museum of the Civil War Soldier, 6125 Boydton Plank Rd., Petersburg, VA, 23803; 1-877-726-7546; www.pamplinpark.org. Open daily; admission charged.*

government that evening. Lee knew that he had to get his now-scattered troops all to the same place, at the same time, to avoid the army's destruction. At 3 PM he issued the instructions for withdrawal to all his generals. All forces were to head for Amelia Court House, west of Petersburg, at 8 PM. Lee would order a supply train to meet them there, and they would then march south to combine with the Confederate army led by Major General Joseph Johnston in the Carolinas.

As the Confederates left Richmond, an order to burn anything of military value was issued. Soon the neighboring tobacco warehouses were also aflame, and mobs of hungry citizens, who had been living on short rations, began to loot the warehouses, looking for food. The fires of Richmond alerted Grant that the Confederate army was gone, and he immediately occupied the city and began to restore order, putting out the fires and receiving its surrender at 8:15 the next morning. He was also making preparations to move west. He could not let the Confederate army get away.

Appomattox

Although battles were still occurring across the country, and Confederate and Union forces would still maneuver around each other for another two months, the Confederate surrender at Appomattox, for all intents and purposes, signaled the end of the Civil War. Even though President Jefferson Davis tried to continue the fight, after the mighty Robert E. Lee surrendered, all other Confederate military leaders in the country took their cue, and the fighting stopped. The entire country knew that Lee's surrender meant that the terrible nightmare of the American Civil War was about to end.

Lee's army, after evacuating Petersburg on the night of April 2, 1865, had not stopped moving. Lee's intention was to find a way south to combine with Joseph Johnston's army, which was still fighting Sherman's army in North Carolina. But Grant would not let it happen. Grant's huge army pursued Lee doggedly, attacking Lee's rear with infantry while keeping the Federal cavalry south, blocking every possible route to North Carolina. The Confederates were forced to march through the nights and without rations, and many of them fell by the wayside. By the time Lee got to Appomattox Court House on April 8, his army numbered under 32,000, having lost almost half its men along the way. Now, at Appomattox, he had Union cavalry in front of him and infantry behind. He had hoped to meet a supply train here, but the Union cavalry dashed all hopes of feeding his men.

Lee knew the end was coming, and so did Grant. Grant sent his first request for Lee's surrender on April 7, and Lee refused. Grant sent another note the next day, offering

Reconstruction of the McLean house, scene of Robert E. Lee's surrender at Appomattox.

SITE DETAILS

Appomattox Court House National Historical Park—Much of the former village of Appomattox Court House survives today, with one notable exception—the McLean House, where the actual surrender took place. Almost immediately after the signing, souvenir seekers began to take pieces of the house, everything from furniture to siding, and it was left in shambles, though not having seen one shot fired in combat. In 1893, after having been repaired, what was left of the house was disassembled, with plans to ship it to Washington for reassembly as a museum. Unfortunately, the company in charge of the house went bankrupt before the move, leaving the house disassembled and lying on the ground for years. Many years later, the National Park Service took on the project, opening the reconstructed home and village in 1954, with the McLean home on its original foundation. Touring the house today is a treat, and even if it's not exactly the same room that the surrender took place in, it is the same airspace. The park's visitor's center is located in the also-reconstructed Appomattox Court House and contains a museum describing the events of the surrender. Walking through the village today, in the quiet countryside, will take you back to that great day in 1865. *Appomattox Court House National Historical Park, intersection of VA 24 and VA 627, Appomattox, VA, 24522; 434-352-8987; www.nps .gov/apco. Open daily; admission charged.*

possible terms for the surrender. Lee responded that the two should meet, but Grant replied that he would not meet unless the Confederates were ready to surrender.

On the night of April 8, Lee met with Generals James Longstreet, John Gordon, and Fitzhugh Lee to discuss their options. Fitz Lee and Gordon thought that the retreat could be continued if only Sheridan's Union cavalry was in their path, but if Sheridan was also supported by infantry, they would not be able to break through. Lee set the attack for 5 AM.

That morning, April 9, while Longstreet held a line facing east, Gordon and Fitz Lee went forward, initially pushing the Federal cavalry back. But they were not pushing; Sheridan was pulling. Behind the Union cavalry lay the infantry corps of Major General John Gibbon. Seeing the infantry in front, both Confederate commanders immediately pulled back. There was no escape. Lee knew now that there was no choice but surrender.

Although he received word that Fitz Lee's cavalry was able to break past the Federals and escape after all, Robert E. Lee ordered his commanders to call for a truce. Lee responded to Grant's message, stating that he was ready to discuss surrender. One of Lee's officers chose the meeting place, the home of Wilbur McLean, who had moved to Appomattox to escape the war. His previous home had been in Manassas,

Virginia. Lee arrived at the home, sat in the parlor, and waited about 30 minutes for Grant to arrive. Lee, as he had been doing often for the past week as he anticipated his possible capture or surrender, was wearing his best uniform, while Grant was wearing a ragged private's uniform with a general's stars on it. After exchanging pleasantries and a few reminiscences about their service in the Mexican War, Grant proposed his surrender terms, which he had already written out to Lee in the note the previous day. Lee asked one other condition: that the men be allowed to keep their horses, which most of them had ridden out to the war and would need for their farms. Grant agreed, and also authorized the immediate transfer of rations to feed Lee's soldiers. The documents were signed, and then the two great generals left, leaving their staffs to work out the details of the proceedings.

On April 12, 1865, Brigadier General Joshua Lawrence Chamberlain formally received the surrender of the Confederates. Both armies behaved with honor, showing mutual respect after four long years of hard fighting. Some 620,000 men were dead, with millions more wounded. But slavery had been abolished, and states, once bitterly divided, again became a nation. The United States of America had survived the Civil War.

» OTHER SITES IN SOUTHERN VIRGINIA

Yellow Tavern—As the Union and Confederate armies were maneuvering around Spotsylvania Court House, Major General Philip Sheridan led 12,000 Union troopers on the first large cavalry raid in over two months. Sheridan's men rode to the east to

Memorial where General J. E. B. Stuart fell at the battle of Yellow Tavern.

get around Spotsylvania, and then went south to cut the Virginia Central Railroad and hit other targets behind Lee's lines. The Federal cavalry took its time as it went, hoping to draw the Confederate cavalry—no longer the fighting force it once was—into an engagement. That engagement came on May 11, 1864, at Yellow Tavern north of Richmond. The Confederates, numbering 5,000 men, were led by their gallant commander, J. E. B. Stuart. They formed a line of battle, and repeated Union charges were unable to budge them, until Brigadier General George Armstrong Custer finally broke the center of the line. As the Confederates counterattacked, Stuart, as he always did, rode with them. He was mortally wounded and died the next day. Sheridan returned to the Army of the Potomac on May 24.

A large memorial marks the spot near where Stuart fell, in the town of Glen Allen. A Virginia Civil War Trails interpretive sign is also at the site. In addition, the National Park Service has developed a driving tour outlining the sites of the battle; the tour is very good, although most of the sites have now been lost to development. The brochure is available at the Fredericksburg & Spotsylvania National Military Park, as well as on the park's Web site. *J. E. B. Stuart Memorial, intersection of Harmony Rd. and Telegraph Rd., Glen Allen, VA, 23059. Open daily. Driving tour, Battle of Yellow Tavern, Fredericksburg & Spotsylvania National Military Park, 1013 Lafayette Blvd., Fredericksburg, VA, 22401; 540-373-6122; www.nps.gov/frsp/yellow.htm. Open daily.*

North Anna—The Confederate army left Spotsylvania Court House on May 21, 1864, to protect the Telegraph Road, a major artery that led to Richmond. Robert E. Lee had

Part of the trail at North Anna Battlefield Park.

expected the Union army to do what it had done on every previous occasion: stop to rest and recuperate. But Ulysses S. Grant would have none of it and pursued Lee's army, reaching Lee's position on the North Anna River on May 23. Lee, thinking that it was only an advance party, did not commit his entire force, allowing the Federals to capture the Telegraph Road bridge to his east that night with relative ease, while also crossing at Jericho Mills to the west. Left with few options, Lee brilliantly constructed a defensive line that formed a V with its angle on the river at Ox Ford, and the two wings of his army close enough together that either could support the other easily if needed. At the same time it would force Grant to split his army three ways, one on each flank of the Confederate line and one in the middle; one side trying to support the other would have to cross the North Anna River twice. Unfortunately for the Confederates, Lee also became extremely ill with dysentery that night and was unable to command. The next morning, May 24, the Federals attacked. The Confederates' earthworks were extremely strong, and Union assaults were driven back at Ox Ford in the center and at the Doswell House on the Union left. The attack at Ox Ford was particularly brutal, due in great part to the insistence of Brigadier General James Ledlie, who was extremely drunk, to repeatedly assault an obviously strong Confederate position. Both sides skirmished for the next two days before Grant moved south on the night of May 26, threatening Richmond. Union losses were 2,623, and Confederate, 2,517.

The site of the heaviest fighting of the battle of the North Anna, Ox Ford, has been preserved at North Anna Battlefield Park. The walking tour contains extremely well done interpretive signs and takes you right through the heart of the battlefield. Although the trails can be a bit confusing, your walk through the peaceful woods will be enjoyable. One note: There is no indication at the site of the trail's length, which is considerable. If you visit, be sure that you come prepared for a decent hike (water, insect repellent, etc.) and have set enough time aside to complete the trail, which is not strenuous but does pass through some hilly terrain. For the other battlefield sites, the National Park Service has a driving tour brochure available at the Fredericksburg & Spotsylvania National Military Park, and also downloadable from the park's Web site. *North Anna Battlefield Park, 0.1 mile north of Verdon Rd. and New Market Mill Rd., Doswell, VA, 23047; 804-365-4695; www.co.hanover.va.us/parksrec/park info_nabp.htm. Open daily. Driving tour, Battle of North Anna, Fredericksburg & Spotsylvania National Military Park, 1013 Lafayette Blvd., Fredericksburg, VA, 22401; 540-373-6122; www.nps.gov/frsp/nanna.htm. Open daily.*

Hanover Court House—On May 27, 1862, McClellan, sensing a threat on his right flank, ordered a Union force to Hanover Court House northeast of Richmond. A Confederate brigade of 4,000 men was in the area and attacked the Federals, who were commanded by Brigadier General Fitz John Porter. The Union troops were able to drive the Confederates off quickly, and left a small detachment behind to guard

Peake's Crossing in their rear. When the Confederates went after the crossing, Porter wheeled his entire command of 12,000 men around and hit them again.

Hanover Tavern, present at the time of the battle, is still there and is the site of a Virginia Civil War Trails sign describing the battle. The courthouse itself is also still standing, as are several other small buildings from the original village. The tavern is now home to a fine restaurant and dinner theater and is also open for tours. *Virginia Civil War Trails—Hanover Tavern, 13181 Hanover Courthouse Rd., Hanover, VA, 23069. Sign accessible daily.*

Haw's Shop—Attempting to gain possession of a crossroads at Haw's Shop on May 28, 1864, Union cavalry under Brigadier Generals David Gregg and Alfred Torbert attacked cavalry led by Major Generals Wade Hampton and Fitzhugh Lee, arranged in a defensive line near Enon Church. Although the Confederates were initially able to resist the assaults, the line was broken late in the day with the arrival of Brigadier General George Custer's brigade, and the Federals were able to seize the crossroads.

Enon Church still stands, dating back to the time of the battle, and two Virginia Civil War Trails interpretive signs describe the action. The area is rural, and the battlefield is still easily recognizable with the help of the signs. *Virginia Civil War Trails— Salem Church / Haw's Shop & Enon Church, 6156 Studley Rd., Mechanicsville, VA, 23116. Signs accessible daily.*

Totopotomoy Creek—General Grant, trying to outmaneuver Robert E. Lee's Army of Northern Virginia and lure it into the open to fight, began to move east of Richmond. The Federals soon found the Confederates, who had fortified a line along Totopotomoy Creek. On May 29, 1864, the Federals attempted several crossings of the creek but were denied each time. Grant sent a unit around the Confederate right in an attempt to outflank Lee, but Lee, knowing the importance of not letting the Union troops approach Richmond, sent Major General Jubal Early against the advancing Union left. Although the Confederates were initially able to push the Federals back at Bethesda Church, a counterattack quickly drove the Confederates back to their original position.

Virginia Civil War Trails interpretive signs are located at the Rural Point Elementary School and at Polegreen Church Historic Site. The historic site, a newly developed public park, has a short trail leading through a steel skeleton of the re-created church; the original, built in 1748, was destroyed by artillery fire in the days following the battle at Totopotomoy Creek. Finally, there is a large memorial to the 36th Wisconsin Volunteer Infantry; it is located on a busy road, so use caution in viewing it. *Virginia Civil War Trails—Fighting at the Totopotomoy, Rural Point Elementary School, 7161 Studley Rd.; Polegreen Church Historic Site, intersection of Rural Point Rd. and Heatherwood Dr.; 36th Wisconsin Volunteer Infantry Monument, intersection of Pole Green Rd. and Sherrington Dr., Mechanicsville, VA, 23116; 804-266-6186; www .historicpolegreen.org. Open daily.*

Old Church—Seeking to gain the important crossroads at Old Cold Harbor, the Union sent cavalry led by Brigadier General Alfred Torbert against the crossroads, guarded by Major General Wade Hampton's Confederates, on May 30, 1864. After a brisk fight at Matadequin Creek, the Federals were able to drive the Confederates back, forcing them to withdraw toward the crossroads.

The site of Old Church, very near the Cold Harbor battlefield, is marked with a historical highway marker, although it does not mention the Civil War. Information can be found at the Cold Harbor Visitor Center of Richmond National Battlefield Park. *Historical highway marker—APVA Hanover Chapter (Old Church), intersection of Old Church Rd. and McClellan Rd., Mechanicsville, VA, 23111. Site accessible daily.*

Walkerton—In late February 1864 the Union launched a large cavalry raid against the Virginia Central Railroad leading into Richmond. The raid was led by Brigadier General H. Judson Kilpatrick, commanding almost 4,000 men, including 460 men under Colonel Ulric Dahlgren, son of Rear Admiral John Dahlgren. Colonel Dahlgren led an advance party whose goal was to release Union prisoners kept at the large Belle Isle prison camp in Richmond. As Kilpatrick attacked the Richmond defenses, then withdrew to the south, Dahlgren and 100 other troopers were forced to head east to avoid capture. On March 2 Dahlgren's party was ambushed near Walkerton; the entire force was captured with the exception of Dahlgren, who was shot dead. Found in Dahlgren's pocket were orders to penetrate the Richmond defenses, assassinate President Jefferson Davis and his cabinet, and torch the city. While the U.S. government denied having anything to do with the order, debate over the facts remains to this day.

A historical highway marker has been placed near the site of the ambush and Dahlgren's death. Information can also be found at the King and Queen County Courthouse Tavern Museum in the town of King and Queen Courthouse. *Historical highway marker OB-6—Virginia Historic Landmarks Commission (Where Dahlgren Died), 0.1 mile south of intersection of Hockley Neck Rd. and Stevensville Rd., Stevensville, VA, 23161. King and Queen County Courthouse Tavern Museum, 400 Court House Landing Rd., King and Queen Court House, VA, 23085; 804-785-9558; www.kingandqueenmuseum.com. Sign accessible daily; museum open Fri.–Sun., admission charged.*

Eltham's Landing—When the Confederates left the York River open by withdrawing up the Virginia Peninsula, Union troops came up by boat and landed at Eltham's Landing at West Point on May 6. General Joseph Johnston, who had his Confederate army only 5 miles beyond the landing site, ordered Major General John Bell Hood to keep the Federals off his back. Hood's rearguard action became an attack, and he was able to scatter the Federals during his maneuver on May 7, 1862, withdrawing when Union reinforcements arrived.

A historical highway marker has been placed near the site of the fighting, about 1 mile inland of the landing site. *Historical highway marker WO-31—Conservation &*

Development Commission (Peninsular Campaign), intersection of Eltham Rd. and Virginia Ave., West Point, VA, 23181. Sign accessible daily.

Saint Mary's Church—Following the cavalry battle at Trevilian Station, Major General Philip Sheridan's Union cavalry headed east, then south to protect a wagon train to the James River supply base. On June 24, 1864, elements of Sheridan's cavalry led by Brigadier General David Gregg were attacked by Confederate forces near Saint Mary's Church on the Virginia Peninsula. Overwhelmed, the Federals were able to hold for a time but were ultimately put on the retreat.

A historical highway marker near the battlefield, referring to the battle by its alternative name of Nance's Shop, is located in Charles City. *Historical highway marker PH-6—Virginia Conservation and Development Commission (Action of Nance's Shop), 0.8 mile west of intersection of Barnett's Rd. and Old Union Rd., Charles City, VA, 23030. Sign accessible daily.*

Yorktown—George McClellan's first Confederate encounter as he marched up the Virginia Peninsula was Major General John Magruder's earthworks at Yorktown. The Confederate trenches stretched across the entire width of the peninsula, from the York River to the James River, and included the works left over from the great British surrender that had ended the fighting in the American Revolution 81 years before. Magruder had only 11,000 men to the Union's 118,000 when McClellan approached on April 5, 1862, but through deception and tactics resembling those seen in a bad movie, Magruder was able to move his troops around and be seen in such a manner that led McClellan to believe that he had many more. One Confederate lieutenant recalled that during the siege that McClellan decided upon, which would last a month, his unit marched from one river to the other and back six times. During that month the Confederates not only were able to add men to Magruder's force, bringing it to 55,000 by the end of the siege, but, more important, had time to greatly improve the Richmond defenses. McClellan finally decided that he had had enough and planned to assault the Confederate trenches on May 6, after a heavy bombardment of the works. The Confederates withdrew on the night of May 3.

The historians at Colonial National Historical Park, obviously experts on Cornwallis's surrender during the American Revolution, are also well versed in the Civil War activity in the area. Many of the earthworks within the park were also used by the Confederates, and the materials and interpretive signs help point out which were used. *Colonial National Historical Park, intersection of Colonial National Historical Parkway and Ballard St., Yorktown, VA, 23690; 757-898-3400; www.nps.gov/colo. Open daily; admission charged.*

Williamsburg—As the Confederates withdrew up the Virginia Peninsula after leaving the Yorktown defenses, the Union was able to hit the rear guard at Williamsburg on May 5, 1862. The Confederates took cover in and around the earthwork they had named Fort Magruder and were able to repulse the Union attack. Occupying some of the Confederates' abandoned works as they moved forward, Union troops assaulted the Confederate left in midafternoon and were able to repulse a Confederate counterattack later in the day. The Confederates eventually fell back after performing their duty, allowing the rest of the army to continue toward Richmond undisturbed.

The site of Fort Magruder has been marked with memorials and a Virginia Civil War Trails interpretive sign. Although the area is fenced off, it is accessible. One of the heaviest areas of fighting, Bloody Ravine, is also marked by a VCWT sign. Parts of the battlefield also lie within Colonial National Historical Park. *Virginia Civil War Trails— Fort Magruder, intersection of Penniman Rd. and Queens Creek Rd.; Virginia Civil War Trails—Battle of Williamsburg, 7135 Pocahontas Trail, Williamsburg, VA, 23185. Signs accessible daily.*

Wilson's Wharf—When Major General Benjamin Butler began his Bermuda Hundred campaign, he established several fortified bases along the way, including one called Fort Pocahontas at Wilson's Wharf. On May 24, 1864, a force of 2,500 Confederate cavalry under Major General Fitzhugh Lee assaulted the fort, but the Union garrison of 1,100, with the help of a gunboat in the James River, was able to hold the position.

Fort Pocahontas is on private property but is open by private appointment and, occasionally, for public viewing and reenactments. Tours are generally reserved for large groups, but it doesn't hurt to try. There is also a historical highway marker near the site. *Fort Pocahontas at Wilson's Wharf, 13150 Sturgeon Point Rd.; historical highway marker V-34—Department of Historic Resources (Fort Pocahontas), 0.2 mile east of VA 614 and Sturgeon Point Rd., Charles City, VA, 23030; 804-829-9722; www.fortpoca hontas.org. Fort open by appointment; sign accessible daily.*

Beaver Dam Creek—The day after Major General George McClellan opened the Seven Days Battles, new Confederate commander Robert E. Lee decided to seize the initiative from him. On what became the first of his two famous "Rides around McClellan," Brigadier General J. E. B. Stuart's cavalry had discovered that the Union right was exposed. Expecting Major General Thomas "Stonewall" Jackson to arrive in time from his Shenandoah Valley campaign, Lee had planned on him to be in position to begin the attack. But Jackson did not show up until late in the day, so instead, on June 26, 1862, Major General A. P. Hill began the attack, assaulting the Union front at 3 PM. Although the Union troops, under Brigadier General Fitz John Porter, were quickly driven through the town of Mechanicsville, they soon found their entrenchments at Beaver Dam Creek and were able to hold their position, repulsing every Confederate assault. The Confederates had suffered an inordinate amount of casualties, 1,484 to the Union's 361. However, when Stonewall Jackson finally arrived, his men encamped near the Union right, threatening the Federal supply line from the Richmond & York River Railroad. McClellan suddenly decided that he now needed to use the much farther away James River as his supply base instead, which meant that his plans for besieging Richmond were over.

The Union army, almost three months into the campaign but only one day after beginning its siege, began to withdraw from Richmond and head for home.

The site of the Beaver Dam Creek fight, as well as the nearby Chickahominy Bluffs from which Lee observed troop movements, are part of the Richmond National Battlefield Park. Interpretive signs detailing the fighting are at both locations. *Richmond National Battlefield—Beaver Dam Creek, 0.2 mile east of intersection of Cold Harbor Rd. and Catlin Rd., Mechanicsville, VA, 23111; 804-226-1981; www.nps.gov/rich. Open daily.*

Garnett's and Golding's Farms—As most of Robert E. Lee's army was north of the Chickahominy River, only a few divisions were left south of the river to protect the capital at Richmond. Brigadier General Robert Toombs, a Georgia politician turned military leader, unwisely went on the attack against several Union units in the area. Late in the day on June 27, 1862, Toombs attacked the Federals at Garnett's Farm and was heavily repulsed. Ordered the next morning to find the Union line, he again attacked, this time at Golding's Farm, and was again quickly driven back.

A historical highway marker has been placed close to the site of Golding's Farm, the scene of the fighting on June 28, although the sign refers to the fighting of the 27th. There is no marker indicating the site of the Garnett farm. *Historical highway marker PA-125—Conservation & Development Commission (Seven Days Battles—Golding's Farm), intersection of N. Airport Dr. and Hanover Rd., Richmond, VA, 23075. Sign accessible daily.*

Savage's Station—The Union Army of the Potomac, trying to reach safety as quickly as possible, had Robert E. Lee's army on its tail. Knowing this, Union commander George McClellan had left strict orders for the rear guard; unfortunately, he did not put anyone in command of the rear guard. As the Federals retreated to the James River, Confederates led by Major General John Magruder hit Union forces under Major General Edwin Sumner, leading a de facto rear guard, at Savage's Station on June 29, 1862. Later in the day another Confederate unit, under Major General Lafayette McLaws, attacked Union troops led by Brigadier General John Sedgwick in the same vicinity. Before darkness ended the fight, the Confederates had inflicted 919 casualties to their own 444.

Two historical highway markers—one old, one new—are near the location of the Savage's Station battlefield. From the location of the older sign, one can actually see the battleground itself, somewhat of a rarity for the Richmond battlefields in this area. *Historical highway marker W-12—Department of Historic Resources (Battle of Savage's Station), intersection of Williamsburg Rd. and Technology Dr.; historical highway marker—Conservation and Development Commission (Seven Days Battles—Savage's Station), intersection of Meadow Rd. and Grapevine Rd., Sandston, VA, 23150. Signs accessible daily.*

Seven Pines—On both sides of the fighting, just about everybody (except for President Jefferson Davis) considered Joseph E. Johnston a premier field general, so when

Johnston was wounded at the battle of Seven Pines, everyone in the Confederacy was extremely concerned. Johnston, seeing an opportunity to attack an isolated portion of McClellan's army advancing upon Richmond, had ordered Major General James Longstreet to attack the Union right. Through confusion of orders, only a portion of Longstreet's command, led by Major General A. P. Hill, attacked, and did so five hours late. But Hill's assault was successful, and he was able to penetrate the Union line, forcing the Federals to fall back. Johnston rode out to watch the fighting and was seriously wounded. Late in the day, the Federals were able to inflict heavy casualties on the Confederates. The attack resumed the next day, with the Union commanders having reformed their line to a more defensible position. They were able to repulse all the Confederate assaults, and the battle was over by noon. Of the battles of McClellan's Peninsula campaign before the Seven Days, this was by far the costliest for both sides, with the Confederates suffering 6,100 casualties and the Union 5,000. Johnston, whose loss was deeply regretted at the time, was replaced in command by Robert E. Lee, who renamed his army the Army of Northern Virginia.

Seven Pines National Cemetery occupies only a very small portion of the battlefield, which has been almost completely lost to development. There is no interpretation of the battle at the cemetery itself, but just down the street, in the parking lot of the Hanover County Public Library, is a Virginia Civil War Trails sign that explains the battle. *Seven Pines National Cemetery, intersection of E. Williamsburg Rd. and VA 33; Virginia Civil War Trails—Seven Pines, 23 E. Williamsburg Rd., Sandston, VA, 23150. Open daily.*

Oak Grove—In mid-June 1862, after two and a half months of preparations, the Union army was finally ready to begin the siege of Richmond. On June 25 McClellan initiated what would become the Seven Days Battles, attempting to gain high ground from which his artillery could fire on the Confederate defense lines. The battle, near the White Oak Swamp, lasted the entire day, with the Confederates repulsing most of the Union advance but then pulling back into their lines. McClellan did not make the gains he was looking for, and his last chance of advancing on Richmond went with the day.

The Oak Grove battlefield is now the Richmond International Airport. Nothing is left to commemorate the battle, except for a small monument in front of the Virginia Aviation Museum at the airport regarding the Richmond defenses. If you do want to view the monument, use caution, as it is along a busy road. *Monument—Richmond Defenses, in front of Virginia Aviation Museum, 5701 Huntsman Rd., Richmond, VA, 23250. Monument accessible daily.*

Darbytown Road, New Market Heights, and Fair Oaks—This region east of Richmond saw a great deal of action in October 1864 related to Grant's siege of Petersburg and Richmond. On October 7 Confederate cavalry attacked their counterparts on the Union right, driving the horsemen along the Darbytown Road and back to the Union lines. The Confederates then assaulted the lines along the New Market Road but were repulsed heavily, losing Brigadier General John Gregg in the process. Less than a week later, on October 13, Union infantry returned the favor. Testing the Richmond defenses, the troops were repulsed at the Confederate lines, and they then returned to their original positions along the New Market Road. Finally, on October 27, as the Union made another attempt at the South Side Railroad leading into Petersburg, Grant launched another diversion to draw Confederate troops away from the action and north of the James River. The movement, directed by Major General Benjamin Butler, marched Union troops north up the Williamsburg Road in an attempt to get around the left flank of the long Confederate defense line. However, Butler had a new adversary: the skilled and experienced Lieutenant General James Longstreet, who had just returned to action after being severely wounded at the battle of the Wilderness almost six months before. Longstreet anticipated Butler's movements and shifted his troops accordingly, thwarting the Union assaults and launching counterattacks of his own. The Federals suffered 1,603 casualties to the Confederates' 100, and no reinforcements from the Petersburg lines were necessary.

At least part of the action of all three of these battles took place in and around Dorey Park, a public park along the Darbytown Road. Unfortunately, the only reminder of any of the action that took place there is one Virginia Civil War Trails sign telling the story of the first battle. The fields are open, and it is a very nice public park, but soccer and softball fields have probably altered the landscape a bit. *Virginia Civil War Trails—Battle of Darbytown Rd., Dorey Park, 7100 Dorey Park Dr., Richmond, VA, 23231. Open daily.*

Glendale and White Oak Swamp—Although they happened on the same day only a couple of miles apart, White Oak Swamp and Glendale are considered two separate battles, as they involved two separate Confederate forces. The Union army, in its retreat during the sixth of the Seven Days, was heading for the critical crossroads near the Glendale farm that would lead them safely to the James River. If Robert E. Lee's Confederates could stop the Federals, he had a good chance of destroying them. The Union army's route was via the White Oak Bridge, the only road crossing of the White Oak Swamp. Lee ordered Major General Thomas "Stonewall" Jackson to pursue the Federals across the bridge and hit their rear, while Major General James Longstreet would attack the Union army from the west. Jackson, with 20,000 men, arrived at the bridge after the Union had already crossed, and they had burned the bridge behind them. Rather than find another crossing, Jackson inexplicably started an artillery duel with the Union rear guard of 17,000 under Major General William Franklin. The duel went nowhere, and neither did Jackson, and thus not much came of the battle of White Oak Swamp.

Farther south, Longstreet and Major General A. P. Hill awaited the sound of Confederate guns—not Jackson's, but Major General Benjamin Huger's, who was to attack north of the main assault. Longstreet and Hill were in position by 11 AM, but no firing was heard until 2:30 PM. Longstreet commanded his artillery to open fire, thinking that he was attacking in concert with Huger, but he had not heard Confederate guns; it was Federal artillery, and it was firing at them. When the Confederates realized they were under fire, Longstreet ordered assaults on the six Union batteries at 4 PM. The attacks were uncoordinated and ineffective and were too late; the Union artillery had protected most of the army, which had headed south toward Malvern Hill, not only a commanding position but also close to the James River and under the covering fire of Union gunboats. Although the Federals holding the final line did finally break, and the Union lost many men when the fighting grew particularly heavy late in the day, most of their men were able to join the rest of the army at Malvern Hill. At the end of the day's fighting, the Union had suffered 2,700 casualties to the Confederates' 3,600; more important, Lee had lost his chance to destroy the Army of the Potomac. He would, however, take them on one more time the next day at Malvern Hill.

Glendale National Cemetery is located within the Richmond National Battlefield Park, and the park operates a visitor's center there seasonally. Information on both the Glendale and White Oak Swamp battles can be found here. An electric-light map illustrates not only the two battles, but also the next day's battle at Malvern Hill. There is also a Virginia Civil War Trails sign at the site of the bridge over the White Oak Swamp. *Richmond National Battlefield Park—Glendale Visitor's Center, 8301 Willis Church Rd., Richmond, VA, 23231; Virginia Civil War Trails—White Oak Swamp, bridge near intersection of VA 156 and Hughes Rd., Richmond, VA, 23150; 804-226-1981; www.nps.gov/rich. Site open daily; visitor's center open June–Aug.*

Deep Bottom—Part of Grant's strategy to take Petersburg and Richmond was to threaten both cities and their supply lines simultaneously, not only forcing the Confederates to stretch their defense lines thin with their limited manpower, but also keeping Lee guessing as to where to concentrate his troops. Two efforts to draw Confederate troops north of the James River occurred at Deep Bottom, southeast of Richmond. The first instance was on July 27, 1864, and was intended to divert Confederate troops away from Petersburg while Union troops detonated explosives underneath the Confederate lines at what became the battle of the Crater. Union troops under Major General Winfield Scott Hancock crossed the James on a pontoon bridge at Deep Bottom and then assaulted the Confederate positions near New Market Heights and Fussell's Mill. The diversion worked; Lee sent 16,500 troops to meet the new threat, leaving only 18,000 men at the Petersburg lines. When Lee sent most of his men back to Petersburg, the Federals withdrew back across the James, leaving only a small group to hold the bridgehead at Deep Bottom.

The second assault at Deep Bottom, two weeks later, was not so successful for the Union. After crossing the pontoon bridge on the night of August 13, Hancock led Union troops from Deep Bottom and again assaulted the Confederate lines, attempting to turn the enemy's left. Union cavalry, meanwhile, headed north around the Confederate flank. The initial Union assaults were successful, driving the Confederates back to a strong defensive position on the New Market Heights. After a day and a half of repositioning, the Federals assaulted the new Confederate position, initially meeting success. But Confederate reinforcements flooded the fresh break in the line, and the Federals were driven off with heavy casualties. The Confederates, however, did suffer two great losses: Brigadier General Victor Girardey, one of Lee's favorite young officers, was killed in the assaults at New Market Heights; and Brigadier General John Chambliss, helping the Confederate cavalry defend against the Union cavalry's push to the north, was also killed on the field. In addition, the removal of troops from the Petersburg lines enabled Grant to take possession of the Weldon Railroad at the battle of Globe Tavern.

The battlefields of Deep Bottom are now privately owned. The landing itself, now a county park and boat ramp, contains a Virginia Civil War Trails sign that interprets Deep Bottom Landing and, to some extent, the battles of Deep Bottom. *Virginia Civil War Trails—Deep Bottom Landing, Deep Bottom County Park, 9401 Deep Bottom Rd., Richmond, VA, 23231. Open daily.*

Chaffin's Farm and New Market Heights—Major General Benjamin Butler, now "unbottled" from his position at Bermuda Hundred, was directed by Ulysses S. Grant to advance on the Confederate lines of defense just north of the James River, with the aim of weakening the Petersburg defenses and possibly opening an avenue to Richmond. The Confederates had constructed a system of heavy fortifications running from the James River north through an area known as Chaffin's Farm, consisting of Forts Hoke, Harrison, Johnson, Gregg, and Gilmer. The line faced east and had an open field of fire. Of the fortifications, Fort Harrison was the strongest, but it was manned by only 300 men, while the rest of the line held more than 4,000 other troops. Not far to the east, the Confederates had also set up a strong line running along the New Market Heights, a commanding ridge facing south; in addition to the excellent defensive position, the Confederates had set abatis in front of the line. This line was manned by only 1,800 men. On the morning of September 29, 1864, Butler sent Major General Edward Ord and 8,000 Union troops to Chaffin's Farm, focusing on Fort Harrison, while Major General David Birney assaulted New Market Heights with 13,000 men. Ord's attack began shortly after 6 AM, with the Union troops overwhelming the defenders. The neighboring Confederate forts, however, repulsed all assaults made against them, some in hand-to-hand fighting. At New Market Heights the infantry assaults against the Confederate lines had begun at 5:30 and continued for two hours, all of them being repulsed with heavy losses. Suddenly, though, the Confederate fire slowed noticeably at 7:30, and the Union attackers had possession of New Market Heights by 8. The Confederates had been so worried about their positions at the forts to the west that they pulled most of their troops to that area, leaving the heights open for the taking. In the two assaults the Federals suffered 4,150 casualties, and the Confederates, 1,750.

The forts at Chaffin's Farm are still well preserved and are part of Richmond National Battlefield Park. A visitor's center, at Fort Harrison, is open only during the summer, but the short walking trail through the fort is full of interpretive signs telling of the battle. As for New Market Heights, the battlefield is now privately owned, although the area is rural and the battlefield can be viewed from a distance. *Richmond National Battlefield Park—Fort Harrison, visitor's center at 8621 Battlefield Park Rd., Richmond, VA, 23231; 804-226-1981; www.nps.gov/rich. Site open daily; visitor's center open summer months only.*

Drewry's Bluff and Proctor's Creek—The site of Drewry's Bluff factored into both McClellan's Peninsula campaign of 1862 and Benjamin Butler's Bermuda Hundred campaign of 1864. In 1862, as the Union army approached Richmond, part of McClellan's plan was to be able to shell the Confederate capital from the river, and the battery on Drewry's Bluff, 8 miles south of the capital, was the last line of defense. But on May 15, 1862, when five Union gunboats, including the ironclads USS *Monitor* and USS *Galena*, approached the 90-foot-high bluff, a combination of accurate artillery fire, Confederate sharpshooting, and the inability of the *Monitor* to elevate her guns high enough to threaten the position was enough to drive the ships off for good. Almost two years later, on May 12, 1864, in an attempt to divert attention from a cavalry

A long view of the James River from the Confederate artillery position at Drewry's Bluff.

raid, Major General Benjamin Butler ordered an attack against the position on the bluff. After the initial assault, the Federals received reinforcements and attacked again the next day, only to find that the Confederates had withdrawn to nearby Fort Stevens, a much stronger position. After the Confederates withdrew again, Major General P. G. T. Beauregard, in charge of the Richmond defenses, personally took command and drew a new defensive line. After building up his forces, Beauregard launched his own attack on May 16, ultimately leading to Butler's decision to withdraw back to Bermuda Hundred, where he remained bottled up until Grant's army arrived in the area.

Both Drewry's Bluff and Fort Stevens are part of the Richmond National Battlefield Park. They are in isolated sites south of the city but are easy to get to and worth the trip. If you wondered at all how five ships, two of them ironclads, could not pass the river battery and advance to Richmond, one look off the top of the bluff at the miles of river below will tell you. Interpretive signs and short walking trails at both locations will take you through the well-preserved earthworks. *Richmond National Battlefield Park—Drewry's Bluff, north of intersection of Fort Darling Rd. and Bellwood Rd.; Fort Stevens, intersection of Pams Ave. and Norcliff Rd., Richmond, VA, 23237; 804-226-1981; www.nps.gov/rich. Open daily.*

Chester Station—On May 10, 1864, Major General Benjamin Butler's troops were still tearing up the railroad track of the Richmond & Petersburg Railroad when they were attacked by Confederates. After receiving reinforcements from Swift Creek, the Federals were easily able to drive the Confederates off. However, when the fighting was over, the Union troops withdrew into their lines at Bermuda Hundred, and the Confederates were able to reopen the supply line between Richmond and Petersburg.

A Virginia Civil War Trails sign discussing the battle of Chester Station has been placed in the parking lot of a YMCA in Chester. The adjacent cemetery was also the scene of fighting during the battle. *Virginia Civil War Trails—Battle of Chester Station, 3011 W. Hundred Rd., Chester, VA, 23831. Sign accessible daily.*

Ware Bottom Church—It is hard to discuss the Bermuda Hundred campaign without describing the Union army as being "bottled up"; the battle of Ware Bottom Church is where the Confederates put the cap on the bottle. The region called Bermuda Hundred is a peninsula with the James River to the north and the Appomattox River to the south. On May 20, 1864, Major General Benjamin Butler had his Union army at Bermuda Hundred after being driven back at the battle of Proctor's Creek. The Federals were in an entrenched position across Bermuda Hundred when they were attacked by Confederate forces. Although the Union army was ultimately able to repulse the attacks, the Confederates withdrew to the "neck" of the bottle and constructed a very strong defensive line known as the Howlett Line, thus "bottling up" Butler's army.

Part of the Richmond National Battlefield Park, the Parker's Battery unit in Chester preserves some of the battlefield, as well as remaining earthworks from the famous Howlett Line. The park contains a short walking trail that leads through the earthworks. *Richmond National Battlefield Park—Parker's Battery, intersection of Ware Bottom Springs Rd. and Old Stage Rd., Chester, VA, 23836; 804-226-1981; www.nps .gov/rich. Open daily.*

Port Walthall Junction—While Ulysses S. Grant was leading the Union army into the Wilderness in northern Virginia, Major General Benjamin Butler landed 39,000 Union troops between the James and Appomattox Rivers at a location known as Bermuda Hundred. The object of Butler's campaign was to destroy the Richmond & Petersburg Railroad, a lifeline between the two cities. On May 6, 1864, Butler sent men against Confederates defending the railroad at Port Walthall Junction, just north of Petersburg. The Federals attacked late in the day but soon called off the attack after thinking they were outnumbered. Butler renewed the attack the next day and captured the junction, while the Confederates withdrew behind the protection of Swift Creek.

Two historical highway markers have been placed near the railroad junction. One describes the fighting at Port Walthall Junction, while the other one generally describes Butler's Bermuda Hundred campaign. *Historical highway markers—Virginia Department of Historic Resources: S-20 (Union Army Railroad Raids) and S-24 (Advance on Petersburg), 16411 Jefferson Davis Hgwy., Colonial Heights, VA, 23834. Signs accessible daily.*

Swift Creek—Major General Benjamin Butler, having driven the Confederates behind Swift Creek after the battle of Port Walthall Junction, attacked their line on May 9, 1862. The Confederates launched a counterattack but failed to move the Union line; Butler resumed tearing up the Richmond & Petersburg Railroad. Meanwhile, several miles away at the mouth of Swift Creek, the Confederate Fort Clifton was being bombarded by Union gunboats in the Appomattox River. One of the gunboats was sunk, and the Federals withdrew.

Both portions of the Swift Creek battlefield have been remembered. A Virginia Civil War Trails marker has been placed at the site of the attack on the Confederate line, in the parking lot of the historic Swift Creek Mill Theatre. The massive Fort Clifton still exists and is part of Berberich Park along the river. There is virtually no interpretation at the park, but the earthworks here are nicely preserved. *Virginia Civil War Trails—Battle of Swift Creek, 17401 Jefferson Davis Hgwy.; Berberich Park, behind Tussing Elementary School, intersection of Brockwell Lane and Conduit Rd., Colonial Heights, VA, 23834. Open daily.*

Petersburg (Old Men and Young Boys)—While the Confederate army was still in its lines at Cold Harbor, General Ulysses S. Grant was preparing to withdraw his army to Petersburg. Major General Benjamin Butler, who still held the majority of his army at Bermuda Hundred, sent a force of 6,500 infantry and cavalry south across the Appomattox River to probe the Petersburg defenses and take the city, if possible. Petersburg was only lightly defended by 2,500 Confederates, but heavy fortifications—

known as the Dimmock Line—had already been constructed to protect the vital rail center. On June 9, 1864, the Union forces, under the command of Major General Quincy Gillmore, began to probe the Petersburg works, 10 miles of entrenchments capped with 55 artillery batteries. Not knowing how few Confederates actually manned the works, most of the Union units, infantry and cavalry alike, approached with extreme caution and concluded that the defenses were too strong for an assault. Southeast of Petersburg, the cavalry did begin to push back the Petersburg Home Guard (125 old men and young boys, unable to join the Confederate army), but their advance was stopped by Confederate regulars at the main defensive line.

A Virginia Civil War Trails interpretive sign has been placed at the site where the Federal advance was stopped. The sign also tells the story of the Petersburg Home Guard and the rest of the first battle of Petersburg. *Virginia Civil War Trails—First Battle of Petersburg, intersection of Graham Rd. and Jefferson Place, Petersburg, VA, 23803. Sign accessible daily.*

Jerusalem Plank Road—While the Union had failed to take the city of Petersburg when it had the chance, it did take control of all but two of the railroads leading into the city—the South Side Railroad and the Weldon & Petersburg. The Weldon led to Wilmington, North Carolina, the only remaining open port for the Confederacy, making it a critical supply line for Lee's army. On June 21, 1864, Union infantry and cavalry began to move toward the Weldon Railroad. One of the defending Confederate units was led by Major General William Mahone, who before the war had surveyed the area as a railroad engineer. Mahone knew of a ravine from which the Confederates could, undetected, approach a gap in the Union line that had grown between two corps. On June 22, while one Confederate division held in place the corps of Major General Horatio Wright, Mahone's men sprang out of the ravine at the Jerusalem Plank Road and inflicted heavy damage on the right flank of Major General David Birney's corps, taking 1,742 prisoners. The next day, after the Confederates fell back to better defend the railroad, the Federals were able to extend their siege lines to the Jerusalem Plank Road.

The Jerusalem Plank Road is now known as Crater Road. It has been completely developed, and there are no reminders of the battle anywhere near the road. Interpretation can be found at Petersburg National Battlefield. *Petersburg National Battlefield, 5001 Siege Rd., Petersburg, VA, 23803; 804-732-3531; www.nps.gov/pete. Open daily.*

Globe Tavern—While Confederate troops were north of the James River fighting the battle of Deep Bottom, General Ulysses S. Grant sent Major General Gouverneur Warren west to take possession of the Weldon & Petersburg Railroad. On August 18, 1864, Warren's men went 6 miles south of Petersburg to Globe Tavern, where they began to tear up railroad track. That afternoon Confederates attacked the Federals, driving them back, but the Union troops maintained a position along the railroad north of Globe Tavern and entrenched. They were, however, separated from the rest of the Union forces, and the next day Lieutenant General A. P. Hill led an attack on the Union right with 14,000 troops. Although the Confederates were able to take 2,700 prisoners, a Federal counterattack stopped the attack, and Warren withdrew to the south and entrenched, staying alongside the railroad. On August 21 the Confederates assaulted Warren's men one more time, this time on the Union left, but the attacks across open fields were repulsed by Union artillery. The Union had successfully cut the Weldon & Petersburg Railroad, with Grant extending his siege lines to the new position. Only one railroad—the South Side Railroad—still supplied Petersburg.

Although massive Fort Wadsworth was constructed afterward to secure the Union's hold on the Weldon & Petersburg, portions of the battle of Globe Tavern were fought on the same ground. The fort is preserved as part of Petersburg National Battlefield and is one of the driving tour stops outside the main park. There are interpretive signs discussing the battle of Globe Tavern, as well as a memorial to General Johnson Hagood's Confederate brigade, which suffered heavily on the last day of the battle. *Petersburg National Battlefield—Fort Wadsworth, intersection of Halifax Rd. and Flank Rd., Petersburg, VA, 23805; 804-732-3531; www.nps.gov/pete. Open daily.*

Ream's Station—Two battles occurred at Ream's Station, and both were Union disasters. The first occurred on June 29, 1864, as Brigadier Generals James Wilson and August Kautz were attempting to hook up with Union infantry following their long cavalry raid behind Confederate lines. Instead of Union troops, however, they found Confederates, and they immediately came under attack. Wilson was forced to burn their wagons and abandon his artillery before heading south, then back toward Petersburg in a wide loop around the Confederate force.

The second battle of Ream's Station was even more costly. The Union had just taken possession of the Weldon & Petersburg Railroad just south of Petersburg at the battle of Globe Tavern. The railroad ran to the Confederate port at Wilmington, North Carolina, and even though the line no longer reached Petersburg, the Confederates could still meet trains from Wilmington south of the city, load their supplies onto wagons, and carry them around the Union lines. The farther south the Union army could force that transfer point to be, the farther the wagons would have to travel, and the more vulnerable they would be. So shortly after the battle of Globe Tavern, Major General Winfield Scott Hancock was given the task of destroying the railroad from Globe Tavern south to Rowanty Creek, 14 miles down the line. Hancock's 7,000 troops had gotten 9 miles down the line when, on August 25, 1864, they were attacked by A. P. Hill's corps of 14,000, commanded by Major General Henry Heth because Hill was sick. Hancock withdrew to the same earthworks that Wilson's cavalry had made during the first battle of Ream's Station, which were extremely shallow and inadequate.

The lines were poorly formed, and when Heth's troops, along with Confederate cavalry led by Wade Hampton, launched their main assault on the Union formation at 5:30 PM, they could not be stopped. Hancock was able to gain control of his troops and escape when darkness fell, but not before losing 2,742 men, mostly captured.

Two Virginia Civil War Trails signs interpreting the first battle of Ream's Station can be found at the Oak Grove Methodist Church. The second battle was in the same area, and not far from the church. The Civil War Preservation Trust is in the process of developing the Ream's Station Battlefield. A gravel parking area and some interpretive signs have been placed along what will be a walking trail, but the trail itself has yet to be finished. The site is a bit rough at the moment, but it promises to be just as good as the other wonderful sites that the CWPT has developed. *Virginia Civil War Trails— Ream's Station, Oak Grove Methodist Church, 12715 Acorn Dr.; Ream's Station Battlefield—Civil War Preservation Trust, intersection of Halifax Rd. and Ream's Rd., Petersburg, VA, 23805. Signs accessible daily; Ream's Station Battlefield under development.*

Sappony Church—On their way back to Petersburg, Union cavalry led by Brigadier Generals James Wilson and August Kautz stopped to tear up parts of the Weldon Railroad near Sappony Church on June 28, 1864. The Federals were met by Confederate cavalry, who stopped the operation and forced Wilson to move north to his expected rendezvous with Union infantry at Ream's Station.

A Virginia Civil War Trails sign interprets the action at Sappony Church, a newer version of which stands at the crossroads where the cavalry fought. *Virginia Civil War Trails—Sappony Church, intersection of Sussex Dr. and Concord Sappony Rd., Stony Creek, VA, 23882. Sign accessible daily.*

Peebles Farm—In a push to take possession of the South Side Railroad, the last railroad leading into Petersburg, Grant ordered Major General Gouverneur Warren west to extend the siege lines. The Confederates had just sent 10,000 troops north in the wake of the battle of Chaffin's Farm and New Market Heights, weakening the Petersburg defenses as Grant had intended. On September 30, 1864, Warren ran into Major General Wade Hampton's cavalry, and a back-and-forth fight ran along the Confederate defenses, with the Federals eventually withdrawing to a defensive position near Peebles Farm. The next day Lieutenant General A. P. Hill's men assaulted the Union position, finding some success initially but in the end being repulsed. However, the Federals were prevented from reaching the railroad and returned to their lines, having suffered 2,869 casualties to the Confederates' 1,300.

Confederate Fort Archer, later renamed Fort Wheaton by the Union, is part of Petersburg Battlefield Park but at present is not open to visitors. The Peebles Farm site is now private property, although one can drive around the area and see what little is left of the battlefield. Information can be found at Poplar Grove National Cemetery, where the Union troops massed before their movements on September 30. *Peebles*

Farm site, near intersection of Wheaton Rd. and Squirrel Level Rd., Petersburg, VA, 23803; 804-732-3531; www.nps.gov/pete. Private property.

Hatcher's Run—With only a few notable exceptions in history up to this time, armies did not generally fight in the winter. Wet roads and cold temperatures tended to bog down operations, so even in mild climates, armies went into winter camp to recuperate and prepare for the spring, when conditions for effective operations would be better. But when the weather in February 1865 turned out to be relatively mild, Major General George Meade saw an opportunity to surprise the Confederates under siege at Petersburg. The Federals had made several unsuccessful attempts the previous fall to extend their siege lines westward to the Boydton Plank Road, the Confederates' supply link to the distant Weldon & Petersburg Railroad. On February 5 they tried again, with Major Generals Gouverneur Warren and David Gregg using Union infantry and cavalry to move south of Hatcher's Run and take control of Dinwiddie Court House along the road. Another Union corps, led by Major General Andrew Humphreys, headed north of Hatcher's Run, and after Humphreys fought off a Confederate attack, both Warren and Gregg moved north to support him. The next day, when Confederates led by Major General John Pegram began to probe the Union line, fighting broke out that went back and forth for four hours, until the Confederates finally forced the Federals to withdraw and reform along Hatcher's Run; Pegram was killed during the fight. On February 7 Warren assaulted the Confederate line, driving it back and recapturing the ground the Federals had lost, but going no farther. The Union army once again could not gain the Boydton Plank Road, but it was able to extend its lines westward, forcing the Confederates to do the same, which they could ill afford.

The Civil War Preservation Trust has acquired part of the Hatcher's Run battlefield and has already installed several interpretive signs. The site is right in the heart of the battlefield of February 6 and 7. A monument to General Pegram also stands at the site to mark the spot where he was killed. *Hatcher's Run Battlefield—Civil War Preservation Trust, 0.6 mile east of intersection of Dabney Mill Rd. and Steers Rd., Petersburg, VA, 23803. Open daily.*

Dinwiddie Court House—As Union infantry prepared to take possession of the Boydton Plank Road to the north, cavalry led by Major General Philip Sheridan was trying to do the same to the south at Dinwiddie Court House. Sheridan took possession of the town on March 29 and then moved northwest to probe the Confederate lines the next day. Finding the Confederates, Sheridan moved back to Dinwiddie Court House that night, while the Confederates gathered forces to meet him in battle. At 2 PM on March 31, 1865, a combined infantry and cavalry force under Major Generals George Pickett, W. H. F. "Rooney" Lee, and Thomas Rosser attempted to drive Sheridan from the Boydton Plank Road. The Confederates were able to split the Federal forces, but Sheridan managed to rally them north of the town. Unable to push

Sheridan away from the road, and learning that the Federals were moving west after the battle of White Oak Road, Pickett withdrew to Five Forks early the next morning.

A stone monument to the Confederates who fought in the battle of Dinwiddie Court House stands on the courthouse lawn. *Memorial, Battle of Dinwiddie Court House, 14016 Boydton Plank Rd., Dinwiddie, VA, 23841. Monument accessible daily.*

Lewis's Farm—After the Confederates' failed assault on Fort Stedman on March 25 and his meeting with President Lincoln and General Sherman two days later, Grant decided to act immediately before Lee's army could escape from the Petersburg defenses. On March 29, 1865, while cavalry under Major General Philip Sheridan advanced to Dinwiddie Court House, Union infantry commanded by Major Generals Gouverneur Warren and Andrew Humphreys extended the siege lines westward toward the Boydton Plank Road. The advance unit of Warren's corps, moving north on the Quaker Road, met Confederate resistance at the Lewis farm, near the the Boydton Plank Road intersection. Lieutenant General Richard Anderson ordered an attack on the Federals, who were commanded by Brigadier General Joshua Chamberlain. Although the Union left was pressed and Chamberlain was wounded, he was able to rally his troops and counterattack, forcing the Confederates to retreat north to the White Oak Road, where they entrenched.

The battle site, at the intersection of the Quaker Road and the Boydton Plank Road, is still mostly surrounded by farms and remains private property; there are no markers related to the action. Some information on the battle can be found at the Civil War Preservation Trust's White Oak Road battlefield. *Lewis's Farm battlefield, intersection of Boydton Plank Rd. and Quaker Rd., Dinwiddie, VA, 23841. Private property.*

White Oak Road—After the battle of Lewis's Farm, the Confederates entrenched along the south side of the White Oak Road. Major General Gouverneur Warren planned an assault on their line on March 31, 1865, but operations for the day were suspended by Major General George Meade on account of the rain and poor road conditions. At the same time, Lee planned an attack from the White Oak Road toward the Union left. As the Federal troops spread out to the west when the rain began to let up, the Confederates launched their attack, bursting out of the woods and sending the Federals back in a panic. However, as the Confederates began to extend their already thin lines, they became vulnerable to a counterattack, and Warren quickly organized one. Although the Confederates were able to hold their ground for some time, their thin line became endangered when troops from Major General Andrew Humphreys's corps attacked the Confederate left at 1 PM. The Confederates withdrew into their previous entrenchments along the White Oak Road in the late afternoon. The Federals had lost 1,781 men to the Confederates' 1,235. Warren abandoned his position and marched west to Five Forks.

The Civil War Preservation Trust's White Oak Road Battlefield preserves some of

Trailhead at the Civil War Preservation Trust's White Oak Road Battlefield.

the earthworks from the battle. A walking trail through the battlefield, complete with interpretive signs, fully explains the action, as well as the nearby battle of Lewis's Farm two days previous. The park is extremely well done and is worth a visit. One note of caution: The park contains land on both sides of the White Oak Road, which is a major artery through the area. Although traffic may not be heavy, it is moving quickly, so be careful as you cross. *White Oak Road Battlefield—Civil War Preservation Trust, intersection of White Oak Rd. and Claiborne Rd., Sutherland, VA, 23803. Open daily.*

Boydton Plank Road—The winter of 1864–65 was fast approaching, and the Union army hoped to capture the South Side Railroad and the Boydton Plank Road into Petersburg before it was too late. On October 27, 1864, a grand Union offensive of almost 43,000, involving Major Generals Winfield Scott Hancock, Gouverneur Warren, and Ambrose Burnside, was launched. Warren and Burnside were to brush aside the Confederate defenses along Hatcher's Run, while Hancock, in a dangerous movement that would briefly isolate his command, swung far around the Confederate right, approaching from the west to link up with his fellow commanders. However, the day opened with rain, and both Burnside and Warren had trouble maneuvering in the weather. Neither was able to perform his assigned task, and Hancock was left to fend for himself. But he was up to the challenge. Hancock moved eastward to cross Hatcher's Run, with Brigadier General David Gregg's cavalry screening his movements on his left. When Hancock reached the Boydton Plank Road he began to advance on the Confederates, but he was then ordered to halt after Grant called off the offensive.

Although Warren tried to close the large gap between his and Hancock's men, Hancock became trapped by men from Lieutenant General A. P. Hill's corps (again commanded by Brigadier General Henry Heth because Hill was sick) and Major General Wade Hampton's cavalry, just as he had been four months before at Ream's Station. The Confederates launched an assault across Hatcher's Run against Hancock's exposed right, but Hancock, showing remarkable coolness, ordered his men to surround the overextended Confederates on three sides, almost capturing them and forcing them back with heavy losses. Although Hancock considered staying on the field for the night (he did, after all, still possess the Boydton Plank Road), his judgment got the better of him, and his men withdrew during the night. Union casualties came to 1,758, with Hancock preventing what could have been a disaster; Confederate casualties came to 1,300.

Only a historical highway marker remains of the battle of Boydton Plank Road. The area around the battle is all private property, although driving through the area will take you through the battlefield, and the roads on which the armies fought are still present today. *Historical highway marker S-51—Virginia Conservation Commission (Burgess' Mill), 0.3 mile north of intersection of Boydton Plank Rd. and Fort Powers Dr., Petersburg, VA, 23803. Signs accessible daily.*

Sutherland's Station—Although access to the South Side Railroad into Petersburg was opened to the Union with their victory at Five Forks on April 1, 1865, there still remained the technicality of actually capturing it. On April 2, as the final battle of Petersburg raged to the east, a Union division commanded by Brigadier General Nelson Miles assaulted a Confederate position at Sutherland's Station, just south of the railroad. The Union assault began at 1 PM, and although the Federals were repulsed two times, they broke the Confederate left on the third try, capturing 600 men and the railroad.

A Virginia Civil War Trails interpretive sign, along with a memorial to the Confederates who fought at the battle, is located at the former location of the Sutherland Tavern, around which the fighting took place. *Virginia Civil War Trails—Sutherland Station; Confederate Memorial, intersection of US 460 and Namozine Rd., Sutherland, VA, 23885. Site accessible daily.*

Namozine Church—After the fall of Petersburg, Major General Philip Sheridan's cavalry was still pursuing the Confederates who had defended Five Forks and the White Oak Road west of the city. On April 3, 1865, at Namozine Church, one of the Federal cavalry units caught up with some of the fleeing Confederates, outflanking them and capturing 350 of them.

The Namozine Church, built in 1847, survived the battle and still stands. A Virginia Civil War Trails interpretive sign stands in front of it. *Virginia Civil War Trails— Namozine Church, intersection of Namozine Rd. and Greenes Rd., Ford, VA, 23850. Sign accessible daily.*

Amelia Springs—When the Confederates evacuated the Petersburg defenses, General Robert E. Lee had ordered all his forces to meet at Amelia Court House. He also ordered food to be sent there to meet the retreating army. Unfortunately, the trains arrived loaded with ammunition instead, and the men were forced to forage. Meanwhile, the Union infantry was right behind them, and the Union cavalry was to their south, preventing their movement to North Carolina to join with Joseph Johnston's army. On April 5, 1865, part of Philip Sheridan's force moved north, where it captured and burned a Confederate wagon train. Before the Federals could advance any farther, though, Confederate infantry, soon reinforced by cavalry, drove them off.

A Virginia Civil War Trails sign has been placed near the action at Amelia Springs. The location is remote but easy to find. *Virginia Civil War Trails—Amelia Springs, intersection of Amelia Springs Rd. and St. James Rd., Jetersville, VA, 23083. Sign accessible daily.*

Sayler's Creek—The retreating Confederate army, hoping to turn south down the Richmond & Danville Railroad, found its path blocked by Union infantry and cavalry at Jetersville, and turned toward Farmville to the west. As the Confederate soldiers moved on, Lieutenant General Richard Anderson's men could not keep up with Lieutenant General James Longstreet's troops in front of him, and a gap developed in the column. On April 6, 1865, Union cavalry under Brigadier General George Armstrong Custer charged into the gap, cutting off Anderson and all the units behind him at Sayler's Creek. Union infantry under Major General Horatio Wright came into the fight

Part of the field at Sailor's Creek Battlefield State Park.

and attacked the corps of Lieutenant General Richard Ewell. Lieutenant General John Gordon, who was the rear guard, had Union infantry under Major General Andrew Humphreys on his tail and went north with the Confederate wagon train. Ewell decided to make a stand southwest of the creek and was able to repulse the first attack. But the Federal troops were double his number, and when Ewell counterattacked, the Union troops easily repulsed and then followed the Confederates. More than 3,000 of them were captured. Meanwhile, in another part of the field, Humphreys caught up with Gordon and the wagon train, and although Gordon tried to make a stand to protect the train, Humphreys's charge forced him to retreat, and the wagons, along with 1,700 more Confederates, were captured. Finally, Anderson's force was attacked by Union cavalry, who captured another 2,600 Confederates. The rest of the Confederates fled to Rice's Station to the west, reassembling and marching on through the night. The Confederates had lost 7,700 men, including eight generals, at Sayler's Creek, to the Union's 1,148.

Sailor's Creek Battlefield State Park (the name has a number of variants, including Saylor, Sayler, and Sailor) occupies the ground where Ewell's men were captured. The park contains interpretive signs and memorials describing the battle, and the Overton-Hillsman House, used as a field hospital during the battle, is open during the summer. *Sailor's Creek Battlefield State Park, north of intersection of VA 617 and VA 307, Rice, VA, 23966; 434-315-0349; www.dcr.virginia.gov/state_parks/sai.shtml. Open daily.*

Rice's Station—Immediately following the battle of Sayler's Creek, what was left of Lieutenant General John Gordon's Confederate corps retreated toward the High Bridge over the Appomattox River. On the evening of April 6, 1865, Lieutenant General James Longstreet, hearing that Union troops were quickly advancing on the High Bridge, dug in at Rice's Station to stall any advancing Federals, to give Gordon time to cross the bridge. Union troops advanced on Longstreet's position, which he held until Gordon was safely across and then withdrew toward Farmville.

A Virginia Civil War Trails interpretive sign is located near where Longstreet dug in at Rice's Station. *Virginia Civil War Trails—Rice's Depot, intersection of VA 600 and VA 735, Rice, VA, 23966. Sign accessible daily.*

High Bridge—On the evening of April 6, 1865, as Lieutenant General Longstreet held out at Rice's Station to stall Union infantry advancing toward High Bridge, he also sent 1,200 cavalry to the bridge to secure it for the retreating Confederates. The Federals got there first, capturing the south end of the bridge, and when the cavalry sent by Longstreet arrived, the Federal cavalry charged them. After first being pushed back, the Confederates countercharged, separating the Union cavalry from their infantry and surrounding them. Most of the Federals were captured, and the Confederates gained control of the bridge in time for Lieutenant General John Gordon's survivors from the battle of Sayler's Creek to cross during the night. The Confederates then attempted to burn the bridge, but pursuing Union infantry under Major

General Andrew Humphreys was able to put the fire out and cross. This enabled the Federals to force Lee's troops at Farmville, who were just receiving the first rations they had had in days, to continue their retreat and abandon their supply trains. Lee ordered the trains to meet the army at Appomattox Station.

Two Virginia Civil War Trails interpretive signs tell the story of High Bridge. One is located south of the bridge, and the other north; at the north location you can see, far in the distance, the modern railroad bridge crossing where the original used to pass. *Virginia Civil War Trails—Cavalry Battle at High Bridge, intersection of VA 406 and VA 601, Rice, VA, 23966; Virginia Civil War Trails—High Bridge, 1 mile east of intersection of River Rd. and Jamestown Rd., Farmville, VA, 23901. Signs accessible daily.*

Cumberland Church—On April 7, 1865, Confederates at Cumberland Church entrenched to act as a rear guard for the rest of their retreating army. Brigadier General Nelson Miles attacked the Confederate line, which was made up of men from the units of Major General William Mahone and Lieutenant Generals James Longstreet and John Gordon. The Confederates were able to repulse the Union assault, allowing the rest of the Confederate army to head west to Appomattox Court House. Leaving on another night march, which the retreating Confederates had been repeatedly forced to do, Gordon's men took the vanguard of the column, and Longstreet's acted as the rear guard.

A Virginia Civil War Trails sign has been placed at Cumberland Church, still an active parish in the Virginia countryside. The ridge of the battle can still be seen from the church parking lot. *Virginia Civil War Trails—Cumberland Church, 1895 Cumberland Rd., Farmville, VA, 23901. Sign accessible daily.*

Appomattox Station—Robert E. Lee's weary and hungry troops, on the run for almost a week, approached Appomattox Station, expecting to meet their wagon trains and eat. But the Federals got there first. On the evening of April 8, 1865, Major General Philip Sheridan's cavalry got ahead of Lee's column, and Brigadier General George Custer entered Appomattox Station and captured the Confederate supply trains. Custer rode on toward the town of Appomattox Court House, where Confederate artillery and more wagons awaited. Although the Confederates held out for a few hours, Custer's men finally overwhelmed them at 9 PM, capturing the wagons and 25 pieces of artillery. Union units were now ahead of Lee, and all his routes of retreat were blocked. Furthermore, he had no food for his starving men.

A Virginia Civil War Trails interpretive sign discussing Custer's capture of the wagon trains and the artillery has been placed at the Appomattox Visitor Information Center, which stands on the same ground as the former rail depot. More information can be found inside the center. *Virginia Civil War Trails—Battle of Appomattox Station, Appomattox Visitor Information Center, intersection of Main St. and Lee St., Appomattox, VA, 24522; 434-352-8106; www.tourappomattox.com. Open daily.*

Lynchburg—While the Confederates were occupied at the battle of Cold Harbor, President Jefferson Davis persuaded General Robert E. Lee, against his better judgment, to release 9,000 men under Lieutenant General Jubal Early. The Union had just won the battle of Piedmont in the Shenandoah Valley, and Davis wanted to keep the valley in Confederate hands. As Early made his way east by rail, the victor of Piedmont, Major General David Hunter, had just crossed the Blue Ridge Mountains with 18,000 men to attack the Confederate rail center at Lynchburg. On June 17, 1864, Hunter drove the 4,000 Confederates under Major General John Breckenridge back into the Lynchburg defenses, planning to attack in force the next day. However, that night, Early's train arrived in Lynchburg, boosting the Confederate defenses to 13,000. Hunter's attacks the next morning were easily repulsed, and the Union force retreated west after dark. Early's men followed for a short distance, then headed north down the Shenandoah Valley. The victory at Lynchburg gave Early the opportunity to use the valley as an avenue of invasion and led to his advance upon Washington the next month.

Much of the battle of Lynchburg remains today, including Jubal Early himself. An audio driving tour of the battle can be obtained from the Lynchburg Visitor Center.

The Confederate Fort Early at Lynchburg, Virginia.

Among the sites on the tour are Fort Early, one of the main Confederate defenses; Historic Sandusky, Hunter's headquarters and now a Civil War museum; and Spring Hill Cemetery, which not only saw action during the battle but is also Early's final resting place—he is buried very near the point from which he led the Confederates in battle. *Driving tour—Battle of Lynchburg, Lynchburg Visitor Center, 216 12th St.; Historic Sandusky, 757 Sandusky Dr., Lynchburg, VA, 24502; Fort Early, intersection of Fort Ave. and Memorial Ave.; Spring Hill Cemetery, 3000 Fort Ave., Lynchburg, VA, 24501; 434-832-0162; www.discoverlynchburg.org. Open daily.*

Staunton River Bridge—Early in the siege of Petersburg, the Union developed plans to disrupt and eventually take the railroads leading into the city. A large cavalry raid led by Brigadier Generals James Wilson and August Kautz went deep into Confederate territory, tearing up track along the South Side Railroad for several days before approaching the Staunton River Bridge on June 25, 1864. The bridge was defended by a Confederate force of 900 men, made up mostly of a Home Guard consisting of old men and young boys. The 5,500 Union cavalrymen attacked the fortifications at the bridge but were unable to take them. Wilson withdrew to head back to Petersburg, leaving the bridge intact.

Staunton River Battlefield State Park is located in south central Virginia, some distance away from many of the other battlefields. But its remoteness and the development at the park make it a great destination for a pleasant drive. The park has two visitor's centers, one on each side of the Roanoke River, and the two sides are connected by the still-standing Staunton River Bridge, which has been converted into a walking trail. Most of the trail and the well-preserved earthworks are on the west side of the river, where the Clover Visitor Center tells the story of the battle and displays relevant artifacts. The park also has two wildlife observation towers, as well as full picnic facilities. *Staunton River Battlefield State Park, intersection of Black Walnut Rd. and Fort Hill Trail, Clover, VA, 24534; 434-454-4312; www.stauntonriverbattlefield.org. Open daily.*

» WHERE TO STAY IN SOUTHERN VIRGINIA

Richmond and Petersburg offer numerous options for lodging, and you won't have any trouble finding a place to stay. The rich history of the area provides many opportunities for bed-and-breakfasts in older homes, but few of them have direct ties to the Civil War.

An exception can be found in Petersburg. The **Walker House Bed and Breakfast**, built in 1815, was the home of a planter and during the war served as a location for Union planning. After the debacle of the battle of the Crater, a federal court of inquiry was called, and it met on the home's front lawn. *Walker House Bed and Breakfast, 3280 S. Crater Rd., Petersburg, VA, 23805; 804-861-5822; www.walker-house.com.*

SEDGWICK

MAJ. GENL. JOHN SEDGWICK
BORN CORNWALL LITCHFIELD CO. CONN.
SEPTEMBER 13, 1813

6TH. ARMY CORPS

8

The War for the Capitals: Washington

OVERVIEW

Throughout the Civil War and in retrospect, most of the focus of the public at large had been and probably always will be in between the two capitals of Washington, D.C., and Richmond, Virginia. Although the battles of the West were just as important, were fought just as hard, and held just as much drama, people have always been fascinated by this portion of the war.

Perhaps the reason is the battles themselves. The names of the battles that took place here are familiar: Bull Run (or maybe Manassas to you), Fredericksburg, Chancellorsville, and the Wilderness all come to mind when discussing the war's great battles. Or perhaps it is because all these battles took place in the same small area of the country; there is no doubt that northern Virginia saw more blood spilled than any other region. It could also be the names, as well as their ghosts: Robert E. Lee, Ulysses S. Grant, Stonewall Jackson, George McClellan, J. E. B. Stuart, and Philip Sheridan. These are the names that people think of when they think of the Civil War.

As far as the men who fought it were concerned, simple geography was the primary reason that the area was the focus of attention. Only 100 miles separated the two capitals, and whoever controlled the area in between had the upper hand. When Manassas, so close to the federal capital, was threatened, it brought on the first major battle of the war. Robert E. Lee was constantly maneuvering his army to protect the capital at Richmond, and the various commanders of the Army of the Potomac were constantly maneuvering to find a way to capture it. "On to Richmond!" was the cry

---

Site of the death of Union General John Sedgwick during the battle of Spotsylvania Court House.

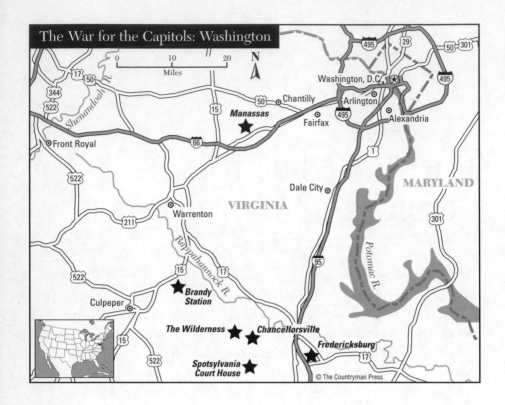

The War for the Capitols: Washington

0   10   20
Miles

N

© The Countryman Press

of so many in the North, and although the victories at Corinth, Vicksburg, and Atlanta were vitally important to the Union, everyone seemed to know that when Richmond fell, the war would end.

The battles in this chapter represent three years of mighty struggle, two great armies working around and about each other, constantly probing for weaknesses, anticipating movements, and trying to gain an advantage. These battles are, rightfully so, in the center spotlight of the Civil War, and they are still sources of wonder and discovery for historians and military analysts and tacticians. Any visitor to these sites will experience the same wonder and discovery.

» PEOPLE TO KNOW

James Longstreet—Although James Longstreet had his critics, Robert E. Lee was not one of them. After the death of Stonewall Jackson, Lee considered Longstreet his most important general, and time and again Longstreet proved himself to be an exceptional field general, although he lacked the skills necessary for independent command.

Longstreet was with the Confederates from the time of the first battle of Manassas to the surrender at Appomattox, although he did have a couple of unexpected detours. Performing well at second Manassas, Antietam, and Fredericksburg, Longstreet was soon promoted to lieutenant general. Given command of Richmond and the Carolinas while Lee prepared to march north in early 1863, Longstreet accomplished little but to provide forage for Lee's army, taking no initiative against the Federal troops all along the Carolina coast. But Longstreet soon returned to Lee's side, in time for the battle at Gettysburg. In the fall of 1863 Longstreet and his corps were rushed to northern Georgia to fight at Chickamauga, where their overnight arrival in the middle of the battle helped to turn the tide. He then marched north to Knoxville but was unable to take the city, despite its small defensive force. Soon he was serving under Lee again when Ulysses S. Grant opened his campaign for Richmond. During the battle of the Wilderness, Longstreet was hit by friendly fire, taking him out of action for six months. He returned to service while Lee's army was besieged at Petersburg, and he remained with Lee until the end. After the war, Longstreet, much to the dismay of many in the South, accepted political appointments offered to him by Grant, a longtime friend, and even supported the Republican Party.

Joseph Hooker—"Fighting Joe" Hooker, as he was known, was indeed an aggressive military man and never one to back down from a fight. His long military career before the Civil War included tough assignments in the Mexican War, the Seminole War, and serving on the frontier, and although many disliked him, he had a reputation for toughness. This reputation is what propelled him to the top of the heap when it was again time to find a new leader for the Army of the Potomac.

Hooker took command of the army after Major General Ambrose Burnside's disaster at Fredericksburg, and he openly criticized Burnside. When Burnside was relieved and Hooker put in his place, Hooker immediately began to restore discipline and morale in the beaten army. His men grew to revere him and would fight for him. Unfortunately for Hooker, his first fight was against Robert E. Lee at Chancellorsville, a battle considered by many to be Lee's masterpiece. Hooker was uncharacteristically cautious during the battle, and his army was soundly beaten. When Hooker asked for more troops after he suspected Lee was on his way to invade Pennsylvania (which he was), his request was denied, and he resigned his command, three days before the battle of Gettysburg. Hooker went on to serve in the western theater and remained in the military until a stroke three years after the war hampered his abilities. He died in 1879.

» THINGS TO KNOW

The highways around the Washington, D.C., area can get pretty crowded, so don't be surprised if you get stuck in traffic, no matter how isolated you think the road is. In fact, the traffic can get particularly thick around Manassas, so as you visit the sites in the area, make sure you are looking both ways before you cross the street, whether driving or walking.

THE TRIP

This tour is arranged more or less chronologically, with the exception of the battle of Brandy Station. All the sites are within an easy drive of the major population centers of the Washington metro area, Fredericksburg, or Richmond, Virginia, so you won't have any issues with finding good food or lodging.

Not a lot of area is covered here—in fact, six of the seven major battles outlined are all within the boundaries of only two national parks. But make sure you allow ample time at each of the sites to get the full experience from them. You may also want to consider some of the other sites in the area, more than a few of which were fairly large battles. A little exploration of the Virginia countryside (particularly of the cavalry battlefields to the west) can make a great drive.

One way to approach the tour in this chapter would be to pick a base and stick to it. The best choice in that regard is undoubtedly Fredericksburg, Virginia. The city has a fantastic wealth of history and is quaint without falling too far into the tourist-trap category. Not only is Fredericksburg centrally located, but it is beyond the D.C. traffic zone, and just outside the small city are plenty of hotels and restaurants.

» THE CAN'T-MISS SITES

Manassas (Bull Run)

In July 1861, even though fighting had occurred and the states that had seceded months ago had not shown any indication of coming back, Americans still had a hard

Henry Hill, the main battleground during First Manassas.

time believing that a war had begun. Surely, something was happening, a major event even, but not a war, not the kind of conflict they had read about in history books and seen in grand paintings, with masses of men clashing and banners flying. But in July of 1861 America would get its wake-up call. This was indeed a war and would in fact become the most terrible war in history to date. And it would start at Manassas.

It would come back to Manassas, too, several times. This was not just by chance. Manassas Junction was a major rail center, with the Orange & Alexandria Railroad meeting the Manassas Gap Railroad. It also happened to be near the capital of Washington, while at the same time being in the seceded state of Virginia. For the Union especially, Manassas Junction could be an important supply base. Naturally, both armies wanted to control this vital junction.

Early in the war both armies concentrated forces near Washington; the Union wanted to protect it, and the Confederates wanted the Federals to know that they could pose a threat to it, as well as protect their railroad at Manassas. While the Union held the towns of Arlington and Alexandria across the river from Washington, everything south of those points was Confederate territory. For months neither army blinked, but as the Confederates' presence at Manassas grew, Washington began to become nervous, and public and political pressure to drive them away increased.

The Confederates were commanded by Brigadier General P. G. T. Beauregard and were 21,000 strong. Finally, someone decided that enough was enough, and it was time to stop this rebellion once and for all. Brigadier General Irvin McDowell, in charge of the Union troops gathered in the Washington defenses, struck out on July 16 to meet the Confederates, even though he did not think his men were ready. Taking his time, McDowell and his army of 35,000—the largest army ever assembled on the continent—slowly and cautiously moved through northern Virginia, looking for a place to cross Bull Run. McDowell's plan was to outflank the Confederate right with his trained but inexperienced soldiers.

McDowell had another worry. The Confederates had another army, 11,000 men under Joseph Johnston in the Shenandoah Valley. They were being held in place by a Union force under Major General Robert Patterson, but if they were able to reach Manassas, McDowell would have a much harder time overrunning the Confederates.

The Federals' first test came on July 18, 1861, at the battle of Blackburn's Ford. A small group of Union troops went to explore the crossing at the ford and found that it was guarded. Disobeying orders, the Union commander attacked the Confederates, who were commanded by Brigadier General James Longstreet and Colonel Jubal Early. The Confederates easily drove the Union troops off. The brash action by the Federals necessitated a new plan; McDowell now had to find a crossing beyond the Confederate left. The army waited for three more days while McDowell came up with a new plan of attack.

The three-day delay would prove fatal. On July 18 Johnston, fooling the Federals by running cavalry between his army and the Union troops, left Winchester, Virginia, at the north end of the valley and put his army on a train—the Manassas Gap Railroad. Over the next two days, almost all of Johnston's troops joined Beauregard. The Confederate army at Manassas was now 33,000 strong, and the Union did not know it. Johnston, the ranking officer, took command of the field.

On the morning of July 21, McDowell ordered the Union troops forward, moving around the Confederate left. Colonel Nathan Evans, receiving word that the Federals might be moving around his flank, sent for reinforcements and moved his 900 troops onto Matthews Hill, directly in the path of the 6,000 Union troops who were crossing Bull Run at Sudley Ford to the north. Evans received the reinforcements he had requested, and they were able to slow the Federals down, but they were pushed off the hill by the much larger Union force. Evans retreated to Henry Hill, where the rest of the Confederate force was waiting. Brigadier General Bernard Bee, part of the group that had reinforced Evans, noticed Brigadier General Thomas J. Jackson's brigade atop the hill and shouted, "There stands Jackson like a stone wall! Rally behind the Virginians!" Rally they did, and soon 7,000 men were ready to meet the Federals on Henry Hill.

McDowell, meanwhile, was still being cautious, taking his time in preparing his attack. By the time the Union troops finally assaulted the hill, the Confederates had been able to bring up reinforcements and completely reorganize their lines. The fighting started again around 1 PM, going back and forth across Henry Hill. After four hours of intense combat, the tide suddenly turned. A Federal battery on the right side of the line was left virtually unprotected, and Confederate reinforcements, screened by the nearby woods, ran for the guns and took them easily. Fresh Confederate troops had been streaming to the battlefield all afternoon, and the Union troops could hold out no longer. The collapse started slowly, but soon the entire Union army was on the retreat, each man for himself, literally running for Washington, despite the best efforts of McDowell and his officers to rally them. The Confederates held their position; although they had scattered the Federals, nobody had expected a fight like this, and they had had enough. The Confederate loss was 1,982 casualties. The Union had suffered far worse—not only 2,896 casualties, but a sharp and demoralizing defeat, both for the troops and for the North as a whole. Although the great battles to follow would be far more devastating than this one, the first battle of Manassas convinced most people, both in the North and the South, that this would be a terrible and perhaps long war.

By August of 1862, no one needed convincing. With the country now over a year into the war, Wilson's Creek, Shiloh, the Seven Days, and scores of other battles had already taken the lives of tens of thousands of men. Much had happened in that time, but still the focus of the country was on the battleground between Washington and Richmond. Major General George McClellan's Peninsula campaign against the Confederate

The stone house, site of General John Pope's headquarters during Second Manassas.

capital had failed. Fearing for Washington, Union generals soon organized a new army under Major General John Pope, christening it the Army of Virginia. It was formed mostly from the troops that had been defeated soundly during Stonewall Jackson's Shenandoah Valley campaign earlier in the year. Now there were two Union armies operating in Virginia, and the ideal for the Union would be for McClellan and Pope to join forces and crush the Confederates.

Robert E. Lee, now in command of the Confederate Army of Northern Virginia after Joe Johnston had been wounded during the battles for Richmond, knew that this could not be allowed to happen. Convinced that McClellan was no longer a threat to Richmond, Lee devised a plan to threaten Washington and defeat Pope's army, hopefully dissolving it.

In mid-August Lee moved his entire army north toward Pope. Creating some good fortune during a raid on Pope's headquarters wagon train, Brigadier General J. E. B. Stuart had captured valuable intelligence, and Lee quickly devised a plan to crush the new Union army. Lee split his army into two wings, one commanded by Stonewall Jackson (now a major general) and the other by Major General James Longstreet. The plan was for Longstreet's force to pin Pope's army against the Rappahannock River, while Jackson's wing swung around Pope's right, passed through the Thoroughfare Gap, and destroyed the Federal supply base at Manassas, cutting Pope's supply line.

It could not have worked any better. From August 23 to 25, during what became known as the battles of Rappahannock River, Longstreet, with Lee at his side, kept Pope busy while Jackson moved his army to Manassas Junction, covering 54 miles in 36 hours. Arriving at Manassas Junction on August 26, Jackson's men gleefully proceeded for the next two days to either destroy or help themselves to everything they could lay their hands on. Pope was forced to leave his position on the Rappahannock and fall back to Manassas. Longstreet immediately marched north to pass through the Thoroughfare Gap, just as Jackson had done, to join him and reunite Lee's army.

After their work at the supply depot was finished, Jackson took his men back to the old battlefield at Manassas. Finding cover behind an unfinished railroad embankment, Jackson waited for Pope and for Longstreet, both of whom he knew were coming.

Like clockwork, late in the day on August 28, 1862, Pope's army appeared, marching north on the Warrenton Turnpike, which ran straight through the heart of the former battlefield and just south of Jackson's position. As the Federals marched, they were suddenly met with a barrage of artillery and rifle fire. The Union men, now much more experienced than they were a year ago, quickly ran for cover, but then formed a line and counterattacked across the open field before them. The two lines battled for two hours, with the fighting ending only with the darkness. Neither side had gained the advantage.

John Pope thought otherwise. He had bragged that he would capture Stonewall Jackson, and he saw this as his chance. The next morning Pope launched an assault on the Confederate line. Jackson set his men behind the protection of the unfinished rail-road, with his back to a low rise known as Stony Ridge, where his artillery had command of the field. Pope directed four assaults against the Confederate line, but all of them were uncoordinated. Each of the Union assaults—two against the Confederate center, and two against the left—met with some success, breaking the Confederate line

SITE DETAILS

Manassas National Battlefield Park—The battlefields at Manassas, not far from Washington, are fairly intact, although there has been a great deal of development around them. Although the two battlefields overlap somewhat, the park's organiza-tion makes separate interpretation of the two battles very simple. The visitor's center is the place to start, with a light-map and an explanation of the significance of the first battle. You can then walk out the back door to explore the battlefield of First Manassas on foot. The walking tour covers the entire Henry Hill area, and Matthews Hill and most of the rest of the battlefield can be seen in the distance. Following the walking tour, you can take a self-guided driving tour of the sites in-volved in the second battle. Although some of these sites have been lost, enough is still left of the much larger second battlefield to make interpretation simple, in-cluding the unfinished railroad, which was never finished and still stands virtually undisturbed. One note of caution: The Warrenton Turnpike down which Pope's army marched to meet Jackson is still used and is a very busy road; the intersections around the park are also very well-traveled. When driving around the park, use cau-tion, and remember that most of the people flying down these roads are not tourists but are just trying to get home, probably after sitting in D.C. metro-area traffic. Don't get in their way. *Manassas National Battlefield Park, 6511 Sudley Rd., Manassas, VA, 20109; 703-361-1339; www.nps.gov/mana. Open daily; admission charged.*

Blackburn's Ford—The site of the Blackburn's Ford battle that preceded the first battle of Manassas has had a Virginia Civil War Trails interpretive sign placed there. It is at the ford, on the west side of the bridge crossing Bull Run. *Virginia Civil War Trails—Blackburn's Ford, intersection of VA 28 and Centreville Rd. (west side of bridge), Centreville, VA, 20121. Site accessible daily.*

Manassas Station Operations—Several Virginia Civil War Trails signs have been placed through downtown Manassas highlighting Jackson's operations preceding the second battle, and both walking and driving tours to view them are available at the Manassas Museum. The museum itself, presenting the history of the town and the railroad junction both before and after the battle, contains a great deal of infor-mation on wartime Manassas. If you happen to catch the museum on its off-hours, the map of the tours is mounted right outside the museum doors. *Manassas Mu-seum, 9101 Prince William St., Manassas, VA, 20110; 703-368-1873; www.manassas museum.org. Sites accessible daily; museum closed Mon.*

several times, but the time and distance between each assault allowed Jackson to seal each breach and turn the Federals back.

Meanwhile, unknown to Pope, Lee and Longstreet had arrived late in the day. Lee directed Longstreet to set up on Jackson's right. The new Confederate line, extended by more than a mile, reached far beyond the Union left. The line formed an angle—two jaws that would snap shut on Pope's army.

The next morning, Pope renewed the assaults on Jackson's men behind the unfinished railroad. After a series of small attacks, Pope decided to break the Confederates once and for all, gathering 10,000 troops at a deep cut in the railroad bed. The assault was launched at 3 PM and was a slaughter. The Confederates, remaining behind the protection of the embankment, mowed down the charging Federals with rifle and artillery fire. The assault lasted 30 minutes before being called off.

Lee saw that the time had come. He immediately ordered Longstreet's 30,000 men to advance against the Union left. Overlapping the Union line by a great distance, the Confederates marched right over the Union defenders. Pope quickly organized a defense on a small rise called Chinn Ridge and was able to slow the Confederates enough to form another line on Henry Hill, where the first battle of Manassas had ended. Although Longstreet pushed hard against this line, it did not break before nightfall, and Pope was able to retreat toward Washington overnight. The Union had suffered a staggering 13,826 casualties to the Confederates' 8,353. It was a total defeat. With the decisive Confederate victory, costly though it was, Lee was able to plan his invasion of the North, which ended at the battle of Antietam. Pope's appalling losses led to his reassignment to Minnesota, where trouble was brewing between settlers and the Dakota tribes.

Fredericksburg

The first battle of Fredericksburg was without a doubt one of the most terrible tragedies of the war. Although both armies learned hard lessons from the battle, the recklessness with which the Union soldiers were used and the loss of life that resulted from that recklessness gave pause to the entire country. Fredericksburg and the area around it would see a lot of fighting during the war, but there were few scenes anywhere in the country that could match the senseless carnage seen at Fredericksburg.

Even though the Union had won a great victory at Antietam, nearly everyone in Washington was disappointed that the Union commander, Major General George McClellan, had subsequently hesitated, losing out on a chance to destroy the Confederate Army of Northern Virginia. Several weeks after the battle, McClellan was replaced with a man who had gained success in other areas of fighting and who was almost universally liked—Major General Ambrose Burnside. Burnside's campaign in North Carolina had established Union control of much of that state's coast, and furthermore,

The sunken road at Fredericksburg, from which well-protected Confederate soldiers mowed down wave after wave of Union attackers.

his plans for the Army of the Potomac met with almost unanimous approval. Unlike the commanders before him, he was willing to march straight for the Confederate capital at Richmond and take it.

After the devastating loss at Antietam, Robert E. Lee needed time. The Confederate forces, although still intact, had taken a beating and were scattered. It would require coordination and planning to bring his army back together again. Once Lee had determined where Burnside's army would move, he could begin to gather his forces and organize a defense. He knew that the Federals would have to cross the Rappahannock somewhere, and among the choices, the most obvious place seemed to be at the town of Fredericksburg.

Fredericksburg was indeed Burnside's choice. His plan was to cross the river as quickly as possible, strike Lee's army while it was still separated, and march on to Richmond. Almost immediately after Burnside took command of the army, on November 15, 1862, his four divisions began their march to Fredericksburg, where they intended to quickly build pontoon bridges and continue their advance. They reached

The battle-scarred Innis House, one of the few existing structures beneath Marye's Heights during the battle of Fredericksburg.

Fredericksburg in good time, with the first division occupying the high ground across from the town on November 17. But they did not cross the Rappahannock. Bureaucracy prevented the pontoon bridges from reaching the army for over a week, and when they did arrive, conditions were not ideal for assembling the bridges, and Burnside held his men north of the Rappahannock for almost three weeks.

Three weeks was plenty of time for Robert E. Lee. Over the next few weeks, Lee was able to get both wings of his army, commanded by Major Generals Stonewall Jackson and James Longstreet, to Fredericksburg and into position. Lee put Jackson's men on the right side of the line, extending far south of the town to guard against any other points of crossing. Longstreet's men stayed on the heights west of Fredericksburg—Marye's Heights—and set their positions, with the artillery along the hillsides and the infantry in line in front of them, in a sunken road behind a stone wall. Union attackers would have to climb a steep hill across open ground for 400 yards before they could reach the Confederate line. It was a strong position. The Confederates also placed men in the houses along the Rappahannock, hidden in basements and well protected for when the initial assault came.

On December 11, early in the morning darkness and under a heavy mist, Union carpenters began building the pontoon bridges from the north bank of the river, muffling the sounds of their work as best they could. But they were detected by the Confederates, and as soon as the sunlight burned off the fog, the Confederates along the river opened fire, scattering the carpenters and leaving the pontoon bridges partially finished. The Federal response was a heavy bombardment of the town using the 150 artillery pieces they had assembled across the river. The guns blasted away at Fredericksburg for 90 minutes, destroying much of the town and setting many homes and other buildings ablaze. But when the carpenters came back out to work after the bombardment, they were again chased off by the Confederate sharpshooters. The Federals would have to take the town before the entire army could cross.

Shortly, Union soldiers, using pieces of the pontoon bridge as boats, hurried across the Rappahannock and took a position behind the high shelter of the riverbank. Emerging and fighting from house to house, the Union troops kept the Confederates busy, driving them out of the town in fierce fighting that lasted for hours. Meanwhile, the Union carpenters resumed their work on the pontoon bridges. As

Salem Church, Fredericksburg & Spotsylvania National Military Park.

SITE DETAILS

Fredericksburg & Spotsylvania National Military Park—The Fredericksburg unit of the park lies at the base of Marye's Heights, just at the end of the sunken road. The visitor's center here is nicely done, and although the clear fields that the Union troops ran up are now mostly developed, the landscape is intact, and the sunken road and the stone wall, most of which had been lost, are now rebuilt (some portions of the original wall remain). One of the homes present during the battle still stands, and it still bears the scars of the day's terrible fighting. There is also a memorial to Confederate soldier Richard Kirkland, the "Angel of Marye's Heights," who brought water to the wounded Union soldiers during the cold night of December 13. The sites of Jackson's line and the Union attack south of the town are also part of the park and are only a short drive away. *Fredericksburg & Spotsylvania National Military Park—Fredericksburg Unit, 1013 Lafayette Blvd., Fredericksburg, VA, 22401; 540-373-6122; www.nps.gov/frsp. Open daily; admission charged.*

Battle of Fredericksburg walking tours—Fredericksburg's tourism department has put together two outstanding walking tours of the town that will take you not only through the fight on Marye's Heights, but also to the site of the action on December 11, when the Federals began to cross the river. The two brochures are very descriptive and can be picked up at the Fredericksburg Visitor Center. *Fredericksburg, December 1862: A Walking Tour, Fredericksburg Tourism and Business Development Visitor's Center, 706 Caroline St., Fredericksburg, VA, 22401; 1-800-678-4748; www.visitfred.com. Open daily.*

darkness fell, the Federals had gained most of the town, and the Confederates were ordered to withdraw to the defensive lines. Overnight and into the next day, as the bridges were completed, Union troops streamed into Fredericksburg. Unfortunately, the combination of open, destroyed homes and a hatred of anything Southern led many of the troops to ransack the town's homes. The Confederate troops watched in anger as the looting went on into the night and next day.

By the end of the day on December 12, the Union troops were back under control and were readied for their assault. South of the town, on the Union left, 60,000 men under Major General William Franklin were massed to face Jackson's Confederates, who had been brought closer to the Confederate center. The remaining troops under Burnside would emerge from the town and attack the Confederates on Marye's Heights. On the morning of December 13, the action began on the left side of the line, with Major General George Meade advancing first; but because Franklin misread the orders, only 4,500 men under Meade were used in the assault. The Federals were crossing an open field when suddenly Confederate artillery opened on their left rear. It was only two guns commanded Major John Pelham, who had left his position dangerously exposed, but it was enough to stop the Union advance for 30 minutes before Pelham ran out of ammunition and withdrew. Meade's troops continued their assault, finding a huge gap in the Confederate line, but a fierce counterattack was launched by Jackson, driving the Federals back to their original position.

At noon Burnside ordered the Union troops in the town to charge Marye's Heights. The first wave of attackers went up the hill and was immediately met with a devastating fire from both infantry and artillery. Reaching the safety of a canal ditch in the hillside, the attackers paused, and then resumed their assault, with the same result. While some were able to find shelter in the handful of buildings or low ridges on the hillside, most were left in the open field and were cut to pieces. Still, wave after wave of Union soldiers was thrown against the Confederate position behind the stone wall, each assault resulting in the same carnage. Soon the ditch, the buildings, and every other possible shelter from the storm of bullets were full, and every man left was exposed to the Confederates' terrible fire. The assaults lasted until dusk, even though the Federals never came close to reaching the Confederate line. Many of those who were still alive on the hillside froze to death in the cold December night. Burnside considered renewing the assault but was talked out of it. After maintaining its position for several days, the Union army withdrew back across the Rappahannock on the night of December 15. The battle of Fredericksburg was over, and the losses, even for this war, were shocking. The Union had lost 12,600 men, more than two-thirds of them on the hillside beneath Marye's Heights. The Confederates suffered 5,300 casualties, still unaffordable but nothing compared to the Union toll.

Chancellorsville

Lee's greatest victory. It is hard to describe the battle of Chancellorsville without using those words, as it is almost universally described as such. It certainly was a brilliant military victory, with the Confederates soundly defeating a Union army more than twice their size. But the critical loss of Major General Thomas "Stonewall" Jackson, the brilliant field commander, was a crippling blow to the Confederate cause. In terms of strategy and tactics, it certainly was Robert E. Lee's masterpiece. But it had cost him, and the Confederacy, dearly.

Following the Union disaster at Fredericksburg, the two armies for the most part stayed in place, each on opposite sides of the Rappahannock River near Fredericksburg. In January 1863 Union commander Major General Ambrose Burnside was replaced by Major General Joseph "Fighting Joe" Hooker. Hooker had a reputation as a man of action, one who would not back down from a fight. Hooker immediately began drilling and retraining his men, quickly restoring the morale of the Union troops that had been so low after their sound defeat a few months back.

As soon as the winter weather left and the dirt roads once again became usable,

Hooker took most of his army away from Fredericksburg, over 100,000 men, leading them north along the Rappahannock, then crossing both that river and the Rapidan. Hooker left 25,000 troops under Major General John Sedgwick at Fredericksburg to cross back into the town and hold Lee in place. Hooker's intention was to come up in the rear of the Confederate army, which he did.

The Federals reached the village of Chancellorsville, west of Fredericksburg and Lee's Army of Northern Virginia, on April 30, 1863. The region around the crossroads at Chancellorsville had long been known as the Wilderness because of the thick brush and undergrowth of the forests. They were nearly impassable, especially by a large army, and so Hooker's men advanced on Chancellorsville by the Orange Turnpike, then split onto two roads, one group staying on the turnpike and the other going down the Plank Road.

Lee was quickly convinced that Sedgwick's men in Fredericksburg were nothing more than a ruse. Hooker was coming up in his rear, so Lee would turn around. Going against the grain of every previous school of military tactics, Lee divided his relatively small army of 60,000, leaving 12,000 men under Major General Jubal Early in Fredericksburg to counter Sedgwick and bringing the rest to bear against Hooker at Chancellorsville. On May 1, as Hooker's men proceeded down the two roads, Jackson attacked up the Plank Road, and Major General Lafayette McLaws attacked up the

Stonewall Jackson Shrine, site of the general's death, Guinea, Virginia.

Lee-Jackson bivouac, site of the last meeting between the two great Confederate generals.

Orange Turnpike. The Federals put up a good fight, but the surprised Hooker withdrew his men to the crossroads at the Chancellorsville Tavern, taking up a defensive position in an angle around the crossroads, with his right extending westward down the Orange Turnpike.

When Major General J. E. B. Stuart returned with the intelligence about Hooker's disposition, Lee again made a remarkable decision that was backward to all previous military thought. He would divide his forces again. Lee would keep 17,000 men, under McLaws and Major General Richard Anderson, in front of Hooker to keep him occupied. He would send 30,000 men with Jackson, who would go on a long, winding route around the Union army and attack its right. On the morning of May 2, Jackson began his march, covering 12 miles on a series of back roads, then approaching the Federal right through the thick trees of the Wilderness. He did not go unnoticed; several Union commanders saw Jackson's movements through the thick trees, and his rear was attacked as he moved. Most of the Federal command, however, was convinced that Jackson was retreating and that Lee was trying to find a way out of this battle against overwhelming numbers.

At 6 PM the Union soldiers stretched out along the Orange Turnpike were at rest, most eating dinner or generally passing time. They were convinced that they were far away from the fight. Suddenly, the woods around the far Union right exploded. Jackson's men came rushing out of the trees, routing the Federals and quickly fighting their way down the turnpike, rolling up the Union line. Finally hampered by darkness, the terrain, and a stubborn Union resistance several miles down the road, the Confederate advance slowed.

Tragedy then struck the Confederates. In the dusk, Jackson, still exploring the front for a way to isolate parts of Hooker's army, came upon some of his own men, who did not recognize him in the dark and began firing. Although the 10 or so men with Jackson shouted that the soldiers were firing into their own men, the North Carolinians did not believe them and kept firing. Jackson was shot twice in the left arm and once in the right hand. He was rushed to a field hospital, where his arm was amputated, and the next day he was sent south of the battlefield by ambulance. He died eight days later. Major General A. P. Hill, who was with Jackson's men, was wounded shortly after Jackson was shot, and all action on the west end of the battlefield ground to a halt.

The next day, May 3, Hooker, still unaware that Lee's army was split, withdrew to another defensive position north of Chancellorsville. Hooker's movements could easily be seen by J. E. B. Stuart, who held a commanding and clear field of fire from a high position known as Hazel Grove. As Stuart opened on the Federals with 50 guns, Confederate infantry pressed through the thick forest and clashed with the Federals north of Chancellorsville. At the same time Lee directed McLaws and Anderson to attack the Union left. The Confederate army, soon and suddenly reunited, was pushing the Federals back when word came that Union troops were approaching Lee's rear.

It was known as the second battle of Fredericksburg. Sedgwick, who had been left in the town by Hooker, attacked the Confederate troops under Early on the same ground, Marye's Heights, that had been so bloodied the previous December. Early had put most of his troops on the line south of the town and had not expected the Union attack to come here. Still, the 600 Confederates were able to hold off two Union assaults from their commanding position atop the hill. Only after the Federals called for a truce to regain their wounded did they realize that they outnumbered the Confederates by more than ten to one; now instilled with great confidence, the Union troops finally strode up the hill and captured Marye's Heights. They immediately advanced westward toward the fighting at Chancellorsville. Sedgwick was able to push the Confederates back several miles to a ridge east of Chancellorsville, atop which sat Salem Church.

Early in the battle of Salem Church, the Union troops were able to continue their advance, but the Confederates formed a mile-long line on the ridge and were able to hold the Federals until reinforcements arrived from Lee. Both armies slept on the field that night. The next morning, May 4, the attack was renewed. Lee, seeing a chance to destroy Sedgwick and then turn his attention back to the entrenched Hooker, rushed men to the east. But Sedgwick, already fighting hard, had seen the writing on the wall. When Lee's

SITE DETAILS

Fredericksburg & Spotsylvania National Military Park (Chancellorsville Unit)—The Chancellorsville unit of the Fredericksburg & Spotsylvania National Military Park is an extension of the driving tour that began at Fredericksburg. The tour begins at the Chancellorsville visitor's center, which contains an excellent museum, as well as a very short walking trail to the location where Stonewall Jackson was mortally wounded. The driving tour continues on to, among other sites, the remains of the Chancellorsville Tavern, Hazel Grove, the point where Jackson started his famous attack on the Union right, and the Lee-Jackson bivouac, where the two great generals met for the last time. Also close by is the Ellwood Farm, where Stonewall Jackson's arm is buried, complete with its own gravestone, in one of the odder memorials of the war. *Fredericksburg & Spotsylvania National Military Park—Chancellorsville Unit, 9001 Plank Rd., Spotsylvania, VA, 22553; 540-786-2880; www.nps.gov /frsp. Open daily; admission charged.*

Second battle of Fredericksburg—The battlefield at Second Fredericksburg is the same as the site of the terrible part of the first battle—Marye's Heights, west of the town. Information and a brochure on the second battlefield of Fredericksburg can be found at the Fredericksburg unit of the national park. *Fredericksburg & Spotsylvania National Military Park—Fredericksburg Unit, 1013 Lafayette Blvd., Fredericksburg, VA, 22401; 540-373-6122; www.nps.gov/frsp. Open daily; admission charged.*

Salem Church—Salem Church is also maintained by the Fredericksburg & Spotsylvania National Military Park. Now completely surrounded by development, the church itself still stands, still bearing the scars and bullet holes from the action of May 3–4, 1863. Brochures about the church, complete with a description of the action and a short walking trail around the grounds, can be found in a stand at the site or, if they're out, at the Fredericksburg unit of the park. *Salem Church, intersection of Old Salem Church Rd. and Norris Dr., Fredericksburg, VA, 22407; 540-373-6122; www.nps.gov/frsp. Open daily; admission charged.*

Stonewall Jackson Shrine—The town of Guinea Station, well south of the battle lines and close to the railroad, was where Stonewall Jackson was taken after his arm was amputated. Jackson arrived at Fairfield Plantation on May 4 and was tended to in one of the plantation's office buildings. Shortly after he arrived, however, he caught pneumonia, and he died on May 8. Today the building is part of Fredericksburg & Spotsylvania National Military Park. It has been restored and is open daily during the summer. Outside the building are several interpretive signs and memorials if you happen to catch it during off-hours. *Stonewall Jackson Shrine, 12019 Stonewall Jackson Rd., Woodford, VA, 22580; 804-633-6076; www.nps.gov/frsp. Open daily, Memorial Day through Labor Day; closed Sun., Oct.–May; admission charged.*

men began to push him back toward the river, Sedgwick withdrew across the Rappahannock at Scott's Ford, which he had thoughtfully secured the previous day.

The next day Lee turned back toward Hooker and prepared for an assault the following morning, but he was too late. Fighting Joe had had enough and was already in the process of retreating north of the Rappahannock. The Union had suffered another staggering defeat, losing 18,000 men between the three battles of Chancellorsville, Second Fredericksburg, and Salem Church. The Confederates had won the day but had lost 12,800 of their own, including the irreplaceable Stonewall Jackson.

The Wilderness

In the spring of 1864, Abraham Lincoln appointed Ulysses S. Grant general-in-chief of the United States Army. No one had held the post since George Washington, but there had been no war this important since Washington's time. Grant's tenacity at Fort Donelson, Vicksburg, and Chattanooga showed that he was a man who would fight and win.

Grant's first step was to set a plan in action to restart the war on all fronts. Sherman would go south to destroy Atlanta. Nathaniel Banks would advance up the

Saunders Field, scene of first fighting at the battle of the Wilderness.

Red River and invade Texas. The Shenandoah Valley would be swept clean. George Meade, who had commanded the Army of the Potomac for nine months since his victory at Gettysburg, would take on Robert E. Lee's Army of Northern Virginia. And Grant, rather than sit in a Washington office, would be in the field with him. Grant's plan for the Union army was simple: engage Lee and keep him from upsetting any of the other armies' plans.

Lee's winter camp had been near Orange, Virginia, west of Fredericksburg. Lee knew that the Union army was building up its numbers north of the Rapidan River and would soon begin its spring campaign. Soon Lee realized where they were going, and he was elated. They would cross near Chancellorsville, into the Wilderness where they had fought a year ago. Lee knew that trying to move that large of an army through the entanglement of brush and undergrowth that characterized the area would greatly diminish, if not eliminate, the vast numerical superiority the Union army held. The moment Lee heard of Grant's crossing, he raced his army of 60,000 men toward the Wilderness. One corps, led by Lieutenant General Richard Ewell, would advance east down the Orange Turnpike, and a second, led by Lieutenant General A. P. Hill, would also head east, but down the Orange Plank Road. Lee's third corps, commanded by Lieutenant General James Longstreet, would come behind both of them.

The Union army of 115,000 crossed the Rapidan at Ely's Ford, north of Chancellorsville, and also used the Germanna Ford Road from the northwest. Grant and Meade tried to get the Union army through the Wilderness as quickly as possible, but it was not easy, and not quick enough. On May 5, 1864, after seeing that Ewell's corps was approaching down the Orange Turnpike, Grant ordered Major General Gouverneur Warren to confront them. In the early afternoon Ewell formed a line on the west side of a clearing known as Saunders Field, and the two units clashed head-on, opening the battle of the Wilderness. Warren launched the first assault and met success, but a Confederate counterattack drove his men back to their original position. Although Warren was later supported by Major General John Sedgwick on his right, the fighting raged across the field for the rest of the day, with neither side gaining an advantage.

To the south, on the Orange Plank Road, A. P. Hill was not as fortunate. Union troops under Major General Winfield Scott Hancock had formed a line in front of the vital intersection with the Brock Road. As the Confederates started to come forward, Hancock's Union troops advanced in a rush, badly mauling Hill's men and driving them away from the crossroads. Hill's men were so torn apart that he begged Lee for a chance to fall back and regroup. But Lee refused the order, expecting Longstreet to arrive shortly.

Longstreet did not make it to the battlefield by morning, and Hill paid dearly for it. The Federals renewed their attack all across the line at dawn, and Hancock quickly and easily started to drive the Confederates back at the south end of the line. At the north end, on the Union right, the previous day's terrible fighting resumed, again with each side making no headway.

Suddenly, Hancock's men on the Union left were the recipients of an overwhelming and vicious counterattack. Longstreet had arrived on the field, just in time to save the Confederate right, and the Federals were thrown backward. Lee, with a fire in his eyes, became swept up in the moment and was ready to lead a group of Texans in a charge of his own. But the Texans, fearing for their beloved commander's safety, shouted for him to go to the rear, or they would not advance. After some gentle coaxing, one of the Texans took Lee's horse by the bridle and led him to the rear. Longstreet followed up the attack with a flank attack that forced Hancock to fall back and once again defend the Brock Road and Orange Plank Road intersection.

Soon after, an unfortunate and strange tragedy struck the Confederates in an event that must have seemed too awful to be true. Only a few miles from where Stonewall Jackson had been killed by friendly fire at Chancellorsville a year before, James Longstreet was suddenly severely wounded, also by friendly fire. Longstreet was quickly carried to the rear, much to the horror of his troops.

Near the end of the day, the Confederates launched a final assault on both Union flanks, and although the Union right was momentarily broken, both sides were holding firm when darkness came. Overnight, brush fires caused by shot and shell igniting the thick undergrowth were passing between the armies, burning alive many of the wounded and cremating the remains of the dead. It was to be remembered by all who were there as one of the ghastliest moments of the war.

On May 7 both armies held their positions but did not fight. When night fell, the Union army, which had suffered 18,000 casualties to the Confederates' 12,800, did what no other Union army before them had done. After defeats at both battles of Manassas, the army had retreated north to Washington. After defeats at Fredericksburg and at Chancellorsville, the army had also moved north, retreating to the other side of the Rappahannock. But despite his heavy losses, Grant did the opposite. Much to the amazement and delight of his men, Grant went south. The morale of the weary Union Army of the Potomac spiked instantly, and they raced, as did Robert E. Lee, to the next vital strategic position—the crossroads at Spotsylvania Court House.

Spotsylvania Court House

After the hard fighting of May 5–6, 1864, Ulysses S. Grant looked at the Confederate lines across from him and concluded that they were too strong for a frontal assault. That night he directed his army to move south to Spotsylvania Court House, the location of an important set of crossroads. While Major General Winfield Scott Hancock held his place on the south end of the line, the other units passed behind him, taking various roads to the town. Finally, Hancock also slipped south.

Meanwhile, the Confederates also began to move south, with two of their three corps now under different commanders. Lieutenant General James Longstreet, who had been wounded, was replaced by Major General Richard Anderson, while Lieutenant

Monuments at the Bloody Angle, Spotsylvania Court House battlefield.

General A. P. Hill, who was sick, was replaced by Major General Jubal Early. Lee also knew the importance of the crossroads and sent his cavalry ahead to hold it while his infantry advanced.

The day that the armies started moving, May 8, 1864, was also the day the battle began, meaning that neither army got any chance to rest before the battle that would last for nearly two weeks around Spotsylvania Court House. Major General Gouverneur Warren, heading down the Brock Road, was met by Anderson as soon as he came into open ground. Two lines formed across the road, and while Warren and Anderson fought it out, troops from both armies filed into the area, with the Confederates forming a line north of Spotsylvania Court House. The movements and the fighting continued into the next day, with the Confederates forming a large V-shaped line and the Union troops filing in across its front. As Major General John Sedgwick set his men along the Union right, his troops were dodging the occasional and seemingly random Confederate bullet. Sedgwick chided his men, saying that the Confederates "couldn't hit an elephant at this distance." He had misjudged not only the Confederates' marksmanship, but also the distance, and he was presently killed by a sharpshooter.

Union attacks continued all along the entire line on May 10, but the Confederates had put a strong defensive position together. Both Warren and Wright decided to conduct attacks on the Confederate left, with Wright concentrating on the angle of the Confederate V, known later as the Mule Shoe because of its shape. Although some of the Union attackers were able to reach the Confederate defenses, they were ultimately repulsed. The next day was mostly made up of troop movement. As Major General Ambrose Burnside took his corps and set up on the Confederate right, Grant had decided on an assault of the Confederate works to begin the next morning, May 12. Burnside would attack from his position along the eastern face of the Confederate line, while the rest of the Union troops would concentrate their attack on the angle.

Just after 4:30 AM on May 12, Hancock led the attack on the angle. His men, concentrated into a thick mass, charged through the morning fog and darkness and swept over the surprised Confederates. They were able to push the Confederates back to a second line, but a counterattack stopped their advance. The Confederates slowly pushed the Federals back to the edges of the Mule Shoe, but no farther. Hand-to-hand combat ensued in the small area for almost 24 full hours before the Confederates could withdraw to a new line behind their original position, forever after known as the Bloody Angle. By almost all accounts it was the most intense and fierce fight of the entire Civil War.

Not much occurred on May 13, as both armies were exhausted. Over the next few days, the armies repositioned themselves again, with Grant bringing most of the units on the right side of his line around to Burnside's left, so that the Union line was now running north to south, facing west toward the Confederates. Lee shifted his men accordingly, meeting the new Union threat. Early on May 19 one final large assault was made by the Confederates, hoping to find and surprise the Union right, but after a hard fight, no ground was gained by either side. The battle was over. Over the two weeks at Spotsylvania Court House, the Federals had again lost many more men than the Confederates had, 18,000 to about 10,000. But again Grant moved south after the battle, heading for the North Anna River and, beyond it, Richmond.

Brandy Station

The great cavalry battle at Brandy Station, Virginia, was a harbinger of things to come. The Confederate cavalry had been completely dominant up to this point in the war. They had conducted daring raids, took "Rides around McClellan," and committed other amazing feats behind enemy lines, and had demonstrated that pound for pound, they were far superior to their Union counterparts. But as the war went on and the Confederate numbers dwindled, the Southerners began to lose their advantage. At the same time, the Federal cavalry became bolder, stronger, and smarter. Brandy Station, the opening battle of the Gettysburg campaign that turned the tide of the war in the Union's favor in the eastern theater, was also the first battle where Union cavalry proved that they could ride with the Confederates.

Following his great victory at Chancellorsville, Robert E. Lee decided that the time was right to attempt to invade the North once more. Commanding three corps of infantry, Lee left one corps at Fredericksburg, Virginia, while he took the other two corps northwest to Culpeper to prepare them for the campaign. Confederate cavalry, commanded by the daring Major General J. E. B. Stuart, would stay between Lee and

The Graffiti House, home of the Brandy Station Battlefield Foundation.

the Union Army of the Potomac, commanded by Major General "Fighting Joe" Hooker, to screen Lee's movements.

Hooker, indeed, did not know what the Confederates were up to. He knew that Confederates were in Culpeper, but according to the information he had, it was just cavalry, and Lee's entire army was still in front of him on the opposite side of the Rappahannock. Hooker thought that the Confederate cavalry was about to launch a raid to cut his supply lines, so he commanded Brigadier General Alfred Pleasonton to break the raid up before it started.

On the morning of June 9, 1863, two groups of Pleasonton's cavalry crossed the Rappahannock in the early morning hours. Brigadier General John Buford crossed at Beverly's Ford, just north of Brandy Station, while Brigadier General David Gregg crossed at Kelly's Ford, 6 miles downriver. They were to meet at Brandy Station, then advance to Culpeper, where the Confederates were supposed to be.

Buford tore across the ford and surprised the small Confederate guard there, many of whom were still asleep. Not far away, though, were Brigadier General William "Grumble" Jones's Confederate cavalry, who were also asleep but were awakened by the gunfire. Jones quickly assembled his men, as well as those of Brigadier General Wade Hampton, and they formed a line on a ridge around the St. James Church, with Jones on the left, Hampton on the right, and artillery in the middle. At the same time, Confederates under Brigadier General W. H. F. "Rooney" Lee fell back to a position behind a low stone wall at the Green Farm on the far Confederate left. Alerted to what was happening, J. E. B. Stuart had left his headquarters, on Fleetwood Hill well behind the lines, to take command at the front.

Quickly organizing his men, Buford decided first to charge the Confederate positions at St. James Church. Several spectacular cavalry charges were launched at the position, and fierce hand-to-hand fighting occurred, but the Confederates held. After some time Buford shifted his weight to the Confederate left, attacking Rooney Lee at the stone wall. Lee held but was eventually driven back to another stone wall on the Green Farm, where his men again held for a time. But suddenly another surprise arrived on the battlefield, and all the Confederate forces immediately and hurriedly fell back.

Gregg's Union cavalry had crossed at Kelly's Ford, but finding Confederates in their front, they simply went the long way around to get to Brandy Station. They

SITE DETAILS

Brandy Station Battlefield—The Civil War Preservation Trust has been able to obtain some of the Brandy Station battlefield, mostly near Beverly Ford and what is now known as Buford's Knoll, and also near the old St. James Church. Like the other CWPT properties, the park provides an excellent interpretation of the battle, with walking trails and signs throughout. The trails are 2 miles and 1 mile long, respectively, and although they are not strenuous, they do cross some hilly terrain, so be prepared if you go. *Brandy Station Battlefield, intersection of St. James Church Rd. and Beverly Ford Rd., Brandy Station, VA, 22714; 202-367-1861; www.civilwar.org/ travelandevents/t_vs_brandystation.htm. Open daily.*

Battle of Brandy Station driving tour—two separate driving tours of the Brandy Station battlefield have been developed, and both are excellent, but they cover slightly different ground. Both cover all the most important sites, so the best suggestion may be to combine the two and make your own tour. One has been developed by the Civil War Preservation Trust, and the other by the National Park Service. The CWPT brochure is available through local tourism offices, including the Graffiti House, home of the Brandy Station Battlefield Foundation. The National Park Service brochure can be picked up at the Fredericksburg & Spotsylvania National Military Park. Both are also available on the Internet, CWPT's by mail order and the National Park Service's by download. *Driving Tour, Battle of Brandy Station, Civil War Preservation Trust, available at Graffiti House, 19484 Brandy Rd., Brandy Station, VA, 22714; 540-727-7718; www.civilwar.org or www.brandystationfoundation.com. Driving Tour, Battle of Brandy Station, Fredericksburg & Spotsylvania National Military Park, 1013 Lafayette Blvd., Fredericksburg, VA, 22401; 540-373-6122; www.nps.gov/ frsp/brandy.htm. Both open daily.*

emerged south of the battlefield, at Fleetwood Hill, which not only held Stuart's lightly guarded headquarters but also a commanding position on the field. Stuart ordered Hampton and Jones to Fleetwood Hill, while commanding Lee to fall back once more.

While Buford followed the Confederates' rear, Gregg's cavalry charged up the southern slope of Fleetwood Hill just as Jones's and Hampton's brigades arrived. What resulted was a spectacular cavalry battle, sabers flashing and pistols firing. The battle on the hill raged all along a 2-mile front, until the Confederates finally drove the Federal troopers off. As a finish, Stuart ordered Rooney Lee to counterattack Buford's men, who fought a rearguard action as they withdrew back across Beverly's Ford.

At day's end the Confederates held the field, having lost 515 men to the Union's 868. But the Federal cavalry had fought well and would continue to do so for the rest of the war. Just as important, Joe Hooker was now convinced that not only was most of Lee's army in Culpeper, but they were not just preparing for another raid; they were preparing for an invasion of the North. He was right, and he would resign his position within the month, citing lack of support to counter what he knew was coming. Lee did invade, but his army met disastrous defeat at Gettysburg less than one month later.

» OTHER SITES IN NORTHERN VIRGINIA

Dranesville—On December 20, 1861, Brigadier General George Ord headed toward Dranesville, Virginia, looking for Confederate activity in the area. A Confederate foraging party commanded by Brigadier General J. E. B. Stuart was indeed heading that way, and Ord formed a defensive line along the Georgetown Pike. Stuart's men assaulted the Union line, pushing it back but not breaking it, and the assault was eventually called off after the Confederates had completed their forage mission.

The Dranesville Tavern, close to the battle site but not exactly in the middle of it (the building has been moved since the battle), has a Virginia Civil War Trails sign in its parking lot. There is a very small park around the tavern, which is open for tours daily. Inside the tavern, however, there is little interpretation of the battle. *Dranesville Tavern Park, intersection of VA 7 and Dranesville Manor Dr., Herndon, VA, 20170. Sign accessible daily.*

Ball's Bluff—A close friend and supporter of Abraham Lincoln, Senator Edward Baker of Oregon was given a commission as a colonel in the Union army when the war broke out, despite his lack of military experience. On October 21, 1861, Baker led troops against a well-positioned Confederate force at Leesburg, Virginia. Baker, however, had not done his homework and did not know the terrain well. Confident of a decisive Union victory, the Federals crossed the Potomac River and approached the Confederate position, which was on a high bluff overlooking the river. The Confederates were surprised, but when they quickly organized an effective counterattack, the Union troops, now stuck atop a steep 70-foot bluff with a mighty river at their backs,

Bottom of the steep riverbank at Ball's Bluff.

were quickly thrown into disarray, a situation that was made even worse when Baker was killed on the field. Many Union soldiers simply jumped off the bluff down to the riverbank, where they were easy targets for the Confederates. Others, frantically trying to escape a desperate situation, drowned trying to recross the Potomac. More than 700 Union soldiers were captured. When the bodies of Union troops began floating past the capital at Washington, the outrage prompted creation of the Congressional Joint Committee on the Conduct of the War, an oversight committee for the military.

Ball's Bluff Battlefield Regional Park has the distinction of holding the nation's smallest national cemetery, with only 54 graves—53 of them unknown. There are trails, interpretive signs, and monuments on the battlefield, including one at the spot where Colonel Baker fell. The park is in a quiet location behind a residential area, and seeing the tall bluff and the river rushing past it is enough to get a sense of the panic that the Federals must have felt. Not too large to take in nor too small to understand, the park does an excellent job of interpreting this relatively small but important battle. *Ball's Bluff Battlefield Regional Park, 17500 Balls Bluff Rd. NE, Leesburg, VA, 20176; 703-737-7800; www.nvrpa.org/parks/ballsbluff. Open daily.*

Aldie—As Robert E. Lee led the Confederate army north to invade Pennsylvania, Major General J. E. B. Stuart stayed between Lee and the Federals. On June 17, 1863,

Union cavalry under Brigadier General H. Judson Kilpatrick went west to reconnoiter Lee's position as part of a greater effort commanded by Brigadier General Alfred Pleasonton. Kilpatrick's men ran into one of Stuart's brigades at Aldie, Virginia, and a four-hour battle ensued. The Confederates were able to hold the Union troopers in place before Stuart finally gave them orders to withdraw west to nearby Middleburg, where other Federal units under Pleasonton were simultaneously attacking.

The battlefield at Aldie is still rolling pasture, and although it is on private property, it has not been forgotten. On the roadside near the battle site are interpretive signs, as well as a monument to the First Massachusetts Cavalry dating back to 1888. More information on the battle can also be found at the Aldie Mill Historic Park, a living history site focused on the history of the town. *Aldie battlefield, 0.1 mile north of intersection of Snickersville Turnpike and Oatlands Rd.; Aldie Mill Historic Park, 39401 John Mosby Hgwy., Aldie, VA, 20105; 703-327-9777; www.nvrpa.org/parks/aldiemill. Signs accessible daily; historic site open weekends Apr.–Oct.*

Middleburg—Major General J. E. B. Stuart, whose task was to stay between the Union army and the main Confederate force invading Pennsylvania, had placed his headquarters at Middleburg, Virginia. Meanwhile, Union cavalry under Brigadier General Alfred Pleasonton headed west in an effort to find Lee. On June 17, 1863, while one unit battled Confederate cavalry at Aldie, another Federal unit, commanded by Colonel Alfred Duffie, met the Confederates at Middleburg. While Stuart moved his headquarters west, he left Confederate cavalry at Middleburg to fight it out and explore the Federal strength. Although the Confederates drove the Union troops out of the town and had some success over the next two days, Union reinforcements arrived on June 19, and the Confederates were forced back.

The Information Center of Historic Middleburg, in a small building known as the Pink Box, contains some information on the battle. A Virginia Civil War Trails sign is outside the museum across the street. Finally, there is also a small private park in the town, marking one of the ridges where fighting took place, but no interpretive information can be found there. *Information Center of Historic Middleburg, 12 N. Madison St.; Battle of Middleburg Park, intersection of John Mosby Hgwy. and Zulla Rd., Middleburg, VA, 20117; 540-687-8888. Open daily.*

Upperville—Having fought Confederate cavalry for three days at Aldie and Middleburg, the Union cavalry now knew the size and location of the Confederate cavalry well. What they did not know, and were trying to find out, was the location of Robert E. Lee's army, which was on its way north to invade Pennsylvania. On June 21, 1863, in an attempt to break through Major General J. E. B. Stuart's screening movement and find Lee, Union forces launched a two-pronged attack against the Confederate cavalry. Although the Confederates were able to repulse the Union assaults, Stuart pulled his units back to Upperville, where they were surprised by Union forces under Brigadier General David Gregg. Gregg pushed the Confederates west for nearly 5 miles until Confederate infantry from Lee's army was forced to support them.

A Virginia Civil War Trails sign is posted in a field in the town of Upperville on the south side of the John Mosby Highway. The sign is located on Vineyard Hill, a prominent landmark of the battle. *Virginia Civil War Trails—Upperville, intersection of John S. Mosby Hgwy. and Crofton Lane, Upperville, VA, 20184. Site accessible daily.*

Chantilly—As Union troops retreated toward Washington after the second battle of Manassas, the Confederates attempted to trap them. On September 1, 1862, General Stonewall Jackson occupied a small rise known as Ox Hill, near the Chantilly plantation, and waited for the Federals. That afternoon, in the middle of a terrible thunderstorm, Union troops under Major General Jesse Reno surprised Jackson's men but were ultimately driven back after a fierce fight. Two Union generals, Brigadier General Isaac Stevens and Major General Philip Kearny, were killed leading assaults against the Confederate line. Union casualties were high at 1,300, but the Federals were able to continue their retreat. The Confederates lost 800 men.

An island oasis in the midst of office buildings and apartment complexes, Ox Hill Battlefield Park sits at a busy intersection in Fairfax, Virginia. The park is small, but it just received a major face-lift and was recently enhanced with additional interpretive signs, informational kiosks, and a much-needed parking area. There are also two monuments, placed long ago, to the two Union commanders who fell here. The park is full of trees and shaded, and it is surprising how isolated it feels from the surrounding sprawl once you step into it. If you don't mind the traffic getting there, it's worth a visit. *Ox Hill Battlefield Park, 4134 W. Ox Rd., Fairfax, VA, 22033; 703-324-8702; www.fairfaxcounty.gov/parks/oxhill/. Open daily.*

Bristoe Station—General George Meade, wary of the movements of Robert E. Lee's Army of Northern Virginia, was moving his entire Army of the Potomac north toward Manassas and Washington, D.C. Lee, however, hoped to strike the Federals before they reached Manassas. On October 14, 1863, as a large force of Union troops marched along the Orange & Alexandria Railroad, Confederates under Lieutenant General A. P. Hill formed a line across the Greenwich Road and began an artillery assault. Unfortunately for the Confederates, Hill had seen only one of the two Union corps moving through the area, the other being hidden by the railroad embankment. When the firing started, the hidden Union corps, commanded by Major General Gouverneur Warren, patiently took a strong position behind the embankment, set themselves, and waited for the Confederate line to move. As soon as Hill's line began to charge the exposed Union troops, the hidden Union soldiers rose and directed a devastating enfilading fire into the Confederates at close range. After being thrown back, the Confederates were able to launch a counterattack, but it too ended in disaster. Hill was eventually reinforced by a Confederate corps under Lieutenant General Richard

Ewell, after which an artillery duel commenced, but the Union had been able to gain better position and took advantage of it. Darkness ended the fighting, and overnight the Federals commenced their march toward Manassas, leaving the Confederates with the field but also 1,380 casualties to the Union's 540. The battle at Bristoe Station effectively ended Lee's attempt at an offensive campaign.

A Civil War Preservation Trust site now holds part of the Bristoe Station battlefield, and development continues. For now, there is parking, extensive walking trails, and some interpretive signs. Although part of the area around the battlefield has been developed as housing, much of the area is still rural, and visualizing the action among the rolling hills of the battlefield is not difficult. *Bristoe Station Battlefield, Civil War Preservation Trust, intersection of Iron Brigade Unit Ave. and Bristow Rd., Bristow, VA, 20136; 202-367-1861; www.civilwar.org. Open daily.*

Thoroughfare Gap—On August 28, 1862, as Major General Thomas "Stonewall" Jackson's Confederates were starting to fight at Manassas, the second wing of the Confederate army, led by Major General James Longstreet, encountered Union resistance near Chapman's Mill at the Thoroughfare Gap. After the Federals were outflanked, they left the gap open for Longstreet's force to advance through. Longstreet continued, virtually unopposed, to reunite with Jackson and Robert E. Lee's Army of Northern Virginia, leading to the decisive victory at the second battle of Manassas.

Virginia Civil War Trails and historical highway markers at Thoroughfare Gap explain the action that happened there. Chapman's Mill is also still standing after all these years, but just barely. The mill was vandalized and nearly burned down several years ago, but an ongoing effort to restore it and the surrounding land has gained some traction. *Virginia Civil War Trails—Thoroughfare Gap; historical highway marker C-50—Department of Historical Resources (Thoroughfare Gap), and 1-FA (Campaign of Second Manassas), intersection of VA 55 and Beverly Mills Rd.; Chapman's Mill, Beverly Mill Rd. and Mountain Rd., Broad Run, VA, 20137; 530-253-5888; www.chap mansmill.org. Sign accessible daily; mill under development.*

Buckland Mills—J. E. B. Stuart's cavalry, waiting at Buckland, Virginia, for the Confederate army to maneuver, saw an opportunity to trap Brigadier General H. Judson Kilpatrick's Union cavalry, which had been pursuing him. Knowing that Major General Fitzhugh Lee's cavalry would be moving into a perfect position to trap Kilpatrick, Stuart planned to lure him as far as Buckland, after which Fitz Lee's men would be able to come up on Kilpatrick's rear on the Warrenton Turnpike. Kilpatrick did indeed ride into Stuart's trap, and the Federal cavalry quickly turned around and flew north up the turnpike; the event was forever after known by Confederates as the Buckland Races. Fitz Lee, however, was not able to close the trap; Union cavalry under Brigadier General George Custer, also in the vicinity, was able to hold Lee back until the rest of Kilpatrick's men reached safety.

At Chestnut Hill, the site of Stuart's ambush, a Virginia Civil War Trails sign has been placed in the parking lot of a commuter station. Even with all the development and congestion around it, the hill is easily discernible, and the old Warrenton Turnpike (now the Lee Highway) is the same road that Kilpatrick's cavalry raced down after its surprise. *Virginia Civil War Trails—Buckland Races, parking lot of commuter station at intersection of Lee Hgwy. and Dumfries Rd., Warrenton, VA, 20187. Signs accessible daily.*

Auburn—Following the battle of Gettysburg, neither the Union nor the Confederate armies in northern Virginia were very active. They were so inactive, in fact, that both were able to send men west to Tennessee to fight at Chickamauga and Chattanooga. Robert E. Lee, knowing that George Meade's Union army had also reduced its strength, finally decided that the time was right to go back on the offensive. Lee planned to come between the Army of the Potomac and the capital at Washington, preventing the Federals from sending more troops to the critically important front in Tennessee. On October 13, 1863, in what was known as the first battle of Auburn, Major General J. E. B. Stuart, riding ahead of Lee's army, had a brief fight with a small group of Federals guarding a supply train. Seeing that the train was heavily guarded, Stuart's men hid in the thick brush to await an opportunity. Before they knew it, however, they were all but surrounded by Union infantry, who were completely unaware of their presence. The next morning Stuart initiated the second battle of Auburn, now fighting to escape. Although it was a close call, Stuart was able to gather intelligence about the Federal troops who had literally been moving all around him.

Each of the two battles of Auburn is represented by its own historical highway marker erected in the area of the battles. They are somewhat difficult to find in the thick growth of the rural roads, and one was recently found partially knocked down, but they are there—just keep your eyes peeled. *First battle of Auburn, historical highway marker CL-8—Department of Historic Resources (Stuart's Bivouac), intersection of Old Dumfries Rd. and Old Auburn Rd.; historical highway marker CL-9— Department of Historic Resources (Battle of Coffee Hill [Second Battle of Auburn]), intersection of Old Auburn Rd. and Rogues Rd., Catlett, VA, 20119. Signs accessible daily.*

Rappahannock River—The Confederates, knowing that the Union armies of Generals George McClellan and John Pope were attempting to join forces, were maneuvering to prevent them from uniting. On August 22, 1862, Major General J. E. B. Stuart led his cavalry against Pope's headquarters supply train, capturing valuable intelligence information for Robert E. Lee. Lee split his army into two wings, ordering Major General James Longstreet to continue the attacks against Pope and keep him in place along the Rappahannock River while Major General Thomas "Stonewall" Jackson took the other wing around Pope, heading for Manassas. Longstreet's small actions at Waterloo Bridge, Freeman's Ford, Beverly's Ford, Sulphur Springs, and other locations kept Pope pinned against the river for three more days while Jackson reached Manassas unopposed.

Historical highway markers commemorate Stuart's initial attack on Pope's train and the attack at Waterloo Bridge. They are both along a busy stretch of highway, so use caution as you pull over and pull back out. *Historical highway marker C-58— Virginia Department of Historical Resources (Second Manassas Campaign, Stuart's Catlett Station Raid), intersection of US 211 and Holtzclaw Rd.; historical highway marker C-60—Virginia Department of Historical Resources (Second Manassas Campaign, Strategic Rappahannock River Crossings), intersection of US 211 and Sturgis Lane, Warrenton, VA, 20186. Signs accessible daily.*

Rappahannock Station—As Robert E. Lee moved the Confederate army south of the Rappahannock River to go into winter camp, the Union army was still on his tail. The Confederates left a fortified position at the town of Rappahannock Station, where they had used a pontoon bridge to cross the river. On November 7, 1863, Major General John Sedgwick led 2,100 men against the position, while another Federal force took the nearby crossing at Kelly's Ford. After pushing the Confederates into their defenses and gaining an excellent artillery position in the afternoon, Sedgwick began bombarding the Confederate earthworks successfully, ceasing when darkness fell. Lee, now convinced that the action at Rappahannock Station was a diversion to cover a larger Union movement at Kelly's Ford, turned his attention to the east and prepared to attack there. But using the cover of darkness and a railroad embankment, Sedgwick's men approached the Confederate works and surprised them, quickly overrunning their positions and capturing most of them. The action here, along with the smaller one at Kelly's Ford, netted 2,041 Confederate casualties to the Union's 461. Lee was ultimately forced to move his entire army south of the Rapidan River for the winter.

The former town of Rappahannock Station is now Remington, and the National Park Service has created a driving tour brochure that points out the distinctive features of the battle. The brochure, along with driving tours for other local battles, can be picked up at Fredericksburg & Spotsylvania National Military Park and can also be downloaded on the park's Web site. *Driving tour, Battle of Rappahannock Station, Fredericksburg & Spotsylvania National Military Park, 1013 Lafayette Blvd., Fredericksburg, VA, 22401; 540-373-6122; www.nps.gov/frsp/rapp.htm. Open daily.*

Kelly's Ford—On March 17, 1863, while the Confederate army was still in its winter camp, Union cavalry under Brigadier General William Averell crossed the Rappahannock River and picked a fight. Crossing at Kelly's Ford, Averell quickly encountered resistance from Brigadier General Fitzhugh Lee and put his 2,100 Union troopers into a defensive line. Lee sent his cavalry, under a promising young major, John Pelham, against the Union right. They were repulsed, and Pelham was mortally wounded. Averell then attacked the Confederates' right, using his superior force to break their line and throw them backward. Reforming his line, Lee directed a successful counterattack against the Union right. Hearing that reinforcements were coming, Averell called off the attack and withdrew back across the Rappahannock.

Kelly's Ford is another one of the cavalry battles in the area for which the National Park Service has created a very nice driving tour. Starting at the ford and including some walking along the way (the short hike to the site where Pelham fell will take you through the heart of the battlefield), it is, like the other tours, well done. The brochure for the tour can be picked up at the Fredericksburg & Spotsylvania National Military Park and can also be downloaded on the park's Web site. The town where the battle occurred is Remington, Virginia. *Driving tour, Battle of Kelly's Ford, Fredericksburg & Spotsylvania National Military Park, 1013 Lafayette Blvd., Fredericksburg, VA, 22401; 540-373-6122; www.nps.gov/frsp/kelly.htm. Open daily.*

Mine Run—In late 1863 Major General George Meade wanted to hit the Confederate army before it went into its winter camps. The Confederates were holding a long defensive line south of the Rapidan River; Meade planned to cross the river east of the line and strike the Confederate right with the entire Army of the Potomac. Meade began to move his army on November 26, 1863, and Confederate commander Robert E. Lee responded instantly by shifting troops to the east and, after fighting several defensive actions, forming a strong line along the west side of a north-south creek of the Rapidan called Mine Run. The position ran for 7 miles and allowed the Confederates a clear field of fire to any possible frontal assault. Meade entrenched and began an artillery bombardment of the Confederate line on November 30, planning to launch attacks on both flanks the next day. But after reassessing the situation with his generals, remembering the disasters at Fredericksburg and Pickett's Charge and the results of assaulting a heavily fortified position across open ground, Meade called off the action. The Federals withdrew on the night of December 1, leaving the Confederates in their lines. Over the week's maneuvering, the Union had lost 1,633 men to the Confederates' 795.

The National Park Service has developed a driving tour of the Mine Run campaign. The tour brochure describes the battle in detail and highlights some of the locations of the lines and the fighting, with a handful of interpretive signs along the way. The brochure can be picked up at the Fredericksburg & Spotsylvania National Military Park and can also be downloaded on the park's Web site. Most of the tour is within the town of Locust Grove. *Driving tour, Battle of Mine Run, Fredericksburg & Spotsylvania National Military Park, 1013 Lafayette Blvd., Fredericksburg, VA, 22401; 540-373-6122; www.nps.gov/frsp/mine.htm. Open daily.*

Morton's Ford—A campaign to free Union prisoners held in Richmond was about to be launched by Major General Benjamin Butler, who would originate his movements from Williamsburg, Virginia, to the southeast. As a diversion he sent Union troops northwest of the city to attempt to draw Confederate soldiers away from their capital. On February 6, 1864, the Federals fought with Confederates at various fords of the Rapidan, including Raccoon Ford, Robertson's Ford, and Morton's Ford.

No signs of the battle of Morton's Ford remain today. The location where the Zachary Taylor Highway crosses the Rapidan River is probably the most accessible location near any of the battle sites, but there is nothing there to indicate that. Information can be found at the Fredericksburg & Spotsylvania National Military Park. *Morton's Ford Site, 0.1 mile southeast of intersection of Zachary Taylor Hgwy. and Algonquin Trail, Raccoon Ford, VA, 22701.*

Cedar Mountain—After the Federals had been driven away from Richmond during the Seven Days Battles, another Union army was forming to the north under Major General John Pope. Major General Thomas "Stonewall" Jackson went north looking for opportunities to strike Pope's forces, which were divided across the Rapidan River. After several days of making little progress, Jackson saw his opportunity on August 9, 1862. A Union force of 12,000 men under Major General Nathaniel Banks was in a position near the Orange-Culpeper Road, close to Cedar Mountain. The 22,000 Confederates formed a line across the road, with the right, commanded by Brigadier General Jubal Early, near the base of Cedar Mountain to the south. The Confederate left, commanded by Brigadier General Charles Winder, was near the gate of the Crittenden farm to the road. An artillery duel that lasted for several hours began the battle, killing General Winder but otherwise achieving little. During the exchange, infantry from both sides took positions for an assault. At 5 PM Banks's men assaulted both flanks of the Confederate line, pushing them back even though the Union troops were heavily outnumbered. As the Confederates fled, Jackson rode directly into the thick of the fighting, waving his sword and rallying his troops to hold. (Few of them probably noticed that the sword was still in its sheath, rusted into place because it had never been drawn before.) At almost the same time, Confederate reinforcements from Brigadier General A. P. Hill arrived, and the Federals were sent reeling, eventually being driven off the field. Jackson's force, almost double the Union number, had come away with a victory but had only narrowly escaped disaster. The Federals had suffered 2,500 casualties; the Confederates, who held the field and carried the day, had lost 1,400 men.

The Civil War Preservation Trust has preserved part of the Cedar Mountain Battlefield. A walking trail, along with interpretive signs and monuments that predate the park, make interpretation of the battle very easy, and the surrounding rural landscape only enhances the experience. In addition, the National Park Service has created a driving tour of the Cedar Mountain battlefield that nicely complements the Preservation Trust's site. As with the other National Park Service driving tours in the area, the brochure can be obtained at the Fredericksburg & Spotsylvania National Military Park and can also be downloaded on the park's Web site. *Cedar Mountain Battlefield, Civil War Preservation Trust, intersection of US 15 and General Winder Rd., Rapidan, VA, 22733; 202-367-1861; www.civilwar.org/travelandevents/t_vs_cedar mountain.htm. Open daily. Driving tour, Battle of Cedar Mountain, Fredericksburg &*

Spotsylvania National Military Park, 1013 Lafayette Blvd., Fredericksburg, VA, 22401; 540-373-6122; www.nps.gov/frsp/cedar.htm. Open daily.

Trevilian Station—General-in-Chief Ulysses S. Grant had decided to leave Cold Harbor, where he had been repeatedly repulsed by the Confederates for over a week. Intending to move south to take Petersburg, he directed Major General Philip Sheridan to get around Robert E. Lee's army, link up with Major General David Hunter coming from the Shenandoah Valley, and threaten the Confederate capital from the west, cutting the Virginia Central Railroad in the process and hopefully diverting Lee's attention. Two divisions of Confederate cavalry under Generals Wade Hampton and Fitzhugh Lee pursued Sheridan, approaching the Union camp at Clayton's Store near Trevilian Station. On June 11, 1864, the Confederates attacked the camp, pushing most of the Federal units back. At the same time Brigadier General George Custer found a gap between Hampton and Lee's divisions and took his men through it, capturing the Confederate wagon train. However, Custer had isolated himself from the rest of the Union force and soon found himself surrounded on three sides at Trevilian Station. In what became known later as Custer's First Last Stand, his men only barely held out until rescued by Brigadier General Alfred Torbert's division. Darkness ended the fighting, with Sheridan's force at Trevilian Station and the Confederates at Louisa Court House. Overnight, Hampton formed a line west of Trevilian, with Lee joining him by noon the next day. Sheridan, meanwhile, had been tearing up the track of the railroad. In the early afternoon Sheridan headed west and attacked the Confederate lines but was repulsed seven times, each one a hard fight. Later in the day the Confederates launched a counterattack on the Union right, driving it back but not breaking it. The fighting finally ended at 10 PM, with Sheridan finally calling it off. He took his troops back to the Army of the Potomac the next day, having lost 1,007 men. The Confederates, though they had suffered 1,071 casualties, held the field and prevented the Federals from approaching Richmond from the west.

The driving tour created by the National Park Service for Trevilian Station is excellent and is much enhanced by the presence of several Virginia Civil War Trails signs scattered along the route. The brochure for the tour can be picked up at the Fredericksburg & Spotsylvania National Military Park and can also be downloaded on the park's Web site. *Driving tour, Battle of Trevilian Station, Fredericksburg & Spotsylvania National Military Park, 1013 Lafayette Blvd., Fredericksburg, VA, 22401; 540-373-6122; www.nps.gov/frsp/trev.htm. Open daily.*

Garrett Farm—On April 24, 1865, John Wilkes Booth stopped by a farmhouse near Port Royal, Virginia, owned by the Garrett family, looking for a place to spend the night. Booth had been hard on the run since the night he had shot President Abraham Lincoln, and was traveling with David Herold, one of his co-conspirators in the assassination. Federal troops, hot on his trail, received a tip that he was at the farm, and

A simple highway marker denotes the former location of the Garrett farm, scene of the death of John Wilkes Booth.

two days later Booth was cornered in a barn on the property. After a failed attempt to talk Booth out of the barn, it was set on fire in an attempt to smoke him out. Suddenly, a shot rang out; a Union soldier, Boston Corbett, had shot Booth through an opening in the barn, inexplicably and against orders. Booth was brought to the porch of the Garrett house, where he died shortly.

Virtually no trace is left of the Garrett farm today. The site of the former farm lies in the thick trees of the median of U.S. Highway 301, just south of Port Royal. A historical highway marker, which can be seen only from the northbound lanes, is near the spot, and an additional sign has now been placed in the median, where a very short and mostly undeveloped trail leads to the former site of the farmhouse. At the site there is a small memorial to Booth, placed by the Twenty-First Century Confederate Legion. If you do pull over, use great caution, as the cars that use the highway tend to fly down the road pretty quickly. *Historical highway marker EP-20—Virginia Conservation and Development Commission (John Wilkes Booth) and Garrett farm site, near milepost 122 in northbound lanes of US 301, 2.2 miles south of intersection of US 301 and US 17, Port Royal, VA, 22535. Site accessible daily.*

Stratford Hall—Almost 200 years of Virginia's history is inextricably tied to the Lee family. In the 1730s, Thomas Lee, member of the House of Burgesses and future acting royal governor of Virginia, began to build a large home, which he named Stratford

Hall, at his plantation along the Potomac River. Thomas's sons, Richard and Francis, went on to sign the Declaration of Independence. Stratford Hall was passed down to his son Philip, who gave it to his eldest daughter Matilda upon his death. Matilda married cousin and Revolutionary War hero Henry "Light-Horse Harry" Lee, who kept the home when she died. Henry remarried, and among their children was son Robert, who would go on to command the Confederate Army of Northern Virginia.

Stratford Hall, an imposing redbrick home and plantation, is well cared for, and guided tours are available. The visitor's center should be visited first to gain some understanding of the wealth of history here (along with the somewhat dizzying Lee family tree). After that, the vast grounds and gardens are free to explore, and you can easily be lost in the peace and quiet. But the tour of the home is a must. Although revered as the birthplace of the much-admired general, the home offers much more to see, and the tour guides do an excellent job, mixing in entertaining stories of the Lee family's exploits in the home (my favorite was the one about Robert's angel in the fireplace), while pointing out how closely today's life is tied to the past; you can't help but leave feeling educated. It's a little out of the way but is worth the drive. (If you're looking for other things to do in the area, the birthplace of another Lee relative, George Washington, is only a few miles away.) *Stratford Hall, 483 Great House Rd., Montross, VA, 22520; 804-493-8038; www.stratfordhall.org. Open daily; admission charged.*

Stratford Hall, birthplace of Robert E. Lee.

Aquia Creek—The Confederates had built artillery batteries along the south bank of the Potomac River to attempt to close the river to Union shipping. One of the batteries, at the mouth of the wide Aquia Creek, had the additional responsibility of protecting the Richmond, Fredericksburg & Potomac Railroad. On May 29, 1861, a Union gunboat shelled the battery at Aquia Creek, then returned on May 31 with additional boats, resuming the shelling that day and the next. Neither side suffered any casualties. When the Confederates abandoned the position the next year, the Union army used the location, with its proximity to the railroad, as a supply base for future operations.

Aquia Landing County Park is home to a Virginia Civil War Trails sign, as well as a historical highway marker; both are mostly related to the large Union supply base that was established here but also briefly mention the battle of Aquia Creek. Although nothing remains of the battery, you get a clear view of the mouth of Aquia Creek and the Potomac River. The park contains full facilities, including a public beach. *Aquia Landing County Park, intersection of Brooke Rd. and Canterbury Dr., Stafford, VA, 22554; 540-658-4871. Open daily.*

Cockpit Point—In late 1861 the Confederates had command of most of northern Virginia and had built a series of artillery positions along 6 miles of the Potomac River in an attempt to control it. The Potomac, however, is very wide below Washington, and most boats were able to pass the batteries by traveling at night and staying close to the Maryland side. On January 3, 1862, two Union gunboats shelled the Confederate battery at Cockpit Point; the engagement ended without casualties when one of the gunboats was damaged. Within a few months, when the Confederate army retreated south to counter the Union's drive on the capital at Richmond, all the batteries were abandoned.

The old earthworks are still around and are preserved as part of Leesylvania State Park. A short walking trail at the end of the main road will take you the site of the batteries, where a few interpretive signs have been erected. You will also have a full, grand view of the river from this point and see the untouched battlefield, which was on the water. The park is also a full-facility recreational area, with camping, boating, fishing, and other activities. *Leesylvania State Park, 1201 Daniel K. Ludwig Dr., Woodbridge, VA, 22191; 703-730-8205; www.dcr.virginia.gov/state_parks/lee.shtml. Open daily; admission charged.*

» WHERE TO STAY IN NORTHERN VIRGINIA

There is no shortage of places to stay in northern Virginia, and the towns of Arlington, Alexandria, and Manassas offer many options. But if you're looking for a home with direct ties to the battlegrounds, you will have to travel out a bit.

The **Briar Patch Bed and Breakfast**, located to the west in Middleburg, was in the thick of the fighting during the battle of Middleburg and still bears the scars of that day. The home was built in 1805 and saw Union and Confederate troops continually passing by as they waged war over the land all around. *Briar Patch Bed and Breakfast, 23130 Briar Patch Lane, Middleburg, VA, 20117; 1-866-327-5911; www.briarpatch-bandb.com.*

In Fredericksburg there is no better place to stay than the **Richard Johnston Inn**, within the small downtown area. The building was one of many along the Rappahannock River to sustain damage when the Union army began to shell the town; the beams of the attic room are still charred from the fires that spread throughout the town that night. Confederate sharpshooters were scattered throughout the buildings along the river, and the ghost of one has been reported in the home. Like much of Fredericksburg, the home's history dates to well before the Civil War. If you're visiting the many battlefields around Fredericksburg, this makes for an excellent base and a complete experience. *Richard Johnston Inn, 711 Caroline St., Fredericksburg, VA, 22401; 1-877-557-0770; www.therichardjohnstoninn.com.*

9

Confederate Invasions of the North

OVERVIEW

Unlike the United States' war plan for returning the seceded states to the Union, which was very clearly laid out in the Anaconda Plan, the Confederate war plan was extremely simple. It was the same war plan as that of virtually every successful rebellion in history, and the same as that of the Continental Army during the American Revolution. The Confederacy did not have to win the Civil War. It simply had to not lose it. If the Confederate States of America could keep up the fight until the United States grew weary of war and fighting, it held a good chance of surviving and becoming a new nation.

Still, both militarily and politically, there were occasionally good reasons to venture into the Northern states and pick a fight. In the case of the western theater, the reason was evident—hope still remained that the border states of Kentucky and Missouri could be induced to join the Confederacy. In the East, however, the reasons had to be not only solid, but the plan had to be feasible and the cause necessary. And so, during the Civil War, the Confederacy conducted only two primary invasions of the Northern states in the eastern theater. Both ended in disaster for the South.

The first invasion was out of necessity. Even after a string of Confederate victories in the spring and summer of 1862, driving the Union army away from the Confederate capital at Richmond and then defeating it soundly at the second battle of Manassas, Robert E. Lee's Army of Northern Virginia was literally hungry. Rather than tax the war-weary farmers of Virginia, Lee decided that he could step into Maryland, gather the supplies he desperately needed, and put a scare into the Northern states only months before

Visitors survey the battlefield from Little Round Top, Gettysburg National Military Park.

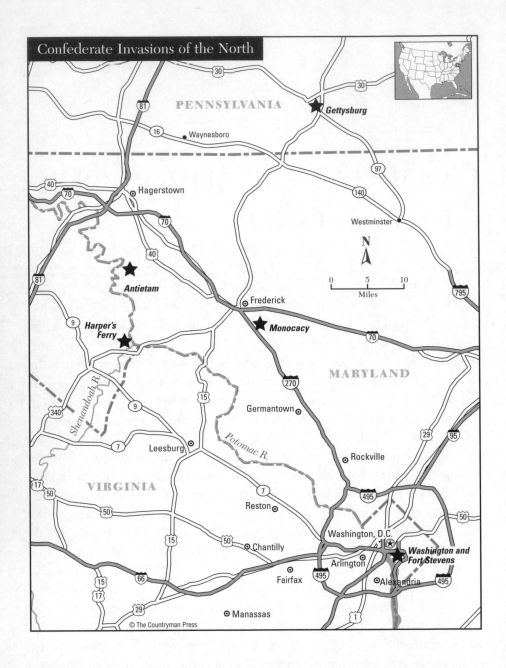

Confederate Invasions of the North

the upcoming elections. After a quick victory at Harpers Ferry, Lee fell into deep trouble and, through some extremely bad luck, almost lost his entire army at the battle of Antietam. While the Union army also suffered greatly at the battle, it held the field, and the Army of Northern Virginia was forced to return south in haste across the Potomac River.

The following year Lee again decided the time was right for invasion. In the summer of 1863, again after decisive Confederate victories, this time at Fredericksburg and Chancellorsville, Lee sought to move the war out of Virginia and into the North. His army was strong and large, and he saw a chance to crush not only the Union Army of the Potomac, but Northern morale as well. He got his chance at Gettysburg, Pennsylvania, on July 1. Three days of battle ensued, the most incredible battle ever to occur on the continent. As the battle, and possibly the war, lay in the balance, Lee ordered a fateful charge on the afternoon of the third day of fighting. Pickett's charge would devastate the Confederate Army, and once more Lee was forced to quickly take his men back to Virginia. The Army of Northern Virginia would never cross into the Northern states again.

That is not to say that the war in the North was over; there was still a chapter left to be written. In the summer of 1864, Lee needed to relieve pressure on his army as it was being squeezed into Petersburg, Virginia. He ordered Major General Jubal Early, commander of the Army of the Valley, to leave the protection of the Shenandoah Valley and threaten Washington, D.C., forcing General Ulysses S. Grant to take troops away from Petersburg and send them to the capital. But Major General Lew Wallace was able to stall Early at the battle of Monocacy, forever known as "the battle that saved Washington." Wallace's tactics, along with timely troop movement by Grant, alleviated any threat to the national capital.

Although they were few, the Confederate invasions of the North always resulted in dramatic and decisive results. These are the battles that to Americans epitomize the Civil War.

» PEOPLE TO KNOW

George G. Meade—Given command of the Army of the Potomac three days before the battle of Gettysburg, George Gordon Meade had served under Zachary Taylor and then Winfield Scott in the Mexican War. Other than those grand experiences, his military career was mostly as a cartographer. But when the Civil War broke out, Meade quickly began to rise through the ranks, establishing himself as a capable field commander.

Meade was wounded during the Seven Days Battles but recovered in time to fight at the second battle of Manassas and Antietam. Soon after, he was promoted to major general and served under Joe Hooker. But when Hooker stalled after the battle of Chancellorsville, President Lincoln quickly replaced him with Meade. Only days later Meade faced Robert E. Lee at Gettysburg, winning a critical but costly victory. After the battle, however, as Union generals had previously done after victories, Meade did not pursue and sat inactive, with the exception of a few maneuvers designed to track Lee southward. When Ulysses S. Grant was given the rank of lieutenant general, he chose to travel with the Army of the Potomac rather than sit in Washington. Meade retained the command of the Army of the Potomac, but with Grant literally over his shoulder, the two and their staffs were often at odds, although they ended up getting the job done. Meade stayed in the army after the war, serving in the East until his death in 1872.

Jubal A. Early—Although the Civil War produced many colorful characters, "Old Jube" Early was certainly one of the standouts. Despite a reputation for feistiness, hard drinking, and abrasiveness, Early was loved by those who fought for him, and also happened to be a very good general.

Early came from a wealthy Virginia family, attended West Point, and went on to fight in the Mexican War and the Seminole War. Like many others who fought for the Confederacy, Early did not support the secession of Virginia and voted against it during the state's convention. But duty called, and he returned to the military after a long absence. Early fought in most of the major battles of the eastern theater but really made a name for himself when he swept through the Shenandoah Valley in June 1864 and threatened to capture the capital at Washington, behind the back of the Union forces nearing Petersburg. Although his invasion was checked, Early went on to fight in the valley until driven out by Major General Philip Sheridan. After fleeing to Texas and then Mexico when the war ended, Early eventually returned to Virginia and later worked for the Louisiana state lottery—operated by his former colleague P. G. T. Beauregard. He died in Virginia in 1894.

» THINGS TO KNOW

Because these historic sites are so well known, they are also extremely popular and well visited. With the exception of perhaps Monocacy National Battlefield, expect at least a decent-size crowd when you visit any of these sites, particularly during the summer months. In fact, some of the sites require a lot of advance planning, and even reservations, so be sure to call ahead.

When in Washington, obviously there is a lot more to see and do than just the Civil War–related sites listed here. The city is not only full of history, but also provides a great chance to see your government in action, all around you. Without a doubt, your best travel agent or tour guide in Washington, D.C., is absolutely free (sort of—you've paid for it with your taxes): Call the office of your senators or congressional representative to get any tours or information; they are the folks who can get you gallery passes to see Congress, intimate guided tours of the Capitol without having to wait in line for hours, and even into the White House.

As stated in previous chapters, driving around the greater Washington area can be incredibly frustrating. Make sure you drive cautiously, and expect slow going around the city.

THE TRIP

No matter where you come from, Washington is the best place to enter and exit this tour. All the sites are close together, and all are near interstates and major cities. You will have no problem finding food or lodging.

Although there aren't many sites on this tour, you will likely want to set aside plenty of time to visit each one. Don't expect to see Gettysburg in an hour; it can't be done. Be sure to give yourself enough time to soak it all in.

» THE CAN'T-MISS SITES

Fort Stevens and Washington

Although Washington, D.C., had certainly grown over the 60 or so years since its founding, by the time of the Civil War it still had the marks of a developing city. Poor sanitation, crowded streets, and a large population of transients, politicians, office seekers, and unsavory characters gave the city a poor reputation. But it was still the political center of the nation, even if it had not yet completely embraced the idea of Union.

Marker indicating where Lincoln came under Confederate fire, Fort Stevens, Washington, D.C.

John Ericsson National Memorial, at the west end of the National Mall in Washington.

Throughout much of the war, fear remained of a Confederate attack and occupation of the city. Washington was always full of Union troops—partly because of the amount of fighting in nearby Virginia, but also because of the vast system of defenses that had been built around the city. Forming a giant ring around the capital, the Washington earthworks covered virtually every possible avenue of invasion, by land or by sea. There were 68 forts, interspersed with breastworks and batteries. Washington was a very well-defended city.

Although occasional threats to the capital were good for throwing a scare into the Northern population, there was really no logical reason for the Confederates to attack Washington. Strategically and politically, it was against the South's stated policy of simply wanting "to be left alone." And in fact there was only one real attempt to threaten Washington during the war, and its purpose was simply to serve as a diversion.

Robert E. Lee's army was being penned into Richmond and Petersburg. Major General Jubal Early was sent from the Shenandoah Valley to threaten Washington, which Lee hoped would force Ulysses S. Grant to send troops north to defend the capital. After Early was stalled at the battle of Monocacy, and Union troops flooded the capital, Early could not do much at Washington. Still, he had come this far; he might as well make a show of it and test the Washington defenses.

On July 11, 1864, Early approached the city from the north, centering on Fort

Stevens, the northernmost fort in the ring of defenses. Some skirmishing took place, and although the fort was only lightly manned, it was enough to convince Early that an assault would be unwise. The action continued into the next day, but Early eventually retreated west back to the Shenandoah Valley.

But Early's withdrawal did not occur before some history was made at Fort Stevens. President Lincoln, who was staying at the Soldiers' Home nearby, decided to come out to the fort and watch the battle himself. Although plenty of myth seems to surround the event, it is said that at one point, Lincoln, standing conspicuously atop the earthworks with his already tall and recognizable frame topped by his stovepipe hat, had to be quickly pulled off the ramparts. Some choice words about the president being a fool and asking if he wanted to get himself shot were allegedly said, and Lincoln apparently took it with his usual humility. Although in later years many a soldier—probably more than were actually at Fort Stevens—claimed the honor of uttering those words, it is likely that there is some truth to the story.

Obviously there is a lot to see in Washington besides Fort Stevens. Because of the Civil War, the city grew not only in size, but in stature and reputation. Among the many historical sites and memorials in our nation's capital, the Civil War looms large.

Ford's Theatre National Historic Site, site of Lincoln's assassination.

SITE DETAILS

Fort Stevens—Although the National Park System's Rock Creek Park preserves many of Washington's Civil War–era fortifications, the only one of them that saw any significant action was Fort Stevens. Although the fort is a unit of the park, it does seem a bit lonely, taking up part of a city block, with no interpretive center and very few signs. (If you do want more information, you can go to the park's Web site and download a self-guided tour of Fort Stevens in the form of a podcast.) What is left is fairly well preserved, and there is a monument near the spot where Lincoln was allegedly standing when he came so close to enemy fire. There may be better examples of Washington's defenses, but Fort Stevens is a nice piece of history. *Fort Stevens, Rock Creek Park, intersection of 13th St. and Quackenbos St. NW, Washington, DC, 20011; 202-895-6070; www.nps.gov/rocr. Open daily.*

President Lincoln's Cottage at the Soldiers' Home—During the summers of 1862 through 1864, the Lincolns (as had the Buchanans before them, and several other presidential families afterward) temporarily moved to a cottage at the Soldiers' Home north of the city. Close enough for a reasonable commute to the White House but far removed from the heat and unpleasantness of the crowded downtown, the home made a perfect evening retreat for the family, particularly after their son Willie died in 1862. The home is set upon a high hill, able to catch the cool summer breezes, and at the time offered a commanding view of the entire city. The Soldiers' Home surrounding the cottage was founded shortly before the war, and every day the Lincolns were reminded of the terrible toll of the fighting as soldiers were buried in the cemetery in front of the home. The Soldiers' Home continued to operate after the war, and over time the cottage served various administrative functions. While many realized the historic importance of the building, funding to preserve it was scarce. Finally, a major project was undertaken, and the Lincoln Cottage, still sparsely furnished but wonderfully restored, opened to the public in 2008. Tours of the home are given daily, and the interpretive center across from the cottage is completely up-to-date, including multimedia presentations displaying Lincoln's life at the home. The interactive program challenging visitors to make the same decisions that Lincoln made is particularly enlightening. Thank goodness this home was finally opened to the public; it is a wonderful piece of history. When you plan your visit, be sure to call at least several days in advance; reservations are required, and it is becoming a very popular destination. Also be aware that what is now the U.S. Soldiers' and Airmen's Home still serves America's veterans as a retirement community, so do not stray from the grounds around the cottage. *President Lincoln's Cottage at the Soldiers' Home, intersection of Rock Creek Church Rd. NW and Upshur St. NW, Washington, DC, 20011; 202-829-0436; www.lincolncottage.org. Open daily; admission charged.*

Ulysses S. Grant Memorial—Absolutely huge but often unnoticed in the shadow of the Capitol building, the Grant Memorial is passed by millions every year who don't even seem to know what it is. Begun in 1909, it was not finished until 1922 with the completion of the statue of Grant on horseback, standing almost 40 feet high between the west front of the Capitol and the Reflecting Pool. Today, unfortunately, the memorial is often viewed as just another part of the landscape of the National Mall. There are other memorials to Grant, but this is certainly the finest and most elaborate in Washington. *Ulysses S. Grant Memorial, near intersection of Third St. SW and Maryland Ave. SW, Washington, DC, 20024; 202-426-6841; www.nps.gov/nama. Open daily.*

Ford's Theatre National Historic Site—On April 14, 1865, five days after Robert E. Lee surrendered his army at Appomattox, President Abraham Lincoln, attending the play Our American Cousin at Ford's Theatre, was shot and killed by the assassin John Wilkes Booth. The story of the assassination is obviously much more complicated than that, but the gravity and consequences of that event are enough to make Ford's Theatre National Historic Site overwhelmingly powerful. The theater, still in operation, has changed some over the years, but walking into the auditorium and looking up at the balcony still makes for a stunning moment. The basement of the theater, undergoing a massive restoration project beginning in 2008, serves as a museum containing an amazing collection of artifacts, including Booth's derringer pistol and the coat Lincoln was wearing that fateful night. Also part of the park is the Petersen House, immediately across from the theater. After Lincoln was shot he was carried outside and directly into the tiny back bedroom of the home, where he was laid on a bed that was far too short for his giant frame. As doctors tended to him, Secretary of War Edwin M. Stanton began an investigation in the back parlor, interviewing witnesses and giving orders, while in the front parlor others tried to somehow comfort Lincoln's traumatized wife. At 7:22 the following morning Lincoln died, finally at peace after four terrible years of the worst war the nation had ever known. *Ford's Theatre National Historic Site, 511 10th St. NW, Washington, DC, 20004; 202-426-6924; www.nps.gov/foth. Open daily.*

Lincoln Memorial—Not a lot of description is needed for the Lincoln Memorial; we've all seen it on television and on the backs of our pennies. But visiting the Lincoln Memorial is a different experience entirely. Dedicated in 1922 after eight years of work, the imposing monument, with its 36 marble columns, the great steps leading to it, and Lincoln's words carved into the walls, is awe-inspiring. But it is the 19-foot-tall Daniel Chester French sculpture of the seated Lincoln, commanding and solemn, that leaves the lasting impression. If there were a short list of sites that all Americans must see, this monument would surely make it. *Lincoln Memorial, Lincoln Memorial Circle SW, Washington, DC, 20037; 202-485-9889; www.nps.gov/linc. Open daily.*

John Ericsson National Memorial—Very near the Lincoln Memorial is another monument to a very important figure in the Civil War, John Ericsson. Ericsson, a Swedish immigrant, came up with a revolutionary design for steamship propulsion, the twin-screw propeller. It was an amazing invention, and when it debuted in 1843, the United States Navy was very pleased to have it—but because of the chicanery of a naval official, Ericsson was never paid for it. As most would, he became resentful of the government, and went around the world to sell his inventions elsewhere. In the early 1860s, putting aside his personal feelings, Ericsson was persuaded to come work for the U.S. Navy again. Rumors had been swirling that the Confederates were building an ironclad gunboat. Ericsson had dabbled with this before, and this time the Navy put its complete faith in him, even as many scoffed at his new design. It proved worthy, however, and Ericsson's "monitor" design was duplicated many times over. Upon his death in 1889, a truly grateful U.S. Navy transported Ericsson's body back to his homeland of Sweden. John Ericsson's memorial is almost as obscure to Washington, D.C., visitors as his name, yet Ericsson's inventions completely modernized naval operations and warfare, and his engineering feats had as much to do with Union victory as any general or weapon. The memorial sits in the middle of an intersection; if you visit, be careful crossing the street, as most cars whiz past the site as if it were just another piece of public art. *John Ericsson National Memorial, intersection of Independence Ave. SW and 23rd St. SW, Washington, DC, 20037; 202-426-6841; www.nps.gov/joer. Open daily.*

Arlington House, the Robert E. Lee Memorial—In April 1861 General Robert E. Lee waited anxiously at his home for word from Richmond. Fort Sumter had been bombarded, and the state of Virginia was likely to secede. Lee had lived in the home overlooking Washington for 30 years; it had been in his family for decades more, a memorial to his forebears, the Custis and Washington families. Finally, the news did come; Virginia had seceded. Several days later, Lee, who abhorred the idea of secession, decided to serve his state over his country and left Arlington House for Richmond. He would never return. Over the next few years, the home and the estate would be ransacked and eventually possessed by the United States because the Lees did not pay their taxes. Ultimately, the army began burying Union soldiers on the property, and the graves soon numbered in the thousands. Today, Arlington House, also known as the Custis-Lee Mansion, still stands atop the high hill overlooking the dead of Arlington National Cemetery but is now a memorial to Robert E. Lee and his life. The home has just begun a major restoration, and although it will stay open to visitors on most days, it will be closed on others; be sure to call ahead to make sure the home is open if you plan to visit. *Arlington House—the Robert E. Lee Memorial, Arlington National Cemetery, Arlington, VA, 22304; 703-838-4848; www.nps.gov/arho. Open daily, but check for construction schedule.*

Fort Ward Museum and Historic Site—One of the many existing examples of the Civil War defenses surrounding Washington, the Fort Ward site contains a museum regarding the entire system of earthworks. Located in Alexandria, Virginia, Fort Ward was one of the larger installations, mounting 36 guns. While the museum's collection is not large, it is impressive, and the restored earthworks are wonderful. *Fort Ward Museum and Historic Site, 4301 W. Braddock Rd., Alexandria, VA, 22211; 703-557-0613; oha.alexandriava.gov/fortward. Park open daily; museum closed Mon.*

Frederick Douglass National Historic Site—There are some men whose presence in appearance, even in a photograph, command instant respect. This can certainly be said of Frederick Douglass. Born a slave in 1818, he was able to escape in 1838 and eventually became one of the world's most eloquent and respected speakers on the subject of slavery. His writings, in the form of several autobiographies and abolitionist newspapers, were equally influential. Douglass fought for decades against slavery and was a close personal adviser to Lincoln as he crafted the Emancipation Proclamation. Following the war Douglass continued his fight for equal rights for African Americans and eventually lent his power and influence to other movements for freedom, including women's rights. In 1872 Douglass moved to Washington, and in 1878 he purchased the impressive home in Washington's Anacostia neighborhood that is now the Frederick Douglass National Historic Site. Douglass's story is remarkable, and even though he spent much of the time until his death in 1895 outside the home, his ghost is still here. If you plan on visiting, be sure to make your reservations very early; the tours fill up quickly and are somewhat limited. *Frederick Douglass National Historic Site, 1411 W St. SE, Washington, DC, 20020; 202-426-5961; www.nps.gov/frdo. Open daily; admission charged.*

Clara Barton National Historic Site—Clara Barton was a 39-year-old woman working in the patent office in Washington, D.C., when the Civil War began. Soon Barton was arranging for humanitarian supplies to be sent from the North and was tending to the wounded of both sides after battles, sometimes even on the field, remarkable for a woman of her time. Her efforts and courage soon became well known, and generals and political leaders began to call for her presence *before* the beginnings of major campaigns and battles. Following the war Barton became a popular speaker and was involved in both the suffrage and civil rights movements, while continuing to serve as a nurse anytime the need was seen. After touring Europe and learning of the International Red Cross, Barton returned to America and lobbied for the creation of the American Association of the Red Cross, which was founded in 1881. In 1891 a headquarters building and home, just outside Washington, D.C., was built as a gift for her and the Red Cross. She remained in it until her death in 1912. The home's remarkable design for dual function as a residence and a warehouse is extremely interesting. Although the home postdates the war by almost three decades, it is the best place to explore Clara Barton's fascinating legacy, which began with the American Civil War. *Clara Barton National Historic Site, 5801 Oxford Rd., Glen Echo, MD, 20812; 301-492-6245; www.nps.gov/clba. Open daily.*

Monocacy

In July 1864 the Confederate Army of Northern Virginia was facing a new enemy in Ulysses S. Grant. Unlike the Union generals who had gone before him, Grant moved south toward Richmond after every battle, win, lose or draw. Robert E. Lee was forced to fall back to protect his capital and was soon dug in around Richmond and Petersburg. As an attempt to relieve the pressure on his army, he ordered Lieutenant General Jubal Early, commanding the Army of the Valley, to leave the Shenandoah Valley and threaten the capital at Washington. Lee hoped that Grant would be forced to either transfer troops north from Richmond or, in the best case, return north with his army to protect the capital.

Early responded quickly and was soon on the move east toward Washington. Lee had correctly predicted that there would not be a lot of opposition in Early's way, and the 14,000 Confederates marched unopposed through Maryland. The move had surprised the Federals, and nobody really knew whether Early's target was Washington or Baltimore, or even the size of Early's army. Grant would need time to move forces north, but something had to be done quickly, so the task fell upon Major General Lew Wallace to gather information on Early and slow the Confederates long enough for the Union to plan a more effective defense.

Visitor's center, Monocacy National Battlefield.

Wallace, with only 5,800 soldiers, quickly set up a defensive line just east of Frederick, Maryland, on the east bank of the Monocacy River and at critical crossing points. From this position he could stall the Confederates, whether Early wanted to take the National Road to Baltimore or the Georgetown Pike to Washington. Wallace's force was pieced together from whatever soldiers he could find, and some of them had even arrived overnight by train from Petersburg. But they were all he had, and he used them to cover every possible movement on the roads or railroad, as well as the crossings of the Monocacy.

On the morning of July 9, 1864, as the Confederates approached the river, they could see the Union defenses laid out before them. First contact was made early, near the Georgetown Pike crossing of the river. Although the Federals at the crossing were quickly pushed across the river, their strong defensive position and artillery were able to make the Confederates think twice about crossing the river here. Meanwhile, much the same was happening along the National Road. Early had sent troops in both directions, confident that he had the advantage. Soon, however, it became clear that the Confederates would have to find another way across the river.

Later in the morning, Confederate cavalry crossed the Monocacy at the Worthington-McKinney Ford, seemingly well south of the fighting. Just across the river were two farms, the Worthington farm and, behind it, the Thomas farm. It looked like an easy passage. Unfortunately for the Confederates, though, the Union had seen this coming. Brigadier General James Ricketts had moved men into the cornfields, stationing them behind a fence than ran between the two farms. The surprised Confederates ran into a wall of fire and were forced to fall back and regroup. A second attempt on the Union line in the early afternoon also failed, as Wallace had shifted troops to his left to strengthen the position.

Seeing that taking the Union left was the key to the battle, Early also shifted more troops to the south end of the battlefield, while keeping troops at the Georgetown Pike and National Road to hold some of the Union troops in place. At 3:30 the Confederates made a charge through the Thomas farm, and after bitter fighting and continuous reinforcement, the Federals slowly began to give ground. In the end the Confederate numbers were too many to stop, and Wallace ordered a withdrawal down the National Road. Early and his much larger force did not pursue, much to the subsequent disappointment of Early's superiors.

The Union had been driven from the field and suffered almost 1,300 casualties, but the battle of Monocacy became known to many as the battle that saved Washington. In the hours that Early spent fighting Wallace, he could easily have advanced to the outskirts of the capital. Instead, while Early was stuck, Grant had been able to move Union troops north by rail in time to strengthen the Washington defenses before Early's arrival. Wallace was an instant hero, and even if he had not gone on to write the epic novel *Ben-Hur*, one of the best-selling books of all time, his fame as a Union general would be assured.

Gettysburg

It's hard even to think of the Civil War without Gettysburg immediately coming to mind. Thousands of books have been written about the battle, and virtually every minute of those three days in July 1863, along with the days immediately preceding and following, have been dissected and studied by historians and military analysts. Yet as much as we read about it, hear about it, and learn about it, the battle of Gettysburg—as well as the simple but brilliant oratory it inspired—will never cease to be a source of interest. The importance of this moment in history will be discussed as long as the American Civil War is remembered.

Robert E. Lee's Army of Northern Virginia, despite its recent triumphs, was in need of a big victory. Lee had soundly defeated the Union Army of the Potomac at Fredericksburg in December 1862 and at Chancellorsville in May 1863, but the victories hardly seemed to make a dent. It was true that Northern morale was damaged, and the Union could not seem to find a suitable leader for its army—the latest choice, in a line of many, was Major General George Meade—but still the Federals kept on coming, the two armies in a continuing dance between the capitals at Washington and Richmond. Lee had been constantly on the defensive. Now, he decided, the time was right to move north. He would make a second attempt to reach the farms and open fields of Pennsylvania and was confident that bringing the battle there would assure him a decisive victory, one that could crush the Army of the Potomac for good. In

General Lee inspects the field at Gettysburg from atop the Virginia Monument on Seminary Ridge.

early June of 1863, Lee began to move his army out of Fredericksburg, Virginia, into the Shenandoah Valley to the west, then north into Pennsylvania.

The Union army, meanwhile, was piecing itself together again. Its recent commander, Major General Joseph Hooker, had surmised that the Confederates were moving north, and had started to move the Army of the Potomac with them. But when he requested more men to counter the movement and was refused by the War Department, he asked to be relieved of command. He was replaced with Meade, who received his orders on June 28 as the Union army continued to move north, keeping between Lee and the capital at Washington.

Lee's plan was to capture Harrisburg, the capital of Pennsylvania, then move east to one of the major cities—Washington, or perhaps Baltimore or even Philadelphia. But Lee suddenly had a severe, unexpected deficiency—he had lost his eyes and ears. Cavalry general J. E. B. Stuart had been given the task of keeping between Lee and the

Federals, reporting on their position, size, and strength. Now, Stuart had disappeared. Operating on the little intelligence available to him, Lee began to mass his army for battle in Cashtown, Pennsylvania, west of Gettysburg.

Meade, meanwhile, knew of the Confederates' movements through Pennsylvania and was also preparing for battle. Still moving north, the Federals began to mass in northern Maryland, just south of Gettysburg. Meade sent Union troops north to see what the Confederates were up to. At the same time, Confederates under Major General A. P. Hill, still east of Lee's main force, began to advance along the Chambersburg Road toward Gettysburg with 14,000 men. The date was July 1, 1863, and one of the most monumental battles in history was about to commence by a chance engagement.

Northwest of Gettysburg, a small college town set in the rolling hills of Pennsylvania, Hill's force met Union pickets in the early morning. The much smaller Federal force was brought up quickly and started to form a line. While the Confederates pushed them back, the Federals began receiving reinforcements and soon formed a strong line on what is now known as McPherson Ridge. The number of soldiers on both sides grew, and by the time the afternoon came, the chance encounter had decidedly grown into a major battle. Hill's men, now joined by Generals Jubal Early and Robert Rodes, eventually began to outnumber the Union troops on the ridge and pushed them off of

The magnificent Pennsylvania monument, Gettysburg.

it, driving them into the town. In the late afternoon fresh Federal troops under Major General Oliver Howard finally stopped the Confederate advance at Cemetery Hill, just southeast of the town. It had been a hard day of fighting, and both armies stopped to maneuver into better positions.

Overnight, the rest of the Union and Confederate armies poured into Gettysburg. The Union line, a strong defensive position, kept Cemetery Hill as its center, then formed a "fishhook" around it; the barb of the hook curved to the east, taking in the commanding position of Culp's Hill. The shaft of the hook, meanwhile, went south along Cemetery Ridge, facing west, and went for 2 miles, ending at the base of two mountains known as Big and Little Round Top. Opposite the Union line on Cemetery Ridge and across an open field was Seminary Ridge, and the Confederates formed their line of battle in the tree line atop this ridge, facing east. Their left, on the north end, curved with the Union line, going beyond the town of Gettysburg and slightly past the Union right at Culp's Hill. The Confederate right also extended south, slightly past the Union left.

By noon on the second day of the battle, July 2, the armies had settled into their positions. After some debate between Lee and one of his most respected advisers, Lieutenant General James Longstreet, Lee decided to attack both flanks of the Union line, Culp's Hill on the Union right and near Little Round Top on the left. As Longstreet advanced on Little Round Top, the Union chief of engineers, Major General Gouverneur K. Warren, realized that Little Round Top was virtually unoccupied by Union troops and that the Confederates were advancing on it. Seeing that the small mountain could command virtually the entire southern portion of the vast battlefield, Warren sent Union troops sprinting to the top of the mountain just as the Confederates began to ascend the southern slope. It became a race to the top, and only after bitter hand-to-hand fighting did the Federals claim this important piece of real estate.

Slowly, the rest of Longstreet's men began to work northward up the Union line. For four hours, fighting moved along the line, in places now forever recognizable by their simple names: Devil's Den. The Wheatfield. The Peach Orchard. In most of these places, the Federals were pushed back, but the line did not break. In all of them, thousands of dead and wounded were left on the field.

At Culp's Hill at the north end of the field, an extended artillery duel began the action, and the accuracy of the Federal fire delayed a Confederate infantry assault for hours. Finally, near the end of the day, a charge was made on the Union position that lasted into the night, but no ground was gained. At the end of the second day, the Union fishhook, although slightly bent, was still intact.

The morning of July 3 opened with a renewal of the attack on Culp's Hill. The Confederates, under Lieutenant General Richard Ewell, made three valiant attempts on the Union position. Each time, they were repulsed, and were eventually driven off.

Stuart's cavalry, which had arrived the previous afternoon after being missing for days, went north to protect the Confederate left, coming out into an open field 3 miles east of Gettysburg. There they were met by Federal cavalry under Brigadier General David Gregg. In what was one of the war's largest cavalry battles, the smaller Union force was able to hold against repeated, fierce mounted attacks by Stuart's Confederates, who were exhausted from their days of riding and recent battle at Hanover, Pennsylvania. The rest of the battlefield, however, was silent.

Overnight, Meade and his generals had decided to maintain their defensive position on Cemetery Ridge. Lee, convinced that another flank attack would be too costly, decided on a direct assault on the Union center. Throughout the morning the Confederates readied themselves on Seminary Ridge, moving fresh units up and placing their artillery. The Federals opposite the field watched, knowing what was coming.

At 1 PM the battlefield exploded. Lee had ordered an artillery bombardment of the Union line, and 180 pieces of Confederate artillery opened fire. They were quickly countered by the Union artillery, and the guns raged for two hours, clouding the battlefield with thick smoke. Meanwhile, Major General George Pickett's Confederates, who had just arrived late the day before, were readied for an assault. At 3 PM the Union fire slowed; the Federals decided to cool their guns and save ammunition for the pending Confederate assault. The Confederates also slowed their fire, and the order was given for Pickett, commanding 15,000 troops, to advance across the mile-wide open field toward the Union center. Picking as their landmark a small copse of trees at the Union line, the units advanced, slowly coming together as one giant mass of men.

The Federals opened fire on them with grape and canister shot as they crossed. Once the Confederates reached the Emmitsburg Road running through the middle of the battlefield, they were within rifle range, and they started to take fire from the Union infantry as well. But they kept coming, and their pace quickened. As Pickett's charge commenced as one wave of Confederate soldiers, the Federal infantry and artillery to the north and south aimed into their flanks, tearing at them from every angle and boxing them in. Pickett's men were able to reach the Union line, but by the time they got there, they had been torn to pieces. The farthest point of their advance, not far from the copse of trees, would later be known as the high-water mark of the Confederacy. Pickett's charge had failed, and before long, those men who were left began stumbling back to Seminary Ridge. The Confederate army's second attempt to invade the North had again ended in disaster. On the afternoon of the next day, July 4, 1863, Lee started his retreat south. He had lost a staggering 28,000 men. The Union, although they had won a great victory, had lost 23,000 of their own.

Over three days, more than 52,000 Americans were dead, wounded, or missing. A massive effort to clean up after the battle was necessary, and it was too much for the suddenly war-torn town of Gettysburg, population 2,400. Soon, the state of Pennsyl-

SITE DETAILS

Gettysburg National Military Park—Even if you have been to Gettysburg, if you have not visited since 2008, you must go. The battlefield itself has not changed much, with the exception of the removal of some of the more unsightly features that were erected after the battle (namely, the old observation tower and the former, somewhat dilapidated and intrusive visitor's center). In early 2008 a new interpretive center was opened, including a new home for the Gettysburg Cyclorama painting later in the year. Gettysburg, because of its history, has always been the most valued and ideal site for people to discover the Civil War. With its new facilities, it has been raised to a whole new level and is without a doubt the premier Civil War site in the country. The new center makes it easy for even the most uninterested visitor to understand and appreciate what happened here. An inspired 22-minute film, A New Birth of Freedom, provides orientation to the battle and the war and should not be skipped, even by the most knowledgeable of visitors. The museum, which already held an incredible collection, is now laid out in a way that vividly illustrates the battle and the reasons for it. A special exhibit hall also holds temporary displays. Licensed tour guides, who have always been accessible to visitors, are now easily arranged through the park service, as are larger guided tours of the battlefield by bus. Interpretive programs and an educational center are also part of the facility, and the bookstore is stocked with an impressive assortment of books and souvenirs. Even the Cyclorama, in a new home designed to better preserve it, has a new audiovisual program. (The old Cyclorama building is at the center of its own preservation battle, as it was built by a student of Frank Lloyd Wright. The building is not only ugly, but is also notoriously leaky, as many of Wright's buildings are; hopefully it will soon be removed, presenting an even more unblemished view of the battlefield.) In addition to the new interpretive center, the east cavalry battlefield, recently saved from being turned into a casino, is now part of the park. While it is true that visitors now pay a bit more for these programs (although the self-guided auto tour route is still free, as is the museum), they are worth every penny. All the while, the vast battlefield itself is still wonderfully interpreted and is a better experience than it has ever been. You must go. *Gettysburg National Military Park, 1195 Baltimore Pike, Gettysburg, PA, 17325; 717-334-1124; www.nps.gov/gett. Open daily; admission charged for parts of interpretive center.*

vania took up the task of creating a cemetery, enlisting the other states not only to contribute but also to memorialize their own native sons. After the layout of the cemetery had been finalized, a dedication ceremony was planned for November 19, 1863, a day that permitted the honored speaker, Edward Everett, a famed orator, to attend and consecrate the ground. President Lincoln was also invited, and to everyone's great surprise he accepted the invitation. Since it was thought improper to deny him a place on the program, a request for the president to give a few short remarks was made, and again Lincoln accepted.

On the day of the ceremony, a grand procession made its way to the cemetery, where all then waited as the proceedings were delayed for an hour by Everett, who was touring the battlefield. When Everett did arrive, he spoke for nearly two hours, and by all accounts it was a great (if long) speech. Then, after a short hymn, Lincoln arose and offered his words. Some thought them plain and boring, while others found them brilliant. Over time, Lincoln's Gettysburg Address has come to be seen as one of the most eloquent statements ever made on the founding principles of our nation. A great tragedy and a great triumph, terrible and inspiring at the same time, Gettysburg will forever remain, as Lincoln stated, consecrated by the men who fought there.

Antietam

The battle at Antietam, a name well-known today even among non-history buffs, meant a lot of different things to different people, but at the time appeared to most as a collection of missed opportunities. The invasion of Maryland by the Confederacy was seen as a necessity for the survival of the Army of Northern Virginia; although the army survived, it was not able to get the food and supplies it needed. The battle was also regarded by many in the South as a lost opportunity to strike a great blow to Northern morale. For the North, conversely, it was regarded as a missed opportunity to crush Lee's army, perhaps dealing a death blow to the rebellion. One thing that everyone did agree upon was that it was a terrible day—and it is still the bloodiest day in American history. But the Union victory at Antietam did give Abraham Lincoln the opportunity and political ability to issue the Emancipation Proclamation, the first real step down the road to ending slavery in America. The tragedy of Antietam, contrasted with the historic significance of its consequences, ultimately embody the debate as to the value, necessity, and justification of war.

Robert E. Lee's Confederates had just won a major victory at the second battle at Manassas. The Union leader—this time, Major General John Pope—had been replaced again, this time by Major General George McClellan, in his second go-around with the Army of the Potomac. Despite the South's recent triumph, Lee faced a problem: His army needed to be fed and supplied. Harvest time was fast approaching, but Lee intended to let the farmers of Virginia gather their crops in peace. Instead, he saw an opportunity to resupply his army at the enemy's expense, while striking a great blow to Northern support of the war just before the coming elections. The Army of Northern Virginia would move north to Maryland and Pennsylvania, gather what it needed, stay long enough to put a scare in the Northern states, and then withdraw back into Virginia. The time was right for an invasion, if it was ever to happen.

Often, even the best laid plans don't work out; this is especially true in military operations. But if you lay out your plans on paper and then let them fall into enemy hands, they don't stand a chance. Unbelievably, this is exactly what happened to the Confederates. As the Federal army trailed Lee, a Union soldier walking through a field near Frederick, Maryland, looked down and saw something interesting, wrapped in paper. He picked it up and, to his delight, found three cigars, unwittingly dropped by some other soldier. It was a grand prize indeed. When he looked at the paper the cigars were wrapped in, he immediately ran to his superior. The paper was marked Special Orders No. 191 and seemed to be Confederate. The paper was delivered to McClellan's staff and discussed. After one of the staff was able to verify some handwriting on the order (remember, many of the men fighting each other had served together or attended West Point together), it was decided that the paper was authentic. The Union commanders had just had Lee's invasion campaign plans handed to them, with a gift of three cigars.

A stunned but elated George McClellan immediately followed up. The Northerners now knew Lee's size, strength, and disposition. They rode hard on his heels, chasing him toward the town of Sharpsburg, Maryland, eager to give battle. The Union had the upper hand.

Robert E. Lee agreed; many of his men were laying siege to Harpers Ferry, and the Union had seized the initiative. But after learning that Stonewall Jackson had taken Harpers Ferry more quickly than expected, Lee decided that now was the time to

Bloody Lane, Antietam National Battlefield.

make a stand and face McClellan's army, which he had been able to defeat time and again. Lee set his men in a long line of battle at Sharpsburg, running roughly north-south behind Antietam Creek, and waited for McClellan.

As McClellan approached the Confederates, he saw that Lee had been able to use the creek to his advantage. After a quick survey of the rest of the field, McClelland was clear on his plan of attack: His army would put most of its weight on the Confederate left, at the north end of the battlefield, where the terrain was more forgiving and Lee's men were more exposed. Other troops were placed along the line to hold the rest of the Confederates in place.

At dawn on September 17, 1862, Union troops under Major General Joseph Hooker opened the attack on the Confederate left—Stonewall Jackson's men—with an artillery assault followed by an advance. The Confederates were massed in the woods to the west, centered on a small building known as the Dunker Church. In between the two armies was a small cornfield, and the two forces went back and forth across the field in fierce fighting for three hours. In the end no one possessed what simply became known to history as the Cornfield, but 13,000 men were killed or wounded trying to take it.

Four hours into the battle, after it became clear that taking the Confederate left would be a difficult proposition, the Federals advanced on the Confederate center. Major General D. H. Hill held the position, posting his men in a sunken road running east to west in the middle of the battlefield. As Major General Edwin Sumner's Federals advanced, they could barely see what was ahead of them because of the rolling terrain. Suddenly they came upon the road, etched deep in the ground after years of use. It was full of Confederates, and it was only yards in front of them. Another fierce fight began at the sunken road, forever afterward known as Bloody Lane. The Confederates held the road for almost four hours before McClellan called off the advance on the center. In this part of the battlefield, another 5,000 men fell.

At the south end of the battlefield, on the Confederate right, not much had happened to this point in the day. The Union men, commanded by Major General Ambrose Burnside, held one end of a stone bridge across Antietam Creek but could not get across the creek due to the Confederate pressure. Their task had been to hold the Confederate right in place while the main attack came at the other end of the field. Now, with the day growing long, it was imperative that the Union take the initiative. After repeated attempts to cross the bridge all day, a desperate charge was made by the Federals, and they finally got to the other side of the creek. Because Confederate troops had been pulled to other parts of the field during the fighting, what was left of Major General James Longstreet's men was not enough; they were quickly pushed back into the town of Sharpsburg. The rest of Lee's army was exhausted, wounded, or dead. Then, just as it appeared that the Confederates would be crushed, Major General A. P. Hill, who had been cleaning up after the victory at Harpers Ferry, arrived with fresh troops at the perfect time. Colliding head-on with Burnside's men, his counterattack pushed the Federals back to what is now known as Burnside's Bridge.

Darkness fell, and the fight was over. The armies stayed in their positions the next day, but neither commander felt he had the strength to launch another assault. Lee was probably right; even with A. P. Hill's timely reinforcement, he was still outnumbered. McClellan, however, probably could have crushed Lee's army with another assault. But it did not come, and Lee was not followed as he retreated back into Virginia. McClellan let him get away. Perhaps the weight of 12,400 Union casualties, along with 10,300 Confederate casualties, was too much for the cautious general. In any case, President Lincoln, who visited the field several days later, dismissed McClellan from service within two months, replacing him with Burnside.

Despite the enormous losses, the Union had won the battle, and Lincoln finally had what he had been hoping for. Months before, Lincoln had shocked his cabinet by telling them that he had decided to emancipate the slaves of the South. After much debate among the cabinet, Lincoln had been persuaded (primarily by Secretary of State William Seward) to wait for a significant battlefield victory before revealing his plans. It could not get more significant than this. Lincoln shortly announced his policy, and on January 1, 1863, the Emancipation Proclamation took effect, freeing slaves in the rebellious states. The bloodiest day in American history—22,700 men dead, wounded, or missing—had been able to bring about the beginning of the end of America's most terrible affliction.

SITE DETAILS

Antietam National Battlefield—The Antietam battlefield, close to Washington, D.C., is one of the most visited battlefields in the National Park System, and although it doesn't receive quite the attention that nearby Gettysburg does, the facilities and interpretation here make it an excellent place to visit. The countryside around the park, for the most part, has not been developed, and you can easily visualize the entire battle, even though it happened over many square miles. An observation tower, much less obtrusive than the one formerly at Gettysburg, also gives a great bird's-eye view of the landscape. The driving tour through the park is well laid out, essentially taking the visitor through the action in chronological order, and the preservation of the sites is excellent—the Cornfield, Bloody Lane, and Burnside's Bridge are all still there. The visitor's center offers a film on the battle, and interpretive programs and ranger-led tours are constantly going on at the park. Excellent planning and an excellent staff make this one a must-visit. *Antietam National Battlefield, 5831 Dunker Church Rd., Sharpsburg, MD, 21782; 301-432-5124; www.nps .gov/anti. Open daily; admission charged.*

Harpers Ferry

Since the time it was selected by George Washington as the location for one of the nation's two armories (along with Springfield, Massachusetts), Harpers Ferry, Virginia, had been well known across the country. But it was not until the late 1850s that Harpers Ferry became the center of a national debate that was about to explode. This peaceful place at the confluence of the Shenandoah and Potomac Rivers became not only a battlefield, but also a powerful symbol for both sides in this great conflict known as the Civil War.

The topic of slavery had been a powder keg for the United States of America since the nation's inception. The founding fathers had worked around it, and Congress had compromised its way through it ever since. Eventually, it was one man's attempt to be the spark that ignited that keg that brought the issue to the military, and within a year and a half the nation had launched into the greatest war it had ever known.

That man was John Brown, and although he was not exactly well known, he was not completely unknown, either. Born in Connecticut and raised in Ohio, Brown had embraced the abolitionist cause at an early age. Even among the radicals that made up the abolitionist movement, Brown was at the fringe, outspoken and even advocating violence to bring about the end of slavery. When the issue of statehood for

"John Brown's Fort," the firehouse at the former Harpers Ferry arsenal.

Kansas arose, Brown and his sons were among the many who moved there in order to tip the balance to ensure that Kansas entered the Union as a free state. Before long Brown was in the middle of the Bleeding Kansas whirlwind, and some would even say that he did his best to direct it. He was allegedly involved in several murderous incidents, including one massacre of five pro-slavery settlers in 1856. Soon after, Brown began raising funds for a much larger and ambitious mission than securing the fate of Kansas: Brown wanted to start a war.

For three years Brown raised money to buy weapons in order to begin an insurrection among the slaves of the South. He was not alone; he had many supporters gathering weapons, raising funds, and quietly spreading the word. Many abolitionists disagreed with his violent practices, and he often met resistance, especially among the more prominent leaders of the movement, Frederick Douglass among them. Ultimately, Brown's plan was to seize the arsenal at Harpers Ferry, take its weapons into the surrounding hills, and fight a war from the mountains, spreading freedom across the land by force. Eventually the time came, and Brown moved to Harpers Ferry in the summer of 1859. Over the course of the next few months, men joined him—several of his sons, several black men, and a number of men who had fought with him in Kansas. On October 16, 1859, Brown and his men surprised the guards at the Harpers Ferry arsenal and attempted to seize it. The raid did not go well, however, and before long most of Brown's men were killed or wounded, although they were able to keep up the fight for 36 hours. After negotiations between Brown and and a U.S. Army lieutenant named J. E. B. Stuart failed, a colonel by the name of Robert E. Lee ordered an assault on the firehouse in which Brown had been cornered. Within three minutes it was all over; although a few men were able to escape, Brown had been captured.

Brown was tried in nearby Charles Town, Virginia, and found guilty of murder, conspiracy to start a rebellion, and treason against the state of Virginia. On December 2, 1859, Brown was hanged and instantly became a martyr for the anti-slavery movement. Many around the world had viewed him as a political prisoner; books and propaganda were written about him, and songs were sung in his honor. Although John Brown's mission had failed, he had succeeded in his ultimate goal—the powder keg was about to blow. He knew as much, as he wrote on the day of his death: "I, John Brown, am now quite certain that the crimes of this guilty land will never be purged away but with blood." Among the controversial figures connected to the war, John Brown will forever remain foremost.

Once the war began, Harpers Ferry was not forgotten. Immediately after Virginia's secession in April 1861, the state seized the arsenal and moved its manufacturing equipment to a safer location in the Deep South. Harpers Ferry was still strategically important, however, and the town changed hands several times. In September 1862 it was garrisoned by 14,000 Union troops when General Robert E. Lee began his first invasion of the North. Lee, wanting to use the Shenandoah Valley as a supply line, needed Harpers Ferry.

Nobody knew the valley and Harpers Ferry better than Major General Thomas "Stonewall" Jackson. Jackson had been the Confederate commander at Harpers Ferry at the beginning of the war, and in June of 1862 he had just completed his brilliant Shenandoah Valley campaign. As Lee moved north, Jackson descended on Harpers Ferry with 24,000 troops in three columns: one at Maryland Heights northeast of the town, one at Loudoun Heights to the southeast, and the largest, 14,000 men, at Bolivar Heights to the west. On September 12, 1862, Jackson's men began their assault on the Federal garrison commanded by Colonel Dixon Miles. Within two days Maryland Heights and Loudoun Heights were in Confederate hands, and on the morning of September 14, Confederate artillery began bombarding the town. An entire day of shelling went by, but the town and Bolivar Heights were still held by the Federals. Overnight, Jackson rearranged his troops, setting up artillery on the south bank of the Shenandoah River that put it in a position behind the Union left. When the bombardment continued the next morning, it was soon clear that Miles had no choice but to surrender. At 8 AM the white flag was raised, and Harpers Ferry belonged to the Confederates. At a loss of 12,500 men, it was the largest Union surrender of the war. Although an important victory, it was virtually wiped out three days later after the decisive Union triumph at Antietam.

SITE DETAILS

Harpers Ferry National Historical Park—The wealth of history that has occurred in this small town is captured at Harpers Ferry National Historical Park. Although it is possible to drive down into the town, to better your experience (and for the locals' sake), park at the visitor's center and take the shuttle into town, where you can explore at your leisure. There is plenty on John Brown here, including the firehouse, now known as John Brown's Fort, where he was finally captured. A museum discussing Brown and how he was seen in the past and today is near the building, as are several other museums concerning the arsenal, the town, and the early history of the area. Several historic buildings still stand, and you can still climb "Jefferson Rock," from which Thomas Jefferson viewed the area and declared it "one of the most stupendous scenes in nature." It's a hard point to argue. The town, the mountains, and the river combine to form a magnificent setting, and the Appalachian Trail runs through town as well. To the west of the town, you can drive to the site of the Confederate and Union lines on Bolivar Heights, and interpretive signs there tell of the battle. Besides the historical park, the town itself contains many restaurants and shops, making it a visitor's paradise. *Harpers Ferry National Historical Park, visitor's center at intersection of US 340 and Shoreline Dr., Harpers Ferry, WV, 25425; 304-535-6029; www.nps.gov/hafe. Open daily; admission charged.*

» OTHER SITES IN MARYLAND AND PENNSYLVANIA

Surratt House Museum—By the beginning of the Civil War, the Surratt House had been well established as a local tavern and meeting place. When the owner, John Surratt, died in 1862, his wife, Mary, took over, and the meetings continued. The border state of Maryland had its share of Confederate sympathizers, and many of these meetings were not sympathetic to the Union cause. One frequent visitor to the tavern was the famous actor John Wilkes Booth. Although many of the details are still debated, it is undisputed that the Surratt family knew Booth and that much of the planning of the assassination of President Abraham Lincoln took place at the Surratt Tavern. How involved Mrs. Surratt was in the conspiracy remains a mystery, but on the night of the murder, Booth did stop at the house and likely picked up weapons and supplies. Even though she was in Washington when these events occurred, Surratt was arrested. In the ensuing trial Mary Surratt was found guilty, and she was hanged along with three others.

You can tour Surratt Tavern today and hear the Surratt side of the story. The mysteries surrounding the Lincoln assassination still make for good debate, and despite what your version of the facts is, it's always entertaining to hear someone else's. Besides, the site is certainly a historic spot, and those who run the property obviously care about it very much. There is also a small museum on the site. *Surratt House Museum, 9118 Brandywine Rd., Clinton, MD, 20735; 301-868-1121; www.surratt.org. Open Wed.–Sun., July–Sep.; Thu.–Sun. rest of year; admission charged.*

Dr. Samuel A. Mudd House—Even more mysterious than the involvement of Mary Surratt in the Lincoln assassination is that of Dr. Samuel A. Mudd. Again, there are some indisputable truths: During his escape, Booth did visit the home, received treatment for his broken leg from Dr. Mudd, and stayed the night. The argument as to how well Mudd knew Booth before that fateful night will likely go on for a long time. Regardless, Mudd was arrested, found guilty, and imprisoned at Fort Jefferson in the Florida Keys. While at the fort, Mudd played a valuable part in treating the sick during a yellow fever epidemic after the fort's doctor died, thereby gaining favor and respect with the fort staff. Soon after, he received a pardon from President Andrew Johnson and returned to his Maryland home.

The Dr. Samuel A. Mudd House, like the Surratt House, is open for tours and presents another interesting angle on the Lincoln assassination. Although the home does keep set hours, it is also available by appointment, and the staff is very dedicated not only to preserving the home, but also to telling Dr. Mudd's story. *Dr. Samuel A. Mudd House, 3725 Doctor Samuel Mudd Rd., Waldorf, MD, 20601; 301-274-9358; www.somd.lib.md.us/MUSEUMS/Mudd.htm. Open Wed., Sat., and Sun., Apr.–Nov. and by appointment; admission charged.*

National Museum of Civil War Medicine—While the Civil War is often referred to as the beginning of modern warfare, it was also a watershed moment in medicine. Never before had so many men needed care at the same time, not only from wounds from bullets and cannonballs, but also from disease. Two-thirds of the 620,000 fatalities that occurred during the war came not from battlefield wounds, but from disease. Unsanitary conditions, poor diets, and the failure to weed out sick soldiers from healthy ones created unbelievably high casualty lists. However, out of this chaos came order and new discoveries. Both armies created new plans for treating the wounded of the battlefield, and evacuation of wounded soldiers was vastly improved. Field doctors learned much about how to treat ghastly wounds, as well as disease outbreaks. Hospitals really didn't exist until the war began, but out of necessity there were many of them at the war's end, and they had only an 8 percent overall mortality rate.

The National Museum of Civil War Medicine pays tribute to the doctors and officers who revolutionized medicine during this period and clearly illustrates how sickness and disease ravaged both armies much worse than any battle. While many museums have the occasional field medical tool, the lessons here are not only in the artifacts (of which there are many), but also in the presentation and storytelling. There is a wealth of information here, and anyone who wants to truly understand the war should visit—this is a chapter of the Civil War that is too often overlooked. *National Museum of Civil War Medicine, 48 E. Patrick St., Frederick, MD, 21705; 301-695-1864; www.civilwarmed.org. Open daily; admission charged.*

Hanover—As Lee moved his armies north into Pennsylvania, Major General J. E. B. Stuart had the job of protecting the Confederate right, keeping in contact with Lee but staying between the Confederates and the Union army. It seemed like a simple order, but Stuart thought he saw an opportunity to do additional damage and rode around the entire Union army to capture a wagon train. Emerging at Hanover, Pennsylvania, on June 30, 1863, Stuart attacked the Union cavalry he found there and drove it through the town, fighting from street to street. However, there was a lot of other Union cavalry in the area, and when two other brigades arrived, the two sides slugged it out for hours, with the Confederates eventually withdrawing to the northeast. Stuart's ambition had prevented him from joining Lee's other forces at Gettysburg until late on the second day of the battle.

Hanover has developed a walking tour through the town, complete with plenty of interpretive signs explaining the action, most of which occurred within the downtown. Although there is an accompanying brochure for the tour, you won't necessarily need it; the signs are easy to find and explain the battle in great detail. The brochure is also available online. *Battle of Hanover Walking Tour, brochures available at Chamber of Commerce, 146 Carlisle St.; tour begins in downtown Hanover, intersection of Frederick St. and Carlisle St., Hanover, PA, 17331; 717-637-6130; www.hanoverchamber.com. Sites accessible daily.*

Williamsport—Three days after Gettysburg, as Lee retreated southward, Union cavalry got between the Confederate infantry and the supply train, which were taking two different routes. At Williamsport, Maryland, on July 6, 1863, the Union troopers attacked the wagon train, but Confederate cavalry was able to hold them back. Although the Federals made several attempts, the appearance of Confederate reinforcements under Brigadier General Fitzhugh Lee forced them to withdraw.

A Maryland Civil War Trails sign has been placed in the Williamsport unit of the Chesapeake & Ohio Canal National Historical Park. The park is located along the old canal, set aside from the town of Williamsport, and provides a picturesque stop. The battle site itself is a bit downstream of the visitor's center. *Chesapeake & Ohio Canal National Historical Park—Williamsport Unit, 205 W. Potomac St., Williamsport, MD, 21795; 301-582-0813; www.nps.gov/choh. Open daily.*

Boonsboro—With Union forces still on Lee's tail the entire way from Gettysburg, Major General J. E. B. Stuart kept cover on the Confederate rear while a pontoon bridge could be built across the Potomac River. Beginning July 8, 1863, after taking several strong defensive positions, Stuart was able to keep Union troops occupied at Boonsboro and the river crossings. Finally, on July 13, the bridge was completed, and the last of Lee's army was across the Potomac on the 24th. Although much of Stuart's guard had been captured, they had protected Lee's rear.

A Maryland Civil War Trails interpretive sign, located along the Old National Pike where the two forces fought, tells of the battle of Boonsboro. Also in Boonsboro is the Boonsborough Museum of History, which contains a fine collection of memorabilia; it's best to make an appointment if you want to go. *Maryland Civil War Trails—Battle of Boonsboro, 7704 Old National Pike; Boonsborough Museum of History, 113 N. Main St., Boonsboro, MD, 21713; 301-432-6969. Sign accessible daily; museum open Sun. from May–Sep. and by appointment.*

South Mountain—While Union troops were under siege at Harpers Ferry, the Federals had just gained the distinct upper hand by stumbling upon the plans for the Confederate invasion of the North. Seeing that Lee's army would be divided into three parts while crossing South Mountain in Maryland, Major General George McClellan had a unique opportunity to deal a death blow to the Confederacy. Three gaps ran through the long ridge: Crampton's Gap to the south, Turner's Gap to the north, and Fox Gap in between. The main Union thrust was to come at Crampton's Gap, the most direct route to Harpers Ferry and the one that would cut Lee's army off from his supplies. Furthermore, the Confederates, still unaware that the Federals had their invasion plans, left only 500 men in the gap as a rear guard. On the afternoon of September 14, 1862, after careful preparation, 12,000 Union soldiers led by Major General William Franklin flooded the gap and quickly overwhelmed the Confederate rear. And then they stopped. Franklin somehow was convinced that he was vastly outnumbered, and halted the fighting. Meanwhile, McClellan ordered assaults at the other gaps, and the Federals were able to break the Confederate right at Fox Gap and pressed hard at the Confederate left north of Turner Gap. However, with the rough, mountainous terrain slowing the Union troops, most of the Confederates had time to withdraw or escape intact. Although the Confederates were pushed out of all three gaps, McClellan's failure to crush Lee's army at South Mountain was an incredibly large wasted opportunity.

Just as the battle took place at several different locations, you have several places to visit when exploring the South Mountain battlefield. They are all contained within what is known as South Mountain State Battlefield—a designation for scattered locations divided between Gathland State Park and Washington Monument State Park, which are themselves a bit split up. Although there are visitor's centers and facilities, you won't find a lot of interpretation of the battle, although several monuments and interpretive signs can be seen at the locations themselves. Seeing the different mountain gaps fought

The giant War Correspondents' Memorial Arch dominates Crampton's Gap, South Mountain State Battlefield.

over in the battle takes a little time, but it's worth the patience. Although the Maryland State Parks page has all the necessary information, your best bet is to check out the Web site of the Friends of South Mountain Battlefield. *South Mountain State Battlefield— Crampton's Gap, 900 Arnoldstown Rd., Jefferson, MD, 21755; Turner Gap, 6132 Old National Pike, Boonsboro, MD, 21713; 301-791-4767; www.fsmsb.org. Open daily.*

Shepherdstown—After the disaster at Antietam, Lee's army withdrew to the south, mostly uncontested. At Botelar's Ford, a crossing of the Potomac River near Shepherdstown, Virginia, a rear guard had been set up to protect the Confederate army, most of which had already crossed. On September 19, 1862, the rear guard was attacked by 2,000 Union troops, who were able to cross the ford and capture several cannon. The next morning, as the Federals were withdrawing because they had found no one else to fight, the Confederates attacked their rear, sending them scurrying back across the ford.

A fight to preserve part of the Shepherdstown battlefield is ongoing, but for now there are plenty of historical markers near the river crossing that tell the story of the Confederates' retreat. Shepherdstown itself has a rich history, going back to colonial days, and is worth spending some time in. *Interpretive signs, intersection of River Rd. and Trough Rd., Shepherdstown, WV, 25443; www.batleofshepherdstown.org. Signs accessible daily.*

Hoke's Run—Before the massed Union and Confederate armies would meet for the first time at the battle of Manassas, Union troops under Major General Robert Patterson were tasked with keeping Brigadier General Joseph Johnston's 11,000 men in the Shenandoah Valley away from the action. Patterson's men entered Martinsburg, Virginia (now West Virginia), on July 2, 1861, and near Hoke's Run ran into a Confederate unit commanded by Colonel Thomas J. Jackson. Jackson delayed the Federals, allowing Johnston to escape from the valley in time to join Brigadier General P. G. T. Beauregard at Manassas.

Although preservationists have been fighting for this ground for some time, much of the Hoke's Run battlefield has been developed, and the site of the main fight is now a parking lot. The Falling Waters Battlefield Association continues the fight, and it is working on restoring some of the surrounding homes that existed at the time of the battle. *Hoke's Run Battlefield, near intersection of US 11 and WV 901, Martinsburg, WV, 25401. Entire battlefield is developed or is private property.*

Hancock—In January 1862 Major General Thomas "Stonewall" Jackson led his Confederates out of Winchester, Virginia, on an expedition to disrupt operations on the Baltimore & Ohio Railroad. On January 5 his troops shelled the town of Hancock, Maryland, from across the Potomac River. They exchanged fire with the Union garrison there for two days before moving on, doing little damage. Although the Confederates were able to burn one of the railroad's bridges in the days after the battle at Hancock, the onset of harsh winter weather prevented Jackson from accomplishing more.

The Hancock unit of the Chesapeake & Ohio Canal National Historical Park, located right along the Potomac, is home to several Maryland Civil War Trails interpretive signs regarding the action at Hancock. From the park you can see not only where the Confederate artillery positions would have been, but also the entire layout of the town, which spreads out on the hillside above you. *Chesapeake & Ohio Canal Historical Park—Hancock Unit, intersection of Main St. and Church St., Hancock, MD, 21750; 301-739-4200; www.nps.gov/choh. Open daily.*

Folck's Mill—Even though Lieutenant General Jubal Early's Army of the Valley had been driven away from Washington once, Early didn't just disappear. Withdrawing west to the Shenandoah Valley, Early was half-heartedly pursued by Union forces until he turned and drove the Federals off the field at the second battle of Kernstown. A week later Early sent parts of his army to wreak havoc all over the area. One of these groups proceeded to Chambersburg, Pennsylvania, to demand a ransom from the town and ended up burning it down when the money was not produced. As the Confederates were on their way back into Maryland, Brigadier General Benjamin Kelley, commanding the Union garrison in Cumberland, Maryland, was ready for them. On August 1, 1864, near Folck's Mill north of town, Kelley stationed his men on a hill when the Confederates approached. A small battle erupted, but when Union cavalry who had been chasing them appeared, the Confederates left the field and crossed back into West Virginia.

A historical marker stands in the parking lot of a restaurant and inn located near the center of the fighting. Although the inn was standing during the battle and was used as a field hospital, it is not open for touring. However, if you eat a meal at the restaurant, a paper describing the inn's history, including the battle, is available. Except for the sign outside, it's about all you'll find regarding the battle of Folck's Mill. *Historical marker—Maryland Civil War Centennial Commission (Folck's Mill), 12901 Ali Ghan Rd. NE, Cumberland, MD, 21502. Sign accessible daily.*

Moorefield—The Confederate cavalry who had burned Chambersburg, Pennsylvania, and escaped at Folck's Mill went into camp near Moorefield, West Virginia, soon after. On August 7, 1864, Union cavalry under Brigadier General William Averell, who had been chasing the Confederates for weeks, finally caught them off guard. After capturing the Confederate pickets without having to fire a shot, Averell's troopers were able to ride into the camp in complete surprise, driving the Confederates across the South Branch of the Potomac River. The Confederates were never able to form up, and those who did not flee were captured.

The Confederates had camped in and about the town of Moorefield, although the sites of the camps are now private property. A short walk through the small town will reveal several buildings that existed during the battle, but the only place providing any interpretation of the events that took place here is the McCoy-McMechen Museum and Theater. The museum is open only by appointment, so if you decide to go, plan ahead. *McCoy-McMechen Museum and Theater, 117 N. Main St., Moorefield, WV, 26836; 304-538-6560. Open by appointment only.*

» WHERE TO STAY IN MARYLAND AND PENNSYLVANIA

Because the Civil War is so closely tied to this part of the country, there are a lot of great options for lodging here. Besides bed-and-breakfasts, there are cities with hotels all along the route, and of course the Washington metropolitan area provides almost unlimited options.

Gettysburg, Pennsylvania, contains a wealth of unique places to stay. The **Lightner Farmhouse**, which was used as a field hospital, was built only a year before the battle. The grounds cover 19 acres near the battlefield, and the bed-and-breakfast offers a comfortable fireplace and some good stories, with a resident storyteller who spins yarns about the ghosts of the battlefield. *Lightner Farmhouse, 2350 Baltimore Pike, Gettysburg, PA, 17325; 1-866-337-9508; www.lightnerfarmhouse.com.*

The **Brickhouse Inn Bed and Breakfast** wasn't built until 1898, but on its property is the **Welty House**, which sustained battle damage, much of which is still visible. Five rooms are available in the Welty House, and it is only steps from the town square. *Brickhouse Inn Bed and Breakfast, 452 Baltimore St., Gettysburg, PA, 17325; 1-800-864-3464; www.brickhouseinn.com.*

Finally, the **Gettysburg Battlefield Bed and Breakfast**, located on 30 acres of the eastern cavalry battlefield, not only provides a place to sleep, but has interactive demonstrations throughout showcasing the battle and Civil War–era life. The home is allegedly haunted, and ghost and other stories are told nightly. *Gettysburg Battlefield Bed and Breakfast, 2264 Emmittsburg Rd., Gettysburg, PA, 17325; 1-888-766-3897; www.gettysburgbattlefield.com.*

In Sharpsburg, near the Antietam battlefield, is the **Historic Jacob Rohrbach Inn**. The inn was damaged during the battle and was used as a field hospital afterward. In the ensuing years, Mosby's Rangers frequented the inn and killed a man inside the home; his ghost is said to still haunt the historic inn. *Historic Jacob Rohrbach Inn, 138 W. Main St., Sharpsburg, MD, 21782; 1-877-839-4242; www.jacob-rohrbach-inn.com.*

Near Harpers Ferry, in the county seat of Charles Town, is the **Carriage Inn**. Although Charles Town was not the focus of any battles, it was the center of attention of the entire nation when John Brown was tried and executed there in 1859. The home was built in 1836 by the man who served as the foreman of the grand jury that sent Brown to trial. In 1864, in the home's dining room, a meeting took place between Ulysses S. Grant and Philip Sheridan, where they mapped out Sheridan's famous Shenandoah Valley campaign. *The Carriage Inn, 417 E. Washington St., Charles Town, WV, 25414; 1-800-867-9830; www.carriageinn.com.*

JACKSON
1824—1863

10

The Shenandoah Valley

OVERVIEW

It was called the breadbasket of the Confederacy. Situated in the western, mountainous region of Virginia, the Shenandoah Valley was known, both then and now, as lush, beautiful country that was ideal for farming. During the Civil War this fertile land would be a major objective of both armies.

The Shenandoah Valley was of critical importance to the Confederate cause and the survival of Robert E. Lee's Army of Northern Virginia. It not only served as a primary source of food and supplies to Lee's army, but its location between the Blue Ridge mountain range to the east and the Shenandoah Mountains to the west made it an ideal protected route to the north.

The valley was the scene of two significant campaigns during the war: one by the Confederacy to keep it, and another by the Union to destroy it. In 1862 General Thomas J. "Stonewall" Jackson fought a brilliant campaign to defend the valley for the Confederacy, crushing the forces he encountered while skillfully evading the traps that the Union army set for him. For the next two years, despite several Union attempts to gain control of the valley, the Confederacy continued to dominate the land and to reap its bountiful harvest, as well as use it for an avenue of invasion when needed. However, in 1864, with Lee's armies being backed slowly into Richmond and Petersburg, the Union recognized the need to close the valley once and for all, particularly after Jubal Early used it to threaten the capital at Washington. General Philip Sheridan was given the task of clearing the valley of Confederates and destroying its capacity to

Grave of Thomas J. "Stonewall" Jackson, near his beloved Virginia Military Institute in Lexington.

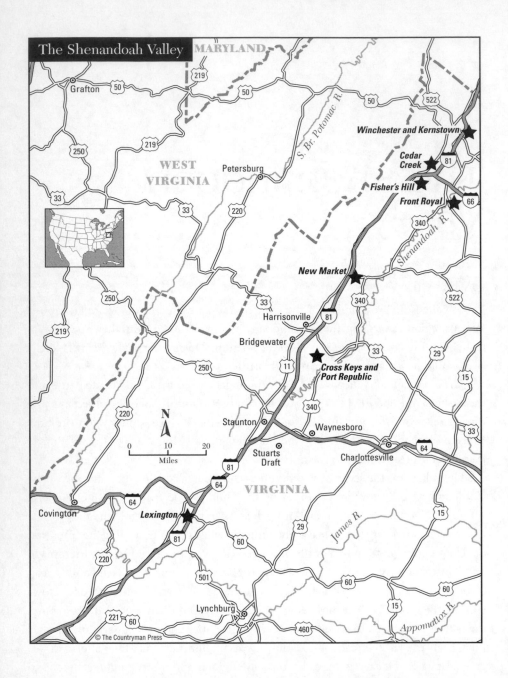

The Shenandoah Valley

MARYLAND

Grafton

WEST VIRGINIA

Petersburg

Winchester and Kernstown

Cedar Creek

Fisher's Hill

Front Royal

New Market

Harrisonville

Bridgewater

Cross Keys and Port Republic

Staunton

Waynesboro

Stuarts Draft

Charlottesville

N

0   10   20
Miles

Covington

Lexington

VIRGINIA

Lynchburg

Appomattox R.

James R.

S. Br. Potomac R.

Shenandoah R.

© The Countryman Press

supply Lee's army. Sheridan oversaw several important battlefield victories and, just as important, destroyed the farms he found in his path, thereby eliminating a major supply of food to the Confederates now under siege around their capital.

Today the Shenandoah Valley is peaceful, but reminders of its past are everywhere. While some of the major battlefield sites have been altered, the valley's historical legacy remains, offering a wonderful opportunity to explore an important part of the war. And you'll also enjoy a great drive.

» PEOPLE TO KNOW

Thomas J. "Stonewall" Jackson—Stonewall Jackson may have earned his nickname at Manassas, but the Shenandoah Valley is where he cemented his legend. Before the war, however, there were some questions. After graduating at West Point and seeing action in the Seminole Indian Wars and the Mexican War, Thomas Jonathan Jackson, a native Virginian, became an instructor at the Virginia Military Institute in Lexington in 1851. Here his students knew him as "Fool Tom," and his eccentric personal habits drew him some ridicule: He did not smoke or drink, was an extremely devout Presbyterian, and was a strict disciplinarian. Nevertheless, when war came, Jackson proved himself one of the most successful, brilliant, and beloved leaders in the Confederacy.

In October of 1861 Jackson was placed in charge of Confederate forces in the Shenandoah Valley. Although he initially suffered defeat at First Kernstown in March 1862, he was soon striking the Union forces effectively and when and where they least expected it. His work in the next few months not only held the valley for the Confederates, but drained critical support from General George McClellan's assault on Richmond during the Peninsula campaign. Jackson's Shenandoah Valley campaign of 1862 is still widely studied for its boldness and genius. Jackson went on to fight with Robert E. Lee for one more year, until he was mortally wounded by friendly fire at the battle of Chancellorsville in May of 1863. Jackson's death was a devastating loss to the Confederacy, but his legend and spirit lived on.

Philip Sheridan—A man known to have a short fuse and a fighting spirit, Philip Henry Sheridan was barely 30 years old when the Civil War broke out. He graduated low in his class at West Point, and his stint there included time off for attacking another cadet with a bayonet. When war came, Sheridan bounced around the army with different duties, until he proved his mettle at Corinth—where he was serving as quartermaster. He was soon advancing quickly up the ranks, distinguishing himself at Perryville, Stones River, and Chattanooga. General Grant soon chose "Little Phil" Sheridan to lead his cavalry in Virginia, where a daring raid on Richmond resulted not only in disrupting Confederate activity at a critical time in Grant's Overland campaign, but also in the death of Confederate hero J. E. B. Stuart at the Battle of Yellow Tavern.

In August of 1864 Grant decided that it was finally time to shut the door to the Shenandoah Valley. He placed Sheridan in command of the Army of the Shenandoah, with orders not only to catch Jubal Early's army, but to destroy the valley's war-making capacity. Sheridan's successes here made him a legend, and his name is often included in the short list of the Union's great generals. After the war Sheridan was general-in-chief of the entire United States Army (replacing William T. Sherman) and remained with the army until his death in 1888.

» THINGS TO KNOW

The bookends of this tour of the valley are Winchester, Virginia, at the northern end, and Lexington, Virginia, at the southern end. Whichever end you start at, don't get caught going the wrong way. The elevation of the valley is higher at the southern end, so if you are heading south, you are moving "up" the valley, and if you are heading north, you are going "down" the valley.

If you do get mixed up somewhere along your journey, be sure to pull over and ask somebody. In fact, pull over whenever you can and talk to someone, explore some of the small towns along the way, and make a few new friends. The locals here are friendly and welcoming, not to mention proud of their history and appreciative of tourists, and you are sure to create some memorable moments.

THE TRIP

Starting the trip at the north end of the valley in Winchester is usually the easiest option. Winchester is approximately a one-and-a-half-hour drive west of Washington, D.C., and about an hour west of Dulles Airport. Remember that driving through any part of the greater Washington metropolitan area can be slow going. If you plan on starting from the south end of the valley, your nearest major city is Richmond, approximately two and one-half hours to the east.

As far as distance, a straight shot from Winchester to Lexington is not a long trip and can be driven in a little over two hours, covering about 130 miles. But you are going to want to make a lot of stops to see this beautiful country up close, so be sure to give yourself plenty of time to wander.

» THE CAN'T-MISS SITES

Winchester and Kernstown

Anchoring the northern end of the valley, Winchester is the site of several critical battles from both Jackson's 1862 campaign and Sheridan's 1864 campaign, including the Class A battles of First Winchester and Opequon (also known as Third Winchester). Although many of the areas where action occurred have been lost to development, enough landmarks and enough of the land is left to get a good idea of how things hap-

Earthworks at Fort Collier, site of the final scene of the battle of Opequon.

pened here. Also adding to the interest is the fact that this town of 25,000 lives and breathes its history. In addition to what is left of the battle sites, there are several excellent historical sites, museums, and resource centers to help you get oriented to the valley and learn its importance during the war, not to mention the rest of Winchester's rich history, which dates to George Washington's time. The town also frequently holds historical festivals and reenactments, and it's not unlikely that you will visit during one of those celebrations. Be sure to check and see if any of these events will be coming up when you plan your trip.

Winchester's first taste of fighting during the Civil War was the first battle of Kernstown, just south of the city. Major General Nathaniel Banks had occupied the northern end of the valley with 38,000 Union troops, but in March of 1862 Major General George McClellan began his ill-fated Peninsula campaign to attempt to capture Richmond. Banks sent two of his three divisions to support McClellan, leaving the remaining division under the command of Brigadier General James Shields. Stonewall Jackson, receiving faulty intelligence that all of Banks's army was leaving, conducted a two-day forced march to catch them by the tail. He caught up with the Federals on March 23, 1862, in the then-small village of Kernstown, with what looked like a small number of Union guns lined up against him. Jackson sent most of his force against the Union right and quickly gained a strong position behind a stone wall. Unknown to Jackson, however, 5,000 Union soldiers were waiting for him, with two of the three Union brigades having been kept hidden from the view of the Confederates. Although the Confederates held the stone wall for two hours, they ran out of ammunition and abandoned their position, retreating to the south. Jackson's first battle in the Shenandoah Valley had ended in defeat, with a loss of the battlefield and 718 casualties to the Union's 590. However, it was also Jackson's last defeat in the valley, and his actions caused the Union forces to return Banks's other two divisions to the area, ultimately taking 60,000 troops from McClellan's drive against Richmond.

Less than two months later, Jackson had scored several important victories and was very active throughout the valley, and it was more than enough to stoke fears of a Confederate invasion of Washington, at the same time that the Union was trying to take Richmond. After Jackson's maneuvering surprised the Federals at Front Royal on

The Pritchard house, caught in the middle of the fighting during both battles of Kernstown.

May 23, 1862, all the Union forces in the valley headed for Winchester to regroup, with Jackson's army in hot pursuit. Banks's troops got to Winchester first and formed a line of battle south of the city, but early on the morning of May 25, Jackson's army met the Union force of 6,000 with 16,000 Confederates, hungry for further victory. In what would be known as the first battle of Winchester, Jackson directed most of his force against the Union right, and within three hours the Federals had been routed and headed north to Harpers Ferry. Jackson held the valley and would score several more important victories before moving east to Richmond to help Robert E. Lee defend the Confederate capital.

One year later, in June 1863, Lee was planning his second invasion of the North. Needing a route to supply his army as it crossed into Maryland, he sent General Richard Ewell to open the Shenandoah Valley. Union forces in the valley, still preoccupied with preventing a raid on the capital at Washington, were concentrated in fortifications at Winchester, totaling approximately 9,000 men under the command of Major General Robert Milroy. On June 13, 1863, the Confederates attacked, beginning the second battle of Winchester. Losing ground and seeing his army in danger of being surrounded, Milroy began a retreat on the night of the 14th. The Confederates cut him off north of the city at Stephenson's Depot early on the morning of the 15th, and after heavy fighting, much of Milroy's force was forced to surrender. Lee later referred to the victory as the "Thermoplae of my campaign," which was to ultimately end in disaster less than one month later at Gettysburg.

By July of 1864 Ulysses S. Grant had forced Lee into siege lines around Richmond and Petersburg. Attempting to relieve the pressure on his army, Lee sent Lieutenant General Jubal Early and 14,000 men through the Shenandoah Valley to feint a raid against Washington, D.C. After being repulsed at Fort Stevens north of Washington, Early began a retreat back through the valley, with a Federal force under General Horatio Wright closely pursuing. As Wright caught up with Early at the battle of Cool Spring on July 17–18, Union forces under General David Hunter were approaching from West Virginia. On July 20, 1863, just north of Winchester, the battle of Rutherford's Farm occurred when elements of Hunter's command met with one of Early's divisions. The Confederates were driven back to Winchester, and Early's forces consolidated. Thinking that the Confederate threat was over, Wright took most of his forces back to Washington, leaving only 9,500 men under Brigadier General George Crook.

Wright's move proved premature. Crook, who had initially settled in Winchester, was forced to send his forces south to meet a growing threat. Crook drove the Confederates out of Kernstown on July 23 and left only a token force while he returned to Winchester. The next day, Early, after realizing his advantage, sent his forces northward against what was left of the Union line, with his infantry driving at the center and cavalry at both flanks. Crook hurried his force back to Kernstown to meet the threat, but the Union infantry was soon being driven backward all along the line. Eventually Crook was forced to quickly retreat back toward Winchester, and eventually to Harpers Ferry. This time the Confederates held the field at Kernstown, and they again held the Shenandoah Valley. The Union army suffered 1,185 casualties to the Confederates' 600.

Although the Confederates had regained the valley with their victory at Second

SITE DETAILS

Shenandoah Valley Civil War Orientation Center—Perhaps the best place to start any tour of the valley, this site, the result of a partnership between Shenandoah University and the Shenandoah Valley Battlefields Foundation, not only explores the history of the wartime Shenandoah Valley, but will also help you get to what still remains. The displays are interactive and very educational. Note, however, that the center is not open on weekends, so plan accordingly. *Shenandoah Valley Civil War Orientation Center, 20 S. Cameron St., Winchester, VA, 22601; 540-722-6367; www.theknowledgepoint.org. Open Mon.–Fri.*

Old Court House Civil War Museum—This courthouse was used as both a prison and a hospital during the war and now houses a museum about the battles around Winchester as well as the Civil War in general. *Old Court House Civil War Museum, 20 N. Loudoun St., Winchester, VA, 22601; 540-542-1145; www.civilwarmuseum.org. Open Wed.–Sun.; admission charged.*

First Winchester historical markers—There are two markers associated with the first battle of Winchester. One is a detailed pair of signs showing troop movements and briefly describing the battle; the other is a historical highway marker near the initial location of one of Banks's two brigades. *First Winchester interpretive signs, located at 2147 Valley Ave.; historical highway marker A-5 (First Battle of Winchester), Virginia Department of Conservation and Historic Resources, located at 1000 Valley Ave.; Winchester, VA, 22601. Both signs accessible daily.*

Second Winchester historical markers—Two Virginia Civil War Trails interpretive signs regarding the second battle of Winchester have been placed, one at Stephenson's Depot, and the other near the location of West Fort. There is also a memorial near the Stephenson's Depot site, as well as a historical highway marker. *Virginia Civil War Trails—Second Battle of Winchester, 1881 N. Frederick Pike, Winchester, VA, 22603; Virginia Civil War Trails—Stephenson's Depot, south of intersection of Old Charles Town Rd. and Milburn Rd., Stephenson, VA, 22656; Stephenson's Depot Memorial and historical highway marker A-1 (Action at Stephenson's Depot), Virginia Department of Conservation and Historic Resources, intersection of US 11 and Stephenson Rd., Stephenson, VA, 22656. Sites accessible daily.*

Fort Collier—Fort Collier was the target as Custer led the grand cavalry charge that

Kernstown, their dominance was short-lived. Tired of the constant threat against Washington distracting his efforts against Lee, Grant ordered Major General Philip Sheridan to clear the Shenandoah Valley for good. Sheridan and his Army of the Shenandoah went right to work, not only pursuing Confederate forces, but also destroying the ability of the valley to supply Lee's army. After Sheridan hit Early's force during several smaller battles through August and September, he realized the nu-

effectively ended the battle of Opequon. The site is small but well preserved, and funding is being gathered to open the Fort Collier Civil War Center on the site. Interpretive signs have already been installed around the earthworks. Although the site is easily accessible to the public, for the moment it sits on private property, so please call ahead if you plan to visit. *Fort Collier, 922 Martinsburg Pike, Winchester, VA, 22601; 540-667-5572; www.fortcollier.com. Site accessible, but please call ahead.*

Third Winchester Battlefield—This portion of the battlefield, maintained by the Civil War Preservation Trust, includes numerous interpretive signs and covers much of the ground fought over. However, if you go, bring your hiking boots, and maybe even your mountain bike. The trail is extensive and may be somewhat strenuous for some. But the effort is worth the walk. The trailhead is behind the Millbrook High School and might be difficult to find, so just drive around the back and keep your eyes peeled. The trust has also recently purchased several other sizable portions of the battlefield, with plans for developing an extensive trail system and further interpretive displays. It seems that this extremely important battlefield, thanks to tireless preservation efforts, will finally be getting the attention it deserves. *Third Winchester Battlefield, 251 First Woods Dr., Winchester, VA, 22603; www.civilwar.org. Open daily.*

Kernstown Battlefield Park—With its large expanse and rural surroundings, the Kernstown Battlefield Park is certainly the best-preserved and best-interpreted battlefield in the area. This was the scene of much of both the First and Second Kernstown battles, and the site contains a museum and visitor's center (open seasonally on weekends only), tours of the Pritchard home, and walking trails across the core of the battlefield. Maintained by the Kernstown Battlefield Association, this one is a must-see, even when unstaffed. *Kernstown Battlefield Park, entrance at intersection of US 11 and Saratoga Dr., Winchester, VA, 22601; 540-869-2896; www.kernstownbattle.org. Site open daily; visitor's center and interpretation during weekends May–Oct.*

Rutherford's Farm—All that remains of this action, prelude to Second Kernstown, is a historical highway marker. The marker was not in place for a time, so if you have a hard time finding it, then it was never replaced. *Historical highway marker A-2 (Action of Rutherford's Farm), Virginia Department of Conservation and Historic Resources, intersection of US 11 and Nulton Lane, Winchester, VA, 22603. Accessible daily.*

merical advantage that he held and readied his army to complete the task. On September 19, 1864, Sheridan launched his force at Early's army, which was still concentrated in Winchester. In the battle known both as Opequon (for a creek running through the area) and Third Winchester, Sheridan attempted to hit Early in several different places, but confusion and slow going among the Union forces allowed Early's army, separated at the beginning of the day, to consolidate. When the battle finally commenced around noon, the fighting was hard and heavy. The Confederates were slowly driven back but held firm until a massive cavalry charge—composed of five brigades led by General George Armstrong Custer—was launched at the Confederate left. The Confederates retreated to Fisher's Hill after suffering 3,610 casualties, a great loss to Early's already reduced force. Union casualties numbered just over 5,000, but they had many more men to spare, having entered the battle with 37,000. Sheridan's victory allowed him the freedom to conduct his campaign to clear out the Shenandoah Valley, a time referred to by the inhabitants as "The Great Burning."

As the northern cap to the Shenandoah Valley, Winchester was the scene of some of the most heated action of the war. It seems as if every corner of this small town was witness to fighting.

Cedar Creek

By mid-October of 1864, the destruction of the Shenandoah Valley was complete. The Union army, led by Major General Philip Sheridan, had waged "total warfare" on the area, laying waste to everything in sight. Furthermore, the Confederate army, led by Lieutenant General Jubal Early, had been driven southward after devastating defeats at Opequon and Fisher's Hill and was no longer considered a threat. The Federals, thinking their job done, had given themselves room to rest. Or so they thought.

Early, never one to lie idle, had been reinforced, with General Robert E. Lee sending a division to the valley from his lines at Petersburg. Early's force, reeling from recent losses, now numbered 21,000. Wasting no time, Early moved north toward Sheridan's army, taking a position across from the Union lines, which had formed along Cedar Creek, just north of Strasburg. Early probed up and down the line, looking for a chance to break the Union force of 32,000. Sheridan, meanwhile, had departed for a war conference in Washington, leaving Major General Horatio Wright in command.

After determining the positions of the Union forces, which were somewhat scattered, Early decided that the time was right for a surprise assault. On the night of October 18, 1864, three Confederate divisions moved around the Union left, forming a line perpendicular to the Federal left flank only one-half mile from the Union encampment. The rest of Early's army would face the center of the Union line. Early in the morning on October 19, the Confederates attacked, quickly driving the surprised Federals back in retreat. The Confederates pushed hard, and almost all the Union forces

Cedar Creek Visitor's Center, home to the Cedar Creek Battlefield Foundation.

were north of the small hamlet of Middletown before long. The Confederate advance was so rapid in most places that Early himself could not keep track of all his forces.

Heavy fighting occurred around the plantation at Belle Grove and a cemetery northwest of the town while the rest of the Union army was withdrawing. Resistance here—although these troops were eventually driven back, too—stalled the Confederate advance enough that the Union army was able to reorganize and form a line north of the town. Meanwhile, Early reorganized his men in an opposite line, stretching west of Middletown and preparing to advance on the demoralized Federals.

What happened next cemented Sheridan's name in the history books forever. He had returned to Winchester from his conference in Washington and on the morning of the battle was riding south to rejoin his army. When he began to come across the routed remnants of his force, he quickly rode south, rallying his men as he went and turning them back toward the fight. When he reached the reformed Union line, his men were not only shocked to see him, but inspired, and they were ready not only to hold, but to advance.

SITE DETAILS

Cedar Creek Battlefield Foundation Visitor's Center—Although technically a unit of the Cedar Creek and Belle Grove National Historic Park, the facilities at the Cedar Creek Battlefield are locally run. A visitor's center, operated by the Cedar Creek Battlefield Foundation, provides interpretation of the battle, and a good view of much of the battlefield can be had from this location. Tours are available when the center is open, and outdoor interpretive signs help out for the off hours. *Cedar Creek Battlefield Foundation Visitor's Center, 8437 Valley Pike, Middletown, VA, 22645; 1-888-628-1864; www.cedarcreekbattlefield.org. Open daily Apr.–Oct.*

Belle Grove Plantation—The plantation at Belle Grove, also part of the Cedar Creek and Belle Grove National Historic Park, was the center of much of the fighting at Cedar Creek. A self-guided tour of the grounds is available, as well as a guided tour of the mansion. The land surrounding the mansion remains much as it was during the battle. *Belle Grove Plantation, 336 Belle Grove Rd., Middletown, VA, 22645; 540-869-2028; www.bellegrove.org. Guided tours available Apr.–Oct., grounds open Mar.–Dec.; admission charged.*

While Early took his time, Sheridan planned a counterattack. At 4 PM, with his rallied troops hungry to regain the field, Sheridan launched a direct assault at Early's forces. This time it was the Confederates who were surprised, and they were quickly routed. What was left of Early's troops gathered at Fisher's Hill, where they had begun the day, and the next morning they headed south. Although the Union had suffered many more casualties—5,672 to the Confederates' 2,910—they had destroyed the morale of Early's army, most of which was soon sent to Robert E. Lee at Petersburg.

Fisher's Hill

Two days after being driven out of Winchester at the battle of Opequon, Lieutenant General Jubal Early entrenched his army near Strasburg, 20 miles south of Winchester, across the Valley Pike. After the disaster at Opequon, Early's force numbered only 12,000 men, and his line was thin. The place he chose for his stand was Fisher's Hill, a strong, elevated position just south of Strasburg, at one of the narrowest points of the valley. Expecting the Union attack to come against his right, Early strengthened this part of the line and strung the rest of his men across the valley as best he could.

After Opequon, Major General Philip Sheridan sent a force of 20,000 after Early in an attempt to crush him. While Sheridan set his infantry in position against the Confederate lines, he sent his cavalry south to New Market to attempt to cut off Early's escape route. On September 21, 1864, two days after Opequon, the action at Fisher's Hill opened when the Federals took advantage of high ground close to the

The battlefield at Fisher's Hill, maintained by the Shenandoah Valley Battlefields Foundation.

Confederate lines. The position offered a commanding field of fire for artillery and a good view of the Confederate positions. Seeing that Early had concentrated his strength on the Confederate right, Sheridan decided to move on the west side of the line, Early's left.

Late in the day on September 22, Brigadier General George Crook sent two divisions against the western part of Early's line. The Confederates could not hold, and after Crook's men broke the line, Major General Horatio Wright sent one of his divi-

SITE DETAILS

Fisher's Hill Battlefield—Although some back roads are needed to get there, the battlefield at Fisher's Hill, particularly where the Confederate line crumbled at Ramseur's Hill on the west end, is well preserved and interpreted. Although much of the battlefield is still privately owned, the site, operated by the Shenandoah Valley Battlefields Foundation, contains extensive walking trails and interpretive signs. The terrain is still open for the most part, and it is very easy to imagine what happened during the battle. *Fisher's Hill Battlefield, Ramseur's Hill Site, east of intersection of Battlefield Rd. and Tumbling Run Lane, Strasburg, VA, 22657. Open daily.*

sions to continue the eastward flanking movement that was crumbling the Confederate position. It was not long before the entire Confederate line was routed. Had Early's cavalry not kept the Union cavalry occupied, thus keeping his avenue of retreat open, his army would have been doomed. Instead Early was able to collect his army near Waynesboro, Virginia, at the southern end of the valley.

Following the battle, Sheridan's forces began to tear up the countryside, eliminating the Shenandoah Valley as a supplier for Lee's army under siege in Petersburg. However, the Union had not fully accomplished its mission; Early's army had taken another beating but still survived, and one more major battle at Cedar Creek remained before the Federals could claim the valley as their own.

Front Royal

After the first battle at Kernstown, General Nathaniel Banks received more help in the valley and proceeded to occupy most of it. However, Stonewall Jackson remained on the move and had built his army back up. After receiving further reinforcements from Robert E. Lee, who was under pressure in Richmond, Jackson's force was now 17,000 strong, compared to Banks's 9,000. Jackson decided to make his move down the valley and confront Banks, who had concentrated most of his force at Strasburg. After moving north, though, toward the main Union force, Jackson suddenly swung east toward the Manassas Gap and the town of Front Royal, where 1,500 Federal troops were stationed to protect the gap. Jackson sent Brigadier General Turner Ashby to feint against Banks.

On May 23, 1862, as Jackson planned his assault at Front Royal, an event occurred that is still retold with much pride in the South. Belle Boyd, a woman who lived in the town, raced toward Jackson's army, found a face she recognized, and told him that Jackson must attack now. Boyd told the soldier that the Union force was very small (information she had gotten while mingling with the Union soldiers) and that Jackson would be able to ride right over them. Whether this was news to Jackson is debatable, but either way it makes for a good story, and Boyd's further exploits made her the most celebrated Confederate spy of the Civil War.

Boyd was correct; compared to Jackson's army, the Union force holding the town was nothing. Early in the afternoon the Confederate army rode into Front Royal from the south and surprised the Federals, driving them through the town with ease. Although the Union troops made a couple of stands, they were soon in full retreat. Jackson took almost 900 prisoners.

The victory at Front Royal was in itself an important achievement for Jackson, and the story of Belle Boyd is legendary. But the strategic implications of the battle proved to be enormous. Banks, who was suddenly in danger of being trapped, raced to his supply depot at Winchester, where he would be soundly defeated two days later at First

Winchester. Meanwhile, as McClellan was approaching Richmond, Brigadier General Irvin McDowell was at Fredericksburg, preparing to reinforce him. However, after the news from Front Royal reached Washington, McDowell was ordered to hold, and also to send part of his army to the valley. The Confederate strategy was working; Jackson was easing pressure on Richmond by threatening Washington, buying time for the army defending the Confederate capital and reducing the force brought against them.

New Market

The battle of New Market was important in many respects. Strategically, the Confederate victory here was critical in delaying Union efforts in the Shenandoah Valley. It was the first battle in the Union's attempt to take the valley, and it led to the eventual appointment of new leadership on the Union side. But regardless of the battle's significance in the grand scope of the war in Virginia, it will forever be remembered and have its story retold proudly because of the participation and sacrifice of 257 young men enrolled at the Virginia Military Institute.

In May of 1864, while Grant and Lee were just starting their fight to the east, the Shenandoah Valley was still an important source of men and supplies for the Confederates, and although Union forces had a presence here, they had not yet made their mark. The Union commander in the area was Major General Franz Sigel, who had his troops scattered throughout the middle of the valley. On the Confederate side, Major General John Breckenridge was in command of a small number of troops that held the southern end of the valley. Because of the importance of the valley, Lee authorized Breckenridge to muster in the cadets at the Virginia Military Institute in Lexington, sorely needed soldiers who, while having no combat experience, were being groomed to help lead in the war effort.

The two forces began to converge near the town of New Market, Virginia, strategically important because of its proximity to the New Market Gap, the only passage over Massanutten Mountain to the east. After several days of skirmishing and positioning, Breckenridge decided to confront the disorganized Union forces north of the town. Early on the morning of May 15, 1864, Breckenridge positioned his artillery on high ground south of the town, while putting his infantry behind them and sending his cavalry to the east in an attempt to flank the Union left. At approximately 11 AM, as Union forces were still arriving, Breckenridge's infantry advanced, pushing through the town

The Bushong farm, site of pitched action during the battle of New Market.

and the scattered Union troops that had been formed around it. By 12:30 the Confederates had established a position near the Bushong farm, 2 miles north of New Market.

Sigel, having arrived after the action began, recognized that his lines were scattered and formed a new, stronger position, just north of the farm. As the Confederates pushed northward, they met Sigel's artillery, and soon their advance stalled. Unable to gain any ground, Breckenridge brought up his reserves, which included the VMI cadets. Fighting around the farm was fierce, and the cadets suffered 57 casualties.

As the Confederates were hung up around the farm, the Union forces attempted several disorganized charges. The confusion was recognized quickly by Breckenridge, who ordered a general advance toward the Union position. The Union line broke and was soon moving northward, covered by artillery. By evening Sigel's army had reorganized near Cedar Creek, well north of the battlefield, having suffered 841 casualties out of an initial force of 8,940. The much smaller Confederate force had lost 520, with over 10 percent of them being the VMI cadets. The cadets' bravery, the tragedy of their losses, and their sacrifice for a dying cause live on as a source of pride and a symbol of the effects of war.

Cross Keys and Port Republic

The battles of Cross Keys and Port Republic, fought on consecutive days in June of 1862, serve as a fitting end to Stonewall Jackson's celebrated 1862 Shenandoah Valley campaign. Jackson's use of the valley's terrain left two Union armies, less than 10 miles apart, unable to assist each other in a movement that should have produced the destruction of Jackson's army. Instead, Jackson's army not only survived, but defeated both armies, severely impacting Union strategy not only in the valley, but in the entire eastern theater.

After Jackson drove Major General Nathaniel Banks's Federals out of Winchester, he soon realized that two other Union forces, led by Major General John Frémont and

The peaceful Shenandoah Valley at Cross Keys battlefield.

Brigadier General James Shields, would attempt to cut off his escape route and trap him in the valley, forcing him to fight. While Jackson raced his soldiers south toward the town of Strasburg, Frémont's force pursued him through the valley, while Shields's force moved parallel to Jackson's but on the opposite (east) side of Massanutten Mountain. The plan was for both Union armies to come together south of the Confederates and crush them. However, Shields's army was on the east side of the south fork of the Shenandoah River. Knowing this, Jackson sent his cavalry to burn all the bridges over the south fork from Front Royal south to the town of Port Republic. Jackson turned his army toward Port Republic and crossed the remaining bridge to face Shields, while Frémont's army pursued him.

Jackson ordered Major General Richard Ewell to confront Frémont's army. Commanding 5,000 men, Ewell formed a line running roughly east to west, near a tavern known as Cross Keys. On the morning of June 8, 1864, Frémont approached Ewell's force and formed a line opposite, more than twice the strength of Ewell's. Frémont moved on Ewell's right and chased an advance Confederate force through an open field. However, Ewell had concealed an entire brigade behind a fence at the opposite end of the field. When Frémont's men neared the fence, the Confederates opened up on them, and the Federals were soon retreating in confusion. Seizing the opportunity, the Confederates pursued them, eventually pushing them back into the rest of the line. On the opposite end of the line, the Confederate left, fighting was much harder, and the outcome was uncertain until Frémont, after seeing his own left crumple, pulled his entire force back. Night fell, and Ewell withdrew under cover of darkness to join the rest of Jackson's force at Port Republic. When Frémont realized this the next morning, he immediately pursued Ewell's force but was stopped in his tracks when he realized that Ewell had burned the only bridge available to cross over to Port Republic. Stuck on the west side of the river, Frémont's troops were helpless bystanders as Jackson and Ewell confronted Shields.

Jackson and Shields had skirmished around the town of Port Republic the day before, and at the end of that day, while Ewell and Frémont were fighting at Cross Keys, the Union troops, commanded by Brigadier General Erastus Tyler, had formed a strong position east of Port Republic. The line was only half a mile long but was anchored on the right by the South Fork of the Shenandoah and on the left by a towering hill known as the Coaling (the name came from the fact that charcoal was produced on the hill). Union artillery placed on the hill held a commanding view of the open ground below, and the short line was packed with 3,000 infantry.

Jackson attacked at dawn with a frontal assault through the open field, but the Confederates quickly came under heavy fire, first from the artillery at the Coaling, then from the infantry below. In the meantime, Jackson sent another brigade through the thick woods in front of the Union left, the location of the Coaling. The Confederate

The view from atop the Coaling, Port Republic Battlefield.

SITE DETAILS

Cross Keys and Port Republic driving tour—This driving tour, created by the Virginia Civil War Trails group, will take you through most of the area of both days' battles, highlighting the key landmarks. Although virtually the entirety of both battlefields is privately owned, the landscape is unblemished, and it is very easy to interpret the events of these two brilliantly fought battles. The brochure for the driving tour can be picked up either at the Harrisonburg Visitor Center or at a kiosk at the beginning of the Cross Keys tour. *Harrisonburg Visitor Center, 212 S. Main St., Harrisonburg, VA, 22801; 540-432-8935. Virginia Civil War Trails Kiosk, 6625 Port Republic Rd., Harrisonburg, VA, 22801. Both sites open daily.*

The Coaling—The Civil War Preservation Trust has acquired the famed hill known as the Coaling that was the focus of much of the battle of Port Republic. The site is also part of the driving tour. There are interpretive signs on the hill, and the climb to the top (it is a trail, with some steps, but is not too strenuous) will give you a commanding view of the Port Republic battlefield. *The Coaling, Civil War Preservation Trust, intersection of US 340 and Ore Bank Rd., Harrisonburg, VA, 24471. Open daily.*

infantry assaulted the Union line again but was again repulsed, this time into retreat, pursued by the eager Federals. However, just as the Union infantry were well into the open field, the Confederate brigade assaulting the Coaling had made it through the woods and seized the Federal artillery. At nearly the same time, Ewell's men arrived from their fighting at Cross Keys, flanking the Union infantry's left. It was a perfect storm: The Union force, in an instant, went from charging pursuers to being assaulted on two sides, as well as now receiving fire from the captured artillery at the Coaling. Soon the Federals were in full retreat, fighting a running battle for 5 miles.

After two days of heavy fighting against two different pursuing forces, Jackson had capped his Shenandoah Valley campaign with a pair of brilliant victories, set up by careful use of the landscape. The valley campaign, particularly his maneuvering at Cross Keys and Port Republic, is still a source of study for military tacticians everywhere.

Lexington

No significant battles occurred in Lexington, Virginia, although Virginia Military Institute, still located here, was burned by Union troops during the war. But Lexington is nevertheless a must-see for Civil War buffs visiting the Shenandoah Valley. Stonewall Jackson was an instructor at his much-beloved VMI, and it is here that he is buried. Washington University was also here, right next to VMI. It was named after George Washington, the father of our country and not-so-distant relative to Robert E. Lee. Lee became president of the university after the war, and it is now called Washington and Lee University. He, too, is buried here, in a chapel that once held his office and now bears his name.

The ghosts of Lee and Jackson, two great icons of the Confederate cause, can be felt throughout this quaint college town. It is quiet, a place of peace, and its position at the southern end of the Shenandoah Valley serves as a perfect place to end this tour.

Lee Chapel, final resting place of Robert E. Lee, Lexington.

SITE DETAILS

Lee Chapel and Museum at Washington and Lee University—This is where Robert E. Lee, after serving his beloved state of Virginia and the university that would later bear his name, chose to rest. Several other members of his family, including his famous father, Revolutionary War hero "Light-Horse Harry" Lee, are also here, as is Lee's horse, Traveller, buried on the grounds just outside the chapel. On the main floor of the chapel is the famous sculpture of Lee lying in repose, while the family crypt is beneath, along with a museum and Lee's former office. This is still a working chapel, and weddings and other events are still held here, so please enter and leave quietly, showing the respect due any place of worship. *Lee Chapel and Museum at Washington and Lee University, parking available near intersection of N. Jefferson St. and Henry St., Lexington, VA, 24450; 540-463-8768; chapelapps.wvu.edu. Open daily.*

Virginia Military Institute—This institution, where Stonewall Jackson once taught, is steeped in history and tradition, and its museum predates the Civil War. Take the time to walk the grounds if you can; if not, visit the recently expanded and renovated museum, which includes Jackson's famous horse, Little Sorrel, as well as the uniform he was wearing when he was mortally wounded at Chancellorsville. *Virginia Military Institute, 415 Letcher Ave., Lexington, VA, 24450; 540-464-7334; www.vmi.edu. Open daily.*

Stonewall Jackson Memorial Cemetery—This is the final resting place of Thomas J. "Stonewall" Jackson, near his beloved VMI. Also buried here are several other generals from the war, congressmen, and governors. But looming over them all is the statue above Jackson's grave, still a commanding presence. *Stonewall Jackson Memorial Cemetery, intersection of S. Main St. and White St., Lexington, VA, 24450. Open daily.*

Time in Lexington would be well used to reflect on the reasons why this great Civil War, which caused so much suffering, was fought, and why so many good people thought that their cause was just enough that they were dedicated to fight for it, despite the terrible consequences.

» OTHER SITES IN THE SHENANDOAH VALLEY

Smithfield Crossing—For several days, skirmishing had occurred between Sheridan's Union force based at Charles Town, West Virginia, and Early's Confederates west of Opequon Creek. Cavalry from both sides met at Smithfield Crossing on August 28, 1864. The fight continued for two days, with Confederate infantry being brought in to take the crossing, but the Union cavalry was able to hold them off until Union infantry arrived. The Confederates retired across the creek, and the Union force held the crossing.

There is no marker at the site of the battle, which occurred where West Virginia Highway 51 crosses Opequon Creek. Interpretation of the battle can be found at the Jefferson County Museum in Charles Town, which has excellent exhibits on local history, including the trial and execution of John Brown for his raid at Harpers Ferry. *Battle site, near intersection of WV 51 and Opequon Lane, Kearneysville, WV, 25430; Jefferson County Museum, 200 E. Washington St., Charles Town, WV, 25414; 304-725-8616; www.jeffctywvmuseum.org. Museum open Tue.–Sat., mid-Mar. to mid-Dec.; admission charged.*

Summit Point—With Sheridan at Charles Town, West Virginia, after the battle at Guard Hill, Early moved first back into Winchester, then toward the Union army with three converging columns. On August 21, 1864, one of the columns, commanded by Lieutenant General Richard Anderson, encountered Union cavalry at the town of Summit Point and was prevented from joining the rest of Early's force. Early, his plan foiled, withdrew back to the west.

All that exists at the battle site is a lone concrete marker, part of a historical trail created long ago by a local historian. There is no interpretation on the marker, simply its identification as point number 13 on the tour. Information on the battle can be found at the Jefferson County Museum in Charles Town. *Marker, intersection of Summit Point Pike and Hawthorne Ave., Summit Point, WV, 25446; Jefferson County Museum, 200 E. Washington St., Charles Town, WV, 25414; 304-725-8616; www.jeffctywvmuseum.org. Site accessible daily; museum open Tue.–Sat., Mar.–Dec.; admission charged.*

Berryville—Following the battles of Guard Hill, Summit Point, and Smithfield Crossing, Sheridan had a good understanding of the opposing Confederate force under General Jubal Early. In early September, Sheridan decided to move toward Early, who was still positioned in Winchester. On the evening of September 3, 1864, while a Union division was going into camp at Berryville, Virginia, east of Winchester, a Confederate division attacked, driving the Federals back before nightfall. Overnight both sides reinforced and drew lines, but when Early saw the Union defenses, he decided to withdraw back toward Winchester. This would be the last significant meeting of the two armies before the Federals drove Early out of Winchester at the battle of Opequon.

There is a historical highway marker in front of a school just west of the town of Berryville. The Clarke County Historical Association Museum in Berryville also has information about the battle. *Historical highway marker J-30 (Battle of Berryville), Virginia Department of Conservation and Historic Resources, 34 Westwood Rd., Berryville, VA, 22611; Clarke County Historical Association Museum, 32 E. Main St., Berryville, VA, 22611; 540-955-2600; www.clarkehistory.org. Marker accessible daily; museum open afternoons Mon.–Fri. and by appointment; admission charged.*

Cool Spring—After General Jubal Early's raid on Washington was ended at the battle of Fort Stevens, he retreated westward toward the Shenandoah Valley. Early was pursued by General Horatio Wright and 10,500 Federals, and as Early's men tried to cross the Shenandoah River on July 17, Union cavalry tried to pin them down. Early repulsed Union efforts to flank his army, and at the Cool Spring farm, near Snicker's Ford, he drove the Federals back to the river.

The battle site at Cool Spring is now part of Holy Cross Abbey, which operates a bakery and confectionery and encourages visitors to enjoy the grounds. However, no interpretation exists here. There is a Virginia Civil War Trails marker near the site. *Holy Cross Abbey, 901 Cool Spring Lane; Virginia Civil War Trails—Battle of Cool Spring, intersection of VA 7 and Castleman Rd., Berryville, VA, 22611. Open daily.*

Guard Hill—In August of 1864 Ulysses S. Grant put Major General Philip Sheridan in charge of all Union forces in and around the valley, creating what was to be known as the Army of the Shenandoah. The Confederates' Jubal Early was still in Winchester, recently reinforced, but he moved south to Front Royal when Sheridan's army approached from Harpers Ferry to the north. On August 16, just north of Front Royal, a cavalry fight broke out at the Shenandoah River crossings near a prominent high point known as Guard Hill. Union infantry became involved, taking 300 prisoners, but eventually withdrew northward.

A historical highway marker stands at a busy intersection on Guard Hill; be very careful if you pull over to see it. Information on the battle can be found at the Warren Rifles Confederate Museum in Front Royal. *Historical highway marker J-11 (Guard Hill Engagement), Virginia Department of Conservation and Historic Resources, intersection of Winchester Rd. and Guard Hill Rd., Front Royal, VA, 22630. Accessible daily.*

Manassas Gap—Following the battle of Gettysburg, General Robert E. Lee quickly retreated south through Maryland and back into Virginia. Although several battles occurred, the movement went largely uncontested. On July 23, 1863, a final attempt to catch Lee's army before it reached Richmond was made at Manassas Gap in the Blue Ridge Mountains. Although the Union force launched several effective attacks, the Confederate rear guard was able to hold and later withdraw successfully with the rest of the army.

Unfortunately, nothing remains at the battle site; there are no markers or interpretation. To see the battle area, travel east from Front Royal on Interstate 66, get off at exit 13, and take a look around. That's Manassas Gap. For information on and interpretation of the battle, your best bet is to visit the Warren Rifles Confederate Museum in Front Royal. *Manassas Gap, around intersection of John Marshall Hgwy. and Apple Mountain Rd. (I-66 exit 13), Linden, VA, 22642.*

Tom's Brook—After the Confederates were defeated at Fisher's Hill, Robert E. Lee sent troops to General Early to try to hold out in the Shenandoah Valley for as long as possible. This included Brigadier General Thomas Rosser's brigade, which had been part of the siege line at Petersburg. Rosser was immediately put in command of two divisions of Early's cavalry. Meanwhile, Sheridan was moving the Union army northward through the valley, destroying everything in sight. When he learned that Rosser's men were following him and were 26 miles north of the rest of Early's army, Sheridan chose to strike. On October 9, 1864, Union cavalry attacked Rosser's encampment at Tom's Brook. After two hours of fighting, the Confederates fled south toward the rest of Early's army in what became known as the Woodstock Races.

A Virginia Civil War Trails interpretive sign in Shenandoah County Park, at the site of Rosser's encampment, tells the story of the battle of Tom's Brook. When you enter the park, follow the VCWT markers to the site, located behind the tennis courts. *Virginia Civil War Trails—Tom's Brook, in Shenandoah County Park, intersection of US 11 and Park Lane, Maurertown, VA, 22644. Accessible daily.*

McDowell—After his defeat at Kernstown, Stonewall Jackson reformed his army in the Shenandoah Valley and headed west from Staunton, Virginia toward McDowell, a town surrounded by high, rugged terrain. He knew that an advance unit of Major General John Frémont's Federals was heading east toward the valley, and he meant to confront it. On May 8, 1862, Jackson's army took a position on clear ground atop Sitlington's Hill, a rocky ridge just east of the town. But before Jackson was able to plan an attack, the Union force, commanded by Brigadier General Robert Milroy, assaulted his position, climbing the steep and difficult hill from the west. Using the thick forest as cover, the Union troops were able to inflict damage, but none of the units were able to make the crest. Still, the Union force of 6,000 men suffered only 256 killed and wounded, while the Confederates, larger in number and holding the high ground, took 500 casualties. Milroy withdrew westward after the battle, and Jackson occupied the town of McDowell.

Visiting the battlefield at McDowell is rewarding but takes some effort, so *please* read this before you head out, so that you know what you're getting into. Heading west from the valley, the drive to McDowell will take you through beautiful mountainous country, but it's slow going; take your time and use caution on the winding roads. Once you get there, you will come upon the McDowell Battlefield, with the trailhead at a roadside pull-off. Owned and maintained by the Civil War Preservation Trust, the battlefield is pristine, and the interpretation is excellent. However, if you want to see it, be prepared to climb. The hill is steep, and the trail is rugged, about 1.5 miles to the top, and signs advise that you'll need two hours to get to the top and back. If you can make the climb, it is certainly worth it. *McDowell Battlefield, on US 250 east of intersection of US 250 and VA 656, McDowell, VA, 24458; www.civilwar.org. Open daily.*

Piedmont—After his defeat at New Market, Major General Franz Sigel was removed from command and replaced by Major General David Hunter. Hunter wasted no time in getting his Federals moving from their position at Cedar Creek toward the Confederate forces to the south. On June 5, 1864, just north of the town of Piedmont, Virginia,

Hunter confronted Brigadier General William "Grumble" Jones's force of 5,600, beginning with a cavalry scuffle early in the morning. The Confederates were soon forced back, and a gap was created between Jones's infantry and cavalry. When the Union forces pressed and tried to flank Jones's infantry, the gap was found, and the fighting grew fierce around the Confederate right. When Jones was killed on the field, the Confederate lines collapsed, and the entire force quickly retreated southward. Hunter tried to pursue but was held back by the Confederate rear guard. The Confederates suffered heavy casualties, losing 1,600 men, but more important, lost their once-firm grip on the Shenandoah Valley.

Although this was an important battle, not much is left of it to see. A monument has been placed along the east side of Battlefield Road, north of the still-tiny town, near where the Confederate lines were located and where Jones was killed. There is also a Virginia Civil War Trails interpretive sign just south of town in front of the New Hope Community Center, which shares a parking lot with the New Hope Fire Department. *Memorial marker, north of intersection of Battlefield Rd. and Patterson Mill Rd., Grottoes, VA, 24441; Virginia Civil War Trails—Battle of Piedmont, parking lot of New Hope Community Center and New Hope Fire Department, 691 Battlefield Rd., Fort Defiance, VA, 24437. Accessible daily.*

Waynesboro—Although most of his army was sent to Petersburg, Lieutenant General Jubal Early still commanded 2,000 Confederates in the Shenandoah Valley in 1865. General Sheridan rode south with 10,000 Federals to drive them out, and on March 2, 1865, Early's force dug in at the town of Waynesboro. Early had so few troops that he could not even cover his front, leaving a large gap in his line. General George Armstrong Custer found the gap and drove into it, breaking the Confederate position. Except for Jubal Early, virtually all the Confederates were captured, while the Federals suffered only 30 casualties. Sheridan, destroying railroad track along the way, rode on to join Grant in his final assault on Petersburg. The Shenandoah Valley, devastated by war, would finally see peace.

A Virginia Civil War Trails interpretive sign at the Plumb house, in the center of the fighting, tells of Custer's charge through the town. *Virginia Civil War Trails—Waynesboro (The Plumb House), 1012 W. Main St., Waynesboro, VA, 22980. Accessible daily.*

» WHERE TO STAY IN THE SHENANDOAH VALLEY

When Sheridan's Federals tore through the Shenandoah Valley in 1864, they didn't leave much behind. Most of the now-existing homes were built after "the Great Burning." But the valley is still a pretty, quiet place, and there is no shortage of excellent bed-and-breakfasts. Most of them can be found through the Bed and Breakfasts of the Historic Shenandoah Valley organization. Their Internet site contains not only a listing of quality B&Bs throughout the entire valley, but also the Web links, phone numbers, and e-mail contacts for each of the inns. The information is also available in a brochure that you can order through the Web site. *Bed and Breakfasts of the Historic Shenandoah Valley, www.bbhsv.com.*

There is one bed-and-breakfast inn in the valley that didn't merely miss Sheridan's torches; it resisted them and won: **By the Side of the Road**, located in Harrisonburg, near the Cross Keys and Port Republic battlefields, dates back to 1790 and was used as a field hospital during the war. Sheridan's men did try to burn the home down, but after four unsuccessful attempts to put the building's fire-resistant timbers to the torch, they gave up and moved on. *By the Side of the Road, 491 Garbers Church Rd., Harrisonburg, VA, 22801; 1-866-274-4887; www.bythesideoftheroad.com.*

Because Interstate 81 runs straight through the heart of the valley, there is no shortage of motels at any of the exits, and you will never be far from lodging. However, there is one other option for those who are more adventurous. **Shenandoah National Park** runs the length of the valley from Front Royal to Waynesboro, and although the focus of the park is recreational and not historic, its natural beauty makes it a wonderful place to visit. The park contains numerous campsites, some with nearly full facilities, and backcountry and wilderness camping is also permitted. The park also has some lodges and cabins, along with several full-service restaurants. *Shenandoah National Park; entrances to park at Front Royal (I-66 and VA 340), Thornton Gap (VA 211), Swift Run Gap (VA 33), and Rockfish Gap (I-64 and VA 250); 540-999-3500; www.nps.gov/shen. Open daily; admission charged.*

PART FOUR

The Wide-Ranging War

11

Other Civil War Sites

OVERVIEW

The battles of the Civil War were fought mostly south of the Mason-Dixon Line. But this great conflict touched every part of America. This chapter gathers the significant Civil War–related sites found in far-flung corners of the nation, from New England to New Mexico to Idaho. It also includes some of the many battles fought right in the heart of the nation but that either weren't part of a critical campaign or were not designated by the Civil War Sites Advisory Commission as Class A battles (in other words, they did not have a direct impact on the course of the war). This is not a chapter of leftovers. These sites are as important as some of the major battlefields in gaining a true understanding of the Civil War.

» THINGS TO KNOW

This chapter isn't organized into tours. Instead, the sites here are gathered into seven themes that end up near each other geographically. Some of the sites can easily be worked into any of the earlier trips, while others might be more difficult to get to. But every one is worth the effort.

The New Mexico Campaign

In the infancy of the Confederacy, the new would-be nation, like the United States, believed that expansion to the west was its manifest destiny and held hopes that this expansion would occur as soon as the issue of the war had been settled. These hopes were not completely unfounded. Slavery was permitted in the territories of New Mexico and Utah, and the state of California had been admitted as a free state by only

General Grant National Memorial, in Riverside Park in Manhattan.

two votes. Many in the Confederacy, including President Jefferson Davis, strongly believed that Confederate influence in the territories, and even California, could bring those areas around to support the effort to forge this new nation.

The Confederacy had other, more practical needs in the West as well. In 1859 gold had been discovered in Colorado, and the possession of these mines would bring in much-needed cash. In addition, the United States Navy, spending so much of its resources on the blockade of the Atlantic and Gulf Coasts, had only a handful of ships in the Pacific. Opening a route to California, albeit a long one, could mean new ports for the import of war materials and, more important, the export of Southern cotton. So, in 1861, the Confederate government authorized an expedition into the far West to win those areas for the Confederacy and help establish its legitimacy as a new nation.

Early in 1862 some 2,500 Texans commanded by Brigadier General Henry Hopkins Sibley headed west, bound for the territorial capital of Santa Fe, New Mexico. It was Sibley who had requested approval for the expedition, and he was confident of its success, believing that the slaveholding citizens of New Mexico would flock to the cause. Sibley also believed that his army would be able to live off the land as it traveled and would not meet much resistance from Union troops, who were widely scattered throughout the New Mexico Territory in various fortifications to guard mail routes and protect settlements.

Sibley's Texans traveled along the west bank of the Rio Grande, capturing several small fortifications near El Paso early in the campaign and then stopping for a short period. The Union commander of the Department of New Mexico, Colonel Edward Canby, had pulled all his approximately 3,800 troops into Fort Craig, 100 miles south of Albuquerque, to await Sibley's approach. Canby knew that Sibley's expedition would have a very hard time finding forage in the harsh desert of the Southwest, and he likely also knew that the locals were not as pro-Confederate as Sibley might have thought. New Mexico, slave territory that it was, had fewer than 100 enslaved persons among its population, and was mostly Hispanic—former Mexicans who had recently had a border dispute with Texas while Texas was still an independent republic.

Sibley's New Mexico campaign had only two large engagements, but they make up one of the most interesting campaigns of the entire war and should not be forgotten. In fact, the battle at Glorieta Pass was determined to have a direct impact on the outcome of the war and was given a Class A designation by the Civil War Sites Advisory Commission—remarkable for a battle so far removed from the rest of the action. The battlefields themselves are also unique, and visiting them is really the only way to gain a full perspective on this strange but important expedition.

Valverde—In early February Sibley left his base and began to make his way up the Rio Grande. He knew that Colonel Edward Canby had moved virtually all his troops and supplies to Fort Craig, along the west bank of the river and directly blocking

Sibley's path to Santa Fe. He also knew that Canby had superior numbers, and that any attempt to take Fort Craig would be futile. Still, Sibley needed the supplies in the fort and did not like the idea of leaving Canby in his rear as he advanced northward. Sibley decided to try to lure Canby's forces out into the open, where the odds would be evened. On February 20, 1862, Sibley's Confederates camped across the river from the fort, and the two sides exchanged shots, with the Confederates eventually withdrawing back into the hills. The next day the Confederates marched to Valverde Crossing, 6 miles north of the fort. Canby, knowing exactly where Sibley was headed, sent his men to the ford and formed lines of battle on both sides of the river. After some heavy fighting near Valverde, the Confederates were able to penetrate the Union center, owing to confusion in Canby's lines. Canby's men retreated to the fort, and when the Confederates asked for surrender, the Federals refused. Still knowing that an assault on the fort would not succeed, and badly needing to move on to find supplies, the Confederates marched north to Santa Fe. They occupied Santa Fe on March 10, only to find that Canby had sent word for all supplies of military use to be evacuated from the city.

Fort Craig National Historic Site is maintained by the Socorro Resource Area of the Bureau of Land Management. What is left of the fort is in ruin, the adobe melted away by years of erosion and human treasure-hunting—but the site is pure gold. This is an isolated area of the New Mexico desert, and there is truly nothing around to spoil your view or imagination of the happenings at the fort in 1862. Enough of the fort is left to determine where the primary areas were, and the foundations of the buildings that were built of stone still remain. The walls of the fort, although not what they used to be, are still easily discernible. A visitor's center offers interpretation of the battle and covers the history of the site and archaeological finds there, and picnic and other facilities are available. The site is not far from Interstate 25, and although the access road is not paved, it is well-maintained and always passable. As for the ford at Valverde itself, it is on private property and cannot be viewed; however, there is a monument just behind the gates of a ranch, directly west of the ford. *Fort Craig National Historic Site, Bureau of Land Management—Socorro Resource Area, 4.5 miles east of intersection of Fort Craig Rd. and NM 1; Battle of Valverde Monument, behind ranch gate at I-25 exit 124, Magdalena, NM 87825; 505-835-0412; www.blm.gov/nm/st/en/prog/recreation/ socorro/fort_craig.html. Open daily.*

Glorieta Pass—While in Santa Fe, Brigadier General Henry Sibley's Confederates gathered what supplies they could for the next phase of their campaign: pushing up the Santa Fe Trail toward Fort Union, where plentiful supplies were being held. Sibley himself preferred to remain in Albuquerque for the time being; quite simply, he was a notorious drunk, and there was more liquor there. Sibley sent a force of 400, led by Major Charles Pyron, up the Santa Fe Trail to scout the enemy on March 25, and Peyron's men camped at Johnson's Ranch near Cañoncito, just west of Glorieta Pass, the narrowest point on the Santa Fe Trail. Meanwhile, Colorado volunteers led by Colonel John Slough had left Fort Union on March 22, moving down the trail toward the Confederates. The Union volunteers, mostly miners, had just barely recovered from a harsh march through blizzard conditions from Denver City, Colorado, and were ready for action. They stopped to camp at Kozlowski's Ranch on March 25, just east of the pass.

The next morning, March 26, 1862, Pyron's Confederates collided with Slough's advance party, 420 men led by Major John Chivington, on the trail at Apache Canyon. Chivington, after setting a line of battle across the trail, conducted a series of three flanking maneuvers by running his men up the steep hills of the canyon and firing down on the Confederates. Each maneuver was successful in driving the Confederates back, and when a cavalry charge was finally organized after several attempts, the Confederates were routed. Seventy of the Confederates were trapped in the canyon, with the rest retreating back to Johnson's Ranch. Chivington, in turn, took his men back to the Union camp at Kozlowski's Ranch, and both sides prepared to bring up the whole of their forces.   On the following day, March 27, no action took place, as the two armies each expected to be attacked. Slough, however, had developed a plan: He would lead 800 men down the Santa Fe Trail directly toward the Confederate front, while Chivington would take 400 men across Glorieta Mesa south of the trail and

Cañoncito and Glorieta Mesa, site of the destruction of the Confederate wagon train at the battle of Glorieta Pass, Pecos National Historical Park.

come up in the Confederate rear, remaining close enough to the edge of the mesa to hear when the fighting would begin. The Confederates would be trapped in the canyon, with no escape. Meanwhile, Pyron had additional forces brought up from Galisteo, 15 miles away. The sides were at about equal strength.

The Confederates marched out of Cañoncito on the morning of March 28 and headed east, leaving their entire supply train of 80 wagons behind, guarded by only a handful of men. They were now under the command of the ranking officer, Lieutenant Colonel William Scurry. First contact came at approximately 11 AM, near Pigeon's Ranch at Glorieta Pass. Slough formed a line across the Santa Fe Trail, and the fighting raged for three hours, with Chivington never coming to the Union aid. He and his men had gotten slowed and lost in the thick brush at the top of the mesa and did not hear the battle begin. Eventually the Union line was driven back after being outflanked, and a second, then a third line was set up. The fighting ended with the darkness, and victory at Glorieta Pass belonged to the Confederates, who had repeatedly pushed the Federals back and held the field.

But where was Chivington? Although the Confederates had won the battle, their campaign in New Mexico was over. During the action, Chivington's men had come out at a location on the mesa overlooking Cañoncito and the lightly guarded Confederate wagon train. After waiting for some time to make sure that they were not being led into a trap (which, with the light guard, was not out of the question), the Union force raced down the side of the mesa, surprising the Confederates, who ran in every direction. Unable to bring the wagons back up the mesa or through the Santa Fe Trail, Chivington's men burned them, leaving the Confederates without food, supplies, or ammunition. Within weeks Sibley was forced to return to Texas. Although casualties at Glorieta Pass were relatively light, Sibley returned with only about half the men he had left with, many of them having deserted.

Much of the battlefield at Glorieta Pass is within Pecos National Historical Park, just east of Santa Fe. Unfortunately, for now, virtually the entire battlefield must be viewed from a distance; although the land has been acquired by the park, little interpretation has been installed. However, the park still provides a great opportunity to experience the battlefield. Once a week, and twice during the summer months, guided tours of the battlefield sites are given by park rangers, and they are exceptional. The tour stops at all the major scenes of action, including Pigeon's Ranch, Kozlowski's Ranch, and Cañoncito. This personal, up-close, two-hour chauffeured tour of the battlefield by an extremely knowledgeable park ranger costs a whopping $5—possibly the best value of any major battlefield park in America. Because the tour groups are so small, be sure to call well ahead of your visit, but do not pass it up. For those who can't make the tour, information on the battle and what can be seen is available at the park's visitor's center, which is geared primarily toward the impressive Pecos Pueblo ruins at the site; future plans include the possible development of a second visitor's center specifically for the battle near the Pigeon's Ranch site. *Pecos National Historical Park, 1 mile south of intersection of NM 63 and Camino Valencia, Pecos, NM, 87552; 505-835-0412; www.nps.gov/peco. Open daily; admission charged.*

The Deep South

Although just what area the "Deep South" encompasses may be open for discussion, certainly many people's first thoughts would include the states of Alabama and Mississippi. However, it may come as a surprise that other than the large actions around Mobile Bay, no major military campaigns occurred in Alabama, and almost all the action in Mississippi happened either around Vicksburg in the west or around Corinth and Tupelo in the northeast corner of the state. There were several reasons for this. For one, both states were primarily agrarian and contained relatively little heavy industry, apart from ironworks in Alabama, meaning that the scarce military targets were usually not worth a major campaign. In addition, while the largest cities in the area, such as Montgomery and Birmingham, were certainly important, they were not comparable in population to the other major cities of the South, nor were they as important as centers of trade, transportation, or industry. Finally, by the time campaigns for targets in this part of the country did begin to take shape, the war was virtually over.

This does not mean that the Deep South, the Confederacy's first political center, rich in cotton, and a great source of manpower for the Southern armies, was able to emerge from the war unscathed, or that it retains little historical interest. On the contrary, battles were fought in northern and central Alabama and eastern Mississippi, many of them cavalry actions or raids to disrupt military operations in other parts of the country. In addition, the first capital of the Confederacy, the location where the Confederate States of America declared itself a sovereign nation, and the place where Jefferson Davis was sworn in as its first president, was Montgomery, Alabama, where the Capitol building is still in use today. Plenty of interesting Civil War sites remain to be explored in today's Deep South.

Athens—The Union garrison of 100 soldiers at the town of Athens, Alabama, was raided by 600 Confederates on January 26, 1864. Although greatly outnumbered, the Union troops were able to hold the off the attackers for two hours, and the Confederates eventually left without taking the railroad center. Federal casualties totaled 20 to the Confederates' 30.

A memorial marker on the courthouse square in Athens commemorates the battle. More conspicuous, however, and more notable in the minds of its citizens, is the memorial to when Major General Nathan Bedford Forrest's cavalry recaptured the town in September of the same year. *Memorial marker—Battle of Athens, intersection of Washington St. and Marion St., Athens, AL, 35611; 1-866-953-6565. Accessible daily.*

Decatur—After Major General John Bell Hood had been unable to protect Atlanta, he eventually decided to lead his men in a desperate mission to capture Nashville. On October 26 Hood led his army through Decatur, Alabama, where 5,000 Federals were garrisoned to guard the crossing of the Tennessee River. After three days of testing the Union strength, Hood eventually moved on, deciding to save his army for the fighting that lay ahead.

The Decatur Convention and Visitor's Bureau has created a very good walking tour of the Civil War sites. The tour makes for a pleasant stroll through this quaint river city, and the interpretive signs along the way are very good. There are also additional driving stops for those who want to explore Hood's actions further. The brochure is also available online. *Civil War Walking Tour, Decatur Visitor's Bureau, 719 6th Ave. SE, Decatur, AL, 35602; 1-800-524-6181; www.decaturcvb.org. Open daily.*

Day's Gap—As the Union prepared to take Vicksburg and secure the Mississippi River, Major General Ulysses S. Grant created a number of diversionary missions in the form of cavalry raids to occupy the Confederates. One of these raids was led by Colonel Abel Streight, who took 1,500 troops to Georgia to destroy the Western & Atlantic Railroad. Just as important was keeping Brigadier General Nathan Bedford Forrest away from Grant. Mission accomplished—but probably not in the fashion that Streight had hoped. On April 30, 1863, Forrest caught Streight at Day's Gap on Sand Mountain in northern Alabama. The Federals put up a good fight, even capturing some of Forrest's artillery. But as Streight headed east toward the railroad, Forrest dogged him for the next several days. On May 3 Streight's men had had enough and surrendered. Unfortunately for them, they had surrendered to only 600 men, another victim of Forrest's inventive ruses. But they had kept Forrest occupied, and as Streight was leading Forrest east, Grant's men were crossing the river into Mississippi.

The battlefield at Day's Gap is one of those gems of a site that is easy to get to but that few know about. It has been struggling for some recognition but unfortunately has received little help. The owner of the site had not realized for some time that he held a piece of history; in addition to being a Civil War battlefield, the land contains remnants of the road on which Davy Crockett traveled on his way to fight with Andrew Jackson at Horseshoe Bend during the War of 1812. The Crooked Creek Civil War Museum contains an excellent display of artifacts that have been found on the land, and paying your small admission fee gets you a personal guided tour of the battlefield and other historic features on the property. The site has even renovated an 1830s cabin that is now available as a bed-and-breakfast. *Crooked Creek Civil War Museum & Park, 516 County Road 1127, Vinemont, AL, 35179; 256-739-2741. Open daily; admission charged.*

Tannehill Iron Works State Park—One of the Confederacy's valued industrial works in its interior, the ironworks at Tannehill, near Birmingham, Alabama, played a major role in supplying the Confederacy with war products. The works operated virtually uninterrupted until near the war's end, producing 22 tons of iron per day. Finally, on March 31, 1865, Union troops under Brigadier General James Wilson occupied the works and destroyed them.

Tannehill Iron Works State Park operates today as a complete living history center. Not only presenting a picture of a Civil War historical site, the park is probably the best location in the country to learn how iron was produced during the war. The Alabama Iron and Steel Museum is dedicated to the works, and it also contains a fine Civil War collection. Also on site is a complete living history village, along with a restaurant and camping, picnic, and hiking facilities. Although the park is open daily, not all the attractions are, so call ahead if you want to see something particular. *Tannehill Iron Works State Park, 12632 Confederate Pkwy., McCalla, AL, 35111; 205-477-5711; www.tannehill.org. Open daily; admission charged.*

Alabama State Capitol—After the secession of the first seven states in late 1860 and early 1861, a convention was held at Montgomery, Alabama, to form a new nation.

The Alabama State Capitol in Montgomery, first capital of the Confederate States of America.

The convention met in the Alabama State Capitol building and, in February 1861, created the Confederate States of America. The convention also ratified a new constitution for the new nation, declared Montgomery its temporary capital, and elected its first president, Jefferson Davis of Mississippi. Davis took the oath of office on the Capitol steps on February 18.

The same Alabama State Capitol building is still used by the state today, and it is open for visitors to view. A gold star on the west steps of the building marks the spot where Jefferson Davis took the oath of office as president. Inside the building are the original legislative chambers, although today's state government sits in the Alabama Statehouse across the street. It was in the old Senate Chamber that the convention ratified the constitution of the Confederacy, and a mural depicting the events of that historic month, along with other moments in Alabama's history, is displayed under the Capitol dome. *Alabama State Capitol, 600 Dexter Ave., Montgomery, AL, 36104; 334-242-3935; www.preserveala.org/capitoltour.htm. Open Mon.–Sat.*

First White House of the Confederacy—While the Confederate capital remained at Montgomery, Alabama, for three months in early 1861, Jefferson Davis lived in a large home just down the street from the Capitol building. The home has since been moved to a location directly across the street from the Capitol. The First White House of the Confederacy has been restored to the appearance of the period when the Davis family inhabited the home, and guided tours are available. The hours for the home can be somewhat irregular, so be sure to call first. *First White House of the Confederacy, 644 Washington Ave., Montgomery, AL, 36130; 334-242-1861. Open Mon.–Fri.*

Selma—In April of 1865, although Robert E. Lee's Confederates were preparing to pull out of their siege defense lines and abandon the capital in Virginia, the war was not over in Alabama, which was still operating ironworks and other industries. One of the major ironworks was in Selma, and a Union cavalry raid led by Brigadier General James Wilson was launched in order to shut it down. After several days of fighting off Confederate cavalry led by Lieutenant General Nathan Bedford Forrest, Wilson's Federals finally approached Selma on April 2, 1865. The city was defended by 3,000 Confederates, including Forrest's men and troops commanded by Lieutenant General Richard Taylor. But Wilson had 9,000 men with him and took the town quickly, splitting his troops into three groups. Selma was forced to surrender (although Forrest and Taylor escaped), and the ironworks and warehouses were taken. Wilson went on to occupy the state capital at Montgomery, destroy the Confederate shipyard at Columbus, Georgia, and eventually capture Jefferson Davis, who was fleeing through Georgia.

The battlefield at Selma has been mostly lost to development; the remaining areas are on private property. The Old Depot Museum in Selma has limited information on the battle, including several maps of where the original battlefield was. Several of the buildings from the ironworks that were the target of the raid are still standing, just outside the front door of the museum. *Old Depot Museum, 4 Martin Luther King St., Selma, AL, 36703; 334-874-2197. Closed Sun.; admission charged.*

Meridian—Meridian, Mississippi, a railroad center with connections to Selma and Mobile, Alabama, was the objective of a Union expedition ordered by Major General William T. Sherman in early 1864 in anticipation of his Atlanta campaign. Some 7,000 Union cavalry left Memphis on February 1, and two days later Sherman left Vicksburg with 26,000 infantry; the two forces were to meet at Meridian, take the railroad center, and push through Mississippi, causing as much damage as possible. However, by the time Sherman reached Meridian, almost all the Confederates were gone, having evacuated their troops and supplies in the days before. The only real success of the Meridian operation was that it led Jefferson Davis to order additional troops to the area, weakening Major General Joseph Johnston's army north of Atlanta.

Today, the only remnant of the battle of Meridian is the railroad depot, which has been turned into the Meridian Railroad Museum. Although there isn't much coverage here of the battle, this depot was the actual objective of Sherman's expedition and the scene of much desperate activity in the days before he arrived. Note that the museum is open infrequently; it may be best to make an appointment. *Meridian Railroad Museum, 1805 Front St., Meridian, MS, 39301; 601-485-7245; www.meridian-railroad-museum.org. Open first and third Sat. of the month and by appointment.*

The Battle for the Heartland:
Eastern Kentucky and Eastern Tennessee

For much of the early part of the war, eastern Kentucky and eastern Tennessee were very much up for grabs. Strategically, the extremely important Cumberland Gap, on the Virginia-Kentucky border, was a critical passage through the mountains. Perhaps more important, the population of the area was not committed to one side or the other. Although Tennessee had seceded, the eastern part of the state was home to many Unionists; even their favorite-son U.S. senator, Andrew Johnson, had not gone with the state when it seceded, remaining loyal to the Union. The entire state of Kentucky was in a similar condition. Although it was a slave state, Kentucky did not secede, and secessionists were in the minority, albeit a large minority. The main reason in the east was that few of the mostly mountain-dwelling residents were slaveholders, and they saw little point in supporting a cause that did not affect them.

Eastern Kentucky was an important battleground for the first two years of the war. The Confederates, who held the Cumberland Gap at the time, made several attempts to drive into Kentucky and establish a presence there, hoping to bring the state into the Confederate fold. However, repeated military disasters prevented them from ever gaining a foothold, and all hopes were dashed after the battle of Mill Springs in January 1862. After that, Kentucky was virtually locked up for the Union, although a major

Confederate invasion in late 1862 attempted to establish a new government in the state. Lack of local support and a major Union victory at Perryville on October 8, 1862, drove the Confederacy out for good, with the exception of an occasional cavalry raid.

Although Union forces gained much of Tennessee early in the war, it was not until Major General Ambrose Burnside occupied the region in August of 1863 that Union forces held any territory in the eastern part of the state. However, soon after Burnside's arrival, the Confederates won a major victory at Chickamauga, not far from Chattanooga, Tennessee, and a Confederate army under Major General James Longstreet was sent to recapture Knoxville. For several months no one knew which side would gain the upper hand, until Union victories at Fort Sanders in Knoxville and at Chattanooga gave the Federals momentum to drive the Confederates out of the region.

The battles in this region of the country had major consequences, and for two periods of time eastern Kentucky and eastern Tennessee became critically important battlegrounds. The battles fought here, small in name, had a measurable impact on the outcome of the Civil War.

Ulysses S. Grant Birthplace State Memorial—On April 27, 1822, Hiram Ulysses Grant was born on the banks of the Ohio River in the small town of Point Pleasant,

The humble birthplace of Hiram Ulysses Grant, along the banks of the Ohio River at Point Pleasant, Ohio.

Ohio. (The S. would not appear in Grant's name until he went to West Point; he liked it much better than his original name.) The first of six children, Ulysses would move with his family to a larger home in a nearby town within two years.

Although the home actually went on tour for a number of years, being displayed at fairs and other events, the Ulysses S. Grant Birthplace State Memorial is back in its original location. The tiny house is open for guided tours, and the area also contains a lovely park overlooking the river, as well as an adjacent memorial bridge dedicated to Grant. *Ulysses S. Grant Birthplace State Memorial, 1591 OH 232, New Richmond, OH, 45153; 513-553-4911; http://ohsweb.ohiohistory.org/. Open daily, Apr.–Oct.; closed Sun. and Mon., Nov.–Mar.; admission charged.*

Cynthiana—On June 11, 1864, the famed Confederate raider Brigadier General John Hunt Morgan swooped into Cynthiana, Kentucky, with 1,400 men. It was his second raid into Cynthiana, a Union supply center. Although the town was garrisoned by only 500 Federals, Brigadier General Stephen Burbridge and 5,200 Union troops had been on Morgan's tail, and they were close behind. Morgan quickly drove off the Union garrison, burned much of the town, and decided to make his stand against Burbridge here. At 2:30 AM the next day, June 12, Burbridge attacked, eventually capturing a number of Morgan's men. Morgan himself was able to escape—again.

The battle of Cynthiana driving tour was developed several years ago and will take you, in a roundabout way, to all the areas of importance of both battles. Although many of the sites of interest have been developed, the area around Kellar's Bridge is still relatively untouched, although it is on private property and should be viewed from the roadside. The brochure and information can be found at the Cynthiana Chamber of Commerce or the Cynthiana-Harrison County Museum. *Driving Tour—Morgan's Raids at Cynthiana, KY, Cynthiana Chamber of Commerce, 201 S. Main St.; Cynthiana-Harrison County Museum, 13 S. Walnut St., Cynthiana, KY, 41031; 859-234-5236; www.cynthianaky.com. Chamber of Commerce open daily; museum open Fri. and Sat.*

Richmond—As part of Major General Braxton Bragg's plan to invade Kentucky for the Confederacy, Major General Kirby Smith, stationed in Knoxville, Tennessee, moved north toward the town of Richmond, not far south of Lexington. On August 29, 1862, Confederate cavalry made first contact with Union defenders south of the town, then pulled back to join the main force. The next day, after a two-hour artillery exchange, the Confederates advanced, steadily pushing the Federals north toward Richmond. Eventually the Confederates took the Union right and sent the Federals into retreat, finally catching them and forcing them to surrender. Smith's victory here, along with Bragg's victory at Munfordville to the west two weeks later, allowed the Confederates to penetrate deep into Kentucky, setting up the decisive battle at Perryville.

Richmond, Kentucky, has realized the potential for interpreting its battlefield, and there is a lot to see here. Currently, a driving tour is available that will take you through the major points of the battle. The highlights are the Herndon and Rogers homes, which were focal points of the fighting. The Herndon home is also the location of the Battle of Richmond Park, which contains a trail system complete with interpretive signs. Future plans include development of the Rogers home as a museum focusing on the battle. The brochure for the tour is available from the Richmond Tourist Commission, and a recap of the tour is available online. *Battle of Richmond Driving Tour, brochures available at Richmond Tourist Commission, 345 Lancaster Ave., Richmond, KY, 40475; 1-800-866-3705; www.battleofrichmond.org. Open daily.*

Mill Springs—Since the beginning of the war, the Confederates had been trying to hold a presence in eastern Kentucky, a slaveholding border state that might, with some influence, swing over into the Confederacy. Brigadier General Felix Zollicoffer, after holding the important Cumberland Gap for the Confederates but making little headway elsewhere, moved most of his men northwest to Mill Springs, Kentucky, to establish a foothold in the Kentucky interior. As Union troops under Brigadier General George Thomas were approaching, Major General George Crittenden arrived to take command of the Confederates. With the Federals advancing quickly, Crittenden decided that he would have to face the enemy and fight with the Cumberland River to his back rather than risk his force being caught while crossing the swollen river. Crittenden marched north to meet the Union threat, and on January 19, 1862, in a rainy, foggy haze, opened the battle of Mill Springs, initially driving the Federals back. In the bad visibility and confusion of the battle, two groups of officers speaking to one another suddenly realized that the other was the enemy. One of these men was General Zollicoffer, and he was killed on the field. Although Crittenden was able to briefly rally the Confederates, they were driven back when Union reinforcements arrived. After the Federals took both flanks of the Confederate line, Crittenden was forced to pull his men south across the Cumberland in disarray. The Confederates had lost 529 casualties to the Union's 262, as well as their best chance to gain Kentucky.

A visitor's center for the Mill Springs Battlefield National Historic Landmark opened in 2006. It contains a museum that interprets the battle and associated campaigns. There is a film on the battle, plus a small Civil War research library. The center, located next to Mill Springs National Cemetery, is the starting point for a driving tour that has been developed to interpret the battle, and the stops offer interpretive signs and, in some cases, complete park facilities. In case you can't make it to the museum during its regular hours, the driving tour is also available online. This is an excellent site to visit, and there are plans to develop it even further. *Mill Springs Battlefield, 9020 West KY 80, Nancy, KY, 42544; 606-636-4045; www.millsprings.net. Open daily; admission charged for museum.*

Camp Wild Cat—In the struggle for control of the Cumberland Gap, Union troops set up camp at Wildcat Mountain along the Wilderness Road. On October 21, 1861,

Brigadier General Felix Zollicoffer led 7,500 Confederates from his position at the gap to Wildcat Mountain and attacked the 5,400 Federals. The Union troops, with their commanding position, were able to stop each of the Confederate assaults. The Confederates withdrew during the night, and the scene of the heaviest fighting, which had been defended by the 33rd Indiana Infantry, became known as Hoosier Knob.

The Camp Wild Cat site, which is contained within Daniel Boone National Forest, has undergone big changes within the last few years. An interpretive kiosk has been built that explains the importance of the battle and the campaigns for Kentucky, and several trails take visitors to the major scenes of battle (although some of them are a bit strenuous). The road to the site is gravel but is well maintained, and although it takes a while to get up the mountain, the reward is a paved lot with picnic, restroom, and interpretive facilities. *Camp Wildcat Civil War Battlefield, Daniel Boone National Forest, 3.1 miles north of intersection of N. Laurel Rd. and Hazel Patch Rd., East Bernstadt, KY, 40729; 606-864-4163; www.fs.fed.us/r8/boone/districts/london/wildcat.shtml. Open daily.*

Barbourville—Early in the war, Barbourville, Kentucky, was the site of a training camp for Union recruits from eastern Kentucky and Tennessee. The camp was named Camp Andrew Johnson after the Tennessee senator (and future president) who had defied his state and left after its secession. On September 19, 1861, a Confederate force of 800 attacked the camp, only to find that most of the recruits had moved to another camp, leaving only a small home guard in the town. The Confederates easily routed the guard, destroyed the camp, and left.

In downtown Barbourville is a small park dedicated to the first Civil War battle that took place on Kentucky soil. Only recently completed, the park contains numerous interpretive signs explaining the battle and the war in eastern Kentucky very thoroughly. While it may not be substantial in size, it is well done, and the town's historic status is obviously a source of pride for the locals. Information can also be found at the Knox County Historical Museum. *Barbourville Civil War Interpretive Park, intersection of Cumberland Ave. and Daniel Boone Dr.; Knox County Historical Museum, 196 Daniel Boone Dr.; Barbourville, KY, 40906; 606-546-4300. Park open daily; museum open Mon., Wed., and Fri. during summer, Wed. only rest of year.*

Cumberland Gap National Historical Park—The best and most important gap through the Appalachian Mountains, as it had been for centuries, was Cumberland Gap, and for this reason both armies were constantly grappling for control of it. Not only did the Wilderness Road run through it, but so did the East Tennessee & Virginia Railroad, a major artery for getting supplies from the west to the east. Although no large battles were fought here, many of the battles fought within 100 miles of it had something to do with control of the Cumberland Gap, which changed hands several times.

Make the trip to Cumberland Gap if for no other reason than the views, but so much more is available here. The visitor's center contains information on the

Commanding view from the mountains at the all-important Cumberland Gap.

importance of the gap not only during the Civil War but for all the people who have used it over time. There are some remaining earthworks and battery locations in the park, but the real highlights are the scenery, the extensive outdoor activities, and the realization that this small gap in the mountains has had a prominent place in human history for as long as we can measure. *Cumberland Gap National Historical Park, intersection of Clydesdale Ave. and Pinnacle Rd., Middlesboro, KY, 40965; 606-248-2817; www.nps.gov/cuga. Open daily.*

Campbell's Station—After the Confederate victory at Chickamauga, Major General Braxton Bragg was able to besiege the Union forces at Chattanooga and sent Major General James Longstreet north to take the Union positions in eastern Tennessee. Ulysses S. Grant, now in command at Chattanooga, ordered Major General Ambrose Burnside, who held Knoxville, to keep Longstreet busy until Grant could manage to cut the Confederate supply lines. On November 16, 1863, Burnside, trying to get into the Knoxville defenses as quickly as possible, reached the vital crossroads at Campbell's Station only minutes ahead of Longstreet's advance units. A hard fight broke out, and although the Confederates tried to cut Burnside off from Knoxville, the attempt failed. The Federals filed into their Knoxville earthworks overnight.

Campbell's Station also happens to be the home of Civil War hero David Glasgow Farragut, the U.S. Navy's first admiral. The town's Farragut Folklife Museum also contains information on the battle of Campbell's Station, including exhibits and artifacts.

A historical highway marker is in the town near the center of the action. *Farragut Museum, 11408 Municipal Center Dr.; historical highway marker—Tennessee Historical Commission 1E-73 (Battle of Campbell's Station), intersection of Lendon Welch Way and Kingston Pike, Farragut, TN, 37934; 865-966- 7057; www.farraguttn.com. Museum open Mon.–Fri.; site accessible daily.*

Fort Sanders—Major General Ambrose Burnside and his Federals had won the race to Knoxville, occupying the existing defenses on November 17, but he was immediately

United Daughters of the Confederacy monument, the only remaining sign of Fort Sanders, Knoxville, Tennessee.

surrounded by Major General James Longstreet's large Confederate force. The defenses around the city were strong, with earthworks running along the eastern slopes of the rolling terrain. One of the primary positions was Fort Sanders, an earthwork atop a large hill, with high walls and a deep moat surrounding it. On November 29, 1863, Longstreet commanded three brigades to take the fort. The results were devastating for the Confederates. Union obstructions made slow going for the attackers, and when they finally advanced to the moat, they became trapped in it, having thought it was much shallower. The Confederates were like fish in a barrel, and the moat later became known as the death pit. The Confederates suffered 800 casualties during the assault, to the Union's mere 15. Following the battle, word reached Longstreet that Grant had unexpectedly defeated Braxton Bragg at Chattanooga. After several more days, Longstreet was forced to end the siege of Knoxville and retreat toward Virginia.

An outstanding driving tour of the siege of Knoxville and the battle of Fort Sanders has been developed by the Knoxville Civil War Round Table, and a second driving tour is offered by the Knoxville Tourism & Sports Corporation. Both tours cover much the same ground, although the Round Table's tour covers more of the minor locations. Although many of the sites of interest have been obscured by development, the descriptions of the locations and what was there are vivid, and picturing the events is made very easy, aided by Knoxville's beautiful rolling landscape. A few of the sites do still exist, and Fort Dickinson, across the Tennessee River from the city, not only preserves some of the historic earthworks from the siege, but also provides a wonderful vista of the city (and the battlefield). Several historic homes related to the battle are also accessible. The site of Fort Sanders has been developed, but signs and memorials there, along with the brochure, make it worth the stop. While many other driving tours through existing cities have a difficult time describing battles and battlefields around strip malls and suburban growth, both these tours are definite exceptions to that rule. The Round Table's tour is available online only; the Tourism & Sports Corporation's tour is in a brochure that can be picked up in the city. *Civil War Knoxville: A Driving Tour, Knoxville Civil War Round Table, www.discoveret.org/kcwrt/ sites/sd-text.htm; Divided Loyalties: A Civil War Driving Tour of Knoxville, Knoxville Tourism & Sports Corp., 301 S. Gay St., Knoxville, TN, 37902; 1-800-727-8045; www.knoxville.org. Tour sites accessible daily.*

Fair Garden—After being forced out of their winter camp, Major General James Longstreet's Confederates had to forage in the eastern Tennessee countryside. On January 27, 1864, Union troops prevented two Confederate parties from converging at the Fair Garden Road and drove them off, pursuing them through the next day. The Confederates eventually retreated into a fortified position and were able to outlast the Federals, who were also short on supplies.

Not much evidence is left of the battle of Fair Garden, which occurred near

Sevierville, Tennessee; no commemorative signs can be found on the battlefield. Although some information about the battle and the war years is available at the Sevier County Museum, it is not much. If you do happen to go, be aware that Sevierville is a gateway to the Smoky Mountains and is a hot tourist spot. Summer traffic, especially on the weekends, can be extremely heavy. *Sevier County Museum, 167 Bruce St., Sevierville, TN, 37862; 865-453-4058. Closed Wed. and Sun.*

Dandridge—General Ulysses S. Grant, having driven the Confederates away from Chattanooga and Knoxville, wanted Major General James Longstreet's Confederate army driven out of its winter camp in eastern Tennessee and into Virginia. Major General John Parke's Union forces parried with the Confederates for several days, and on the afternoon of January 17, 1864, Longstreet's men counterattacked at Dandridge, Tennessee. Although the fighting was stalemated as darkness fell, the Federals were short on supplies and were forced to fall back overnight.

Dandridge is a cute little remote town in eastern Tennessee, but there are few reminders left that a battle occurred here. A historical highway marker in town commemorates the action. *Historical highway marker—Tennessee Historical Commission 1C-49 (Battle of Dandridge), 1221 Gay St., Dandridge, TN, 37725. Site accessible daily.*

Mossy Creek—On December 29, 1863, while most of the Confederates went into winter camp after their failed attempt to capture Knoxville, a Union party was attacked by Confederate cavalry at Mossy Creek, west of Dandridge. Although the Confederates were able to push the Union force back, other Federal troops soon arrived, and the Confederates were driven off.

Just east of Mossy Creek, a historical highway marker has been erected in front of the Tennessee National Guard station. Because the area contains a lot of open space, including a large public park, the landscape is very visible from this point, and you can see virtually the entire battlefield. *Historical highway marker—Tennessee Historical Commission 1C-83 (Battle of Mossy Creek December 29, 1863), 270 E. Old Andrew Johnson Hgwy., Jefferson City, TN, 37760. Site accessible daily.*

Bean's Station—As Major General James Longstreet retreated toward Virginia following his short, unsuccessful siege at Knoxville, he was pursued by Union forces, suddenly free to maneuver following the Union victories at Fort Sanders and Chattanooga. On December 14, 1863, Longstreet turned to face his pursuers and tried to trap them, but two of the three Confederate columns failed to get into position in time. Although the Confederates did launch a successful assault, they were forced to continue their withdrawal toward Virginia.

Bean's Station is one of the handful of unfortunate battlefields lost to the Tennessee Valley Authority; the site lies at the depths of the artificial Cherokee Lake. That does not mean that the battle has been forgotten, however. A well-developed pull-off, called Veterans' Overlook, offers a scenic view of the lake and takes in the entire valley below; a historical highway marker regarding the battle has been erected at the overlook, which itself is dedicated to veterans of all wars. *Historical highway marker—Bean Station, Veterans' Overlook, intersection of US 25E and Old Mountain Rd., Bean Station, TN, 37708. Site accessible daily.*

Bull's Gap—Over the course of several weeks, Bull's Gap, through which both the East Tennessee & Virginia Railroad and the Knoxville Road passed, became a heavily contested piece of real estate. The Federals needed the roads and railroads open; the Confederates needed the area's abundant supplies. On November 11, 1864, the gap was held by 2,500 Union troops, and 3,000 Confederates under Major General John Breckenridge attacked their position. Breckenridge held the Federals in place while sending another force to get behind them. Eventually running low on ammunition, the Union troops attempted to withdraw on the night of November 13, only to be caught in the rear by the Confederates. Most of the Federals were able to make it to safety, although 300 were forced to surrender.

The railroad has always been important to this small town, and its history will be told at the Bulls Gap Railroad Museum, still under development. The museum is working to include the history of the battle in its exhibits; the railroad, of course, is why the battle was fought in the first place. The railroad still passes through the town, and the gap is clearly discernible. *Bulls Gap Railroad Museum, 139 S. Main St., Bulls Gap, TN, 37711; www.bullsgaprailroadmuseum.org. Site not yet open; check Web site for details.*

Blue Springs—After word of the Union disaster at Chickamauga reached Major General Ambrose Burnside, he recalled to Knoxville most of his forces, which had recently taken control of much of eastern Tennessee. Consequently the Confederates retook much of the ground they had lost, advancing as far west as the town of Blue Springs. On October 10, 1863, Burnside's 20,000 Union troops faced a Confederate force under Brigadier General John Williams. Through some deception, Williams convinced Burnside that the Confederate force was much larger than the 3,200 actually under his command. The Federals advanced cautiously at dawn, with cavalry sent to go around Williams and attack him from the rear. Skirmishing continued throughout the day, with little advantage gained by either side. Finally, at 5 PM, a Federal division caught the Confederates at the right place at the right time, and they were forced back into their earthworks, eventually retreating before the Union cavalry could find them.

Although a large reenactment occurs in the town every year, not much is left in Blue Springs itself that tells of the battle, although fighting probably occurred all along the hills and ridges surrounding the present-day town. Some information about the battle can be found at the Nathanael Greene Museum in nearby Greeneville. *Nathanael Greene Museum, 101 W. McKee St., Greeneville, TN, 37743; 423-636-1558; www.nathanaelgreenemuseum.com. Open Tue.–Sat.*

Andrew Johnson National Historic Site—Born in North Carolina in 1808, Andrew Johnson, apprenticed to a tailor, broke the apprenticeship agreement and ran to Greeneville, Tennessee, in 1826, where he opened his own shop, married, and became a respected citizen. Within three years he was elected an alderman, and his political career would go on to include mayor of Greeneville, state representative, state senator, United States congressman, governor of Tennessee, and United States senator—and that was all before the Civil War broke out. When Tennessee seceded, Johnson kept his seat in the U.S. Senate and ran for vice president on Abraham Lincoln's ticket in 1864; with Lincoln's assassination in 1865, Johnson became president. After his presidency he went on to be elected to the Senate again, the only man to ever do so. All the while his home remained in Greeneville, Tennessee, and it is here that he and his family are buried.

Two of the homes that Johnson owned are preserved at the Andrew Johnson National Historic Site, as is his tailor shop. A visitor's center housed in a separate building tells the details of Johnson's very interesting life and includes artifacts and an interpretive film. Guided tours of the later Johnson home, which remained in the family

Andrew Johnson's tailor shop, preserved at Andrew Johnson National Historic Site.

until 1956, are available, while the other buildings are open and house other exhibits. Johnson's burial site, atop a small hill within what is now Andrew Johnson National Cemetery, is open for public visits. *Andrew Johnson National Historic Site, intersection of N. College and E. Depot Sts., Greeneville, TN, 37743; 423-638-3551; www.nps.gov/anjo. Open daily.*

Blountville—With much of Tennessee under Union control in 1863, it became a Union priority to gain control of the eastern part of the state, where although many of the residents supported the Union cause, the Confederates had retained military control. Major General Ambrose Burnside's Army of the Ohio marched for eastern Tennessee in August 1863, eventually taking Knoxville and the Cumberland Gap, then quickly cleaning up the rest of the area with smaller forces. On September 22, 1863, some 1,500 Union cavalry under Colonel John Foster attacked Confederates at Blountville, Tennessee, first exchanging artillery fire, then driving them southward out of the town.

A lot of work has gone into bringing Blountville's history to life. Historic downtown Blountville provides interpretation not only of the Civil War battle, but also of other events in the town's long and rich history. Among the attractions are the Anderson House and the Deery Inn, both of which took artillery fire during the battle. Although several historical markers in the town give information on the battle, try to visit during regular daytime hours, when the locals are around to answer questions about the town's history. *Historic Downtown Blountville, intersection of TN 394 and County Hill Rd., Blountville, TN, 37617; 423-323-8661. Open daily.*

Ivy Mountain—On November 8, 1861, Union troops approached a smaller Confederate force of about 1,000 men near Pikesville, Kentucky. Knowing that his Confederates were outnumbered, Colonel John Williams sent out his cavalry to meet the Federals to buy time for the rest of his force to retreat to Virginia. The following day, although the Confederates caught Brigadier General William Nelson's Federals in an ambush, the fighting came to a stalemate. Williams managed to withdraw his men successfully.

Along the highway in the small town of Ivel, Kentucky, is a monument to the action at Ivy Mountain, along with two interpretive signs. Behind the monument, although obscured by bushes and on private property, is the mouth of Ivy Creek, where the fighting took place. Ivel is a bit out of the way, but the drive through the mountains to get here (and to nearby Middle Creek battlefield) is great. *Battle of Ivy Mountain monument, north of Ivel Post Office at 6367 US 23, Ivel, KY, 41642; 606-886-1341. Site accessible daily.*

Middle Creek—Eager to maintain a presence in eastern Kentucky but repeatedly losing ground, Confederates set up a recruitment and training camp in the region in late 1861, eventually gathering 2,200 volunteers. Union troops under Colonel James A. Garfield (future president of the United States) drove the Confederates out of their camp and over the mountains over the course of three days. On January 10, 1862, at the battle of Middle Creek, the Federals were finally able to hit the Confederates in the open, eventually sending them back into Virginia.

The official name of the site is Middle Creek National Battlefield. Don't let the name throw you—it is *not* part of the national park system—but some exciting things *are* happening here. To date, extensive interpretive signs, along with two short trails, have been completed, as well as a small parking lot. Work continues on developing a visitor's center and other facilities that would interpret the battle. Although a glance at a road atlas may make Middle Creek seem a bit isolated, the battle site is along the intersection of major highways and is not difficult to get to, and you will wind through some beautiful country. *Middle Creek National Battlefield, intersection of KY 114 and KY 104, Prestonsburg, KY, 41653; 606-886-1312; www.middlecreek.org. Open daily.*

The Battle for the Heartland: West Virginia and Ohio

Like the fighting in eastern Kentucky and Tennessee, the battles of western Virginia were only partly for the strategic value of the territory; they were also for the hearts and minds of the people in those regions. In Virginia, however, the story was somewhat simpler. The mountainous Appalachian region in the western part of the state was much less affluent than the rest of Virginia, and few of the citizens owned or could afford to own slaves. So when the Commonwealth of Virginia seceded from the Union in 1861, most of the western counties were not supportive of the effort. Although several important battles took place in the region to control roads and passages through the mountains, most of the people of western Virginia were not prepared to support secession. Instead, with the help of political wrangling and several Union victories in the area, a number of counties seceded from Virginia and formed the new state of West Virginia in 1863.

There was one resource in western Virginia that was extremely important to the Confederacy: salt. Used for curing and preserving the supply of meat and other foods for its men in the field, salt was a necessary commodity, and without the ability to import it, the Confederacy needed to defend the salt furnaces of western Virginia. Just how crucial the supply of salt became was evidenced by the extensive network of earthworks and forts that surrounded the town of Saltville, as well as the number of Confederate troops stationed there. Union attempts to disrupt activities in this region were frequent.

There is another story to be told here, just outside the West Virginia border and over the Ohio River to the northwest. Brigadier General John Hunt Morgan had bedeviled Union military leaders and terrorized the citizenry of Ohio and Indiana into believing that Confederate invasion was a constant threat. The last of his great raids, in July of 1863, concluded along the banks of the Ohio in two small battles that spelled the end of the last of his men after a long trip into the region. Although Morgan's intriguing story did not end here—he was able to escape from his jail in Ohio and return to the South to conduct other smaller raids, only to be captured, killed, and allegedly have his body dragged through the streets of Greeneville, Tennessee—the two battlefields here, one of them representing the northernmost battle of the Civil War, are worth visiting.

Appalachia is unique, one of the most charming and fascinating regions in America. The countryside is beautiful, and you should give yourself ample time when you visit—not only because of the scenery, but also because getting from stop to stop will take you on winding roads up, down, and around the mountains. Be sure to stop and visit the small towns along the way, talk with the locals, and enjoy the mountain music on the radio.

Salineville—Brigadier General John Hunt Morgan had been riding with his Confederate raiders through Indiana and Ohio for over three weeks, and he had just barely escaped capture at the battle of Buffington Island, where 900 of his men were taken prisoner. Now he was running for his life, along with 400 others who had been able thus far to elude Union forces. After Buffington Island Morgan headed north, looking for a safe place to cross the Ohio River. All the while, he and his men were pursued by Union cavalry eager to prevent his recrossing into Kentucky. Finally, on July 26, 1863, Morgan and his raiders ran out of luck near Salineville, Ohio. Making a mad dash for the river, he and his men were cut off by Union cavalry, and Morgan was forced to surrender.

Just west of the town of Salineville, a memorial has been erected in a small park by the Carroll County Historical Society. The memorial only briefly describes the battle but does indicate its significance as the northernmost battle of the war. *Morgan's Raid memorial marker, 0.2 mile west of intersection of Salineville Rd. NE and Ocean Rd. NE, Salineville, OH, 43945. Open daily.*

Buffington Island—After crossing into Indiana on July 2, 1863, and fighting a small battle at Corydon on July 9, Brigadier General John Hunt Morgan, leading 2,500 Confederate troopers in what would become the longest cavalry raid of the war, headed east into Ohio. All the while, Morgan's force was being pursued by cavalry sent by Major General Ambrose Burnside, who had been preparing to march into Tennessee from his base in Cincinnati. Morgan, unable to stop, was desperate for a river crossing to get back into friendly territory and thought he had found one near Portland, Ohio, at Buffington Island. Unfortunately for Morgan, Union troops anticipated his move, and the pursuing cavalry was right on his heels. On the morning of July 19, Morgan attempted to take the crossing, only to find a Union gunboat in his path and Federal cavalry in his rear. Some 900 Confederates were forced to surrender, and although Morgan and 400 others were able to escape, they ultimately were captured at Salineville a week later.

Portland, Ohio, is the home of the Buffington Island State Memorial, honoring the soldiers who fought here. The 1.5-acre site contains several monuments, including one that describes the battle, although there is little interpretive information. Picnic

Buffington Island State Memorial, where famed Confederate raider John Hunt Morgan only narrowly avoided capture.

and restroom facilities are available, and an ancient Native American mound is also at the site. On the roadside not far south of the site is another memorial, this one to Daniel McCook, one of "the fighting McCooks" and an Ohio resident who died in the battle. *Buffington Island State Memorial, 0.1 mile south of intersection of OH 124 and McKelvey Rd.; Daniel McCook Memorial, 0.8 mile south of intersection, Portland, OH, 45770; 614-297-2630; http://ohsweb.ohiohistory.org/places/se03. Open daily.*

Philippi—The battle of Philippi, also known as the Philippi Races, is considered by most to be the first land battle of the Civil War. In May of 1861 Confederate troops in the area (at this time still part of the state of Virginia) seized and burned several railroad bridges. In the eyes of the commander of the Union Department of the Ohio, Major General George B. McClellan, this was an act of war and justification enough to initiate military action. The Confederates camped in Philippi, just east of the covered bridge that linked the town to all points west. On June 3 a coordinated surprise attack on the Confederate camp, involving Federal artillery on the hill opposite the town and a Union force moving south of the town, sent the rebels into flight. Telegrams, authorized by McClellan, immediately went out east to inform the world

Barbour County Museum, located in the midst of the first battleground of the Civil War at Philippi.

of the spectacular Union victory at Philippi, Virginia, a sure confirmation that this "war" would be a very short affair.

The small town of Philippi has seen a lot of interesting happenings throughout its history, and it is all very nicely summed up at the Barbour County Museum. Not only will the staff tell you the complete story of the battle, but their collection, for a small local museum, is very impressive. Right next to the museum is the covered bridge that the Union troops swarmed over when the races began, although it had to be partially restored after a fire. At both ends of the bridge are interpretive signs describing the battle, and on the west end, a monument flying all five of the different flags present during the battle is testament to the town's longstanding role as a center for reconciliation between North and South. *Barbour County Museum, 200 N. Main St., Philippi, WV, 26416; 304-457-8846. Signs accessible daily; museum open daily May–Oct., by appointment Nov.–Apr.*

Rich Mountain—As western Virginia began to take the steps necessary to secede from the rest of the state and form a new state within the Union, 20,000 Federal troops under Major General George McClellan began to occupy the region as a sign of protection. The Confederates in the area totaled about 4,600 men, commanded by Brigadier General Robert Garnett. After the battle at Philippi, the Confederates were pushed toward the town of Beverly, a stop on the important Staunton–Parkersburg turnpike. To guard the turnpike, Garnett placed 1,300 troops on the pass over Rich

Mountain, just west of Beverly, under Colonel John Pegram. On July 11, 1861, a brigade of McClellan's men, commanded by General William Rosecrans, was able to flank Pegram's position, scattering the entire camp down the mountain. Garnett, hearing of Pegram's defeat, began to move his troops out of the area. Two days later, while fighting a small rearguard action, Garnett became the Civil War's first general to be killed in combat.

The Rich Mountain Battlefield Foundation, along with other local organizations in the town of Beverly, has worked very hard to preserve and interpret this important early battle. In the town of Beverly, the Rich Mountain Battlefield Visitor Interpretive Center describes the battle, the politics of western Virginia at the outset of the war, and the other many local ties to the Civil War, including the importance of the Staunton–Parkersburg Turnpike. Several other locations throughout the town are also dedicated to interpreting Beverly's Civil War history. After seeing the visitor's center, you can travel just west of the town to the Rich Mountain Battlefield Civil War Site, which follows the old turnpike and has numerous interpretive signs set up for not only the Rich Mountain battlefield but also Confederate Camp Garnett. The road is gravel for the last few miles but is well maintained. An area has been set aside for reenactments of the battle, which happen every two years. The foundation is still trying to improve its site by adding more visitor facilities, but the efforts already made have produced a great battlefield experience. *Rich Mountain Battlefield Visitor Interpretive Center, intersection of Court St. and Walnut St.; Rich Mountain Battlefield Civil War Site, 4.9 miles west of intersection of Main St. and Rich Mountain Rd., Beverly, WV, 26253; 304-637-7424; www.richmountain.org. Battlefield open daily; visitor's center open daily during summer, closed Sat. and Sun. during winter.*

Cheat Mountain—The Staunton–Parkersburg Turnpike was a vital passage through the mountains of western Virginia, and Union forces built a fort atop Cheat Mountain, alongside the turnpike, to protect it. The Federal force of 3,000 men was commanded by Brigadier General Joseph Reynolds. Meanwhile, Brigadier General William Loring, assisted by the newly appointed head of the Confederate Army of the Northwest, Major General Robert E. Lee, devised a plan to take control of Cheat Summit Fort and the turnpike. On September 12, 1861, Confederates under Colonel Albert Rust approached the fort, only to lose the element of surprise when they stumbled into a passing Federal wagon train. After three days of minor engagements around the fort, the Confederates eventually withdrew.

Cheat Summit Fort is located within Monongahela National Forest. The 2-mile gravel road to the site is accessed from US Highway 250 where the highway crosses a set of railroad tracks; the signs indicating the beginning of the road, 12.8 miles south of the town of Huttonsville, are very easy to see. (The Forest Service's detailed maps of the area are excellent and clearly show how to get to the many Civil War–related sites in and around the national forest; they are available at either of Monongahela's visitor's centers.) Once you get to the site, there are several interpretive signs, including an explanation of the battle and what remains of the fort, which was damaged by strip mining before it became part of the national forest. *Cheat Summit Fort—Monongahela National Forest, gravel road entrance on US 250, 12.8 miles south of intersection of US 250 and US 219, Huttonsville, WV, 26273; 304-636-1800; www.fs.fed.us/r9/mnf. Open daily.*

Greenbrier River—Confederates under Brigadier General Henry Jackson were camped along the Staunton–Parkersburg Turnpike at its crossing of the Greenbrier River. On October 3, 1861, two Union brigades from Cheat Summit Fort attacked the Confederate camp, shelling it from across the river while the infantry made several attempts to take it. After several efforts to outflank Jackson's Confederates were repulsed, the Federals withdrew back to Cheat Mountain.

The Confederate Camp Bartow, the focus of the Union attack, was located around the Traveler's Repose Inn, which is now a private home. The site is at a busy intersection in Bartow, and several interpretive signs have been installed in the area. *Interpretive signs, Camp Bartow / Traveler's Repose, intersection of WV 28 and Old Pike Rd., Bartow, WV, 24920. Signs accessible daily.*

Camp Alleghany—Confederate Camp Alleghany was established at the summit of Allegheny Mountain as the Confederates' last hold on the Staunton–Parkersburg Turnpike. On December 13, 1861, a Union brigade under General Robert Milroy attacked the camp, but attempts at coordinated assaults were thwarted by the terrain, and the Confederates were able to repulse each one. The Federals were forced to withdraw, having done little damage.

Like the Cheat Mountain site, Camp Alleghany is within Monongahela National Forest. Unlike at Cheat Mountain, however, the gravel-and-dirt road is not in perfect condition, so be sure that if you go to the site, you are either in a vehicle that can handle the road or you visit on a day when the road is dry. (Your cell phone will *not* work in this area, so you don't want to get stuck.) The road to the site is southeast of the town of Bartow, right on the Virginia–West Virginia state line; the Forest Service maps can help you get to the site easily. Once you're there, an interpretive sign explains the battle and the site. There isn't much of a trail here, so if you plan on exploring, make sure you are properly equipped for the outdoors—this is wilderness country. *Camp Alleghany—Monongahela National Forest, gravel road entrance on US 250, 7.0 miles south of intersection of US 250 and WV 28, Bartow, WV, 24920; 304-636-1800; www.fs.fed.us/r9/mnf. Open daily.*

Droop Mountain—A combined Union force, targeting the Virginia & Tennessee Railroad, met 600 Confederates in the newly formed state of West Virginia and drove them to Droop Mountain, where reinforcements swelled the Confederates' numbers to 1,700. The Confederates held a commanding position on the mountain, but on November 6, 1863, some 4,000 Federals led by Brigadier General William Averell stormed the mountaintop, taking the Confederate left and driving the defenders out of their position. The Federals had suffered 140 casualties, the smaller Confederate force, 275. Although the exhausting battle took the fight out of the Union forces and they were not able to continue their expedition to the railroad, the victory effectively ended Confederate resistance in West Virginia.

Droop Mountain Battlefield State Park contains extensive trails and a small museum that interprets the battle. Informative signs are located along the trails, and the park brochure is very descriptive regarding the length of each trail, what you'll see, and how strenuous it is. For those who don't want to explore the mountain on foot, you can drive to the park's observation tower, which offers a wonderful view of the surrounding mountains. A sign at the top of the tower explains where the various units involved in the battle were relative to the landscape. *Droop Mountain Battlefield State Park, intersection of Park Rd. and Russell Scott Rd., Hillsboro, WV, 24946; 304-653-4254; www.droopmountainbattlefield.com. Park open daily; museum open weekends Memorial Day through Labor Day.*

Kessler's Cross Lanes—Near the important crossing of the Gauley River at Carnifex Ferry, a Confederate brigade under John Floyd, a former Virginia governor, attacked a Union regiment at Kessler's Cross Lanes on August 26, 1861. The Confederates easily drove the Federals off and occupied the river crossing, setting up the battle of Carnifex Ferry two weeks later.

Two historical highway markers at the crossroads briefly explain the battle. More information can be obtained from Carnifex Ferry Battlefield State Park. *Historical highway markers—Nicholas County Historic Landmark Commission, West Virginia Division of Archives and History (Kessler's Cross Lanes), West Virginia Historic Commission (Cross Lanes Battle), intersection of WV 129 and Cooper Creek Rd., Keslers Cross Lanes, WV, 26675. Site accessible daily.*

Carnifex Ferry—After the small Union force at Kessler's Cross Lanes was routed, Brigadier General William Rosecrans, taking command of the region when General George McClellan was named head of the Army of the Potomac, sent 5,000 Union troops to recapture the crossing of the Gauley River at Carnifex Ferry. On September 10, 1861, Brigadier General John Floyd's 1,740 Confederates were in a defensive position at the Patterson House near the ferry when the Federals approached. Although the Confederates were driven back and eventually trapped in a bend in the river, they were able to drive off several Union assaults on their line and eventually escaped.

Carnifex Ferry Battlefield State Park covers much of the battlefield, including the original Patterson House at the center of the action. A museum and visitor's center is located in the home, and if you venture upstairs to see the exhibits, you can see some

Overlook of the Gauley River, Carnifex Ferry Battlefield State Park.

Whitestone Hill dominates the far-reaching prairie of North Dakota.

of the damage the home sustained during the fighting. The park also contains a re-constructed breastwork, as well as a beautiful vista of the Gauley River valley. Several walking trails have been laid out within the park, each of which is well described in the park brochure. *Carnifex Ferry Battlefield State Park, entrance 0.7 mile south of in-tersection of WV 129 and Carnifex Ferry Crossing, Keslers Cross Lanes, WV, 26675; 304-872-0825; www.carnifexferrybattlefieldstatepark.com. Park open daily; museum open weekends Memorial Day through Labor Day.*

Princeton Courthouse—On May 15, 1862, Union forces under Brigadier General Jacob Cox were attacked by Confederates commanded by Brigadier General Humphrey Marshall at Princeton, Virginia (now West Virginia). The Federals, who were threatening the East Tennessee & Virginia Railroad, were driven off by Marshall's Confederates over a three-day running battle.

A historical highway marker on Princeton's Courthouse Square briefly mentions the fighting that took place there. For a slightly more in-depth exploration of the battle, across from the courthouse is the Those Who Served War Museum, which dis-plays artifacts dating from the battle all the way through today's military. *Those Who Served War Museum, 1500 W. Main St.; historical highway marker—State of West Vir-ginia (Princeton), intersection of W. Main St. and Scott St., Princeton, WV, 24740; 304-487-8397. Museum open Mon.–Fri.; marker accessible daily.*

Cloyd's Mountain—The Virginia & Tennessee Railroad had long been a target of Union expeditions, but most expeditions had met with little success. By May of 1864, however, with Ulysses S. Grant now directing Union forces and facing off with Robert E. Lee to the east, taking the railroad suddenly became a much higher priority. Brigadier General George Crook set out with 6,500 men to destroy the railroad, starting with the New River Bridge near the town of Dublin, Virginia. On May 9 Crook approached Cloyd's Mountain and 2,400 Confederates who had hastily been gathered by Brigadier General Albert Jenkins. Jenkins had been named commander of Confederate forces in the region only four days earlier and was still recovering from a wound received at Gettysburg. With his far superior numbers, Crook decided to at-tack the Confederate right, and his men were able to get within 20 yards of the Con-federate line before being stopped cold, taking heavy casualties in the open field. As Jenkins massed his men on the right to counter the attack, a Union colonel (and fu-ture president of the United States) named Rutherford B. Hayes saw a weakness in the center of the line and charged it, leading a desperate hand-to-hand fight. The battle raged until Jenkins was wounded and the Confederates withdrew, leaving the Union with possession of the field. In a ferocious battle that lasted only an hour, the Federals had suffered 688 casualties and the Confederates 538. Jenkins, whose arm had to be amputated, eventually died from the wound. Crook was able to destroy the railroad, a vital supply line for Lee's army.

Two locations north of the town of Dublin are worth visiting if you would like to explore this battle. The first is a historical highway marker, placed near Back Creek, which was very near the center of the lines. The marker, however, is in the median of a highway, so use caution when visiting it. The second site is the Cleburne Wayside, which contains a memorial to Captain Christopher Cleburne of Kentucky, who died in the battle. Another historical highway marker and a picnic area are also at the site. *Cleburne Wayside, intersection of VA 100 and Laboratory St.; historical highway marker K-38—Virginia Department of Resources (Battle of Cloyd's Mountain), 0.1 mile south of intersection of VA 100 and Horton Rd., Dublin, VA, 24084. Sites accessible daily.*

Cove Mountain—While Brigadier General George Crook led his men against the Confederates at Cloyd's Mountain, Brigadier General William Averell, hoping eventually to unite with Crook, was just approaching his objective, the Confederate salt works at Saltville, Virginia. Not far from Averell's path to Saltville was the town of Wytheville, which supplied lead for the Confederate forces. Brigadier General John Hunt Morgan, who had been waiting for Averell at Saltville, found out about a diversion to the Union mission and raced east to Wytheville, which was being defended by men commanded by Brigadier General William "Grumble" Jones. On May 10, 1864, at Cove Mountain northeast of the town, Jones's troops held the Federals back until Morgan arrived. The combined Confederate force counterattacked and drove Averell's men from the mountain.

The battle of Cove Mountain took place northeast of Wytheville, but there are no markers related to the battle. Information can be found at the Thomas J. Boyd Museum, part of the Museums of Wytheville, where several displays highlight various Civil War action in Wythe County. Virginia Civil War Trails signs are scattered around Wytheville, but none of them has any information on the battle of Cove Mountain. *Thomas J. Boyd Museum, 295 Tazewell St., Wytheville, VA, 24382; 276-233-3330; www.museums.wytheville.org. Open Mon.–Fri.; admission charged.*

Marion—In late 1864 the far southwest tip of Virginia, although far removed from most of the fighting, became very important. Besides being a supply line for Lee's army under siege at Petersburg, the region was prized for its lead and salt mines. On December 16 a small Confederate force at Marion, Virginia, guarding the lead mines there, was overrun by Union cavalry. The next day Major General John Breckenridge arrived with Confederate reinforcements, and they attacked the Union force of 1,500. After two days of fighting and Union reinforcement, Breckenridge was forced to withdraw, leaving the works at Saltville exposed.

Near the battlefield is a Virginia Civil War Trails interpretive sign that nicely lays out the battle and the surrounding landscape and also tells of the heroic deeds of two of the town's young women during the battle. Information can also be found at the Smyth County Historical Museum and Society, but call before you go; the museum is in the process of moving. *Virginia Civil War Trails—Engagement at Marion, 0.4 mile east of intersection of N. Main St. and Wassona Circle; Smyth County Historical Museum and Society, 109 W. Strother St., Marion, VA, 24354; 276-783-7067. Sign accessible daily; museum open by appointment.*

Saltville—Salt was needed by campaigning armies to preserve meat and other foods. When the Union army and the naval blockade cut off all other sources of this vital commodity, the Confederacy relied on its last remaining saltworks at Saltville, Virginia, in the far southwest of the state. Knowing this, the Federals were eager to capture it, but the Confederates heavily fortified the town. The first Union attempt on Saltville occurred on October 2, 1864, when Brigadier General Stephen Burbridge led 5,200 soldiers to take the works from the west end of the town. Following several delaying actions, the Confederates were able to muster a defensive force of 2,800 men at Saltville. The Federals were repulsed with each assault, and Burbridge was forced to retreat, leaving many of his wounded on the field. What happened next is still the subject of debate and conflicting stories, but it is still known to most as the Saltville Massacre. Many of the Union troops were from the Fifth U.S. Colored Cavalry, and they took heavy losses during the battle. Confederates led by Champ Ferguson allegedly killed more than 100 of the wounded black soldiers, although claims were made that the killings were much fewer and that they were retaliation for a local murder. Still, when Major General John Breckenridge arrived at the scene, he immediately had Ferguson arrested. After the war Ferguson was hanged for his crimes.

Less than three months later, following their victory at Marion 12 miles to the east, Union forces led by Major General George Stoneman made another assault on the saltworks. On December 20, 1864, facing only 400 Confederates, the Federals were able to take the town easily, destroying the saltworks and taking a great amount of ammunition, artillery, and other weapons that had been stored there. Although the saltworks were soon open again, the loss of the supplies at Saltville, coupled with the disruption of the supply line, dealt a devastating blow to Lee's army.

The two battles of Saltville occurred on opposite sides of town, but areas are set aside for both of them. But before you visit the sites, stop at the Museum of the Middle Appalachians in downtown Saltville, which explains both of the battles and displays artifacts of some of the region's unique history (including a very impressive collection of mammoth and mastodon fossils). The first battle of Saltville occurred east of town, and an overlook on one of the mountainsides, with an interpretive sign, provides a fine view of the battle area, including remnants of the original earthworks. West of town, you can see what's left of the original salt furnaces, the primary objective of both battles. At the furnace site, a Virginia Civil War Trails interpretive sign tells the story of the second battle of Saltville. As an added bonus, just down the street from the salt furnace is the Stuart House, where the widow of famed General J. E. B.

Stuart lived for a short period after her husband's death at the battle of Yellow Tavern. (The general's brother owned the saltworks.) *Civil War Battlefield Overlook, on Buckeye Rd. 0.3 mile east of intersection of Buckeye Rd. and E. Main St.; Salt Furnaces, intersection of W. Main St. and King Ave.; Stuart House, intersection of W. Main St. and Stuart Ave.; Museum of the Middle Appalachians, 123 Palmer St., Saltville, VA, 24370; 276-496-3633; www.museum-mid-app.org. Sites accessible daily; museum open daily, admission charged.*

The Indian Wars

The Civil War Sites Advisory Commission's list of primary Civil War battles includes nine battles in which no Confederate soldiers fought. These nine battles occurred far north and west of the rest of the action but still made a measurable impact on the war. They were actions involving the United States Army and various Native American tribes, most notably the tribes of the Great Plains. Although the names of these nine sites are not familiar to many, they include two of the worst massacres committed in American history and the seeds of what would become the war with the Dakota that ultimately led to the battle of the Little Bighorn and the tragedy at Wounded Knee.

So why were these battles included on the list? Because during the period of the Civil War, the westward expansion of the nation, although slowed, did not stop. Settlers had already established themselves in Minnesota and Utah, and relations with the neighboring tribes were often contentious. The issues that were raised could not be ignored, and the U.S. Army was often called in to settle disputes. This led directly to thousands of additional troops being stationed on the frontier, keeping them off the front lines of the Civil War. Although frontier life for a soldier was often boring, these were moments of great importance not only to the Civil War but to the growth of America, not to mention having great impact on the Indian nations of the West.

Fort Ridgely—In 1853 the Dakota Indian tribes agreed to treaties with the United States government to settle in reservations along the Minnesota River. Soon afterward Fort Ridgely was established at the edge of the new Lower Sioux Agency, and white settlers soon followed, depending upon the protection of the fort. Meanwhile, the treaties that the government had established with the Dakota were not being honored. Politically appointed Indian agents, in charge of providing the tribes with food and supplies, were often corrupt, not only neglecting their duties but often dealing with the tribes in an unfair and often cruel manner. The army often rightfully viewed these agents as the seeds of much of the trouble that was experienced with many of the tribes over the coming decades.

In 1862 many of the Dakota were starving, victims of another rash of corrupt agents, including one who boasted that if the Dakota were hungry, "let them eat grass." The lid finally blew off in the late summer, when a band of Dakota led by Little Crow began attacking white settlements in the area, resulting in the deaths of over 350 white settlers. (This included the aforementioned agent, whose body was found with its mouth full of grass.) The remaining settlers fled to Fort Ridgely, seeking the protection of the Minnesota volunteers now manning the fort after the regulars had been sent to the Civil War. On August 20, 1862, Little Crow attacked the fort, and two days later the Dakota tried another assault. Both assaults were repulsed largely by skilled artillery fire; the fort had served as an artillery school for training Civil War troops.

Today only one building of the original fort remains, but archaeological excavations have outlined the traces of the foundations of the buildings. The building that remains serves as a museum, run by the Minnesota Historical Society, for Fort Ridgely State Park. The grounds are stocked with excellent interpretive signs, and the surrounding landscape makes the battle easy to interpret. The site is also due to receive funds for improvements that will restore the fort's parade grounds to their former condition. The park has many of the usual amenities, including camping, hiking and horseback trails, and even a nine-hole golf course. Note, though, that there are separate admission charges for the state park and the museum. *Fort Ridgely State Park, intersection of MN 4 and CR-21, Lafayette, MN, 56054; 507-426-7840; www.dnr.state .mn.us/state_parks. Open daily; admissions charged for both the park and the museum.*

Wood Lake—Following the battle at Fort Ridgely and an attack on the town of New Ulm, Minnesota, Little Crow's small band of Dakota held a number of captive settlers. Although urged by the many noncombative Dakota to return the captives, Little Crow refused. A former Minnesota governor and now colonel in the state militia, Henry Hastings Sibley (not to be confused with Henry Hopkins Sibley, a Confederate general), led 1,600 soldiers to find Little Crow. At the battle of Wood Lake on September 23, 1862, Sibley's force, instead of walking into a trap set by Little Crow's band, routed the Dakota, who fled to the north. Over the next few weeks Sibley captured thousands of Dakota in the area, many of whom were against the uprising. A military tribunal was set up, and 307 of the Dakota were sentenced to hang. Although President Lincoln intervened and the number was reduced to 38, it is still regarded as the largest mass execution ever to occur on United States soil. Sibley was named head of the Military District of Minnesota and was promoted to brigadier general.

A small park with a monument has been set up at the site by the Wood Lake Battlefield Preservation Association. A historical highway marker explains some of the action. *Wood Lake Battlefield, 0.7 miles west of intersection of MN 67 and CR-18, Echo, MN, 56237; 507-280-9970; www.woodlakebattlefield.com. Open daily.*

Big Mound, Dead Buffalo Lake, and Stony Lake—In 1863, although the Dakota had been expelled from the state of Minnesota, it was felt that a punitive action for the 1862 uprising was necessary. A two-pronged assault into the Dakota Territory was organized, with one group led by Brigadier General Henry Hastings Sibley and the other by Brigadier General Alfred Sully. On July 24, 1863, Sibley's force found a large Dakota village near what is now Tappen, North Dakota. Most of the Dakota here had nothing to do with the previous year's troubles in Minnesota. However, when Sibley's scouts met with scouts from the Dakota camp, one of the Dakota inexplicably shot Dr. Joseph Weiser, who was serving as a translator for the army, and the battle of Big Mound erupted. Many of the Dakota fought, while most went back to the village to prepare their families to move. At the end of the day the Dakota retreated, moving into camp near Dead Buffalo Lake. On July 26 Sibley's command approached the Dakota, who were now with some Lakota tribes. The Indians showed some resistance but largely retreated. The final battle occurred on July 28, at Stony Lake, where Sibley, along with a small group from his camp, came over a hilltop only to surprise a group of Dakota preparing to attack. Again the Dakota were no match for Sibley's cavalry, and they were driven west of the Missouri River. It is notable that these Dakota, many of whom drowned and lost equipment and food for the upcoming winter, very likely included the great Dakota warriors Gall and Sitting Bull, who had just had their first encounters with the United States Army.

A visitor's center located in the town of Dawson, North Dakota, contains brochures for the Redline History Tour, which starts in Tappen and finishes near Dawson. The visitor's center also contains mounted maps and the stories of the battles. The trail, which consists of six stops along a 35-mile driving route, includes the Big Mound, Dead Buffalo Lake, and Stony Lake battlefields. Although almost the entire route is on gravel roads, and virtually all the land is private property, and there is no interpretation at the stops (with the exception of Dead Buffalo Lake), the brochure and the tour are excellent, and the surrounding scenery, consisting of vast cattle farms, is virtually unblemished for almost as far as the eye can see. If you don't go for the battles, go for the view. *Redline History Tour, brochures located at the Dawson Area Visitor's Center, I-94 and ND 3 (exit 208), Dawson, ND, 58428. Open daily.*

Whitestone Hill—While Brigadier General Henry Sibley had quickly found the Dakota, Brigadier General Alfred Sully had missed his mark. Soon after Sibley returned to Minnesota, the Dakota had recrossed the Missouri River to the east side. On September 3, 1863, one of Sully's scouting parties found a camp of Dakota at Whitestone Hill and rode into them. As the scouts were talking with the Dakota, who had surrounded them, the rest of Sully's force was summoned, and they charged into the camp. After a brief fight in which the Dakota were quickly overwhelmed, most of the Indians managed to escape, but they had to leave behind not only their lodging and supplies, but also their food supply for the winter. Sully's men spent several days destroying the Dakotas' supplies, burning hundreds of thousands of pounds of buffalo meat.

Whitestone Battlefield State Historic Site contains a small museum with displays on the battle and the development of the site. The hill itself, where most of the fighting took place, is a prominent feature of the landscape, and the short climb presents a wonderful vista of the surrounding plains. There are monuments to both the soldiers and the Dakota warriors who fought here. Note that the site is open only from mid-May to mid-September and is closed Tuesday and Wednesday. *Whitestone Hill Battlefield State Historic Site, intersection of 86th St. SE and 73rd St. SE, Kulm, ND, 58456; 701-396-7731; www.nd.gov/hist/whitestone. Open May 16—Sep. 15, Thu.–Mon.*

Killdeer Mountain—By the summer of 1864, white settlers were pouring through lands granted to the Indians, and the Lakota tribes responded with raids and attacks on settlements and travelers passing through the area. Brigadier General Alfred Sully led 2,200 soldiers into the Dakota and Montana Territories to provide protection for the settlers, as well as punish the Lakota. A camp of Lakota and Dakota was located in the Killdeer Mountains, and on July 28 and 29, 1864, Sully attacked. The tribes were again outfought and fled, once more being forced to abandon their equipment and food stores. Although this was the last major battle between the plains tribes and the U.S. Army during the Civil War period, Killdeer Mountain, along with the other battles in Minnesota and North Dakota, was only the beginning of the conflict. Custer's last stand at Little Bighorn in 1876, the surrender by Sitting Bull and the Lakota in 1881, and the massacre at Wounded Knee in 1890 were still to come.

Killdeer Mountain Battlefield State Historic Site, northwest of the town of Killdeer, is very remote and accessible only by dirt roads. Before you go, you should know that finding the site may try your patience; there are signs to direct you, but when I visited, several had been knocked down. The site, which is surrounded by private property, contains the graves of two Minnesota cavalrymen, as well as several monuments and signs explaining the conflict. From North Dakota Highway 22, go west on First St. SW for 4.9 miles until you come to an open gate marked NO TRESPASSING. Turn right (north) on this unnamed road and proceed for 1.0 miles. You will then turn left (west) on another unnamed road and drive another 1.6 miles to the site, passing through the entrance to a ranch on the way. The roads are not paved, so use some caution. *Killdeer Mountain Battlefield State Historic Site, west then north of intersection of ND 22 and First St. SW, Killdeer, ND, 58640; 701-328-2666; www.nd.gov/hist. Open daily.*

Bear River—Many Americans are familiar with the names of a scant few of the battles and massacres involving American Indians: Tippecanoe, Little Bighorn, Wounded Knee. But virtually no one has heard about the worst massacre of the American Indian to have ever occurred, and that is the massacre at Bear River. The main reason for this, of course, is that it occurred during the war, but at the time the attack by Federal soldiers was, to some, justified. The Shoshone tribes had been attempting to learn to live with the settlers around them, mostly of Mormon faith in northeastern Utah. An agreement was eventually reached with the church, which agreed to provide the Shoshone with food, as the lands of the Shoshone were being depleted by the settlers.

Relics are left as solemn reminders of the massacre at Bear River, Idaho.

However, no agreement was made with the many pioneers who were passing through the area, and Shoshone attacks on these parties, along with the mail routes, were frequent. Following one of these incidents, an arrest warrant was issued for a Shoshone leader named Bear Hunter. Learning that he was in camp with a large band of Shoshone led by Chief Sagwitch near the Bear River, near present-day Preston, Idaho, a combined force of U.S. Army infantry and cavalry led by Colonel Patrick Connor left in the cold January snows to attack the camp. On the morning of January 29, 1863, Connor's approximately 280 men charged the camp, and although the Shoshone detected them coming and attempted to put up a fight, they were soon overwhelmed. The military result was decisive, but the horror that followed would burn into the culture of the Shoshone forever. None of the warriors survived except for those who were able to escape the camp. Women and children were also slaughtered and mutilated, and their tepees and provisions were destroyed. In all, approximately 250 Shoshone were killed, the worst massacre of Native Americans in history. As for Connor's men, they suffered 65 casualties, many of them from exposure to the harsh winter, which the surviving Shoshone now had to endure without provisions or shelter.

Area groups have been trying very hard for years to develop the site into a proper and fitting memorial to the massacre. The Northwest Band of the Shoshone Nation has been successful at buying some of the land where the massacre occurred, although none of it has been developed to date. At present there is a marker, erected many years ago, that holds several plaques commemorating the battle. Unfortunately, the plaques are dated and one-sided, and one even refers to the Shoshone "combatant women and children." Another larger sign briefly explaining the battle has been erected by the Idaho State Historical Society. Perhaps the most telling element of the site is behind the sign, where numerous anonymous Native American tributes and relics hang silently from a tree. (Please respect these as you would any cemetery or other sacred site, and do not disturb the items.) From the parking lot of the area, you can see the entire battlefield, including the creek and the bluff that Connor's soldiers rode down into the village. Just north of the small town of Preston, Idaho, the site is easy to find, and it deserves your attention. *Bear River Massacre historical marker, on US 91 3.9 miles north of intersection with ID 34, Preston, ID, 83263; 1-888-716-5172; www.nwb shoshone-nsn.gov. Site accessible daily.*

Sand Creek—There is no logical explanation for the massacre at Sand Creek. In general terms, it was a product of the plan for Colorado statehood, but personal political ambition is likely closer to the truth. The governor of the territory, John Evans, and Colonel John Chivington, the U.S. Army hero of the battle of Glorieta Pass, believed that in order to ensure the safety of the territory, guarantee Colorado statehood,

Trail through the grasslands to the site of the Sand Creek Massacre, Colorado.

and advance their own political goals, the American Indian, no matter what tribe, needed to be exterminated. Chivington issued orders in April of 1864 to kill all Cheyenne Indians, and many of the tribes responded with raids and other uprisings. In September some of the tribes had negotiated peace at Fort Lyon in southeast Colorado, including the Southern Cheyenne, led by Black Kettle, and the Southern Arapaho, led by Left Hand. After peace was negotiated, the tribes camped at Sand Creek on the Colorado plains, as they had been ordered to by the military. On the morning of November 29, 1864, as the Indians were still sleeping, Chivington led 700 soldiers into the camp with orders to take no prisoners. The surprised Indians did not put up much resistance; many were killed trying to surrender, and even Chief Black Kettle stood in front of his tepee waving an American flag, along with a white flag of truce, telling his people that the soldiers were not there to harm them. It did not stop Chivington, whose men pursued the Indians up the creek for several hours, killing many women and children. It is estimated that over 160 Indians were killed, many of them mutilated and scalped, and the camp's winter stores were destroyed. Several officers and units at Sand Creek had refused to fight, viewing the actions of Chivington's men as barbaric. Even in its day, a time when many Americans held a fear and hatred of all Indians, the general public was outraged at the massacre. A congressional investigation was held, with Governor Evans being forced to resign, and Chivington was essentially run out of the army before he could be court-martialed.

Sand Creek Massacre National Historic Site is still very much in its infancy, having opened to the public only in 2007. The site does not yet have a visitor's center, and the development of trails and other interpretation is ongoing. Future plans include an interpretive center, additional trails, and the installation of more public facilities (restrooms are available, but potable water is not). However, a visit to the site is still rewarding. Like the site at Bear River, a small monument, on which numerous personal tributes have been placed, is extremely moving, especially amid the silence of the prairie atop the bluff, and in sight of the entire scene of the massacre and miles and miles of open land. If you do go, know that you will have to travel on several gravel or dirt roads to get there; but they are well maintained. The trail, while easily walkable, is a bit long, and no water is available at the site, so stop in one of the nearby towns (the closest is Eads, approximately 20 miles away) and bring water, especially for those hot summer days. *Sand Creek National Historic Site, 1.3 miles east of intersection of CR-W and CR-54, Eads, CO, 81036; 719-813-5051; www.nps.gov/sand. Open daily.*

New England and the Northeast

Although well out of the picture as far as combat was concerned, the Northeast played a major role in the war effort. Much more than now, the population of the United States was concentrated in the East; and New England, in particular, besides providing the Union with hundreds of thousands of soldiers, was home to most of America's industrial might.

New England was also the hotbed of the anti-slavery movement. Many northeasterners still heartily embraced the spirit of liberty, and less than a century after the Declaration of Independence decreed that all men were created equal, Boston was undeniably ground zero for abolitionists, as well as the home of many free blacks. This was made evident by the early push from this part of the country to use black soldiers to help fight the war.

Although it was far from the theaters of action, the Northeast did witness fighting and other violence during the Civil War. New York City (along with many other major cities) was the scene of major riots over United States draft policy. And along the Canadian border, in the town of St. Albans, Vermont, one of the oddest invasions in our history occurred, when the United States was raided by Confederates from across the Canadian border. New England, although not in the middle of the fighting, was still very much in the middle of the war.

Boston African American National Historic Site and Robert Gould Shaw Memorial—Since before the American Revolution, Boston, Massachusetts, had been known as the cradle of liberty because of the willingness of its inhabitants to question the status quo and ask what truly defined freedom. This attitude among its citizens, along with a sizable and active black population, made Boston not only the center of the abolitionist movement but also an example of an integrated society (even if somewhat limited by today's standards) for cities nationwide. One of the first colonists killed in the name of America was a black man, Crispus Attucks, in the Boston Massacre in 1770; Massachusetts had been the first state to outlaw slavery, in 1783; and Boston public schools were integrated as early as 1855. Naturally, the anti-slavery movement was able to gain traction quickly in Boston. In 1826 a black abolitionist group called the Massachusetts General Coloured Association was formed, and in 1831 William Lloyd Garrison began to publish *The Liberator*, an anti-slavery newspaper that gained wide circulation.

When the Civil War broke out, the call quickly went up from the citizens of Boston to arm black men and allow them to fight for the Union. In 1863 the nation's first all-black regiment, the 54th Massachusetts Volunteer Infantry, was formed. Quickly organized and trained, the regiment was led by Colonel Robert Gould Shaw, son of a prominent Boston family and an ardent abolitionist himself. The unit saw heavy action during the war and grew to be well respected; it included the first African American to earn the Congressional Medal of Honor, at the battle of Fort Fisher. The 54th, of course, was featured in the extremely popular movie *Glory*, possibly the finest and most well-known Civil War battle film ever made.

Beginning near the same point as Boston's Freedom Trail, the Boston African

Memorial to Robert Gould Shaw, commander of the 54th Massachusetts Volunteer Infantry, part of Boston African American National Historic Site.

American National Historic Site is a trail that winds through the northern slope of Beacon Hill and passes a number of still-existing buildings that featured prominently in the progression of black society in Boston and in America, including the locations where slavery was debated, where African Americans began to integrate into white society, and where fugitive slaves found shelter on the Underground Railroad. The walking trail begins on Boston Common across from the Massachusetts State House, and the first stop is the now very famous memorial to Robert Gould Shaw and the 54th Massachusetts, created by the great sculptor Augustus Saint-Gaudens and dedicated in 1897. But be sure to take the entire trail; while most of the buildings are privately owned, the story of Boston's African American community and its fight for equality still echoes in these streets. Note that driving around Boston and finding free or cheap parking can be difficult, so if you do visit, try to take public transportation if at all possible. *Boston African American National Historic Site, Black Heritage Trail begins at intersection of Park St. and Beacon St., Boston, MA, 02108; 617-742-5415; www.nps.gov/boaf. Open daily.*

Springfield Armory National Historic Site—Early in the country's history, it was understood that before the United States could be recognized, respected, and completely independent from the influence of foreign powers, it would need to be able to manufacture its own weapons. To that end, in 1794 Congress approved the establishment of two federal armories: one in Harpers Ferry, Virginia, to serve the southern states, and another in Springfield, Massachusetts. Soon the Springfield Armory became well known for technological innovation and a leader in what was eventually termed the "American style" of manufacturing: many units, quickly produced, with great precision. This mass production of field arms continued until the armory was closed in 1968, and of course one period of peak production was the Civil War.

During the Civil War the armory produced up to 1,000 muskets each day. These were almost entirely the percussion rifled musket, first produced at Springfield in 1855 and continued through the end of the war. While the Confederacy was able to obtain a number of these through what state arsenals had accumulated, the advantage clearly went to the Union, which was able to continuously produce large numbers of precision-machined weapons, rather than rely on the outdated smoothbore civilian or imported arms used by most Confederate soldiers. (While the Confederate states did have several small armories, they virtually all served their own states, not the Confederate States of America, and in total produced only 107,000 weapons.).

The Springfield Armory National Historic Site is home to the world's largest collection of shoulder arms, including the largest collection of Confederate shoulder arms, and the display is truly impressive. The museum, which is located in the former Main Arsenal Building, also shows a film explaining the creation and development of the armory. Exhibits are split between the incredible collection of weapons and the impressive history of industrial research and development performed at the site. While only a portion of the former grounds belongs to the National Historic Site, many of the original buildings remain, now part of the Springfield Technical Community College, making for a nice walk through the campus. *Springfield Armory National Historic Site, One Armory Square, Springfield, MA, 01105; 413-734-8551; www.nps.gov/spar. Open daily.*

St. Albans Historical Museum—Toward the end of the Civil War, one of the oddest events of the war occurred far north of every previous shot fired in battle. Twenty-two armed men gathered in Canada and, determined to strike a terroristic blow to the United States and gather some much-needed cash for the Confederacy, crossed the border and entered the small town of St. Albans, Vermont. A railroad town, St. Albans was home to three banks at the time, and so on the afternoon of October 19, 1864, the men entered town and proceeded to rob all three of them at gunpoint. The residents of the town were forced to gather on the town square, and one was killed. As an additional humiliation, some citizens were allegedly forced to recite

The St. Albans Historical Museum, Vermont.

the Confederate oath of allegiance. Within a half hour of the beginning of the raid, the men stole a number of horses and headed for Canada. They were pursued across the border by the townsmen, and many were captured, but after Canadian authorities stepped in, the Vermonters returned to their homes. Eventually Canadian courts ruled that the men were soldiers conducting an act of war, and they were freed, although the tens of thousands of dollars they stole was returned to the town. It is alleged and suspected that the raiders were acting on the part of the Confederate government, although there is debate over this even today.

Only one of the three banks in St. Albans that day still stands, but complete information on the raid, as well as several books containing original records and eyewitness accounts, can be found in the St. Albans Historical Museum. The museum is on the village green, which remains virtually unchanged from that day in 1864, with the exception of the addition of a monument or two. A peaceful little Vermont town, St. Albans is certainly remote, but it is charming, and the drive to its location near the shores of Lake Champlain is beautiful. *St. Albans Historical Museum, 9 Church St., St. Albans, VT, 05478; 802-527-7933; www.stamuseum.com. Open Tue.–Sat., May–Oct.; admission charged.*

General Grant National Memorial—By the time of his death in 1885, Ulysses S. Grant was undoubtedly a world figure and a national hero. He had risen from humble beginnings to earn a reputation as one of history's greatest military leaders, had been elected president of the United States, and later toured the world as a celebrity. Soon after Grant died in upstate New York, a commission was formed and plans were started for a grand mausoleum along the Hudson River. Construction, although delayed, finally began in 1892 in New York City's Riverside Park, which at the time was a quiet, peaceful part of Manhattan. The tomb was modeled after some of the grandest mausoleums in the world, and when it was finished in 1897, it was (and remains) the largest in the United States, with a height of 150 feet and over 8,000 tons of granite.

Grant's tomb holds the remains of both the general and his wife, Julia. The crypt is viewable from above, and visitors may descend to where the two sarcophagi are surrounded by large busts of some of Grant's greatest generals. The main floor of the memorial contains some small displays on Grant's life, along with a number of interesting artifacts, and the stone walls are decorated with several scenes of Grant's wartime heroics. The memorial may be somewhat imposing for such a humble man, but it is certainly fitting of his accomplishments. Note that only street parking is available in

Grant's most trusted generals stand guard over his sarcophagus at the General Grant National Memorial.

the area, and while it can be found with some patience, public transportation to the site is available and should be used if possible. *General Grant National Memorial, intersection of 122nd St. and Riverside Dr., New York, NY, 10003; 212-666-1640; www.nps.gov/gegr. Open daily.*

Lincoln and Grant

It is indisputable that the two great leaders of the Union cause—one politically, one on the field of battle—were Abraham Lincoln and Ulysses S. Grant. Both men began their lives in the humblest circumstances, and both overcame great personal demons and obstacles to become among the most revered leaders in our country's history. In fact, in many cases (particularly with Lincoln), it has become increasingly difficult to separate myth from fact. The best way to do this is to walk in their footsteps.

While sites devoted to both men are scattered throughout the chapters of this book, there is one region of the country where Lincoln and Grant share some common ground: the Midwest. Although the paths of their lives took them to all sorts of different places, Illinois will always be the Land of Lincoln, and Grant also spent considerable time in and around this state. Following are a number of sites related to both men that are within a very short drive of one another.

Ulysses S. Grant National Historic Site—Julia Dent, born in St. Louis, Missouri, in 1826, grew up on a sizable farm outside the city known as White Haven. Although she came from a wealthy, slave-owning family, Julia grew up to be, for the most part, a very typical young woman of the time. After she returned home from boarding school one year, she met her brother Fred's West Point roommate, Ulysses, who was staying at the Jefferson Barracks in St. Louis. Ulysses S. Grant became a frequent visitor to the Dent home, and the two were married in 1848. The couple stayed at White Haven, with a sizable gift of farmland from her father. Although they went on to live in Illinois and later at the White House and then upstate New York, and took an extended world tour, White Haven remained home in the hearts of the Grant family for many years after their departure.

The site today is only a small portion of the former homestead, but what is left contains the home itself, as well as several of the outbuildings (including the slaves' quarters), a restored barn, and a brand-new visitor's center. The home has been restored to its original condition and is available for guided tours. The barn was recently turned into a fantastic museum of Grant's life, featuring not only the high points of his military and political career, but also asking (and forcing visitors to ask) some tough questions about his actions—and what they would do in his place. Although there are plans for even more at this site, what is already here is worth a visit. *Ulysses S. Grant National Historic Site, 7400 Grant Rd., St. Louis, MO 63123; 314-842-3298; www.nps.gov/ulsg. Open daily.*

Abraham Lincoln Presidential Library and Museum—Dedicated in 2005, the Lincoln Presidential Library and Museum is the new jewel of the city of Springfield, Illinois. The library is enormous (it has to be, considering that Lincoln is one of the most written-about human beings ever to have lived), and is becoming a major center of scholarly study (it is open only by appointment to those performing research). For the historical tourist, however, the new museum is an eyeful. Multimedia presentations, numerous artifacts from Lincoln's life, and an absolutely beautifully built set of buildings combine to create a wonderful experience. In addition, the city of Springfield has really cleaned up its act in recent years, giving its downtown a complete face-lift to go along with the new facilities.

To be fair, the new museum has received some criticism, striking some as a bit "simple" and not presenting as thoroughly detailed a picture of Lincoln as some would like. This might be true for the jaded historian; and for Lincoln devotees, much of what is presented could even be dismissed as eye candy. However, if you are either

Reproduction of the White House, Abraham Lincoln Presidential Library and Museum in Springfield.

of the above, I would suggest that you go just to see the artifacts. For the rest of us, the incredible presentations engage all senses at once in a very impressive display and paint a moving picture of our great leader, while at the same time doing an excellent job of separating the facts from the myth. It may be eye candy, but it's worth the experience. Furthermore, if you've been looking for that place where you can take your children to experience history without boring them out of their minds within 15 minutes, I assure you that this is it. They will be wowed, and will hopefully come away realizing why history is something to be cherished, not dreaded. *Abraham Lincoln Presidential Library and Museum, 112 N. 6th St., Springfield, IL, 62701; 1-800-610-2094; www.alplm.org. Open daily; admission charged.*

Lincoln Home National Historic Site—In 1844 Abraham Lincoln purchased a family home near the new Illinois state capital of Springfield for the then considerable sum of $1,500. It was a considerable home to match, but Lincoln was doing well. His law practice had been extremely successful, and he was serving in the Illinois General Assembly. His family was still small, with his wife, Mary, and young son, Robert, but the Lincoln family, home, and legend would grow. Over the next 16 years the Lincolns would have three more sons, only to lose one of them to tuberculosis; celebrate

Home of the Lincoln family for 16 years, now the Lincoln Home National Historic Site, Springfield.

Abraham's election to the United States Congress; watch his political star rise during his famous debates with Senator Stephen Douglas, only to see him suffer defeat in their 1858 race; and receive the news that he had been elected 16th president of the United States during the nation's most trying time—all from this house in downtown Springfield.

The Lincoln Home National Historic Site preserves the house in its 1860 state, along with most of the surrounding homes in the neighborhood. In fact, a walk down that Springfield street today offers much the same view as Lincoln had 150 years ago. Several of the surrounding houses have been turned into exhibit halls regarding the Lincolns, the city of Springfield, and Lincoln's life before the presidency. While these homes are open to the public, the Lincoln home itself is accessible only by guided tour, and timed-entry tickets must be obtained in advance. With all the monuments to Lincoln, the homes that have been preserved, and the myths surrounding the man, a visit to the Lincoln home in Springfield, imagining him roughhousing with his sons on the living room floor, is perhaps the most personal way to attempt to get in touch with Lincoln as a human being. *Lincoln Home National Historic Site, 413 South 8th St., Springfield, IL, 62701; 217-492-4241; www.nps.gov/liho. Open daily; no admission charged.*

Lincoln Tomb—Immediately upon Lincoln's death in 1865, a public cry went out to build a proper tomb for the man who had saved the Union. After a lengthy national rail tour, Lincoln's body was returned to Springfield, Illinois, and temporarily held in a receiving vault at Oak Ridge Cemetery while the grand tomb was designed and built. Construction issues, along with an attempt to steal Lincoln's body, delayed work. Finally, in 1874, the tomb was completed, and Lincoln was permanently laid to rest, joined by his sons Edward and Willie, who had gone before him, and Tad, who had died in 1871. Lincoln was later joined by his wife, Mary, who died in 1882.

The exterior of the Lincoln Tomb is grand, standing atop a large hill and surmounted with a 117-foot-high obelisk. Staircases lead to the top of the base of the granite tomb, which provides a far-reaching view of the peaceful cemetery below. Also atop the base is a copy of a famous Gutzon Borglum bust of Lincoln, the nose of which is often rubbed for good luck, despite the admonishment of those who maintain the tomb. (Borglum sculpted a much larger and more famous bust of Lincoln atop Mount Rushmore in South Dakota.) But for all the tomb's size and ornamentation, the part of it that leaves the greatest impression is in the interior. After entering the chamber and walking through a small hallway, passing miniature versions of some of the more famous sculptures of Lincoln, you come to the marble-and-bronze walls of the burial chamber, where Lincoln's body lies beneath 10 feet of granite and a large cenotaph. Along the walls on the way in, the visitor has already seen some of Lincoln's more famous words. But etched in bronze upon the back wall of the burial chamber is the simple but perhaps most moving summation, uttered by Secretary of War

Edwin Stanton upon Lincoln's death: "Now he belongs to the ages." *Lincoln Tomb, Oak Ridge Cemetery, 1500 Monument Ave., Springfield, IL, 62702; 217-782-2717; www.illinoishistory.gov/hs/lincoln_tomb.htm. Cemetery open daily; interior open Tue.–Sat.*

U. S. Grant Home State Historic Site—In 1860 Ulysses S. Grant and his family, in a desperate financial situation, moved to Galena, Illinois, so that Grant could work with his father and brothers in their store. War broke out soon after, and Grant would go on to become the celebrated war hero we know today. Upon leaving the army at the end of the war, Grant was presented a large new home in Galena by its grateful citizens. The family lived in the home until Grant was elected president of the United States in 1868; Grant received the news of his election in the home's living room. Although Grant visited several times over the years, the last time in 1880, the family never permanently moved back into the home.

Galena is a beautiful little river town along the Mississippi, in the far northwestern corner of Illinois. The U.S. Grant Home State Historic Site is staffed by volunteers, and guided tours are available. Besides the Grant home, several of the surrounding houses have been developed to demonstrate the town's history and how the town has changed over the years. There are plenty of other things to see and do in Galena, so while it is a bit of a drive, it makes for an interesting visit. *U. S. Grant Home State Historic Site, 500 Bouthillier St., Galena, IL, 61036; 815-777-0248; www.illinoishistory.gov/ hs/grant_home.htm. Open Wed.–Sun., but hours change seasonally.*

ACKNOWLEDGMENTS

THIS BOOK COVERS A LOT OF TERRITORY and represents a journey of tens of thousands of miles across many states. Trying to list the names of all the people who assisted me as I went searching for site after site in town after town would be folly. But to all the volunteers who help keep our Civil War heritage alive through site staffing, serving on local committees, fund-raising, and performing the countless other thankless efforts required to keep these places running, on behalf of every citizen of the world, who all benefit from your efforts whether they know it or not, thank you. Thank you also to the countless gas station attendants, convenience store owners, and townsfolk who shared cups of coffee with me and helped me find my way.

In particular, the employees of the National Park Service, whether in person, by telephone, or by e-mail, have always gone out of their way to assist at every park I've ever visited, whether it was for this book or along some other journey. They have always been willing to go the extra mile for their visitors, despite drastic cutbacks in funding over the last few years; they are sustained by their passion for the service they perform, and we are a better nation for it.

The staff at The Countryman Press, Kermit Hummel, Jennifer Thompson, and Lisa Sacks in particular, have been extraordinarily helpful as I made my way through my first book, and I am eternally grateful for their guidance, their questions, and their interest in this project. I am also deeply indebted to Glenn Novak, whose passion for and knowledge of the subject proved invaluable as we went through the editing process.

From the very beginning, the support of my family and friends has been an absolute necessity. Many thanks go out to those who encouraged me that this was a project worth pursuing, especially John Fountain, who assisted me in my initial research and provided great insight for the first chapters, and Shannon Gaffney, who not only reviewed some of my early material, but also gave me a boost when I most needed it. To all those who offered and gave food, shelter, a couch to crash on, and a cold beer at the end of a week's worth of driving—particularly Carter Ficklen, Laurie Vivekanand, and Darrell Hollowell—thank you for helping me refuel and keep traveling.

Finally, unending thanks go to my wife, Charlotte, who put up with books and pamphlets piled up all over the house, maps hung on every wall, and countless trips away from home. Her support and encouragement did more to keep me going than any other force. I love you very much.

EXCEPT FOR THE FEW CRITICAL EXAMPLES listed here, much of the information presented in this book was gleaned from interpretive signs, faded highway markers, pamphlets, brochures, Internet sites, wandering exploration, and, most important, the many wonderful volunteers who keep the sites listed in this book on the map. Each battle-field and historical site in the book lists contact, site, and/or location information, and each of them should be considered references.

In addition, the following books were used as sources:

Cantor, George. *Confederate Generals: Life Portraits.* Dallas: Taylor Trade Publishing, 2000.

Civil War Sites Advisory Commission Report on the Nation's Civil War Battlefields. Prepared for the United States Senate Committee on Energy and Natural Resources, the United States House of Representatives Committee on Natural Resources, and the Secretary of the Interior. Washington, DC: National Park Service, Civil War Sites Advisory Commission, 1993.

The Civil War Society's Encyclopedia of the Civil War: The Complete and Comprehensive Guide to the American Civil War. Princeton, NJ: The Philip Lief Group, 1997.

Eicher, David. *Civil War Battlefields: A Touring Guide.* Dallas: Taylor Publishing Co., 1995.

Esposito, Brigadier General Vincent J., ed. *The West Point Atlas of War: The Civil War.* New York: Tess Press, 1995.

Foote, Shelby. *The Civil War: A Narrative* (3 vols.). New York: Random House, 1963.

Kennedy, Frances H., ed. *The Civil War Battlefield Guide, Second Edition.* New York: The Conservation Fund, Houghton-Mifflin Co., 1998.

Lamb, Brian, et al. *Who's Buried in Grant's Tomb?: A Tour of Presidential Gravesites.* Washington, DC: National Cable Satellite Corp., 2000.

Richards, Sarah, ed. *Civil War Sites: The Official Guide to Battlefields, Monuments, and More.* Guilford, CT: Globe Pequot Press, 2003.

Shively, Julie. *The Ideals Guide to American Civil War Places.* Nashville: Ideals Publications Inc., 1999.

The Civil War Sites Advisory Commission
List of Principal Battles—by State

The Civil War Sites Advisory Commission, tasked by Congress to assess the condition of the nation's Civil War battlefields, reviewed over 10,500 actions that occurred during the war and created a list of 384 principal battles. The battles were further distinguished into the following classes:

A—Having a decisive influence on a campaign and a direct impact on the course of the war

B—Having a direct and decisive influence on their campaign

C—Having observable influence on the outcome of a campaign

D—Having a limited influence on the outcome of their campaign or operation but achieving or affecting important local objectives

The following list, organized by state, is the CWSAC's list of primary battlefields. The number designation given to each battle (OK001, OK002, etc.) is, in most cases, in chronological order, though there are some exceptions. Alternative names for the battle, if any, are shown in parentheses.

BATTLE	CWSAC DESIGNATION	CLASS
Alabama		
Athens	AL002	D
Day's Gap (Sand Mountain)	AL001	C
Decatur	AL004	C
Fort Blakely	AL006	A
Mobile Bay (Passing of Forts Morgan and Gaines)	AL003	A
Selma	AL007	B
Spanish Fort	AL005	B
Arkansas		
Arkansas Post (Fort Hindman)	AR006	C
Bayou Fourche (Little Rock)	AR010a	B
Cane Hill (Canehill, Boston Mountains)	AR004	C
Chalk Bluff	AR007	D
Devil's Backbone (Backbone Mountain)	AR009	C
Elkin's Ferry (Okolona)	AR012	C
Helena	AR008	B
Hill's Plantation (Cache River, Cotton Plant, Round Hill)	AR003	D
Jenkins' Ferry	AR016	C
Marks' Mills	AR015	D
Old River Lake (Ditch Bayou, Lake Chicot, Lake Village, Furlough, Fish Bayou, Grand Lake)	AR017	D
Pea Ridge (Elkhorn Tavern)	AR001	A
Pine Bluff	AR011	D
Poison Spring	AR014	C
Prairie D'Ane (Gum Grove, Moscow)	AR013	B
Prairie Grove (Fayetteville)	AR005	B
St. Charles	AR002	C
Colorado		
Sand Creek (Chivington Massacre)	CO001	B

BATTLE	CWSAC DESIGNATION	CLASS
District of Columbia		
Fort Stevens (Washington)	DC001	B
Florida		
Fort Brooke	FL004	D
Natural Bridge	FL006	C
Olustee (Ocean Pond)	FL005	B
St. John's Bluff	FL003	D
Santa Rosa Island	FL001	C
Tampa (Yankee Outrage at Tampa)	FL002	D
Georgia		
Adairsville	GA009	C
Allatoona	GA023	B
Atlanta	GA017	B
Buck Head Creek	GA026	C
Chickamauga	GA004	A
Dallas (New Hope Church, Pumpkinvine Creek)	GA011	C
Dalton I	GA006	C
Dalton II	GA020	D
Davis' Cross Roads (Dug Gap)	GA003	C
Ezra Church (Battle of the Poor House)	GA018	B
Fort McAllister I	GA002	C
Fort McAllister II	GA028	B
Fort Pulaski	GA001	B
Gilgal Church (Marietta Operations)	GA013b	B
Griswoldville	GA025	B
Jonesborough	GA022	A
Kennesaw Mountain	GA015	B
Kolb's Farm	GA014	C
Lovejoy's Station	GA021	D
New Hope Church	GA010	C
Noonday Creek (Marietta Operations)	GA013c	B
Peachtree Creek	GA016	B
Pickett's Mill (New Hope, New Hope Church)	GA012	C
Pine Mountain (Marietta Operations)	GA013a	B
Resaca	GA008	C
Ringgold Gap (Taylor's Ridge)	GA005	B
Rocky Face Ridge (Combats at Buzzard Roost, Mill Creek, Dug Gap)	GA007	C
Ruff's Mill (Marietta Operations)	GA013d	B
Utoy Creek	GA019	C
Waynesborough	GA027	C
Idaho		
Bear River (Massacre at Boa Ogoi)	ID001	C
Indiana		
Corydon	IN001	C
Kansas		
Baxter Springs (Baxter Springs Massacre)	KS002	C
Lawrence (Lawrence Massacre)	KS001	C
Marais des Cygnes (Battle of Osage, Battle of Trading Post)	KS004	C
Mine Creek (Battle of the Osage)	KS003	C
Kentucky		
Barbourville	KY001	D
Camp Wild Cat (Wildcat Mountain)	KY002	C
Cynthiana (Kellar's Bridge)	KY011	C
Ivy Mountain (Ivy Creek, Ivy Narrows)	KY003	D
Middle Creek	KY005	C
Mill Springs (Logan's Cross-Roads, Fishing Creek)	KY006	B
Munfordville (Green River Bridge)	KY008	B
Paducah	KY010	C

BATTLE	CWSAC DESIGNATION	CLASS
Perryville	KY009	A
Richmond	KY007	B
Rowlett's Station (Woodsonville, Green River)	KY004	D
Louisiana		
Baton Rouge (Magnolia Cemetery)	LA003	B
Blair's Landing (Pleasant Hill Landing)	LA020	C
Donaldsonville	LA004	D
Donaldsonville	LA013	D
Fort Bisland (Bethel Place)	LA006	D
Fort DeRussy	LA017	B
Forts Jackson & St. Philip	LA001	A
Georgia Landing (Labadieville)	LA005	C
Goodrich's Landing (The Mounds, Lake Providence)	LA014	D
Irish Bend (Nerson's Woods, Franklin)	LA007	C
Kock's Plantation (Cox's Plantation)	LA015	C
LaFourche Crossing (Lafourche Crossing)	LA012	D
Mansfield (Sabine Cross Roads, Pleasant Grove)	LA018	A
Mansura (Smith's Place, Marksville)	LA022	C
Milliken's Bend	LA011	C
Monett's Ferry (Cane River Crossing)	LA021	D
New Orleans	LA002	B
Plains Store (Springfield Road)	LA009	C
Pleasant Hill	LA019	B
Port Hudson	LA010	A
Stirling's Plantation (Fordoche Bridge)	LA016	D
Vermilion Bayou	LA008	D
Yellow Bayou (Norwood's Plantation)	LA023	C
Maryland		
Antietam (Sharpsburg)	MD003	A
Boonsboro	MD006	D
Folck's Mill (Cumberland)	MD008	D
Hancock (Romney Campaign)	MD001	D
Monocacy (Battle That Saved Washington)	MD007	B
South Mountain (Crampton's, Turner's, and Fox's Gaps)	MD002	B
Williamsport (Hagerstown, Falling Waters)	MD004	C
Minnesota		
Fort Ridgely	MN001	C
Wood Lake	MN002	C
Mississippi		
Big Black River Bridge (Big Black)	MS010	B
Brices Cross Roads (Tishomingo Creek)	MS014	B
Champion Hill (Bakers Creek)	MS009	A
Chickasaw Bayou (Chickasaw Bluffs, Walnut Hills)	MS003	B
Corinth	MS002	A
Corinth	MS016	B
Grand Gulf	MS004	C
Iuka	MS001	C
Jackson	MS008	B
Meridian	MS012	C
Okolona	MS013	B
Port Gibson (Thompson's Hill)	MS006	B
Raymond	MS007	B
Snyder's Bluff (Snyder's Hill)	MS005	D
Tupelo (Harrisburg)	MS015	B
Vicksburg	MS011	A
Missouri		
Belmont	MO009	C
Boonville (First Battle of Boonville)	MO001	C

BATTLE	CWSAC DESIGNATION	CLASS
Byram's Ford (Big Blue River)	M0026	B
Cape Girardeau	M0020	D
Carthage	M0002	C
Clark's Mill (Vera Cruz)	M0017	D
Dry Wood Creek (Big Dry Wood Creek, Battle of the Mules)	M0005	D
Fort Davidson (Pilot Knob)	M0021	B
Fredericktown	M0007	D
Glasgow	M0022	C
Hartville	M0019	D
Independence	M0025	C
Independence	M0014	D
Kirksville	M0013	D
Lexington (Battle of the Hemp Bales)	M0006	C
Lexington	M0023	D
Liberty (Blue Mills Landing, Blue Mills)	M0003	D
Little Blue River (Westport)	M0024	D
Lone Jack	M0015	D
Marmiton River (Shiloh Creek, Charlot's Farm)	M0028	D
Mount Zion Church	M0010	D
New Madrid / Island No. 10	M0012	A
Newtonia	M0029	B
Newtonia	M0016	C
Roan's Tan Yard (Silver Creek)	M0011	D
Springfield (Zagonyi's Charge)	M0008	D
Springfield	M0018	D
Westport	M0027	A
Wilson's Creek (Oak Hills)	M0004	A
New Mexico		
Glorieta Pass (La Glorieta Pass)	NM002	A
Valverde	NM001	B
North Carolina		
Albemarle Sound	NC013	C
Averasborough (Taylor's Hole Creek, Smithville, Smiths Ferry, Black River)	NC019	C
Bentonville (Bentonsville)	NC020	A
Fort Anderson (Deep Gully)	NC010	D
Fort Fisher	NC014	C
Fort Fisher	NC015	A
Fort Macon	NC004	C
Goldsborough Bridge	NC009	C
Hatteras Inlet Batteries (Forts Clark and Hatteras)	NC001	C
Kinston	NC007	D
Monroe's Cross Roads (Fayetteville Road, Blue's Farm)	NC018	D
New Berne	NC003	B
Plymouth	NC012	C
Roanoke Island (Fort Huger)	NC002	B
South Mills (Camden)	NC005	D
Tranter's Creek	NC006	D
Washington	NC011	D
White Hall (Whitehall, White Hall Ferry)	NC008	D
Wilmington (Fort Anderson, Town Creek, Forks Road, Sugar Loaf Hill)	NC016	D
Wyse Fork (Wilcox's Bridge, Wise's Fork, Second Kinston, Second Southwest Creek, Kelly's Mill Pond)	NC017	D
North Dakota		
Big Mound	ND001	C
Dead Buffalo Lake	ND002	D
Killdeer Mountain (Tahkahokuty Mountain)	ND005	C
Stony Lake	ND003	D
Whitestone Hill	ND004	D

BATTLE	CWSAC DESIGNATION	CLASS
Ohio		
Buffington Island (St. Georges Creek)	OH001	C
Salineville (New Lisbon, New Lisbon Road, Wellsville)	OH002	D
Oklahoma		
Cabin Creek	OK006	C
Chustenahlah	OK003	B
Chusto-Talasah (Caving Banks)	OK002	D
Honey Springs (Elk Creek, Shaw's Inn)	OK007	B
Middle Boggy Depot (Middle Boggy)	OK005	D
Old Fort Wayne (Beatties Prairie, Beaty's Prairie)	OK004	D
Round Mountain (Round Mountains)	OK001	D
Pennsylvania		
Gettysburg	PA002	A
Hanover	PA001	C
South Carolina		
Charleston Harbor (Fort Sumter)	SC004	C
Charleston Harbor (Battery Gregg, Fort Wagner, Morris Island, Fort Sumter)	SC009	B
Fort Sumter	SC001	A
Fort Sumter (Charleston Harbor, Morris Island)	SC008	B
Fort Wagner (First Assault, Morris Island)	SC005	D
Fort Wagner / Morris Island (Second Assault, Morris Island)	SC007	B
Grimball's Landing (Secessionville, James Island)	SC006	D
Honey Hill	SC010	C
Rivers' Bridge (Salkahatchie River, Hickory Hill, Owens' Crossroads, Lawtonville, Duck Creek)	SC011	D
Secessionville (Fort Lamar, James Island)	SC002	B
Simmon's Bluff	SC003	D
Tennessee		
Bean's Station	TN026	D
Blountville	TN019	D
Blue Springs	TN020	D
Brentwood	TN015	D
Bull's Gap	TN033	D
Campbell's Station	TN023	D
Chattanooga	TN018	D
Chattanooga	TN005	D
Chattanooga	TN024	A
Collierville	TN022	D
Columbia	TN034	C
Dandridge	TN028	C
Dover (Fort Donelson)	TN012	D
Fair Garden	TN029	C
Fort Donelson	TN002	A
Fort Henry	TN001	B
Fort Pillow	TN030	B
Fort Sanders (Fort Loudon)	TN025	B
Franklin	TN016	D
Franklin	TN036	A
Hartsville	TN008	C
Hatchie's Bridge (Davis Bridge, Matamora)	TN007	C
Hoover's Gap	TN017	C
Jackson	TN009	D
Johnsonville	TN032	B
Memphis	TN031	C
Memphis	TN004	B
Mossy Creek	TN027	D
Murfreesboro (Wilkinson Pike, Cedars)	TN037	D
Murfreesboro	TN006	C

BATTLE	CWSAC DESIGNATION	CLASS
Nashville	TN038	A
Parker's Cross Roads	TN011	C
Shiloh (Pittsburg Landing)	TN003	A
Spring Hill	TN035	B
Stones River (Murfreesboro)	TN010	A
Thompson's Station	TN013	C
Vaught's Hill (Milton)	TN014	D
Wauhatchie (Brown's Ferry)	TN021	B
Texas		
Galveston	TX002	D
Galveston	TX003	B
Palmito Ranch (Palmito Hill)	TX005	D
Sabine Pass	TX001	C
Sabine Pass II	TX006	B
Virginia		
Aldie	VA036	C
Amelia Springs	VA091	C
Appomattox Courthouse	VA097	A
Appomattox Station	VA096	B
Aquia Creek	VA002	D
Auburn (Catlett's Station, St. Stephen's Church)	VA039	D
Auburn (Coffee Hill)	VA041	D
Ball's Bluff (Harrison's Landing, Leesburg)	VA006	B
Beaver Dam Creek (Mechanicsville, Ellerson's Mill)	VA016	B
Berryville	VA118	C
Big Bethel (Bethel Church, Great Bethel)	VA003	C
Blackburn's Ford (Bull Run)	VA004	C
Boydton Plank Road (Hatcher's Run, Burgess' Mill)	VA079	B
Brandy Station (Fleetwood Hill)	VA035	B
Bristoe Station	VA040	B
Buckland Mills (Buckland Races, Chestnut Hill)	VA042	D
Cedar Creek (Belle Grove)	VA122	A
Cedar Mountain (Slaughter's Mountain, Cedar Run)	VA022	B
Chaffin's Farm / New Market Heights (Combats at New Market Heights, Forts Harrison, Johnson, and Gilmer, Laurel Hill)	VA075	B
Chancellorsville	VA032	A
Chantilly (Ox Hill)	VA027	B
Chester Station	VA051	D
Cloyd's Mountain	VA049	C
Cockpit Point (Batteries at Evansport, Freestone Point, Shipping Point)	VA100	C
Cold Harbor (Second Cold Harbor)	VA062	A
Cool Spring (Island Ford, Parkers Ford, Snickers Ferry, Castleman's Ferry)	VA114	C
Cove Mountain	VA109	D
Crater (The Mine)	VA070	A
Cross Keys	VA105	B
Cumberland Church (Farmville)	VA094	C
Darbytown and New Market Roads (Johnson's Farm, Fourmile Creek)	VA077	C
Darbytown Road (Alms House)	VA078	D
Deep Bottom I (Darbytown, Strawberry Plains, New Market Road, Gravel Hill)	VA069	C
Deep Bottom II (New Market Road, Fussell's Mill, Bailey's Creek, Charles City Road, White's Tavern)	VA071	B
Dinwiddie Court House	VA086	C
Dranesville	VA007	C
Drewry's Bluff (Fort Darling, Fort Drewry)	VA012	B
Eltham's Landing (Barhamsville, West Point)	VA011	D
Fair Oaks & Darbytown Road (Second Fair Oaks)	VA080	C
Fisher's Hill	VA120	B
Five Forks	VA088	A

BATTLE	CWSAC DESIGNATION	CLASS
Fort Stedman	VA084	A
Fredericksburg I (Marye's Heights)	VA028	A
Fredericksburg II (Marye's Heights)	VA034	B
Front Royal (Guard Hill, Cedarville)	VA103	C
Gaines' Mill (First Cold Harbor)	VA017	A
Garnett's & Golding's Farms	VA018	D
Glendale (Nelson's Farm, Frayser's Farm, Charles City Crossroads, White Oak Swamp, New Market Road, Riddell's Shop)	VA020b	B
Globe Tavern (Second Battle of Weldon Railroad, Yellow Tavern, Yellow House, Blick's Station)	VA072	B
Guard Hill (Front Royal, Cedarville)	VA117	C
Hampton Roads (*Monitor* vs. *Virginia* (*Merrimack*), Battle of the Ironclads)	VA008	B
Hanover Courthouse (Slash Church)	VA013	C
Hatcher's Run (Dabney's Mill, Rowanty Creek, Armstrong's Mill, Vaughan Road)	VA083	B
Haw's Shop (Enon Church)	VA058	C
High Bridge	VA095	C
Jerusalem Plank Road (First Battle of Weldon Railroad)	VA065	B
Kelly's Ford (Kellysville)	VA029	C
Kernstown, First	VA101	B
Kernstown, Second	VA116	B
Lewis's Farm (Quaker Road, Military Road, Gravelly Run)	VA085	C
Lynchburg	VA064	B
Malvern Hill (Poindexter's Farm)	VA021	A
Manassas, First (First Bull Run)	VA005	A
Manassas, Second (Manassas, Second Bull Run, Manassas Plains, Groveton, Gainesville, Brawner's Farm)	VA026	A
Manassas Gap (Wapping Heights)	VA108	D
Manassas Station Operations (Bristoe Station, Kettle Run, Bull Run Bridge, Union Mills)	VA024	B
Marion	VA081	D
McDowell (Sitlington's Hill)	VA102	C
Middleburg	VA037	C
Mine Run (Payne's Farm, New Hope Church)	VA044	B
Morton's Ford (Rapidan River)	VA045	D
Namozine Church	VA124	D
New Market	VA110	B
North Anna (Telegraph Road Bridge, Jericho Mill [May 23]; Ox Ford, Quarles Mill, Hanover Junction [May 24])	VA055	B
Oak Grove (French's Field, King's School House)	VA015	D
Old Church (Matadequin Creek)	VA059	C
Opequon (Third Winchester)	VA119	A
Peebles Farm (Poplar Springs Church, Wyatt's Farm, Chappell's House, Pegram's Farm, Vaughn Road)	VA074	B
Petersburg (Old Men and Young Boys)	VA098	D
Petersburg (Assault on Petersburg)	VA063	A
Petersburg (The Breakthrough)	VA089	A
Piedmont	VA111	B
Port Republic	VA106	B
Port Walthall Junction	VA047	C
Proctor's Creek (Drewry's Bluff, Fort Darling)	VA053	B
Rappahannock Station (Waterloo Bridge, White Sulphur Springs, Lee Springs, Freeman's Ford)	VA023	D
Rappahannock Station	VA043	B
Ream's Station (Reams' Station)	VA068	C
Ream's Station (Reams' Station)	VA073	B
Rice's Station (Rice's Depot)	VA092	D
Rutherford's Farm	VA115	D

BATTLE	CWSAC DESIGNATION	CLASS
St. Mary's Church (Nance's Shop)	VA066	D
Salem Church (Banks' Ford)	VA033	B
Saltville	VA082	C
Saltville	VA076	C
Sappony Church (Stony Creek Depot)	VA067	D
Savage's Station	VA019	C
Sailor's Creek (Hillsman Farm, Lockett Farm)	VA093	B
Seven Pines (Fair Oaks, Fair Oaks Station)	VA014	B
Sewell's Point	VA001	D
Spotsylvania Court House (Combats at Laurel Hill and Corbin's Bridge [May 8]; Ni River [May 9]; Laurel Hill, Po River, and Bloody Angle [May 10]; Salient or Bloody Angle [May 12-13]; Piney Branch Church [May 15]; Harrison House [May 18]; Harris Farm [May 19])	VA048	A
Staunton River Bridge (Blacks and Whites, Old Men and Young Boys)	VA113	C
Suffolk (Fort Huger, Hill's Point)	VA031	C
Suffolk (Norfleet House Battery)	VA030	C
Sutherland's Station	VA090	C
Swift Creek (Arrowfield Church)	VA050	C
Thoroughfare Gap (Chapman's Mill)	VA025	C
Tom's Brook (Woodstock Races)	VA121	C
Totopotomy Creek (Bethesda Church, Crumps Creek, Matadequin Creek, Shady Grove, Hanovertown)	VA057	B
Trevilian Station (Trevilians)	VA099	B
Upperville	VA038	C
Walkerton (Mantapike Hill)	VA125	C
Ware Bottom Church	VA054	C
Waynesborough	VA123	B
White Oak Road (Hatcher's Run, Gravelly Run, Boydton Plank Road, White Oak Ridge)	VA087	B
White Oak Swamp	VA020a	C
Wilderness (Combats at Parker's Store, Craig's Meeting House, Todd's Tavern, Brock Road, the Furnaces)	VA046	A
Williamsburg (Fort Magruder)	VA010	B
Wilson's Wharf (Fort Pocahontas)	VA056	D
Winchester, First (Bowers Hill)	VA104	A
Winchester, Second	VA107	B
Yellow Tavern	VA052	C
Yorktown	VA009	B
West Virginia		
Camp Alleghany (Allegheny Mountain)	WV008	C
Carnifex Ferry	WV006	B
Cheat Mountain (Cheat Mountain Summit)	WV005	B
Droop Mountain	WV012	C
Greenbrier River (Camp Bartow)	WV007	D
Harpers Ferry	WV010	B
Hoke's Run (Falling Waters, Hainesville)	WV002	D
Kessler's Cross Lanes (Cross Lanes)	WV004	D
Moorefield (Oldfields)	WV013	C
Philippi (Philippi Races)	WV001	D
Princeton Courthouse (Actions at Wolf Creek)	WV009	C
Rich Mountain	WV003	B
Shepherdstown (Boteler's Ford)	WV016	C
Smithfield Crossing	WV015	D
Summit Point (Flowing Springs, Cameron's Depot)	WV014	D

The Civil War Sites Advisory Commission List of Principal Battles—by Class

The Civil War Sites Advisory Commission, tasked by Congress to assess the condition of the nation's Civil War battlefields, reviewed over 10,500 actions that occurred during the war and created a list of 384 principal battles. The battles were further distinguished into the following classes:

A—Having a decisive influence on a campaign and a direct impact on the course of the war

B—Having a direct and decisive influence on their campaign

C—Having observable influence on the outcome of a campaign

D—Having a limited influence on the outcome of their campaign or operation but achieving or affecting important local objectives

The following list, organized by class, is the CWSAC's list of primary battlefields. The number designation given to each battle (OK001, OK002, etc.) is, in most cases, in chronological order, though there are some exceptions. Alternative names for the battle, if any, are shown in parentheses.

BATTLE	STATE	CWSAC DESIGNATION	CHAPTER
Class A			
Fort Blakely	Alabama	AL006	5
Mobile Bay (Passing of Forts Morgan and Gaines)	Alabama	AL003	5
Pea Ridge (Elkhorn Tavern)	Arkansas	AR001	1
Chickamauga	Georgia	GA004	4
Jonesborough	Georgia	GA022	4
Perryville	Kentucky	KY009	4
Forts Jackson & St. Philip	Louisiana	LA001	5
Mansfield (Sabine Cross Roads, Pleasant Grove)	Louisiana	LA018	3
Port Hudson	Louisiana	LA010	3
Antietam (Sharpsburg)	Maryland	MD003	9
Champion Hill (Bakers Creek)	Mississippi	MS009	3
Corinth	Mississippi	MS002	2
Vicksburg	Mississippi	MS011	3
New Madrid / Island No. 10	Missouri	MO012	2
Westport	Missouri	MO027	1
Wilson's Creek (Oak Hills)	Missouri	MO004	1
Glorieta Pass (La Glorieta Pass)	New Mexico	NM002	11
Bentonville (Bentonsville)	North Carolina	NC020	6
Fort Fisher	North Carolina	NC015	6
Gettysburg	Pennsylvania	PA002	9
Fort Sumter	South Carolina	SC001	6
Chattanooga	Tennessee	TN024	4
Fort Donelson	Tennessee	TN002	2
Franklin	Tennessee	TN036	4
Nashville	Tennessee	TN038	4
Shiloh (Pittsburg Landing)	Tennessee	TN003	2
Stones River (Murfreesboro)	Tennessee	TN010	4

BATTLE	STATE	CWSAC DESIGNATION	CHAPTER
Appomattox Courthouse	Virginia	VA097	7
Cedar Creek (Belle Grove)	Virginia	VA122	10
Chancellorsville	Virginia	VA032	8
Cold Harbor (Second Cold Harbor)	Virginia	VA062	7
Crater (The Mine)	Virginia	VA070	7
Five Forks	Virginia	VA088	7
Fort Stedman	Virginia	VA084	7
Fredericksburg I (Marye's Heights)	Virginia	VA028	8
Gaines' Mill (First Cold Harbor)	Virginia	VA017	7
Malvern Hill (Poindexter's Farm)	Virginia	VA021	7
Manassas, First (First Bull Run)	Virginia	VA005	8
Manassas, Second (Manassas, Second Bull Run, Manassas Plains, Groveton, Gainesville, Brawner's Farm)	Virginia	VA026	8
Opequon (Third Winchester)	Virginia	VA119	10
Petersburg (Assault on Petersburg)	Virginia	VA063	7
Petersburg (The Breakthrough)	Virginia	VA089	7
Spotsylvania Court House (Combats at Laurel Hill and Corbin's Bridge [May 8]; Ni River [May 9]; Laurel Hill, Po River, and Bloody Angle [May 10]; Salient or Bloody Angle [May 12-13]; Piney Branch Church [May 15]; Harrison House [May 18]; Harris Farm [May 19])	Virginia	VA048	8
Wilderness (Combats at Parker's Store, Craig's Meeting House, Todd's Tavern, Brock Road, the Furnaces)	Virginia	VA046	8
Winchester, First (Bowers Hill)	Virginia	VA104	10
Class B			
Selma	Alabama	AL007	11
Spanish Fort	Alabama	AL005	5
Bayou Fourche (Little Rock)	Arkansas	AR010a	3
Helena	Arkansas	AR008	3
Prairie D'Ane (Gum Grove, Moscow)	Arkansas	AR013	3
Prairie Grove (Fayetteville)	Arkansas	AR005	1
Sand Creek (Chivington Massacre)	Colorado	C0001	11
Fort Stevens (Washington)	District of Columbia	DC001	9
Olustee (Ocean Pond)	Florida	FL005	6
Allatoona	Georgia	GA023	4
Atlanta	Georgia	GA017	4
Ezra Church (Battle of the Poor House)	Georgia	GA018	4
Fort McAllister II	Georgia	GA028	6
Fort Pulaski	Georgia	GA001	6
Gilgal Church (Marietta Operations)	Georgia	GA013b	4
Griswoldville	Georgia	GA025	4
Kennesaw Mountain	Georgia	GA015	4
Noonday Creek (Marietta Operations)	Georgia	GA013c	4
Peachtree Creek	Georgia	GA016	4
Pine Mountain (Marietta Operations)	Georgia	GA013a	4
Ringgold Gap (Taylor's Ridge)	Georgia	GA005	4
Ruff's Mill (Marietta Operations)	Georgia	GA013d	4
Mill Springs (Logan's Cross-Roads, Fishing Creek)	Kentucky	KY006	11
Munfordville (Green River Bridge)	Kentucky	KY008	4
Richmond	Kentucky	KY007	11
Baton Rouge (Magnolia Cemetery)	Louisiana	LA003	5
Fort DeRussy	Louisiana	LA017	3
New Orleans	Louisiana	LA002	5
Pleasant Hill	Louisiana	LA019	3
Monocacy (Battle That Saved Washington)	Maryland	MD007	9

BATTLE	STATE	CWSAC DESIGNATION	CHAPTER
South Mountain (Crampton's, Turner's, and Fox's Gaps)	Maryland	MD002	9
Big Black River Bridge (Big Black)	Mississippi	MS010	3
Brices Cross Roads (Tishomingo Creek)	Mississippi	MS014	2
Chickasaw Bayou (Chickasaw Bluffs, Walnut Hills)	Mississippi	MS003	3
Corinth	Mississippi	MS016	2
Jackson	Mississippi	MS008	3
Okolona	Mississippi	MS013	2
Port Gibson (Thompson's Hill)	Mississippi	MS006	3
Raymond	Mississippi	MS007	3
Tupelo (Harrisburg)	Mississippi	MS015	2
Byram's Ford (Big Blue River)	Missouri	MO026	1
Fort Davidson (Pilot Knob)	Missouri	MO021	2
Newtonia	Missouri	MO029	1
Valverde	New Mexico	NM001	11
New Bern	North Carolina	NC003	6
Roanoke Island (Fort Huger)	North Carolina	NC002	6
Chustenahlah	Oklahoma	OK003	1
Honey Springs (Elk Creek, Shaw's Inn)	Oklahoma	OK007	1
Charleston Harbor (Battery Gregg, Fort Wagner, Morris Island, Fort Sumter)	South Carolina	SC009	6
Fort Sumter (Charleston Harbor, Morris Island)	South Carolina	SC008	6
Fort Wagner / Morris Island (Second Assault, Morris Island)	South Carolina	SC007	6
Secessionville (Fort Lamar, James Island)	South Carolina	SC002	6
Fort Henry	Tennessee	TN001	2
Fort Pillow	Tennessee	TN030	2
Fort Sanders (Fort Loudon)	Tennessee	TN025	11
Johnsonville	Tennessee	TN032	2
Memphis	Tennessee	TN004	2
Spring Hill	Tennessee	TN035	4
Wauhatchie (Brown's Ferry)	Tennessee	TN021	4
Galveston	Texas	TX003	5
Sabine Pass II	Texas	TX006	5
Appomattox Station	Virginia	VA096	7
Ball's Bluff (Harrison's Landing, Leesburg)	Virginia	VA006	8
Beaver Dam Creek (Mechanicsville, Ellerson's Mill)	Virginia	VA016	7
Boydton Plank Road (Hatcher's Run, Burgess' Mill)	Virginia	VA079	7
Brandy Station (Fleetwood Hill)	Virginia	VA035	8
Bristoe Station	Virginia	VA040	8
Cedar Mountain (Slaughter's Mountain, Cedar Run)	Virginia	VA022	8
Chaffin's Farm / New Market Heights (Combats at New Market Heights, Forts Harrison, Johnson, and Gilmer, Laurel Hill)	Virginia	VA075	7
Chantilly (Ox Hill)	Virginia	VA027	8
Cross Keys	Virginia	VA105	10
Deep Bottom II (New Market Road, Fussell's Mill, Bailey's Creek, Charles City Road, White's Tavern)	Virginia	VA071	7
Drewry's Bluff (Fort Darling, Fort Drewry)	Virginia	VA012	7
Fisher's Hill	Virginia	VA120	10
Fredericksburg II (Marye's Heights)	Virginia	VA034	8
Glendale (Nelson's Farm, Frayser's Farm, Charles City Crossroads, White Oak Swamp, New Market Road, Riddell's Shop)	Virginia	VA020b	7
Globe Tavern (Second Battle of Weldon Railroad, Yellow Tavern, Yellow House, Blick's Station)	Virginia	VA072	7
Hampton Roads (*Monitor* vs. *Virginia* (*Merrimack*), Battle of the Ironclads)	Virginia	VA008	6

BATTLE	STATE	CWSAC DESIGNATION	CHAPTER
Hatcher's Run (Dabney's Mill, Rowanty Creek, Armstrong's Mill, Vaughan Road)	Virginia	VA083	7
Jerusalem Plank Road (First Battle of Weldon Railroad)	Virginia	VA065	7
Kernstown, First	Virginia	VA101	10
Kernstown, Second	Virginia	VA116	10
Lynchburg	Virginia	VA064	7
Manassas Station Operations (Bristoe Station, Kettle Run, Bull Run Bridge, Union Mills)	Virginia	VA024	8
Mine Run (Payne's Farm, New Hope Church)	Virginia	VA044	8
New Market	Virginia	VA110	10
North Anna (Telegraph Road Bridge, Jericho Mill [May 23]; Ox Ford, Quarles Mill, Hanover Junction [May 24])	Virginia	VA055	7
Peebles' Farm (Poplar Springs Church, Wyatt's Farm, Chappell's House, Pegram's Farm, Vaughn Road)	Virginia	VA074	7
Piedmont	Virginia	VA111	10
Port Republic	Virginia	VA106	10
Proctor's Creek (Drewry's Bluff, Fort Darling)	Virginia	VA053	7
Rappahannock Station	Virginia	VA043	8
Ream's Station (Reams' Station)	Virginia	VA073	7
Sailor's Creek (Hillsman Farm, Lockett Farm)	Virginia	VA093	7
Salem Church (Banks' Ford)	Virginia	VA033	8
Seven Pines (Fair Oaks, Fair Oaks Station)	Virginia	VA014	7
Totopotomy Creek (Bethesda Church, Crumps Creek, Matadequin Creek, Shady Grove, Hanovertown)	Virginia	VA057	7
Trevilian Station (Trevilians)	Virginia	VA099	8
Waynesborough	Virginia	VA123	10
White Oak Road (Hatcher's Run, Gravelly Run, Boydton Plank Road, White Oak Ridge)	Virginia	VA087	7
Williamsburg (Fort Magruder)	Virginia	VA010	7
Winchester, Second	Virginia	VA107	10
Yorktown	Virginia	VA009	7
Carnifex Ferry	West Virginia	WV006	11
Cheat Mountain (Cheat Mountain Summit)	West Virginia	WV005	11
Harpers Ferry	West Virginia	WV010	9
Rich Mountain	West Virginia	WV003	11
Class C			
Day's Gap (Sand Mountain)	Alabama	AL001	11
Decatur	Alabama	AL004	11
Arkansas Post (Fort Hindman)	Arkansas	AR006	3
Cane Hill (Canehill, Boston Mountains)	Arkansas	AR004	1
Devil's Backbone (Backbone Mountain)	Arkansas	AR009	1
Elkin's Ferry (Okolona)	Arkansas	AR012	3
Jenkins' Ferry	Arkansas	AR016	3
Poison Spring	Arkansas	AR014	3
St. Charles	Arkansas	AR002	3
Natural Bridge	Florida	FL006	5
Santa Rosa Island	Florida	FL001	5
Adairsville	Georgia	GA009	4
Buck Head Creek	Georgia	GA026	6
Dallas (New Hope Church, Pumpkinvine Creek)	Georgia	GA011	4
Dalton I	Georgia	GA006	4
Davis' Cross-Roads (Dug Gap)	Georgia	GA003	4
Fort McAllister I	Georgia	GA002	6
Kolb's Farm	Georgia	GA014	4
New Hope Church	Georgia	GA010	4
Pickett's Mill (New Hope, New Hope Church)	Georgia	GA012	4

BATTLE	STATE	CWSAC DESIGNATION	CHAPTER
Resaca	Georgia	GA008	4
Rocky Face Ridge (Combats at Buzzard Roost, Mill Creek, Dug Gap)	Georgia	GA007	4
Utoy Creek	Georgia	GA019	4
Waynesborough	Georgia	GA027	6
Bear River (Massacre at Boa Ogoi)	Idaho	ID001	11
Corydon	Indiana	IN001	4
Baxter Springs (Baxter Springs Massacre)	Kansas	KS002	1
Lawrence (Lawrence Massacre)	Kansas	KS001	1
Marais des Cygnes (Battle of Osage, Battle of Trading Post)	Kansas	KS004	1
Mine Creek (Battle of the Osage)	Kansas	KS003	1
Camp Wild Cat (Wildcat Mountain)	Kentucky	KY002	11
Cynthiana (Kellar's Bridge)	Kentucky	KY011	11
Middle Creek	Kentucky	KY005	11
Paducah	Kentucky	KY010	2
Blair's Landing (Pleasant Hill Landing)	Louisiana	LA020	3
Georgia Landing (Labadieville)	Louisiana	LA005	5
Irish Bend (Nerson's Woods, Franklin)	Louisiana	LA007	5
Kock's Plantation (Cox's Plantation)	Louisiana	LA015	5
Mansura (Smith's Place, Marksville)	Louisiana	LA022	3
Milliken's Bend	Louisiana	LA011	3
Plains Store (Springfield Road)	Louisiana	LA009	3
Yellow Bayou (Norwood's Plantation)	Louisiana	LA023	3
Williamsport (Hagerstown, Falling Waters)	Maryland	MD004	9
Fort Ridgely	Minnesota	MN001	11
Wood Lake	Minnesota	MN002	11
Grand Gulf	Mississippi	MS004	3
Iuka	Mississippi	MS001	2
Meridian	Mississippi	MS012	11
Belmont	Missouri	MO009	2
Boonville (First Battle of Boonville)	Missouri	MO001	1
Carthage	Missouri	MO002	1
Glasgow	Missouri	MO022	1
Independence	Missouri	MO025	1
Lexington (Battle of the Hemp Bales)	Missouri	MO006	1
Newtonia	Missouri	MO016	1
Albemarle Sound	North Carolina	NC013	6
Averasborough (Taylor's Hole Creek, Smithville, Smiths Ferry, Black River)	North Carolina	NC019	6
Fort Fisher	North Carolina	NC014	6
Fort Macon	North Carolina	NC004	6
Goldsborough Bridge	North Carolina	NC009	6
Hatteras Inlet Batteries (Forts Clark and Hatteras)	North Carolina	NC001	6
Plymouth	North Carolina	NC012	6
Big Mound	North Dakota	ND001	11
Killdeer Mountain (Tahkahokuty Mountain)	North Dakota	ND005	11
Buffington Island (St. Georges Creek)	Ohio	OH001	11
Cabin Creek	Oklahoma	OK006	1
Hanover	Pennsylvania	PA001	9
Charleston Harbor (Fort Sumter)	South Carolina	SC004	6
Honey Hill	South Carolina	SC010	6
Columbia	Tennessee	TN034	4
Dandridge	Tennessee	TN028	11
Fair Garden	Tennessee	TN029	11
Hartsville	Tennessee	TN008	4
Hatchie's Bridge (Davis Bridge, Matamora)	Tennessee	TN007	2
Hoover's Gap	Tennessee	TN017	4

BATTLE	STATE	CWSAC DESIGNATION	CHAPTER
Memphis	Tennessee	TN031	2
Murfreesboro	Tennessee	TN006	4
Parker's Cross Roads	Tennessee	TN011	2
Thompson's Station	Tennessee	TN013	4
Sabine Pass	Texas	TX001	5
Aldie	Virginia	VA036	8
Amelia Springs	Virginia	VA091	7
Berryville	Virginia	VA118	10
Big Bethel (Bethel Church, Great Bethel)	Virginia	VA003	6
Blackburn's Ford (Bull Run)	Virginia	VA004	8
Cloyd's Mountain	Virginia	VA049	11
Cockpit Point (Batteries at Evansport, Freestone Point, Shipping Point)	Virginia	VA100	8
Cool Spring (Island Ford, Parkers Ford, Snickers Ferry, Castleman's Ferry)	Virginia	VA114	10
Cumberland Church (Farmville)	Virginia	VA094	7
Darbytown and New Market Roads (Johnson's Farm, Fourmile Creek)	Virginia	VA077	7
Deep Bottom I (Darbytown, Strawberry Plains, New Market Road, Gravel Hill)	Virginia	VA069	7
Dinwiddie Court House	Virginia	VA086	7
Dranesville	Virginia	VA007	8
Fair Oaks & Darbytown Road (Second Fair Oaks)	Virginia	VA080	7
Front Royal (Guard Hill, Cedarville)	Virginia	VA103	10
Guard Hill (Front Royal, Cedarville)	Virginia	VA117	10
Hanover Courthouse (Slash Church)	Virginia	VA013	7
Haw's Shop (Enon Church)	Virginia	VA058	7
High Bridge	Virginia	VA095	7
Kelly's Ford (Kellysville)	Virginia	VA029	8
Lewis's Farm (Quaker Road, Military Road, Gravelly Run)	Virginia	VA085	7
McDowell (Sitlington's Hill)	Virginia	VA102	10
Middleburg	Virginia	VA037	8
Old Church (Matadequin Creek)	Virginia	VA059	7
Port Walthall Junction	Virginia	VA047	7
Ream's Station (Reams' Station)	Virginia	VA068	7
Saltville	Virginia	VA082	11
Saltville	Virginia	VA076	11
Savage's Station	Virginia	VA019	7
Staunton River Bridge (Blacks and Whites, Old Men and Young Boys)	Virginia	VA113	7
Suffolk (Fort Huger, Hill's Point)	Virginia	VA031	6
Suffolk (Norfleet House Battery)	Virginia	VA030	6
Sutherland's Station	Virginia	VA090	7
Swift Creek (Arrowfield Church)	Virginia	VA050	7
Thoroughfare Gap (Chapman's Mill)	Virginia	VA025	8
Tom's Brook (Woodstock Races)	Virginia	VA121	10
Upperville	Virginia	VA038	8
Walkerton (Mantapike Hill)	Virginia	VA125	7
Ware Bottom Church	Virginia	VA054	7
White Oak Swamp	Virginia	VA020a	7
Yellow Tavern	Virginia	VA052	7
Camp Alleghany (Allegheny Mountain)	West Virginia	WV008	11
Droop Mountain	West Virginia	WV012	11
Moorefield (Oldfields)	West Virginia	WV013	9
Princeton Courthouse (Actions at Wolf Creek)	West Virginia	WV009	11
Shepherdstown (Boteler's Ford)	West Virginia	WV016	9

Class D

Athens	Alabama	AL002	11

BATTLE	STATE	CWSAC DESIGNATION	CHAPTER
Chalk Bluff	Arkansas	AR007	2
Hill's Plantation (Cache River, Cotton Plant, Round Hill)	Arkansas	AR003	3
Marks' Mills	Arkansas	AR015	3
Old River Lake (Ditch Bayou, Lake Chicot, Lake Village, Furlough, Fish Bayou, Grand Lake)	Arkansas	AR017	3
Pine Bluff	Arkansas	AR011	3
Fort Brooke	Florida	FL004	5
St. John's Bluff	Florida	FL003	6
Tampa (Yankee Outrage at Tampa)	Florida	FL002	5
Dalton II	Georgia	GA020	4
Lovejoy's Station	Georgia	GA021	4
Barbourville	Kentucky	KY001	11
Ivy Mountain (Ivy Creek, Ivy Narrows)	Kentucky	KY003	11
Rowlett's Station (Woodsonville, Green River)	Kentucky	KY004	4
Donaldsonville	Louisiana	LA004	5
Donaldsonville	Louisiana	LA013	5
Fort Bisland (Bethel Place)	Louisiana	LA006	5
Goodrich's Landing (The Mounds, Lake Providence)	Louisiana	LA014	3
LaFourche Crossing (Lafourche Crossing)	Louisiana	LA012	5
Monett's Ferry (Cane River Crossing)	Louisiana	LA021	3
Stirling's Plantation (Fordoche Bridge)	Louisiana	LA016	5
Vermilion Bayou	Louisiana	LA008	5
Boonsboro	Maryland	MD006	9
Folck's Mill (Cumberland)	Maryland	MD008	9
Hancock (Romney Campaign)	Maryland	MD001	9
Snyder's Bluff (Snyder's Hill)	Mississippi	MS005	3
Cape Girardeau	Missouri	MO020	2
Clark's Mill (Vera Cruz)	Missouri	MO017	1
Dry Wood Creek (Big Dry Wood Creek, Battle of the Mules)	Missouri	MO005	1
Fredericktown	Missouri	MO007	2
Hartville	Missouri	MO019	1
Independence	Missouri	MO014	1
Kirksville	Missouri	MO013	1
Lexington	Missouri	MO023	1
Liberty (Blue Mills Landing, Blue Mills)	Missouri	MO003	1
Little Blue River (Westport)	Missouri	MO024	1
Lone Jack	Missouri	MO015	1
Marmaton River (Shiloh Creek, Charlot's Farm)	Missouri	MO028	1
Mount Zion Church	Missouri	MO010	1
Roan's Tan Yard (Silver Creek)	Missouri	MO011	1
Springfield	Missouri	MO018	1
Springfield (Zagonyi's Charge)	Missouri	MO008	1
Fort Anderson (Deep Gully)	North Carolina	NC010	6
Kinston	North Carolina	NC007	6
Monroe's Cross Roads (Fayetteville Road, Blue's Farm)	North Carolina	NC018	6
South Mills (Camden)	North Carolina	NC005	6
Tranter's Creek	North Carolina	NC006	6
Washington	North Carolina	NC011	6
White Hall (Whitehall, White Hall Ferry)	North Carolina	NC008	6
Wilmington (Fort Anderson, Town Creek, Forks Road, Sugar Loaf Hill)	North Carolina	NC016	6
Wyse Fork (Wilcox's Bridge, Wise's Fork, Second Kinston, Second Southwest Creek, Kelly's Mill Pond)	North Carolina	NC017	6
Dead Buffalo Lake	North Dakota	ND002	11

BATTLE	STATE	CWSAC DESIGNATION	CHAPTER
Stony Lake	North Dakota	ND003	11
Whitestone Hill	North Dakota	ND004	11
Salineville (New Lisbon, New Lisbon Road, Wellsville)	Ohio	OH002	11
Chusto-Talasah (Caving Banks)	Oklahoma	OK002	1
Middle Boggy Depot (Middle Boggy)	Oklahoma	OK005	1
Old Fort Wayne (Beatties Prairie, Beaty's Prairie)	Oklahoma	OK004	1
Round Mountain (Round Mountains)	Oklahoma	OK001	1
Fort Wagner (First Assault, Morris Island)	South Carolina	SC005	6
Grimball's Landing (Secessionville, James Island)	South Carolina	SC006	6
Rivers' Bridge (Salkahatchie River, Hickory Hill, Owens' Crossroads, Lawtonville, Duck Creek)	South Carolina	SC011	6
Simmon's Bluff	South Carolina	SC003	6
Bean's Station	Tennessee	TN026	11
Blountville	Tennessee	TN019	11
Blue Springs	Tennessee	TN020	11
Brentwood	Tennessee	TN015	
Bull's Gap	Tennessee	TN033	11
Campbell's Station	Tennessee	TN023	11
Chattanooga	Tennessee	TN018	4
Chattanooga	Tennessee	TN005	4
Collierville	Tennessee	TN022	2
Dover (Fort Donelson)	Tennessee	TN012	2
Franklin	Tennessee	TN016	4
Jackson	Tennessee	TN009	2
Mossy Creek	Tennessee	TN027	11
Murfreesboro (Wilkinson Pike, Cedars)	Tennessee	TN037	4
Vaught's Hill (Milton)	Tennessee	TN014	4
Galveston	Texas	TX002	5
Palmito Ranch (Palmito Hill)	Texas	TX005	5
Aquia Creek	Virginia	VA002	8
Auburn (Catlett's Station, St. Stephen's Church)	Virginia	VA039	8
Auburn (Coffee Hill)	Virginia	VA041	8
Buckland Mills (Buckland Races, Chestnut Hill)	Virginia	VA042	8
Chester Station	Virginia	VA051	7
Cove Mountain	Virginia	VA109	11
Darbytown Road (Alms House)	Virginia	VA078	7
Eltham's Landing (Barhamsville, West Point)	Virginia	VA011	7
Garnett's & Golding's Farms	Virginia	VA018	7
Manassas Gap (Wapping Heights)	Virginia	VA108	10
Marion	Virginia	VA081	11
Morton's Ford (Rapidan River)	Virginia	VA045	8
Namozine Church	Virginia	VA124	7
Oak Grove (French's Field, King's School House)	Virginia	VA015	7
Petersburg (Old Men and Young Boys)	Virginia	VA098	7
Rappahannock River (Waterloo Bridge, White Sulphur Springs, Lee Springs, Freeman's Ford)	Virginia	VA023	8
Rice's Station (Rice's Depot)	Virginia	VA092	7
Rutherford's Farm	Virginia	VA115	10
St. Mary's Church (Nance's Shop)	Virginia	VA066	7
Sappony Church (Stony Creek Depot)	Virginia	VA067	7
Sewell's Point	Virginia	VA001	6
Wilson's Wharf (Fort Pocahontas)	Virginia	VA056	7
Greenbrier River (Camp Bartow)	West Virginia	WV007	11
Hoke's Run (Falling Waters, Hainesville)	West Virginia	WV002	9
Kessler's Cross Lanes (Cross Lanes)	West Virginia	WV004	11
Philippi (Philippi Races)	West Virginia	WV001	11
Smithfield Crossing	West Virginia	WV015	10
Summit Point (Flowing Springs, Cameron's Depot)	West Virginia	WV014	10

Cross-Index of Alternative Battle Names

The battles of the Civil War often had two or more names attributed to them. The name of a battle could be based on that of a nearby town, a creek or other body of water, a building, or any number of other reference points, and the common name of the battle could be determined by who won or who thought they did. In either case, even the most well-known battles often have alternative and sometimes colorful names.

The list below is a cross-index of the battles discussed in this book. The name referenced in the body of the book, which is the primary name used by the Civil War Sites Advisory Commission, is in bold type.

BATTLE NAME	STATE	CWSAC DESIGNATION	ALTERNATIVE NAMES	CHAPTER
Athens	Alabama	AL002		11
Day's Gap	Alabama	AL001	Sand Mountain	11
Decatur	Alabama	AL004		11
Fort Blakely	Alabama	AL006		5
Forts Morgan and Gaines	Alabama	AL003	**Mobile Bay**	5
Mobile Bay	Alabama	AL003	Forts Morgan and Gaines	5
Sand Mountain	Alabama	AL001	**Day's Gap**	11
Selma	Alabama	AL007		11
Spanish Fort	Alabama	AL005		5
Arkansas Post	Arkansas	AR006	Fort Hindman	3
Backbone Mountain	Arkansas	AR009	**Devil's Backbone**	1
Bayou Fourche	Arkansas	AR010a	Little Rock	3
Boston Mountains	Arkansas	AR004	**Cane Hill**	1
Cache River	Arkansas	AR003	**Hill's Plantation**, Cotton Plant, Round Hill	3
Cane Hill	Arkansas	AR004	Boston Mountains	1
Chalk Bluff	Arkansas	AR007		2
Cotton Plant	Arkansas	AR003	**Hill's Plantation**, Cache River, Round Hill	3
Devil's Backbone	Arkansas	AR009	Backbone Mountain	1
Ditch Bayou	Arkansas	AR017	**Old River Lake**, Lake Chicot, Lake Village, Furlough, Fish Bayou, Grand Lake	3
Elkhorn Tavern	Arkansas	AR001	**Pea Ridge**	1
Elkin's Ferry	Arkansas	AR012	Okolona	3
Fayetteville	Arkansas	AR005	**Prairie Grove**	1
Fish Bayou	Arkansas	AR017	**Old River Lake**, Ditch Bayou, Lake Chicot, Lake Village, Furlough, Grand Lake	3
Fort Hindman	Arkansas	AR006	**Arkansas Post**	3
Furlough	Arkansas	AR017	**Old River Lake**, Ditch Bayou, Lake Chicot, Lake Village, Fish Bayou, Grand Lake	3

BATTLE NAME	STATE	CWSAC DESIGNATION	ALTERNATIVE NAMES	CHAPTER
Grand Lake	Arkansas	AR017	**Old River Lake**, Ditch Bayou, Lake Chicot, Lake Village, Furlough, Fish Bayou	3
Gum Grove	Arkansas	AR013	**Prairie D'Ane**, Moscow	3
Helena	Arkansas	AR008		3
Hill's Plantation	Arkansas	AR003	Cache River, Cotton Plant, Round Hill	3
Jenkins' Ferry	Arkansas	AR016		3
Lake Chicot	Arkansas	AR017	**Old River Lake**, Ditch Bayou, Lake Village, Furlough, Fish Bayou, Grand Lake	3
Lake Village	Arkansas	AR017	**Old River Lake**, Ditch Bayou, Lake Chicot, Furlough, Fish Bayou, Grand Lake	3
Little Rock	Arkansas	AR010a	**Bayou Fourche**	3
Marks' Mills	Arkansas	AR015		3
Moscow	Arkansas	AR013	**Prairie D'Ane**, Gum Grove	3
Okolona	Arkansas	AR012	**Elkin's Ferry**	3
Old River Lake	Arkansas	AR017	Ditch Bayou, Lake Chicot, Lake Village, Furlough, Fish Bayou, Grand Lake	3
Pea Ridge	Arkansas	AR001	Elkhorn Tavern	1
Pine Bluff	Arkansas	AR011		3
Poison Spring	Arkansas	AR014		3
Prairie D'Ane	Arkansas	AR013	Gum Grove, Moscow	3
Prairie Grove	Arkansas	AR005	Fayetteville	1
Round Hill	Arkansas	AR003	**Hill's Plantation**, Cache River, Cotton Plant	3
St. Charles	Arkansas	AR002		3
Chivington Massacre	Colorado	CO001	**Sand Creek**	11
Sand Creek	Colorado	CO001	Chivington Massacre	11
Fort Stevens	District of Columbia	DC001	Washington	9
Washington	District of Columbia	DC001	**Fort Stevens**	9
Fort Brooke	Florida	FL004		5
Natural Bridge	Florida	FL006		5
Ocean Pond	Florida	FL005	**Olustee**	6
Olustee	Florida	FL005	Ocean Pond	6
St. John's Bluff	Florida	FL003		6
Santa Rosa Island	Florida	FL001		5
Tampa	Florida	FL002	Yankee Outrage at Tampa	5
Yankee Outrage at Tampa	Florida	FL002	Tampa	5
Adairsville	Georgia	GA009		4
Allatoona	Georgia	GA023		4
Atlanta	Georgia	GA017		4
Battle of the Poor House	Georgia	GA018	**Ezra Church**	4
Buck Head Creek	Georgia	GA026		6
Buzzard Roost	Georgia	GA007	**Rocky Face Ridge**, Mill Creek, Dug Gap	4
Chickamauga	Georgia	GA004		4
Dallas	Georgia	GA011	New Hope Church, Pumpkinvine Creek	4
Dalton I	Georgia	GA006		4
Dalton II	Georgia	GA020		4
Davis Cross-Roads	Georgia	GA003	Dug Gap	4
Dug Gap	Georgia	GA003	**Davis' Cross-Roads**	4
Dug Gap	Georgia	GA007	**Rocky Face Ridge,** Buzzard Roost, Mill Creek	4
Ezra Church	Georgia	GA018	Battle of the Poor House	4
Fort McAllister I	Georgia	GA002		6

BATTLE NAME	STATE	CWSAC DESIGNATION	ALTERNATIVE NAMES	CHAPTER
Fort McAllister II	Georgia	GA028		6
Fort Pulaski	Georgia	GA001		6
Gilgal Church	Georgia	GA013b	Marietta Operations	4
Griswoldville	Georgia	GA025		4
Jonesborough	Georgia	GA022		4
Kennesaw Mountain	Georgia	GA015		4
Kolb's Farm	Georgia	GA014		4
Lovejoy's Station	Georgia	GA021		4
Marietta Operations	Georgia	GA013b	**Gilgal Church**	4
Marietta Operations	Georgia	GA013c	**Noonday Creek**	4
Marietta Operations	Georgia	GA013a	**Pine Mountain**	4
Marietta Operations	Georgia	GA013d	**Ruff's Mill**	4
Mill Creek	Georgia	GA007	**Rocky Face Ridge,** Buzzard Roost, Dug Gap	4
New Hope	Georgia	GA012	**Pickett's Mill**, New Hope Church	4
New Hope Church	Georgia	GA011	**Dallas**, Pumpkinvine Creek	4
New Hope Church	Georgia	GA012	**Pickett's Mill**, New Hope	4
New Hope Church	Georgia	GA010		4
Noonday Creek	Georgia	GA013c	Marietta Operations	4
Peachtree Creek	Georgia	GA016		4
Pickett's Mill	Georgia	GA012	New Hope, New Hope Church	4
Pine Mountain	Georgia	GA013a	Marietta Operations	4
Pumpkinvine Creek	Georgia	GA011	**Dallas**, New Hope Church	4
Resaca	Georgia	GA008		4
Ringgold Gap	Georgia	GA005	Taylor's Ridge	4
Rocky Face Ridge	Georgia	GA007	Buzzard Roost, Mill Creek, Dug Gap	4
Ruff's Mill	Georgia	GA013d	Marietta Operations	4
Taylor's Ridge	Georgia	GA005	Ringgold Gap	4
Utoy Creek	Georgia	GA019		4
Waynesborough	Georgia	GA027		6
Bear River	Idaho	ID001	Massacre at Boa Ogoi	11
Massacre at Boa Ogoi	Idaho	ID001	**Bear River**	11
Corydon	Indiana	IN001		4
Battle of the Osage	Kansas	KS004	**Marais des Cygnes**, Battle of Trading Post	1
Battle of the Osage	Kansas	KS003	**Mine Creek**	1
Battle of Trading Post	Kansas	KS004	**Marais des Cygnes**, Battle of the Osage	1
Baxter Springs	Kansas	KS002	Baxter Springs Massacre	1
Baxter Springs Massacre	Kansas	KS002	**Baxter Springs**	1
Lawrence	Kansas	KS001	Lawrence Massacre	1
Lawrence Massacre	Kansas	KS001	**Lawrence**	1
Marais des Cygnes	Kansas	KS004	Battle of the Osage, Battle of Trading Post	1
Mine Creek	Kansas	KS003	Battle of the Osage	1
Barbourville	Kentucky	KY001		11
Camp Wild Cat	Kentucky	KY002	Wildcat Mountain	11
Cynthiana	Kentucky	KY011	Kellar's Bridge	11
Fishing Creek	Kentucky	KY006	**Mill Springs**, Logan's Cross Roads	11
Green River	Kentucky	KY004	**Rowlett's Station**, Woodsonville	4
Green River Bridge	Kentucky	KY008	**Munfordville**	4
Ivy Creek	Kentucky	KY003	**Ivy Mountain**, Ivy Narrows	11
Ivy Mountain	Kentucky	KY003	Ivy Creek, Ivy Narrows	11
Ivy Narrows	Kentucky	KY003	**Ivy Mountain**, Ivy Creek	11
Kellar's Bridge	Kentucky	KY011	**Cynthiana**	11
Logan's Cross Roads	Kentucky	KY006	**Mill Springs**, Fishing Creek	11
Middle Creek	Kentucky	KY005		11

BATTLE NAME	STATE	CWSAC DESIGNATION	ALTERNATIVE NAMES	CHAPTER
Mill Springs	Kentucky	KY006	Logan's Cross Roads, Fishing Creek	11
Munfordville	Kentucky	KY008	Green River Bridge	4
Paducah	Kentucky	KY010		2
Perryville	Kentucky	KY009		4
Richmond	Kentucky	KY007		11
Rowlett's Station	Kentucky	KY004	Woodsonville, Green River	4
Wildcat Mountain	Kentucky	KY002	Camp Wild Cat	11
Woodsonville	Kentucky	KY004	Rowlett's Station, Green River	4
Baton Rouge	Louisiana	LA003	Magnolia Cemetery	5
Bethel Place	Louisiana	LA006	Fort Bisland	5
Blair's Landing	Louisiana	LA020	Pleasant Hill Landing	3
Cane River Crossing	Louisiana	LA021	Monett's Ferry	3
Cox's Plantation	Louisiana	LA015	Kock's Plantaton	5
Donaldsonville	Louisiana	LA004		5
Donaldsonville	Louisiana	LA013		5
Fordoche Bridge	Louisiana	LA016	Stirling's Plantation	5
Fort Bisland	Louisiana	LA006	Bethel Place	5
Fort DeRussy	Louisiana	LA017		3
Forts Jackson & St. Philip	Louisiana	LA001		5
Franklin	Louisiana	LA007	Irish Bend, Nerson's Woods	5
Georgia Landing	Louisiana	LA005	Labadieville	5
Goodrich's Landing	Louisiana	LA014	The Mounds, Lake Providence	3
Irish Bend	Louisiana	LA007	Nerson's Woods, Franklin	5
Kock's Plantation	Louisiana	LA015	Cox's Plantation	5
Labadieville	Louisiana	LA005	Georgia Landing	5
LaFourche Crossing	Louisiana	LA012		5
Lake Providence	Louisiana	LA014	Goodrich's Landing, The Mounds	3
Magnolia Cemetery	Louisiana	LA003	Baton Rouge	5
Mansfield	Louisiana	LA018	Sabine Cross Roads, Pleasant Grove	3
Mansura	Louisiana	LA022	Smith's Place, Marksville	3
Marksville	Louisiana	LA022	Mansura, Smith's Place	3
Milliken's Bend	Louisiana	LA011		3
Monett's Ferry	Louisiana	LA021	Cane River Crossing	3
Nerson's Woods	Louisiana	LA007	Irish Bend, Franklin	5
New Orleans	Louisiana	LA002		5
Norwood's Plantation	Louisiana	LA023	Yellow Bayou	3
Plains Store	Louisiana	LA009	Springfield Road	3
Pleasant Grove	Louisiana	LA018	Mansfield, Sabine Cross Roads	3
Pleasant Hill	Louisiana	LA019		3
Pleasant Hill Landing	Louisiana	LA020	Blair's Landing	3
Port Hudson	Louisiana	LA010		3
Sabine Cross Roads	Louisiana	LA018	Mansfield, Pleasant Grove	3
Smith's Place	Louisiana	LA022	Mansura, Marksville	3
Springfield Road	Louisiana	LA009	Plains Store	3
Stirling's Plantation	Louisiana	LA016	Fordoche Bridge	5
The Mounds	Louisiana	LA014	Goodrich's Landing, Lake Providence	3
Vermilion Bayou	Louisiana	LA008		5
Yellow Bayou	Louisiana	LA023	Norwood's Plantation	3
Antietam	Maryland	MD003	Sharpsburg	9
Battle That Saved Washington	Maryland	MD007	Monocacy	9
Boonsboro	Maryland	MD006		9
Crampton's Gap	Maryland	MD002	South Mountain, Fox's Gap, Turner's Gap	9
Cumberland	Maryland	MD008	Folck's Mill	9
Falling Waters	Maryland	MD004	Williamsport, Hagerstown	9

BATTLE NAME	STATE	CWSAC DESIGNATION	ALTERNATIVE NAMES	CHAPTER
Folck's Mill	Maryland	MD008	Cumberland	9
Fox's Gap	Maryland	MD002	**South Mountain**, Crampton's Gap, Turner's Gap	9
Hagerstown	Maryland	MD004	**Williamsport**, Falling Waters	9
Hancock	Maryland	MD001	Romney Campaign	9
Monocacy	Maryland	MD007	Battle That Saved Washington	9
Romney Campaign	Maryland	MD001	**Hancock**	9
Sharpsburg	Maryland	MD003	**Antietam**	9
South Mountain	Maryland	MD002	Crampton's Gap, Fox's Gap, Turner's Gap	9
Turner's Gap	Maryland	MD002	**South Mountain**, Crampton's Gap, Fox's Gap	9
Williamsport	Maryland	MD004	Hagerstown, Falling Waters	9
Fort Ridgely	Minnesota	MN001		11
Wood Lake	Minnesota	MN002		11
Bakers Creek	Mississippi	MS009	**Champion Hill**	3
Big Black	Mississippi	MS010	**Big Black River Bridge**	3
Big Black River Bridge	Mississippi	MS010	Big Black	3
Brices Cross Roads	Mississippi	MS014	Tishomingo Creek	3
Champion Hill	Mississippi	MS009	Bakers Creek	3
Chickasaw Bayou	Mississippi	MS003	Chickasaw Bluffs, Walnut Hills	3
Chickasaw Bluffs	Mississippi	MS003	**Chickasaw Bayou**, Walnut Hills	3
Corinth	Mississippi	MS002		2
Corinth	Mississippi	MS016		2
Grand Gulf	Mississippi	MS004		3
Harrisburg	Mississippi	MS015	**Tupelo**	2
Iuka	Mississippi	MS001		2
Jackson	Mississippi	MS008		3
Meridian	Mississippi	MS012		11
Okolona	Mississippi	MS013		2
Port Gibson	Mississippi	MS006	Thompson's Hill	3
Raymond	Mississippi	MS007		3
Snyder's Bluff	Mississippi	MS005	Snyder's Hill	3
Snyder's Hill	Mississippi	MS005	**Snyder's Bluff**	3
Thompson's Hill	Mississippi	MS006	**Port Gibson**	3
Tishomingo Creek	Mississippi	MS014	**Brices Cross Roads**	3
Tupelo	Mississippi	MS015	Harrisburg	2
Vicksburg	Mississippi	MS011		3
Walnut Hills	Mississippi	MS003	**Chickasaw Bayou**, Chickasaw Bluffs	3
Battle of the Hemp Bales	Missouri	MO006	**Lexington**	1
Battle of the Mules	Missouri	MO005	**Dry Wood Creek**, Big Dry Wood Creek	1
Belmont	Missouri	MO009		2
Big Blue River	Missouri	MO026	**Byram's Ford**	1
Big Dry Wood Creek	Missouri	MO005	**Dry Wood Creek**, Battle of the Mules	1
Blue Mills	Missouri	MO003	**Liberty**, Blue Mills Landing	1
Blue Mills Landing	Missouri	MO003	**Liberty**, Blue Mills	1
Boonville	Missouri	MO001		1
Byram's Ford	Missouri	MO026	Big Blue River	1
Cape Girardeau	Missouri	MO020		2
Carthage	Missouri	MO002		1
Charlot's Farm	Missouri	MO028	**Marmaton River**, Shiloh Creek	1
Clark's Mill	Missouri	MO017	Vera Cruz	1
Dry Wood Creek	Missouri	MO005	Big Dry Wood Creek, Battle of the Mules	1
Fort Davidson	Missouri	MO021	Pilot Knob	2
Fredericktown	Missouri	MO007		2
Glasgow	Missouri	MO022		1

BATTLE NAME	STATE	CWSAC DESIGNATION	ALTERNATIVE NAMES	CHAPTER
Hartville	Missouri	M0019		1
Independence	Missouri	M0025		1
Independence	Missouri	M0014		1
Kirksville	Missouri	M0013		1
Lexington	Missouri	M0006	Battle of the Hemp Bales	1
Lexington	Missouri	M0023		1
Liberty	Missouri	M0003	Blue Mills, Blue Mills Landing	1
Little Blue River	Missouri	M0024	Westport	1
Lone Jack	Missouri	M0015		1
Marmaton River	Missouri	M0028	Shiloh Creek, Charlot's Farm	1
Mount Zion Church	Missouri	M0010		1
New Madrid / Island No. 10	Missouri	M0012		2
Newtonia	Missouri	M0029		1
Newtonia	Missouri	M0016		1
Oak Hills	Missouri	M0004	**Wilson's Creek**	1
Pilot Knob	Missouri	M0021	**Fort Davidson**	2
Roan's Tan Yard	Missouri	M0011	Silver Creek	1
Shiloh Creek	Missouri	M0028	**Marmaton River**, Charlot's Farm	1
Silver Creek	Missouri	M0011	**Roan's Tan Yard**	1
Springfield	Missouri	M0008	Zagonyi's Charge	1
Springfield	Missouri	M0018		1
Vera Cruz	Missouri	M0017	**Clark's Mill**	1
Westport	Missouri	M0024	**Little Blue River**	1
Westport	Missouri	M0027		1
Wilson's Creek	Missouri	M0004	Oak Hills	1
Zagonyi's Charge	Missouri	M0008	**Springfield**	1
Glorieta Pass	New Mexico	NM002		11
Valverde	New Mexico	NM001		11
Albemarle Sound	North Carolina	NC013		6
Averasborough	North Carolina	NC019	Taylor's Hole Creek, Smithville, Smith's Ferry, Black River	6
Bentonville	North Carolina	NC020		6
Black River	North Carolina	NC019	**Averasborough**, Smithville, Taylor's Hole Creek, Smith's Ferry	6
Blue's Farm	North Carolina	NC018	**Monroe's Cross Roads**, Fayetteville Road	6
Camden	North Carolina	NC005	**South Mills**	6
Deep Gully	North Carolina	NC010	**Fort Anderson**	6
Fayetteville Road	North Carolina	NC018	**Monroe's Cross Roads**, Blue's Farm	6
Forks Road	North Carolina	NC016	**Wilmington**, Fort Anderson, Town Creek, Sugar Loaf Hill	6
Fort Anderson	North Carolina	NC010	Deep Gully	6
Fort Anderson	North Carolina	NC016	**Wilmington**, Town Creek, Forks Road, Sugar Loaf Hill	6
Fort Fisher	North Carolina	NC014		6
Fort Fisher	North Carolina	NC015		6
Fort Huger	North Carolina	NC002	**Roanoke Island**	6
Fort Macon	North Carolina	NC004		6
Forts Clark and Hatteras	North Carolina	NC001	**Hatteras Inlet Batteries**	6
Goldsborough Bridge	North Carolina	NC009		6
Hatteras Inlet Batteries	North Carolina	NC001	Forts Clark and Hatteras	6
Kelly's Mill Pond	North Carolina	NC017	**Wyse Fork**, Wilcox's Bridge, Wise's Fork, Second Kinston, Second Southwest Creek	6

BATTLE NAME	STATE	CWSAC DESIGNATION	ALTERNATIVE NAMES	CHAPTER
Kinston	North Carolina	NC007		6
Monroe's Cross Roads	North Carolina	NC018	Fayetteville Road, Blue's Farm	6
New Bern	North Carolina	NC003		6
Plymouth	North Carolina	NC012		6
Roanoke Island	North Carolina	NC002	Fort Huger	6
Second Kinston	North Carolina	NC017	**Wyse Fork**, Wilcox's Bridge, Wise's Fork, Second Southwest Creek, Kelly's Mill Pond	6
Second Southwest Creek	North Carolina	NC017	**Wyse Fork**, Wilcox's Bridge, Wise's Fork, Second Kinston, Kelly's Mill Pond	6
Smith's Ferry	North Carolina	NC019	**Averasborough**, Smithville, Taylor's Hole Creek, Black River	6
Smithville	North Carolina	NC019	**Averasborough**, Taylor's Hole Creek, Smith's Ferry, Black River	6
South Mills	North Carolina	NC005	Camden	6
Sugar Loaf Hill	North Carolina	NC016	**Wilmington**, Fort Anderson, Town Creek, Forks Road	6
Taylor's Hole Creek	North Carolina	NC019	**Averasborough**, Smithville, Smith's Ferry, Black River	6
Town Creek	North Carolina	NC016	**Wilmington**, Fort Anderson, Forks Road, Sugar Loaf Hill	6
Tranter's Creek	North Carolina	NC006		6
Washington	North Carolina	NC011		6
White Hall	North Carolina	NC008	White Hall Ferry	6
White Hall Ferry	North Carolina	NC008	**White Hall**	6
Wilcox's Bridge	North Carolina	NC017	**Wyse Fork**, Wise's Fork, Second Kinston, Second Southwest Creek, Kelly's Mill Pond	6
Wilmington	North Carolina	NC016	Fort Anderson, Town Creek, Forks Road, Sugar Loaf Hill	6
Wise's Fork	North Carolina	NC017	**Wyse Fork**, Wilcox's Bridge, Second Kinston, Second Southwest Creek, Kelly's Mill Pond	6
Wyse Fork	North Carolina	NC017	Wilcox's Bridge, Wise's Fork, Second Kinston, Second Southwest Creek, Kelly's Mill Pond	6
Big Mound	North Dakota	ND001		11
Dead Buffalo Lake	North Dakota	ND002		11
Killdeer Mountain	North Dakota	ND005	Tahkahokuty Mountain	11
Stony Lake	North Dakota	ND003		11
Tahkahokuty Mountain	North Dakota	ND005	**Killdeer Mountain**	11
Whitestone Hill	North Dakota	ND004		11
Buffington Island	Ohio	OH001	St. George's Creek	11
New Lisbon	Ohio	OH002	**Salineville**, New Lisbon Road, Wellsville	11
New Lisbon Road	Ohio	OH002	**Salineville**, New Lisbon, Wellsville	11
Salineville	Ohio	OH002	New Lisbon, New Lisbon Road, Wellsville	11
St. George's Creek	Ohio	OH001	**Buffington Island**	11
Wellsville	Ohio	OH002	**Salineville**, New Lisbon, New Lisbon Road	11
Beattie's Prairie	Oklahoma	OK004	**Old Fort Wayne**, Beaty's Prairie	1
Beaty's Prairie	Oklahoma	OK004	**Old Fort Wayne**, Beattie's Prairie	1

BATTLE NAME	STATE	CWSAC DESIGNATION	ALTERNATIVE NAMES	CHAPTER
Cabin Creek	Oklahoma	OK006		1
Caving Banks	Oklahoma	OK002	**Chusto-Talasah**	1
Chustenahlah	Oklahoma	OK003		1
Chusto-Talasah	Oklahoma	OK002	Caving Banks	1
Elk Creek	Oklahoma	OK007	**Honey Springs**, Shaw's Inn	1
Honey Springs	Oklahoma	OK007	Elk Creek, Shaw's Inn	1
Middle Boggy Depot	Oklahoma	OK005		1
Old Fort Wayne	Oklahoma	OK004	Beattie's Prairie, Beaty's Prairie	1
Round Mountain	Oklahoma	OK001		1
Shaw's Inn	Oklahoma	OK007	**Honey Springs**, Elk Creek	1
Gettysburg	Pennsylvania	PA002		9
Hanover	Pennsylvania	PA001		9
Battery Gregg	South Carolina	SC009	**Charleston Harbor**, Fort Wagner, Morris Island, Fort Sumter	6
Charleston Harbor	South Carolina	SC009	Battery Gregg, Fort Wagner, Morris Island, Fort Sumter	6
Charleston Harbor	South Carolina	SC004	Fort Sumter	6
Charleston Harbor	South Carolina	SC008	**Fort Sumter**, Morris Island	6
Duck Creek	South Carolina	SC011	**River's Bridge**, Salkahatchie River, Hickory Hill, Owens' Crossroads, Lawtonville	6
First Assault on Morris Island	South Carolina	SC005	**Fort Wagner**	6
Fort Lamar	South Carolina	SC002	**Secessionville**, James Island	6
Fort Sumter	South Carolina	SC004	**Charleston Harbor**	6
Fort Sumter	South Carolina	SC009	**Charleston Harbor**, Battery Gregg, Fort Wagner, Morris Island	6
Fort Sumter	South Carolina	SC008	Charleston Harbor, Morris Island	6
Fort Sumter	South Carolina	SC001		6
Fort Wagner	South Carolina	SC009	**Charleston Harbor**, Battery Gregg, Morris Island, Fort Sumter	6
Fort Wagner	South Carolina	SC005	First Assault on Morris Island	6
Fort Wagner / Morris Island	South Carolina	SC007	Second Assault on Morris Island	6
Grimball's Landing	South Carolina	SC006	Secessionville, James Island	6
Hickory Hill	South Carolina	SC011	**River's Bridge**, Salkahatchie River, Owens' Crossroads, Lawtonville, Duck Creek	6
Honey Hill	South Carolina	SC010		6
James Island	South Carolina	SC006	**Grimball's Landing**, Secessionville	6
James Island	South Carolina	SC002	**Secessionville**, Fort Lamar	6
Lawtonville	South Carolina	SC011	**River's Bridge**, Salkahatchie River, Hickory Hill, Owens' Crossroads, Duck Creek	6
Morris Island	South Carolina	SC009	**Charleston Harbor**, Battery Gregg, Fort Wagner, Fort Sumter	6
Morris Island	South Carolina	SC008	**Fort Sumter**, Charleston Harbor	6
Owens' Crossroads	South Carolina	SC011	**River's Bridge**, Salkahatchie River, Hickory Hill, Lawtonville, Duck Creek	6
Rivers' Bridge	South Carolina	SC011	Salkahatchie River, Hickory Hill, Owens' Crossroads, Lawtonville, Duck Creek	6
Salkahatchie River	South Carolina	SC011	**River's Bridge**, Hickory Hill, Owens' Crossroads, Lawtonville, Duck Creek	6

BATTLE NAME	STATE	CWSAC DESIGNATION	ALTERNATIVE NAMES	CHAPTER
Secessionville	South Carolina	SC002	Fort Lamar, James Island	6
Secessionville	South Carolina	SC006	**Grimball's Landing**, James Island	6
Second Assault on Morris Island	South Carolina	SC007	**Fort Wagner / Morris Island**	6
Simmon's Bluff	South Carolina	SC003		6
Bean's Station	Tennessee	TN026		11
Blountville	Tennessee	TN019		11
Blue Springs	Tennessee	TN020		11
Brentwood	Tennessee	TN015		4
Brown's Ferry	Tennessee	TN021	**Wauhatchie**	4
Bull's Gap	Tennessee	TN033		11
Campbell's Station	Tennessee	TN023		11
Cedars	Tennessee	TN037	**Murfreesboro**, Wilkinson Pike	4
Chattanooga	Tennessee	TN018		4
Chattanooga	Tennessee	TN005		4
Chattanooga	Tennessee	TN024		4
Collierville	Tennessee	TN022		2
Columbia	Tennessee	TN034		4
Dandridge	Tennessee	TN028		11
Davis Bridge	Tennessee	TN007	**Hatchie's Bridge**, Matamora	2
Dover	Tennessee	TN012	Fort Donelson	2
Fair Garden	Tennessee	TN029		11
Fort Donelson	Tennessee	TN012	**Dover**	2
Fort Donelson	Tennessee	TN002		2
Fort Henry	Tennessee	TN001		2
Fort Loudon	Tennessee	TN025	**Fort Sanders**	11
Fort Pillow	Tennessee	TN030		2
Fort Sanders	Tennessee	TN025	Fort Loudon	11
Franklin	Tennessee	TN016		4
Franklin	Tennessee	TN036		4
Hartsville	Tennessee	TN008		4
Hatchie's Bridge	Tennessee	TN007	Davis Bridge, Matamora	2
Hoover's Gap	Tennessee	TN017		4
Jackson	Tennessee	TN009		2
Johnsonville	Tennessee	TN032		2
Matamora	Tennessee	TN007	**Hatchie's Bridge**, Davis Bridge	2
Memphis	Tennessee	TN031		2
Memphis	Tennessee	TN004		2
Milton	Tennessee	TN014	**Vaught's Hill**	4
Mossy Creek	Tennessee	TN027		11
Murfreesboro	Tennessee	TN010	**Stones River**	4
Murfreesboro	Tennessee	TN037	Wilkinson Pike, Cedars	4
Murfreesboro	Tennessee	TN006		4
Nashville	Tennessee	TN038		4
Parker's Cross Roads	Tennessee	TN011		2
Pittsburg Landing	Tennessee	TN003	**Shiloh**	2
Shiloh	Tennessee	TN003	Pittsburg Landing	2
Spring Hill	Tennessee	TN035		4
Stones River	Tennessee	TN010	Murfreesboro	4
Thompson's Station	Tennessee	TN013		4
Vaught's Hill	Tennessee	TN014	Milton	4
Wauhatchie	Tennessee	TN021	Brown's Ferry	4
Wilkinson Pike	Tennessee	TN037	**Murfreesboro**, Cedars	4
Galveston	Texas	TX002		5
Galveston	Texas	TX003		5
Palmito Hill	Texas	TX005	**Palmito Ranch**	5

BATTLE NAME	STATE	CWSAC DESIGNATION	ALTERNATIVE NAMES	CHAPTER
Palmito Ranch	Texas	TX005	Palmito Hill	5
Sabine Pass	Texas	TX001		5
Sabine Pass II	Texas	TX006		5
Aldie	Virginia	VA036		8
Alms House	Virginia	VA078	**Darbytown Road**	7
Amelia Springs	Virginia	VA091		7
Appomattox Courthouse	Virginia	VA097		7
Appomattox Station	Virginia	VA096		7
Aquia Creek	Virginia	VA002		8
Armstrong's Mill	Virginia	VA083	**Hatcher's Run**, Dabney's Mill, Rowanty Creek, Vaughan Road	7
Arrowfield Church	Virginia	VA050	**Swift Creek**	7
Auburn	Virginia	VA039	Catlett's Station, St. Stephens Church	8
Auburn	Virginia	VA041	Coffee Hill	8
Bailey's Creek	Virginia	VA071	**Deep Bottom II**, New Market Road, Fussell's Mill, Charles City Road, White's Tavern	7
Ball's Bluff	Virginia	VA006	Harrison's Landing, Leesburg	8
Banks' Ford	Virginia	VA033	**Salem Church**	8
Barhamsville	Virginia	VA011	**Eltham's Landing**, West Point	7
Batteries at Evansport	Virginia	VA100	**Cockpit Point**, Freestone Point, Shipping Point	8
Battle of the Ironclads	Virginia	VA008	**Hampton Roads**, *Monitor* vs. *Virginia* (*Merrimack*)	6
Beaver Dam Creek	Virginia	VA016	Mechanicsville, Ellerson's Mill	7
Belle Grove	Virginia	VA122	**Cedar Creek**	10
Berryville	Virginia	VA118		10
Bethel Church	Virginia	VA003	**Big Bethel**, Great Bethel	6
Bethesda Church	Virginia	VA057	**Totopotomoy Creek**, Crumps Creek, Matadequin Creek, Shady Grove, Hanovertown	7
Big Bethel	Virginia	VA003	Bethel Church, Great Bethel	6
Blackburn's Ford	Virginia	VA004	Bull Run	8
Blacks and Whites	Virginia	VA113	**Staunton River Bridge**, Old Men and Young Boys	7
Blick's Station	Virginia	VA072	**Globe Tavern**, Second Battle of Weldon Railroad, Yellow Tavern, Yellow House	7
Bloody Angle	Virginia	VA048	**Spotsylvania Court House**, Laurel Hill, Corbin's Bridge, Ni River, Po River, Piney Branch Church, Harrison House, Harris Farm	8
Bowers Hill	Virginia	VA104	**Winchester, First**	10
Boydton Plank Road	Virginia	VA079	Hatcher's Run, Burgess' Mill	7
Boydton Plank Road	Virginia	VA087	**White Oak Road**, Hatcher's Run, Gravelly Run, White Oak Ridge	7
Brandy Station	Virginia	VA035	Fleetwood Hill	8
Brawner's Farm	Virginia	VA026	**Manassas Second**, Second Bull Run, Manassas Plains, Groveton, Gainesville	8
Bristoe Station	Virginia	VA024	**Manassas Station Operations**, Kettle Run, Bull Run Bridge, Union Mills	8
Bristoe Station	Virginia	VA040		8
Brock Road	Virginia	VA046	**Wilderness**, Combats at Parker's Store, Craig's Meeting House, Todd's Tavern, The Furnaces	8
Buckland Mills	Virginia	VA042	Buckland Races, Chestnut Hill	8
Buckland Races	Virginia	VA042	**Buckland Mills**, Chestnut Hill	8
Bull Run	Virginia	VA004	**Blackburn's Ford**	8

BATTLE NAME	STATE	CWSAC DESIGNATION	ALTERNATIVE NAMES	CHAPTER
Bull Run Bridge	Virginia	VA024	**Manassas Station Operations**, Bristoe Station, Kettle Run, Union Mills	8
Burgess' Mill	Virginia	VA079	**Boydton Plank Road**, Hatcher's Run	7
Castleman's Ferry	Virginia	VA114	**Cool Spring**, Island Ford, Parker's Ford, Snickers Ferry	10
Catlett's Station	Virginia	VA039	**Auburn**, St. Stephens Church	8
Cedar Creek	Virginia	VA122	Belle Grove	10
Cedar Mountain	Virginia	VA022	Slaughter's Mountain, Cedar Run	8
Cedar Run	Virginia	VA022	**Cedar Mountain**, Slaughter's Mountain	8
Cedarville	Virginia	VA103	**Front Royal**, Guard Hill	10
Cedarville	Virginia	VA117	**Guard Hill**, Front Royal	10
Chaffin's Farm / New Market Heights	Virginia	VA075	Combats at New Market Heights, Forts Harrison, Johnson, and Gilmer, Laurel Hill	7
Chancellorsville	Virginia	VA032		8
Chantilly	Virginia	VA027	Ox Hill	8
Chapman's Mill	Virginia	VA025	**Thoroughfare Gap**	8
Chappell's House	Virginia	VA074	**Peebles' Farm**, Poplar Springs Church, Wyatt's Farm, Pegram's Farm, Vaughn Road	7
Charles City Crossroads	Virginia	VA020b	**Glendale**, Nelson's Farm, Frayser's Farm, White Oak Swamp, New Market Road, Riddell's Shop	7
Charles City Road	Virginia	VA071	**Deep Bottom II**, New Market Road, Fussell's Mill, Bailey's Creek, White's Tavern	7
Chester Station	Virginia	VA051		7
Chestnut Hill	Virginia	VA042	**Buckland Mills**, Buckland Races	8
Cloyd's Mountain	Virginia	VA049		11
Cockpit Point	Virginia	VA100	Batteries at Evansport, Freestone Point, Shipping Point	8
Coffee Hill	Virginia	VA041	**Auburn**	8
Cold Harbor	Virginia	VA062	Second Cold Harbor	7
Combats at New Market Heights	Virginia	VA075	**Chaffin's Farm / New Market Heights**, Forts Harrison, Johnson, and Gilmer, Laurel Hill	7
Combats at Parker's Store	Virginia	VA046	**Wilderness**, Craig's Meeting House, Todd's Tavern, Brock Road, The Furnaces	8
Cool Spring	Virginia	VA114	Island Ford, Parkers Ford, Snickers Ferry, Castleman's Ferry	10
Corbin's Bridge	Virginia	VA048	**Spotsylvania Court House**, Laurel Hill, Ni River, Po River, Bloody Angle, Piney Branch Church, Harrison House, Harris Farm	8
Cove Mountain	Virginia	VA109		11
Craig's Meeting House	Virginia	VA046	**Wilderness**, Combats at Parker's Store, Todd's Tavern, Brock Road, The Furnaces	8
Crater (The Mine)	Virginia	VA070	The Mine	7
Cross Keys	Virginia	VA105		10
Crump's Creek	Virginia	VA057	**Totopotomoy Creek**, Bethesda Church, Matadequin Creek, Shady Grove, Hanovertown	7

BATTLE NAME	STATE	CWSAC DESIGNATION	ALTERNATIVE NAMES	CHAPTER
Cumberland Church	Virginia	VA094	Farmville	7
Dabney's Mill	Virginia	VA083	**Hatcher's Run**, Rowanty Creek, Armstrong's Mill, Vaughan Road	7
Darbytown	Virginia	VA069	**Deep Bottom I**, Strawberry Plains, New Market Road, Gravel Hill	7
Darbytown and New Market Roads	Virginia	VA077	Johnson's Farm, Fourmile Creek	7
Darbytown Road	Virginia	VA078	Alms House	7
Deep Bottom I	Virginia	VA069	Darbytown, Strawberry Plains, New Market Road, Gravel Hill	7
Deep Bottom II	Virginia	VA071	New Market Road, Fussell's Mill, Bailey's Creek, Charles City Road, White's Tavern	7
Dinwiddie Court House	Virginia	VA086		7
Dranesville	Virginia	VA007		8
Drewry's Bluff	Virginia	VA012	Fort Darling, Fort Drewry	7
Drewry's Bluff	Virginia	VA053	**Proctor's Creek**, Fort Darling	7
Ellerson's Mill	Virginia	VA016	**Beaver Dam Creek**, Mechanicsville	7
Eltham's Landing	Virginia	VA011	Barhamsville, West Point	7
Enon Church	Virginia	VA058	**Haw's Shop**	7
Fair Oaks	Virginia	VA014	**Seven Pines**, Fair Oaks Station	7
Fair Oaks & Darbytown Road	Virginia	VA080	Second Fair Oaks	7
Fair Oaks Station	Virginia	VA014	**Seven Pines**, Fair Oaks	7
Farmville	Virginia	VA094	**Cumberland Church**	7
First Battle of Weldon Railroad	Virginia	VA065	**Jerusalem Plank Road**	7
First Bull Run	Virginia	VA005	**Manassas, First**	8
First Cold Harbor	Virginia	VA017	**Gaines' Mill**	7
Fisher's Hill	Virginia	VA120		10
Five Forks	Virginia	VA088		7
Fleetwood Hill	Virginia	VA035	**Brandy Station**	8
Fort Darling	Virginia	VA012	**Drewry's Bluff**, Fort Drewry	7
Fort Darling	Virginia	VA053	**Proctor's Creek**, Drewry's Bluff	7
Fort Drewry	Virginia	VA012	**Drewry's Bluff**, Fort Darling	7
Fort Huger	Virginia	VA031	**Suffolk**, Hill's Point	6
Fort Magruder	Virginia	VA010	**Williamsburg**	7
Fort Pocahontas	Virginia	VA056	**Wilson's Wharf**	7
Fort Stedman	Virginia	VA084		7
Forts Harrison, Johnson and Gilmer	Virginia	VA075	**Chaffin's Farm / New Market Heights**, Combats at New Market Heights, Laurel Hill	7
Fourmile Creek	Virginia	VA077	**Darbytown and New Market Roads**, Johnson's Farm	7
Frayser's Farm	Virginia	VA020b	**Glendale**, Nelson's Farm, Charles City Crossroads, White Oak Swamp, New Market Road, Riddell's Shop	7
Fredericksburg I	Virginia	VA028	Marye's Heights	8
Fredericksburg II	Virginia	VA034	Marye's Heights	8
Freeman's Ford	Virginia	VA023	**Rappahannock River**, Waterloo Bridge, White Sulphur Springs, Lee Springs	8
Freestone Point	Virginia	VA100	**Cockpit Point**, Batteries at Evansport, Shipping Point	8
French's Field	Virginia	VA015	**Oak Grove**, King's School House	7
Front Royal	Virginia	VA103	Guard Hill, Cedarville	10

BATTLE NAME	STATE	CWSAC DESIGNATION	ALTERNATIVE NAMES	CHAPTER
Front Royal	Virginia	VA117	**Guard Hill**, Cedarville	10
Fussell's Mill	Virginia	VA071	**Deep Bottom II**, New Market Road, Bailey's Creek, Charles City Road, White's Tavern	7
Gaines' Mill	Virginia	VA017	First Cold Harbor	7
Gainesville	Virginia	VA026	**Manassas Second**, Second Bull Run, Manassas Plains, Groveton, Brawner's Farm	8
Garnett's & Golding's Farms	Virginia	VA018		7
Glendale	Virginia	VA020b	Nelson's Farm, Frayser's Farm, Charles City Crossroads, White Oak Swamp, New Market Road, Riddell's Shop	7
Globe Tavern	Virginia	VA072	Second Battle of Weldon Railroad, Yellow Tavern, Yellow House, Blick's Station	7
Gravel Hill	Virginia	VA069	**Deep Bottom I**, Darbytown, Strawberry Plains, New Market Road	7
Gravelly Run	Virginia	VA085	**Lewis' Farm**, Quaker Road, Military Road	7
Gravelly Run	Virginia	VA087	**White Oak Road**, Hatcher's Run, Boydton Plank Road, White Oak Ridge	7
Great Bethel	Virginia	VA003	**Big Bethel**, Bethel Church	6
Groveton	Virginia	VA026	**Manassas Second**, Second Bull Run, Manassas Plains, Gainesville, Brawner's Farm	8
Guard Hill	Virginia	VA103	**Front Royal**, Cedarville	10
Guard Hill	Virginia	VA117	Front Royal, Cedarville	10
Hampton Roads	Virginia	VA008	*Monitor* vs. *Virginia* (*Merrimack*), Battle of the Ironclads	6
Hanover Courthouse	Virginia	VA013	Slash Church	7
Hanover Junction	Virginia	VA055	**North Anna**, Telegraph Road Bridge, Jericho Mill, Ox Ford, Quarles Mill	7
Hanovertown	Virginia	VA057	**Totopotomoy Creek**, Bethesda Church, Crump's Creek, Matadequin Creek, Shady Grove	7
Harris Farm	Virginia	VA048	**Spotsylvania Court House**, Laurel Hill, Corbin's Bridge, Ni River, Po River, Bloody Angle, Piney Branch Church, Harrison House	8
Harrison House	Virginia	VA048	**Spotsylvania Court House**, Laurel Hill, Corbin's Bridge, Ni River, Po River, Bloody Angle, Piney Branch Church, Harris Farm	8
Harrison's Landing	Virginia	VA006	**Ball's Bluff**, Leesburg	8
Hatcher's Run	Virginia	VA079	**Boydton Plank Road**, Burgess' Mill	7
Hatcher's Run	Virginia	VA083	Dabney's Mill, Rowanty Creek, Armstrong's Mill, Vaughan Road	7
Hatcher's Run	Virginia	VA087	**White Oak Road**, Gravelly Run, Boydton Plank Road, White Oak Ridge	7
Haw's Shop	Virginia	VA058	Enon Church	7
High Bridge	Virginia	VA095		7
Hill's Point	Virginia	VA031	**Suffolk**, Fort Huger	6
Hillsman Farm	Virginia	VA093	**Saylor's Creek**, Lockett Farm	7
Island Ford	Virginia	VA114	**Cool Spring**, Parker's Ford, Snickers Ferry, Castleman's Ferry	10
Jericho Mill	Virginia	VA055	**North Anna**, Telegraph Road Bridge, Ox Ford, Quarles Mill, Hanover Junction	7
Jerusalem Plank Road	Virginia	VA065	First Battle of Weldon Railroad	7

BATTLE NAME	STATE	CWSAC DESIGNATION	ALTERNATIVE NAMES	CHAPTER
Johnson's Farm	Virginia	VA077	**Darbytown and New Market Roads**, ourmile Creek	7
Kelly's Ford	Virginia	VA029	Kellysville	8
Kellysville	Virginia	VA029	**Kelly's Ford**	8
Kernstown, First	Virginia	VA101		10
Kernstown, Second	Virginia	VA116		10
Kettle Run	Virginia	VA024	**Manassas Station Operations**, Bristoe Station, Bull Run Bridge, Union Mills	8
King's School House	Virginia	VA015	**Oak Grove**, French's Field	7
Laurel Hill	Virginia	VA075	**Chaffin's Farm / New Market Heights**, Combats at New Market Heights, Forts Harrison, Johnson and Gilmer	7
Laurel Hill	Virginia	VA048	**Spotsylvania Court House**, Corbin's Bridge, Ni River, Po River, Bloody Angle, Piney Branch Church, Harrison House, Harris Farm	8
Lee Springs	Virginia	VA023	**Rappahannock River**, Waterloo Bridge, White Sulphur Springs, Freeman's Ford	8
Leesburg	Virginia	VA006	**Ball's Bluff**, Harrison's Landing	8
Lewis' Farm	Virginia	VA085	Quaker Road, Military Road, Gravelly Run	7
Lockett Farm	Virginia	VA093	**Saylor's Creek**, Hillsman Farm	7
Lynchburg	Virginia	VA064		7
Malvern Hill	Virginia	VA021	Poindexter's Farm	7
Manassas Gap	Virginia	VA108	Wapping Heights	10
Manassas Plains	Virginia	VA026	**Manassas Second**, Second Bull Run, Groveton, Gainesville, Brawner's Farm	8
Manassas Station Operations	Virginia	VA024	Bristoe Station, Kettle Run, Bull Run Bridge, Union Mills	8
Manassas, First	Virginia	VA005	First Bull Run	8
Manassas, Second	Virginia	VA026	Second Bull Run, Manassas Plains, Groveton, Gainesville, Brawner's Farm	8
Mantapike Hill	Virginia	VA125	**Walkerton**	7
Marion	Virginia	VA081		11
Marye's Heights	Virginia	VA028	**Fredericksburg I**	8
Marye's Heights	Virginia	VA034	**Fredericksburg II**	8
Matadequin Creek	Virginia	VA059	**Old Church**	7
Matadequin Creek	Virginia	VA057	**Totopotomoy Creek**, Bethesda Church, Crump's Creek, Shady Grove, Hanovertown	7
McDowell	Virginia	VA102	Sitlington's Hill	10
Mechanicsville	Virginia	VA016	**Beaver Dam Creek**, Ellerson's Mill	7
Middleburg	Virginia	VA037		8
Military Road	Virginia	VA085	**Lewis' Farm**, Quaker Road, Gravelly Run	7
Mine Run	Virginia	VA044	Payne's Farm, New Hope Church	8
Monitor vs. Virginia (Merrimack)	Virginia	VA008	**Hampton Roads**, Battle of the Ironclads	6
Morton's Ford	Virginia	VA045	Rapidan River	8
Namozine Church	Virginia	VA124		7
Nance's Shop	Virginia	VA066	**St. Mary's Church**	7
Nelson's Farm	Virginia	VA020b	**Glendale**, Frayser's Farm, Charles City Crossroads, White Oak Swamp, New Market Road, Riddell's Shop	7
New Hope Church	Virginia	VA044	**Mine Run**, Payne's Farm	8
New Market	Virginia	VA110		10
New Market Road	Virginia	VA069	**Deep Bottom I**, Darbytown, Strawberry Plains, Gravel Hill	7
New Market Road	Virginia	VA071	**Deep Bottom II**, Fussell's Mill, Bailey's Creek, Charles City Road, White's Tavern	7

BATTLE NAME	STATE	CWSAC DESIGNATION	ALTERNATIVE NAMES	CHAPTER
New Market Road	Virginia	VA020b	**Glendale**, Nelson's Farm, Frayser's Farm, Charles City Crossroads, White Oak Swamp, Riddell's Shop	7
Ni River	Virginia	VA048	**Spotsylvania Court House**, Laurel Hill, Corbin's Bridge, Po River, Bloody Angle, Piney Branch Church, Harrison House, Harris Farm	8
Norfleet House Battery	Virginia	VA030	**Suffolk**	6
North Anna	Virginia	VA055	Telegraph Road Bridge, Jericho Mill, Ox Ford, Quarles Mill, Hanover Junction	7
Oak Grove	Virginia	VA015	French's Field, King's School House	7
Old Church	Virginia	VA059	Matadequin Creek	7
Old Men and Young Boys	Virginia	VA113	**Staunton River Bridge**, Blacks and Whites	7
Opequon	Virginia	VA119	Winchester, Third	10
Ox Ford	Virginia	VA055	**North Anna**, Telegraph Road Bridge, Jericho Mill, Quarles Mill, Hanover Junction	7
Ox Hill	Virginia	VA027	**Chantilly**	8
Parker's Ford	Virginia	VA114	**Cool Spring**, Island Ford, Snickers Ferry, Castleman's Ferry	10
Payne's Farm	Virginia	VA044	**Mine Run**, New Hope Church	8
Peebles' Farm	Virginia	VA074	Poplar Springs Church, Wyatt's Farm, Chappell's House, Pegram's Farm, Vaughn Road	7
Pegram's Farm	Virginia	VA074	**Peebles' Farm**, Poplar Springs Church, Wyatt's Farm, Chappell's House, Vaughn Road	7
Petersburg (Assault on Petersburg)	Virginia	VA063		7
Petersburg (Old Men and Young Boys)	Virginia	VA098		7
Petersburg (The Breakthrough)	Virginia	VA089		7
Piedmont	Virginia	VA111		10
Piney Branch Church	Virginia	VA048	**Spotsylvania Court House**, Laurel Hill, Corbin's Bridge, Ni River, Po River, Bloody Angle, Harrison House, Harris Farm	8
Po River	Virginia	VA048	**Spotsylvania Court House**, Laurel Hill, Corbin's Bridge, Ni River, Bloody Angle, Piney Branch Church, Harrison House, Harris Farm	8
Poindexter's Farm	Virginia	VA021	**Malvern Hill**	7
Poplar Springs Church	Virginia	VA074	**Peebles' Farm**, Wyatt's Farm, Chappell's House, Pegram's Farm, Vaughn Road	7
Port Republic	Virginia	VA106		10
Port Walthall Junction	Virginia	VA047		7
Proctor's Creek	Virginia	VA053	Drewry's Bluff, Fort Darling	7
Quaker Road	Virginia	VA085	**Lewis' Farm**, Military Road, Gravelly Run	7
Quarles Mill	Virginia	VA055	**North Anna**, Telegraph Road Bridge, Jericho Mill, Ox Ford, Hanover Junction	7
Rapidan River	Virginia	VA045	**Morton's Ford**	8
Rappahannock River	Virginia	VA023	Waterloo Bridge, White Sulphur Springs, Lee Springs, Freeman's Ford	8
Rappahannock Station	Virginia	VA043		8

BATTLE NAME	STATE	CWSAC DESIGNATION	ALTERNATIVE NAMES	CHAPTER
Ream's Station	Virginia	VA068		7
Ream's Station	Virginia	VA073		7
Rice's Depot	Virginia	VA092	**Rice's Station**	7
Rice's Station	Virginia	VA092	Rice's Depot	7
Riddell's Shop	Virginia	VA020b	**Glendale**, Nelson's Farm, Frayser's Farm, Charles City Crossroads, White Oak Swamp, New Market Road	7
Rowanty Creek	Virginia	VA083	**Hatcher's Run**, Dabney's Mill, Armstrong's Mill, Vaughan Road	7
Rutherford's Farm	Virginia	VA115		10
St. Mary's Church	Virginia	VA066	Nance's Shop	7
Salem Church	Virginia	VA033	Banks' Ford	8
Saltville	Virginia	VA082		11
Saltville	Virginia	VA076		11
Sappony Church	Virginia	VA067	Stony Creek Depot	7
Savage's Station	Virginia	VA019		7
Saylor's Creek	Virginia	VA093	Hillsman Farm, Lockett Farm	7
Second Battle of Weldon Railroad	Virginia	VA072	**Globe Tavern**, Yellow Tavern, Yellow House, Blick's Station	7
Second Bull Run	Virginia	VA026	**Manassas Second**, Manassas Plains, Groveton, Gainesville, Brawner's Farm	8
Second Cold Harbor	Virginia	VA062	**Cold Harbor**	7
Second Fair Oaks	Virginia	VA080	**Fair Oaks & Darbytown Road**	7
Seven Pines	Virginia	VA014	Fair Oaks, Fair Oaks Station	7
Sewell's Point	Virginia	VA001		6
Shady Grove	Virginia	VA057	**Totopotomoy Creek**, Bethesda Church, Crump's Creek, Matadequin Creek, Hanovertown	7
Shipping Point	Virginia	VA100	**Cockpit Point**, Batteries at Evansport, Freestone Point	8
Sitlington's Hill	Virginia	VA102	**McDowell**	10
Slash Church	Virginia	VA013	**Hanover Courthouse**	7
Slaughter's Mountain	Virginia	VA022	**Cedar Mountain**, Cedar Run	8
Snickers Ferry	Virginia	VA114	**Cool Spring**, Island Ford, Parker's Ford, Castleman's Ferry	10
Spotsylvania Court House	Virginia	VA048	Laurel Hill, Corbin's Bridge, Ni River, Po River, Bloody Angle, Piney Branch Church, Harrison House, Harris Farm	8
St. Stephen's Church	Virginia	VA039	**Auburn**, Catlett's Station	8
Staunton River Bridge	Virginia	VA113	Blacks and Whites, Old Men and Young Boys	7
Stony Creek Depot	Virginia	VA067	**Sappony Church**	7
Strawberry Plains	Virginia	VA069	**Deep Bottom I**, Darbytown, New Market Road, Gravel Hill	7
Suffolk	Virginia	VA031	Fort Huger, Hill's Point	6
Suffolk	Virginia	VA030	Norfleet House Battery	6
Sutherland's Station	Virginia	VA090		7
Swift Creek	Virginia	VA050	Arrowfield Church	7
Telegraph Road Bridge	Virginia	VA055	**North Anna**, Jericho Mill, Ox Ford, Quarles Mill, Hanover Junction	7
The Furnaces	Virginia	VA046	**Wilderness**, Combats at Parker's Store, Craig's Meeting House, Todd's Tavern, Brock Road	8
The Mine	Virginia	VA070	**Crater**	7
Thoroughfare Gap	Virginia	VA025	Chapman's Mill	8

BATTLE NAME	STATE	CWSAC DESIGNATION	ALTERNATIVE NAMES	CHAPTER
Todd's Tavern	Virginia	VA046	**Wilderness**, Combats at Parker's Store, Craig's Meeting House, Brock Road, The Furnaces	8
Tom's Brook	Virginia	VA121	Woodstock Races	10
Totopotomy Creek	Virginia	VA057	Bethesda Church, Crumps Creek, Matadequin Creek, Shady Grove, Hanovertown	7
Trevilian Station	Virginia	VA099	Trevilians	8
Trevilians	Virginia	VA099	**Trevilian Station**	8
Union Mills	Virginia	VA024	**Manassas Station Operations**, Bristoe Station, Kettle Run, Bull Run Bridge	8
Upperville	Virginia	VA038		8
Vaughn Road	Virginia	VA083	**Hatcher's Run**, Dabney's Mill, Rowanty Creek, Armstrong's Mill	7
Vaughn Road	Virginia	VA074	**Peebles' Farm**, Poplar Springs Church, Wyatt's Farm, Chappell's House, Pegram's Farm	7
Walkerton	Virginia	VA125	Mantapike Hill	7
Wapping Heights	Virginia	VA108	**Manassas Gap**	10
Ware Bottom Church	Virginia	VA054		7
Waterloo Bridge	Virginia	VA023	**Rappahannock River**, White Sulphur Springs, Lee Springs, Freeman's Ford	8
Waynesborough	Virginia	VA123		10
West Point	Virginia	VA011	**Eltham's Landing**, Barhamsville	7
White Oak Ridge	Virginia	VA087	**White Oak Road**, Hatcher's Run, Gravelly Run, Boydton Plank Road	7
White Oak Road	Virginia	VA087	Hatcher's Run, Gravelly Run, Boydton Plank Road, White Oak Ridge	7
White Oak Swamp	Virginia	VA020b	**Glendale**, Nelson's Farm, Frayser's Farm, Charles City Crossroads, New Market Road, Riddell's Shop	7
White Oak Swamp	Virginia	VA020a		7
White Sulphur Springs	Virginia	VA023	**Rappahannock River**, Waterloo Bridge, Lee Springs, Freeman's Ford	8
White's Tavern	Virginia	VA071	**Deep Bottom II**, New Market Road, Fussell's Mill, Bailey's Creek, Charles City Road	7
Wilderness	Virginia	VA046	Combats at Parker's Store, Craig's Meeting House, Todd's Tavern, Brock Road, The Furnaces	8
Williamsburg	Virginia	VA010	Fort Magruder	7
Wilson's Wharf	Virginia	VA056	Fort Pocahontas	7
Winchester, First	Virginia	VA104	Bowers Hill	10
Winchester, Second	Virginia	VA107		10
Winchester, Third	Virginia	VA119	**Opequon**	10
Woodstock Races	Virginia	VA121	**Tom's Brook**	10
Wyatt's Farm	Virginia	VA074	**Peebles' Farm**, Poplar Springs Church, Chappell's House, Pegram's Farm, Vaughn Road	7
Yellow House	Virginia	VA072	**Globe Tavern**, Second Battle of Weldon Railroad, Yellow Tavern, Blick's Station	7
Yellow Tavern	Virginia	VA072	**Globe Tavern**, Second Battle of Weldon Railroad, Yellow House, Blick's Station	7
Yellow Tavern	Virginia	VA052		7
Yorktown	Virginia	VA009		7
Actions at Wolf Creek	West Virginia	WV009	**Princeton Courthouse**	11

BATTLE NAME	STATE	CWSAC DESIGNATION	ALTERNATIVE NAMES	CHAPTER
Allegheny Mountain	West Virginia	WV008	**Camp Alleghany**	11
Boteler's Ford	West Virginia	WV016	**Shepherdstown**	9
Cameron's Depot	West Virginia	WV014	**Summit Point**, Flowing Springs	10
Camp Alleghany	West Virginia	WV008	Allegheny Mountain	11
Camp Bartow	West Virginia	WV007	**Greenbrier River**	11
Carnifex Ferry	West Virginia	WV006		11
Cheat Mountain	West Virginia	WV005	Cheat Mountain Summit	11
Cheat Mountain Summit	West Virginia	WV005	**Cheat Mountain**	11
Cross Lanes	West Virginia	WV004	**Kessler's Cross Lanes**	11
Droop Mountain	West Virginia	WV012		11
Falling Waters	West Virginia	WV002	**Hoke's Run**, Hainesville	10
Flowing Springs	West Virginia	WV014	**Summit Point**, Cameron's Depot	10
Greenbrier River	West Virginia	WV007	Camp Bartow	11
Hainesville	West Virginia	WV002	**Hoke's Run**, Falling Waters	10
Harper's Ferry	West Virginia	WV010		9
Hoke's Run	West Virginia	WV002	Falling Waters, Hainesville	10
Kessler's Cross Lanes	West Virginia	WV004	Cross Lanes	11
Moorefield	West Virginia	WV013	Oldfields	9
Oldfields	West Virginia	WV013	**Moorefield**	9
Philippi	West Virginia	WV001	Philippi Races	11
Philippi Races	West Virginia	WV001	**Philippi**	11
Princeton Courthouse	West Virginia	WV009	Actions at Wolf Creek	11
Rich Mountain	West Virginia	WV003		11
Shepherdstown	West Virginia	WV016	Boteler's Ford	9
Smithfield Crossing	West Virginia	WV015		10
Summit Point	West Virginia	WV014	Flowing Springs, Cameron's Depot	10